Handbook of Research on Microfinancial Impacts on Women Empowerment, Poverty, and Inequality

Ramesh Chandra Das
Katwa College, India

A volume in the Advances in Finance, Accounting, and Economics (AFAE) Book Series

IGI Global
DISSEMINATOR OF KNOWLEDGE

Published in the United States of America by
IGI Global
Business Science Reference (an imprint of IGI Global)
701 E. Chocolate Avenue
Hershey PA, USA 17033
Tel: 717-533-8845
Fax: 717-533-8661
E-mail: cust@igi-global.com
Web site: http://www.igi-global.com

Library of Congress Cataloging-in-Publication Data

Names: Das, Ramesh Chandra, 1973- editor.
Title: Handbook of research on microfinancial impacts on women empowerment, poverty, and inequality / Ramesh Chandra Das, editor.
Description: Hershey : Business Science Reference, [2018]
Identifiers: LCCN 2017037844| ISBN 9781522552406 (hardcover) | ISBN 9781522552413 (ebook)
Subjects: LCSH: Women--Economic conditions. | Women--Social conditions. | Microfinance.
Classification: LCC HQ1381 .M53 2018 | DDC 305.42--dc23 LC record available at https://lccn.loc.gov/2017037844

This book is published in the IGI Global book series Advances in Finance, Accounting, and Economics (AFAE) (ISSN: 2327-5677; eISSN: 2327-5685)

British Cataloguing in Publication Data
A Cataloguing in Publication record for this book is available from the British Library.

Advances in Finance, Accounting, and Economics (AFAE) Book Series

Ahmed Driouchi
Al Akhawayn University, Morocco

ISSN:2327-5677
EISSN:2327-5685

Mission

In our changing economic and business environment, it is important to consider the financial changes occurring internationally as well as within individual organizations and business environments. Understanding these changes as well as the factors that influence them is crucial in preparing for our financial future and ensuring economic sustainability and growth.

The **Advances in Finance, Accounting, and Economics (AFAE)** book series aims to publish comprehensive and informative titles in all areas of economics and economic theory, finance, and accounting to assist in advancing the available knowledge and providing for further research development in these dynamic fields.

Coverage

- Internet Banking
- Public Finance
- Risk Analysis and Management
- Microfinance
- Applied economics
- Applied Accounting
- Managerial Accounting
- Health Economics
- Economic Downturn
- Statistical Analysis

IGI Global is currently accepting manuscripts for publication within this series. To submit a proposal for a volume in this series, please contact our Acquisition Editors at Acquisitions@igi-global.com or visit: http://www.igi-global.com/publish/.

The Advances in Finance, Accounting, and Economics (AFAE) Book Series (ISSN 2327-5677) is published by IGI Global, 701 E. Chocolate Avenue, Hershey, PA 17033-1240, USA, www.igi-global.com. This series is composed of titles available for purchase individually; each title is edited to be contextually exclusive from any other title within the series. For pricing and ordering information please visit http://www.igi-global.com/book-series/advances-finance-accounting-economics/73685. Postmaster: Send all address changes to above address.

Titles in this Series

For a list of additional titles in this series, please visit: www.igi-global.com/book-series

Agricultural Finance and Opportunities for Investment and Expansion
Augustine Odinakachukwu Ejiogu (Imo State University, Nigeria)
Business Science Reference • copyright 2018 • 236pp • H/C (ISBN: 9781522530596) • US $195.00 (our price)

Regaining Global Stability After the Financial Crisis
Bruno Sergi (Harvard University, USA) Filip Fidanoski (University of New South Wales, Australia) Magdalena Ziolo (University of Szczecin, Poland) and Vladimir Naumovski (University American College Skopje, Macedonia)
Business Science Reference • copyright 2018 • 383pp • H/C (ISBN: 9781522540267) • US $215.00 (our price)

Employment Protection Legislation in Emerging Economies
Samir Amine (Universite du Quebec en Outaouais, Canada)
Business Science Reference • copyright 2018 • 301pp • H/C (ISBN: 9781522541349) • US $195.00 (our price)

Fractal Approaches for Modeling Financial Assets and Predicting Crises
Inna Nekrasova (Southern Federal University, Russia) Oxana Karnaukhova (Southern Federal University, Russia) and Bryan Christiansen (PryMarke, LLC, USA)
Business Science Reference • copyright 2018 • 306pp • H/C (ISBN: 9781522537670) • US $215.00 (our price)

Regulation and Structure in Economic Virtualization Emerging Research and Opportunities
Denis Ushakov (Suan Sunandha Rajabhat University, Thailand)
Business Science Reference • copyright 2018 • 238pp • H/C (ISBN: 9781522549666) • US $145.00 (our price)

Accountancy and the Changing Landscape of Integrated Reporting
Ioana Dragu (Babes-Bolyai University, Romania)
Business Science Reference • copyright 2018 • 303pp • H/C (ISBN: 9781522536222) • US $195.00 (our price)

Foreign Direct Investments (FDIs) and Opportunities for Developing Economies in the World Market
Venkataramanaiah Malepati (University of Gondar, Ethiopia) and C. Mangala Gowri (University of Gondar, Ethiopia)
Business Science Reference • copyright 2018 • 315pp • H/C (ISBN: 9781522530268) • US $215.00 (our price)

Economic Growth in Latin America and the Impact of the Global Financial Crisis
Mauricio Garita (Universidad del Valle de Guatemala, Guatemala) and Celso Fernando Cerezo Bregni (Universidad del Valle de Guatemala, Guatemala)
Business Science Reference • copyright 2018 • 240pp • H/C (ISBN: 9781522549819) • US $180.00 (our price)

IGI Global
DISSEMINATOR OF KNOWLEDGE

701 East Chocolate Avenue, Hershey, PA 17033, USA
Tel: 717-533-8845 x100 • Fax: 717-533-8661
E-Mail: cust@igi-global.com • www.igi-global.com

Editorial Advisory Board

List of Contributors

Table of Contents

Detailed Table of Contents

The present chapter analyzes two cases of a joint venture stage to determine the successes and failures undertaken by the PROMUSAG and Uber as a model and strategies of collaborative economies to improve the quality of life. First, it is analyzed PROMUSAG as a program to finance women entrepreneurship aimed to improve the quality of life and the second case aims to analyze the different strategies taken by Uber to join the global market successfully, positioning itself in different countries. The analysis concludes that the empirical knowledge of entrepreneurs, in this case were not sufficient to direct the business to success, and that the lack of structured knowledge and adequate scientific support for this project strongly directed towards the non-permanence on the market. Taking terms as work global, it is considered Uber as a technology-based company and sees it from an overall, same strategy refers to a strategy that follows the company having a worldwide standardized product, another issue that would revise the importance of the theory of institutions.

Microfinance is considered as one of the most potential and successful tools which battle against poverty in the way of financing people with small financial need and helping poor women financially in less developed countries like India. It is a well-recognized notion that without upliftment of the condition of women in a society a nation cannot be developed in a competitive world. Microfinance may in fact help women to gain respect in her family and realize more self-confidence in socially defined roles. The chapter discusses the conceptual framework of microfinance growth of SHG-linked microfinance program and different types of microfinance services in India. Also, this chapter depicts how women are financially benefitted from microfinance institution through self-help groups and measured state-wise microfinance penetration index (MPI) in India. The findings of this study show that there have been favorable changes in the microfinance variables considered.

Empowerment of women is a comprehensive issue and it is a dynamic, multi-dimensional process which enables women to realize their full distinctiveness and power in all spheres of life. In order to achieve it, mobilization and organization of women into self-reliant groups is indispensable for gaining solidarity and strength and inducing collective actions in right time. Against this backdrop, the chapter is conducted through a questionnaire-based survey on the members from a representative sample of the women-run SHGs under the aegis of Sandeshkhali Large-Sized Multipurpose Co-Operative Societies (LAMPS), West Bengal Tribal Development Co-operative Corporation Ltd. (WBTDCC) under Backward Classes Welfare Department, Government of West Bengal in the backward class-dominated, economically

This chapter analyzes the impact of microfinance on poverty, in general, and female-headed households, in particular, for Ghana. The analysis shows that there are three types of microfinance institutions in Ghana, and successive governments have identified and upheld microfinance as the means to reduce national poverty rates and close the gender gap in the country. The analysis also demonstrates that microfinance has both positive and negative impacts on poverty and female-headed households. Microfinance has contributed to narrowing the poverty gap between the female and male gender, and improving the quality of their lives. However, on its own, it is not sufficient and necessary means to poverty reduction, growth, and development. The extent to which microfinance impacts on poverty is not conclusive. This necessitates remedial measures such as regulation and monitoring, proper balance between needs of clients and commercial interest of institutions, incentives to microfinance institutions, and capacitation of the poor and institutions.

Economic development in the truest sense remains far from the development targets and millennium development goals in many less developed and developing countries of the world particularly because of the perennial problems of poverty and inequality in the distribution of income and wealth. The trajectory of planned economic development of India has also experienced the said problem. One of the escape routes for the poverty trap particularly in the rural areas of India has been the formation of self-help groups (SHGs) and the provision of microfinance to the SHGs. The present study tries to analyze the intensity of poverty and inequality among the rural households of some of the backward regions of West Bengal. This study indicates that the incidence of poverty remains less among the SHG members in comparison with the non-SHG households in both drought prone and non-drought prone areas of rural West Bengal. Further, the inequalities in the distribution of income and expenditure among the SHG members are also found to be more prominent in non-drought prone areas compared to drought prone areas.

Policymakers throughout the world have actively been in pursuit of improvements of financial markets in the developing regions, but often with disappointing results. In this background, this chapter claims that microfinance can play a significant role in financial development, and that by concentrating on microfinance, development policy can consolidate the links between financial development, growth, and thus inequality reduction. The inequality computation used is based on the generalized entropy index (standard assumption of weight equal to 2 is applicable). Panel cointegration and panel causality are the

examined using vulnerability index, which is constructed considering different quantitative and subjective issues. For this, the micro level data have been collected from the state of West Bengal (India). The index value in the study shows that female is 56% more vulnerable than male even after joining in SHG and, therefore, requires large policy attention and intervention from different agencies to minimize such discrimination.

The chapter aims at finding the microfinance effect on households' shocks easing of Nigerians, and estimating the inequality in the use of MFIs' services under the backdrop that rural farmers do not have access to credits to boost productivity and this affects their income and widens inequality. Based upon the World Bank microdata on financial inclusion survey for 2014 (the Global Fundex survey data set), the study employed the Heckman selection model and concentration index. The results show that households in urban areas have more access to MFIs services than rural households in terms of mobile money accounts, emergency funds, and receiving remittances to smooth their consumption shocks. The results also show wide disparities in deprivation of owning accounts, in loans for apartment, in trend of saving habits, in capacity to participate in MFIs services between the rich and the poor. The study, therefore, recommends that more MFIs can be established in rural areas and more awareness campaign be carried to reach out to the targeted households.

The microfinance program has now been recognized as an effective tool to empower economically the rural women folk. The earning is the most important direct outcome of micro finance participation unlike acquiring empowerment. Participation in the program helps women to inculcate their saving habit. It gives access to the formal credit to them. All these have direct impact on their economic condition. This study explores the impact of microfinance program on the income of the program participants of Birbhum District in West Bengal in India. The study also focuses on how participation helps in reducing inequality in income of the participants. The major finding of the study is that women self-help group (SHG) members have the higher level of income compared to that of non-SHG members. The study also shows that SHG participation also helps them in reducing inequalities in their income. Gini coefficient and Lorenz curve technique has been used to assess the income distribution of the respondents.

This chapter explores the penetration of SHGs and assesses socio-economic status and its inequality for the SHG-member households in North Andaman Island in the union territory Andaman and Nicobar Islands of India. The authors have used the Gini coefficients for computing inequalities and log-linear model for estimating the impact of borrowing on food and non-food expenditure. It is revealed that the incidence and intensity of poverty of the sample households is not so serious. Majority of the sample women under SHG schemes actively participate in group activities and have obtained micro credit. Inequality in household income is lower than the inequality in per capita income. Moreover, inequality for health expenditure is higher compared to the inequality in food expenditure. Borrowing through SHGs accelerates non-food expenditures not investment in income generating activities. However, SHGs inculcates empowerment of the participations.

In India, 70% of population lives in rural area and 60% of population earn their livelihood from agriculture which implies a high rate of underemployment and poverty. The root cause of poverty is the low access to credit facilities. Micro finance in this respect can play a vital role in providing financial services to the poor. In India Micro finance is dominated by self-help groups (SHGs), bank linkage programs aimed at providing a cost effective mechanism for providing financial services to unreached poor to fight against poverty. The chapter, thus, aims at identifying the current status, role, and performance of microfinance in Char areas of Assam in India. The chapter is concluded with the stress that more and more number of SHGs should be encouraged to form among the poor household in the study area to avail the benefit and cross poverty line.

Foreword

One of the important goals of microfinance activities is to empower women by providing them financial assistance and allowing them to earn independent incomes and contribute financially to their households and generate self-employment. This economic independence is expected to improve the overall development of the country. The millennium developmental goal of the United Nations is to posit the empowerment of women to decrease the gender gap to zero and poverty in the society so that an equitable development of a country as well as restoring the world. Microfinance system has been projected as one of the good options for attaining the equitable development where the financial inclusion mission is targeted through the empowerment of the woman members of the families. In the countries of the developing or underdeveloped zones, it has been proved to be an ideal way of reducing poverty and making consumption smoothened.

The present book titled *Handbook of Research on Microfinancial Impacts on Women Empowerment, Poverty, and Inequality* edited by Dr. Ramesh Chandra Das has rightly commenced this issue in the objective of further survey across different countries and zones whether the microfinance activities have been capable of increasing women empowerment, reducing poverty, and reducing inter-country or inter-class inequality. The book covers studies related to the countries from Africa, Asia and other Emerging Economies. Therefore, this book is recommended for researchers, practitioners, policymakers, and students of economics, finance and related social sciences.

It is a praiseworthy work and I hope it will be read by a lot of people, not only in the countries targeted by the book, but also in the other countries of the world.

Murat Akbalık
Marmara University, Turkey

Murat Akbalık *is the Professor and Head of Capital Markets Department, School of Banking and Insurance, Marmara University, Turkey. He completed both Masters and PhD, in the field of Banking, in the years of 1993 and 2001, respectively at Marmara University, Institute of Banking and Insurance. His main research interests are Capital Markets and Banking; however, he has lately been focusing on Behavioral Finance and new financial asset valuation. Dr. Akbalik has many papers and articles, both in national and in international journals as well as some chapters in books.*

Preface

INTRODUCTION

One of the major tools of attaining proper development all around the world is complete financial inclusion in the way that all classes of people are capable of securing their life styles through access to financial services from formal sector. At the same time, it is also required to ensure the empowerment of the women in all respect to minimize gender inequality in particular and overall inequality in general, which can further boost up the magnitudes of developments in all classes of economies. Microfinance is considered by the world policy makers as having such potential to incorporate maximum number of women in different countries to enter into the financial sectors' umbrella to make them empowered through developments of entrepreneurial activities.

Influenced by this mode of transformation into women empowerment, inclusive growth and development and complemented by the publisher, IGI Global, it was in mind to construct such a research outcome in mutual manner so that the said financial activities can be highlighted and their impacts and implications are explained. After a series of screening by the expert teams of the IGI Global the ultimate title of the book was first-rated as *Microfinancial Impacts on Women Empowerment, Poverty, and Inequality* that would be expected to be capable of covering the original thoughts.

The Classical School of Thought led by Adam Smith did not belief in the role of the monetary and financial sectors in deciding the real variables like output and employment of an economy. The opposite group led by Joseph Schumpeter and later by J. M. Keynes believed in the active role of the formal monetary and financial sectors in explaining real variables. The formal monetary and financial sectors are controlled and managed by the central banks of the countries. But, one of the major limitations of such formal monetary and financial sectors is their reluctance to cater the so called backward classes of the population of the country leading to weak financial inclusion. Over the last three decades, there has been a tremendous development in this area which tried to connect most of the poor and backward classes with the formal sector credit net to ensure the magnitude of financial inclusion mission and inducing the overall growth and development of a country. This particular process of developments in this head is known as Microfinance or Microcredit which is operated by the NGOs who act as Self Help Groups and make link between the common people and the formal financial institutions.

One of the important goals of MF activities is to empower women by providing them financial assistance and allowing them to earn an independent income, contribute financially to their households and generate self-employment. This economic independence is expected to improve the overall development of the country. Again, microfinance activity, as an instrument of financial inclusion in a country, is considered as a well-designed institutional innovation to ensure a substantial flow of credit to poor households with no or less stringent collateral. However, it is widely believed that microfinance programme is not a universal remedy for poverty alleviation from grass root level; rather it is considered only as a means to address the issue, particularly to the countries of emerging and less developed groups. Microfinance intervention expand the access to resources, increase self-employment opportunities and thereby, reduce poverty, provided a proper government initiatives are taken in the direction of social mobilization, capital formation, capacity building and pro-poor programme design. Without an effective intervention in a pro-poor macro policy environment, no such micro policy intervention can be successful in alleviating poverty. The World Summit for Social Development (WSSD) in March 1995 articulated a global commitment by Governments to eradicate poverty as an ethical, social, political and economic imperative. Poverty eradication was one of three core themes of WSSD. The Programme of Action affirmed the primacy of national responsibility for social development, including poverty eradication, but also called for international support to assist governments in developing strategies. The Programme of Action suggested ways to involve civil society in social development and to strengthen their capacities. It called on Governments to mobilize resources for social development, including poverty alleviation. The WSSD Programme of Action was to be implemented within the framework of international cooperation that integrated the follow-up to recent and planned UN conferences relating to social development. The UN organizations' mandates in the area of microfinance primarily lie in the area of technical assistance and demonstration of models that contribute effectively to poverty alleviation. The responsibility for provision of capital rests with governments, with support from bilateral donors and international financial institutions (Report of United Nations, 1995).

ORGANIZATION OF THE BOOK

After invitation to the potential authors through the official website of the IGI Global and my personal networks for contributions to the said mission through chapter submission on the recommended topics, a number of chapters have been ultimately selected. All the chapters have attempted to justify their positions in terms of standard quantitative analysis at per their capabilities. After a double blind peer review system and additional review by me, as editor, the number of chapters in revised form ultimately turned out to be 19 with a standard volume. The entire book has been arranged by two different sections in the content to cover the basic themes as addressed in the title.

Section 1, covering Chapters 1 to 8, highlights the discussions on the effects of microfinance upon women empowerment across countries. In particular, the club of studies in this section covers the impact studies for the countries like India, Nigeria, Ghana and Mexico and the South Asian, European and Middle East and African regions. The studies covered the impact of microfinance on gender inequality issue in particular and women empowerment in general. Section 2, constituting Chapters 9 to 19, throws lights on the micro financial activities as a weapon to fight against poverty and inequality in overall sense across different countries. Most of the chapters have been deeply based on empirical observations through primary data with modern tools of quantitative economics to have concrete research outputs. A brief outcome of the chapter contributions are addressed below sequentially.

A brief outcome of the chapter contributions included in Section 1 is addressed below sequentially.

Chapter 1 concentrates to determine how microfinance has empowered women in Nigeria. It employed propensity score matching and logit model to estimate the effect of microfinance on women empowerment and welfare. The results show that age of women, education, belonging to saving association, and operating an account are the determinants of women empowerment and welfare as they access finance from the microfinance banks. It was also observed that there is disparity among women who have access to liquidity. It is recommended that more microfinance banks be cited in the rural sector where the majority of the poor reside, policies like low interest rates, national awareness, and incentives for more women to access micro-credits.

Chapter 2 attempts to analyze the concept of women empowerment and its various indices such as GDI, GEM, and Women's Empowerment Index (WEI)for India in detail. The study tries to explore the linkage between the role of microfinance and the empowerment of women in rural and urban areas of the country. The study reveals that though micro finance is supposed to provide an effective tool for financial and social upliftment of the poorer sections of the society, particularly women, but its penetration depends on a multifaceted and integrated network and so both the self-help bank model and the MFI model may have achieved some positive growth, but their performances are not quite deterministic when compared with other countries of the world.

Chapter 3 examines empirically the role of microfinance access on women empowerment by using primary data on women borrowers from different microfinance institutions in Nadia and Murshidabad districts of West Bengal in India. Microfinance institutions play an important role in strategies related to gender and development due to their active relationships with women empowerment and poverty alleviation. The various programmes under microfinance like self help groups (SHGs) are promoted and inspired for their significant economic impacts on empowerment of women. It investigates the impact of microfinance access on three dimensions of women empowerment, which make influence upon decision making on the issues of credit, expenditure and children. Using primary data on about eight hundred respondents of women borrowers from different microfinance institutions and applying multivariate probit estimation, the study reveals that the greater access to microfinance credit negatively impacts on economic empowerment i.e. decisions on credit and expenditure related issues.

Chapter 4, under the background that the aim of development policies of any country around the world is to include the marginalized people into development process and microfinance is among one such development strategies to alleviate poverty, aims to evaluate the contribution of microfinance as a weapon to gain empowerment of women on a case study in Nabagram Block of West Bengal, India. It is observed from the study that 73 per cent of respondents have reported that they have utilized their loan on such income generating activities which are different from the prime occupation of the family. Also the study reveals that members of SHGs seek for greater assistance from facilitators as well as funding authority regarding information, skill development training, raw material supply and process of marketization of their products.

Chapter 5 analyzes two cases of a joint venture stage to determine the successes and failures undertaken by the PROMUSAG and Uber as a model and strategies of collaborative economies to improve the quality of life. First, it is analyzed PROMUSAG as a program to finance women entrepreneurship aimed to improve the quality of life and the second case aims to analyze the different strategies taken by Uber to join the global market successfully, positioning itself in different countries. The analysis concludes that the empirical knowledge of entrepreneurs, in this case were not sufficient to direct the business to success, and that the lack of structured knowledge and adequate scientific support for this project strongly directed towards the non-permanence on the market. Taking terms as work global, it is considered Uber as a technology-based company and sees it from an overall, same strategy refers to a strategy that follows the company having a worldwide standardized product, another issue that would revise the importance of the theory of institutions.

Chapter 6 discusses the conceptual framework of microfinance growth of SHG linked microfinance programme and different types of microfinance services in India. Also this chapter depicts how women are financially benefitted from microfinance institution through Self Help Groups and measured state wise microfinance penetration index (MPI) in India. The findings of this study show that there have been favourable changes in the microfinance variables considered.

Chapter 7 throws light on economic empowerment of women through SHGs in Sunderban Delta Areas of India which is conducted through a questionnaire-based survey on the members from a representative sample of the women-run SHGs under the aegis of Sandeshkhali Large Sized Multipurpose Co-operative Societies (LAMPS), West Bengal Tribal Development Co-operative Corporation Ltd. (WBTDCC) under Backward Classes Welfare Department, Government of West Bengal in the backward class-dominated, economically-backward and naturally-disadvantageous thirteen Mouzas in two Blocks of Sandeshkhaliagainst the backdrop that empowerment of women is a comprehensive issue and it is a dynamic, multi-dimensional process which enables women to realize their full distinctiveness and power in all spheres of life. It is revealed from the survey that, since joining the SHG movement, the economic condition, decision-making power relating to expenditure, status within the family and the society has increased favorably for the women members.

Chapter 8 analyzes the viability of social responsibility of microfinancing by the Compartamos banco of Mexico for the period 2002-2015. The results show that microfinance working on social responsibility by the Compartamos Banco is not viable as there are the results of inverse correlation results, although, the banco served some social responsibility by means of pulling people out of poverty. It further concludes that these organizations fulfill their main objective, which is to benefit the people of the base of the pyramid in Mexico.

Let us present the chapter information covered in Section 2 of the present book title.

Chapter 9 spells on microfinance as becoming the latest buzzword in the credit markets where it shoulders the responsibility of alleviating poverty coupled with socio-economic development. Dealing with microfinance coupled with the issue of poverty reduction, the first concern is to handle the twin objectives of poverty alleviation and achievement of financial self-sufficiency, which are often at loggerheads. The chapter constructs a five dimensional Human Poverty Index (HPI) in terms of the rate of unemployment, state wise illiteracy rate, state wise infant mortality rate, state wise percentage of population below the poverty line and the percentage of population not having an access to electricity for the states across India. Thus, this will serve as an index for the extent of poverty. Consequently, a fall in the value of the index actually implies poverty alleviation. This empirical model does not justify the hypothesis that "microfinance reduces poverty" at the macro level using cross-state panel data for India.

Chapter 10 throws light on the economy of Ghana and analyzes the impact of microfinance on poverty, in general, and female-headed households, in particular for the country. The analysis shows that there are three types of microfinance institutions in Ghana, and successive governments have identified and upheld microfinance as the means to reduce national poverty rates and close the gender gap in the country. The analysis also demonstrates that microfinance has both positive and negative impacts on poverty and female-headed households. Microfinance has contributed to narrowing the poverty gap between the female and male gender, and improving the quality of their lives. However, on its own, it is not sufficient and necessary means to poverty reduction, growth and development. The extent to which microfinance impacts on poverty, is not conclusive. This necessitates remedial measures such as regulation and monitoring, proper balance between needs of clients and commercial interest of institutions, incentives to microfinance institutions, and capacitation of the poor and institutions.

Chapter 11 aims to analyze the intensity of poverty and inequality among the rural households under the SHGs of some of the backward regions of West Bengal in India. This study indicates that the incidence of poverty remains less among the SHG members in comparison with the non-SHG households in both drought pronc and non-drought pronc arcas of rural Wcst Bcngal. Furthcr, thc incqualitics in thc distribution of income and expenditure among the SHG members are also found to be more prominent in non-drought prone areas compared to drought prone areas.

Chapter 12 elucidates that microfinance can play a significant role in financial development, and that by concentrating on microfinance, development policy can consolidate the links between financial development, growth, and thus inequality reduction. The inequality computation used is based on the Generalized Entropy Index. Panel cointegration and Panel causality techniques have been applied in a Vector Error Correction Mechanism (VECM) set-up using panel data for fifteen years across seven South Asian nations, viz., Bhutan, India, Afghanistan, Bangladesh, Nepal, Pakistan and Sri Lanka. The findings validate the existence of a cointegrated relation coupled with a tri-variate causality linking the focus variables in this model in the way that microfinance initiatives, their outreach is beneficial for the reduction of inequality but that inequality reduction does not promote economic growth*per se*.

Chapter 13 aims to study the concept of Microfinance and Microfinance institutions and its impact on financial inclusion in India under the backdrop that the important part of the financial inclusion strategy is to provide access to finance to those people belonging to remote and disadvantaged areas. This study provides recommendations to grow and sustain microfinance institutions to achieve greater financial inclusion.

Chapter 14, under the backdrop that microfinance, is expected to significantly affect macro variables such as inequality, poverty and human development, provides a detailed empirical analysis of the correlation between microfinance and inequality in West Africa sub-region. The correlation coefficient shows that although there is a positive linear connection between the possibilities of microfinance to reduce inequality, it has not contributed significantly to poverty reduction with the independent variables. The findings further suggest that the most robust explanatory variables for inequality reduction are GDP per capita and democracy which are invariably significant with positive sign. Taken together, these findings reinforce the intuition that greater democracy and provision and expansion of financial infrastructures especially in backward countries of the region are necessary for microfinance to thrive and contribute abundantly to inequality reduction.

Chapter 15 examines the extent of vulnerability between male and female SHG members have examined using 'Vulnerability Index' which have constructed considering different quantitative and subjective issues under the framework that gender bias retards economic growth for all the economies including India. For this, the micro level data have been collected from the state of West Bengal (India). The index value in the study shows that female is 56% more vulnerable than male even after joining in Self-Help Groups and therefore, requires large policy attention and intervention from different agencies to minimize such discrimination.

Chapter 16 throws light upon finding the microfinance effect on households' shocks easing of Nigerians, and estimating the inequality in the use of MFIs' services under the backdrop that rural farmers do not have access to credits to boost productivity and this affects their income and widens inequality. Based upon the World Bank micro data on financial inclusion survey for 2014 (the Global Fundex survey data set), the study employed the Heckman Selection model and Concentration Index. The results show that households in urban areas have more access to MFIs services than rural households in terms of mobile money accounts, emergency funds, and receiving remittances to smooth their consumption shocks. The results also show wide disparities in deprivation of owning accounts, in loans for apartment, in trend of saving habits, in capacity to participate in MFIs services between the rich and the poor. The study, therefore, recommends that more MFIs can be established in rural areas and more awareness campaign be carried to reach out to the targeted households.

Chapter 17 explores the impact of micro finance programme on the income of the programme participants of Birbhum District in West Bengal in India. The study also focuses on how participation helps in reducing inequality in income of the participants. The major finding of the study is that women Self Help Group (SHG) members have the higher level of income compared to that of non-SHG members. The study also shows that SHG participation also helps them in reducing inequalities in their income. Gini coefficient and Lorenz curve technique has been used to assess the income distribution of the respondents.

Chapter 18 reconnoiters the penetration of SHGs and assesses socio-economic status and its inequality for the SHG-member households in North Andaman Island in the union territory Andaman and Nicobar Islands of India. It has used the Gini coefficients for computing inequalities and log-linear model for estimating the impact of borrowing on food and non-food expenditure. It is revealed that the incidence and intensity of poverty of the sample households is not so serious. Majority of the sample women under SHG schemes actively participate in group activities and have obtained micro credit. Inequality in household income is lower than the inequality in per capita income. Moreover, inequality for health expenditure is higher compared to the inequality in food expenditure. Borrowing through SHGs accelerates non-food expenditures not investment in income generating activities. However, SHGs instructs empowerment of the participations.

Chapter 19 highlights the concern that the root cause of poverty is the low access to credit facilities and advocates that micro finance in this respect can play a vital role in providing financial services to the poor. The study, thus, aims at identifying the current status, role and performance of microfinance in Char areas of Assam in India. The chapter is concluded with the stress that more and more number of SHGs should be encouraged to form among the poor household in the study area to avail the benefit and cross poverty line.

CONCLUSION

The upshot of the covered studies in the book provides that microfinance activities in general make the women empowered. It also shows that, age of the women member, literacy, savings behavior, etc. are the determinants of women empowerment and microfinance activities have such potential to ensure it. The results also reveal in some country case that, though micro finance is supposed to provide an effective tool for financial and social upliftment of the poorer sections of the society, particularly women, but its penetration depends on a multifaceted and integrated network and so both the self-help bank model and the MFI model may have achieved some positive growth. There are some studies related to the rural belt in India that they reveal that the greater access to microfinance credit negatively impacts on economic empowerment i.e. decisions on credit and expenditure related issues. The outcome of the last section covering the effects of microfinance on reducing poverty and inequality depicts that microfinance has been able to eradicate poverty and reducing inequality in many countries like Nigeria, Ghana, countries from South Asia. But in India, at state levels, one study does not justify the hypothesis that "microfinance reduces poverty" at the macro level using cross-state panel data.

It is now the fact that the proposed project has been going to be grounded. I expect that the said research outcome will lend a hand to the academicians and policy makers all around the world to have a better understanding on the impacts of microfinance programmes all around the world upon women empowerment and fighting against poverty and inequality that the book addressed to.

Ramesh Chandra Das
Katwa College, India

REFERENCES

Report of the United Nations. (1995). Retrieved from: www.laghuudyog.com/schemes/microfinance.htm

Acknowledgment

It is now an inexplicable pleasure to reveal that the proposed book on microfinancial impacts on women empowerment, poverty, and inequality has been eventually unearthed. The ultimate success of developing such a huge volume of the edited book could not be consummated if the contributions of the concerned branch of academicians all around the world were clubbed particularly when the entire work was controlled and managed from a rural belt of Indian subcontinent. Hence, it would be culpable if I do not acknowledge the offerings of the concerned academicians and other members of the society associated to the project.

At the outset, I must acknowledge the IGI Global Team for approving the proposal and continuously guiding me at all stages of developments by means of their cordial and corroborative suggestions. I did not face any kind of encumbrance from their parts and hence their sincere efforts were always praiseworthy. Secondly, I remain grateful to my research guides Professor Soumyen Sikdar of Indian Institute of Management, Calcutta, India and Professor (formerly) Sarmila Banerjee of Calcutta University, India and Dr. Asis Kumar Banerjee, Professor and Vice Chancellor (formerly) of Calcutta University for their continuous encouragement to me to undergo such a project and circulating the message to the potential chapter contributors of the said field. Thirdly, I must express gratitude to Dr. Amaresh Das, Dr. Igwe, E. Udeh and Dr. Frank Martin of College of Business, Southern University at New Orleans, USA, and Dr. Soumyananda Dinda, Dr. Maniklal Adhikary of The University of Burdwan, India, and Dr. Kamal Ray of Katwa College (formerly), India for their uninterrupted efforts in helping review works in higher masses and editing the texts of the book besides added encouragements to me. Fourthly, I should acknowledge the efforts of the editorial advisory board members for reviewing the chapters with greater genuineness and providing me suggestions in an ceaseless manner notwithstanding their busy academic schedules. Fifthly, I must be grateful to Professor Murat Akbalık of Marmara University, Turkey, for spending his valuable time on writing Foreword for the book. Sixthly, I pay due honor to all the contributing authors for their valuable chapter contributions and showing their patience for such a long duration project coming into veracity. I must admit the values they added to the existing literature through this edited volume.

Last but not the least I must be obliged to my parents, wife and daughter and other members of the family for their continuous encouragements, supports and sacrifice in carrying out the long-lasting project. Of course, no one other than me, as the editor, remains completely responsible for the remaining errors, if any, still appear in the book.

Ramesh Chandra Das
Katwa College, India

Section 1

Effects of Microfinance on Women Empowerment Across Countries

Chapter 1
How Does Microfinance Empower Women in Nigeria?
A Study

Ezebuilo R. Ukwueze
University of Nigeria, Nigeria

Henry T. Asogwa
University of Nigeria, Nigeria

Onyinye M. David-Wayas
University of Nigeria, Nigeria

Chisom Emecheta
University of Nigeria, Nigeria

Johnson E. Nchege
University of Nigeria, Nigeria

ABSTRACT

That microfinance institutions empower women has become a heated debate at both theoretical and empirical economics. A large proportion of women in developing countries are characterized by segregation, relegation, poverty, vulnerability; majority of them engaged in agriculture and related economic activities, while a few others have menial jobs. The objective of this chapter is to determine how microfinance has empowered women in Nigeria. It employed propensity score matching and logit model to estimate the effect of microfinance on women empowerment and welfare. The results show that age of women, education, belonging to saving association, and operating an account are the determinants of women empowerment and welfare as they access finance from the microfinance banks. It was also observed that there is disparity among women who have access to liquidity. It is recommended that more microfinance banks be cited in the rural sector where the majority of the poor reside, policies like low interest rates, national awareness, and incentives for more women to access micro-credits.

DOI: 10.4018/978-1-5225-5240-6.ch001

INTRODUCTION

Women play a crucial role in the economic development of their families and communities but certain obstacles such as poverty, unemployment, low household income and societal discriminations mostly in developing countries have hindered their effective performance of that role. Therefore, most of them embark on entrepreneurial activities to support their families. Studies have shown that women entrepreneurship could be an effective strategy for poverty reduction in a country, since women are the worst hit in such situation (Ekpe et al., 2010).

In order to support the women in their attempts to vanquish poverty, several governments in Nigeria have initiated a series of empowerment programmes. Some of these programmes include Peoples' Bank, Family Economic Advancement Programme (FEAP), Better Life for Rural Women, and Poverty Alleviation Programme (PAP). Despite these laudable programmes, they have failed to address the empowerment and poverty reduction among the Nigerian women (Awojobi, 2013).

Microfinance has emerged a major strategy to solve twin problems of poverty and unemployment that continue a major threat to the policy and economy of the developing countries. Some studies, for instance, Qazi (2007), Narender (2007) and Sing (2009) have identified the benefits of microfinance as women empowerment, poverty alleviation and employment opportunities.

From the early 1970s, women's movements in a number of countries, notably India, became increasingly interested in the degree to which women were able to gain access to and benefit from poverty-focused credit programmes and credit cooperatives (Mayoux & Hartl, 2009). The problem of women's access to credit was highlighted at the first International Women's Conference in Mexico in 1975, leading to the setting up of the Women's World Banking network. In the wake of the second International Women's Conference in Nairobi in 1985, there was a mushrooming of government and NGO-sponsored income generating programmes for women, many of which included savings and credit. From that moment, there emerged increasing awakening and interest into the need for women to have more access to financial services at the rural setting, since the greater percentage of women live in the rural areas.

Women empowerment is part of the third Millennium Development Goals (MDG) (MDG Report, 2006). When women are empowered, there appear to be the following impacts: (1) gain more equality and control over their own lives, (2) contributing: (a) directly to their children's human capital (nutrition, health and education) and thereby indirectly to their nation's income growth; (b) directly to the wealth and well-being of their nations, and (c) indirectly to their country's national income growth through their own and their educated daughters by lower fertility (there is an inverse relationship between the fertility rate and national income growth) (Nessa et al. 2012). According to Blumberg, (2005), more female economic power might help reduce corruption, poverty, conflict and violence in nations. It has been observed by Mayoux (2005) that women's empowerment through access to saving and credits, employment income opportunities, consumption, mobility, education, health, control of asset, personal security and political participations increase the wellbeing of women.

Empowerment of women is crucial for the emancipation of poverty and meaningful participation of entrepreneurship development. It is assumed that increasing women's access to micro finance will enable women to make a greater contribution to household income and this, together with other interventions to increase household wellbeing, translate into improved wellbeing for women and ability to bring about wider changes in gender inequality (Biswas, 2008). Micro finance institutions target women with the explicit goal of empowering them. In actuality, the effect of these micro finances intervention and provision of resources include access to and future claims to both material and social resources. They also provide agency such as the process of decision making, negotiations, deception and manipulation; and achievement that are outcomes of well-being.

Micro-finance was introduced in Nigeria in 2005 after a recommendation from the World Bank. The hypothesis that micro-finance reduces poverty and empowers women has been a contentious issue in the academic and the public domain. The validity of the claim that micro-credit empowers women through poverty reduction has been questioned (Schicks, 2010; Schmidt, 2010). The protagonists who are supporting the assumption that loans from micro-finance institutions empower women are (Hashemi et al., 1996; Hunt & Kasynathan, 2002; Asemelash, 2002; Holvoet, 2003; Montgomery & Weiss, 2005; Taha, 2012). However, there are those having pessimistic views on the positive correlation between micro-finance and women's empowerment (see Vengroff & Creevet, 1994; Goetz & Gupta, 1996; Rahman, 1999; Mayoux, 1999) for details.

Based on the foregoing background, it is evident that in Nigeria, women constitute a significant number of entrepreneurs and their main challenge is lack of funds. Micro finance institutions have come up to provide interventions that enable women to overcome some of the obstacles such as access to micro credit to fund their new ventures and / or expand existing ones. However, generally, the concept of women empowerment has not been effectively addressed as the women entrepreneurs continue to remain under represented and their success continue to remain invisible and unacknowledged. It is expected that increased women access to micro finance would increase their income which would in turn translate to improved wellbeing and a wider change as well as enhance gender equality (Basu, 2006).

Although, there have been some studies that have investigated the correlation between microcredit and women's empowerment in Nigeria, yet none of these studies have been able to validate the positive impact of micro-finance on Nigerian women. The limitation of these studies calls for empirical investigation by this paper to examine how microfinance empowers women in Nigeria.

MICROFINANCE: A SURVEY

This section seeks to survey the contributions of microfinance institutions (MFIs) to national economies.

Microfinance Experience in Africa

The microfinance sector in Africa is expanding rapidly and the institutions have increased their activities. African MFIs are among the most productive globally as measured by the number of borrowers and savers. It is also reported that MFIs in Africa also demonstrate higher levels of portfolio quality with an average portfolio at risk of over 30 days of only 4.0 per cent. According to a Poverty Reduction Strategy Paper (PRSP) produced in 1999, a large number of Kenyans derive their livelihood from the Medium and Small Scale Enterprises (MSEs). The development of that sector, therefore, represents an important means of creating employment, promoting growth and reducing poverty in the long term. As the Report notes, "In spite of the importance of the sector, experience shows that provision and delivery of credit and other financial services to the sector by formal financial institutions such as commercial banks has been below expectation…" (Poverty Reduction Strategy Paper, 1999). It has, therefore, according to the author, become difficult for the poor to climb out of poverty due to lack of finance for their productive activities. New, innovative and pro-poor modes of financing low-income households and MSEs based on sound operating principles have become imperative if Kenya is to get out of the woods of poverty. In the past, microfinance institutions (MFIs) that were established using NGOs or savings and credit co-operative society's framework have contributed to a large number of low-income households and MSEs in rural and urban areas of Kenya without appropriate policy and legal framework. Nana (2008) observes the growing competition in the financial services sector in Ghana, hence the need for innovative financial products with emphasis on sale of funds in order to succeed in the dynamic operating financial environment. She further observed that Microfinance Institutions (MFIs) are playing a pivotal role in microfinance service delivery, through innovative product development, and that they render useful financial services to the rural, semi-urban, urban and the informal sectors in the Ghanaian economy due to the increased demand for the microfinance service.

Microfinance Experience in Nigeria

Several researchers have turned their attention to the operations of MFIs in Nigeria. Akintoye and Owoyori (2009) opined that micro-financing has been accepted as a major subsector in the finance sector of the Nigeria economy. The authors are concerned with the performance of the microfinance banks in order that both the clients (the poor of the society) and the owners (shareholders) may attain the objectives of the banks. "Ultimately, satisfactory performance of microfinance banks will lead to poverty alleviation and economic development…" The above contribution by the authors lay emphasis on corporate governance, training of operators, satisfactory regulatory framework and monitoring on the part of policy makers. This contribution is considered as extremely relevant as poor corporate governance, poor training and inconsistent policies were the bane of earlier programmes aimed at alleviating poverty and enhanced economic development. If microfinance will succeed in poverty alleviation and enhance economic development, all the issues raised above must accompany microfinance operations. In a paper on "Microfinance and Developing the Nigerian economy", Onwumere (2009) appraised Nigeria's current microfinance policy within the context of the country's aspiration to join the league of twenty largest economies of the world by the year 2020. After reviewing the number of microfinance banks relative to the population of the country, the author concluded that more microfinance banks and branches would have to be put in place and be more widely spread across the country in order to ensure that their services reach more clients and in more places. According to Kimotho (2007), there has been a high level of mushrooming of microfinance institutions (MFIs) worldwide. The author observes further that despite the growth of the sector over the last couple of years the overall outreach of MFIs remains relatively low. In effect, the entire microfinance activity in Nigeria contributes a meagre 0.2 per cent to the Gross Domestic Product (GDP) and account for only 0.9 per cent of the total credit, compared with about 22 per cent in South Africa. Current efforts are geared towards making micro enterprise activities the engine of growth and economic development in Nigeria, where vibrant microfinance sector and SME programmes have led to significant, noticeable and measurable improvement in the financial well- being of the lives of the poor and has also resulted in sustainable increase in employment generation. Kefas (2006) submitted that Microfinance was often considered one of the most effective and flexible strategies in the fight against global poverty by performing the following functions; Provision of Seed Money, Business training, social rehabilitation, Start Up Funding and Training in Business Practices, Promotion of Socio-Economic Conditions and General Welfare, Literacy Campaigns.

REVIEW OF RELEVANT LITERATURE

Conceptual Literature

Women are unevenly affected by poverty, inequality and discrimination. Though a global phenomenon, it is particularly prevalent in developing countries in general and in Nigeria in particular. Insecure low-paid jobs, limited or no access to education and lack of access to financial services and tools needed for progress are the core characteristics of women and girls at the local, national and global fronts. Supporting this, Holloway, Niazi and Rouse (2017) noted that poverty levels are top-heavy with women as a result of lack of economic resources and inequality in the labour market. This was hinted by an earlier study by the United Nations which notes that most women in developing countries depend on their husbands to the extent that about 33% of women are excluded from most household purchase decisions. They further noted that 10% are not consulted on how their income is spent (United Nations, 2015). Thus, as theories and studies suggest, stakeholders are becoming increasingly conscious of the fact that to achieve sustainable economic growth, human development and poverty eradication, promoting women empowerment is essential. We kick-off this section with a brief definition of the concepts of empowerment, microfinance and women empowerment.

Empowerment

The term empowerment has been used in different fields of study by different scholars and researchers, hence the lack of consensus in the definition of empowerment. In 1996, Paulo Freire was given the credit of discussing 'empowerment' for the first time in his book titled "Padagogy of the Oppressed". Ever since then variant opinions have emerged as to the meaning of the concept of empowerment. In the views of Rowland (1997), empowerment consists of different aspects of power, that is, power over, power to, power with and power from within. According to him, "power over" empowers people to resist manipulation or victimization. It entails getting people who face regular exclusion involved in the decision-making processes. It stresses participation in the political, economic and social spheres. "Power to", on the other hand, refers to the ability to produce or originate new possibilities without fear of domination. "Power with" and "Power from within" were, however, lumped together to mean self-awareness, self-determination, awareness of individual and group interest and ability to influence decisions. From Rowland's point of view, empowerment is the process of dismantling adverse social construction, so that people will recognize their ability and right to influence decisions and act.

The wealth of vocabulary of development agencies and international organizations is with the concept of empowerment. From the lens of some of these organizations and agencies (SDC, CIDA, DFID and Oxfam), empowerment is both a process and outcome. Driving this point home, SDC (2004) conceptualizes empowerment as a process through which the vulnerable and the disadvantaged are empowered to access economic resources, exercise their rights and become activist in the process of both decision making and shaping the society. On the other hand, the United Nations (UNDAW, 2001; UNICEF, 1999) and the Declaration made at the Micro-Credit Summit (RESULTS, 1997), DFID (2000) saw "empowerment as a tool for advocating policies and interventions". Based on the assumption that increased participation could lead to empowerment, they focused more on the process and adopted an instrumentalist view of empowerment.

Drawing from the definitions above, there are four dimensions of empowerment (economic, political, social and cultural). These dimensions focus heavily on access to economic resources, control over one's life and building the capacity to claim one's right and entitlements.

Women Empowerment

There has been a new wave of the concept of empowerment since the decade of the 1990's. Feminism has in recent years taken the front seat in the discourse of empowerment. While many development agencies (CIDA and USAID) associate empowerment with gender: CIDA's (1999) gender policy has it that empowerment is fundamental to the realization of gender equality and helping women to become aware of unequal power relations, to gain control over their lives, and to acquire a greater voice to overcome inequality in their home, workplace and community, DFID and SDC, on the other hand, were distinct in their view that empowerment is not only a gender related issue but that it concerns a whole host of marginalized groups. Taking the feminist perspective, Kumari and Subrahmanyam (2017) see women empowerment as an increase in the social, economic, political, spiritual and cultural strength of women which enhances their self-esteem and confidence, participation in decision making, access to resources and learning. Women's empowerment is a process of social and personal change, which has psychological, social, political, cultural and economic domains, and through which women individually and collectively gain power, meaningful choices and control over their lives (O'Neil et al., 2014). It is not a direct, uncompetitive process rather; it is a journey filled with negotiation and compromise, and whose outcomes are not certain (Cornwall & Edwards, 2016). This paper takes a general approach given by Taylor and Pereznieto (2014) by defining women's economic empowerment as 'a process whereby women's lives are transformed from a situation where they have limited power and access to economic assets to a situation where they experience economic advancement'.

MICROFINANCE AND WOMEN EMPOWERMENT

The agenda of microfinance as a tool for women empowerment was electrified in 2005 in Nigeria as a result of the deficiency and inability of the formal financial institutions to provide credit and other financial services to the poor and vulnerable. Women's access to financial services is fundamental in enhancing women's economic opportunities. However, there seems to be a wide access gap between men and women especially in developing countries. Granting that global access to financial services has increased, gender access gap also increased between 2011 and 2014 in South Asia, MENA and Sub-Saharan Africa (Gonzales et al., 2015). Although Nigeria has a higher level of financial inclusion than Sub-Saharan Africa, the country recorded a higher access gap than that of Sub-Saharan (Word Bank Global Findex, 2014). As a corollary, the government in recent time instituted micro-financing schemes to empower the poor especially women. Traditionally, Nigerians have always provided themselves some kind of micro-financing through Door-to-Door Deposit Collection, Self-Help Groups and Group Based Microfinance Programs among others. But the inherent ambiguities coupled with the problem of information asymmetry in these financial arrangements propelled the Nigerian government in 2005 to introduce some microfinance policies and institutions. These institutions were, however, licensed to operate in 2007 to provide such financial services as credit, micro-leasing, savings, money transfer and payment services (Eboh, 2008). Thus, microfinance can be seen as those informal financial institutions that make access to credit or financial services by rural and poor households easy with little or no collateral. Also, Sahu and Datta (2017) defined microfinance as those institutions that provide financial services to low-income clients, including the self-employed.

Theoretical Literature

In establishing the nexus between women empowerment and microfinance, there has been broad unanimity among development economists and scholars on the promise of two similar but rather distinct theories: the "Social Capital Theory" and the "Group Lending Model". The World Bank (2001) defined the social capital theory "as local forms of association that express trust and norms of reciprocity – can contribute significantly to the alleviation of poverty worldwide". The hypothetical relevance of this theory lies in its bottom up approach to development by recognizing social networks and associations that can speed-up development by offering its members access to financial services by means of social collateral. Findings by one of the proponents of this theory, Putnam (1993), confirmed that associational networks within the society correlate positively with the indicators of economic growth in Italy and North America. He, however, linked the political malaise and economic stagnation that was prevalent in the United States to the declining stocks of social capital in neighborhoods and communities. In lieu of the probably positive outcome, the World Bank and other development agencies are campaigning new approaches to development which is microfinance. The essence is not just for the poor to have access to credit on the basis of their membership in social groups, but also to target women in their services and advancement of loans. A more dominant model which has gained widespread acceptance by mainstream development agencies is the Group Lending Model or what is popularly known as the "Grameen model" pioneered by the Grameen Bank in Bangladesh. Though the model targets unions and solidarity groups, women receive credit by "group guarantee or solidarity". Since women are disadvantaged and lack the collateral to obtain loans from conventional financial institutions, this model therefore implies that women who participate in group lending have greater access to financial services and loan as the financial discipline instilled in them through peer pressure motivates them to repay (Yaron, 1991). Servon (1998), noted that the theory affords the poor both economic payoff (increased access to financial services) and empowerment payoff.

Empirical Literature

With the paradigm shift in approaches to poverty alleviation and women empowerment - from access to credit for male-headed households to microfinance institutions whose target are poor rural women - there has been a proliferation of microfinance programmes in women empowerment in Nigeria. The success stories of micro-finance in women empowerment in Bangladesh and Indonesia triggered the Nigeria governments' series of empowerment programmes; Peoples' Bank, Better Life for Rural Women and Poverty Alleviation Programme (PAP), Family Economic Advancement Programme (FEAP), etc. Though a contentious issue, so many studies have either lent empirical evidence or disputed the validity of the hypothesis that microfinance empowers women.

Recent studies empirically established that microfinancing is fundamental to women empowerment. For instance, Gangadhar, Bhat and Malyadri (2017) studied the impact of microfinance on women's awareness of some empowerment factors (health awareness, political awareness, right to legal protection and property right awareness) in the pre-loan and post-loan period. The study found that contrary to the pre-loan period, women's health awareness and awareness of their right to justice increased exponentially after participation in the microfinance program. They concluded that microfinance (with particular reference to Self-Help Groups) through seminars, workshops and symposiums does not just improve the health condition of women and their family members, but also increase their awareness of right to seek legal protection from abuse and violence. The study, however, found negative results for property right awareness. Also, Saravanan and Dash (2017) in their study established that Self-Help Groups (SHGs) and women labour force participation are complementary in their effect. According to them, women labour force participation, savings rate, literacy rate and per capita income positively influence women's decision to form Self-Help Groups. This in turn encourages the establishment of micro and small enterprises. Furthermore, the study of Roy and Biswas (2016) titled "Women Empowerment through SHGs and Financial Inclusion: A Case Study on Lataguri Region in West Bengal" lends evidence that Self-Help Groups have an enormous impact on financial inclusion and empowerment of rural women. According to them, membership of Self-Help Groups increased the number of savings account opened, the number and magnitude of loans taken for the purchase of such machineries as sewing machines and their involvement in household or family purchases. The women become both economically and socially empowered.

Earlier studies, on the other hand, concentrated on the fact that limited access to financial services could impoverish women. For example, Alila (1993) found low purchasing powers in the rural areas, poor management skills and poor infrastructural facilities as the major setback to women empowerment. Corroborating this, K-REP (1995) identified lack of access to credit and lack of training on the management of borrowed fund as the key inhibitor to women successful venture in business. Taking into consideration the prevalent condition in most developing countries where most women are poor, lack access to education and suffer social discrimination (Porter & Nagarajan, 2005; Roomi & Parrot, 2008), Akanji (2006) and Kuzilwa (2005) found training to be an integral part of micro-finance for women entrepreneurs as it would provide the much-needed skills and experience for business purposes. Alila (1993) further noted that limited or no capital, insufficient working capital, poor infrastructural facilities, lack of managerial and technical skills, etc., are some of the teething problems experienced by women at the early stages of their business life cycle.

On the other hand, Mayoux (2001) linked acquisition of increased assets and improved welfare in housing, food security and health to increased access to micro credit and trainings on management skills. This contrasts his early findings that micro-credit to women does not appreciably cause positive improvement and development (Mayoux, 1997). A plausible explanation for the earlier finding could be misappropriation of funds or channeling of funds into ceremonies. Majoor and Mendes (2009) in a Kenyan study found that 17 out of the 18 women sampled were already empowered. According to one of the women interviewed, micro-finance empowers women, increases their knowledge and education. Also, the empirical evidence from Heshemi et al. (1996), Mayoux (1999), Hunt and Kasynathan (2002), Holvoet (2003), Montgomery and Weiss (2005), Taha (2010), and Awojobi (2013) confirmed the positive relationship between micro-credits and women empowerment.

Contrary to the views of the optimist, Kumar (2006) found that Micro-finance institutions pave way for what seems to be an unending vicious circle of poverty and debt through the imposition of high interest rate, though Julien (2009) and Chun (2013) argued otherwise by linking high interest rates to operational cost, loss of loans and profit maximization. Supporting Kumar, Dobra (2011) found no significant correlation between micro-finance and women's empowerment. Going by the definition of empowerment by McWhirter (1991) - empowerment is a state of awareness of power by people who hitherto lack power; Dobra argues that if empowerment is all about awareness of power, then empowerment has not occurred. Mitra (2005), Rhyne (2001), Shylendra (2006) and Sinha and Matin (1998) lend empirical evidence to Kumar's postulations. Vengroff and Creevet (1994), Goetz and Gupta (1996) and Rahman (1999) suggest that the relationship between micro-finance and women's empowerment is rather negative.

The microfinance cum women empowerment literature known to us in Nigeria concentrated on such issues as impact of microfinance on entrepreneurial development (Carl & Agboola, 2012), the impact of micro-finance banks on women entrepreneurial development in metropolis (Abdulkadir et al., 2012), microfinance banking in Nigeria: problems and prospects (Acha, 2012) and empowering women through micro-finance: evidence from Nigeria (Awojobi, 2014). Carl and Agboola (2012) posit that globally and in Nigeria, in particular, microfinance institutions play a key role in the financial industry. According to them, through the services they offer, individuals, other financial institutions, business enterprises, the government and the economy are positively affected. Awojobi, (2014) found that the quality of life of about 65% of respondents improved. This increased standard of living was linked to employment and income generation. The loan obtained from microfinance banks were used for both establishment of new business and/or for expansion of existing business and these in turn create new income levels. Awojobi also found that 77.5% of the respondents acquired 'power over' lack of economic resources. They therefore do not depend solely on their spouse to provide their children education and to access health facilities.

From the wealth of literature available to us, not much Nigerian studies have been done in the area of microfinance and women empowerment nexus. Most of the studies focused more on the problems and promise of microfinancing. Also, other studies gleaned from literature were met with mixed results. It is therefore against this backdrop that this paper seeks to elucidate the possible impact of microfinancing on women empowerment.

OBJECTIVE OF STUDY

The main objective of this chapter is to determine how microfinance has affected and impacted on the wellbeing of women in Nigeria.

SOURCE OF DATA

The study employs cross sectional secondary data from the World Bank micro data on financial inclusion survey for 2014 (the Global Fundex survey data set) to attain its objectives. The Global Findex database provides in-depth data on how individuals save, borrow, make payments, and manage risks. It is the world's most comprehensive database on financial inclusion that consistently measures people's use of financial services across countries and over time. The 2014 Global Findex consists of over 100 indicators, also shown by gender, income, and age hence, was instrumental to this study.

METHODOLOGY

The method of analysis for this study is the propensity score matching. Propensity score matching technique was used in ascertaining the impact of women access to microfinance and how it has affected their welfare and poverty. Propensity score matching in its simplest form involves predicting the probability of treatment on the basis of observed covariates for both the treatment and the control group samples (Rawlings & Schady, 2002). In propensity score matching, one picks an ideal comparison group from a larger survey and then matches the comparison group to the treatment group on the basis of set of observed characteristics on the predicted probability of participation given observed characteristics (propensity score) (Ravallion, 2001). The observed characteristics are those used in selecting individuals but not affected by programme participation and act as the control variables.

Matching, according to researchers, is a design option that can be used in both experimental and non-experimental studies to: (i) balance data, (ii) reduce or eliminate selection bias, (iii) gain precision in the estimation of an effect measure of interest, (iv) control for variables or covariates that are difficult to measure, and (v) for other practical aspects of data collection such as convenience, time-saving, and cost-saving (Guo & Fraser, 2010; Stuart & Rubin, 2007; Rosenbaum & Rubin, 1983; Rubin, 1974). However, Kleinbaum, Sullivan, and Barker (2007) show that matching (i) can enable data balancing thus reducing or removing the confounding effect of a covariate or variable and (ii) can help in gaining precision by allowing an estimation of a narrower confidence interval around the effect measure that could have been obtained without matching.

Joffe and Rosenbaum, (1999) and D'Agostino (1998) opine that the overall objective of a matching procedure is to reduce sampling bias which emanate from non-random assignment between treatment and control group. This matching exercise helps to draw a comparison group that is as similar as possible to the treatment group except for exposure to the experimental condition(s) (Rubin, 1980; Dehejia & Wahba, 2000; Rosenbaum, 2002).

Those with access to microfinance (treated) are matched to those without (control group) on the basis of the propensity score: (probability of having access to microfinance given observed characteristics)

$$P(x_i) = prob\left(R_i = 1 \mid x_i\right); \left(0 < p(x_i) < 1\right) \quad (1)$$

where xi is a vector of access to microfinance control variables. If the R_i's are independent over all i, and the outcomes are independent of access to microfinance given xi then outcomes are also independent of access to microfinance given p(xi), just as they would be if access to microfinance were transferred randomly.

Propensity score matching is a better methodology for dealing with differences in population characteristics. However, a few tests that have been done suggest that with good data, propensity score matching can greatly reduce the overall bias and outperform regression-based methods (Ravallion, 2001).

The estimation of the average treatment effect on the treated (ATT) based on the propensity score matching for with and without access to microfinance was carried out based on the following procedures:

1. 1. Pooling of two groups of individuals, that is, the treatment and comparison group of those who have access to microfinance and those who do not have access. After the pooling, a logit model of women empowerment due to access to microfinance and non-access to microfinance as a func-

tion of some socio-economic variables will be estimated. Some of the socio-economic variables included are Age, Education of female respondent, saving in informal saving club, Mobile money account, Accounts in other finance institutions, saved for education fees, and Saved for farm/business purpose. The equation is presented thus:

$$P_i = \log\frac{P_i}{1-P_i} = \log O_i = \alpha_i + \beta_1 Age + \qquad (2)$$

2. From the logit regression, a predicted value of the probability of having been empowered through access to microfinance was created. These were the propensity scores and each individual had a propensity score.
3. For each woman empowered through microfinance, a non-empowered woman that has the closest propensity score, as measured by the absolute difference in scores, referred to as nearest neighbor was obtained. For more precise estimate, the nearest five neighbors were used. Thus, the nearest neighbor matching was used.
4. The mean values of the outcome indicator (per capita expenditures) for the nearest neighbors were calculated. The difference between the mean and actual value for the empowered women through microfinance (beneficiaries) is the estimate of the gain due to access to microfinance.
5. The mean of individual gains is calculated to obtain the average overall gain i.e. the average treatment effect on the treated (ATT).

RESULTS AND DISCUSSION

The study therefore proceeded to analyse the results as presented below, with the STATA output.

The results in table 1 show a relatively low Pseudo R^2, but a significant model at 1% level of significance given the chi^2 probability of 0.0000. This means that the overall model is significant and conforms to the Hosmer and Lemeshow's (1989) goodness of fit test. However, the results suggest that out of 8 that were examined, there exist at least three significant indicators that determine how microfinance impact on the wellbeing of women in Nigeria.

The study shows that there is significant relationship between age and women wellbeing in increasing the log of odds that a woman access microfinance. In fact, the study opines that an increase by a woman that access microfinance relative to those that do not increases the log of odds that a woman wellbeing increase by approximately 0.32 given its z-value of 2.89 which is greater than 1.96 and probability value of 0.004 which is less than 0.05, hence significant at 5% significant level.

Education is equally a positive significant indicator of how microfinance according to the results illustrated by Table 1. This means therefore that the higher the educational level, the greater the log of odds that women will have access to microfinance, as expected a priori given that some who do not have access to finance lack information or shy away from exposing their inability to read and/or write (illiteracy) in most cases. The higher the education level of women, the more empowered they are and the more they access finance from microfinance banks. This shows that the level of education positively correlates with women empowerment and access to finance from microfinance banks. Education is therefore an eye-opener for many and a confidence booster to take credits as opportunities and possibilities when all

Table 1. First stage propensity score: Logit regression results

Variables	Coefficient	Z	P>/z/
Age	0.0032997	2.89	0.004
Education level of female respondent	0.1443483	4.33	0.000
Saved in informal saving club	0.0566818	2.55	0.002
Loan from fin insti for apartment	0.0662148	1.19	0.233
Mobile money account– Yes	0.118707	1.29	0.199
Account finance– Yes	0.1253615	3.59	0.000
Saved for education fees	-0.0083915	-0.25	0.806
Saved for farm/business purpose	0.0341137	1.02	0.308
Constant	1.794841	7.83	0.000
Log Likelihood -686.60056			
Pseudo R^2 0.5323			
Prob> chi2 0.0000			

Source: Regression Output from Stata 13 Software

the necessary conditions are satisfied. This also translates to the women wellbeing hence, significantly impact on the woman wellbeing.

The results also suggest that savings in the informal saving club significantly impact on women wellbeing and hence empower them. The findings show that a unit increase in savings in the informal saving club significantly increases the log of odds that women wellbeing improves by 0.0566818. It is a significant determinant given that its z-value is given as 2.55 (greater than 1.96) and its probability value of 0.002 (less than 0.05), hence significant at 5% significant level. Women who belong to local saving associations know more about access to finance apart from their personal saving and therefore are likely to patronize the microfinance banks for credits, due to the fact that they have more awareness of external finance. Through this method (sourcing external finance) they become more empowered and their welfare improved more than their counterparts who do not belong to any such association, thus, remain unaware of possibility of external finance.

Furthermore, the results show that females with functional account have significant opportunity for empowerment than those who do not have and thus have the increase in the log of odds of wellbeing. The account finance variable was recorded as a dummy and was examined as such an important variable because having functional account implies that those who have functional accounts are enlightened and can access micro-credits from microfinance banks. This led to the omission of female with no account finance category as the bench category, and the female with account finance category stipulated to be interpreted with respect to their female counterparts. As women who have functional accounts increase by one unit, the log of odds that a woman improves on her wellbeing increases by 0.1253615, hence, significant at 5% significant level.

However, women who have ever obtained loans from other financial institutions for erecting apartments do not show any significant relationship with women empowerment. For the women who already collect loans from other institutions, they are already empowered and for this reason, the variable does not show any significant relationship with women empowerment and welfare improvement. In the same vein, women who have mobile accounts also are already empowered and may not have any need for microfinance assistance. This may constitute the reason why these variables are not statistically significant, even though they have a positive relationship.

Also, the variable, women who save for the education of their family members, has a positive link with women empowerment, although statistically not significant. This might be that women who save for education are already empowered and need no more empowerment. Similarly, women who save for their business (a variable) has a positive relationship with women empowerment but statistically not significant. It might mean that this group of women may not need the services of the microfinance, having established themselves for businesses.

Presentation of the Average Treatment Result on the Treated

The second stage results show the treatment effect of the treated group (the group that had access to microfinance) on women wellbeing in Nigeria. The results below therefore illustrate the extent microfinance impacted on women empowerment, poverty and inequality in Nigeria.

The results on table 2 suggest that there exists significant impact of microfinance on women empowerment, poverty and inequality in Nigeria. This is implied due to the t-value of the Average Treatment Effect on the Treated (ATT) given as 2.626 which is greater than 1.96 and hence, significant at the standard 5% level of significance. The result showing the average overall gain in welfare per capita due to access to microfinance (step 5 as described in the analytical framework) after the nearest neighbor matches of propensity scores obtained after the logit analysis is presented in Table 2. The result shows that the average treatment effect on the treated (ATT), that is, average gain in welfare per capita by women who have access to microfinance, using nearest neighbor matches is 0.261. This shows that those who have access to microfinance gained by 0.261 improvement in welfare after the matches.

The result in table 3 shows the level of disparity among women decomposed into those that actively participate in financial institution and those with mobile money account for both formal and informal

Table 2. Second stage propensity score: Results of the average treatment effect on the treated (ATT)

No. treated	No. control	ATT	Std.Err.	t
4,481	10,832	0.261	0.161	2.626

Source: Regression Output from Stata 13 Software

Table 3. Pyatt's inequality decomposition result

Design and Groups	Indices	Part
Decomposition		
Between	0.025	10.170
Overlap	0.098	39.775
Within	0.123	50.054
Total Gini	0.246	100.000
Gini coefficient by subgroups of female	0.263	

Source: Regression Output from Stata 13 Software

financial institution. The result shows that access to liquidity helps them meet their welfare needs. This is likely due to the fact that some of the women receive both local and international remittance through their mobile money accounts; hence this makes them better off than those without such interventions. Other ways of access to liquidity also include borrowing, savings, and mobile purchase and payments. This to a large extent is meant to improve women's wellbeing in rural areas through small business, and farming businesses but the evidence from the result showed otherwise as huge disparity exist among the women with such access and those without (given by 0.263 indices) showing the level of disparity that exist among rural women in Nigeria.

CONCLUSION AND POLICY SUGGESTIONS

We have seen from this study that financial services from the microfinance banks empower and improve the welfare of women in Nigeria. Women who benefit from the financial services rendered by these microfinance institutions have been shown to start small businesses, take decisions on household necessities, and contribute to the income increase of households. When women begin to earn income, no matter how little, they contribute to the purchase of household's nutrition needs (without waiting for the household head), take decisions on some things that affect them, contribute to other household's welfare needs. All these are part of what the microfinance banks do to the women, especially when they have access to finance through micro-credits rendered to them by the microfinance banks. Other formal financial institutions (commercial banks) deny poor women access to finance due to the inability of these women to provide collaterals which are required before credits are granted.

The propensity score matching, and the logistic regression show that microfinance institutions (MFIs) empower women and alleviate their poverty. Form the findings of this study, it could be seen that the age of women is a determinant of their access to micro-credits, thus giving them access to finance their businesses or spending. Similarly, it was found that education of women gives them leverage to be able to demand for micro-credits from these MFIs, thus showing that women who are enlightened stand better chances to benefit from the services of MFIs. Also, women who belong to informal savings associations have more chances from accessing finances provided by these MFIs. This is because they might wish to augment the little saving they accumulated from the clubs which they belong. Another determinant of women empowerment and welfare improvement through access to finances from the MFIs is when they have accounts with the banks. When women have transactions with MFIs, they are treated better than those who are somewhat strange to the banks.

The implications of the findings are that policies directed at MFIs so as to be women friendly would attract more women, thus empowering them to support their families, become self-employed, take decisions on family matters, etc. It is therefore recommended that more MFIs should be cited in the rural sector where the majority of the poor reside. This will help empower the rural women, and give them a voice in their families, alleviate their poverty and improve their standard of living. We also recommend that appropriate policies should be put in place to help women have access to finances provided by the MFIs – low interest rates, national orientation programmes to enlighten women, creation of incentives for women who access credits for these MFIs.

REFERENCES

Abdulkadir, F. I., Umar, S., Garba, B. I., & Ibrahim, S. H. (2012). The Impact of Micro-finance Banks on Women Entrepreneurial Development in Metropolis. *Scientific and Academic Publishing.*, *1*(3), 28–38.

Acha, I. A. (2012). Microfinance Banking in Nigeria: Problems and Prospects. *International Journal of Finance and Accounting*, *1*(5), 106–111.

Ackerly, B. A. (1995). Testing the Tools of Development: Credit Programmes, Loan Involvement and Women's Empowerment. In *Getting Institutions Right for Women in Development*. IDS. doi:10.1111/j.1759-5436.1995.mp26003007.x

Akanji, O. O. (2006). Microfinance as A Strategy for Poverty Reduction, *Central Bank of Nigeria Economic and Financial Review*, *39*(4).

Akinsanmi, A. (2005). Working under Constraint: Women, Poverty and Productivity. *Women and Environments International*, *66/67*, 17–18.

Akintoye, I. R., & Owojori, K. (2009), Microfinance Banking System: A Counsel to the Nigerian Populace. *Paper presented at the 6th African Finance Journal Conference*, Cape Town, South Africa. July 16-17.

Albee, A. (1994). Support to Women's Productive and Income Generating Activities. UNICEF Evaluation and Research.

Alila, P. O. (1993). Informed credit and Rural Enterprise Sector Development.

Anjugam, M., & Alagumani, T. (2001). Impact of Micro Finance through Self Help Groups: A Case Study. *Indian Journal of Agricultural Economics*, *56*(3), 458.

Asemelash, B. (2002). The Impact of Microfinance in Ethiopia: The case of DCSI in Ganta Afeshum Woreda of Eastern Tigray. Unpublished MA thesis, Addis Ababa University, Ethiopia.

Awojobi, N. O. (2013). Microfinance as a Strategy for Poverty Reduction: The Nigerian Experience [Master Thesis]. Berlin School of Economics and Law, Berlin, Germany.

Awojobi, N. O. (2014). Empowering women through Micro-finance: Evidence from Nigeria. *Australian Journal of Business and Management Research*, *4*(1), 17–26.

Basu, J. P. (2006). *Microfinance and Women Empowerment: An Empirical Study with special Reference to West Bengal*. Mumbai, India: Indira Gandhi Institute of Development Research.

Batliwala, S. (1994). The Meaning of Women's Empowerment: New Concepts from Action. In G. Sen, A. Germain & L.C. Chen (Eds.), Population Policies Reconsidered: Health, Empowerment and Rights. Cambridge: Harvard University Press.

Biswas, T. (2008). Women Empowerment through Micro Finance: A Boon for Development. *Social Welfare*, *55*(8).

Blumberg, R. L. (2005). Women's Economic Empowerment as the "Magic Potion" of Development? University of Virginia and University of California, San Diego, Paper presented at the 100th Annual Meeting of the American Sociological Association Philadelphia, August 2005.

Bradshaw, Y. W. (1998). Small Enterprises: Flexibility and Networking in an African Context.

Canadian International Development Agency (CIDA). (1999). *CIDA's Policy on Gender Equality*. Quebec: CIDA.

Carrl, O. & Agboola, G.M. (2012) Microfinance and Entrepreneurial Development in Nigeria. *JORIND*, *10*(3).

Chun, S. (2013). Why do Microfinance Institutions Charge High Interest Rates? An Empirical Assessment of the Fixed Cost Theory. Michigan State University.

Cornwall, A., & Edwards, J. (2016). Introduction: Negotiating empowerment. *IDS Bulletin*, *47*(21A). Retrieved from http://bulletin.ids.ac.uk/idsbo/article/view/1355/PDF doi:10.19088/1968-2016.123

D'Agostino, R. B. (1998). Tutorial in Biostatistics: Propensity Score Methods for Bias Reduction in the Comparison of a Treatment to a Non-Randomized Control Group. *Statistics in Medicine*, *17*(19), 2265–2281. doi:10.1002/(SICI)1097-0258(19981015)17:19<2265::AID-SIM918>3.0.CO;2-B PMID:9802183

Dehejia, R. H., & Wahba, S. (2000). Causal Effects in Non-Experimental Studies: Re-evaluating the Evaluation of Training Programmmes. *Journal of the American Statistical Association*, *4*(10), 53–62.

Demirguc-Kunt, A., Klapper, L., Singer, D., & van Oudheusden, P. (2014). Measuring Financial Inclusion around the World. The Global Findex Database 2014. Policy Research Working Paper 7255.

DFID. (2000). *Poverty Elimination and the Empowerment of Women: Strategies for Achieving the International Development Targets*. London: DFID.

Dobra, A. (2011). Microfinance: Champion in Poverty Alleviation and Failure in Female Empowerment. *International Politik und Geseflschaft*, *3*(3), 134-144.

Eboh, E. F. (2008). Changing Development Paradigms via Microfinance Banks. *African Journal of Entrepreneurship*, *1*(1), 52–63.

Ekpe, I., Mat, N.B. & Razaq, R.C. (2010). The Effect of Microfinance Factors on Women Entrepreneurs' Performance in Nigeria: A Conceptual Framework.

Gangadhar, S., Bhat, M. S., & Malyadri, P. (2017). An Empirical Study on Microfinance and Women Empowerment in Karimnagar District of Telangana State, India. *CSCanada International Business and Management*, *14*(2), 65–69.

Goetz, A. M., & Sen Gupta, R. (1996). Who takes the Credit? Gender, Power and Control over Loan use in Rural Credit Programs in Bangladesh. *World Development*, *24*(1), 45–63. doi:10.1016/0305-750X(95)00124-U

Gonzales, C., Jain-Chandra, S., Kochhar, K., Newiak, M., & Zeinullayev, T. (2015). *Catalyst for change: Empowering women and tackling income inequality. Staff Discussion Note*. Washington, DC: IMF.

Guo, S., & Fraser, M. W. (2010). *Propensity Score Analysis: Statistical Methods and Applications*. Sage Publications.

Gurumoorthy, T. R. (2000). Self-Help Groups Empower Rural Women. *Kurukshetra, 48*(5), 31-37.

Hashemi, S. M., Schuler, S. R., & Riley, A. P. (1996). Rural Credit Programs and Women's Empowerment in Bangladesh. *World Development, 24*(4), 635–653. doi:10.1016/0305-750X(95)00159-A

Holloway, K., Niazi, Z. & Rouse, R. (2017). Women's Economic Empowerment Through Financial Inclusion: A Review of Existing Evidence and Remaining Knowledge Gaps. Financial Inclusion Program Innovations for Poverty Action (IPA).

Holt, S. L. (1994). The Village Bank Methodology: Performance and Prospects. In M. Otero & E. Rhyne (Eds.), *The New World of Micro-Enterprise Finance* (pp. 156–204). London: IT Publications.

Holvoet, N. (2003). The Impact of Microfinance on Decision-Making Agency: Evidence from South India. *Development and Change, 36*(1).

Holvoet, N. (2005). The Impact of Microfinance on Decision-Making Agency: Evidence from South India. *Development and Change, 36*(1), 75–102. doi:10.1111/j.0012-155X.2005.00403.x

Hosmer, D. W., & Lemeshow, S. (1989). *Applied Logistic Regression* (2nd ed.). New York: Wiley.

Hunt, J., & Kasynathan, N. (2002). Reflections on Microfinance and Women's Empowerment. *Development Bulletin (Canberra), 57*, 71–75.

Iganiga, B. O. (2008). Much Ado about Nothing: The Case of the Nigerian Microfinance

Jahan, R. (1995). *The Elusive Agenda: Mainstreaming Women in Development.* Atlantic Highlands, NJ: Zed Books Ltd.

Joffe, M. M., & Rosenbaum, P. R. (1999). Propensity Scores. *American Journal of Epidemiology, 150*(4), 327–333. doi:10.1093/oxfordjournals.aje.a010011 PMID:10453808

Julien, K. (2009). A Look at Interest Rates in Microfinance. Retrieved from https://www.academia.edu/1044113/A_Look_at_Interest_Rates_in_Microfinance

K-REP. (1995). Employment and Income in Micro and Small Enterprises in Kenya. Results of a 1995 Survey (Research Paper No. 26).

Kabeer, N. (2001). Discussing Women's Empowerment. SIDA Studies 136 (2001).

Kabeer, N. (2005). Is Microfinance a 'Magic Bullet' for Women's Empowerment? Analysis of Findings from South Asia. *Economic and Political Weekly*, 4709–4718.

Kato, M. P., & Kratze, J. (2013). Empowering Women through Microfinance: Evidence from Tanzania. *ACRN Journal of Entrepreneurship Perspectives, 2*(1), 31-59.

Kefas, S.D. (2006), Fighting Poverty through Empowering Women with Microfinance, *A Quarterly Newsletter of International Year of Microcredit, 2*.

Khandker, S. R., Hussain, S., & Zahed, K. (1998). Income and Employment Effects of Micro-Credit Programmes:Village-level Evidence from Bangladesh. *The Journal of Development Studies, 35*(2), 96–124. doi:10.1080/00220389808422566

Kimotho, M. W. (2007). The Key Success Factors in Microfinance: Wide Outreach and Long-Term Sustainability. The Nigerian Microfinance, 4.

Kleinbaum, D. G., Sullivan, K. M., & Barker, N. D. (2007). *A Pocket Guide to Epidemiology*. New York: Springer Science and Business Media, LLC.

Krishna, A. (2003). Social Capital, Community driven Development and Empowerment: A Short Note on Concepts and Operations (*Working Paper* 33077). *World Bank*.

Kumar, R. (1993). *The History of Doing: An Illustrated Account of Movements for Women's Rights and Feminism in India, 1800-1990*. New York: Verso.

Kumar, S. N. (2006, April 20). The Making of Debt Trap in Andhra Pradesh. The Hindu. Retrieved from www.hindu.com/2006/04/20/stories/2006042005220900.htm

Kumari, G. L., & Subrahmanyam, S. (2017). Women Empowerment through Financial Inclusion – A Study with Reference to YSR Kadapa District of Andhra Pradesh. *International Journal of Applied Research*, *3*(4), 509–513.

Kuzilwa, J. (2005). The role of credit for small business success: A study of the National Entrepreneurship Development Fund in Tanzania. *The Journal of Entrepreneurship*, *14*(2), 131–161. doi:10.1177/097135570501400204

Ledgerwood, J. (1999). *Microfinance Handbook: An Institutional and Financial Perspective*. Washington, DC: World Bank.

Manjoor, H., & Manders, J. (2009). *Women Empowerment: Comparing concepts & Assessment Implications for microfinance*. Commissioned by Oiko Credit.

Marr, A. (2002). Studying Group Dynamics: An Alternative Framework for the Study of Microfinance Impacts on Poverty Reduction. *Journal of International Development, 14(4), 511-534.*

Mayoux, L. (1997). The Magic Ingredient? Microfinance and Women's Empowerment, A Briefing. Paper prepared for the Micro Credit Summit, Washington.

Mayoux, L. (1999). Questioning virtuous Spirals: Microfinance and Women's Empowerment in Africa. *Journal of International Development*.

Mayoux, L. (2001). *Impact assessment of microfinance: Towards a sustainable learning process. Enterprise Development Impact Assessment Service*. EDIAS.

Mayoux, L. (2005). Women Empowerment through Sustainable Micro-Finance: Rethinking Best Practice.

Mayoux, L., & Hartl, M. (2009). Gender and Rural Microfinance: Reaching and Empowering Women, Guide for practitioners. International Fund for Agricultural Development (IFAD), Powerguda, India.

McWhirter, E.H. (1991). Empowerment, in Counselling. *Journal of Counselling and Development, 69*, 222-227.

Mitra, S. K. (2005). Asking Price of Microfinance Loan to Poor Borrowers (Working Paper 191). Institute of Rural Management, Anand, India.

Montgomery, H., & Weiss, J. (2005). Great Expectations: Microfinance and Poverty Reduction in Asia and Latin America (Research Paper Series No. 63). ADB Institute, Manila.

Nana, O. (2008). Microfinance Product Development in Ghana: The Innovative And Unique Dimensions of Kraban Support Foundation's Microloan Products. *Paper presented at the Third Microfinance Conference*, January 10-11, Elmina Beach Resort, Ghana.

Narender, K. (2007). Microfinance for poverty reduction-the Dhan Foundation Experience. In M. Self-employment & P. Alleviation (Eds.), *Kamdar* (pp. 205–226). Mumbai: Himalaya Publishing House.

Nessa, T., Ali, J., & Hakim, R. A. (2012). The Impact of Microcredit Programme on Women Empowerment: Evidence from Bangladesh. Ontario International Development Agency. Retrieved from http://www.ssrn.com/link/OIDA-Intl-JournalSustainable-Dev.html

Nirmala, C. R., & Debasish, B. (2016). Women Empowerment through SHGs and Financial Inclusion: A Case Study on Lataguri Region in West Bengal. *International Journal of Management Research and Review.*, *6*(6), 827–834.

O'Neil, T., Domingo, P., & Valters, C. (2014). *Progress on women's empowerment: From technical fixes to political action*. London: ODI.

Onwumere, J.U.J. (2008). Microfinance and Developing the Nigerian Economy. The Nigerian Banker, October – December.

Otero, M. (1999). Bringing Development Back into Microfinance. Latin America: ACCION International.

Owojori, A. A. & Oladejo, M. O. (2009). Re-engineering cooperative societies for sustainable small and medium business growth and development in Nigeria.

Porter, E. G., & Nagarajan, K. V. (2005). Successful women entrepreneurs as pioneers: Results from a study conducted in Karaikudi, Tamil Nadu, India. *Journal of Small Business and Entrepreneurship*, *18*(1), 39–52. doi:10.1080/08276331.2005.10593331

Putnam, R. (1993). *Making Democracy Work: Civic Traditions in Modern Italy*. Princeton, NJ: Princeton University Press.

Qazi, M. (2007). Microfinance and Woman's Empowerment. In M. Self-Employment & P. Alleviation (Eds.), *Kamdar* (pp. 158–177). Mumbai: Himalaya Publishing House.

Rahman, A. (1999). Micro-Credit Initiatives for Equitable and Sustainable Development. *World Development*, *27*(1), 67–82. Retrieved from http://EconPapers.repec.org/Repec:wdevel:v:27:1999:i:1:67-82 doi:10.1016/S0305-750X(98)00105-3

Ravallion, M. (2001). The Mystery of the Vanishing Benefits: An Introduction to Impact Evaluation. *The World Bank Economic Review*, *15*(1), 115–140. doi:10.1093/wber/15.1.115

Rawlings, L., & Schady, N. R. (2002). Impact Evaluation of Social Funds: An Introduction. *The World Bank Economic Review*, *16*(2), 213–217. doi:10.1093/wber/16.2.213

Rhyne, E. (2001). *Mainstreaming Microfinance: How Lending Began, Grew and Came of Age in Bolivia*. Bloomfield: Kumarian Press.

Roomi, M. A., & Parrot, G. (2008). Barriers to development and progression of women entrepreneurs in Pakistan. *The Journal of Entrepreneurship*, *17*(1), 59–72. doi:10.1177/097135570701700105

Rosenbaum, P. R. (2002). Observational studies (2nd ed.). New York: Springer. doi:10.1007/978-1-4757-3692-2

Rosenbaum, P. R., & Rubin, D. B. (1983). The Central Role of the Propensity Score in Observational Studies for Causal Effects. *Biometrika*, *70*(1), 41–45. doi:10.1093/biomet/70.1.41

Rosenberg, R. (2007). CGAP Reflections on the Compartamos Initial Public Offering: A Case Study on Microfinance Interest Rates and Profits (Focus Note 42). CGAP.

Rowland, Jo. (1997). *Questioning Empowerment.* Oxford: Oxfam. doi:10.3362/9780855988364

Rubin, D. B. (1974). Estimating Causal Effects to Treatments Randomized and Nonrandomized Studies. *Journal of Educational Psychology*, *66*(5), 688–701. doi:10.1037/h0037350

Rubin, D. B. (1980). Bias Reduction using Mahalanobis - Metric Matching. *Biometrics*, *36*(2), 293–298. doi:10.2307/2529981

Sarangi, N. (2007). *Microfinance and Rural Poor: Impact Assessment Based on Field Work in Madhya Pradesh, India.* New Delhi, India: CSRD, Jawhar Lal Nehru University.

Saravanan, S., & Dash, D. P. (2017). Microfinance and Women Empowerment-Empirical Evidence from the Indian States. *Regional and Sectoral Economic Studies.*, *17*(2), 61–74.

Schicks, J. (2010). Microfinance Over-Indebtedness: Understanding its Drivers and Challenging the Common Myths (Working Paper N° 10/048 2010). Centre Emile Bernheim (CEB).

Schmidt, R. (2010). Microfinance, Commercialization and Ethics. *Poverty & Public Policy*, *2*(1). doi:10.2202/1944-2858.1020

Sen, G., & Grown, C. (1987). *Development, Crises, and Alternative Visions: Third World Women's Perspectives*. New York: Monthly Review Press.

Servon, L. J. (1998). Credit and Social Capital: The Community Development Potential of U.S. Microenterprise Programs. *Housing Policy Debate*, *9*(1), 115–149. doi:10.1080/10511482.1998.9521288

Sharma, P. R. (2007). Micro-finance and Women Empowerment. *The Journal of Nepalese Business Studies*, *4*(1), 16–27. doi:10.3126/jnbs.v4i1.1026

Shylendra, H. S. (2006, May 20). Microfinance institutions in Andhra Pradesh: Crisis and diagnosis. *Economic and Political Weekly*, 1959–1963.

Sing, G (2009). Microfinance – An Innovation in Rural Credit System. *Kurukshetra*, Feb., 3-6.

Sinha, S., & Matin, I. (1998). Informal Credit Transactions of Microcredit Borrowers in Bangaldesh. *IDS Bulletin*, *29*(4), 66–80. doi:10.1111/j.1759-5436.1998.mp29004008.x

Stuart, E. A., & Rubin, D. B. (2007). Best Practices in Quasi-Experimental Designs: Matching Methods for Causal Inference. In J. Osborne (Ed.), *Best Practices in Quantitative Social Science* (pp. 155–176). Thousand Oaks, CA: Sage Publications.

Swain, R. B. (2007). Impacting Women through Microfinance. *Dialogue, Appui au Developpement Autonome*, 37.

Swain, R. B., & Wallentin, F. Y. (2009). Does Microfinance Empower Women Evidence from Self-Help Groups in India. *International Review of Applied Economics*, *23*(5), 541–556. doi:10.1080/02692170903007540

Swiss Agency for Development and Cooperation (SDC). (2004). *Creating the Prospect of Living a Life in Dignity – Principles Guiding the SDC in its Commitment to Fighting Poverty*. Berne: SDC.

Taha, S.G.A. (2010). *The Effectiveness of Microcredit Programmes on Alleviating Poverty and Empowering Women in Cairo*.

Taylor, G., & Pereznieto, P. (2014). *Review of evaluation approaches and methods used by interventions on women and girls' economic empowerment*. London: ODI.

Teye, J. K., Teye, I., & Asiedu, M. O. (2015). Financing Housing in Ghana: Challenges to the Development of Formal Mortgage System. *Journal of Housing and the Built Environment*, *30*(1), 1–16. doi:10.100710901-013-9376-z

UN Division for the Advancement of Women (UNDAW), Department of Economic and Social Affairs. (2001). Empowerment of Women Throughout the Life Cycle as a Transformative Strategy for Poverty Eradication. *Report of the Expert Group Meeting*, New Delhi, India, November 26-29.

United Nations. (2001). *Guidelines on Women's Empowerment for the UN Resident Coordinator System. Secretariat of the UN Inter-Agency Task Force on the Implementation of the ICPD Program of Action*. New York: United Nations.

United Nations. (2006). The Millennium Development Goals (MDG) Report (2006).

United Nations. (2015). *The World's Women 2015: Trends and Statistics*. United Nations, Department of Economic and Social Affairs, Statistics Division.

United Nations Children's Fund (UNICEF). (1999). Human rights for children and women: How UNICEF helps make them a reality. Retrieved from http://www.unicef.org/pubsgen/humanrights-children/index.html

Vengroff, R., & Creevey, L. (1994). Evaluation of Project Impact: ACEP Component of the Community Enterprise Development Project (Report to USAID/Dakar).

World Bank. (2001). Social Capital for Development. Retrieved from http://www.worldbank.org/poverty/scapital/

Yaron, J. (1991). *Successful Rural Financial Institutions*. Washington, DC: World Bank.

KEY TERMS AND DEFINITIONS

Empowerment: A management practice of sharing information, rewards and power with employees so that they can take initiative and make decisions to solve problems and improve service performance. Empowerment is the process of becoming stronger and more confident, especially in controlling one's life and claiming one's rights. From this, we can take empowerment in this context to mean when women have a say in making decisions about household matters; whether they can have freedom to buy household needs; and whether they have freedom to move about.

Financial Inclusion: Financial inclusion is the pursuit of making financial services accessible at affordable costs to all individuals and businesses, irrespective of net worth and size respectively. Financial inclusion strives to address and proffer solutions to the constraints that exclude people from participating in the financial sector. Access and usage of a broad range of affordable, quality financial services and products, in a manner convenient to the financially excluded, unbanked and under-banked; in an appropriate but simple and dignified manner with the requisite consideration to client protection. Accessibility should be accompanied by usage which should be supported through the financial education of clients.

Logit Model: Logistic regression is the appropriate regression analysis to conduct when the dependent variable is dichotomous (binary). Like all regression analyses, the logistic regression is a predictive analysis. Logistic regression is used to describe data and to explain the relationship between one dependent binary variable and one or more nominal, ordinal, interval or ratio-level independent variables. Logistic Regression is a type of predictive model that can be used when the target variable is a categorical variable with two categories – for example live/die, has disease/doesn't have disease, purchases product/doesn't purchase, wins race/doesn't win, etc. A logistic regression model does not involve decision trees and is more akin to nonlinear regression such as fitting a polynomial to a set of data values.

Microfinance: Microfinance is a general term used to describe the financial services of credits, savings, insurance, and fund transfers to individuals, entrepreneurs, and small businesses who lack access to the services of the traditional banks. Microfinance is often defined as financial services for poor and low-income clients offered by different types of service providers. The term is often used more narrowly to refer to loans and other services from providers that identify themselves as "microfinance institutions" (MFIs). These institutions are expected to provide these to the poor, and those who do not have access to the formal banking system.

Poverty: Poverty is a condition where people's basic needs for food, clothing, and shelter are not being met. Poverty is generally of two types: Absolute poverty - synonymous with destitution and occurs when people cannot obtain adequate resources (measured in terms of calories or nutrition) to support a minimum level of physical health. Absolute poverty means about the same everywhere and can be eradicated as demonstrated by some countries; relative poverty - occurs when people do not enjoy a certain minimum level of living standards as determined by a government (and enjoyed by the bulk of the population) that vary from country to country, sometimes within the same country. We think of conditions like hunger, homelessness, preventable diseases, unemployment, and illiteracy as elements of poverty.

Propensity Score Matching: A propensity score is the probability that a unit with certain characteristics will be assigned to the treatment group (as opposed to the control group). The scores can be used to reduce or eliminate selection bias in observational studies by balancing covariates (the characteristics of participants) between treated and control groups. Propensity score matching creates sets of participants for treatment and control groups. A matched set consists of at least one participant in the treatment group and one in the control group with similar propensity scores.

Treatment Effect: When discussing propensity score matching, two categories (or populations) stand out: treated group and the control group. The average treatment effect (ATE) is a measure used to compare treatments (or interventions) in randomized experiments, evaluation of policy interventions, and medical trials. The ATE measures the difference in mean (average) outcomes between units assigned to the treatment and units assigned to the control. In a randomized trial (i.e., an experimental study), the average treatment effect can be estimated from a sample using a comparison in mean outcomes for treated and untreated units. However, the ATE is generally understood as a causal parameter (i.e., an estimate or property of a population) that a researcher desires to know, defined without reference to the study design or estimation procedure.

Chapter 2
Microfinance
A Tool for Empowering Women in India

Rajib Bhattacharyya
Hooghly Mohsin College, India

ABSTRACT

In India, microfinance, dominated by Self Help Groups (SHGs), has provided an effective mechanism for providing financial services to the "unreached poor", and also in strengthening underprivileged and discriminated women in the society and thus significantly contributing to gender equality and women empowerment. The present chapter attempts to analyze the concept of women empowerment and its various indices such as GDI, GEM, and Women's Empowerment Index (WEI) in detail for India. The chapter explores the linkage between the role of microfinance and the empowerment of women in rural and urban India. The study reveals that though micro finance is supposed to provide an effective tool for financial and social upliftment of the poorer sections of the society, particularly women, but its penetration depends on a multifaceted and integrated network and so both the self-help bank model and the MFI model may have achieved some positive growth, but their performances are not quite deterministic when compared with other countries of the world.

INTRODUCTION

Realizing deep-rooted gender bias and discrimination in the Indian economy like the confinement of women to the private domestic realm, restrictions on their mobility, poor access to health services, nutrition, education and employment, and exclusion from the public and political sphere, the 12th Five Year Plan (2012-2017) focused strongly on sustainable, equitable and inclusive growth, along with women empowerment, taking into account the needs of all sections of the society. For the first time the Twelfth Five Year Plan Approach Paper identified financial inclusion as a public policy initiative to achieve rural transformation and development through the process of improving access to organized financial market for ordinary households, especially in excluded and underserved areas. In this context, microfinance emerged as a powerful tool for poverty alleviation and financial inclusion in India. Microfinance refers to small savings, credit and insurance services extended to socially and economically disadvantaged segments of

DOI: 10.4018/978-1-5225-5240-6.ch002

society. Microfinance may be defined as provision of thrift, the wide network of the organized banking system deep credit and other financial services and products of very into rural areas. Market and the government both failed to small amounts to the poor in rural, semi urban or urban provide credit access to the poor. In fact, the failure of areas, for enabling them to raise their income levels and institutional initiatives of rural credit and to the improve living standards. Women constitute a vast majority of users of micro-credit and saving services. Microfinance institutions (MFIs) broadly refers to a wide range of organizations dedicated to providing these services through Self-Help Groups (SHGs), NGOs, credit co-operatives, commercial banks, NBFCs and parts of State-owned banks.

In spite of all government and non-governments' efforts, women have been the most underprivileged and discriminated strata of the society in India. In the recent times, microfinance has been emerging as a powerful instrument for empowering women particularly, the rural women. The Indian Constitution in its Preamble, Fundamental Rights and Duties and Directive Principles emphasizes on the principle of gender equality. The Indian Constitution not only ensures gender equality, but also empowers the state to adopt measures for upliftment of the women folk. Empowerment of women means developing them as more aware individuals, who are politically active, economically productive and independent and are able to take part effectively in the decision making. Women empowerment as a concept was introduced at the International Women Conference in 1985 at Nairobi, which defined it as redistribution of social power and control of resources in favour of women. The United Nations Development Fund for Women (UNDFW) includes the following factors in its definition of women empowerment:

1. Acquiring knowledge and understanding of gender relations and the way in which these relations may be changed.
2. Developing a sense of self-worth, a belief in one's ability to secure desired changes and the right to control one's life.

LITERATURE SURVEY

A huge volume of literature has developed over the last two decades discussing and analyzing the issues of microfinance and women empowerment separately as well as collectively, try to address them from various stand points. Here some of these studies are highlighted. Mahanta, Panda and Sreekumar (2012), in their paper three key issues on micro finance are discussed- growth of microfinance in India, role played by National Bank for Agriculture and Rural Development (NABARD) and other National Banks and the role of government. Bharat Micro Finance Report (Sa-Dahn, 2015) of NABARD provides a detailed analysis of the progress of microfinance in India. Mokta (2014) highlighted the constitutional provisions of women empowerment and its various aspects as well as various initiatives taken by Government of India for empowering women by analyzing position of India in Gender Inequality Index and Global Gender Gap Index. Das, Chandra, Kochhar and Kumar (2015) in their paper examines the determinants of female labor force participation in India, against the backdrop of India having one of the lowest participation rates for women among peer countries. Swain (2007) concluded many strides have been made in the right direction and women are in the process of empowering themselves and NGOs that provide support in financial services and specialized training, have a greater ability to make a positive impact on women empowerment. Batliwala (1994) identified three approaches to women's empowerment: the integrated development approach which focused on women's survival and livelihood needs; the economic development approach which aimed to strengthen women's economic position and the consciousness approach which organized women into collectives that address the source of oppression. Kabeer (1999), stresses that women's empowerment is about the process by which those who have been denied the ability to make strategic life choices acquire such ability. He emphasizes that the ability to exercise choice incorporates three interrelated dimensions: resources (defined broadly to include not only access, but also future claims, to both material and human and social resources); agency (including processes of decision-making, as well as less measurable manifestations of agency such as negotiation, deception and manipulation) and achievements (well-being outcomes).Malhotra, Schuler and Carol(2002) constructed a list of the most commonly used dimensions of women's empowerment, drawing from the frameworks developed by various authors in different fields of social sciences. According to Krishna (2003) empowerment means increasing the capacity of individuals or groups to make effective development and life choices and to transform these choices into desired actions and outcomes. Swian (SIDA-2006) provides evidence from the self-help group bank linkage programme in India. The results show a definite economic impact on households, with increases in income and decline in vulnerability. Swain and Wallentin (2014) examined how the impact on women empowerment varies with respect to the location and type of group linkage of the respondent. Using household survey data from five states in India they demonstrated that a significant correlation between women empowerment and autonomy in women's decision-making and network, communication and political participation respectively. Ray and Mahapatra (2014) provides and empirical estimation of the penetration of MFI among Indian states using cross section secondary data and suggested macro level factors are significant in explaining geographical skew. Pokhriyal, Rani and Uniyal (2014) attempted to study the role of microfinance intervention in promoting women empowerment in rural India through various schemes of the commercial banks and the NABARD. It also focuses on the progress of the MFI-Bank linkage programme.

OBJECTIVE OF THE STUDY AND METHODOLOGY

The fundamental objective of this chapter is to examine the relation between micro finance and women employment keeping in the background the government initiative and programmes implemented during the various plan periods. Firstly, it provides a brief historical perspectives of the development of micro finance in India. The chapter examines the recent growth of micro finance in India with its focus on client's outreach and portfolio operations. It provides a comparative analysis of the SBLP- model and MFI model and their relative performances. The performances of micro finance with respect to women empowerment in India has been studied using the standard UNDP international indices like GDI, GEM and GII. The present work also tries to evaluate the success of the linkage between micro finance and women empowerment in India in terms of economic empowerment, political empowerment and employment generation. Finally, an attempt has been made to assess the various policy initiatives of the government of India with regard to micro-credit and women empowerment and one such scheme has been evaluated as a case study. The entire analysis is based on time series data available from the various departments of the government of India and also the NSSO Data (various survey rounds). The ideas of various published papers, journals and Reports have also helped in developing this paper.

HISTORICAL BACKGROUND OF THE GROWTH OF MICRO FINANCE IN INDIA

The historical development of micro finance in India dates to the establishment of Syndicate Bank in 1921 in private sector. In its initial phase of development, Syndicate Bank concentrated on raising micro deposits in the form of daily/weekly basis and sanctioned micro loans to its clients for shorter period of time. But microfinance came to limelight only when Dr. Yunus gave it a mass movement in Grameen Bank experiment of group lending. Later in the 1970s a significant microfinance initiative was undertaken by Shri Mahila (Self Employed Women's Association, SEWA) Sahakari Bank in 1974 for providing banking services to the poor women employed in the unorganized sector in Ahmadabad in Gujarat. Mysore Rehabilitation and Development Agency (MYRADA) of Karnataka was another NGO to start in 1968 to foster a process of ongoing change in favour of the rural poor. But with the establishment of National Bank for Agriculture and Rural Development (NABARD) in 1992 in the field of microcredit, the movement of microfinance got a boost in India. Today we find that the microfinance services are delivered by apex institutions like National Bank for Agriculture and Rural Development (NABARD), Small Industries Development Bank of India (SIDBI) and RMK. At the lower level we have commercial Banks, Regional Rural Banks and cooperatives to provide microfinance services. The private institutions that undertake microfinance services as their main activity are generally referred to as Micro Finance Institutions (MFIs) in Indian context.

PRESENT SITUATION OF MICROFINANCE IN INDIA

The Government of India and the Reserve Bank of India have created conducive policy and regulatory framework for MFIs to operate in the country. Last decade has seen the Indian Microfinance Sector experiencing a phenomenal growth and taking its rightful place in the financial inclusion scenario of the nation, as evidenced by the fact that eight MFIs received RBI's nod for Small Finance Banks and one MFI has already started functioning as a universal bank. The number of institutions providing microfinance services has gone up from a handful to a few hundreds. The quantum of credit made available to the poor and financially excluded clients has crossed `48,882 crore and number of clients benefitted crossed 37 million as of March 2015. The SHG bank linkage program has equally grown to touch the lives of individuals through SHGs with an outstanding loan portfolio of approximately 43,000 crores (The Bharat Microfinance Report, 2015).

In the face of higher risk and higher vulnerability, the poor have come to the center stage of micro-insurance efforts. The Insurance Regulatory and Development Authority (IRDA) has been the standing authority on micro-insurance initiatives over the past decade. They propose to allow Regional Rural Banks or Gramin Banks, Rural and Urban Cooperative Societies to act as micro-insurance agents in rural areas in an effort to increase insurance penetration, particularly in remote areas IRDA has even moved to allow SHGs and NGOs to carry out the distribution of micro-insurance products in rural areas. MFI's contribution to financial inclusion as well as the depth and breadth of financial deepening depends on two key indicators – (i) Client outreach and (ii) loan portfolio.

MFIs currently operate in 28 States, 5 Union Territories and 568 districts in India. Table 1 shows the distribution of MFIs by state. In particular, it shows the number of MFIs operating in each state, their total number of branches in the state and the number of districts with microfinance operations. Twenty-

Table 1. No. of MFIs in Indian States/UTs, No. of Districts and Branches

Name of the States/UTs	No. of MFIs Operating in the State	No. of Districts of the State Where MFI Operates	No. of Branches
Madhya Pradesh	37	48	870
Maharashtra	37	35	980
West Bengal	35	20	1740
Tamil Nadu	34	32	1377
Karnataka	29	30	1185
Bihar	28	38	915
Odisha	26	30	742
Uttar Pradesh	23	70	1063
Gujarat	22	23	386
Rajasthan	21	33	287
Assam	19	24	552
Jharkhand	19	23	231
Chhattisgarh	17	16	248
Delhi	13	7	70
Haryana	13	19	129
Kerala	13	14	220
Uttarakhand	13	10	95
Pondicherry	11	3	17
Andhra Pradesh (Telengana Included)	10	23	776
Manipur	8	9	45
Meghalaya	7	6	26
Punjab	7	17	93
Tripura	6	6	99
Goa	4	2	7
Himachal Pradesh	4	4	6
Mizoram	4	8	34
Arunachal Pradesh	3	7	11
Sikkim	3	3	10
Nagaland	2	4	2
Andaman & Nicobar	1	1	1
Chandigarh	1	1	2
Dadra and Nagar Haveli	1	1	1
Jammu & Kashmir	1	1	1
Total		568	12221

(Source: Sa-Dahn, 2015)

nine MFIs with a large outreach and portfolio have operations in more than five states, out of which five leading MFIs are operating in more than fifteen states.

Table 2 pinpoints the top 10 MFI on the basis of no. of states/ union territories where they operate. Among these MFIs Bandhan Financial Services Ltd has the highest number of branch networks (2022) followed by SKS Microfinance Limited (1273); Spandana Sphoorty Financial Limited (784); Share Microfin Limited (618); Ujjivan Financial Services Private Limited (423).

The total number of clients served by MFIs stood at 371 lakh as on 31 March, 2015. Client outreach of MFIs had grown substantially from 2005 to 2011, reaching a level of 371 lakh. This trend slowed down during 2012 and 2013 and the number of clients slumped to 275 lakh. The trend reversed in 2014 with a growth and reached a level of 330 lakhs. This trend continued in 2015 with an astounding rise in clients/borrowers to an all-time high of 371 lakh (Figure 1). Majority of these clients are being served by NBFC-MFIs (85.18%).

In terms of client's outreach, all the States and Union Territories have grown, except for combined Andhra Pradesh and Telangana, and Andaman and Nicober. Across the board loan waivers announced by both the state governments led to sticky accounts in MFIs' books, which later had to be cleaned up. This could be one of the reasons for the fall in client outreach. The other reason is a deliberate scaling down of operations in both these states by leading MFIs. There has been a reversal of trend in the percentage share of MFI clients in between 2012 and 2015. It has changed from rural-centric to urban-centric. One probable explanation may be minimization of operational expenses and maximization of their operational efficiency for reasonable profitability.

In India, the focus of microfinance has always been on serving women. Women clients constitute 97% of the total clients of MFIs. A trend analysis of women borrowers, SC/ST borrowers and minority borrowers is shown in Figure 3.

As of March 2015, the total loan portfolio of MFIs has reached an all-time high of over Rs.48882 which is a46.89% growth over last year crore that also includes a managed portfolio of nearly Rs.9854 crore. The net loan portfolio or owned portfolio on the books of the MFIs stood at Rs. 39028 crore, which is an increase of 33% over the last year. MFIs have become increasingly prudent to use financial innovations to enhance their income and reduce risk. Securitization model was devised for the purpose of overcoming capital constraints.

Table 2. Top 10 MFI on the basis of No. of States/ Union Territories where they operate

Name of MFI	No. of States/ Union Territories
Ujjivan	24
Bandhan	22
SKS	19
Janalakshmi	17
Basix	15
Share Microfin	14
Spandan	12
Asmitha	12
Satin Credit care	11
NERFL	11

(Source: Sa-Dahn, 2015)

Figure 1. MFIs client outreach expansion trend in India
(Source: Sa-Dahn, 2015)

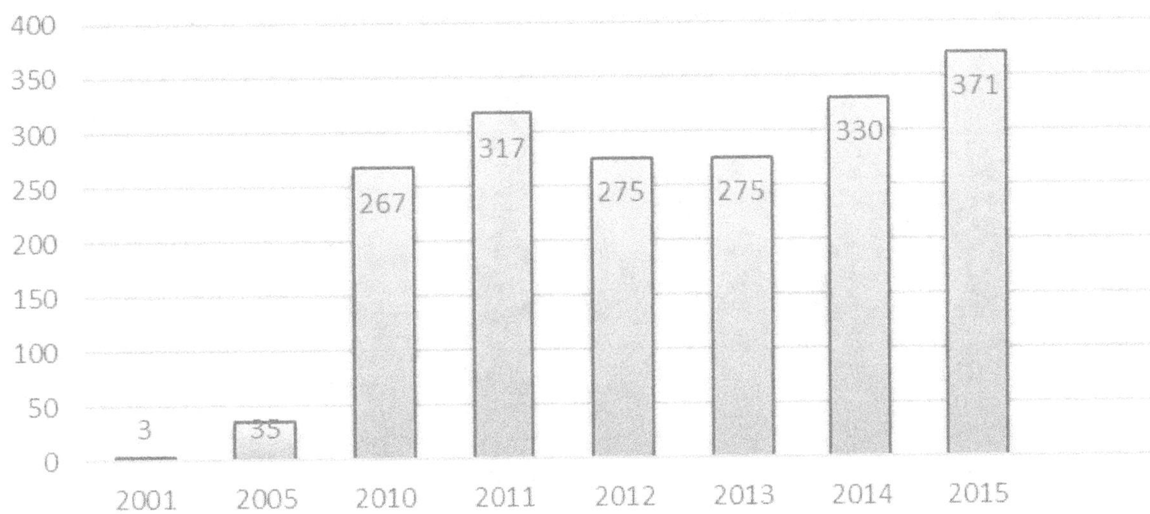

Figure 2. Changes in the rural-urban share of MFI clients
(Source: Author's Construction based on Sa-Dahn, 2015)

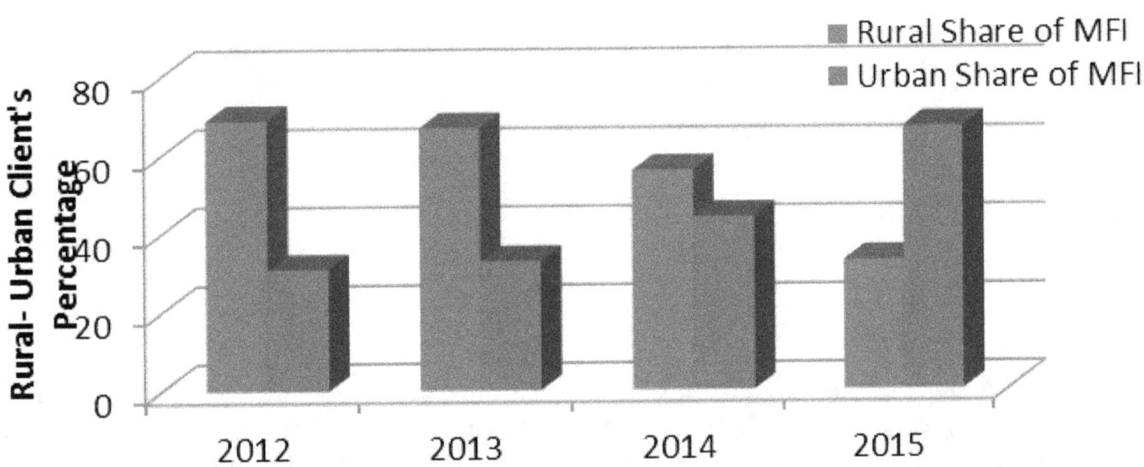

COMPARISON BETWEEN SBLP- MODEL AND MFI MODEL IN INDIAN SCENARIO

In India microfinance operates through two main channels viz. a) banking system through the SHGs under SHG-Bank Linkage Programme (SHG-BLP) and b) through Micro Finance Institutions (MFIs) lending through individual and group approach. In the case of the banking model Self Help Groups (SHGs) are formed and financed by banks. In some cases, SHGs are formed by formal agencies/NGOs and financed by banks. In the MFI model, SHGs are formed and financed by the Microfinance Institutions (MFIs) that obtain resource support from various channels. While the MFI model is growing rapidly, the SBLP

Figure 3. Composition of MFI clients in India
(Source: Author's Construction based on Sa-Dahn, 2015)

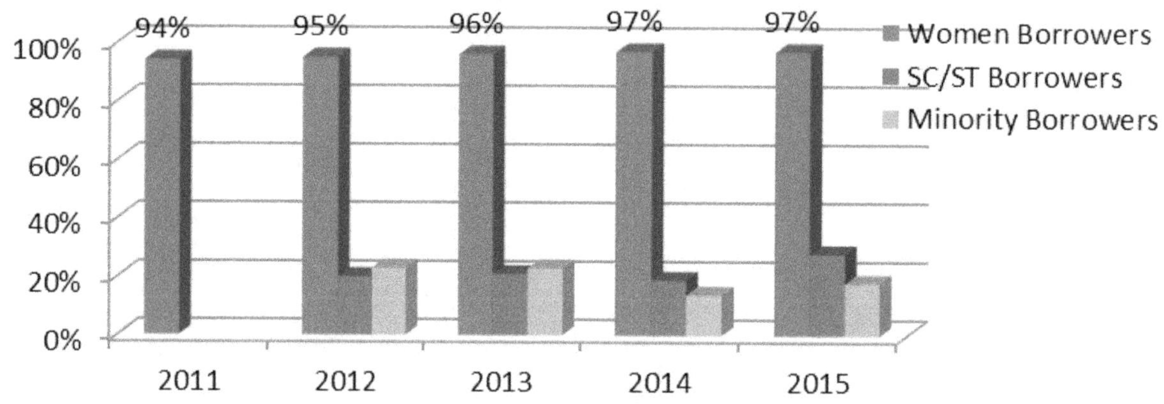

Figure 4. Changes in the managed loan portfolio (in Rs. crores) in Indian MFI
(Source: Author's Construction based on Sa-Dahn, 2015)

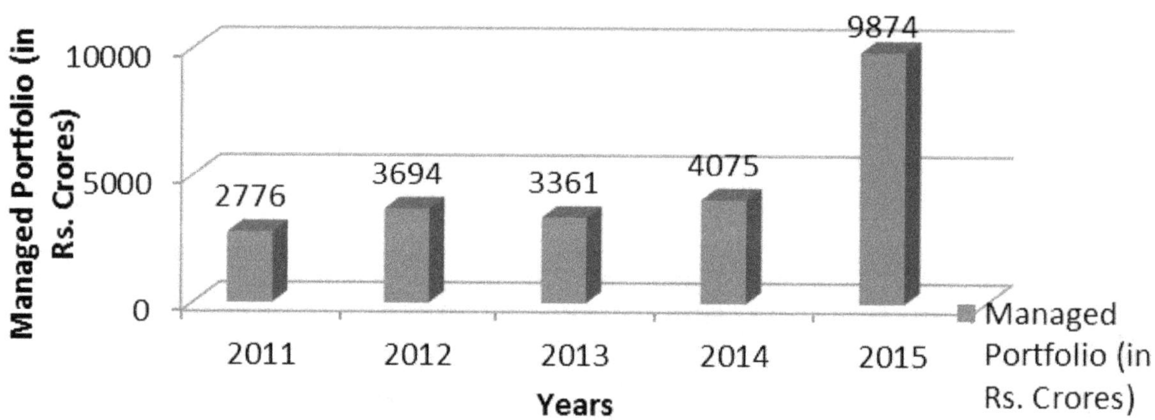

is by far the more dominant model in terms of outreach. Both these models are very different from each other in methodologies adopted and legal forms of institutions involved in service delivery- SBLP is run by the government while the MFI model is privately managed with some institutions being regulated by the Reserve Bank of India.

Microfinance Institutions in India emerged in the late 1980s in response to the gap in availability of banking services for the unserved and underserved rural population. Their business proliferated in 1990s under the open economy regime. Most of the institutions that entered the field were from the social sector and hence they took the legal form of trusts or Societies. These institutions were then registered as NBFC-MFIs under the category created by RBI based on Malegam committee recommendations. While the MFI model reaches microcredit quickly and efficiently to the financially excluded, the SHG-BLP programme besides credit and savings provides wholesome social and economic justice to the excluded and deprived section of the society and has proven itself as an invaluable platform for inclusive growth.

The number of SHGs with savings linkage, loan disbursed and bank loans outstanding as well as the quantum of savings outstanding, loan disbursed during the year and total loan outstanding had shown positive growth during the period 2013-14 to 2015-16 (Figure 5).The MFIs were able to grab higher confidence of banks and financial institutions. The total loans to MFIs by banks and financial institutions increased by over 36.90% during the current year as against 47.73% during the previous year (Figure 6). Though most of the MFIs entered the microfinance arena only after the SHG-Bank linkage programme was well entrenched, business of these institutions grew at a much faster pace than the former.

REGIONAL CONCENTRATION OF MFIS IN INDIA

Microfinance Penetration Index (MPI) denotes a state's share of MFI clients relative to the total MFI clients in the country. One of the striking features of the growth of microfinance institutions in India has been the wide regional disparity. There is huge amount of unevenness in the spread of microfinance across the country. The Inclusive Finance Report (Nair & Tankha, 2014) analyzing the growth of Indian microfinance reveals that MFI's have highest penetration in southern regions, followed by eastern region (Figure 7). The concentration of microfinance in the three southern states of Andhra Pradesh, Karnataka and Tamil Nadu is comparatively much higher than the other states in the country. In fact, a comparison of MPI scores across various states of India reveals that Andhra Pradesh tops the list (3.38), followed by Puducherry (2.87) and then Karnataka (2.27). This represented in Figure 8.

LINK BETWEEN MICRO FINANCE AND WOMEN EMPOWERMENT IN INDIAN SCENARIO

The large proportion of microfinance beneficiaries are the women in the society as they are mostly engaged in unpaid work and they need access to productive resources with financial services being a key resource. Microfinance provides women with the financial backing they need to start business ventures

Figure 5. Performance of SGH-BLP during the period 2013-14 to 2015-16 in India (No. in Lakhs, Amt. in Rs. '000 crores)
(Source: Author's Construction based on NABARD, 2016)

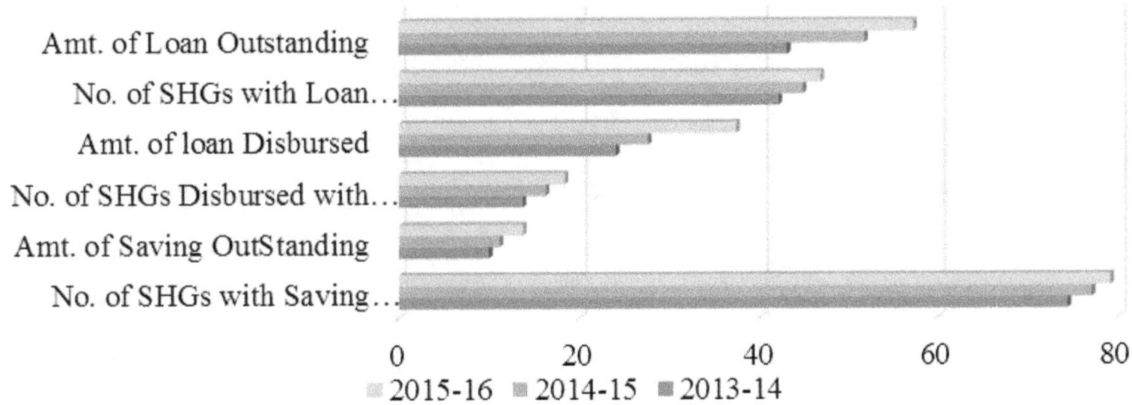

Figure 6. Performance of MFI-Bank Linkage in India (Amt. in Rs. Crores)
(Source: Author's Construction based on NABARD, 2016)

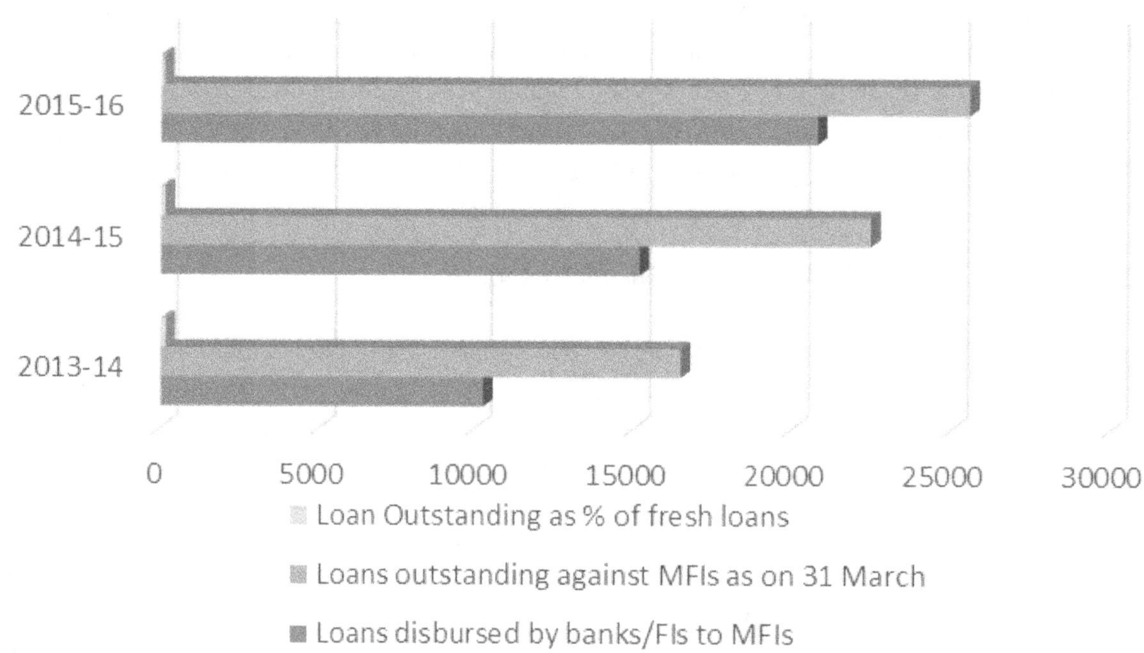

Figure 7. Regional dispersion of MPI across various states of India
(Source: Author's construction based on The Inclusive Finance Report, 2014)

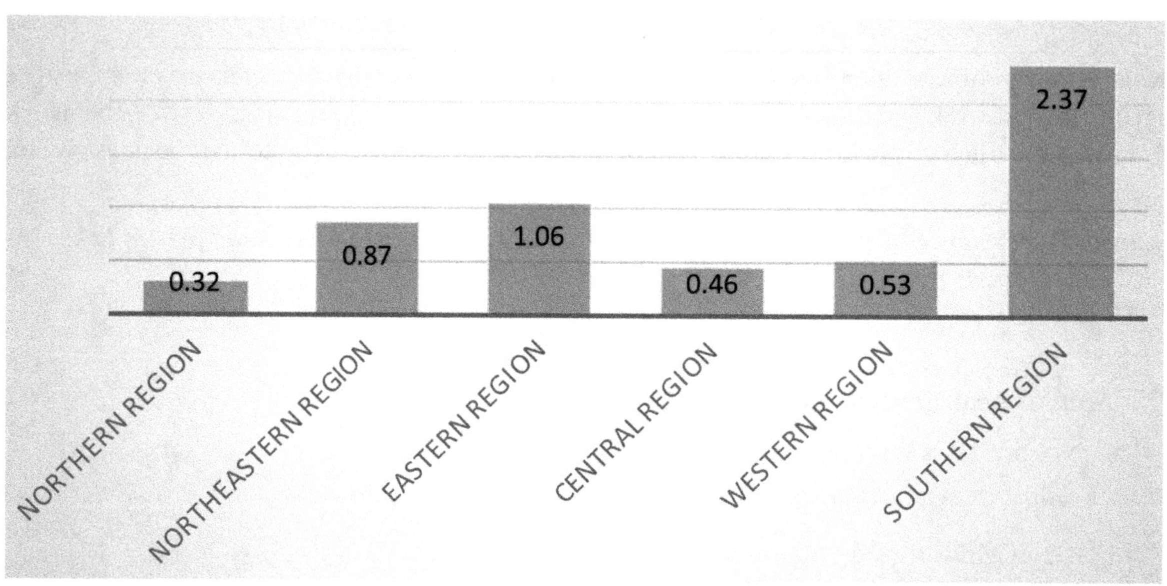

Figure 8. State-wise dispersion of MPI
(Source: Author's construction based on The Inclusive Finance Report, 2014)

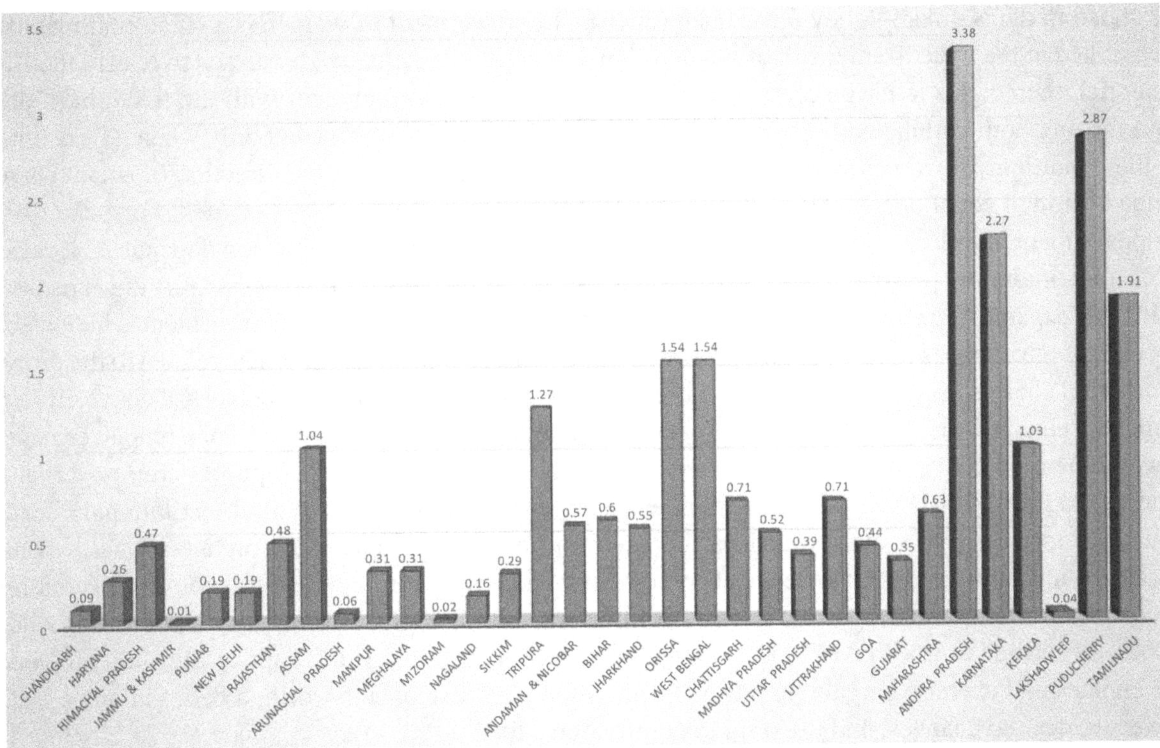

and actively participate in the economy. It gives them confidence, improves their status and makes them more active in decision making, thus promoting gender equality. Microfinance schemes usually lend small short-term loans to very poor micro-entrepreneurs (very poor micro-entrepreneurs are women). Experience reveals that women have a small credit risk, repaying their loans and tend more often to benefit the whole family. Loan repayment is always guaranteed by group members collectively and access to future credit or loans is contingent on successful repayment. Hence peer monitoring and the prospect of subsequent larger loans act as strong incentive for repayment (Ray, 1998). The sector is characterized by women dominance and lack of access to credit from the traditional banking institution due to the inability to offer collateral security. Giving women access to microcredit loans therefore generates a multiplier effect that increases the impact of a microfinance institution's activities, benefiting multiple generations. Therefore, the effectiveness of any microfinance scheme or programme should be assessed based on how it has been able to empower women economically, politically and socially.

Several studies have shown that the impact of microcredit on empowerment of women have been positive effects, with some of these impacts being ripple effects. Microfinance, dominated by SHGs, have been successful in reducing the vulnerability of the poor and unprivileged section of the society, through asset creation, income and consumption smoothing, provision of emergency assistance, and empowering women by giving them control over assets, taking active participation in decision-making and enhancement of self-esteem and knowledge (Zaman, 2001; Simanowitz & Walker, 2002).

CONCEPTS OF WOMEN EMPOWERMENT

As stated in the National Policy for women (2016), "Empowerment of women is a socio-political ideal envisioned in the wider framework of women rights. It is a process that leads women to realize their full potential, their rights to have access to opportunities, resources and choices with the freedom of decision making both within and outside home. Empowerment would be achieved only when advancement in the conditions of women is accompanied by their ability to influence the direction of social change gained through equal opportunities in economic, social and political spheres of life". For Sen (1993), empowerment is reflected in a person's capability set. The 'capability' of a person depends on a variety of factors, including personal characteristics and social arrangements. Empowerment is the capacity to fulfil this capability and not just the choice to do so. Sen's view on women's empowerment is indicated in his discussion on measurement of empowerment (Sen 1990). Empowerment is also related to the process of internal change (Mayoux, 1998) and to the capacity and right to make decisions (Kabeer, 2001). In a policy research report, World Bank (2001) identified both gender equality and women empowerment as development objectives and means to promote growth, reduce poverty and support better governance. The World Bank (2001) also identifies four key elements of empowerment to draft institutional reforms: access to information; inclusion and participation; accountability; and local organizational capacity. Another view of women's empowerment argues that it needs to occur in multiple dimensions: economic, sociocultural, familial/interpersonal, legal, political and psychological (Malhotra, Schuler & Boender, 2002). According to UNIFEM (2000), women's empowerment consists of "gaining the ability to generate choices and exercise bargaining power … developing a sense of self-worth, a belief in one's ability to secure desired changes, and the right to control one's life."

VARIOUS INDICES FOR MEASUREMENT OF WOMEN EMPOWERMENT

The UNDP report of 1995 introduced two new complementary indices: the Gender-related Development Index (GDI) and the Gender Empowerment Measure (GEM). GDI and GEM developed by UNDP need to be recast to realistically capture the gender gaps in development and empowerment in the Third World. The Gender Development Index (GDI) measures gender inequalities in achievement in three basic dimensions of human development: health, measured by female and male life expectancy at birth; education, measured by female and male expected years of schooling for children and female and male mean years of schooling for adults ages 25 years and older; and command over economic resources, measured by female and male estimated earned income.

The GDI groups are based on the absolute deviation of GDI from gender parity, 100 .$|GDI–1|$. Countries with absolute deviation from gender parity of 2.5 percent or less are considered countries with high equality in HDI achievements between women and men and are classified as group 1. Countries with absolute deviation from gender parity of 2.5–5 percent are considered countries with medium-high equality in HDI achievements between women and men and are classified as group 2. Countries with absolute deviation from gender parity of 5–7.5 percent are considered countries with medium equality in HDI achievements between women and men and are classified as group 3.Countries with absolute deviation from gender parity of 7.5–10 percent are considered countries with medium-low equality in HDI achievements between women and men and are classified as group 4. Countries with absolute deviation from gender parity of more than 10 percent are considered countries with low equality in HDI achievements between women and men and are classified as group 5. India falls within the medium HDI group but according to GDI score India falls under group 5 (i.e. with low equality in HDI achievements between women and men) (figure 9).

UNDP's GEM is specifically focused on determining women's relative empowerment, which we consider to be a valuable feature of the measure. GEM contains three components: political representation, representation in senior positions in the economy, and power over economic resources (proxied by earned incomes). Similar to the GDI, it uses the same aversion to inequality procedures that penalizes inequalities in political and economic representation as well as earned incomes. But there are a range of problems associated with the current GEM, which have been discussed in detail by Klasen (2006). Human Development Report (2014) introduced new Gender Development Index (GDI) which is simply the ratio of a female human development index to the male human development index. The main proposal regarding the GDI was to make it a direct gender inequality measure which they called the Gender Gap Measure (GGM) which is simply the geometric mean of the female-male ratios of life expectancy, education, and labor force participation rates, i.e. the GGM is defined as

$$GGM=\left(\frac{LE_f}{LE_M}.\times\frac{ED_F}{ED_M}.\times\frac{LF_F}{LF_M}\right)^{1/3}$$

Where, LE, ED, and LF are the life expectancy index adjusted for a assumed 5 year female longevity advantage, the education index, and labor force participation rates of women and men, respectively.

In the 2010 Human Development Report, UNDP decided to rework its gender-related indices and address some of the shortcomings that had been identified in the literature. As recommended by Klasen and Schüler (2011) and others, the GDI was dropped and also the GEM has been discontinued. Instead a new Gender Inequality Index (GII) has been created and calculated for 137 countries. The new GII contains three dimensions, reproductive health, empowerment, and labor market. The first averages fe-

Figure 9. Changes in India's GDI from 2000 – 2015
Source: Author's compilation based on the HDI Statistics (2000 – 2015)

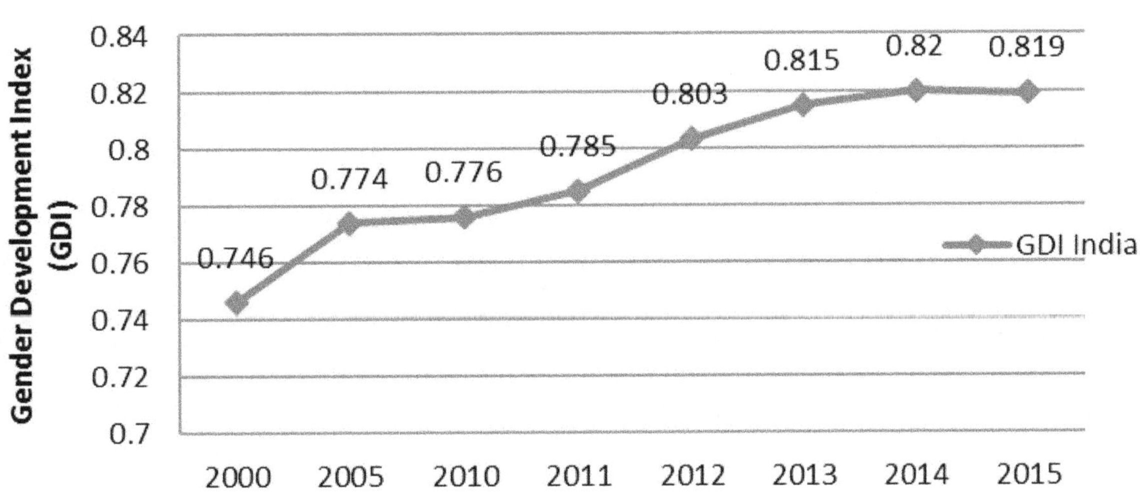

male adolescent fertility and maternal mortality, the second parliamentary representation and educational attainment, and the third just consist of labor force participation. The aggregation is first across dimensions for males and females separately, using the geometric mean. Since the indicators of reproductive health only apply to women, for males a perfect score in reproductive health is assumed and used in the aggregation of geometric mean. In a next step, the aversion to inequality procedure (as in the GDI and GEM) is used to calculate welfare losses associated with the inequalities between males and females and the GII measures the welfare loss of these inequalities, relative to the achievements if perfect equalithad psisted. The GII is an index measuring the welfare loss of gender inequality considering a hybrid of well-being and empowerment outcomes rather than gender-sensitive development or gender inequality directly. The changes in the GII values for India are shown in Figure 10 and has shown a downward trend.

As per the United Nations Development Programme's Human Development Report 2013: India stood at 132nd position out of 187countries on the gender inequality index (GII) —performing worse than Pakistan whose position is 123. All nations in South Asia, except Afghanistan, performed better than India, with Sri Lanka (75) topping them all. Nepal ranked 102nd and Bangladesh 111th. Key factors which put India on such a low position in 2013 are: Only 29 per cent of Indian women above the age of 15 in 2011 were a part of the country's labour force; only 26.6 per cent women above 25 years received a secondary education in 2010, compared to 50.4 per cent of men, about 200 women died every 100,000child births.

Figure 10. Changes in India's GII from 2005 to 2015
Source: Author's compilation based on the HDI Statistics (2005 – 2015)

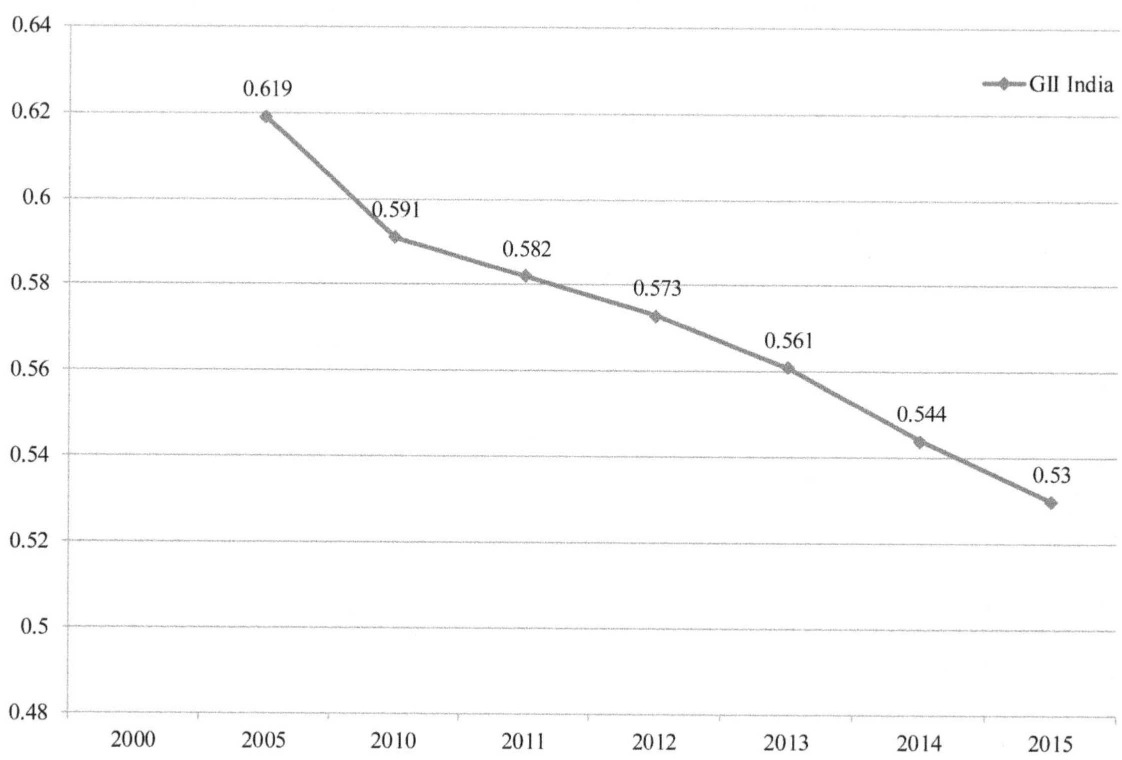

Another index for measurement of empowerment of women is the Women's Empowerment Index (WEI) which is a composite index designed to measure progress in the multi-dimensional aspects of women's empowerment. The Women's Empowerment Index (WEI) is composed of two parts: the women's achievement ratio (WAR) and the gender parity ratio (GPR). WAR measures women's achievement to a pre-defined set of goals, while GPR measures women's achievement in comparison to men's achievement in the same community. WEI is calculated on the scores of five key domains: agency, income, leadership, resources and time.

MICRO FINANCE AND WOMEN EMPOWERMENT

Empowerment through microfinance is identified and measured in various dimensions: impact on decision-making, on self-confidence of women, on their status at home, on family relationships and the incidence of domestic violence, on their involvement in the community, on their political empowerment and rights (Cheston & Kuhn, 2002).Although it is difficult to measure the exact impact of access to microcredit on different dimensions – such as impact on decision-making and on self-confidence –studies have shown that MFIs indeed have a positive effect on each of these different dimensions of women's empowerment. Other studies indicate that the SHGs mediated by microcredit have helped women gain control over assets and subsequently acquire self-esteem, knowledge and power (Zaman, 2001; Simanowitz & Walker, 2002). In India, there is evidence of microfinance programmes leading to women's political empowerment through political mobilization. The linkage between this aspect of empowerment and microfinance was explored by Sanyal (2009) in her study of 59 microfinance groups in West Bengal. She found that economic ties produced through access to microcredit led to improvements in women's social capital and their ability to influence social norms. There are many successful women organizations working for the overall upliftment of the rural women like Shri Mahila Griha Udyog lijjat Papad (1959), Self Employed Women association (SEWA) established in 1972, The Working Women's Forum (WWF) in 1978, RMK, a govt. Organization for women established in 1993, Mann Deshi Mahila Sahakari Bank Ltd. (MDMSB) in 1997 etc. ICTs are increasingly used by rural co-operatives (e.g. Amul) and women enterprises (e.g. SEWA) for enhancing efficiencies and to compete in the domestic and international markets. It also saves lot of time for women who are involved in many of these operations. A successful example of an ICT-enabling business which has access to the Internet and a micro financing component is the use of smart cards by Indian women milk collectors in Rajasthan.

ECONOMIC EMPOWERMENT

Microfinance through SHGs has linked rural poor women with formal credit delivery system, provided micro-loans and has encouraged them to start microenterprises. This programme has helped in increasing self-employment as well as income of the participants and helped them to become economically more empowered than non-participants. The SHG-BLP is also the largest coordinated financial inclusion programme and NABARD has always strived to broad base the ownership of the programme amongst different stakeholders like banks, NGOs, Govt. etc. This saving led model of microfinance is a successful empowerment tool which has covered almost 10 crores households in the country. Among these 86 percent are exclusively women groups which are a big push to the women empowerment programme.

The number of SHGs having savings linkage increased to 79.03 lakh as on 31 March 2016 from 76.97 lakh a year back. There was a net addition of 2.06 lakh SHGs during the year 2015-16. The domain of SHGs consists of 85.6% women groups which play a crucial role in empowerment of the poor rural women. The number of SHGs with savings linkage, credit disbursed during the year and bank loans outstanding as well as the quantum of savings outstanding, loan disbursed during the year and total loan outstanding had shown positive growth during the past four years (table 3).

ROLE OF MGNREGA IN FOSTERING WOMEN EMPOWERMENT

The role of MGNREGA and micro finance in this context is important because it provides an environment of sustainable improvement in the quality of life of rural women folk for equal opportunity in decision making process and to participate in community life by forming SHGs and MFIs.

Utilization of allocated funds and asset creation has been taken as a measure of success for women empowerment (though table 4 shows that the percentage of women days has remained the same).

Table 3. Progress of SHG- Bank Model during 2012-13 to 2015-16 in India (No. in Lakhs./Amt. Rs. Crore)

		2012-13		2013-14		2014-15		2015-16	
		No. of SHGs	Amount	No. of SHGs	Amount	No. of SHGs	Amount	No. of SHGs	Amount
SHG Savings with Banks as on 31st March	Total No. of SHGs	73.18 (- 8.1%)	8217.25 (25.4%)	74.3 (1.53%)	9897.42 (20.45%)	76.97 (3.59%)	11059.84 (11.74%)	79.03 (2.68%)	13691.39 (23.79%)
	All Women SHGs	59.38 (- 5.7%)	6514.86 (27.6%)	62.52 (5.27%)	8012.89 (22.99%)	66.51 (6.38%)	9264.33 (15.61%)	67.63 (1.68%)	12035.78 29.92%)
	% of Women Groups	81.1	79.3	84.15	80.96	86.41	83.77	85.58	87.91
Loans Disbursed to the SHGs during the year	No. of SHGs Extended Loans	12.20 (6.3%)	20585.36 (24.5%)	13.66 (12.02%)	24017.36 (16.67%)	16.26 (19.03%)	27582.31 (14.84%)	18.32 (12.67%)	37286.90 (35.18%)
	All Women SHGs	10.37 (12.4%)	17854.31 (26.3%)	11.52 (11.02%)	21037.97 (17.83%)	14.48 (25.69%)	24419.75 (16.07%)	16.29 (12.50%)	34411.42 (40.92%)
	% of Women Groups	85.1	86.7	84.3	87.6	89.06	83.53	88.92	92.29
Loans Outstanding against SHGs as on 31st March	Total No. of SHGs Linked	44.51 (2.2%)	39375.30 (8.4%)	41.97 (-5.71%)	42927.52 (9.02%)	44.68 (6.46%)	51545.46 (20.06%)	46.73 (4.59%)	57119.23 (10.81%)
	All Women SHGs	32.57 (2.9%)	32840.04 (7.8%)	34.06 (-9.34%)	36151.58 (10.08%)	38.58 (13.27%)	45901.95 (26.97%)	40.36 (4.61%)	51428.91 (12.04%)
	% of Women Groups	84.4	83.3	81.2	84.2	86.35	89.05	86.37	90.04

(Source: Author's Compilation from Sa-Dahn, 2015, 2016; NABARD, 2016)

Table 4. Role of MGNREGA in women empowerment

	Person Days (in Crores), [% of Total Person Days]					
	FY 2006-07	FY 2007-08	FY 2008-09	FY 2009-10	FY 2010-11	FY 2011-12
Total	90.5	143.59	216.32	283.6	257.2	218.6
Women	36.8 (40%)	61.2 (43%)	103.5 (48%)	136.4 (48%)	122.7 (48%)	105.27 (48%)

(Author's Construction based on MGNREGA, 2014)

WOMEN ENTREPRENEURSHIP IN SMALL SCALE INDUSTRIES THROUGH MICROFINANCE

Women Entrepreneurs are the women or a group of women who initiate, organize and operate a business enterprise. The government of India notes women entrepreneurs as "An enterprise owned and controlled by women saving a minimum financial interest of 51 per cent of the capital and giving at least 51 per cent of the employment generated in the enterprise to women" (MSME, Govt. of India, as cited in Sharma, 2013). The share of the units managed by women in terms employment was 7.14. The employment generated per Rs. one lakh investment in the units managed by women was 2.49. Among the small scale industrial units owned by women entrepreneurs in India, Kerala tops the list with over 1.39 lakh units, followed by Tamil Nadu with 1.30 lakh units. Principal Characteristics of SSI units managed by women are presented in the following table 5.

POLITICAL EMPOWERMENT

Table 6 shows the participation of women in the two Houses of Parliament. The data clearly reveals that the percentage of women in decision-making positions always remained low (with a highest of 15%). Women do not share the power of decision-making and are not involved in policy making in Indian democracy in proportion to their numerical strength.

TRENDS IN WOMEN EMPLOYMENT AS PER VARIOUS NSS ROUNDS

The employed persons are categorized into three broad categories according to their status of employment. These broad categories are: (i) self-employed, (ii) regular wage/salaried employee and (iii) casual labour [NSSO Classification]. Figure 11 and Figure 12 shows the all-India employment for usual status (ps+ss) for self-employed and regular employed workers the per 1000 distribution. It clearly shows that in the self-employed category rural-female employment is the highest and not only that the urban females has also better performers than the urban males. This clearly proves that role of microfinance in improvement in women empowerment. But this is opposite when it comes to regular employment

Table 5. Principal characteristics of SSI Units managed by women in India

For Units Managed by Women	No. of Units	Market Value of Fixed Assets	Employment	Gross Output	Exports
Regd. SSI Sector	114362	33624570500	349342	60316833602	3314822655
Percentage to total of the respective category	8.32	3.66	5.67	2.97	2.69
Unregd. SSI Sector	880780	37763317590	1429962	37324824839	53802469
Percentage to total of the respective category	9.63	6.04	7.62	4.72	0.28
Total SSI Sector	995142	71387888090	1779304	97641658441	3368625124
Percentage to total of the respective category	9.46	4.63	7.14	3.46	2.37

(Source: MSME, 2018)

Table 6. Women's empowerment through political participation in Indian parliament

Year	Members in Lok Sabha			Members in Rajya Sabha		
	Total Members	Female	% of Female	Total Members	Female	% of Female
1980	544	28	5.15	244	24	9.84
1984	544	44	8.09	244	28	11.48
1989	517	27	5.22	245	24	9.8
1991	554	39	7.17	245	38	15.51
1996	543	39	7.18	223	19	8.52
1998	543	43	7.92	245	15	6.12
1999	543	49	9	245	19	7.8
2004	539	44	8.2	245	28	11.4
2009	543	58	10.6	245	22	8.98
2014	543	61	11.2	245	29	11.8

(Source: Election Commission of India, 2015)

category (Figure 11). Her urban males performed better but in the 68th round they also coincided with that of urban female in terms of regular employment. Also interesting to note is that the rural urban gap is quite prominent in case of regular employment but it's the reverse gap in case of self-employed.

Figure 11. Changes in the proportion of self-employed in usual status (ps+ss)
(Author's Construction based on IHSN, 2013)

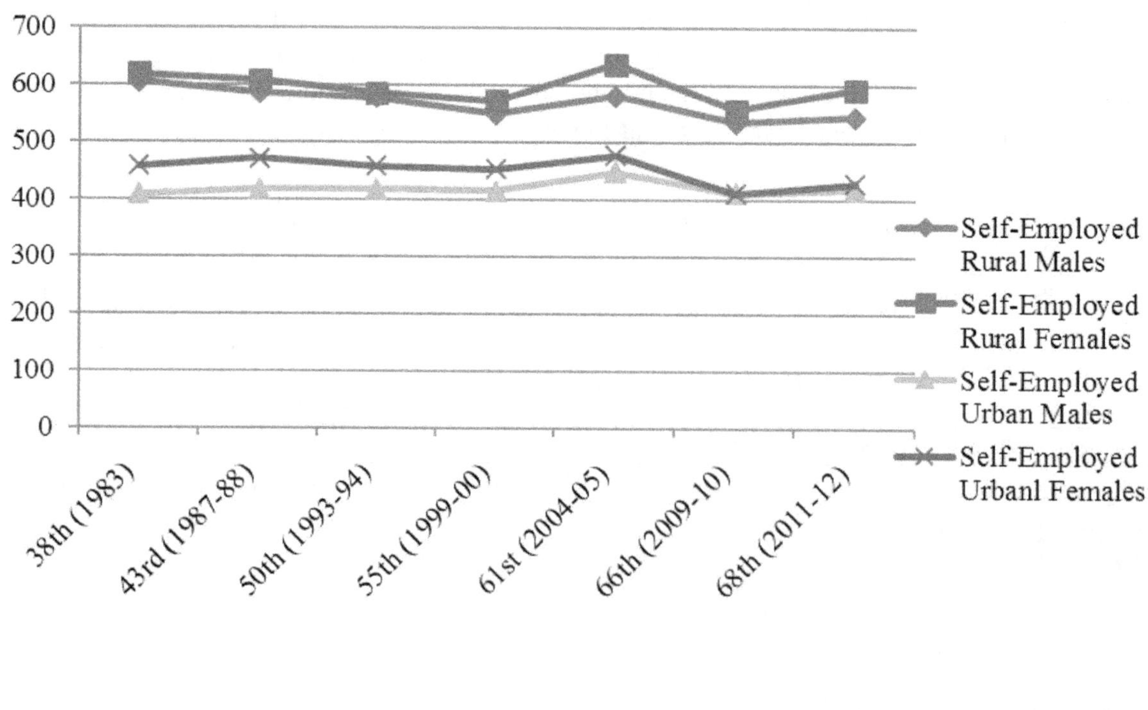

WOMEN EMPOWERMENT AND PROTECTION- GOVERNMENT INITIATIVES

From 30th January, 2006, the Ministry of Women and Child Development, Government of India, started functioning as a separate Ministry. A national apex statutory body in the name of National Commission for Women (NCW) was set up in 1992 for protecting and safeguarding the rights of women. India is a signatory to the Convention on Elimination of all Forms of Discrimination against Women (CEDAW), Sustainable Development Goals (SDGs) for addressing key challenges including gender equity. The Ministry has been administering 'Support to Training and Employment Programme (STEP) for Women' since 1986-87 as a 'Central Sector Scheme'. The STEP Scheme aims to provide skills that give employability to women and to provide competencies and skills that enable women to become self-employed/ entrepreneurs. One of the significant micro-credit schemes has been taken up as a case study below.

CASE STUDY: RASHTRIYA MAHILA KOSH (RMK)

Rashtriya Mahila Kosh (RMK) or 'The National Credit Fund for Women' was set up by the Government of India in 1993 as a national level organization under the Ministry of Women and Child Development, primarily to meet the credit needs of poor and asset-less women who work in the informal sector. As regards its administrative set up, the Governing Board of RMK which administers RMK consists of sixteen members representing various Central Ministries/ Departments, State Governments, Specialists and Representatives of Organizations active in the field of micro credit. RMK provides micro-finance services such as Loans are granted for Income Generating Activities (IGA), housing, micro-enterprises, family needs, etc. Initiatives has also been taken by the RMK for women empowerment by way of micro financing, thrift and credit, capacity building and marketing linkages through SHGs format and also

Figure 12. Changes in the proportion of regular-employed in usual status (ps+ss)
(Author's Construction based on IHSN, 2013)

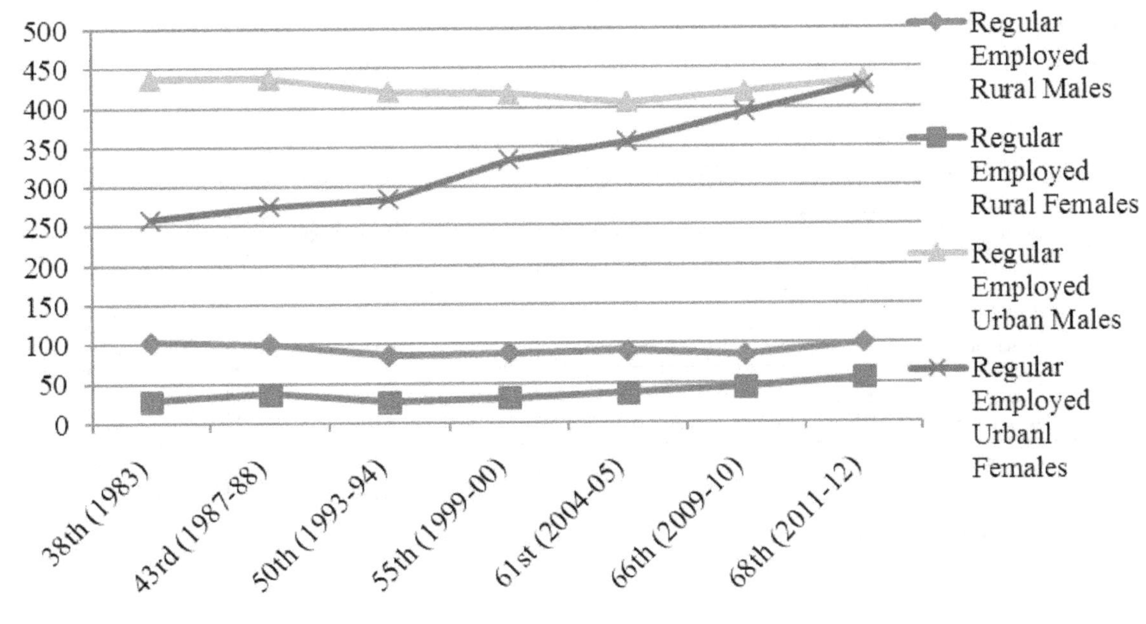

enterprise development for poor women. Credit is provided to the poor women beneficiaries through Intermediary Micro financing Organizations (IMOs) working at grass root level such as NGOs, Women Federations, Cooperatives etc. by following a client friendly procedure, simple, without collateral loan required for livelihood and income generation activities, housing, microenterprises etc. The states in Table 7 are major receivers of micro-credit from RMK:

RMK has a network of large number of IMOs in the country, which helps in creating awareness among the partner organizations. RMK has launched a Nodal Agency Scheme for credit linkages with potential NGOs with a view to expand its outreach in a most cost-effective manner in the remote or un-covered areas of the country. The Ministry of Women & Child Development launched "Mahila E-Haat", a unique direct online digital marketing platform for women entrepreneurs/SHGs/ NGOs on 7th March 2016. This can become a catalyst in strengthening women entrepreneurship.

EMPIRICAL ANALYSIS

Our basic objective is to provide some empirical support to the analysis made using various secondary data. The relationship between the independent and dependent variables is determined using ordinary least squares (OLS) regressions. The model tries to seek explanatory relationships between the independent and dependent variables. Here we have tried to measure women empowerment by means of percentage of self-employment among women (PSELF_EMP) and the independent variables are Per capita State GDP (SGDP), micro finance penetration rate (MPIPR) across states, literacy rate among women (LITRT) across states and state-wise regional rural bank (RRBPR). The microfinance penetration index (MPI) provides estimates of the relative share of the states in microfinance clients as compared to their share in the population (calculated by share of microfinance clients divided by population of the respective state). There are 28 states and 7 union territories in India which provides a scope of 35 observations in a cross-sectional study. However, in our study we have 31 observations which include 26 states and 5 union territories. The states of Jammu and Kashmir, Lakshadweep, Daman and Dui, and Dadra and Nagar Haveli have been omitted because of non-availability of data (Telengana is included in the state of Andhra Pradesh).

This study is based on secondary data from the following sources:

Table 7. Performance of micro-credit through RMK

State	Sanctioned (in Rs. Lakhs.)	Disbursed (in Rs. Lakhs.)	No. of Beneficiaries
Andhra Pradesh	8,138.41	7,153.48	197,760
Tamil Nadu	8,013.84	6,495.77	169,274
West Bengal	2,477.29	2,023.79	54,072
Orissa	2,299.45	2,186.05	39,097
Madhya Pradesh	2,207.30	1,987.40	21,866
Rajasthan	1,963.90	1,819.74	30,285
Maharashtra	1,671.90	1,420.05	35,672

(Source: Ministry of Women and Child Development, 2017)

1. State-wise percentage of self-employed women (taken as a proxy for women empowerment) has been taken from the Annual Report 2016-2017 (Ministry of Child and Women development, 2017).
2. Micro finance penetration rate across states Inclusive Finance India Report, 2014.
3. Per capita State GDP (SGDP), literacy rate among women (LITRT) across states and state-wise regional rural bank (RRBPR) are taken from RBI's Handbook of Statistics on Indian Economy. (RBI, 2017).

The functional specification of the model is as follows:

$$pself\_emp_i = \alpha_1 + \beta_1 sgdp + \beta_2 mfipr\left(-1\right) + \beta_3 mfipr\left(-2\right) + \beta_4 litrt + \beta_5 \, litrt\left(-1\right) + \beta_6 d\left(rrbpr\right)$$

First, we check the stationarity of the data using Augmented Dickey-Fuller (ADF) Test and finally we run the OLS regression to have an estimate of the parameters.

The results of table 8 clearly shows that all the variables are stationary at level except for RRBPR, which is stationary at first difference.

Regression Results

Dependent Variable: PSELF_EMP

The coefficients of regression shows that SGDP has a positive impact on self-employment of women i.e. on women empowerment. But both MFIPR (-2) and LITRT (-1) are lagged functions which have a positive impact on the self -employment of women (Table 9). But the change in the no. of rural bank

Table 8. Results of Unit Root Test (Using Augmented Dickey-Fuller Test)

Variable	t-Statistic	Probability	Critical Value (5% Level)	Series Type
PSELF_EMP	-4.764167	0.0006	-2.963972	S
SGDP	-4.688575	0.0008	-2.963972	S
MFIPR	-3.850841	0.0064	-2.963972	S
LITRT	-4.878424	0.0005	-2.963972	S
RRBPR	-1.762456	0.3880	-3.004861	NS
D(RRBPR)	-5.181940	0.0005	-3.020686	S

Table 9. Results of regression

Variable	Coefficient	Std. Error	t-Statistic	Prob.
C	60.15535	49.16381	1.223570	0.2388
SGDP	0.000645	0.000199	-3.236914	0.0052
MFIPR(-1)	-15.59103	5.333034	-2.923483	0.0099
MFIPR(-2)	1.978889	5.676740	0.348596	0.7319
LITRT	-0.845715	0.475671	-1.777942	0.0944
LITRT(-1)	1.322357	0.447986	2.951781	0.0094
D(RRBPR)	-0.003047	0.004698	-0.648512	0.5259

R-Squared = 0.680615; Durbin-Watson stat= 2.207394

branches across states has a negative impact. The explanatory variables together explain 68 per cent of the variations in the dependent variables. Moreover, the DW statistic value is close to 2, showing non-autocorrelation.

CONCLUSION

In the International Women Conference in 1985 at Nairobi, the concept of women empowerment was introduced, which defined it as redistribution of social power and control of resources in favour of women. In India, empowerment of women has been recognized and accepted as a distinct strategy since the Eighth Five year Plan. In achieving sustainable and inclusive growth along with women empowerment the policy makers found the magic bullet (Kabeer, 2005) of micro finance. But the present study reveals that though micro finance is supposed to provide an effective tool for financial and social upliftment of the poorer sections of the society, particularly women, but its penetration depends on a multifaceted and integrated network and so both the self-help bank model and the MFI model may have achieved some positive growth, but their performances are not quite deterministic when compared with other countries of the world. While the MFI model reaches microcredit quickly and efficiently to the financially excluded, the SHG-BLP programme besides credit and savings provides wholesome social and economic justice to the excluded and deprived section of the society and has proven itself as an invaluable platform for inclusive growth. India falls within the medium HDI group but according to GDI score India falls under group 5 (i.e. with low equality in HDI achievements between women and men). As per the UNDP's Human Development Report 2013: India stood at 132nd position out of 187countries on the gender inequality index (GII) —performing worse than Pakistan whose position is 123. All nations in South Asia, except Afghanistan, performed better than India, with Sri Lanka (75) topping them all. Nepal ranked 102nd and Bangladesh 111th. The Inclusive Finance Report (Nair & Tankha, 2014) analyzing the growth of Indian microfinance reveals that MFI's have highest penetration in southern regions, followed by eastern region (Figure 7a). The concentration of microfinance in the three southern states of Andhra Pradesh, Karnataka and Tamil Nadu is comparatively much higher than the other states in the country. In fact, a comparison of MPI scores across various states of India reveals that Andhra Pradesh tops the list (3.38), followed by Puducherry (2.87) and then Karnataka (2.27). The empirical analysis of the impact of Per capita State GDP (SGDP), micro finance penetration rate (MPIPR) across states, literacy rate among women (LITRT) across states and state-wise regional rural bank (RRBPR) on Women empowerment (proxied by percentage of self-employed women workers) shows SGDP has a positive impact on self-employment of women i.e. on women empowerment. But both MFIPR (-2) and LITRT (-1) are lagged functions which have a positive impact on the self -employment of women. But the change in the number of rural bank branches across states has a negative impact. The explanatory variables together explain 68 per cent of the variations in the dependent variables. Though there are certain criticisms against using these indicators as measures of women empowerment, but still the picture is quite blurred. Micro Finance Institutions (Development and Regulation) Bill 2012 on May 22, 2012 has been introduced by the government of India to establish a regulator under RBI to regulate and supervise the activities of NGOs and MFIs. So the road map of microfinance has miles to go to really achieve something commendable in the field of women empowerment.

REFERENCES

Ministry of Child and Women development, Govt. of India. (2017). Annual Report. 2016-17. Retrieved from http://www.wcd.nic.in/sites/default/files/FINAL%20WCD_AR_English%202016-17.pdf

Sa-Dahn. (2015). Bharat Micro Finance Report 2015. Retrieved from https://www.microfinancegateway.org/library/bharat-microfinance-report-2015

Sa-Dahn. (2016). Bharat Microfinance Report 2016. Retrieved from http://indiamicrofinance.com/wp-content/uploads/2016/09/The-Bharat-Microfinance-Report-2016.pdf

Batliwala, S. (1994). The Meaning of Women's Empowerment: New Concepts from Action.

Townsend, J., Zapata, E., Rowlands, J., Alberti, P. and Mercado, M. (1999). Women and Power: Fighting Patriarchies and Power. London, New York: Zed Books.

Cheston, S., & Kuhn, L. (2002). Empowering Women through Microfinance. In S. Daley-Harris, (Ed.), Pathways out of poverty: Innovations in Microfinance for the Poorest Families (pp. 167-228). Bloomfield, CT: Kumarian Press.

Das, S., Chandra, S., Kochhar, K., & Kumar, N. (2015). Women Workers in India: Why So Few Among So Many? (Working Paper, WP/15/55). IMF.

Kabeer, N. (2005). Is microfinance a magic Bullet for Women's Empowerment? Analysis of Findings in South Asia.

Kabeer, N. (2001). Conflicts over credit: Re-evaluating the empowerment potential of loans to women in rural Bangladesh. *World Development*, *29*(1), 63–84. doi:10.1016/S0305-750X(00)00081-4

Klasen, S. (2006). UNDP's Gender-Related Measures: Some Conceptual Problems and Possible Solutions. *Journal of Human Development*, *7*(2), 243–274. doi:10.1080/14649880600768595

Klasen, S., & Schüler, D. (2011). Reforming the Gender-related Development Index and the Gender Empowerment Measure: Implementing some specific proposals. *Feminist Economics*, *17*(1), 1–30. doi:10.1080/13545701.2010.541860

Krishna, A. (2003). Social Capital, Community Driven Development, and Empowerment: A short note on concepts and operations (*Working Paper* 33077). *World Bank.*

Mahanta, P, & Panda, G. & Sreekumar. (2012). Status of Microfinance in India - A review, International Journal of Marketing. *Financial Services & Management Research*, *1*(11), 142–155.

Malhotra, A., S.R. Schuler & C. Boender (2002.) Measuring women's empowerment as a variable in international development. *Paper for World Bank Workshop on Poverty and Gender: New Perspectives*, May 7.

Mayoux, L. (1998). Participatory learning for women's empowerment in micro-finance programmes: Negotiating complexity, conflict and change. *IDS Bulletin*, *29*(4), 39–51. doi:10.1111/j.1759-5436.1998.mp29004005.x

Mokta, M. (2014). Empowerment of Women in India: A Critical Analysis. *The Indian Journal of Public Administration*, *60*(3), 473–488. doi:10.1177/0019556120140308

Pokhriyal, A. K., Rani, R., & Uniyal, J. (2014). Role of Micro-Finance in the Empowerment of the Women. *Journal of Business and Finance*, *02*(01), 21–31.

Ray, S., & Mahapatra, S. K. (2014). Penetration of MFIs among Indian States: An Understanding through Macro Variables (working paper 2014-01). Centro de Economia e Financas da UP.

Ray, D. (1998). *Development economics*. New Jersey: Princeton University press.

Reserve Bank of India (RBI). (2017, September 15). RBI's Handbook of Statistics on Indian Economy, 2016, 2017. Retrieved from https://rbi.org.in/Scripts/AnnualPublications.aspx?head=Handbook%20of%20Statistics%20on%20Indian%20Economy

Sen, A. K. (1990). Gender and co-operative conflict. In I. Tinker (Ed.), *Persistent inequalities*. New Delhi: Oxford University Press.

Sen, A. K. (1993). Capability and well-being. In: Nussbaum and Sen, eds. The quality of life. Helsinki: World Institute of Development Economics Research. doi:10.1093/0198287976.003.0003

Simanowitz, A., & A. Walker (2002). Ensuring impact: reaching the poorest while building financially self-sufficient institutions, and showing improvement in the lives of the poorest women and their families. *Paper for the Microcredit Summit*, New York, November 10-13.

Sinha, F. (2009). State of Microfinance in India. Retrieved from http://www.inm.org.bd/publication/state_of_micro/India.pdf

Swain. (2007). Can Microfinance Empower Women? Self-Help Groups in India. Retrieved from http://mfg-en-paper-can-microfinance–empower- women-self-help-groups-in-india-may-2007.pdf

Nair, T. S., & Tankha, A. (2014, December). The Inclusive Finance Report. Retrieved from https://www.microfinancegateway.org/library/inclusive-finance-india-report-2014

International Household Survey Network (IHSN). (2013). The NSS Report (68th Round), 2011-12. Retrieved from http://catalog.ihsn.org/index.php/catalog/3281

UNIFEM. (2000). *Progress of the world's women*. New York: United Nations Development Fund for Women.

World Bank. (2001). *Engendering Development: Through Gender Equality in Rights, Resources and Voice, World Bank Policy Research Report*. Oxford: Oxford University Press.

Zaman, H. (2001). *Assessing the poverty and vulnerability impact of micro-credit in Bangladesh: a case study of BRAC. Background paper for World Bank World Development Report 2000/2001*. Washington, DC: World Bank.

The Mahatma Gandhi National Rural Employment Guarantee Act. 2005 (MGNREGA). (2014). Retrieved from http://www.nrega.nic.in/netnrega/home.aspx

Micro, S., & Enterprises, M. (MSME). (2018, March 6). Registered SSI Sector – Review of the results. Retrieved from http://www.dcmsme.gov.in/ssiindia/census/ch2.htm

Election Commission of India. (2015). Retrieved from http://eci.nic.in/eci/eci.html

Sharma, Y. (2013, November-December). Women Entrepreneur in India. *IOSR Journal of Business and Management, 15*(3), 9–14. doi:10.9790/487X-1530914

NABARD. (2016). *Status of Microfinance in India 2015-16*. NABARD.

KEY TERMS AND DEFINITIONS

Cross Section Data Analysis: Cross section data refers to data of variables across cross section of the population at the same point of time or during the same time period. So, Cross-sectional data, or a cross section of a study population, in statistics and econometrics is a type of data collected by observing many subjects (such as individuals, firms, countries, or regions) at the same point of time, or without regard to differences in time. Analysis of cross-sectional data usually consists of comparing the differences among the subjects. Cross-sectional data differs from time series data, in which the same small-scale or aggregate entity is observed at various points in time.

Gender Development Index (GDI): The UNDP Report of 1995 introduced two new complementary indices, of which the most significant is the Gender-related Development Index (GDI). The GDI measures gender inequalities in achievement in three basic dimensions of human development: health, measured by female and male life expectancy at birth; education, measured by female and male expected years of schooling for children and female and male mean years of schooling for adults ages 25 years and older; and command over economic resources, measured by female and male estimated earned income.

Gender Empowerment Measure (GEM): UNDP's GEM is specifically focused on determining women's relative empowerment, which we consider to be a valuable feature of the measure. GEM contains three components: political representation, representation in senior positions in the economy, and power over economic resources (proxied by earned incomes). But there are a range of problems associated with the current GEM, which have been discussed in detail by Klasen (2006). Human Development Report (2014) introduced new Gender Development Index (GDI) which is simply the ratio of a female human development index to the male human development index.

Gender Inequality Index (GII): GII is an index measuring the welfare loss of gender inequality considering a hybrid of well-being and empowerment outcomes rather than gender-sensitive development or gender inequality directly. As per the United Nations Development Programme's Human Development Report 2013: India stood at 132nd position out of 187countries on the GII—performing worse than Pakistan whose position is 123.The new GII contains three dimensions, reproductive health, empowerment, and labor market. The first averages female adolescent fertility and maternal mortality, the second parliamentary representation and educational attainment, and the third just consist of labor force participation. The aggregation is first across dimensions for males and females separately, using the geometric mean.

Microfinance: Microfinance may be defined as "provision of thrift, the wide network of the organized banking system deep credit and other financial services and products of very into rural areas. Market and the government both failed to small amounts to the poor in rural, semi urban or urban provide credit access to the poor. In fact, the failure of areas, for enabling them to raise their income levels and institutional initiatives of rural credit and to the improve living standards". Women constitute a vast majority of users of micro-credit and saving services. Microfinance institutions (MFIs) broadly refers to a wide range of organizations dedicated to providing these services through Self-Help Groups (SHGs), NGOs, credit co-operatives, commercial banks, NBFCs and parts of State-owned banks.

Microfinance Penetration Index (MPI): Denotes a state's share of MFI clients relative to the total MFI clients in the country. The Inclusive Finance Report (2014) analyzing the growth of Indian microfinance reveals that MFI's have highest penetration in southern regions, followed by eastern region (Figure 7a). The concentration of microfinance in the three southern states of Andhra Pradesh, Karnataka and Tamil Nadu is comparatively much higher than the other states in the country. In fact, a comparison of MPI scores across various states of India reveals that Andhra Pradesh tops the list (3.38), followed by Puducherry (2.87) and then Karnataka (2.27).

Self Help Groups (SHGs): Self Help Groups (SHGs) are formed by people from homogenous groups and common social background and occupation voluntarily form the group and pool their savings for the benefit of all the members of the groups. The Self Help Groups (SHGs) is the dominant microfinance methodology in India. In this case the members of SHGs pool their small savings regularly at a prefixed amount on daily or weekly basis and SHGs provide loan to members for a fixed period. SHGs are essentially formal and voluntary association of 15 to 20 people formed to attain common objectives. NABARD has facilitated and extensively supported a program which entails commercial banks' lending directly to SHGs rather than via bulk loan to MFIs.

Women Empowerment: Empowerment of women is a socio-political ideal envisioned in the wider framework of women rights. It is a process that leads women to realize their full potential, their rights to have access to opportunities, resources and choices with the freedom of decision making both within and outside home. Empowerment would be achieved only when advancement in the conditions of women is accompanied by their ability to influence the direction of social change gained through equal opportunities in economic, social and political spheres of life (National Policy for women, 2016). Empowerment of women means developing them as more aware individuals, who are politically active, economically productive and independent and are able to make intelligent discussion in matters that affect them.

APPENDIX

Unit Root Test

Table 10.

Null Hypothesis: PSELF_EMP has a unit root				
Exogenous: Constant				
Lag Length: 0 (Automatic - based on SIC, maxlag=7)				
			t-Statistic	Prob.*
Augmented Dickey-Fuller test statistic			-4.764167	0.0006
Test critical values:	1% level		-3.670170	
	5% level		-2.963972	
	10% level		-2.621007	

*MacKinnon (1996) one-sided p-values

Table 11.

Null Hypothesis: SGDP has a unit root				
Exogenous: Constant				
Lag Length: 0 (Automatic - based on SIC, maxlag=7)				
			t-Statistic	Prob.*
Augmented Dickey-Fuller test statistic			-4.688575	0.0008
Test critical values:	1% level		-3.670170	
	5% level		-2.963972	
	10% level		-2.621007	

*MacKinnon (1996) one-sided p-values

Table 12.

Null Hypothesis: MFIPR has a unit root				
Exogenous: Constant				
Lag Length: 0 (Automatic - based on SIC, maxlag=7)				
			t-Statistic	Prob.*
Augmented Dickey-Fuller test statistic			-3.850841	0.0064
Test critical values:	1% level		-3.670170	
	5% level		-2.963972	
	10% level		-2.621007	

*MacKinnon (1996) one-sided p-values

Table 13.

Null Hypothesis: LITRT has a unit root				
Exogenous: Constant				
Lag Length: 0 (Automatic - based on SIC, max lag = 7)				
			t-Statistic	Prob.*
Augmented Dickey-Fuller test statistic			-4.878424	0.0005
Test critical values:	1% level		-3.670170	
	5% level		-2.963972	
	10% level		-2.621007	

*MacKinnon (1996) one-sided p-values

Table 14.

Null Hypothesis: RRBPR has a unit root				
Exogenous: Constant				
Lag Length: 1 (Automatic - based on SIC, max lag = 6)				
			t-Statistic	Prob.*
Augmented Dickey-Fuller test statistic			-1.762456	0.3880
Test critical values:	1% level		-3.769597	
	5% level		-3.004861	
	10% level		-2.642242	

*MacKinnon (1996) one-sided p-values

Table 15.

Null Hypothesis: D(RRBPR) has a unit root				
Exogenous: Constant				
Lag Length: 1 (Automatic - based on SIC, max lag = 6)				
			t-Statistic	Prob.*
Augmented Dickey-Fuller test statistic			-5.181940	0.0005
Test critical values:	1% level		-3.808546	
	5% level		-3.020686	
	10% level		-2.650413	

*MacKinnon (1996) one-sided p-values

Table 16. Model:pself_emp c sgdpmfipr(-1) mfipr(-2) litrtlitrt(-1) d(rrbpr)

Dependent Variable: PSELF_EMP				
Method: Least Squares				
Date: 07/30/17 Time: 20:26				
Sample (adjusted): 3 27				
Included observations: 23 after adjustments				
Variable	Coefficient	Std. Error	t-Statistic	Prob.
C	60.15535	49.16381	1.223570	0.2388
SGDP	0.000645	0.000199	-3.236914	0.0052
MFIPR(-1)	-15.59103	5.333034	-2.923483	0.0099
MFIPR(-2)	1.978889	5.676740	0.348596	0.7319
LITRT	-0.845715	0.475671	-1.777942	0.0944
LITRT(-1)	1.322357	0.447986	2.951781	0.0094
D(RRBPR)	-0.003047	0.004698	-0.648512	0.5259
R-squared	0.680615	Mean dependent var		58.17391
Adjusted R-squared	0.560845	S.D. dependent var		24.00695
S.E. of regression	15.90911	Akaike info criterion		8.617451
Sum squared resid	4049.596	Schwarz criterion		8.963036
Log likelihood	-92.10069	Hannan-Quinn criter.		8.704365
F-statistic	5.682705	Durbin-Watson stat		2.207394
Prob(F-statistic)	0.002503			

Chapter 3
Microfinance and Women Empowerment: An Empirical Analysis

Madhabendra Sinha
National Institute of Technology Durgapur, India

Sudhansu Sekhar Mahapatra
Sikkim University, Gangtok, India

Abhijit Dutta
Sikkim University, Gangtok, India

Partha Pratim Sengupta
National Institute of Technology Durgapur, India

ABSTRACT

The present chapter empirically examines the role of microfinance access on women empowerment by using primary data on women borrowers from different microfinance institutions in Nadia and Murshidabad districts of West Bengal in India. Microfinance institutions play an important role in strategies related to gender and development due to their active relationships with women empowerment and poverty alleviation. The various programmes under microfinance like self-help groups (SHGs) are promoted and inspired for their significant economic impacts on empowerment of women. We investigate the impact of microfinance access on three dimensions of women empowerment, which make influence upon decision making on the issues of credit, expenditure and children. We conduct a primary survey on about eight hundred respondents of women borrowers from different microfinance institutions and apply multivariate probit estimation. Our findings imply that the greater access to microfinance credit negatively impacts on economic empowerment i.e. decisions on credit and expenditure related issues.

INTRODUCTION

Women empowerment is a global issue. The concept of women empowerment was introduced at the international women conference at Nairobi in 1985. Education is milestone of women empowerment because it enables them to respond to the challenges to confront their traditional role and change their

DOI: 10.4018/978-1-5225-5240-6.ch003

life. The world of humanity has two wings, one is women and other is man. Meet until both wings are equally developed can the bird fly. The process of empowerment is multidimensional, and it enables women to realize their full destiny and powers in all spheres of life. In fact, women's empowerment is central to the achievement of the triple goals of equality, development and social justice.

In recent times, empowerment has emerged as a concept that would liberate women from their unsaved states, and provides them an opportunity to embrace that promised freedom to make choice and contribute to their societies. Requirement of empowering women is felt at the national as well as the international level. In order to bring about a change, women have to develop and nurture the idea of Self-reliance and Self-esteem. Empowerment is a growing process and not an end by itself. It means control over and access of resources and take decision in the matters of her own earned income, saving and expenditures for her household needs and other purpose. The economic empowerment of women is a pre-requisite for sustainable development, pro-poor growth and achievements of all Millennium Development Goals (MDGs).

Since the turn of the century, growing industrialization, globalization, and social legislation have contributed towards changing status of women worldwide. Along with the expansion of education and awareness, women have come out of their kitchens and have reached out to higher level of professional activities. In almost all the developed countries women have successfully equated themselves with men in the corporate field (Nandy & Kumar, 2014). Women-controlled and women-owned enterprises are now seen as vital functional elements of the society and the economy, representing approximately 25.8 to 28.1 percentage of the total entrepreneurship in the world.

India is the fastest growing economy in the world and provides tremendous opportunities to entrepreneurs. However, the scene for women entrepreneurs is not very encouraging because of the percolation of patriarchy into businesses. Though the percentage of women entrepreneurs is increasing constantly from 14% in 1970 to 31% in 2010, motivated women who can really bring a difference are still handfuls. After India has introduce a new law in 2013 and made it mandatory for every company to have at least one woman on board of director, the number of successful women entrepreneurs has raised but not significantly. Participation of women in work and businesses is relatively low in India in comparison to developed countries. Women participation in working India is 31.6% whereas in USA it is 45%, UK 43%, Canada 42%, France 32%, Indonesia 40%, Sri Lanka and Brazil both 35%.

Traditionally in India the role of women has been to look after domestic affairs as housewives. The greatest barriers faced by Indian women in succeeding in their enterprise are expectations from the family and personal commitments and responsibilities. In such circumstances, it is difficult to set priorities and execute their businesses efficiently and effectively. Indian women are highly careful and concerned regarding their obligations and duties in the family and place them above business responsibilities. In Hindu culture, woman is beheld as the epitome of Shakti or power. Using the Shakti, a woman can do all achievable tasks; come what may. In earlier times there existed 3 Ks for the Indian women in an Indian household - Kids, Kitchen and Knitting.

The stepping up of women into corporate realm is considered as an extension to their household chores and kitchen, mainly the 3P's- Pickle, Powder and Pappad. However, along with the expanse of education and passage of time women started shifting from 3P's to the new age 4E's i.e., Electricity, Electronics, Energy and Engineering. Women entrepreneurs are now diversifying from certain standard businesses roles as mentioned above. Normally they were involved in micro and small businesses like beauty product business, or beauty saloon business, or restaurants, or even boutiques. But now the trend is changing and women are directing their attention towards technical, software oriented and technological jobs. In the state of Kerala 30% of factories are registered by the name of women entrepreneurs. In Maharashtra, about 33% of the industries which are registered are run by women (Micro, Small and Medium Enterprises (MSMEs) Report, 2014).

The role of Women entrepreneur in economic as well as social development is very crucial. A next generation of women across the world have undone all negative notions and limitations, and they have proved their mettle beyond doubt in every walk of life, even the most complicated and ever - demanding world of corporate. Our country too has its own pool of smart and confident women who have distinguished themselves within the country as well as on the global platform. Since the middle of 1991, a dramatic change has occurred in Indian Economy. In India, low work participation limits the contribution of women in commercial activities. In recent years, even among of the developed countries like USA and Canada, women's role in terms of their share in small businesses has been increasing. Six out of every ten women in India are not educated. They are far behind men in the field of education. The rapidly growing technology, new methods of production, marketing techniques, and other governmental policy are areas in which women entrepreneurs lack information. On the other hand, there is a continuous pressure from government, regulatory bodies and planning commission to focus on empowering women, especially at the grass roots level and to encourage women in setting up their own micro, small and medium size ventures. This inspired us to analyze the critical success factor of women entrepreneurship in Indian MSMEs.

Against this background this chapter is an attempt to evaluate such an impact of microcredit institutions operating in India by taking the districts of Nadia and Murshidabad in the state of West Bengal as a case study. It tries to explore the impact of giving out small loans to poor women on intra-household decision making. This has been made possible by a design of comprehensive questionnaire in the areas of Nadia and Murshidabad districts specifically to measure the empowerment of microcredit access. This specially designed instrument allows us to identify the treatment effect of microcredit access on the measurement of women empowerment.

We don't have any separate platform for the conflict of interest between men and women members of the household in the traditional views of household behaviour based on the unitary approach to maximize the utility. However different theoretical views have recognized such type of conflict of interest in their efforts to explain the certain backdrops of the process of development namely gender inequality, where is basically less investment in women, child education and health and even gender discrimination in the market place (Manser & Brown, 1980; McElroy & Horney, 1981; Behrman, 1997) Against this background, the microfinance institutions to provide access to credit to women is under investigated upon as an effective tool to resolve the above stated backdrops of the development process and even contribute to achieving the Millennium Development Goals (MDG) on gender equality and women empowerment (Kabeer, 2005). Although it is generally hoped that women's access to credit through the microfinance route can empower women, the empirical evidence so far provided in support of this view is mixed.

Different literature like Hashemi et al. (1996) observed that access to microfinance increases mobility of women, ability to make purchases and take major household decisions, ownership of the productive assets, awareness of legal and political issues etc. Pitt et al. (2006) found the positive effects of microfinance on the autonomy of women in purchasing household decisions, access of women to financial and productive resources, the extent of social networks of women with greater freedom of mobility and greater likelihood that the women can initiate discussion with husband about planning for family. In their study Ashraf et al. (2010) discovered that access to a product of commitment savings leads to the rising purchases of women oriented durable goods and services (e.g. sewing machine, washing machine, micro oven etc.) as opposed to other durables products such as recreational goods, vehicles etc.

Many authors have identified that government policies and schemes directly affect the conditions of women entrepreneurs (Iakovleva et al., 2013). The Government of India has initiated different programs for ladies to begin their endeavours in micro and small level businesses (Farr-Wharton & Brunetto, 2007). Apart from this, different NGOs have supported women entrepreneurship skills. Government of India has organized many training programs for women entrepreneurship (Garg et al., 2017). Government has exercised various policies such as limitations on imports and fares, provisions of insolvency law's passage hindrances, procedural prerequisite for enrolment and authorizing rules and directions representing entrepreneurial manoeuvres, and laws to ensure respectability rights (Michael and Pearce, 2009). Personal skills, competency and capabilities are critical factors for entrepreneurial activities. Combination of knowledge and skills were practiced by the business visionaries that can be utilized to bolster the advancement of those competencies (Walker & Webster, 2006) and can possibly, thus, drive business development. These comprehensive skills support the women-entrepreneurs to manage organizations effectively (Mitchelmore & Rowley, 2013). Additionally, willingness to tune in, individual style and self-advancement capacity to withstand weight, tender loving care and concentration on consistent change, uplifting the state of mind, individual duty and obligations were the inhibited attributes which are required to be a successful entrepreneur.

In India, social issues are very critical for women entrepreneurs. It is difficult for women to use entrepreneurial models, to deal with them, and manage the challenge of social dogma. A business visionary tries to change and address the societal concerns through the production of reasonable financial structures, relations, foundations, associations, and practices that yield and support social advantages (Hasan, 2005). This requires societal support and inspiration especially to women who endeavour to do business. Women entrepreneurship adoption is also influenced by nearness of experienced maori business people, presence of good example inside maori society, existence with maori entrepreneurial qualities, recognition of maori entrepreneurial execution (Clydesdale, 2007). Success of women entrepreneur depends on the acceptance and perception of the society (Welsh & Krueger, 2012). Entrepreneur should be able to control the cost and achieves economy of scale (Amatucci & Crawley, 2011).

Successful businesses require allocating and projecting sufficient resources wherever they are required and utilize them effectively and efficiently (Garg, 2016). Business women are required to be capable enough to arrange sufficient funds for business operations. An entrepreneur must be able to finance business through various financial sources and manage capital budgeting decisions effectively (Kumar, 2013). The success of business firm depends on the market demands of the organizational products and services. Business entrepreneurs were able to address the gaps and generate sufficient demand for their products and services (Prakash & Barua, 2016). Effective marketing efforts are required for MSMEs products and services in order to increase the reach to the customers. Technology and infrastructure is showing up as a vital renderer in enhancement of global economy and cleaner and safer technology adoption is now being used extensively to do away with problems like the case of environmental issues.

Information and Communication Technologies (ICTs) can play a vital role in developing MSMEs through efficient usage and good inclusion of ICTs in entrepreneurial tasks while providing assistance in zeroing down to efficient decisions that are contextually relevant and precise. ICTs can generate the step change among MSMEs and make them competitive, innovative and generate growth (Barba-Sánchez et al., 2007). The success and performance of the firm directly depends on management and strategic decision making. Successful business people can see what other people cannot. They believe in good relationships with their colleagues and sub-ordinates. Their decision making style, skills and competency make them different forms others. Managerial ability and administrative skills provides human asset to the firms such as procedures that comprise the orderly legible proof of key standings which add to the organization's economical bounds, gender equality, the improvement of an ability pool of potent and efficient occupants to complete these parts, talent management and the advancement of a separated human asset engineering to encourage filling these positions with skilled office holders and to guarantee their proceeding with responsibility to the organization (Collings & Mellahi, 2009).

However, some studies have found negative or no effects of microfinance access on women empowerment. Armendáriz and Roome (2008) quoted subjective evidence that women access to microfinance with the exclusion of men might have perverse effects on women empowerment. Pitt et al (1999) identified that access of women to microfinance sometimes can have a positive effect on fertility and no impact on contraceptive use. Rahman (1999) viewed that a major portion of the women borrowers of Grameen Bank have experienced an increased conflict of spousal and aggression in both verbal and physical terms. In his study of two drought prone villages in India, Garikipati (2008) found the negative empowerment impacts on work time allocation of women as well as control over financial resources. Banerjee et al. (2013) did not find any significant impact of microfinance access on different measures of decision making power over issues of household expenditure, savings, investment or education to women.

Given the mixed evidence of the literature on effects of microfinance on women empowerment, more empirical exercise will be helpful to shed light on this issue. Our paper is an attempt to provide additional empirical evidence from the context of India. We investigate against a primary data set collected from women borrowers of different kinds of microfinance institutions like Grameen Banks, Samabay Samiti, Bandhan etc located in the districts of Nadia and Murshidabad in West Bengal, India whether and what way microfinance access leads to women empowerment. We examined women empowerment in three dimensions, which are whether influence over, decisions on credit related matters, decisions on expenditure related matters and decisions on children related matters have increased. The rest of the paper is structured as follows. Section 2 describes about the data and methodology. Section 3 analyses the empirical findings and finally section 4 concludes our paper.

DATA AND METHODOLOGY

We collect the data from women borrowers of different microfinance institutions like Grameen Banks, Samabay Samiti, Bandhan etc located in the districts of Nadia and Murshidabad in West Bengal in India. To focus on the women empowerment, we keep our attention to the adult women who have collected loans for their household purpose. The data has been collected from eight major areas of Nadia and Murshidabad district during the period of March to November 2016, and the areas are Krishnagar, Santipur, Tehatta and Nabadwip in Nadia and Kandi, Nabagram, Jangipur and Farakka in Murshidabad.

In the plan of sample design, the pipeline approach to impact evaluation has been used; it is involving the use of new members to controls the existing members. The longitudinal approach like the difference in difference can be used when random experiment is not possible. The approach can compare the pre and post situations of members and non-members. This technique accounts for the selection bias due to time-invariant unobservable at individual specific. The cross-sectional comparisons of members and non-members may be there. To handle the selection bias in this approach will require selection of simultaneous modelling into the treatment for example via Heckman two stage approach or the instrumental variables approach or the use of semi-parametric methods.

Here as the evaluation has been performed after the interventions of microfinance have been going on for some years, longitudinal approach cannot be feasible. Sufficient interview of non-members in order to form a large enough comparison group is not feasible, thus ruling out the conventional cross-sectional comparisons approach. Given the process of the evaluation, the most suitable approach is the pipeline approach, where new members have been used as controls for existing members. After the restriction in attention to members alone, the pipeline approach is an attempt to get around the selection bias issue, assuming that new and old members have similar unobservable. However, even if this assumption is true, it will not address the issue of timing of the joining decision, an issue that is related to dynamic selection biases (Karlan, 2001). For an example, if the risk loving ambitious members in a locality join first and only after observing their outcomes the risk averse less ambitious members of a locality connect next, then the latter will not be a good control group for the former.

Of the resulting sample of 800 households, 220 households were in the first loan cycle, where households correspond to the control group under the pipeline approach. The remaining 580 households were in second and higher loan cycles, when the households correspond to the treatment group under the pipeline approach. Out of the 800 households sampled, 40 were dropouts i.e., 5% of total sample. The low dropout rate gives us some confidence that incomplete sample bias and attrition bias may not be serious concerns. Data on all households have been collected using a structured questionnaire covering women empowerment measures, enterprise related information, and member and family socio-economic characteristics.

The paper has concentrated on three dimensions of women empowerment; whether women influence over household decisions on credit related matters has increased, whether women influence over household decisions on expenditure related matters has increased and whether women influence over household decisions on child-related matters has increased. All the three variables are binary in nature. Women empowerment is measured based on the responses of the borrowers of different microfinance institutions, not on the basis of responses of other members of the borrower household, and thus reflects the borrower's own feelings about her empowerment status. We ask whether the member's influence over household decisions has increased (i.e. change in influence), as opposed to asking for a measure of the level of influence so as to minimize the problem of selectivity bias in terms of surveying already empowered women and concluding that microfinance has empowered women. If access to microfinance increases women empowerment, then even in the presence of selectivity bias i.e., interviewing already empowered women, we should still expect to see empowerment increasing with duration of access to microfinance.

Since the three dimensions of women empowerment have been captured from the same set of households, an equation by equation estimation structure to explain variation in each of the four dimensions of empowerment may be inefficient due to possible cross-correlation of error terms between equations. In the case of continuous dependent variables, one solution to handle cross-correlation of error terms between equations is to use Seemingly Unrelated Regression model, proposed by Zellner (1962). However, in our case we have binary response dependent variables and therefore use a multivariate probit specification to estimate these equations as a system, taking into account the cross correlations of errors across equations.

The regression specification we use for the analysis is the following multivariate probit model, specified by Cappellari and Jenkins (2003):

$$y^*_{ik} = \beta_k' X_{ik} + \varepsilon_{ik}$$

$$y_{ik} = 1 \text{ if } y^*_{ik} > 0 \text{ and } 0 \text{ otherwise}$$

Where, *k* indexes outcomes and *i* indexes borrowers. In equation system (1) and (2), the errors are distributed as multivariate normal, with mean zero and variance-covariance matrix The diagonal elements of are 1s and the off-diagonal elements are symmetric i.e., $\rho_{jk} = \rho_{kj}$. In equation (1), y^*_{ik} signifies the four measures of women empowerment and X_{ik} includes all independent variables. The estimation is performed using the multivariate probit command of Cappellari and Jenkins (2003), implemented in the Stata software. The estimation is performed both on the entire sample of 800 households (inclusive of dropouts), as well as on a sub-sample of 760 households (excluding dropouts). The discussion of the results that follows refers to the entire sample of 800 households (inclusive of dropouts).

EMPIRICAL RESULTS

We now interpret the results of the multivariate Probit estimation of equation system on the entire sample of 800 households (inclusive of dropouts), as reported in Table 1. The effect of access to microfinance is captured by the coefficients on loan cycle and the square of the loan cycle. We find that access to microfinance is associated with a decreased likelihood of the borrower managing the microfinance backed enterprise. There is no change in the likelihood of increased influence over credit related decisions, and a lower likelihood of increased influence over expenditure related decisions. These results indicate no or negative empowerment effects of access to microfinance on economic dimensions of empowerment. However, we find a higher likelihood of increased influence over child related decisions, seeming to indicate a reallocation of influence between family members along traditional gender lines, rather than an unambiguous narrowing of women's sphere of influence. Our results provide empirical corroboration of the anecdotal evidence cited in Armendáriz and Roome (2008) of the possible perverse effects on women empowerment of female access to microfinance with male exclusion.

Decreased likelihood of the borrower managing the microfinance backed enterprise may be indicative of male capture of control over productive assets. Lower likelihood of increased influence over expenditure related decisions may be indicative of gender conflict over and ultimate male capture of the fruits of productive assets even where women were responsible for the generation or augmentation of these assets through their access to microfinance - a scenario highlighted in Garikipati (2008). Alternatively, women may be simply allowing their husbands to handle the returns from their microfinance backed enterprises - a scenario highlighted in Goetz and Sen Gupta (1996). A third possibility is that a reallocation along traditional gender lines may be a natural process in situations where women access microfinance with the sole objective of improving their family's financial position, not necessarily with the objective of developing a business empire, and therefore have no qualms in returning to their traditional domain of decision making in the household especially child related matters, once the household economic position is suitably stabilized. For example, Mahmud et al. (2012) find in Bangladesh that women in wealthier households are less likely to feel that they should have a say in household decisions.

Table 1. Empirical results of multivariate probit estimation

Explanatory Variables	Credit Related Decisions		Expenditure Related Decisions		Child Related Decisions	
	Coeff	z Value	Coeff	z Value	Coeff	z Value
Constant	1.64**	2.13	1.83**	2.51	3.24***	4.21
Cycle of the loan	0.06	0.07	0.13	1.23	0.18*	1.71
Square of loan cycle	0.01	0.84	0.03**	2.23	0.03**	2.41
Age of woman member	0.07	1.58	0.09**	2.18	0.14***	3.37
Square of age of woman member	0.01	1.43	0.001**	2.06	0.02***	3.55
Whether the member has completed primary education (Yes = 1, No = 0)	0.22*	1.79	0.07	0.55	0.30***	2.57
Whether member has completed secondary education (Yes = 1, No = 0)	0.06	0.55	0.16	1.44	0.1	0.89
Whether highest educated male is less educated than highest educated female (Yes = 1, No = 0)	0.04	0.42	0.19*	1.85	0.06	0.55
Percentage of dependents in family	0.05*	1.89	0.07***	2.8	0.05	0.02
No of informal loan sources accessed	0.02	0.29	0.02	0.36	0.03	0.38
Number of problems faced in use of production credit	0.07***	3.47	0.04**	2.22	0.08***	3.97
Microfinance backed enterprise is engaged in non-farm activity	0.11	0.84	0.28**	2.13	0.03	0.28
Whether household is upper caste (Yes = 1, No = 0)	0.21**	2.04	0.25***	2.49	0.06	0.58
Whether household has a sanitary latrine (Yes = 1, No = 0)	0.05	0.5	0.11	1.15	0.1	1.02
Whether household located in rural area (Yes = 1, No = 0)	0.19	1.61	0.31***	2.59	0.41***	3.55
Whether household is in Nadia (Yes = 1, No = 0)	0.39***	2.59	0.19	1.26	1.01***	6.54
Whether household is in Murshidabad (Yes = 1, No = 0)	0.2	1.07	0.09	0.05	0.04	0.2
No. of obs	800					
Wald Chi^2	298.89					

Note: ***, **and * represent level of significance at 1%, 5% and 10% respectively
Source: Authors' own estimation using primary data in STATA 12 software

CONCLUSION

This paper tries to contribute to the empirical literature on the women empowerment effects of microfinance. We examine the effect of access to microfinance on four dimensions of women empowerment, namely influence over credit related matters, influence over expenditure related matters and influence over children related issues. We use data on a sample of women borrowers of different MFI operating in Nadia and Murshidabad districts of West Bengal in India, a sampling plan based on the modified pipeline approach to impact evaluation taking appropriate precautions to minimize the concomitant incomplete sample bias and attrition bias, and used a multivariate probit regression specification in order to control for correlation of error terms across multiple equations estimated on the same data set.

We find that greater access to microfinance as measured by longer duration of treatment is associated with a decreased likelihood of the borrower managing the enterprise, lower likelihood of increased influence over expenditure related decisions, and higher likelihood of increased influence over child related decisions. Our results seem to indicate a reallocation of influence between family members along traditional gender lines, rather than an unambiguous narrowing of women's sphere of influence. The negative empowerment effects along economic dimensions provide empirical corroboration of the anecdotal evidence cited in Armendáriz and Roome (2008) of the possible perverse effects on women empowerment of female access to microfinance with male exclusion. The observed reallocation of influence merely conforms to existing norms and culture regarding women's traditional roles, rather than challenging them, and therefore may not constitute evidence of increased women empowerment in a South Asian context.

The intent and social perspectives of the lender, which are often captured in the credit-plus approach, can be an important factor affecting the achievement of economic and gender empowerment through micro-finance. If women empowerment is one of the goals of microfinance, then our results illustrate the importance, in the present setting at least, of the need to explicitly design program features in order to promote women empowerment, rather than simply restricting the supply of credit to women, and assuming that improvement of the economic status of the family due to access to microfinance will automatically translate into gains in women empowerment.

REFERENCES

Amatucci, F. M., & Crawley, D. C. (2011). Financial self-efficacy among women entrepreneurs. *International Journal of Gender and Entrepreneurship*, *3*(1), 23–37. doi:10.1108/17566261111114962

Armendáriz, B., & Roome, N. (2008). Gender Empowerment in Microfinance. In *Microfinance: Emerging Trends and Challenges, edited by Sundaresan* (p. 108). New York: Edward Elgar Publishing. doi:10.4337/9781848445178.00011

Ashraf, N., Karlan, D., & Yin, W. (2010). Female Empowerment: Impact of a Commitment Savings Product in the Philippines. *World Development*, *38*(3), 333–344. doi:10.1016/j.worlddev.2009.05.010

Banerjee, A., Chandrasekhar, A. G., Duflo, E., & Jackson, M. O. (2013). The Diffusion of Microfinance. *Science*, *341*(6144), 6144. doi:10.1126cience.1236498 PMID:23888042

Behrman, J. R. (1997). Intrahousehold Distribution and the Family. In M. Rosenzweig & Stark (Eds.), The Handbook of Population and Family Economics (Vol. 1, Part A). Elsevier.

Bhaumik, S. K. (2015). *Principles of Econometrics: A Modern Approach using Eviews*. New Delhi: Oxford University Press.

Cappellari, L., & Jenkins, S. P. (2003). Multivariate Probit Regression Using Simulated Maximum Likelihood. *The Stata Journal*, *3*, 278–294.

Clydesdale, G. (2007). Cultural evolution and economic growth: New Zealand Maori. *Entrepreneurship and Regional Development*, *19*(1), 49–68. doi:10.1080/08985620601002204

Collings, D. G., & Mellahi, K. (2009). Strategic talent management: A review and research agenda. *Human Resource Management Review*, *19*(4), 304–313. doi:10.1016/j.hrmr.2009.04.001

Farr-Wharton, R., & Brunetto, Y. (2007). Women entrepreneurs, opportunity recognition and government-sponsored business networks: A social capital perspective. *Women in Management Review*, *22*(3), 187–207. doi:10.1108/09649420710743653

Garg, C., Sharma, A., & Goyal, G. (2017). A hybrid decision model to evaluate critical factors for successful adoption of GSCM practices under fuzzy environment. *Uncertain Supply Chain Management*, *5*(1), 59–70. doi:10.5267/j.uscm.2016.7.002

Garg, C. P. (2016). A robust hybrid decision model for evaluation and selection of the strategic alliance partner in the airline industry. *Journal of Air Transport Management*, *52*, 55–66. doi:10.1016/j.jairtraman.2015.12.009

Garikipati, S. (2008). The Impact of Lending to Women on Household Vulnerability and Women's Empowerment: Evidence from India. *World Development*, *36*(12), 2620–2642. doi:10.1016/j.worlddev.2007.11.008

Goetz, A. M., & Sen Gupta, R. (1996). Gender, Power, and Control in Rural Credit Programs in Bangladesh. *World Development*, *24*(1), 45–63. doi:10.1016/0305-750X(95)00124-U

Government of India. (2014). Micro, Small and Medium Enterprises (MSMEs) Report 2014.

Hasan, S. (2005). Social capital and social entrepreneurship in Asia: Analysing the links. *Asia Pacific Journal of Public Administration*, *27*(1). doi:10.1080/23276665.2005.10779296

Hashemi, S. M., Schuler, S. R., & Riley, A. P. (1996). Rural Credit Programs and Women's Empowerment in Bangladesh. *World Development*, *24*(4), 635–653. doi:10.1016/0305-750X(95)00159-A

Iakovleva, T., Solesvik, M., & Trifilova, A. (2013). Financial availability and government support for women entrepreneurs in transitional economies: Cases of Russia and Ukraine. *Journal of Small Business and Enterprise Development*, *20*(2), 314–340. doi:10.1108/14626001311326752

Kabeer, N. (2005). Gender Equality and Women's Empowerment: A Critical Analysis of the Third Millennium Development Goal. *Gender and Development*, *13*(1), 13–24. doi:10.1080/13552070512331332273

Karlan, D. S. (2001). Microfinance Impact Assessments: The Perils of Using New Members as a Control Group. *Journal of Microfinance*, *3*(2), 75–85.

Kumar, N. (2013). Financial inclusion and its determinants: Evidence from India. *Journal of Financial Economic Policy*, *5*(1), 4–19. doi:10.1108/17576381311317754

Mahmud, S., Shah, N. M., & Becker, S. (2012). Measurement of Women's Empowerment in Rural Bangladesh. *World Development*, *40*(3), 610–619. doi:10.1016/j.worlddev.2011.08.003 PMID:23637468

Manser, M., & Brown, M. (1980). Marriage and Household Decision-Making: A Bargaining Analysis. *International Economic Review*, *21*(1), 31–44. doi:10.2307/2526238

McElroy, M. B., & Horney, M. J. (1981). Nash-Bargained Household Decisions: Toward a Generalization of the Theory of Demand. *International Economic Review*, *22*(2), 333–349. doi:10.2307/2526280

Michael, S. C., & Pearce, J. A. II. (2009). The need for innovation as a rationale for government involvement in entrepreneurship. *Entrepreneurship and Regional Development*, *21*(3), 285–302. doi:10.1080/08985620802279999

Millennium Development Goals. (MDGs). (2015). The Millennium Development Goals Report 2015. New York: United Nations.

Mitchelmore, S., & Rowley, J. (2013). Entrepreneurial competencies of women entrepreneurs pursuing business growth. *Journal of Small Business and Enterprise Development*, *20*(1), 125–142. doi:10.1108/14626001311298448

Nandy, S., & Kumar, S. (2014). Women entrepreneurship in 21st century India. *Global Journal of Finance and Management*, *6*(9), 967–976.

Pitt, M. M., Khandker, S. R., & Cartwright, J. (2006). Empowering Women with Microfinance: Evidence from Bangladesh. *Economic Development and Cultural Change*, *54*(4), 791–831. doi:10.1086/503580

Pitt, M. M., Khandker, S. R., McKernan, S., & Latif, M. A. (1999). Credit Programs for the Poor and Reproductive Behavior in Low-Income Countries: Are the Reported Causal Relationships the Result of Heterogeneity Bias? *Demography*, *36*(1). doi:10.2307/2648131 PMID:10036590

Prakash, C., & Barua, M. K. (2015). Integration of AHP-TOPSIS method for prioritizing the solutions of reverse logistics adoption to overcome its barriers under fuzzy environment. *Journal of Manufacturing Systems*, *37*, 599–615. doi:10.1016/j.jmsy.2015.03.001

Rahman, A. (1999). Micro-credit Initiatives for Equitable and Sustainable Development: Who pays? *World Development*, *27*(1), 67–82. doi:10.1016/S0305-750X(98)00105-3

Sen, A. (1992). Missing Women. *British Medical Journal*, *304*, 586–587. PMID:1559085

Sinha, M., Sengupta, D., Roy, O., Banerjee, J., & Sengupta, P. P. (2017). Determinants of Participation of Women in Labour Market: An Empirical Evidence from Nadia District of West Bengal in India. *Man in India*, *97*(2), 239–255.

Walker, E., & Webster, B. (2006). Management competencies of women business owners. *The International Entrepreneurship and Management Journal*, *2*(4), 495–508. doi:10.100711365-006-0009-9

Welsh, D. H., & Krueger, N. (2012). The evolution of social entrepreneurship: What have we learned? *Journal of Technology Management in China*, *7*(3), 270–290. doi:10.1108/17468771311325176

Zellner, A. (1962). An Efficient Method of Estimating Seemingly Unrelated Regressions and Tests for Aggregation Bias. *Journal of the American Statistical Association*, *57*(298), 348–368. doi:10.1080/01621459.1962.10480664

KEY TERMS AND DEFINITIONS

Impact Evaluation: Impact evaluation is an assessment of how the intervention being evaluated affects, outcomes, whether these effects are intended or unintended. The proper analysis of impact requires a counterfactual of what those outcomes would have been in the absence of the intervention. There is an important distinction between monitoring outcomes, which is a description of the factual, and utilizing the counterfactual to attribute observed outcomes to the intervention. The International Fund for Agricultural Development (IFAD) impact evaluation guidelines accordingly define impact as the "the attainment of development goals of the project or program, or rather the contributions to their attainment." The Asian Development Bank (ADB) guidelines state the same point as follows: "project impact evaluation establishes whether the intervention had a welfare effect on individuals, households, and communities, and whether this effect can be attributed to the concerned intervention".

Microfinance: Microfinance is a general term for financial services such as debt, savings, insurance and fund transfer for entrepreneurs, small businesses and lack of access to traditional banking services. There were two main mechanisms for providing financial services to such clients: relational banking for individual entrepreneurs and small businesses; and group-based models, where a few entrepreneurs come together to apply for loans and other services as a group. The microfinance service is broad classified, which includes microcredit. Micro credit only provides services for credit services for poor clients; however, financial inclusion is to be increased.

Multivariate Probit Estimation: In statistics and econometrics, the multivariate probit model is a generalization of the probit model used to estimate several correlated binary outcomes jointly with more than two variables. For example, if it is believed that the decisions of sending at least one child to public school and that of voting in favor of a school budget are correlated (both decisions are binary), then the multivariate probit model would be appropriate for jointly predicting these two choices on an individual-specific basis.

Murshidabad District of State of West Bengal, India: Murshidabad is situated on the eastern peripheral plains of the state of West Bengal and it is the northernmost district of Presidency division. It formed the eastern international boundary of state bordering Bangladesh (erstwhile East Pakistan) from 1947 when India became independent. Padma River flows through the entire eastern boundary, separating the district from the districts of Malda and Rajshahi (Bangladesh). Burdwan and Nadia are in the southern side and Birbhum and the Pakur (Jharkhand) are on the western side of the District.

Nadia District of State of West Bengal, India: The district of Nadia is situated in the heart of the Bengal delta held within the arms of the river Ganga, comprising of the Bhagirathi on the west and the Padma on the east bordering Bangladesh. The district has been famous owing to a rich historical background and also for the presence of cottage and small-scale industries, particularly relating to hand woven textile. Nadia was also the last bastion of independent Hindu Kingdom of Bengal before it was annexed by the Muslim invaders from North India towards the end of the twelfth century A.D. The centres of Sanskrit learning situated across the district were well acclaimed throughout the country. Nadia district was the birth place of Sree Chaitanya, who was one of the foremost religious reformers of the country during the middle ages apart from being one of the principal preachers of the Bhakti movement.

Self Help Groups (SHGs): Self-Help Groups associate self-governed, intermediate, informal groups with the same social-economic background and collectively express their desire to accomplish common objectives. Here the poor people willingly come together to save some of which can save conveniently from their income, contribute together a common fund mutually and agree to give loans to the members to meet their productive and emergent needs. SHG is a micro-enterprise comprehensive program under all aspects of self-initiatives, the organization of rural communities of self-reliant groups and their power-maker, employment cluster planning, infrastructure building, technology, credit and marketing. It emphasizes activity clusters based on the resources and occupational efficiency of the people and market availability.

Women Empowerment: Women empowerment mentions spiritual, political rights, social rights, education, judiciary or economic stability of the people and all other rights should be equal to women. There should be no discrimination between men and women. Women now have a basic and social right to get there once they are born. It is advisable that microcredit also offers a way to provide empowerment for women. Many government organizations and individuals financially support women.

Chapter 4
Microfinance as a Weapon to Gain Empowerment:
A Study on Rural Women in Nabagram Block in Murshidabad of West Bengal

Indrani Basu
Berhampore College, India

ABSTRACT

The aim of development policies of any country around the world is to include the marginalised people into development process. Women generally belong to this marginalised group who are struggling over the period of time for their basic sustenance. Microfinance is among one such development strategies to alleviate poverty. However, success of such initiatives depends on the interaction among the several social processes within multi-dimensional society. Aim of this chapter is to evaluate the contribution of microfinance as a weapon to gain empowerment of women on a case study in Nabagram Block of West Bengal, India. It is observed from the study that 73% of respondents have reported that they have utilised their loan on such income generating activities which are different from the prime occupation of the family. Also, the study reveals that members of SHGs seek for greater assistance from facilitators as well as funding authority regarding information, skill development training, raw material supply and process of marketization of their products.

INTRODUCTION

The success of noble idea of Prof. Mahammud Yunus in 1983 in Bangladesh encouraged social innovators and organisers all over the world to commence several micro-finance delivery methods to fetch financial services with ambit of poor. Women, being an integral part of the socio-economic system needs more equitable distribution of income that will lead a greater space in the critical decision-making processes at home as well as in their public sphere. Freedom to lead decent life depends on person's capability set. Promoting microfinance through self-help groups (SHG) has been recognised internationally as the modern means to combat poverty, rural unemployment and womenfolk. Women who are treated as

DOI: 10.4018/978-1-5225-5240-6.ch004

marginalised group are suffering from access to credit which is prerequisite for their gaining opportunity to take part in decision making process. However, women as target group for credit scheme of formal banking system were almost negligible before 1990s. After that the concept of women credit emerged due to references made by several women-oriented studies that analysed the discrimination against women in getting credit facilities from formal banking system. But still there exist a gap between need and availability of financial resources by poor women due to misperception about women that they were not at all bankable. Studies of HGs established womens' managerial capacities in handling credit and finance. So, extending the availability of microfinance through SHGs makes an empower woman who has made her life better by having access of resources.

The present work is organized in different sections as follows. In section 1, an attempt has been made to understand analytically empowerment of women. Section 2 dwells on this issue significance of microfinance to empower women. Chapter 3 deals with the process of methodology that we have followed in this work. This section is followed by section 4 where we have illustrated the major findings of our primary survey. The concluding section 5 summarizes the major findings of the study as far as microfinance as a weapon to gain women empowerment is concerned.

CONCEPT OF WOMEN EMPOWERMENT

'Empowerment' seems to be a modern idea that was not recognized even two centuries ago (Bhadra, 2001). In the twentieth century we observed many examples of political empowerment (Mahatma Gandhi, Martin Luther King, Nelson Mandela, etc.) in different countries over the world. The perspective of such movement was to expand the base of power of low–power groups (Mondal, 2012). Empowerment refers to the process by which power is gained, developed, seized, facilitated or gained. The World Bank (2012) defines the term empowerment as —— "the process of increasing the capacity of individuals or groups to make choices and to transform those choices into desired actions and outcomes." Therefore, the term empowerment refers to a multi-dimensional social process and it helps people gain control/ autonomy over their own lives. Throughout the world women as the other sex are marginalized. one can say that women empowerment indicates a situation where women gain autonomy over their own lives to improve their personal, social, economic, political and legal conditions so as to achieve greater respect in family, society and market. The extent of autonomy that women enjoy varies in terms of differences in their economic-social and regional and cultural groupings.

It was John Stuart Mill, a British Member of Parliament, whose essay "The Subjection of Women" written with his wife Harriet Taylor Mill, made the first attempt in favour of an establishing equality between males and females. Further Mary Wollstonecraft in ——Vindication of the right of Women|| (1792) wrote on the struggle for women equality (as cited in Mazumdar, 2005). For achieving complete equality in the society, it is necessary to eliminate domination, oppression, exploitation and discrimination against fair sex by their stronger counterpart. From the sociological point of view, women empowerment can be defined as ——equal status to women opportunity and freedom to develop herself (Kapur, 2001). Now Economists believe that without economic self-sufficiency, other rights and scopes remain meaningless to women. SEWA (Self Employed Women Association) has emphasized on the economic empowerment of women. It holds that raising voice and visibility is not possible unless there is access to the ownership of economic resources by the poor women.

Economic empowerment gains through equal opportunities, equal organizational benefits and equal working environment (Mandal, 2012). Therefore, in economic development, the empowerment approach focuses on mobilizing the self-help efforts of the poor, rather than providing them with social welfare. Legal expert and lawyers have envisaged the term empowerment as recognition and enforcement of women human right (Kapur, 2001). Through the establishment of equality before the law and equal protection of the law, the legal experts want to ensure women empowerment. We define empowerment as letting this power out (Blanchard et al., 1996). Modern democracy means participatory democracy, where both men and women irrespective of colour, creed, economic and social position should join in the decision-making processes. Without political participation it would be hard for women to increase effectiveness, capacity, challenging the existing power structure and patriarchal ideology (Mandal, 2012).

However, a single indicator is insufficient and incomplete to realize women empowerment, which is considered as a multi-dimensional concept in multiple domains in which a woman generally, functions and discharges her duties. As there are several social processes within society, therefore we have diversified knowledge on women empowerment. Each space defines women empowerment using their discipline. So, the conception also varies across the spaces. Further, the status of women as can be derived from the point of view of empowerment depends upon the strength of social processes which are operating in both public and private spaces. Their positions within households (synonymous as private space) and also in market (synonymous public space) operate as both causes and effects of each other. They mutually constitute each other in overdetermined sense (Fraad, Resnick & Wolff, 2009).

Fradd et al. (1994) introduced a new analysis which shows the mutual interdependence of gender, class, cultural, legal and political processes. Class process is an economic process which concern with the production, appropriation, distribution and receipt of surplus labour. So it is the process concerned with the production and distribution of goods and services. Class is not the name for a group of people. Class is an adjective, which qualify particular economic processes which rooted in processes of surplus labour (Dhar & Dasgupta, 2014). Class processes as a process which could be either exploitative or non-exploitative depending on whether performed surplus labour is appropriated by the performer or by the non-performer. From our class-focused point of view it is clear that unless and until an individual appropriates surplus labour, it is not possible to her/him to construct property and exert power. Society is experiencing simultaneous occurrences of different class processes at a time. Therefore, one's life is shaped by the several class processes which prevails both inside (private sphere) and outside (public sphere) the household.

Economy is a decentred, disaggregated space construed in terms of class as processes of performance, appropriation, distribution and receipt of surplus labour and their associated non-class processes (Dhar & Dasgupta, 2014). A society produces multiple gender processes. Individual are pushed and pulled by the contradictory definitions of identities and standardized lifestyles that are projected by alternative gender processes (Fradd et al., 1994). Political, legal, economical, religious and cultural processes combine to form different gender processes projecting different conceptions of male and female within society. Society as a heterogeneous space does not furnish equal benefits in terms of resources, training, opportunities and entitlements. Such type of socialization ensures separate gender processes that explain the relationship between male and female members within society. Such gender processes teach the members what role she/he should play within family. How the individuals participate in the production, appropriation and distribution of surplus labour within society will be determined by conceptualization of gender. Gender is also a set of processes that are cultural or ideological processes (Barrett, 1980).

As these gender processes are cultural and ideological, therefore, these processes have left deep impression within minds of members of society. Previously, when, women mainly used to do domestic chores and family used to meet her economic needs and provides security; prevailing gender process holds that female are physically, intellectually and morally inferior to male. Females were given burden of housework, child-care and care of older people with the exclusive role of moral and intellectual guides for future generation as a mother, teacher etc. Now, in the recent era of financial crisis, family can no longer perform its role properly that it used to perform in the past. Participation in the market becomes inevitable for all the members of the family irrespective of their sexes. In spite of bearing the biologically determinist notions that they are physically unfit for the outside world, in recent years, the lowering of real wages and the reduction of public services and family assistance, family pushes housewives into the market to earn income from outside family to sustain proper family life. Family now starts to recognize that it is the obligation for women to work hard in the market to support her family and protect it from economic suffering.

However, on-cooperative gender processes and exploitative class processes are obstacles for women to be productive and efficient in society. Studies conducted during the sixties and early seventies highlighted the dual or triple roles of women due to the absence of the facilities of crèche, convenient transport, canteen and help in the family (Desai & Thakkar 2001). Empirical data also showed the sad fact that quite often women impose upon themselves limitation of career enhancement which would entail transfer or more working hours or touring (Krishna Raj, 1991). Cultural processes mean the processes of producing and disseminating meanings in society (Fradd et al., 2009). So, proper womanhood means caring for family and its members while adopting a sub-ordinate, exploited and oppressed position in relationship to the master of the family.

By political conditions of existence, we mean processes of establishing and enforcing rules of family behaviour and adjudicating disputes over those rules. Generally, laws punish physical or sexual assault in the market while treating such assault within family more leniently or not at all. Now the political process of establishing and differentially enforcing laws helps to maintain feudal family pattern in which the rights of women in the family are different from the rights of citizens outside of family. At the same time if laws fail to punish physical and sexual assault in the market widely, then these steps not only encourage the gender-discriminated exploitative class process in the market, it further strengthens the roots of feudal class processes within family. On the other hand, if the woman faces favourable political and legal processes in the market, then it may help her to resist exploitation and oppression within family and also, to transform the existing exploitative and oppressive family structure into non-exploitative and non-oppressive one. However, transformation of family pattern is not quick to occur. Implementation of non-discriminated laws will create favourable environment for women to compete as equal in the labour market (Hewlett, 1986). Evidence suggests that, an individual who has more successful career does less or no housework (Blumenstein & Schwartz, 1983).

Further, surplus labour performed by women in feudal family is determined by the access to property. Being property-less may push women more into feudal class process-based family. Women face discrimination in markets or societal institutions that prevent them from completing their education, entering certain occupations and earning the same income as men. When women farmers lack security of land tenure, the result is lower access to credit and inefficient land use, reducing yields. The, Food and Agricultural Organization (FAO) estimates that equalizing access to productive resources between female and male farmers could increase agricultural outputs in developing countries by as much as 2.5 to 4 per cent (FAO, IFAD and ILO, 2010). If laws and economic condition help women to hold property, then this effort becomes conducive to reduce and/or eliminate exploitative and oppressive surroundings for women. This is by no means that political process of ownership itself undermines feudal family. Whether and to what extent it does so depend on all other processes that produce such family. If sex-gender and cultural processes are such that women have to undertake stress for housework and became pride to do so, then she will perform such chores and produce surplus labour and strengthen the root of exploitation. Here women accept the gender notion of their own incapacity for financial management and free control over their property by male. Sometimes they have done it less willingly out of fear of psychological or physical retaliation from the members of the family. Family exploits her feudally without making any payment from her property. Under such ideology of love of living being, responsibility, self-sacrifice, co-operation, universal brotherhood has been consciously and unconsciously makes her unthinkable to use her political power to withhold property or to demand subsumed class payments for access to it. This ideology constrains the family from making payment to women. This may help to understand why in spite of having joint property ownership, feudal structure of family has not altered. Cultural and environment have created differences in the outlook of male and female with respect to risk aversion, social preferences, attitude and choices.

Persistence differences in power and status between men and women can become internalized in aspirations, behaviour, and preferences that perpetuate the inequalities. So it becomes unjust to measure gender equality as equality of opportunities. By attempting to equalize outcomes one can break the vicious circle of low aspirations and low opportunities (Sen, 1999; Booth & Nolen, 2009; Croson & Gneezy, 2009; World Bank, 2011 as cited in World Development Report, 2012). It is difficult to measure opportunities separately from outcomes. Rather they are interlinked tightly.

The traditional family performed a variety of functions, which may be subsumed as economic, protective, educational, religious, recreational, biological, affection and status giving. This multi-functional pattern no longer exists, except in an attenuated form. The changing society has shifted functions from one institution to the other and has removed first one and then another of its traditional functions from the family, until today it is in many respect a mere shadow of its former self (Madan,1981).

Today, women have stepped her feet into the market to earn income and save the family from economic sufferings. Did the women who initially joined the market due to economic necessity of their families find any alteration in traditional class, gender, political, legal and cultural processes? Or it has created a boon only for a group of women who are educated, highly paid and belongs to urban areas? Or there have been no significant changes that can affect the status of women within family? The answer is both yes and no. It is yes for certain categories of working women today and it is no for the remaining categories of women today.

In all, 136 countries now have explicit guarantees for the equality of all citizens and non-discrimination between men and women in their constitutions. Despite, these positive changes, they now face many challenges in their daily lives. However, it has not come evenly to all women or across all dimensions of gender equality. The gender inequality that persists within society does matter the development process of society. Sometimes, women are suffering from financial crisis at household level could not able to get opportunity to work and earn income.

The World Development Report (2012) argues that there are two reasons to ensure equality for the perspective of social welfare. First, gender equality matters intrinsically, because the ability to live the life of one's own choosing and be spared from absolute deprivation is a basic human right and should be equal for everyone independent of whether one is male or female. Second, gender equality matters instrumentally, because greater gender equality contributes to economic efficiency and the achievement of other key development outcomes. Conversely, when women and men do not have equal chances to be socially and politically active and to influence laws, politics, and policy making, institutions and policies are more likely to systematically favour the interest of those with more influence.

Previously family was the centre of economic activities. Agriculture was the primary occupation which was pursued jointly by the entire family. The family makes the arrangements for an income in an effort to fulfil the economic and noneconomic needs of the family members. Most families also possessed property in the form of house, farm, jewellery etc. The family took care of this property and at times of contingency it also distributed then among the members. What share of property an individual member of family shall receive, who shall look after the property and how – all such decisions were taken by family (Sharma, 1989). In the modern age of explosive population, many of the economic functions which were previously better performed by the family are now being performed by factories, market, government aid and other associations/agencies. With growing pressure of population on arable land, agriculture is no longer the only basic livelihood of the family. Members of the family are forced to join non-agricultural activities which are no longer home-based occupations.

Women who previously used to receive life security from family are now compelled to join the market to earn income to supplement their family income mostly. These women are suffering from financial resources. Several studies have shown that access to financial resources helps women generate income and lessen poverty. keeping our earlier discussion regarding the perception of position of women in society, one can observe that in our society there are certain misconceptions about the women that they need loan at subsidised rates of interest on soft condition, they are suffering from lack of education and proper training, skills, capacity to save and invest, managing credit and finance, and therefore are not bankable at all. Perceptible gap between their need and availability of credit sinks them within exploitative class processes and oppressive non-economic social processes.

Formal banking sector that needs collateral security and follows stringent lending procedure are unable to meet the credit needs of these marginalised women. on the other side, in informal credit market where local money lender, merchants, traders and several agents dominates, they offer lending system with varying terms and conditions which usually go beyond the capacity of poor women.

Various government in India have adopted several development programmes through which grants and subsidies could flow towards these vulnerable sections of society to combat poverty. But such programmes had no such perception to build up women's own capacity so that they can fight against their adverse condition in society. Banking sectors had not fully successful in meeting their social and economic objectives.

Experiences of different anti-poverty and other welfare programmes have shown that the success of these attaining destiny depends on participation of targeted community at the grass root level. Formation of Self-help group(SHG) is one such initiatives have made through which microfinance would be disbursed and bring banking sectors to the door steps of poor women. Simultaneously women can actively participate in credit delivery and recovery process and build up their own managerial capacity in handling credit and finance to get rid from several exploitation and oppression that persist within society for them.

CONTRIBUTION OF MICROFINANCE TO EMPOWER WOMEN

Microfinance is one of among the system through which government is furnishing financial assistance towards poverty-stricken women. It distributes small loans to poor deprived women in order to enable them to generate income and start their own small businesses. This would lessen disadvantageous position of women in society as well as promote entrepreneurship and uphold the social and economic development for them (Lazar, 2008). Poor women do not get the bank loans as they don't have collateral to deposit. Microfinance institutions are not only providing loans to them but as well as at subsidized interest. Access to credit is a useful and quick way for the poor to have the means to pay for food and shelter (Dutta & Mukherjee, 2009). It mostly targets small- scale businesses in rural and agricultural sectors (Sanyal, 2009). MFIs offer a wide range of financial services, such as savings and insurance options also (Premchander, 2009). Microfinance removes the vacuum that created by bank out of their inability to give time for the poor women to be educated and understood about the rules regulations to get loan from bank. In addition, microfinance gives loan without any collateral. Further many microfinance programs use the group-based format and extending loans to members only to keep the group interest intact (World Bank, 2009).

The objective of 21st century is to ensure equality and inclusion of all the marginalized people into development process. The status of Indian women is a complicated due the multidimensional structure of Indian society. Marginalised situation is very common to poor women and their contributions towards society are yet to be recognised. They do not have the same opportunity to get jobs as they are lacking access of better jobs, education, technologies and overall opportunities at all.

We have already mentioned earlier that lack of access of property creates an obstacle for women to uphold their position both in family and in society. Our gender and cultural processes have established some misperception about efficiency of women in handling credit and finance. We think women only seek for a loan at subsidised rate on interest on easy terms, they are inefficient for credit worthiness and have less capacity to save and invest as they are suffering from lack of education and vocational training.

The Government of India has introduced 'Self-Help Group' programme as poverty alleviating programme as well as to promote self-help, savings, micro-enterprise and credit linkage with formal credit institution. It acts as the agent of development at a grass root level. This programme has been initiated with a view to facilitate poor rural women to avail micro-credit from formal banking sector.

The experience of several SHGs reveals that poor women are actually efficient managers of credit and finance. Previously, our banking sector felt burden in serving small frequent borrower loans due to high transaction cost associated with them. This thought actually reflects our oppressive gender, political and cultural social processes. The experience of several SHGs proved that meagre defaults rate in loan repayments rate by women members of these SHGs rather large borrowers with large volume of loans with bank. Availability of timely and adequate credit is essential for them to undertake any economic activity rather than credit subsidy (Raju, Reddy & Reddy, 2009). Actually, societal effort to overlook and undermine their capacity as manager in keeping the household sphere creates several misperceptions about their capacity.

Particularly women inherited by their role as home keeper, they seek not only loan for production need but also demand for composite loan (including consumption and production) to protect members of family from threatening of lower food security. Due to their biasness to disburse production credit, formal banking sector have not been able to reach poor household, especially women.

Experiences of different poverty alleviating welfare as well as development programmes have established the fact that active participation of poor community at grass root level is essential for successful implementation of such programmes. Women's' participation in credit delivery and recovery and linking of formal credit institution to borrowers through formation of SHGs have been recognised as supplementary mechanism for providing micro-finance to the door steps of marginalised women. Some studies (Pitt & Khandker, 1998; Pitt et al., 1999; Pitt, 2000; Pitt et al., 2003) have found that the effects of program participation differ importantly by the gender of program participant. For example, Pitt and Khandker (1998) find that the flow of consumption expenditure increases 18 taka for every 100 taka borrowed by women, but only 11 taka for every 100 taka borrowed by men.

Micro-finance meets both needs of production credit as well as consumption credit. By utilizing the funds of microfinance, marginalised women can earn their own income that assist them to perform their reproductive role with more efficiency, uphold their confidence as independent micro-enterprises and above all, it helps them to gain opportunities and enhance their capacity as a decision maker in family as well as in society also. They become able to get out and /or challenge exploitative class processes that prevails in society. When they apply together for loans and act the members as co-guarantor of repayments and support one another's effort at economic self-advancement that attitude has gained the strength to fight against several types of misperception about their ability as a decision maker as well as challenge the prevailing oppressive social processes against them.

Usually, one can find four major types of microfinance institutions models. These are: i) Self Help Group Model(SHG), ii) The Grameen Model, iii) The Individual Banking Model, and iv) The mixed Model (Dutta & Mukherjee, 2009). In India microfinance operates through two main channels viz. a) banking system through the SHGs under SHG-Bank Linkage Programme (SHG-BLP) and JLG (Joint liability group) bank lending programme and b) through Micro Finance Institutions (MFIs) lending through individual and group approach.

In following Table 1. We have shown the performances of SHG-BLP during the period 2015-16. we can observe from Table:1 that out of total SHGs, women led SHGs constitute 67.63% of total SHGs.

Keeping the objective to strengthen the regulation of MF sector, including RBI guidelines on NBFC-MFIs and inclusion of loans to MFIs by banks under priority sector had performed a world of good for the sector. During 2013- 2016, lending by MFIs exhibited a growth in loans disbursed consecutively from `24017.3 crore to ` 37286.90 crore (as per MFIN data).The number of SHGs with savings linkage, credit disbursed during the year and bank loans outstanding as well as the quantum of savings outstand-

Table 1. Highlights of the SHG-Bank Linkage Programme 2015-16

Sl.No	Particulars	Achievements	
		Physical (No. in lakh)	Financial (` in crore)
1	Total number of SHGs saving linked with banks	79.03	13691.39
2	Out of total SHGs - exclusive Women SHGs	67.63	12035.78
3	Total number of SHGs credit linked during 2015-16	18.32	37286.90
4	Out of total SHGs - exclusive Women SHGs	16.29	34411.42
5	Total number of SHGs having loan outstanding as on31 st March,2016	46.73	57119.23
6	Out of total SHGs - exclusive Women SHGs	40.36	51428.91

Source: Sa-Dahn, 2016

ing, loan disbursed during the year and total loan outstanding had shown positive growth during the past three years (Table.2). The number of SHGs having savings linkage increased to 79.03 lakh as on 31 March 2016 from 76.97 lakh a year back. There was a net addition of 2.06 lakh SHGs during the year. The domain of SHGs consists of 85.6% women groups which play a crucial role in empowerment of the poor rural women.

The most heartening development during the year is improved repayment and reduced NPA in SHG-BLP. The gross NPA of bank loans to SHGs has declined from 7.4% as on 31 March 2015 to 6.4% as on 31 March 2016. This was achieved in a year when there was overall deterioration in quality of assets and mounting NPAs in the banking sector (Sa-Dahn, 2016). One interesting features is that over the past three year the loan outstanding against SHG are trying to be reduced. Though some kind of volatility is appearing it is at the same time clear that SHGs are struggling to reduce amount of loan outstanding against them.

All above mentioned data reveals credit worthiness of women which has made noteworthy alteration in approach of State towards women. So it becomes possible for poor women to get out from oppressive political process that prevailed before in society.

Now we present a short analysis to understand how SHGs are functioning following the guideline 2002 published by the Ministry of Panchayats and Rural Development. According to this guideline, Self-Help Group(SHG) is a small voluntary association of poor people (not more than 20 people) having the same socio –economic background and do not have the capacity to collect financial funds from formal

Table 2. Overall progress under SHG-Bank Linkage Programme during past three years (Numbers in lakh/Amount crore)

Particulars		2013-14		2014-15		2015-16	
		No. of SHGs	Amount	No. of SHGs	Amount	No. of SHGs	Amount
SHG Savings with Banks as on March 31	Total SHG Nos.	74.30 (1.53%)	9897.42 (20.45%)	76.97 (3.59%)	11059.84 (11.74%)	79.03 (2.68%)	13691.39 (23.79%)
	All women SHGs	62.52	8012.89 (22.99%)	66.51 (6.38%)	9264.33 (15.61%	67.63 (1.68%)	12035.78 (29.92%)
	Percentage of Women Groups	84.15	80.96	86.41	83.77	85.58	87.91
Loans Disbursed to SHGs during the year	No of SHG extended loan	13.66 (12.02%)	24017.36 (16.67%)	16.26 (19.03%)	27582.31 (14.84%	18.32 (12.67%)	37286.90 (35.18%)
	All women SHGs	11.52 (11.02%)	21037.97 (17.83%)	14.48 (25.69%	24419.75 (16.07%)	16.29 (12.50%)	34411.42 (40.92%)
	Percentage of Women Groups	84.3	87.6	89.05	83.53	88.92	92.29
Loans Outstanding against SHGs as on 31March	Total No of SHG linked	41.97 (-5.71%)	42927.52 (9.02%)	44.68 (6.46%)	51545.46 (20.06%)	46.73 (4.59%)	57119.23 (10.81%)
	All women SHGs	34.06 (-9.34%)	36151.58 (10.08%)	38.58 (13.27%)	45901.95 (26.97%)	40.36 (4.61%)	51428.91 (12.04%)
	Percentage of Women Groups	81.2	84.2	86.35	89.05	86.37	90.04

(Figures in parentheses indicate increase/decrease over the previous year)
Source: Sa-Dahn, 2016

financial institutions. So the natural bonds and affiliations among the members of the group is pre-requisite to form the "Affinity group' by the facilitators. Majority of the members (at least 70%) should come from the families below poverty line. Remaining may belongs to families marginally above the poverty line but living with former families. This formation is gender neutral. However, several studies have expressed that women's' group performs better. (Datta & Mukherjee, 2009).

Facilitators come from Non-Government Organisations(NGOs), social workers, village level workers, health workers, informal association of local people, development-oriented government departments, banks, farmers' club under the Vikas Volunteer Vahini(VVV) Programme of NABARD, and other development institutions.

Apart from the facilitators, the bank officials are members of The Block / District SGSY committees. According to Guideline, they should play a major role for proper functioning of SHG group by furnishing funds to them and evaluate group activities through grading system.

Initially, the members should build their Corpus fund through regular savings after the formation of group and they also set their Group management norms. They then open a saving accounts in nearest commercial or Regional Rural Bank or cooperative bank. Bank will disburse loan to individual members against application of the member and unanimous resolution of members of concerned group. This is known as "inter-loan". This loan is fully funded out of the saving generated by group members themselves within a short duration of 3-6 months.

After sixth month of operation, they will be going through a process of grading to make it a viable group. Aim of this grading is to judge the affinity among members on various matter. Once the Group has proved its potential as a viable Group, then a Revolving fund of Rs 25000 will sanction by funding authority in favour of Group with a view to build-up further capacity of group. These funds can be utilized either for generating income through some income generation activities or lend to individual members. Members have to earn at least Rs 500 per month by utilizing Revolving fund. Aim behind this funding is to make members aware about the process of banking as well as make them credit worthy and bankable in the eyes of bank.

After six months of getting Revolving fund group can apply for further loan for higher level of investments. In this phase they should qualify the second grading process by assuring that per capita loan amount availed by its members has increased gradually over time and there has been a shift from consumption loans to production loans.

OBJECTIVE

Objective of this chapter is to analyse the positive effect of disbursement of micro-credit through SHGs on women's empowerment in the selected people in the survey.

DATA AND METHODOLOGY

We have selected the District of Murshidabad as our area of studying role of microfinance to empower women. Murshidabad is in the mid-North-Eastern part of West Bengal with its Head Quarter at Berhampur which is located on the left bank of the Bhagirathi River. The river Bhagirathi, flowing from north to south through the district, divides it into two almost equal portions.

Given the physical characteristics of the district it is a predominantly agriculture-based economy and in most of the parts of the district the traditional method of farming is still in vogue due to fragmentation of landholding and the uncertainty in the areas bordering with Bangladesh owing to the frequent erosion of the Padma river bank which has become a normal phenomenon over the years.

Now the pertinent question is why we have chosen the district of Murshidabad out of 19 districts of West Bengal. We have used literacy rate – particularly female literacy rate as the principal criterion for choosing this district. And of late, we know the significance of female literacy in the context of improving quality of life of an individual and also, of a family. P. H. Sethumadhava Rao considers that, "The most important thing is that they (the women) need to be given free and compulsory education so as to make them aware of the rights and duties and possible free legal aid so that they can fight their cases without spending money" (Kapur, 2001).

From the district-wise performance of literacy rate as per the latest Census of India 2011, the four districts in the state of West Bengal have performed quite miserably during 2011 period in terms of improving female literacy rate. The districts which have failed to obtain more than 70% literacy rate are Murshidabad, Purulia, Maldah and Uttar Dinajpur. We have chosen Murshidabad (as one of these four poor performing districts of West Bengal) for our empirical study. It has been analysed that women have faced a wide variety of constraints which interact and reinforce each other. Constraints which are operating at both public and private spheres can hinder their endowment of skills, knowledge, asset, and/or confidence. Through microfinance programme several agencies including Government have been trying to uphold women's productive capacity to alleviate poverty.

In district of Murshidabad, the literacy rate as per the Census of India (2011) is 67.53% (71.02% for male and 63.88% for female) which is below the State average of 77.08% (82.67% for male and 71.16% for female) and stands fourth from below (above Purulia, Maldah and Uttar Dinajpur). Note that the female literacy rate in the district as per the latest Census Report is quite poor when compared with the state level average of 71.16% - implying a difference of almost 8% with the state level figure. The majority of the population in the district as per the latest Census Report believes in Islamic faith and women in general encounter various types of social control and taboos – especially in the rural areas. The district has shown a fast growth rate in female literacy rate in the last one decade.

Murshidabad is an economically backward district in the state. Situation was not so poor in the past. Population density is relatively higher in those places/areas where economic opportunities are more. Percentage of female workers in the main worker category is quite low and share of female marginal workers is very high. A large number of female belongs to non-worker category. As the economy is basically agrarian, a significant number of women are concentrated in agricultural sector as unpaid family labour.

During 1991-2001 percentages of female workers under main worker category in total working population has increased from 12.69% to 17.65% (Census, 2001). Declining percentage under non-working category also reveals that more and more women are now joining labour force. Participations under different jobs like cultivation, agricultural work, household's industries, etc. are all in at increasing trend. So basically, working women in districts are engaged in informal sector where sustenance of acquired job is very poor.

Historically, the district was industrially developed during the pre-colonial days and it was famous for its ivory industry, silk weaving and allied industries, cotton industry, shola (thermocol) industry and conch shell industry and like. Most of these industries have now lost their economic significance. The urbanization process in the district of Murshidabad started waning out during the colonial period as the district lost its glory as the political centre of the region then. During, post-Independent period Murshidabad did not witness any major industrialization attempt. And hence, it still remains a predominantly agrarian economy-based district. The economy of the district is rural agrarian with very little urban development. There are 242 backward villages, the third highest in the State. The men folk mostly are farmers or masons who migrate out. The women stay behind and do petty jobs as agricultural labour, or are involved in rearing of domestic animals, household industrial works including biri binding and like. In 1911 the district had an area of 2143 square miles as per the Census of India Report (1911). The Census of India Report (2001) revealed that usable land area decreased by erosion/ river-shift while increase in the district population in absolute terms caused heavy pressure on land and other natural resources. Analysing sectoral composition of occupational structure, we have observed that the major share of working people is engaged in household industrial activities (Census, 2001).

This district has a continuous trend of tartarisation and in formalisation which allow the people to find out alternative occupations without leaving the place. But production nature in the district, being predominantly agrarian, and it is basically seasonal which fails to create additional gainful employment on a sustained basis. Expansion of biri industries in Dhulian, Aurangabad, and Jangipur etc could engage local working population – especially female working population in household industrial activities.

One source of economic empowerment is the opportunities to inherit property. The inheritance or property laws existing in India are primarily governed by religious and personal laws of different communities. Hindu Succession Act of 1956 makes women absolute owners of the property and daughters are recognized as class I heir to the father's property at par with the sons. In case of Murshidabad, the status of women regarding such right is very poor because majority of the population follows Islamic faith where discrimination against women is very prominent. The Islamic rule of succession is in generally gender biased against women.

We have observed that women of this District have been historically placed as disadvantaged group in access of both material and social resources. Under such background Microcredit programmes which aims to alleviate poverty may have tremendous impact on process of empowerment of women.

For our analytical study we have conducted a primary survey. The reference period for the study was 2017 and the population was all rural females who have availed the microfinance. We have selected 100 clients randomly from the Nabagram block under Lalgola subdivision. Nabagram is located in the relatively economically prosperous western part of river Bhagirathi i.e.; in Rarh. However, one can observe that instead of achieving highest literacy rate (76.44%) according to 2011 census, block performances regarding female literacy rate was much poor compare to the other blocks who have achieved literacy rate more than 70%. We have already stated that society is multi-dimensional heterogeneous space. This kind of finding may help to understand how prevailing cultural and gender processes within society affects efficacy of micro-finance programme which is a political process. The data has been collected by door to door visit and the women were interviewed through structured questionnaire. Medium of instructions was Bengali. At the very beginning, we should mention that we have followed a selective case study approach. However, we have tried to capture as much diversity as possible. The interviews were administered personally as most of the respondents were illiterate. 2 members from 50 Self-Help Group were interviewed. We have ensured that no two SHGs are connected with same facilitator. Among the 50 SHGs, some of them have been formed by NGOs and some by Panchayats. However, we should admit at earlier that we have followed a selective case study approach, so this cannot claim to be statistically representative study.

MAJOR FINDINGS ALONG WITH DISCUSSION

Composition of the Population

The primary data and related information was collected for 100 respondents from Nabagram block. About 20% of the respondents have the male household heads believing in Hindu religion and 80% of the respondents with male heads of the family believing in Islam religion. Among the respondents, 44% of them belongs to the general category, 20% belongs to scheduled castes, 13% belongs to OBC-B category and remaining (23%) belongs to OBC-. These are shown in Figure 1 and Figure 2.

Around 62% of respondents belongs to a family with number of family member is ≤ 3and 21% of them have family member within 4-5. The remaining respondents (17%) belong to the family with

Figure 1. Distribution of respondents according to religion
Source: Author's calculation based on field survey during February,2017.

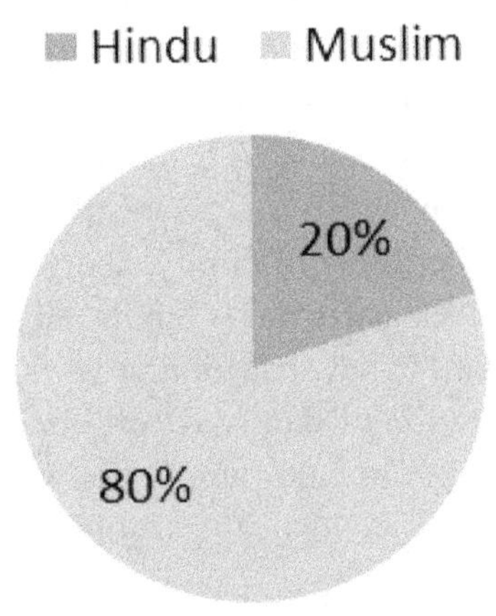

Figure 2. Distribution of respondents along Caste
Source: Author's calculation based on field survey during February,2017

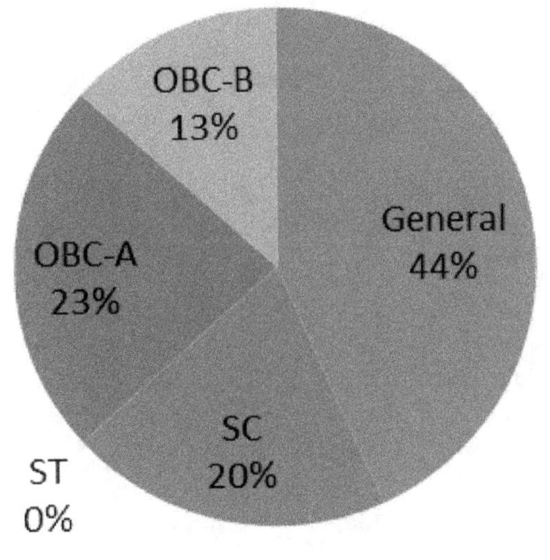

number of members more than 5 (Figure 3). This indicates that during this period of drastic urbanisation, characteristics of rural areas are also changing. We have found that majority of the respondents are residing in nuclear family structure. The various aspects of social life are being continually transformed due to the effects of dynamic social changes always. The form of family, marriage, state, religion, culture, education system, and economic and social structures are continually changing and transforming, as a result of which, a change occurs in the life of the individual and subsequently in his/her relationship with others (Sharma, 1989).

Previously family was the centre of economic activities. Agriculture was the primary occupation which was pursued jointly by the entire family. The family makes the arrangements for an income in an effort to fulfil the economic and noneconomic needs of the family members. In the modern age of explosive population, many of the economic functions which were previously better performed by the family are now being performed by factories, market, government aid and other associations/agencies. With growing pressure of population on arable land, agriculture is no longer the only basic livelihood of the family. Members of the family are forced to join non-agricultural activities which are no longer home-based occupations. Women who previously used to receive life security from family are now compelled to join the market to earn income to supplement their family income mostly. So many of the functions that were previously performed by women, have been taken over by other agencies like hospital, baby clinics, crèches, baby sitters, hotel and restaurants etc. in the emerging urban spaces. This is still not the case in the rural space where women perform still double burden of work – within and outside family. Even if she is confined entirely to family, apart from performing her household chores she is forced provide her labour services as (unpaid) family labour to her husband in the agricultural field and otherwise. Therefore, it is hard to say that joining working force is an indicator of 'empowerment of women'. Concept of disintegration of family is very much relevant to our research problem as because it helps us to understand changes in cultural process which is one of relevant factor to realize over-determined process.

Figure 3. Distribution of respondents along their number of member of family
Source: Author's calculation based on field survey during February,2017

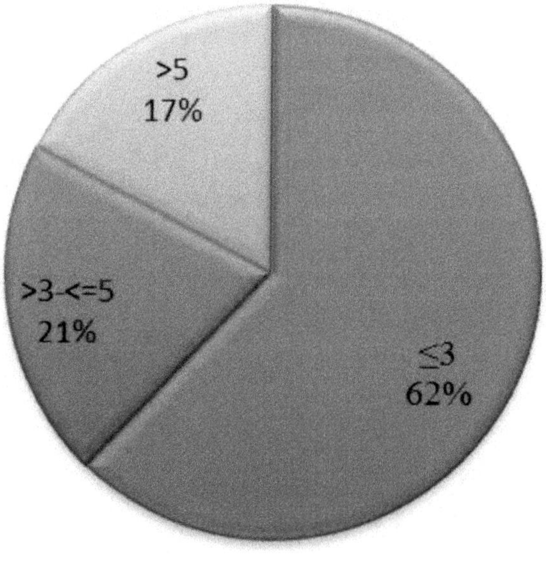

Around 20% of respondents have single child and 30% of the respondents have more than two children. 43% of respondents have 2 children, and 7% of respondents do not have any child (Figure 4). We found that the working women cutting across income groups and religions generally prefer less children due to their dual burden. However, this choice mostly depends on their husbands, not on them as we were informed during our field survey.

Only 7% of the respondents (Figure 5) have more than 10 years of schooling whereas 27% of the respondents are illiterate. The average education level of the members is quite low. 43% of the members are being functionally literate. These statistics consistent with data at District level also. However, these findings ensure that the 'Affinity Groups' are consisting with people of homogeneous group. One of the major aim behind engendering microfinance is to provide opportunities to those women who are suffering from gender inequalities within society. By providing educational and vocational training, microfinance assists in upholding productive capacity of women. Therefore, it is one of the primary requirements of the formation of SHG that members should come from same affinity group. Our facilitators have fulfilled the criteria.

Another interesting feature is that majority of respondents (54%) comes from those family with 10 years of schooling experience. 43% of the family has an experience of 15 years of educational attainment. This is shown in Figure 6. Thus, support of the family members for woman's' SHG involvement is an indicator of real motivation. Here we can notice an existence of co-operative gender processes within the family.

Figure 4. Distribution of respondents according to number of child
Source: Author's calculation based on field survey during February,2017

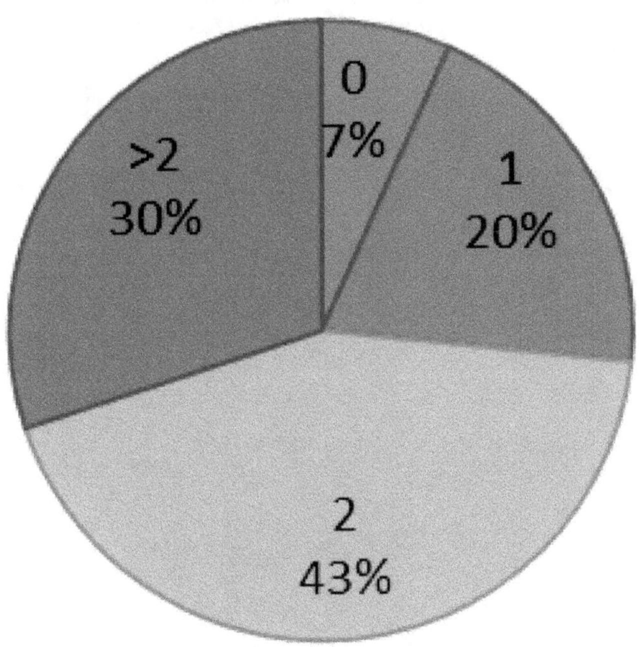

Figure 5. Literacy wise distribution of respondents
Source: Author's calculation based on field survey during February,2017

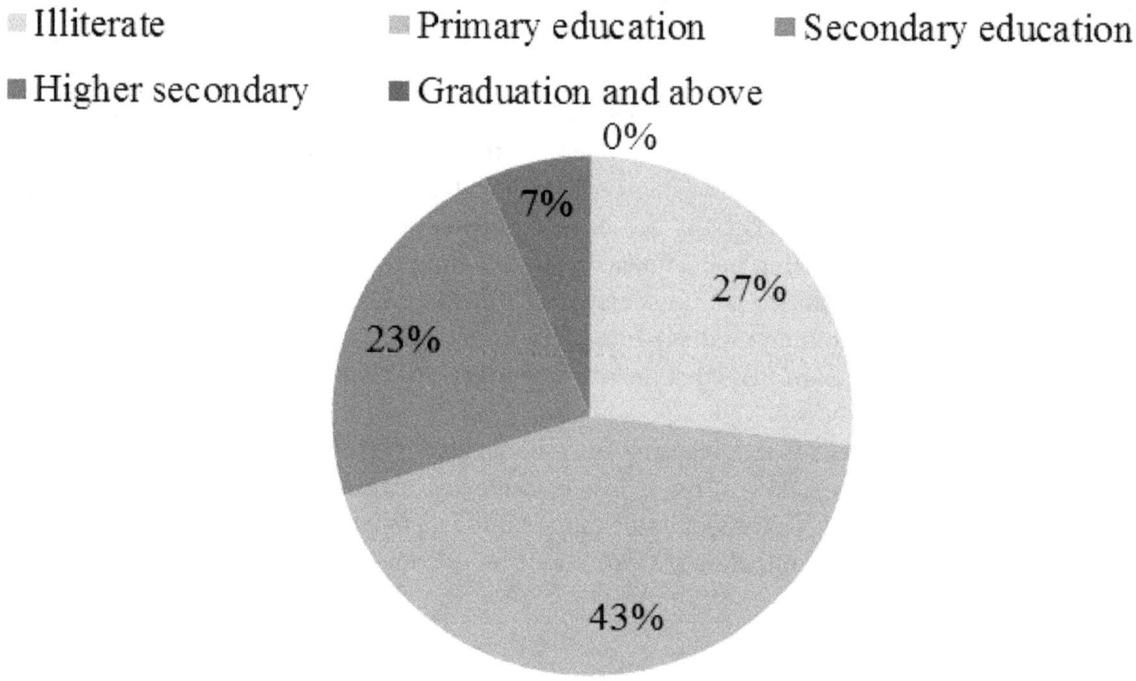

Figure 6. Distribution of respondents along highest year of schooling of family
Source: Author's calculation based on field survey during February,2017

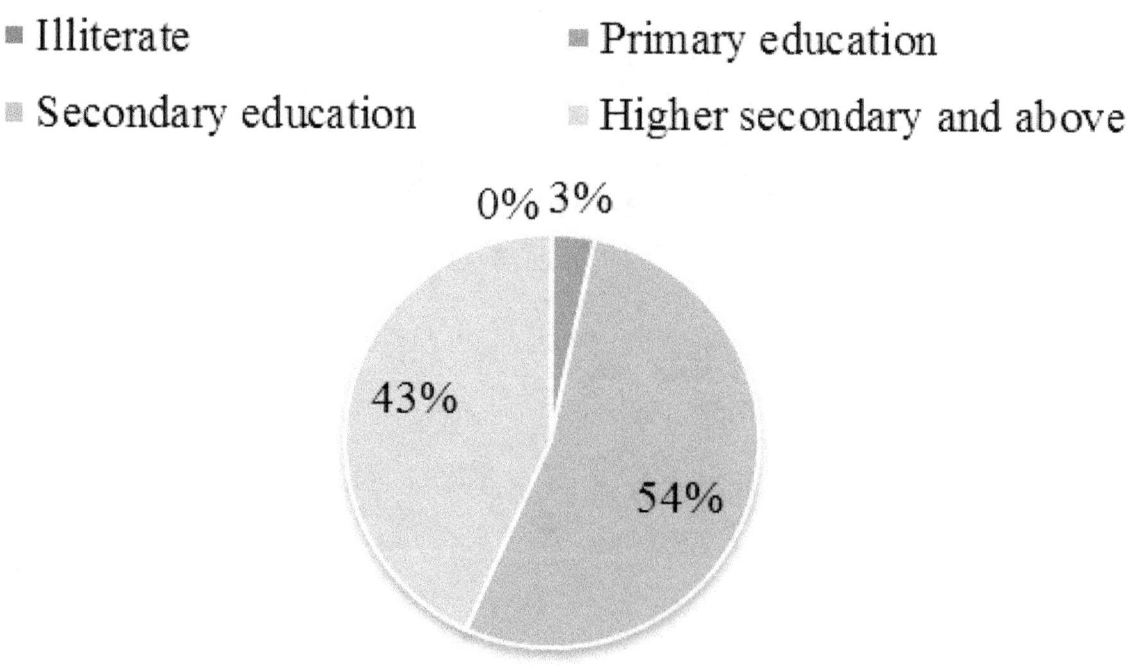

Employment

Women in our sample are basically involved in home keeping services (47%). only 20% of them are wage labour and they have independent source of income. Interestingly, 33% of them are unaware about their contribution to society as a productive unit. These views are matched with our previous finding of low literacy of the members. Figure 7 and 8 represent that women are coming from those families which are operating in informal sectors. 57% of the family of members are involving in crop production, 3% in fishing, 7% are artisans and 20% of them are collecting their basis sustenance by working as wage labour. Therefore, there is similarity in economic background which is one of the criterion of formation of group.

We have already mentioned earlier that during survey, we have observed considerable variety in scale of operation of the groups. Some groups have attained first grading whereas other have entered into the second grading. Apart from that few of them are trying to be proved as a viable group. So, some groups are operating with "inter-loans' and other are at the stage so that they can use "Revolving Fund". Our survey report has revealed that 44% of respondents have used the SHG loan as initial funding for their independent business activities. 33% of them have utilised micro-finance for agricultural activities and another 13% for fishing. Around 10% of respondents have utilised loans for consumption purposes (Figure 9).

Figure 7. Distribution of respondents along various occupation
Source: Author's calculation based on field survey during February,2017

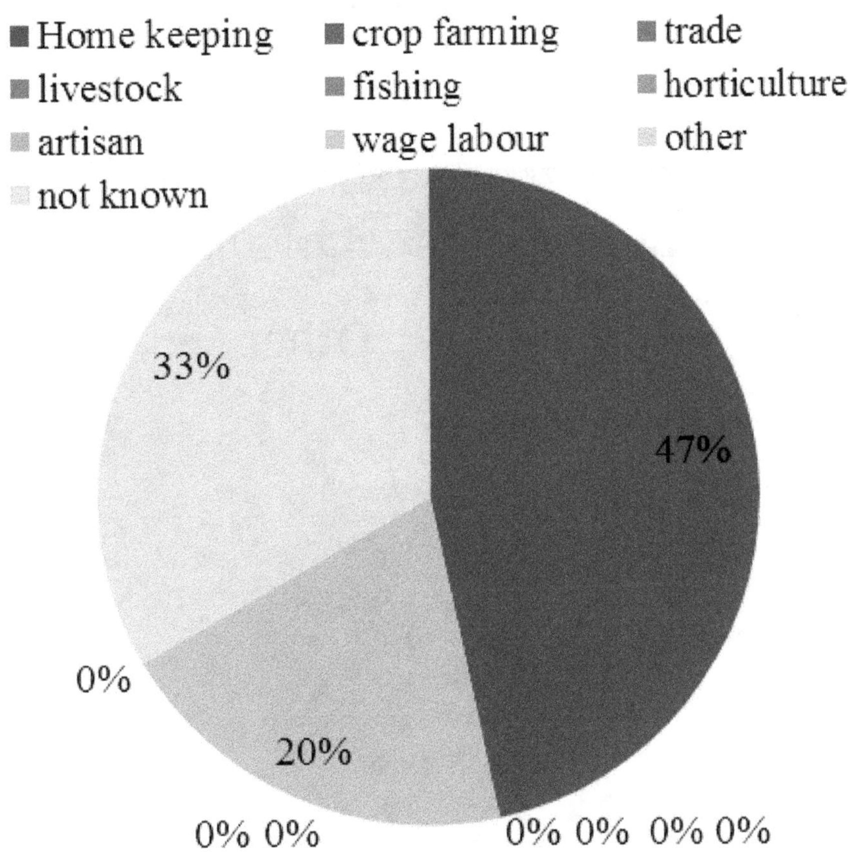

Figure 8. Distribution of respondents along prime occupation of family
Source: Author's calculation based on field survey during February,2017

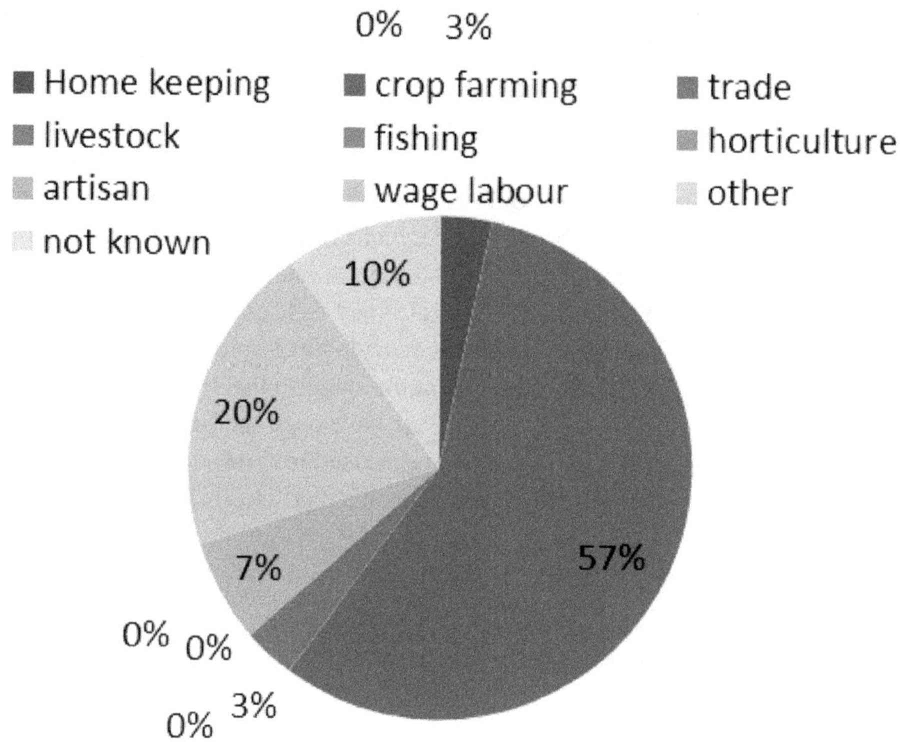

Figure 9. Area of Investment
Source: Author's calculation based on field survey during February,2017

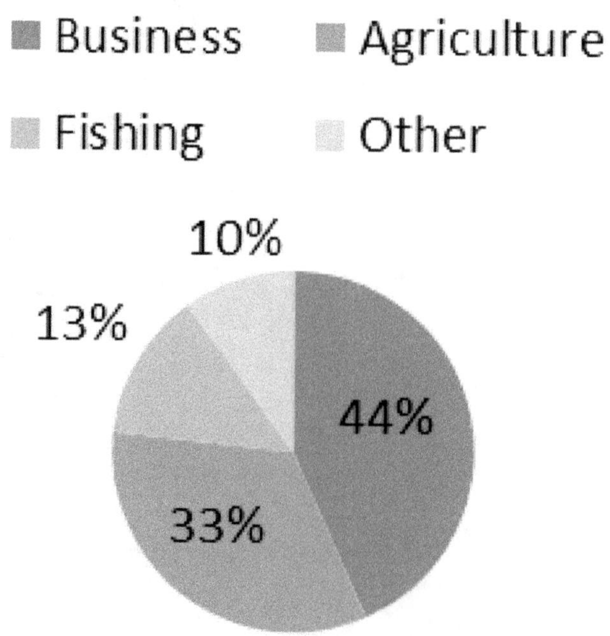

One of the major findings is that when surveyors enquired about the area of investment, 73% of respondents (Figure 10) have reported that they have utilised their loan on such income generating activities which are different from the prime occupation of the family. 27% of them have continued with their prime family occupation. This is an encouraging finding that the members have utilised micro credit for boosting their own income generating activities not their husbands' or fathers' occupations. This feature has supported co-operative gender and cultural processes which assist women to get real motivation and assist them to utilise monetary fund from micro finance institution for generating capabilities.

One of the major objectives of the formation of group is to ensure each member earn at least Rs 500/month by utilising revolving fund. Our survey has found that among the respondents 60% of them can earn Rs 500 or more than that per month by utilising revolving fund, whereas remaining are unable to earn such amount (Figure 11 and 12). Reasons behind that some group are still under grading 1 and in some cases lack of formulation of appropriate project by facilitators is responsible behind these failures.

It is well-known fact that facilitators must form the group with those who are preferably come from same socio-economic background and do not have access to formal financial institutions (Datta & Mukherjee,2009).

So lack of funds is their common problems. We have found that 66% of them have arranged initial capital from personal savings (Figure 12). 7% of them have collected fund from MFIs for generating earning activities. There comes the question of real motivation by facilitators and funding agencies. Apart from few, majority of facilitators did not conduct any market survey to identify the needs that can be catered by microfinance. On their part, majority of them never took any such initiatives so that the willing poor women can get proper financial assistance from MFIs. Funding authorities are also not trying to ascertain the purpose for which the loans are disbursed. They only maintain their accounts. No such real initiatives have taken to explore some new income generating arenas where microfinance can help the willing women to take new challenges. So role of facilitators as capacity building through taking some initiatives for getting required loan amount, conducting vocational training is very much

Figure 10. Difference among area of investment and prime occupation of the family
Source: Author's calculation based on field survey during February,2017

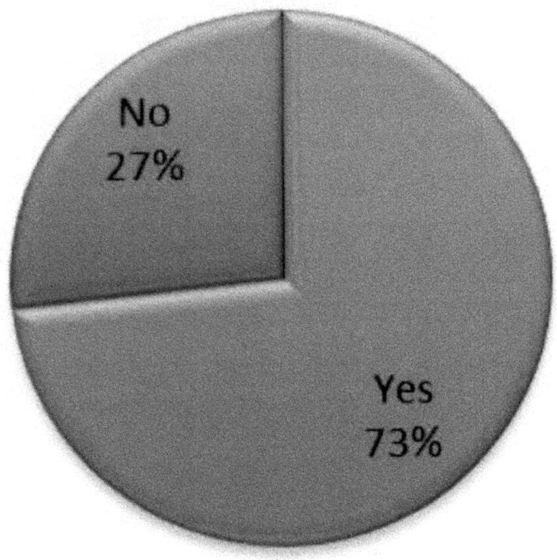

Figure 11. Amount of increased income after entering group
Source: Author's calculation based on field survey during February,2017

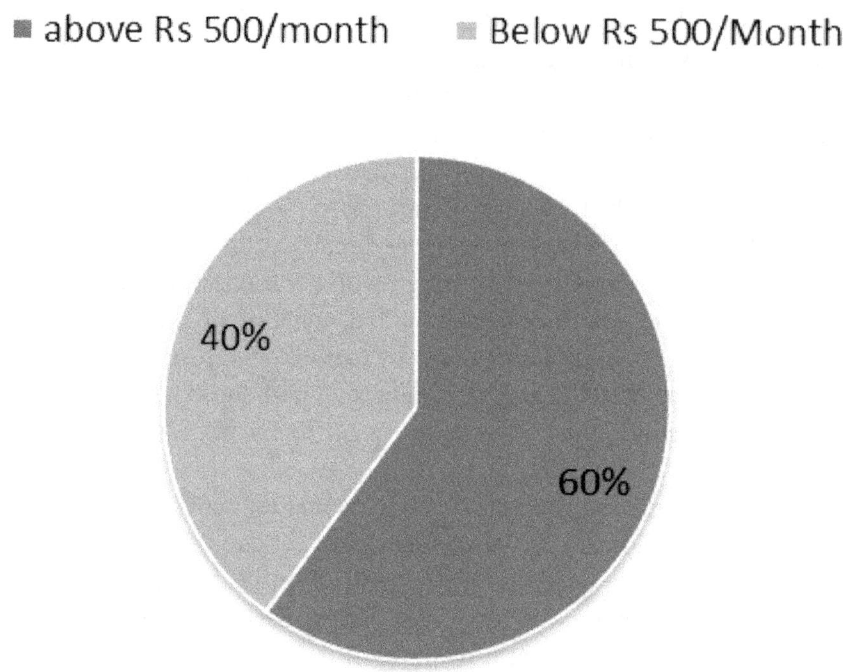

Figure 12. Sources of initial capital
Source: Author's calculation based on field survey during February,2017

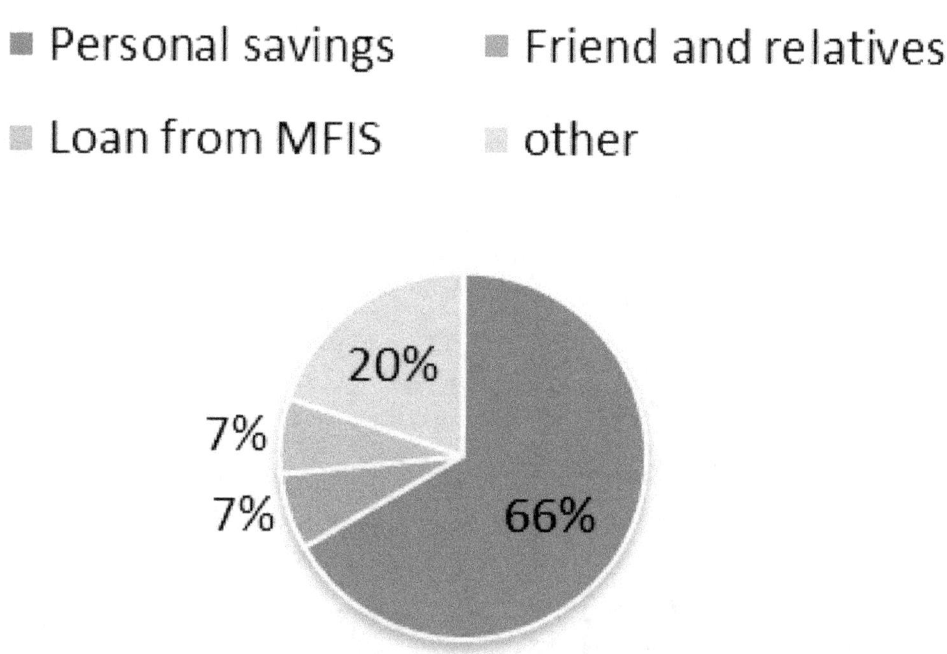

restricted. This lack of efficiency in nurturing the poor women after forming the group leads to under-utilisation of microfinance. There is a huge scope for engendering microfinance if facilitators and funding authority no longer consider the group formation as only a monetary matter. This ambience supports non-cooperative political process.

From figure 13 and 14 it is clear that poor women have taken considerable amount of loan from MFIs quite regularly. Their repayments practices are quite good (Figure 15 and 16). However, as per guideline the repayment periods of loan which are usually within 3-6 month, is not followed by our case studies. Majority of them (41%) repaid loan within 6 month- 12 months. A considerable number of respondents (35%) repaid loan within 12months -24 months. Only 10% of them are following guideline and submitted within 3-6 months.

However, from Figure 17, it is clear that even though 30% of them have made some delayed in repaying loan, but majority of respondents (70%) are not defaulter.

In the case of default, members are facing penalties. Figure 18 shows that in majority cases (47%) defaulter members are rusticated. In some cases, they face penalty and they have faced problems in getting further loan.

All such findings prove that poor women are very much eager to take loan from MFIs. But perspectives of funding authority and facilitators should change. Funding authority should not disburse the loans in accordance with grade attained by group. They must formulate suitable projects that matched with the requirements of credit by poor women. Facilitators should build-up a friendly community contacts with the poor women so that they can formulate requirement specific projects. Poor women need a cooperative political and legal processes so that they can directly involve in credit lending process, but not to get

Figure 13. Amount of loan

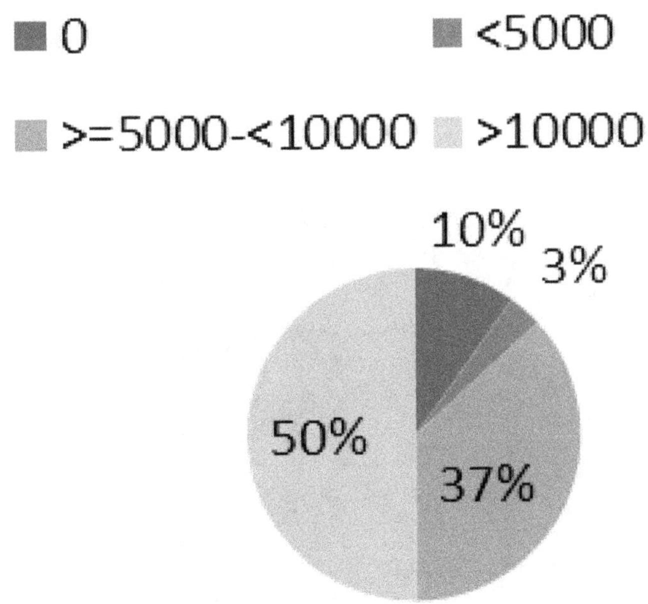

Figure 14. Frequency of loan taking
Source: Author's calculation based on field survey during February,2017

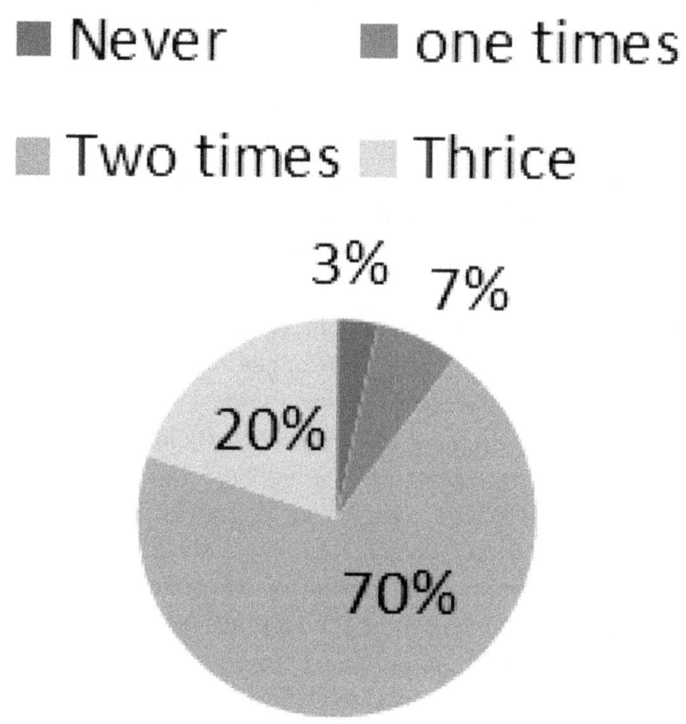

Figure 15. Frequency of repayments of loan

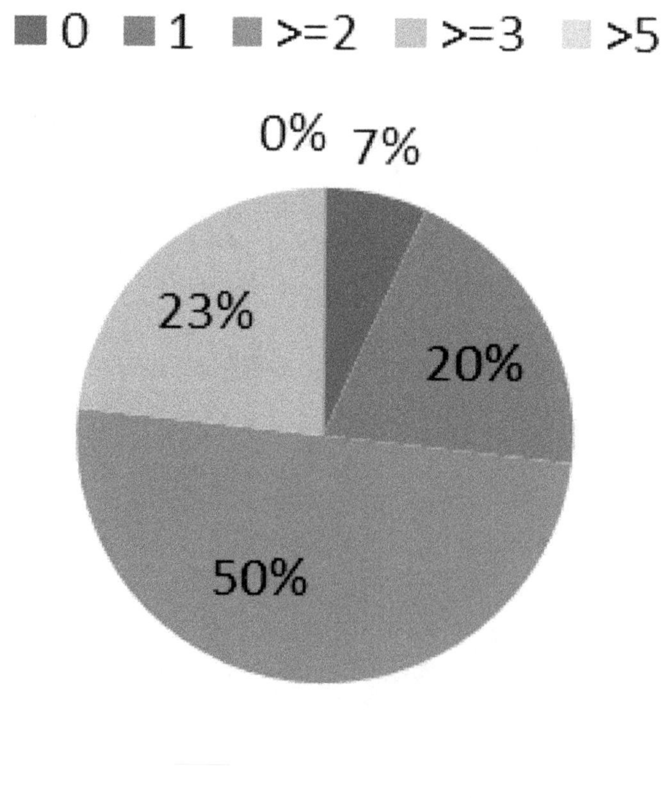

Figure16. Duration of instalments
Source: Author's calculation based on field survey during February,2017

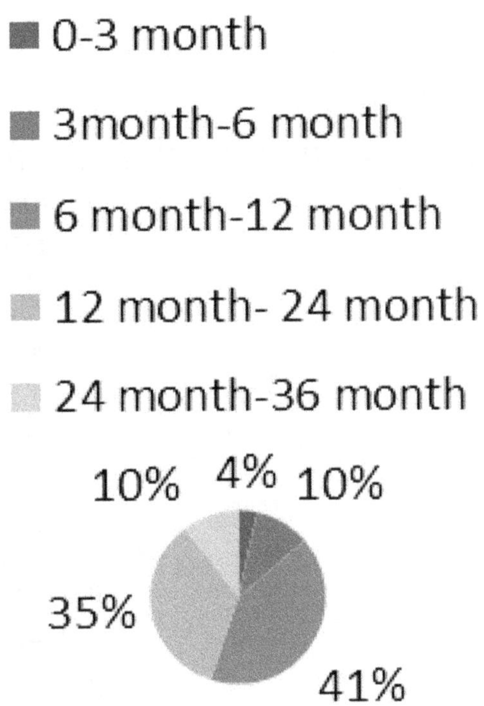

Figure 17. Distribution of respondents for defaulting loan
Source: Author's calculation based on field survey during February,2017

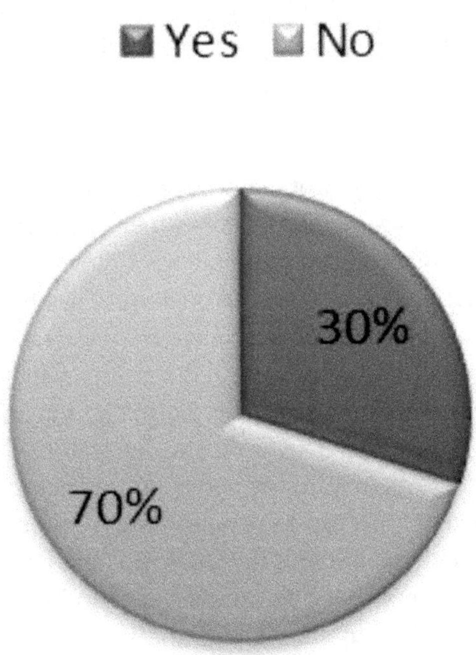

Figure 18. Penalty for defaulting loan
Source: Author's calculation based on field survey during February,2017

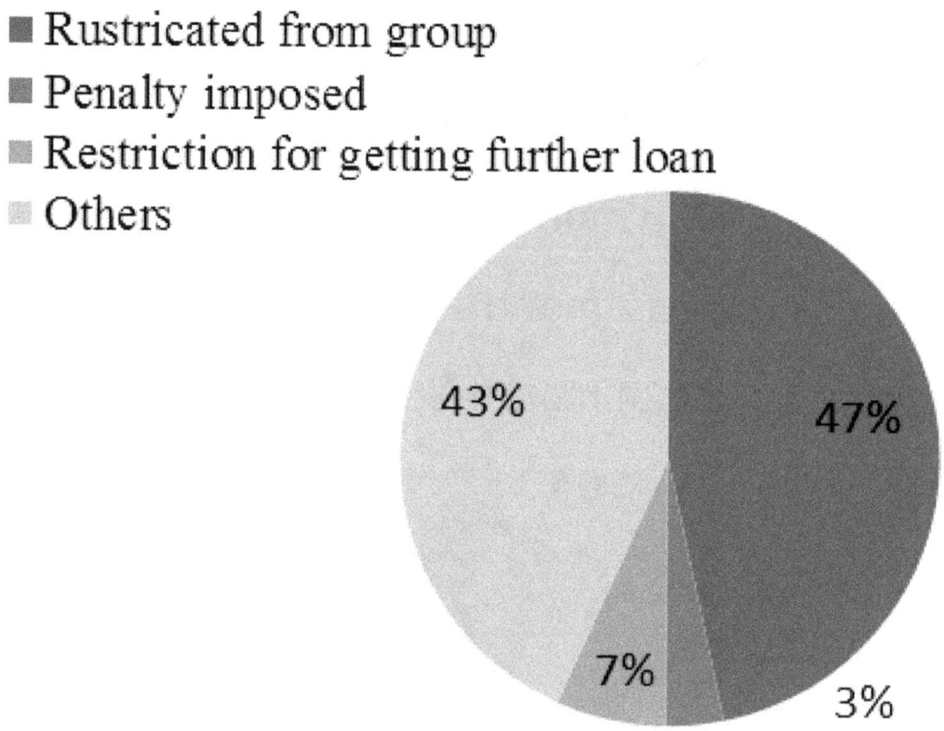

mere sympathy. They are looking for greater assistance from facilitators, funding authority and above all from government who can create a level-playing field for their empowerment. They need strongly motivated and trained personnel who can guide them and bring them on right path.

Marketing the Product

Our survey has revealed that though majority of members are investing in business activities as considering it as independent income generating activities, 60% of them are facing several problems in marketing their product (Figure 19 and 20). Inadequate communication, low quality of product, lack of adequate fund for marketing, etc. make them at disadvantageous position. They have reported that they receive very little marketing assistance and seek for greater assistance from the facilitators for marketwise product.

Our survey in Nabagram block has revealed that all the groups which have constructed for engendering microfinance are belongs to homogeneous socio-economic group and hence construction of Affinity Groups have been satisfied as per as norms. However, one can state that in spite of having great potentiality of microfinance to gain empowerment for the poor illiterate marginalised people, non-cooperative political, legal processes may make this effort in vain. Having a cooperative gender processes in family sphere could not be able to ensure engendering the microfinance programme. From above analysis it is clear that the prime objectives of engendering microfinance to impart credit discipline and financial management skills to the member of group have been satisfied. From Figure 9, we have observed 44% of respondent has started business activities in which they have no previous experience. Apart from

Figure 19. Problem in facing marketing product
Source: Author's calculation based on field survey during February,2017

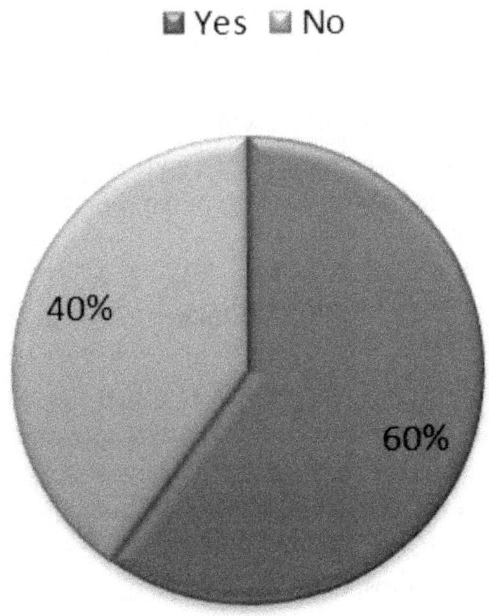

Figure 20. Types of problem in marketing product
Source: Author's calculation based on field survey during February,2017

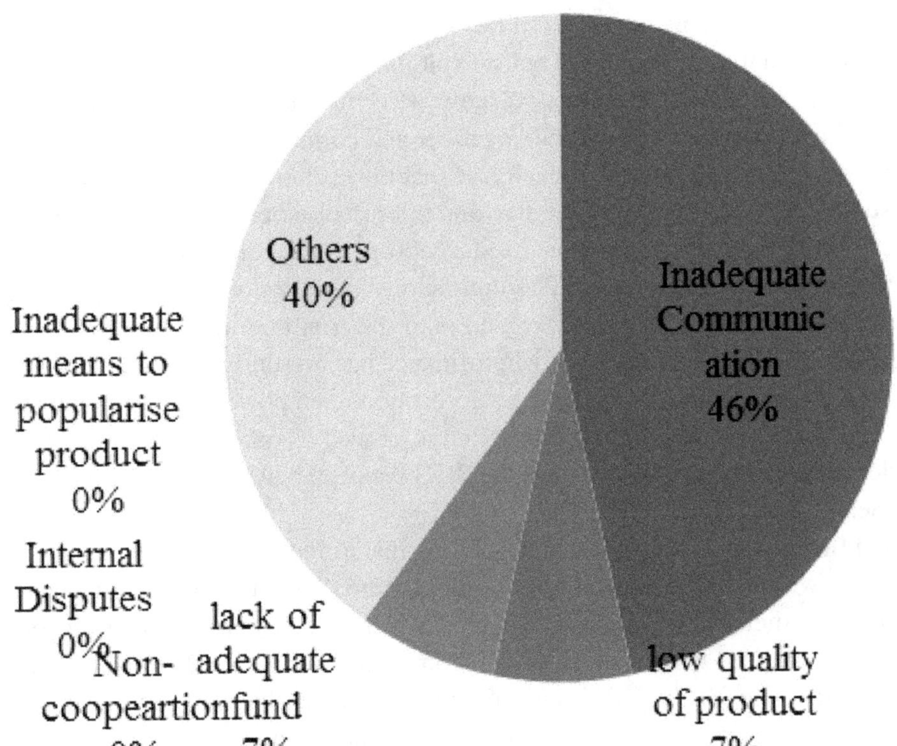

that 73% of total respondents have invested their funds on such activities which are different from their prime occupation of family (Figure 10). 60% of total respondents can earn Rs500 or more than that / month. Data on frequency of taking loans reveals that 70% of respondents have taken loan twice in a year and majority of them (70%) are non-defaulter. These statistics reveal that one of prime objective of microfinance to make poor women credit worthy and bankable has been fulfilled. However, a lack of sincere efforts of facilitators and funding authority for preparing formulation of time, space and need specific projects and their proper implementation with a view to uphold capacity of poor women have lessened the progress of engendering microfinance programme.

CONCLUSION AND POLICY SUGGESTIONS

Objectives of development policy makers in countries around the World in 21st century is to ensure balanced and inclusive economic growth Gains of economic growth are easily accessible to relatively advantaged, who find it easier to involve in the growth process while, poor marginalised women have to wait much longer to reap the benefits. Bringing these sections of society to mainstream economical activities is essential to achieve equitable growth, which is prerequisite for the long-term sustainability of social development and economic prosperity.

We have analysed that degree of women empowerment has been also changing persistently and as a process women empowerment remains an overdetermined process characterized by its multi-faceted heterogeneity. Women face several economic and non-economic social processes within society. Being property-less, women may push women more into feudal class process-based family. Now to bringing up these women on development sphere, presence of co-operative gender, political and legal processes are pre-requisites for proper implementation. If the woman faces favourable political and legal processes in the public sphere, then it may help her to resist exploitation and oppression within family and also, to transform the existing exploitative and oppressive family structure into non-exploitative and non-oppressive one. On the other hand, presence of favourable gender and culture processes in the family sphere (i.e.; private) helps women regain productive capacity, so that they can perform more efficiently in the public sphere and raise their voices against exploitative and oppressive social processes in public sphere.

Programme of microfinance can be visualised as co-operative political process that can ensure the access of women to financial resources. The community-based microfinance approach under SHG-BLP, have the potential to transform poor women onto the frontline in terms of thrift, credit linkage, and livelihood activities. As a consequence, Microfinance has presently a central component of income generation, financial management and overall socio-economic empowerment of many financial institutions, NGOs, civil society organizations, governments as well as other stakeholders. In the past more than two decades, many new initiatives within the SHG concept, have designed and launched as a target driven government programs,

Our empirical findings have illustrated that by using microcredit, women can change the perspective of gender processes within family as well as in public sphere. Such domain that does positively signify their empowerment in their public domain. It is clear from the study that 73% of respondents have reported that they have utilised their loan on such income generating activities which are different from the prime occupation of the family. This is an encouraging finding that the members have utilised micro credit for boosting their own income generating activities not their husbands' or fathers' occupations. This feature has supported co-operative gender and cultural processes which assist women to get real motivation for micro finance involvement from their family. Study has revealed that members of SHGs seek for greater assistance from facilitators as well as funding authority regarding information, skill development training, raw material supply and process of marketization of their products. In several cases inadequate training has just upgrades the skill that have poor women already possess in typical activities like preparing jam, jelly, spices, knitting, tailoring, livestock activities, etc. Failure of bank personnel to formulate suitable projects for expansion of scope to enthusiastic poor women due to their lack of coordination with community hinder the growth of microfinance. Lack of nourishment in capacity building from facilitator's part makes non-co-operative political and legal processes that create obstacle to gain empowerment instead of having favourable gender process within family.

Therefore, to gain real empower for women through providing micro-finance facilities requires favourable economic and non-economic social processes both at private and public sphere. Family's outlook which has altered regarding women's attachment with microfinance programmes, would be sustained if these changes would be supported by the economic and noneconomic social processes at public sphere. More emphasis should be given for building capacity of women in entering several occupational areas as well as ensure facilities to marketwise their products. Facilitators and other related personnel should organise need based projects so that marginalised women along with their family get involve spontaneously under such programmes for their up gradation.

In India the niche area for microfinance along with mainstream institution will continue to exist, not only till the complete eradication of poverty, but to gain empowerment for poor women. In the nook and corner of the country NGO-MFIs, for-profit MFIs, Self Help Groups will keep up their activities, providing services to the needy according to their needs. In this gigantic effort, the spectrum of stakeholders is to nurture and strengthen this institutional infrastructure so that financial services reach the last women in the remotest corner of the country. The design of programmes that foster active participation of marginalised women requires un understanding of local, social, institutional and cultural context and the relevant gender related social patterns. Project needs continuous monitoring by facilitators, proper social and gender assessment, inclusive consultation at community level, ensure active participation of women into credit-lending process and careful monitoring and evaluation system provide second based alternatives for providing microfinance towards marginalised women successfully. In such a way we can "*Save for the present, securing the future.*"

REFERENCES

Barrett, M. (1980). *Women's Oppression Today*. London: Verso.

Bhadra, B. (2001, August). Janani O Prayukti: Lingakaran O Kshamatayaner Sahabastan [Mother and Technology: Co-existence of Sexualisation and Empowerment]. Yojana. (in Bengali)

Blumstein, P., & Schwartz, P. (1983). *American Couples: Money, Work and Sex*. New York: William Morrow.

Datta, S. R., & Mukherjee, S. R. (2009). *Women in the changing world-Global Experiences and Challenges*. Kolkata: Levan Books.

Desai, N., & Usha, T. (2001). *Women in Indian Society*. Delhi: National Book Trust of India.

Dhar, A., & Dasgupta, B. (2014). When Our Lips Speak —genderlabour together. In S. Sen & A. Chakrabarti (Ed.), Development on Trials. Orient Blackswan: New Delhi.

FAO (Food and Agricultural Organization). IFAD (International Fund for Agricultural Development) and ILO (International Labour Organization) (2010). Gender Dimensions of Agricultural and Rural Employment: Differentiated Pathways Out of Poverty. Status, Trends and Gaps; FAO, IFAD and ILO: Rome.

Fraad, H., Resnick, S. A., & Wolff, R. D. (1994). *Bringing it All Back Home: Class, Gender and Power in Modern Household*. London, Boulder, Colorado: Pluto Press.

Fraad, H., Resnick, S. A., & Wolff, R. D. (2009). For Every Knight in Shining Armour, There's a Castle Waiting to be Cleaned. In G. Cassano (Ed.), Class Struggle on the Home Front: Work, Conflict and Exploitation in the Household. London, UK: Palgrave-Macmillan.

Government of West Bengal. (1951). *District Statistical Hand-Books: Murshidabad.*

Government of West Bengal. (1961). *District Statistical Hand-Books: Murshidabad.*

Government of West Bengal. (1971). *District Statistical Hand-Books: Murshidabad.*

Government of West Bengal. (1981). *District Statistical Hand-Books: Murshidabad.*

Government of West Bengal (1991). *District Statistical Hand-Books: Murshidabad.*

Government of West Bengal (2001). *District Statistical Hand-Books: Murshidabad.*

Government of West Bengal (2009). *District Statistical Hand-Books: Murshidabad.*

Hewlett, S. (1986). *A Lesser Life*. New York: William Morrow.

Kapur, P. (2001). *Empowering the Indian Women*. New Delhi: Ministry of Information and Broadcasting, Government of India.

Madan, G. R. (1980). *Indian Social Problem*. Kolkata: Allied Publishers Private Limited.

Mandal, K. (2012). *Gender and Empowerment- A comparative Analysis of India and USA*. Kolkata: Levant Book.

Mazumder, R. (2005). *Introduction to Feminist Theory*. Kolkata: Towards Freedom.

Pitt, M. M., & Khandker, S. R. (1998). The Impact of Group-Based Credit Programs on Poor Households in Bangladesh: Does the Gender of the Participant Matter? *Journal of Political Economy*, *106*(5), 958–996. doi:10.1086/250037

Pitt, M. M., Khandker, S. R., McKernan, S.-M., & Latif, M. A. (1999). Credit Programs for the Poor and Reproductive Behavior in Low Income Countries: Are the Reported Causal Relationships the Result of Heterogeneity Bias? *Demography*, *33*(February). doi:10.2307/2648131 PMID:10036590

Pitt, M. M., Khandker, S. R., McKernan, S.-M., & Latif, M. A. (2000). The Effect of Non-agricultural Self-Employment Credit on Contractual Relations and Employment in Agriculture: The Case of Microcredit Programs in Bangladesh. *Bangladesh Development Studies*, *26*(2–3), 15–48.

Pitt, M. M., Khandker, S. R., Choudhury, O., & Millimet, D. (2003). Credit Programs for the Poor and the Health Status of Children in Rural Bangladesh. *International Economic Review*, *44*(February), 87–118. doi:10.1111/1468-2354.t01-1-00063

Srivastava, R. S. (2001). Women Empowerment: Some Critical issues. In A. Avasti & A.K. Srivastava (Ed.), Modernity, Feminism and Women Empowerment. New Delhi: Rawat Publications.

World Bank. (2012). *World Development Report, (2012)- Gender Equality and Development*. Washington, DC: The World Bank.

Sa-Dahn. (2016). Bharat Microfinance Report 2016. Retrieved from http://indiamicrofinance.com/wp-content/uploads/2016/09/The-Bharat-Microfinance-Report-2016.pdf

NABARD. (2005). *Progress of SHG – Bank Linkage in India, 2004-2005*. Microcredit.

KEY TERMS AND DEFINITIONS

Class Processes: Class process is an economic process which concern with the production, appropriation, distribution and receipt of surplus labour.

Cultural Process: Cultural processes mean the processes of producing and disseminating meanings in society.

Empowerment: Empowerment refers to the process by which power is gained, developed, seized, facilitated or gained.

Gender Process: These processes are cultural and ideological, therefore, these processes have left deep impression within minds of members of society.

Microfinance: Microfinance is one of among the system through which government is furnishing financial assistance towards poverty stricken women.

Political Process: By political conditions of existence, we mean processes of establishing and enforcing rules of family behaviour and adjudicating disputes over those rules.

SHGs: Self-Help Group(SHG) is a small voluntary association of poor people (not more than 20 people) having the same socio –economic background and do not have the capacity to collect financial funds from formal financial institutions.

Women Empowerment: Women's empowerment indicates a situation where women gain autonomy over their own lives to improve their personal, social, economic, political and legal conditions so as to achieve greater self-respect in both private and public spheres.

Chapter 5
Microfinancial Collaborative Economies Business Models and Strategies for Quality of Life Improvement:
Case studies for PROMUSAG and UBER

José G. Vargas-Hernández
University of Guadalajara, Mexico

ABSTRACT

The present chapter analyzes two cases of a joint venture stage to determine the successes and failures undertaken by the PROMUSAG and Uber as a model and strategies of collaborative economies to improve the quality of life. First, it is analyzed PROMUSAG as a program to finance women entrepreneurship aimed to improve the quality of life and the second case aims to analyze the different strategies taken by Uber to join the global market successfully, positioning itself in different countries. The analysis concludes that the empirical knowledge of entrepreneurs, in this case were not sufficient to direct the business to success, and that the lack of structured knowledge and adequate scientific support for this project strongly directed towards the non-permanence on the market. Taking terms as work global, it is considered Uber as a technology-based company and sees it from an overall, same strategy refers to a strategy that follows the company having a worldwide standardized product, another issue that would revise the importance of the theory of institutions.

INTRODUCTION

The Mexican government through the Ministry of Agrarian Reform supports rural entrepreneurship projects. One way is PROMUSAG (program for women in agriculture). This is a support program for rural women entrepreneurs, seeking their integration in the productive sector to earn income to help in the fight against poverty in this rural environment. The support consists of a sum of money to start up

DOI: 10.4018/978-1-5225-5240-6.ch005

the business to undertake, which is repayable, but it is considered at lost funds. In 2009, hundreds of projects have benefited from PROMUSAG, one of which has been analyzed for this report. This case is featuring nine women in the municipality of San Martin de Hidalgo, Jalisco. In that year, nine women was PROMUSAG order required for each project. The team for this project consisted of women with little or no preparation in business, but the team had a leader with knowledge and skills acquired empirically that gave the project some routing to success. PROMUSAG central requirements requested to be eligible for funding to the various proposals were teams of nine members, all participants should be female, a project to undertake the business detailing emphasizing the distribution of grant money, it is sent to be developed by an engineer in the agricultural area and the last requirement was to have an area of land sufficient to carry out the purpose of the enterprise activity. The venture was marked by the fall in leader's illness, which conditioned the project to a resounding lack of profitability, this, coupled with the lack of scientific preparation and support scientists generated a mismanagement of resources and capabilities that had the project, bringing this to its final termination in six months.

For decades the transfer of people from one place to another in large cities has been using public transport, taxis, or those with better economic position and resource allows them to move in their own car. That was the traditional way going from one point to another, but with the different changes that occur in society today, technological, economic or related to the environment issues have been marking new ways of moving from one point to another. These new forms also have to do with issues of passenger safety, comfort and other factors.

As a result of these new ways of moving emerges UBER, which for several years start to mark a new trend in moving people from one point to another, especially in big cities around the world. It has its origins in a revised class concept of Strategic Management as it is born global that refers to those companies that are born in global or international markets and are marking a new trend in the way of doing business, taking advantage of the technological changes that have occurred in the world in which today we live. This company considers having a relationship with the technological-based firms that are characterized by being innovative, enough reason to learn more about the same as it was able to study from approaches such as the theory based on institutions and global strategy.

Uber has its origins in 2008 as it tells the story in its page when Travis Kalanick and Garrett Camp could not get a taxi in Paris, which led to an idea to create an application where with just one button, could have a trip. What started with this simple idea is now changing the way people are transported in large cities? According to the Uber definition, it is the smartest way to move and luxury at low cost.

THEORETICAL BACKGROUND

Entrepreneurial Ventures and Life Quality

Quality of life is considered as the set of factors which contribute to the general well-being of people in terms of personal satisfaction with happiness, health, safety, intellectual and cultural preferences, financial security, family life, job satisfaction, etc. Quality of life has been defined as the level of satisfaction with an individual´s conditions, relationships, and surroundings relative to the available alternatives (McGregor & Goldsmith, 1998).

The Business Dictionary defines quality of life as "Daily living enhanced by wholesome food and clean air and water, enjoyment of unfettered open spaces and bodies of water, conservation of wildlife and natural resources, security from crime, and protection from radiation and toxic substances. It may also be used as a measure of the energy and power a person is endowed with that enable him or her to enjoy life and prevail over life's challenges irrespective of the handicaps he or she may have…" Quality of life has different manifestations, ranging from improvements in health, standards of living, education, work life, etc. Quality of life can be described as a multidimensional phenomenon that cannot be reduced to a few quantitative indicators. Explanations of quality of life include psychological, social, political environmental, economic, issues. Quality of life profiles or analysis of the correlates are different only in the emphasis of the human development approach to social welfare.

Existing concepts of quality of life are wide enough to overcome multidimensional social concerns such as exclusion and poverty explanations that cover much the same territory. However, the improvement in the provision of social services to a specific community or to a specific segment of population, can raise the indicators of quality of life of that society, but fail to deliver services in geographically remote areas or to socially disadvantaged groups as an unfocused goal. The consensus that narrows measures of consumption and quality of life is inadequate and a broader view is needed. Economists concerned with quality of life recognize the importance of income and consumption derived from sources provided by the State, social and private sectors. There are some policies and synergies contained on this approach to quality of life. Economic growth may increase the living standards, benefit the quality of life and reduce poverty. The approach to income and the level of consumption as a quality of life can be criticized when having access to resources by other means. A case is the improvement of the social services, education and health provisions, etc., and taking advantage of opportunities offered by the growth of safety groups and social networks.

The best known of these influences on improvement on quality of life as national welfare strategies derived from postindustrial growth, state structures and economic geography. This institutional welfare state approach focuses more on the content of policies, more universal and less directed social programs at target groups, the requirements to be eligible beneficiary and the quality of the services. These welfare programs benefit the quality of working life and employment, rather than social spending. Thus, it improves the societal quality of life. Societal quality of life is defined as the general state of well-being experienced by society's members (Morris & Lewis, 1991). However, the decline in the terms of quality of life and socioeconomic characteristics of the working class as well as the dismantling of the welfare state, are taking place already.

Entrepreneurship has been found to have an impact on life quality (Morris, 1998b; Pennings, 1982; Sirgy, 1985). The relationship between entrepreneurship and life quality is being studied by the family and consumer sciences focusing on societal and environmental trends (American Association of Family and Consumer Sciences, 2004; Horridge & Craig, 2001; Key & Firebaugh, 1989; Kim, Sharpe & Kim, 2002; McNabb, 2004). Morris (1998b) contends that entrepreneurship has an impact on quality of life dimensions. The perception level of the entrepreneurial efforts has a significant impact on dimensions of quality of life. Entrepreneurs' quality of life and a positive perception of impacts on their families, customers and community sustain their business. Thus, lifestyle entrepreneurship benefits family´s quality of life and community development (Marcketti et al., 2006). Peters, Frehse and Buhalis (2009) continue the analysis of the relationship between entrepreneurial quality of life and tourism business growth. The quality of life perceived motivates and sustains lifestyle and economic status more than growth. Entrepreneurs may be emotionally motivated by their families and quality of life more than workload factors depending upon individual wants and characteristics and personality traits (Marcketti et al., 2006).

Peters, Frehse and Buhalis (2009) have analyzed the relationship between entrepreneurial quality of life and profits and have derived some propositions. Life quality and leisure time decrease determined by entrepreneurial factors during the time of financial risks and expectations for establishing the new business. Lowering or heightening quality of life expectations may be necessary to meet the profits requirement despite that the lifestyle entrepreneurship may have positive effects.

Social Entrepreneurs contribute to enhance the well-being and quality of life (Baden, 2006). Social entrepreneurship at national business system level has an impact on the societal quality of life. At regional/ national business system level, social entrepreneurship improves the objective and subjective indicators the quality of life. Social, organizational and individual interactions and complex inter-organizational relationships at regional/national business system have an impact on quality of life (Koponen, n.d.). Small businesses are formed to improve quality of life conditions by meeting the family's needs and demands (Brush, 1992; Stanforth & Muske, 1999). Social entrepreneurship contributes to the general well-being and societal quality of life balancing social change and social capital in a certain regional or local level. The model of Koponen (n.d.) proposes that the objective parameters of quality of life are sustained on social entrepreneurship, considering social value vs. market mechanism which in turn is the base of business model with its value proposition and exchange. The dimensions of quality of life are the social, material, physical, productive and emotional quality of life. Entrepreneurship has an impact on quality of life economic, physical and mental health, social, technological, job satisfaction, institutional, and ecological dimensions (Morris, 1998b; Rice, 1985).

The objective parameters are the numbers, percentages, total sums, etc. The subjective parameters are the society´s experience, opinion, social norms, traditions, etc. These objective and subjective parameters have social and business effects on the general well-being, the national business system, social capital and change. The economic model of any society is related to the improvement of a societal quality of life (Jordan, 2008). However, there is no unified conclusion on how to achieve a greater level of quality at local, regional or national levels. Few studies have examined the relationship between lifestyle entrepreneurship and life quality (Henderson, 2002; Mhango, Marcketti, & Niehm, 2005; Scarborough & Zimmerer, 2003). From the systems theory, perspective lifestyle entrepreneurship bridges with quality of life. Lifestyle entrepreneurship has an impact on life quality for individual small business owners, their families, and communities. Successful lifestyle entrepreneurs enhance the perception of a better quality of life driven by a mindset and values affecting their families, customers and the community. Life quality of the business owner perceived as an entrepreneurial venture may provide quality of life to employees, consumers, and the community.

Still it is not clear how to measure entrepreneur's quality of life and the effects on new ventures. When creating a new venture, the entrepreneur's quality of life may lower while workloads increase by many personal barriers, worries and financial risks (Shaver et al., 2001; Weiermair & Peters, 1998b) until he reaches a breakeven point where both qualities of life and profits are maximized. As a consequence of this new venture that entrepreneurial effects on quality of life may be positive, although sometimes when creating a new venture, individual quality of life may start to decrease. After lifestyle entrepreneurs reach this breakeven point, they diminish activities and depending of several variables of life quality, their effects start to decrease and to become negatives. The, the lifestyle entrepreneur does not have economic motivations and hinders growth. Although he contributes to economic welfare (Weiermair & Peters, 1998a) he does not lower quality of life.

An exploratory study conducted by Marcketti; Niehm, and Fuloria (2006) found a relationship between lifestyle entrepreneurship and life quality for business owners, families and communities involved. Also, some elements of entrepreneurship such as creativity, innovation, and personal life experiences have long-term effects on the life quality of business owners, their families and communities.

Despite that quality of life is a relevant factor for the location of new business; it is one of the most neglected by policymakers. However, regional variables have an impact on entrepreneurial decisions and policy makers on quality of life, although some variables cannot be controlled such as the impact of weather and geography on quality of life. Quality of life is a livable factor that attracts business and individuals (Endeavor Insight, 2014; McCann, 2000; Pennings, 1982). However, quality of life is not always the main factor in deciding to start a business.Many of the policies that address these concerns at local levels that link quality of life to economic growth may lead to the central dilemma. This dilemma can be represented on an advanced society that may be opposed to materialism. The elevation of a post-industrial expansion of quality of life is related to multi-site decision making on well-being. Also, it is related to a long tradition of social, political and economic welfare policies as much attention to subnational spatial conditions of the economic policy and market geography, rather than simply eliminating territorial influences make them relevant in new ways.

Quality of life is an intangible and subjective variable difficult to measure objectively because individuals have different priorities. The quality of life (QOL) index is an objective measure compiling a variety of objective factors ranging from life expectancy, public education, public safety, recreation, etc. to the share of childhood welfare and poverty. The level of entrepreneurship has a causal effect of the societal quality of life. Morris and Richard J. Lewis (1991) examine the relationship between entrepreneurship and societal quality of life. Morris and Lewis (1991) identified seven quality of life dimensions in terms of costs and benefits produced by entrepreneurship: economic, health, social, technological, work, institutional, and ecological. For example, they found that entrepreneurship may have a positive effect on the ecological dimension of quality of life.

Research has shown that there is significant correlation but not perfect within specific regions. Comparison of QOL measures on regional bases can correlate entrepreneurial decisions and quality of life. Quality-of-life variables can explain new-business formations across the regions, although may not indicate causation. All these variables contribute to increase the standard of living that influence entrepreneurship, new business startups, and decisions of local policymakers. A high quality of life means that people get increased power. The decline in the terms of quality of life and socioeconomic characteristics of the working class as well as the dismantling of the welfare state are being shaped by the advance of economic globalization processes and the deepening of capitalism that benefit from the intensive exploitation of labor. From a public management perspective, it is intended to view government from the bottom up focusing more on quality of life and work in public organizations and seeking to understand and improve organizational elements such as leadership, strategic management, organizational climate, service quality, innovation, performance and customer satisfaction.

Quality of life has been related to satisfaction with management decisions regarding individual goals, physical and emotional improvements and betterment of self, family and community (Edwards, 1991; McGregor & Goldsmith, 1998; Morris, 1998a). Decision-making and management may result in satisfying outcomes and better life quality. The human development index is an indicator of a set of minimum values of the quality of life of a person, such as his educational, health, economic and other. The first concern is with human services agencies being established which provide care, money, education, shelter and support to people, often with significant personal interaction between the agency and the individual client user. A high quality of life for people is the goal of sustainable development. Policies fostering the post-industrial growth have focused increasingly on the economies of cities and regions, and sub national elites have emerged as sectors in these policies. At the same time, space policies explicitly targeted the urban environmental problems with a main impact on local quality of life in general that has proliferated conditions. Especially in the post- industrial urban arrangements, local social movements and parties regularly mobilize people around these concerns on a better quality of life. Women employment contributes to improve the overall quality of life through the formulation of more sustainable development policies.

To determine the relationships between entrepreneurial motivations and realities and the enhancement of quality of life is important to consider for a comprehensive framework for policy making and to design the incentives to motivate entrepreneurs. Incentivizing external growth instead of internal growth of business is required to achieve and breakeven point with the higher rates of quality of life and profits.

An Institutional Approach

One of the aspects that fit for this work was the subject where the importance of institutions is played and whether it can reach affect or influence strategies that take companies to conduct their operations. An aspect that Uber considered is the adaptation to the current legal framework, which call as the theory of institutions, and in this category, it is found in a definition of the Nobel laureate in economics, North (1990) defined an institution as humanly planned restrictions that structure the interaction of people, which is popularly known as rules of the game.

Likewise, the same author classifies 2 different types of institutions and classifies them as follows (North 2005) formal and informal institutions. In the former are the laws, regulations and standards, and on the side of informal talks about rules, culture and ethics, including different ideas, values and attitudes of people in their behavior in society. Moreover, it is possible to distinguish three aspects the authors belonging to the first generation of institutionalisms, neo institutionalisms and the new institutional economics (Urbado & Hernandez, 2007). Moreover, Veblen (1965) also talks about the institutions and gives us another definition that by the end of this work is also acceptable. It is defined as common and predictable patterns of behavior in society, including the habits of thought and action generally shared. One area where have failed Institutions are flaws in the regulations for these type of companies, i.e. not governments had considered the new e-business, category where Uber is characterized. Canals (1994) states that the objective of internationalizing a company are the opening of new markets, lower production costs, and a more efficient structure of production and distribution of the company.

The business model of this type of business is focused on a specific sector of the population and from this part gives a new way to operate, which is not available for all people who want to use the product or service this type of companies offer. The overall and global strategy adopted by these firms have advantages over competitors as it refers to how to compete and focuses on providing standardized products and services worldwide (Peng, 2000). Within the theory of institutions see different regulations that have occurred around the world to allow the application to offer their services. For example, in the United States in the city of Chicago a new category of transportation calls service transport networks, just as in Mexico City was created have made regulations for the operation of the service, in New Orleans you will have to pay the city by permits, something similar happened in New York where the council of citizenship and Uber reached an agreement to set the number of vehicles that can circulate in the city.

Just as there are cities where they operate without any regulation of institutions, there are cases like the above where they operate with certain regulations by the institutions and authorities of the city, but is also the case of Florida in the United States because it does not operate in this city for failing to meet the requirements of city tax. On the other hand, the phenomenon of globalization (Peng, 2012) refers to the close integration of people and countries around the world, and today this concept is applied in different sectors and industries.

Within the theory of institutions are seen different regulations that have occurred around the world to allow the application to offer their services. For example, in the United States in the city of Chicago was created a new category of transportation called service transport networks, just as in Mexico City was created, both have made regulations for the operation of the service. In New Orleans the customer has to pay the city permits. Something similar happened in New York where the council of citizenship and Uber reached an agreement to set the number of vehicles that can circulate in the city. Just as there are cities where they operate without any regulation of institutions, there are cases like the above where they operate with certain regulations by the institutions and authorities of the city. But, it is also the case of Florida in the United States, because it does not operate in this city for failing to meet the requirements of city tax.

On the other hand, the phenomenon of globalization (Peng, 2012) refers to the close integration of people and countries around the world, and today this concept is applied in different sectors and industries.

Collaborative Economies Business Model

Bostman and Rogers (2010) argue that firms like UBER are part of a classic model of collaborative economy, being a disruptive innovation (Christensen & Raynor, 2003) that occurs when individuals share common interests and a common philosophy of life. In this case, they aim to rent cars in shared taxis or whole taxis through a social search and management system (Bostman & Rogers, 2010). So, the emergence of this phenomenon is possible as the evolution of technology allows imitate the exchanges that usually or used to give face to face, on a larger scale thanks to the internet, together with the ability to create trust between strangers. Rifkin (2014) points out that the decline in marginal costs, which tends to be near zero, is resulting in a dichotomous economy, partly capitalist market and on the other hand, collaborative commons gradually drawn out a new economic paradigm. Interian, (2016) argues that the sharing economy is credited with reducing transaction costs, increase efficiency and promote accountability and competence. This model does not require a centralized entity that should have an inventory and therefore is free of logistics, costs associated with maintaining inventory, product and geographic expansion for these purposes.

This model by allowing individuals to take advantage of the ability to take advantage of an asset that already possess, collaborative business model eliminates in an efficient and convenient way transaction costs. The specific characteristics of collaborative consumer of passengers and commuters are little known, although generally, it may try to travelers connected and experts, likely to responsible consumption, characterized by a high level of trust in the other members of the community and familiarity with internet and online commerce, demanding about the quality of its transport and commuting experiences (Russo & Quaglieri, 2014).Despite its purported benefits, companies of collaborative economies have been strongly criticized for the way they operate, and in some cases have been forced to shut down operations. Critics argue that the laws are evading created precisely to regulate certain practices in which their companies are engaged; users sharing platforms become "prosumers" people who consume, like produce (Streitfeld, 2014).

Blurring the line between consumer and producer collaborative economy breaks with the traditional business model that companies own and people consume. On the other hand, the concept of sharing erodes the disinterested public regulation, substituting private regulation or leaving unattended regulated transactions. Because of this, business creation becomes more widespread and may even lead to displace their regulated and established counterparts some time ago. An example of this is Uber, which has become a ubiquitous service in major cities around the world (Interian, 2016). The most important cities in the United States and Europe have begun to implement regulations regarding share or rent cars and have initiated investigations with the goal of bringing the collaborative economy in accordance with existing laws (Chafkin, 2016).

On the other hand, information technologies have facilitated the exchange of user experiences, enabling the comments and product valuation objective and transparent manner. These valuations are perceived in the market as certain and are changing consumer behavior and redefining the role of influence during the buying process by providing more realistic expectations (Cañigueral, 2015). That is when the consumer can know the costs and perceived by others who have commented and valued their consumer experiences, which later will help to make a decision with some confidence, even if the consumer never had before contracted this service, reducing significantly benefits the perceived risk (Wen, 2009).

PROMUSAG PROGRAM: WOMEN ENTREPRENEURSHIP TO IMPROVE THE QUALITY OF LIFE

The Secretary of Agrarian Reform (Secretaría de la Reforma Agraria, SRA) is the institution of the Federal Government that serves women and men who live and work in the rural communities and ejidos or community´s owned land across the country. The SRA provides legal certainty for the owners of the land and promote comprehensive rural development social justice. One of the ways the SRA supports rural development is through the promotion of entrepreneurial and productive projects in ejidos and communities through its programs Support for Productive Projects in Agrarian Nucleolus Fund (Fondo de Apoyo para Proyectos Productivos en Núcleos Agrarios, FAPPA) Program for Women in the Agricultural Sector (Programa de la Mujer en el Sector Agrario, PROMUSAG) and Young Rural Entrepreneur and Land Fund (Joven Emprendedor Rural y Fondo de Tierras, JERFT). PROMUSAG is aimed at women who are organized to develop a productive project that allows them to earn an income and thus help fight poverty in rural areas (PROMUSAG 2012, SAGARPA, 2016).

Within PROMUSAG program, projects can be installed in various areas, such as ecotourism, cattle fattening, rural stores, food production or various services. Women living in the countryside can access the program PROMUSAG women's groups of 3-6 members, over 18 years old, who inhabit agrarian and rural areas owners of community land. The financial support is of $30,000.00 per member provided it does not exceed the amount of $ 180,000.00. Women may be benefiting from the support of PROMUSAG until they have been supported in the past five fiscal years by himself or by the FAPPA PROMUSAG (Fund for supporting productive projects in agrarian).

METHODOLOGY

The methods employed are the analytical and descriptive. The first aims to analyze the case and identify failures and successes which led the company for the ensuing year and the descriptive method to detail the situations experienced by the venture.

Case to Analyze

The history and details of the case were provided by one of the women who undertook this business which in turn is a daughter of the initial principal leader of the enterprise. To gather the information, a personal informal interview was conducted on May 2012. What more motivated the business venture was the fact that the main entrepreneur has a great taste an innate ability for this type of business, her personal qualities and characteristics mostly agree with those of a successful entrepreneur. The main obstacle for this business venture was the lack of funding, which it once existed, the project was launched.

In 2009 the entrepreneurial principal, was blessed with a support of $ 100,000.00 in cash, with the advantageous feature called "sunk" to the implementation of a rural business in the town of San Martin de Hidalgo, Jalisco, which consisted of raising and fattening cattle. Support was received from the government body called Agrarian Reform Secretariat by rural support program to women entrepreneurs "PROMUSAG". PROMUSAG central requirements requested to be eligible for funding to the various proposals were teams of nine members, all participants should be female, a project to undertake the business detailing emphasizing the distribution of grant money, it is sent to an agricultural engineer to develop the agricultural area and the last requirement was to have an area of land sufficient to carry out the purpose of the enterprise activity.

The selection criteria for the formation of the task force were: being female is the PROMUSAG prerequisite required and indispensable, belonging to the family, time available for the project and interest in it. The skills and / or abilities that have the formed team made are the leadership, expertise in law, some livestock knowledge and empirical knowledge of small business management. The way in which it was given the work distribution between women entrepreneurs was by making meeting arrangements, where they defined their roles. The "lady" was the project leader, his daughter is bachelor-in-law and has the role of administrator of financial resources, and the other members would act as support staff, i.e. performing operational tasks of supplies purchase, cleaning stalls, feeding cattle and attention to situations that may arise in the production area.

The business plan prepared was paid before the monetary benefit was granted, it just detail issues relating to investment in equipment and production inputs such as instruments, equipment, food, young livestock, among others. Therefore, only was useful to structure the production plant and neither for business organization or healthy finance to sustain within inside. The way to get to the end customer and more convenient for the type of business, existing resources and the region where they conducted the enterprise, was to sell the product at a much larger broker to sell the product it the final consumer. The project lasted only six months from commissioning to decommissioning, which corresponds to a period of fattening cattle.

Application of the Theories to the Case

It is necessary to analyze the internal aspects of the company to find the main successes and failures committed in undertaking this business, as the main reasons for the success of a company are brewing inside of it. A business venture begins with the idea and the desire of an individual undertaking, which must have certain qualities and characteristics. In this case, for the entrepreneur's main business was a success in life, as she is a person who has the characteristics and qualities of a successful entrepreneur, which are constancy, sense or business opportunity, knowledge, personal responsibility and leadership skills.

The monetary resource was, together with the decision of entrepreneurship, the main trigger of the business. This financial resource was needed for the purchase of instruments and appliances for conditioning the production plant. These acquired assets would be tangible resources with which the company would have to begin to build a road and build competitive advantage. Unfortunately, these were not innovative or special characteristics that could lead the company to take advantage of some sort as cost leadership, differentiation or focus. It really was the most common for a company to take from this type of business. The fact that there was no proper business plan to guide this enterprise in the formation of a solid organizational structure led to the existence of a variety of situations, which the organization was not in a proper way as there is no basis for internal coordination. That is, the organization did not develop intangible resources, neither knowledge nor skills, and also did not took advantage of the existing resources in good way, and there was no strategic plan to guide the company towards a goal through proper orientation of each of the actions to be undertaken. This due to the existing empirical knowledge and not theoretical basis exists. When it happened the disease of the entrepreneurship leader in the early stages, when the project did not even started to run was one of the situations for which the organization had no way to handle properly.

The lack of evidence document-based to guide the integration of the existent resources and capabilities propelled an unsuitable an inadequate knowledge management tied to hand and feet to the organization in terms of the creation and development of competitive advantages. There were three reasons why the venture was short-lived for only six months:

1. Failures in the leadership capability, the main leader fell ill soon after received financing and abandoned the project, not permanently but did not have enough contact to conduct business to success, being at the head of the project the daughter of the main leader. Her daughter is Bachelor-in-Law as a profession, but without certainty in knowledge about business management and effective leadership skills. This created an atmosphere of des governance, which brought conflict among team members and discouragement to work and / or continue in the project.
2. Lack of capacity in the area of procurement, equipment and supplies were bought at high prices, which were not covered by the investment project. This situation created a debt in addition to the already acquired through funding from PROMUSAG, turn in a few days unviable the business that was being undertaken, as the rate of return on investment would hardly be necessary for the project to survive in the short term.
3. Lack of marketing capacity to market the product, at the time it was possible to have a finished product, feedlot cattle in optimum conditions, the price at which it was sold was low. However, it was not possible to recover the investment in the production stage; the money raised was used to pay debts owed to suppliers and creditors, leaving the project without resources and women without encouragement to continue. This happens due to a lack of capacity in the area of negotiation and the lack of market intelligence to analyze the situation and to anticipate future price to implement the actions that were relevant.

UBER STRATEGIES FOR TRANSPORT INCORPORATED PRIVATE MARKET

Background of the Problem

Today globalization plays an important process, because by this concept can be eliminated some barriers between countries. Through technology has been a way these barriers have been eliminated, since technological innovations often come equally to different countries and at different times around the world, so it can be seen different products with similar characteristics, which is called as a standard product, regardless of whether they are produced in different cultures.

The story so before it started this century tells that the common way to establish a company along the story is that the company or the plant reached the place where he would have operations, had a physical place, and was established formally. Now it is seeing a new trend in strategies and ways of doing business in enterprises as a platform generated by its operations, profits, sales and everything related to business dedicated activity. Which have started with this simple idea is now changing the way people are transported in large cities, according to the Uber definition is the smartest way to move and luxury at low cost.

Technology and innovation play an important role in the process of globalization. Adopting a comprehensive strategy for technology companies is essential and addressing new ways of doing business. Nowadays have been emerging these new companies of successful technology-based, born in markets international companies like Netshoes, Netflix, Google, Amazon and many other technological changes that have been created and have managed to be successful in their business segment. The creation of these new companies has diversified options that consumers have to purchase the good or service that require, with new technology and not in the common traditional form.

One problem faced by companies that wanted to provide the services of private transport in the country, were the unions of taxi drivers that prevent or put barriers to companies that wanted to provide these services faced, and who would provide the service had to join the unions of transportation in addition to the permits they had to acquire by the authorities to provide the service. Thus, the institutions were an impediment to a company that wanted to be in this area. But also, an advantage of same weaknesses they could have the same institutions, they have created companies like Uber and reaching nations that did not consider these businesses in their regulations. Taking advantage of those holes is how they have succeeded in entering the global market.Within technology and new ways of doing business in the globalization process, it can be found different definitions and ways in which this process is changing. One of these definitions is that of Friedman (1970) and for example he says that globalization is a phenomenon characterized by technological innovation and its appearance in the world has been consolidated in stages. The initial stage of economic globalization, for some authors, is the industrial revolution the event that gave rise to this phenomenon. Most authors state that consolidation was given to a process of trade integration (Carbaugh, 2005).

In recent years this type of technology-based companies has increased their presence around the world and have led to the emergence of more of this type and have seen more and more not only born but become successful, not only in a nation but in the global market place. A technology-based company can differentiate itself from other companies with the main feature innovation processes, either in the product or service offered. They base their activity on technological research, having scientific and technological knowledge.

For purposes of this research, the case of Uber is studied from the side of the strategies used to enter the global market, and succeeding in many countries, taking into account that each country and culture is different, the use of concepts as work global, technology-based companies, global strategy was considered a factor for growth and establishment of industries or companies of this type. The technology-based companies like Uber have achieved their positioning in the limited control of institutions to such companies, in the absence of regulatory schemes both Uber and other companies have used this to establish their operations. Some features that make them different companies like Uber is that they have fewer staff operating or working for the company, since by creating the online platform and working and operating costs are lower than in a company established in a physical place also presented in the world with a standard or homogenized product. Companies like Uber generate an advantage for users or consumers and have achieved different countries or states to consider making changes to their laws to fit the modus operandi of these companies. States allow or block entry of Uber and other companies in their type, having a power in the region where they arrive with their operations, thus having influence on decisions or regulations made in the laws for operation.

The research of these report wants to answer is on How technology-based companies with a global strategy have succeeded in entering and being successful in the new way of doing business?

The importance comes to have this work of serious research to understand the impact of the strategies of technology-based companies taking specific case of Uber. This is done using the theory of institutions and by applying the concept of global strategy came to succeed. Overall, a case of Uber especially as famous as the raised here in this chapter case where the company has already been established in at least 20 countries, albeit with some adjustments as the nation where the product offering remains standard worldwide reaches, and despite having problems in some cities where he settled.

These problems especially with local competitors, called taxis are mainly due to fact they think it is unfair competition and with innovation that the company Uber made in the product achievement that many people with common form move from side to side in public or private transport, now do differently and have changed the way they use the shuttle. While we know that the group of people or consumers who can access this service is limited, because people who use it so far require at least two basic things to make use of the product. One of them is to have a cell phone where downloading the application, then also required to have a bank account as a credit card or debit card with which to pay the service they have. These basic elements are essential of this new business model and so far, it is fundamental to acquire a service like what Uber offers, because without them they cannot access the transfer from one place to another. Thus, this is being a limiting factor that not all people can consume this good or service, so the service is intended for a specific sector of the population which operates the platform.

In the case of Mexico, so far is not entirely clear the legal fulfillments that must have this company. Mexico is working on making changes to laws, regulations roads and adaptations of the legal framework of the relevant institutions to consider Uber and companies of its kind in formal enterprises. In this case, some state laws are working to make adaptations to their traffic laws, such as the state of Jalisco and Mexico City that having already advanced and concrete proposals as to how to resolve this issue. However, at the time of writing this report, some of the proposals were being approved or published to make them official.

Moreover, companies offering the same service as Uber, in this case the taxis see it as an illegal and unfair to the service competition that for years have been offering and operating in some form as a monopoly. They do not pay taxes and have adopted certain aggressive strategies to try to reach the market to Uber through intimidation or aggression towards users or drivers of the business. Taking advantage of technological changes and the weakness of the institutions not considered. Also, with the emergence years ago of other technology companies and carrying out a global strategy have been incorporated to market, different companies.

One of these technology-based companies with a comprehensive global strategy that has carried out these concepts in a successfully way is Uber because today it is seen with these strategies that has-been established in the market. After seeing this case have emerged more companies with the same features and offer the service of private transport, as are Cabify and City drive to name some of the same sector. Even its operations are similar to the case analyzed in this work. These firms are technology-based companies that offer a private shuttle service to their users through a platform. Although not all companies operate as such in the same cities, their strategies are like. On the other hand, if it is seen the part where it operates each company taking the case of Mexico. For example, in Guadalajara operates Uber and City drive but not Cabify, leading to the conclusion that even with global strategies are not present in the same cities or arrive at the same time. Uber is in Guadalajara and 379 cities worldwide and is aimed at a specific segment of the population that is people with bank account, credit card or debit card to pay for the service they purchase, as well as having the application installed on their cell phone.

Within its business model, Uber does not accept payment in cash so far, this being an important innovation in the model, and this aspect is also part of the diversification of the service. Another important issue is quality standards for these keep the user since the end of each trip it can rate the service and the driver, this being another innovation in the service provided how had offered traditional way. An important issue in such companies as already mentioned is the diversification of product or service offered, as it has been key to succeed and companies like Netshoes, Netflix, Amazon and the company analyzed in this case Uber. These technology-based companies have in common is that they are based on diversification and innovation in what they offer which is considered the most important to have successful operations in a globalized world. Another important segment is the population that has access to the good or service that is launched. when somebody wants to buy a product like shoes, food, books or any other product only they go to the market place where the product is sold and with money in hand it is acquired and anyone who can pay the price can buy it.

In the case of service Uber, this simply fact does not apply because it is a service that only is acquired it from a strict sense by people over 18, who are the people likely to have a bank account to pay for the service. Thus, the target population or that can be client f Uber, are people over 18 years with bank account. Uber on its website states that offers the service in five municipalities of the Metropolitan area of Guadalajara (ZMG), that is Guadalajara, Zapopan, Tlaquepaque, Tonala and Tlajomulco, taking a total of 2,745,260 potential customers broken down as follows the municipalities, and displaying data as much as by men and women.

According to data from the Metropolitan Transportation Institute Jalisco, taxis continue to maintain market power and Uber is positioned in second place in service of private transport as it is concerned. An advantage of Uber, considered by users is mainly the price and greater security.

Analysis of Results

Today many companies seek more customer satisfaction or give greater importance to this issue. Therefore, they carry out different strategies to accomplish this and satisfy their customers. According to the sector where companies unfold will make the appropriate innovations to the product or service offered by adaptations according to geographical area, with strategic advertising, by price or by improving

Table 1. Total population of the metropolitan area of Guadalajara

Municipality	Population 18 and Over	Masculine Population 18 and More	Feminine Population 18 and More
Guadalajara	1,031,902	482,713	549,189
Tlaquepaque	376,022	182,406	193,616
Tlajomulco de Zúñiga	235,703	115,015	120,688
Tonalá	289,679	147,418	142,261
Zapopan	811,954	388,501	423,453

Source: Prepared with data from INEGI 2010 census

product quality. Sometimes what the customer is looking for comfort, closeness or facility to acquire the asset or service. This is what UBER has done to offer its service. Uber implements innovations in the business model.

In finding that customer satisfaction, Uber relies to implement its innovations both in service and customer experience that maximizes utility when using the service. One of those innovations was the automatic payment. Also requesting service by an application installed on the user's phone that easily and at the touch of a button is the means to obtain the service. So, consumers identify this innovation in service and thus the company could exercise monopoly power over its competitors once started. Uber to operate the platform seized market share by displacing the service that for years has been given in different parts of the world called taxis that were intended to transport people who had no car or prefer not to use it.

With all the technological changes that have occurred in recent years, it is common that most of the population have access to a cell where through download the application and use the platform can request their transportation service, regardless of whether they bring cash. Uber main advantages over its competitors and by its strategies just identified the customer, are:

1. Innovation in the way of providing the service.
2. No need cash (automatic payment).
3. The customer requires a cell with the application and a bank account where he will be charged by the service.
4. Cheaper than a taxi fare.
5. Provide a standard or homogenized product.
6. They offer a bonus in addition to transportation, like listening to the music the customer wants during the trip, water, air conditioning in the car.

An important aspect to consider is that many innovations and changes that a company has made if the service or product offered does not meet the quality standards of its customers would not be accepted. Bringing the theoretical aspects to the practice when technological innovations, prices and product quality were bad, Uber would not have achieved success that has today. In this way, it can be seen how by implementing a comprehensive and global strategy, a standardized product and application of technology in its service, Uber achieved to implement a new business model in the field of private transport service, and how this has given rise to emerging technology-based companies in different industries or sectors.

These technology-based companies begin to take an important role by having greater technological resources in their operations, with so many changes that have occurred in the way business enterprises have had to adapt to these technological changes and because of this have emerged companies like Uber.

CONCLUSION AND RECOMMENDATIONS

Empirical knowledge of entrepreneurs, in this case, was not enough to route this business to success and the lack of structured knowledge and appropriate scientific support to this project strongly directed towards not stay in the market.

The recommendation for PROMUSAG is that it needs to call for a strategic plan as a requirement to be eligible for financial support. To start a business, the entrepreneurs should also count on empirical knowledge, a scientific basis, either by the project members, or by external consultants. One of the advantages of technology-based companies like Uber is to reduce costs and adapt to the new way they are giving businesses through different mechanisms and strategies that were studied for this case. It can be concluded that through a global strategy and technological adaptations companies like Uber have been successful and also taking advantage of the gaps that institutions not considering such firms have adapted to the country coming through a standard product offering in the world.

Companies of its kind have well defined characteristics as that base their operations through the use of technological resources, maintains a standard or homogenized product regardless of the region or geographical area and implements global strategies. However, a weakness that can have companies in their type and it is necessary to assess the institutional aspects, as in some countries are making changes to allow operation through restrictions or in some cases block and not allow its operation. It is important to consider carrying out a successful global strategy.

Another advantage that can have the technology-based companies over their competitors is that their operations are based on the use of technological resources, so it can be concluded that through technological innovations and through a global strategy, it is shown that there is an emerging new type of economic system or a new business model that emerged a few years ago and through successful cases like Uber. This new model begins to change the course of business. The elements that the company included and considered fundamental are the implementation of automatic payment, request the service by installed on a cell application because without it cannot access the transfer from one place to another, thus being a limiting so that not all people have free access to the service.

Finally, it should be mentioned that innovations do not reach at the same time to all places. Where the technology-based company starts operations, a company is critical to have a successful experience away from and continue to apply the strategies used to bequeath to success in its home and then expand their horizons.

REFERENCES

American Association of Family and Consumer Sciences. (2004). *A brief history of AAFCS*. Retrieved May 10, 2004, from http://www.aafcs.org/about/history.html

Baden, J. A. (2006). Social Entrepreneurship and Quality of Life. *Posted on June 07, 2006FREE Insights. Topics in Cognitive Science.*

Bostman, R., & Rogers, R. (2010). *What's mine is yours: the rise of collaborative consumption*. New York: Harper Business.

Brush, C. G. (1992). Research on women business owners: Past trends, a new perspective, and future directions. *Entrepreneurship Theory and Practice, 16*(4), 5–30. doi:10.1177/104225879201600401

Canals, J. (1994). *La internacionalización de la empresa*. Madrid: McGraw-Hill.

Cañigueral, A. (2015). Consumo colaborativo. *Leaners Magazine*, 18-22.

Carbaugh, R. J. (2005). La globalización de la actividad económica. In R. J. Carbaugh (Ed.), Economía Internacional (pp. 4-8). Thompson.

Chafkin, M. (12 de 1 de 2016). *Fast Company*. Obtenido de Fastcompany.com: http://www.fastcompany.com/3054873/can-airbnb-unite-the-world

Christensen, C., & Raynor, M. (2003). *The innovator's solution: creating and sustaining successful growth*. Boston: Harvard Business Press.

Edwards, C. H. (1991). Quality of life. In C. Edwards (Ed.), *Human ecology: Interactions of man with his environment* (pp. 97–111). Dubuque, IA: Kendall Hunt.

Endeavor Insight. (2014). What Do the Best Entrepreneurs Want in a City?" *Endeavor Insight*, February 4.

Friedman, M. (1970, September 13). The Social Responsibility of Business Is to Increase Profits. *The New York Times Magazine.*

Henderson, J. (2002). Building the rural economy with high-growth entrepreneurs. *Economic Review (Federal Reserve Bank of Atlanta), 87*(3), 45–70.

Horridge, P. E., & Craig, J. S. (2001). Female business owners in apparel manufacturing: An integrative perspective. *Clothing & Textiles Research Journal, 19*(3), 89–102. doi:10.1177/0887302X0101900301

INEGI. (2010). Mexico en cifras. Retrieved from http://www.inegi.org.mx/Censos

Interian, J. (2016). Up in the air: Harmonizing economy through airbnb regulations. *Boston College International and Comparative Law Review*, 129–161.

Jordan, B. (2008). *Welfare and well-being: social value in public policy*. The Policy Press.

Key, R. J., & Firebaugh, F. M. (1989). Family resource management: Preparing for the 21st century. *Journal of Home Economics, 81*(1), 13–17.

Kim, S. H., Sharpe, D. L., & Kim, H. (2002). Factors influencing the likelihood of leaving self employment in Korea. *Family and Consumer Sciences Research Journal*, *30*(4), 554–569. doi:10.1177/1077727X02030004007

Koponen, D. (n.d.). *Social entrepreneurship perspective for quality of life improvement at national business system level*. Kaunas University of Technology, Lithuania.

Marcketti, S. B., Niehm, L. S., & Fuloria, R. (2006). An Exploratory Study of Lifestyle Entrepreneurship and Its Relationship to Life Quality. *Family and Consumer Sciences Research Journal*, *34*(3), 241–259. doi:10.1177/1077727X05283632

McCann, J. (2000). Quality of Life Scores Highest for Florida Entrepreneurs. University of Florida (2000).

McGregor, S. L., & Goldsmith, E. B. (1998). Expanding our understanding of quality of life, standard of living, and wellbeing. *Journal of Family and Consumer Sciences*, *90*(2), 2–6.

McNabb, T. (2004). FCS students learn how to achieve a balance. *Journal of Family and Consumer Sciences*, *96*(1), 15–16.

Mhango, M. W., Marcketti, S. B., & Niehm, L. S. (2005). Small retailers' integration of e-commerce technology: Personal and business perspectives of Iowa business owners. *Journal of Business and Entrepreneurship*, *17*(2), 70–90.

Morris, M. (1998a, Fall). What is microenterprise development? (Editor's commentary). *Journal of Developmental Entrepreneurship*, *3*(2), 5–8.

Morris, M. (1998b). *Entrepreneurial intensity sustainable advantages for individuals, organizations, and societies*. Westport, CT: Quorum Books.

Morris, M., & Lewis, R. J. (1991). Entrepreneurship as a Significant Factor in Societal Quality of Life (1991). *Journal of Business Research*, *23*(1), 21–36. doi:10.1016/0148-2963(91)90056-4

North, D. C. (1990). *Institutions, institutional Change, and economic performance*. New York: Norton. doi:10.1017/CBO9780511808678

North, D. C. (2005). *Understanding the Process of Economic Change*. Princeton, University Press. doi:10.1515/9781400829484

Peng, M. W. (2000). *Business strategies in transition Economies*. *Thousand Oaks,* CA: Sage.

Peng, M. W. (2012). *Estrategia global*. México: Cengage Learning.

Pennings, J. M. (1982). The Urban Quality of Life and Entrepreneurship. *Academy of Management Journal*, *25*(01), 63–71. doi:10.2307/256024

Peters, M., Frehse, J., & Buhalis, D. (2009). The importance of lifestyle entrepreneurship: A conceptual study of the tourism industry. *Revista de Turismo y Patrimonio Cultural*, *7*(2), 393-405.

PROMUSAG. (2012). *promusagg-fappa-proyectos-sra.blogspot*. Retrieved from www.promusagg-fappa-proyectos-sra.blogspot.mx

Rice, R. W. (1985). Organizational work and the perceived quality of life: Toward a conceptual model. *Academy of Management Review*, *10*, 296–310.

Rifkin, J. (2014). *La sociedad de coste marginal cero: el internet de las cosas, el procomún colaborativo y el eclipse del capitalismo*. Barcelona: Paidós.

Russo, A., & Quaglieri, A. (2014). La lógica espacial del intercambio de casas: una aproximación a las nuevas geografías de lo cotidiano en el turismo contemporáneo. *Revista electrónica de georgrafía y ciencias sociales*, 324-331.

SAGARPA. (2016). Programas fappa y promete. sagarpa. Retrieved from http://www.sagarpa.gob.mx/ProgramasSAGARPA/2014/Documents/Resumen%20de%20ROP%20FAPPA%20y%20PROMETE%202014.pdf

Scarborough, N. M., & Zimmerer, T. W. (2003). *Effective small business management: An entrepreneurial approach* (7th ed.). Upper Saddle River, NJ: Prentice Hall.

Shaver, K. G., Gartner, W. B., Crosby, E., Bakalarova, K., & Gatewood, E. J. (2001). Attributions About Entrepreneurship: A Framework and Process for Analyzing Reasons for Starting a Business. *Entrepreneurship Theory and Practice*, *26*(2), 5–32. doi:10.1177/104225870102600201

Sirgy, M. J., Morris, M., & Samli, K. C. (1985). The question of value in social marketing: Use of a quality of life theory to achieve long-term life satisfaction. *American Journal of Economics and Sociology*, *44*(2), 797–814. doi:10.1111/j.1536-7150.1985.tb02336.x

Stanforth, N., & Muske, G. (1999). Family and consumer science students' interest in entrepreneurship education. *Journal of Family and Consumer Sciences*, *91*(4), 34–38.

Streitfeld, D. (2014, October 15). Airbnb listing mostly illegal. *New York Times*.

Urbado, D., Díaz, J., & Hernández, R. (2007). Evolución y principios de la teoría económica institucional. Una propuesta de aplicación para el análisis de los factores condicionantes de la creación de empresas. *Investigaciones Europeas de Dirección y Economía de la Empresa*, *13*(3), 183–198.

Veblen, T. (1965). *La teoría der la empresa de negocios (1904)*. Buenos Aires: Eudeba.

Villarreal, O. (2005). La internacionalización de la empresa y la empresa multinacional: Una revisión conceptual contemporánea. *Cuadernos de Gestión*, *5*(2), 55–73.

Weiermair, K., & Peters, M. (1998a). Entrepreneurial Small- and Medium Sized Tourism Enterprises. In K. S. Chon (Ed.), *Tourism and Hotel Industry in Indo-China and Southeast Asia: Development, Marketing and Sustainability* (pp. 235–243). Houston: Hilton College.

Weiermair, K., & Peters, M. (1998b). The internationalization behavior of service enterprises. *Asia Pacific Journal of Tourism Research*, *2*(2). doi:10.1080/10941669808721992

Wen, I. (2009). Factors affecting the online travel buying decision: A review. *International Journal of Contemporary Hospitality Management*, *21*(6), 752–765. doi:10.1108/09596110910975990

KEY TERMS AND DEFINITIONS

Business Model: It is a conceptual structure designed as a system to support the methods of business viability, the means to fulfill its purpose and goals, financing, resources, operations, customer base, generation of revenues and profits.

Collaborative Economy: It is a set of initiatives based on horizontal networks with the participation of a community and formed by individuals who have something to share and others who need them with the purpose of giving, swapping, borrowing, trading, renting, and sharing products and services based on distributed trust and decentralized power.

Private Market: The structure of transactions that are negotiated directly between two parties and can take any form the parties agreement.

Strategy: It is the orientation and delimitation given to resources and capabilities of a firm in relation to complex and uncertain competitive market environments in order to accomplish the vision and mission of the firm.

Technology-Based Company: Also known as tech company, it is a firm focusing on the development and manufacturing that uses leading edge scientific and technological knowledge systematically and continuously to produce new goods or services with high added value.

Transport Incorporated: The act or process of moving people or things through different means of transport from one place to another subject to a patronage or ridership refers to the number of people using a transit unit.

Uber: It is an acronym to mean ultimate, best for above in German. It also has the basic meaning of over, beyond, extremely good. As the trade mark and global brand of a private transportation incorporated company, Uber has been changing inner-city transport structure.

Chapter 6
An Overview of Microfinance in India and Its Role in Financing Poor Women

Anindita Neogi
Kandi Raj College, India

ABSTRACT

Microfinance is considered as one of the most potential and successful tools which battle against poverty in the way of financing people with small financial need and helping poor women financially in less developed countries like India. It is a well-recognized notion that without upliftment of the condition of women in a society a nation cannot be developed in a competitive world. Microfinance may in fact help women to gain respect in her family and realize more self-confidence in socially defined roles. The chapter discusses the conceptual framework of microfinance growth of SHG-linked microfinance program and different types of microfinance services in India. Also, this chapter depicts how women are financially benefitted from microfinance institution through self-help groups and measured state-wise microfinance penetration index (MPI) in India. The findings of this study show that there have been favorable changes in the microfinance variables considered.

INTRODUCTION

Man's fight for eradication of poverty ensuring empowerment to the vulnerable class stems from the prehistoric time and possibly exists today at the same level as had been when they deliberately started their struggle. Scientific inventions, political restructurings, all have failed to ensure a poverty free world. The struggle however continues. In the early seventies Prof. Md. Yunus, a Nobel Prize Winner from Bangladesh, who was an eminent economist teaching in the Chittagong University however, felt that poverty could be ended by guaranteeing right to loan to the poor who were so far had been regarded as non-bankable. Microfinance is a way of financing people with small financial need. Literary poor people are deprived of getting banking facilities for their inability to provide valuable security on one hand and on the other hand, micro financing is not cost-effective in the eye of banking sector. That is why micro

DOI: 10.4018/978-1-5225-5240-6.ch006

financing emerged. Microfinance should not be used interchangeably with micro credit. Micro financing covers savings, insurance, training etc. in addition to micro credit.

Gender discrimination is our inborn concept of mind, but human capital (both men and women) is the most important part of a country and the development of a nation is dependent on the quality of its human asset. World is developed not by the physical power of human but by the application of knowledge or education of that. Human civilization has a long history. We have reached from the primitive age to the modern age. In the ancient age men would struggle for collection of food outside the living place and women would struggle for cooking and nursing their children within the residence. Now if we ask ourselves why men and women preferred their work in such a manner when there was no compulsion on them, perhaps it is the nature which is responsible for directing men and women differently. Nature makes men physically stronger than women. In the old age physical power was important as they have to fight with animals continuously to save themselves. From then gradually primitive men tried to understand that the physical energy is not the only way to survive. They started to sharp their Weapons which is the evidence of application of innovative power of their brain. In this way focus is changed from physical power to the power of knowledge. This is the difference between the archaic age and modern age. When muscle power is considered then generally women may be less strong than men but when knowledge is the focal point then men-women division will not be meaningful. As women were used to do work in the home, a habit and custom developed in the mind of people that woman is suitable and safe for home work only and no other power is necessary for them. Thus male people empowered them in every respect keeping female people confined within pavilion. In this way year after year gender discrimination was practiced and hidden power of women remains unutilized. After that the development of education and knowledge helps male people to dream otherwise and instances of female success in different sectors triggered this thinking. Present age of globalization is directing towards formation and development of human capital and not the development of men or women. Women empowerment is providing women the opportunities so that they can apply their inherent power to various creative activities and thereby increasing their efficiencies which in turn boost their creativity.

Microfinance institutions and agencies all over the world direct their endeavor towards the empowerment of women initially by providing financial services. It is observed that women make up large proportion of microfinance recipients. Microfinance lending is often focused on women for a number of reasons. First, gender inequalities in developing societies hamper economic growth and development. The greater the level of gender-based discrimination in a given society, the more likely the society is to experience higher levels of poverty, stagnant economic growth, and weaker governance. Additionally, those within societies where gender discrimination is practiced tend to have a lower standard of living. Second, women are excessively represented among the world's poorest people. Women access to microfinance services will enable them to make a greater contribution to household income. This, in turn, will lead to improved standards of living. Women have meager resources available to them for which they tend to be more vulnerable when economic challenges or unforeseen adverse circumstances arise. By providing access to loans for income-generating activities, microfinance institutions can significantly increase a woman's resources, thereby reducing her overall vulnerability. Furthermore, it is well-documented that women are more likely than men to spend their income on household and family needs. Third, assistance to women has been shown to generate a multiplier effect that improves the welfare of the whole family. MFIs also target women for sustainability reasons. Repayment rates of women are typically far higher than those of men. Fourth, lower arrears and loan loss rates have an important effect on the efficiency and sustainability of the MFI. Many programmers have also found that women tend to be more cooperative in administrative and organizational matters, such as attending group meetings regularly and respecting lending by-laws. Fifth, by providing access to loans for income-generating activities, microfinance institutions can significantly increase a woman's resources, thereby reducing her overall weakness. Finally, one of the most important causes for targeting women by MFIs is that microfinance can be an effective means for empowering women. If the livelihood of a woman is fully dependent on the income generated by the husband, the breakdown of the marriage would mean a terrible consequence for the woman. Because of this, the woman is likely more ready to hold her husband's interests in order to save the marriage from breaking down. This weaker bargaining position of women gives an upper hand to the male counterpart in any decision-making within the household. By putting financial resources in the hands of women, MFIs can promote gender equality.

Microfinance through Self Help Groups (SHGs) has been recognized internationally as the modern tool to combat poverty and for rural development. Microfinance and SHGs are effective in reducing poverty, empowering women and creating awareness which finally results in sustainable development of the nation. The main aim of microfinance is to empower women in the developing countries like India. Giving women access to microcredit loans therefore generates a multiplier effect that increases the impact of a microfinance institution's activities, benefiting multiple generations. The vital purpose of microfinance is to provide financial services to low income people for giving a chance to become self dependent through engaging in productive activities or to start their very small and new business.

REVIEW OF RELEVANT LITERATURE

Microfinance approaches have appeared in India over the past decade, involving the provision of thrift, credit and other financial services and products, with the aim to raise income levels and improve living standards. The most notable among these microfinance approaches is a nationwide attempt, pioneered by Non- Governmental Organizations and now supported by the state, to create links between commercial banks and NGOs and informal local groups. Microfinance through Self Help Groups (SHGs) is accelerating as an alternative system of credit delivery for the poorest of the poor groups. Recognizing their importance, both Reserve Bank of India and National Bank for Agriculture and Rural Development (NABARD) have been spreading the promotion and linkage of SHGs to the banking system through refinance support and initiating other proactive policies and systems. This paper attempts to give a comprehensive overview of all aspects of microfinance in India – its essence, the different institutions involved in its promotion, the different modes of delivery, its weakness and the challenges that lay ahead the programme of microfinance that has made rapid speed in India. Microfinance is a participative model that can address the needs of the poor especially women members. Microfinance has a very important role to play in development according to proponents of microfinance. UNCDF (2004) states that studies have shown that microfinance plays three key roles in development. It helps very poor households and meets basic needs and protects against risks. It is also associated with improvements in household economic welfare and to empower women by supporting women's economic participation that promotes gender equity. One of the key roles microfinance has to play in development is in bringing access to financial services to the poor, to those who are neglected by the formal banking sector. This is their social mission. Mainstream banks target clients that have collateral. The poor do not have assets to act as collateral, therefore they are ignored by the formal financial sector. These banks tend to be found in urban centers while the majority of the poor in the developing world live in rural areas, where financial services are not provided. Therefore, if MFIs are to fill this void they must reach the rural poor. However, according to most studies, microfinance is only reaching a small fraction of the estimated demand of the poor for financial services. Nasir and Farooqi (2016) observed that microfinance facilitates women economically,socioculturally and politically.It also increases the income, savings, skills and confidence of the participants in SHGs. Dhar(2015) studied microfinance penetration in India region-wise by the two models MFIs and SHGs. His analysis revealed the high performance of microfinance penetration in the Southern region comparing to others. While low penetration was observed in the North-Eastern region. Biswas and Rao(2014) argue that microfinance sector has grown rapidly over the past two decades and has helped women to gain economic empowerment and improve quality of their life. According to them development of Micro Entrepreneurship through microfinance can help to reduce the problem of unemployment and several social problems that go with it. Kumar and Chauhan (2015) in their paper "An overview of microfinance in India" highlighted the significance of microfinance for strengthening financial condition of the poor and low income peoples. 1990 onwards poverty alleviation was given top most priority in the developmental process both at national and international level. Economic development of a country largely depends on the financial services available. Microfinance helps in economic development by providing a series of financial services like, savings, loans, money transfers, insurance etc. They also focused on the responsibility of the Government of India for widening the financial services to both rural and urban people in order to attain sustainable and inclusive growth. Microfinance interventions have also been shown to have a positive impact on the education of clients' children. The study of Littlefield, Murduch and Hashemi (2003) states that one of the first things that poor people do with new income from microenterprise activities is to invest in their children's education. Studies show that children of microfinance clients are more likely to go to school and stay longer in school than for children of non-clients. Again, in their study of FOCCAS, client households were found to be investing more in education than non-client households. Nasir (2013) highlighted the insufficiency of the financial services provided by the MFIs in terms of microcredit to the real needy people, regional imbalance and proper regulations etc. He pointed out that if the above shortcomings are removed the objectives of poverty elimination and improving the standards of living of the poor will be achieved. Ranjani, (2012) finds out the need of conceptual outline for the regulation of MFIs in India. If the MFIs are subjected to regulatory framework, it will benefit the members and the industry as a whole. Tiwari,(2012) carried out a comparison between MFIs of India and that of Bangladesh. The study revealed that the profitability and efficiency of the Indian MFIs are better than that of Bangladesh. Arora and Meenu (2012) carried out a study to find the impact of micro financing in removing the financial needs of the rural poor. The study was conducted in the rural areas of the three districts of Punjab. It was observed that saving habits developed in the rural poor people using formal financial sectors. Another observation was that a large percentage of rural poor people utilize bank micro credit. Mahanta, Panda and Kumar (2012) in their article "Status of Microfinance in India-A Review" told that MF with various aspects is operated in an integrated system. Pros and cons are there in the operation of MF services which changes with time. He pointed out the high rate of interest and the harsh way loans are collected which cause the introduction of Microfinance Institutions (Development and Regulation). Bill 2012 highlighted that MF itself cannot provide much result but the technique it is used can be directed to immense opportunities. He also cited the role of Government in providing necessary support to the beneficiaries in the successful implementation of the opportunities. Utmost importance was given on the joint effort of Government and Microfinance Institutions in poverty alleviation. Morses (2011) tried to find out the role of microfinance in poverty alleviation, women empowerment and rural development in India. The author concluded that the microfinance is an excellent way of improving the economic condition of the have-not. It is more effective when group approach is followed for the implementation of the programme. Manoharan (2011) considered the financial activities of the Indian microfinance institutions for a period of five years from 2006 to 2010. From statistical analysis he observed that MFIs must be financially sound in order to continue their performance. Sarumathi and Mohan (2011) observed that microfinance has created more psychosocial empowerment than the much-needed economic empowerment among the rural poor people. Anuradha and Ganesan (2010) observed that microfinance plays dominant role for inclusive growth and sustainable development. It generates employment, reduces gender discrimination and geographical differences which induce economic growth and prosperity. They also highlighted the immense role of Govt. and private sector participation in inclusive growth. Priyadarshee (2010) tried to find out the justification for present level of financial inclusion and the ways of improving financial inclusion mechanisms. The writer suggested that positive political environment helps financial inclusion drives and are used extensively for poverty alleviation. Jothi (2010) gave an impression of the development of microfinance for socio- economic development. Research findings put forward the view that Self Help Groups contribute in the upliftment of poor women and eradicate poverty. Cheston and Kuhn (2001) in their article titled 'Empowering Women through Microfinance' accomplished microfinance has the prospective to have a influential impact on women's empowerment. Santharam (2009) suggested that commercial banks in India have to raise the amount of loans to the SHGs for maintaining better living standard of the rural poor. Swaina and Wallentin (September 2009) in their article 'Does microfinance empower women? Evidence from self-help groups in India' said that their study powerfully indicate that members of SHG are empowered by engaging in microfinance programme so that they have a greater propensity to protect against existing gender discrimination and culture that restrict their ability to build up their own choices independently. Mayoux (1997) argues that the impact of microfinance programmes on women is not always positive. Women that have set up enterprises benefit not only from small increases in income at the cost of heavier workloads and repayment pressures. Sometimes their loans are used by men in the family to set up enterprises, or sometimes women end up being employed as unpaid family workers with little benefit. She further points that in some cases women's increased autonomy has been temporary and has led to the withdrawal of male support. It has also been observed that small increases in women's income are also leading to a decrease in male contribution to certain types of household expenditure. She further discusses that the impact within a programme also varies from woman to woman. These differences arise due to the difference in productive activities or different backgrounds. Sometimes, programmes mainly benefit the women who are already better off, whereas the poor women are either neglected by the programmes or are least able to benefit because of their low resource base, lack of skills and market contacts. However, poorer women can also be more free and motivated to use credit for production. Mayoux's study(1998) on Participatory Learning for Women's Empowerment in Microfinance Programmes proposes a participatory approach for integrating women's empowerment concerns into ongoing programmes learning, which itself would be a contribution to empowerment and microfinance programs for women are currently promoted not only as a strategy for poverty alleviation but also for women's empowerment.

OBJECTIVES OF THE CHAPTER

The objective of the present chapter is to discuss conceptual framework of microfinance, different types of microfinance services in India, region-wise and agency wise growth of SHG linked microfinance programmein India. Also this chapter determines state wise microfinance penetration index (MPI) in India. Lastly this chapter depicts how women are financially benefitted from microfinance institutions through Self Help Groups in India.

DATA AND METHODOLOGY

The present study is descriptive and based on secondary data. Secondary data is collected from different sources such as (a) NGO reports; (b) Status of microfinance in India report, 2015-2016, NABARD(c) Census of India; (d) The Bharat Microfinance Report 2016, Sa-Dhan (e)RBI bulletin; and from different websites which provide microfinance related literature and data.

CONCEPTUAL FRAMEWORK OF MICROFINANCE

The microfinance sector in India has developed a flourishing and sustainable business model which has been able to overcome challenges traditionally faced by the financial services sector in servicing the lower income population. Indian economy is categorized by low growth rate, supremacy of rural population, dependency on agriculture, lack of education, unequal distribution of income and wealth, high incidence of poverty and unemployment. But poverty and unemployment creates major problem to the growth and development of the country. To overcome this problem, some newly developed sectors like microfinance are playing a crucial role in developing countries like India; also the Microfinance world of today is a world of speedy growth in an economy and facing a hard competition. According to the Asian Development Bank (2000), microfinance is the provision of broad range of services such as savings, deposits, loans, payment services, money transfers and insurance to poor and low income households and their micro-enterprises. The SHG (Self Help Group) Bank Linkage Programme of NABARD has emerged as the primary model for providing microfinance services in the country. Promoted by the success of this programme NABARD encouraged the linkage of Microfinance Institutions(MFIs) with the banking sector. The evolution of Indian Microfinance sector can be broadly divided into four different phases Suchas; Phase 1, Phase 2, Phase 3and Phase 4. Phase 1 is known as the Cooperative Movement (1900-1960) and in this period Credit cooperatives were vehicles to enlarge subsidized credit to villages under government funding. Phase 2 which was Subsidized Social Banking (1960s-1990) and it was appeared after failure of cooperatives. The government determined on measures such as nationalization of banks, extension of rural branch networks, organization of Regional Rural Banks (RRBs) and the setting up of apex institutions such as the National Bank for Agriculture and Rural Development (NABARD) and the Small Scale Industries Development Bank of India (SIDBI), including initiation of a government sponsored Integrated Rural Development Programme (IRDP). Phase 3 which was described by SHG-Bank Linkage Programmme and Growth of NGO-MFIs (1990-000). The breakdown of subsidized social banking generated a concept that was a move in delivery of rural credit with NABARD initiating the Self Help Group (SHG) Bank Linkage Programme (SBLP), planning for connection of informal women's groups to formal banks.

The model created a lot of interest among newly promising Microfinance Institutions (MFIs), largely of non-profit origin, to collaborate with NABARD under this programme. The macroeconomic crisis in the early 1990s that led to introduction of the Economic Reforms of 1991 resulted in greater autonomy to the financial sector. This also led to emergence of new generation private sector banks that would become important players in the microfinance sector a decade later. Phase 4 is the Commercialization of Microfinance and here rural markets appeared as the new growth drivers for MFIs and banks. On the demand side, NGO-MFIs increasingly began transforming themselves into more regulated legal entities such as Non Banking Finance Companies (NBFCs) to attract commercial investment.

In Table 1, we see that FY16 witnessed strong growth in the microfinance industry in India, continuing the momentum from the last two years. The microfinance industry shows strong growth in new loan disbursements, loan Portfolio, clients, employees and branches. During FY16, the Microfinance Institution (MFI) industry disbursed new loans of Rs61,860 crore representing a 65% increase over the previous year. This resulted in 84% growth in the total Gross Loan Portfolio (GLP) and the amount reached atRs 53,233 crore. During the same period, the number of clients increased by 44% and stood at 3.25 crore, while the number of people employed by the industry grew by 38% to 85,888 and the number of branches rose by 22% to 9,669.

In contrast to the MFIs, the self-help group ("SHG") portfolio grew by 20% in FY15. The total portfolio outstanding of SHGs as on March 31, 2015 was Rs51,545 crore. The SHG portfolio in the states of Andhra Pradesh, Tamil Nadu, Karnataka and West Bengal is of 76% share out of total 100% share in India. The SHG coverage in these states is given below in theTable2during 2015-2016.

DIFFERENT TYPES OF MICROFINANCE SERVICES

The Microfinance services can be classified into three main groups such as, SHG-Bank linkage Model, Non-Banking Finance Companies and others including trust, Societies, etc.

Primary Agricultural Co-operative Societies numbering 95,663 covering every village in the country. Total number of MFIs in India is in Table 3 at 2015-2016 periods. Here we see that total number of MFIs is 223, out of which MFIs under Society is 78 and it is highest in number. Lowest number of MFIs under Local Area Bank is only 1 which is lowest in number.

The growth of Microfinance loan outstanding and disbursed in India from periods 2009 to 2015 are presented in Table 4. It can be observed from the table below that the outstanding loan portfolio shows an increasing trend, it is highest in 2014-2015, the amount being Rs.48,882 crore and also it is lowest in 2009-2010 as it is only Rs. 22,544 crore. But in case of loan disbursed, it does not show increasing

Table 1. Comparison of growth of microfinance industry for FY16 and FY15

Particulars	FY16	FY15	% Increase
Disbursements (crore)	61,860	37,599	65
Gross Loan Portfolio (crore)	53,233	28,940	84
No. of clients (crore)	3.25	2.26	44
No. of employees	85,888	62,407	38

Source: MFIN Micrometer, 2016

Table 2. SHG portfolio in top 4 states in India during 2015-16

State	SHG Portfolio(%)
Andhra Pradesh	47
Tamil Nadu	12
Karnataka	11
West Bengal	6

Source: Status of Microfinance in India, NABARD, 2016

Table 3. Total number of microfinance institutions in India

Legal Form	No. of MFIs
Society	78
Trust	19
Section 8 (Sec 25) Company	29
MACS/Cooperative	12
Local Area Bank	1
NBFC	13
NBFC-MFI	71
Total	223

Source: The Bharat Microfinance Report, Sa-Dhan, 2016,

Table 4. Growth in microfinance Sector from 2009-2010 to 2014-2015

YEAR	Outstanding Loan Portfolio (Rs crore)	Loan Disbursed (Rs crore)	Client Outreach (in lakhs)
2009-10	22,544	29,330	267
2010-11	24,332	35,176	317
2011-12	24,607	22,635	275
2012-13	25,699	25,635	275
2013-14	33,517	38,558	330
2014-15	48,882	56,860	371

Source: The Bharat Microfinance Report, Sa-Dhan, 2015

trend. Initially, increased but decreased in the year 2011-2012. In this year it was lowest in amount i.e. Rs 22,635 crore. Thereafter, started to increase and the amount reached at Rs 56,860 crore. Also Table 4shows increasing trend of client outreach.In 2009-2010 total number of client was only 267 lakh but in 2014-2015 it reached at 371 lakh.

REGION-WISE AND AGENCY-WISE GROWTH OF SHG LINKED MICROFINANCE PROGRAMME

Distribution of SHGs in India has always continued skewed towards the Southern region which accounts for almost half of the SHGs in the country. From Table 5, it is observed that region wise distribution of number of SHGS with savings linkage is highest in Southern region in India compared to other regions from the period 2013-2014 to 2015-2016.The share of Southern Region in number of SHGs has declined from 49.8% in 2013-14 to 44.9% in 2015-16. Maximum availability of new SHGs and rationalization of data by banks, especially in Kerala, Tamil Nadu and Pondicherry, has resulted in decline in the number of savings linked SHGs in South Region by 4.7% from 37.19 lakh as on 31 March 2015 to 35.46 lakh as on 31 March 2016. North Eastern Region has recorded a 29% rise in number of SHGs during 2015-16 owing to a jump in Tripura, Nagaland and Assam. All states in Northern, North Eastern, Western and Eastern Regions have registered increase in number of SHGs withsavings linkage during the year.

Table 6 shows region-wise status of bank loan outstanding to SHGs during past three years from 2013-14 to 2015-16. Here we see that total outstanding loan for the years were Rs.42.92 lakh, 51.54 lakh and 57.11 lakh respectively. It indicates 20.08% increase in the year 2014-15 and 10.81% increase in the year 2015-16 with respect to previous year. The growth rate of total outstanding loan is highest in case of North Eastern Region which is 39.89% more than the percentage increase in the country. Eastern

Table 5. Region-wise distribution of number of self help groups with savings linkage(%)

Year	North Eastern Region	Northern Region	Central Region	Western Region	Eastern Region	Southern Region
2013-14	4.26	4.92	9.23	12.07	19.77	49.75
2014-15	4.34	4.69	10.62	12.23	19.81	48.32
2015-16	5.44	4.98	10.32	12.88	21.51	44.87

Source: The Bharat Microfinance Report, Sa-Dhan, 2015

Table 6. Region-wise status of bank loan outstanding to self help groups during past three years(total loan o/s in Rs lakh, average loan o/s in Rs / SHG)

Regions	2013-14			2014-15			2015-16		
	No. of SHGs	Total Loan o/s	Average Loan o/s	No. of SHGs	Total Loan o/s	Average Loan o/s	No. of SHGs	Total Loan o/s	Average Loan o/s
North Eastern	183929	110064	59840	176904	153970	87036	150860	88473	58646
Northern	124569	75380	60513	123041	72209	58687	154724	115907	74912
Central	419834	269666	64232	438216	248614	56733	434797	289590	66604
Western	269008	164046	60982	270718	198739	73412	258119	203462	78825
Eastern	978960	494463	50509	1069329	617046	57704	1130902	703767	62231
Southern	2221038	3179133	143137	2389972	3863969	161674	2543219	4310725	169499
All India	4197338	4292752	102273	4468180	5154546	115361	4672621	5711923	122242

Source: The Bharat Microfinance Report, Sa-Dhan, 2015

NB: o/s = Outstanding as on 31 March of the financial year.

Region showed an increase of 24.79%, Southern and Western Region showed an increase of around 21% but Northern and Central Region showed a decline in the amount of total loan outstanding in the year 2014-15. The year 2015-16 observed a fall of 42.54% in total loan outstanding for North Eastern Region but Northern Region observed an increase of 60.52%. The table further shows an increase of 12.80% and 5.96% of the average outstanding loan of SHGs of the country in the year 2014-15 and 2015-16 respectively. Highest increase was observed for North Eastern Region which was 45.45% in 2014-15 but declined in 2015-16 which was 32.62%. Northern Region showed an increase of 27.65% of average outstanding loan in the year 2015-16. Overall growth of the number of SHGs was 6.45% and 4.58% for the year 2014-15 and 2015-16 respectively. Eastern Region showed highest percentage increase in year 2014-15 which was 9.23% and it was 25.75% in the year 2015-16 in case of Northern Region.

Table 7 shows agency-wise distribution of SHG-BLP during 2015-016 and here Commercial

Banks play vital role in case of SHG-BLP. More than 50% of the SHGs in the country preserve their savings account with the Commercial Banks. During 2015-2016, the share of Commercial Banks in terms of SHGs with savings linkage marginally declined, but their share in volume of savings outstanding increased from 60% in the previous year to almost two thirds during 2015-2016.The share of RRBs increased both in terms of number of SHGs and savings balances. Cooperative banks increased their share in number of SHGs but their share in savings declined. During 2015-2016, Commercial banks had disbursed Rs.2518497 lakh to 1132281 number of SHGs, and also Commercial banks accounted for 67.5% of bank loans disbursed to 61.8% SHGs during the year.

STATE WISE MICROFINANCE PENETRATION INDEX IN INDIA

In India there are two types of models adopted for the release of microfinance services to the poor, one is Self Help Groups (SHGs) and other is Microfinance Institutions (MFIs). But the penetration of these two models have been uneven in the country because still now microfinance services remaining concentrated mainly to the Southern region of the country while the North and the North-Eastern region are still lacking the services of both the formal sources of finance and also the microfinance services. Table 8 shows state wise comparison of microfinance penetration index (MPI) in India. The MPI is cal-

Table 7. Agency-wise status of self help group bank linkage program in 2015-16 (Amountin lakh)

Name of the Agency	Total Savings of SHGs with Banks as on 31 March 2016		Loans Disbursed to SHGs by Banks During the Year		Total Outstanding Bank Loans Against SHGs	
	No. Of SHGs	Savings Amount	No. of SHGs	Loans Disbursed	No. of SHGs	Loan Outstanding
Commercial Banks	4140111	903389	1132281	2518497	2626364	3714562
% Share	52.6	66.0	61.8	67.5	56.2	65.0
Regional Rural Banks	2256811	248428	470399	916493	1445476	1610935
% Share	28.56	18.1	25.7	24.6	30.9	28.2
Cooperative Banks	1506080	217322	229643	293700	600781	386426
% Share	19.1	15.9	12.5	7.9	12.9	6.8
Total	7903002	1369139	1832323	3728690	4672621	5711923

Source: Status of Microfinance in India, NABARD, 2016

Table 8. Microfinance penetration index during 2014-15

States	Total No. of SHGs With loan Outstanding	No. Of SHG Members	No. of MFI Clients	Total Microfinance Clients	Share of State to Total	Total Households	Share of House-holds to Total	MPI
Andhra Pradesh	810889	10541557	4600000	15141557	16.62	21024534	8.52	1.95
Arunachal Pradesh	308	4004	10000	14004	0.015	261614	0.11	0.14
Assam	108618	1412034	1200000	2612034	2.868	6367295	2.58	1.11
Bihar	189341	2461433	1700000	4161433	4.569	18940629	7.68	0.60
Chhattisgarh	89765	1166945	400000	1566945	1.720	5622850	2.28	0.75
Delhi	1029	13377	200000	213377	0.234	3143600	1.27	0.18
Goa	3014	39182	9000	48182	0.053	322813	0.13	0.40
Gujarat	65232	848016	700000	1548016	1.700	12181718	4.94	0.34
Haryana	19581	254553	200000	454553	0.499	4717954	1.91	0.26
Himachal Pradesh	18527	240851	0	240851	0.264	1476581	0.60	0.44
Jammu & Kashmir	2243	29159	1000	30159	0.033	2015088	0.82	0.04
Jharkhand	57810	751530	500000	1251530	1.374	6181607	2.51	0.55
Karnataka	529953	6889389	5200000	12089389	13.27	13179911	5.34	2.48
Kerala	143358	1863654	600000	2463654	2.705	7716370	3.13	0.86
Madhya Pradesh	97621	1269073	1600000	2869073	3.150	14967597	6.07	0,52
Maharashtra	202472	2632136	2800000	5432136	5.964	23830580	9.66	0,62
Manipur	2647	34411	60000	94411	0.104	507152	0.21	0.50
Meghalaya	1904	24752	30000	54752	0.060	538299	0.22	0.28
Mizoram	1140	14820	60000	74820	0.082	221077	0.09	0.92
Nagaland	1404	18252	2000	20252	0.022	399965	0.16	0.14
Odisha	236042	3068546	1700000	4768546	5.235	9661085	3.92	1.34
Punjab	15845	205985	200000	405985	0.446	5409699	2.19	0.20
Rajasthan	119607	1554891	600000	2154891	2.366	12581303	5.10	0.46
Sikkim	609	7917	10000	17917	0.020	128131	0.05	0.38
Tamil Nadu	427153	5552989	3800000	9352989	10.26	18493003	7.50	1.37
Tripura	6411	83343	300000	383343	0.421	842781	0.34	1.23
Uttar Pradesh	224165	2914145	2100000	5014145	5.505	32924266	13.35	0.41
Uttarakhand	26665	346645	200000	546645	0.600	1997068	0.81	0.74
West Bengal	585116	7606508	4300000	11906508	13.07	20067299	8.13	1.61
All India	4468180	58086340	33000000	91086340	100	246692667	100	1.00

Source: Status of Microfinance in India, Sa-Dhan, 2015

culated as the relative share of the states in microfinance clients as compared to their share in the total population in a country. All the Southern states have recorded massive number of microfinance clients compared to other states in India and highest MPI among southern states is in Karnataka with an MPI value of 2.48. But all the Northern states recorded low MPI value and among these states lowest MPI value is in Jammu &Kashmir of amount 0.04 only.

FINANCIAL BENEFIT BY POOR WOMEN FROM MICROFINANCEINSTITUTION THROUGH SELF HELP GROUPS

Traditionally women have been confined to household activities keeping their capabilities hidden within themselves. All over the world women cited their efficiency in various sectors. There are numerous examples where women showed their skills. Ignoring the skills and efficiency of women a nation cannot boost its developmental process. Empowering women may be thought in terms of financial, educational, family planning, decision making, cultural participation, self-reliance, self-esteem etc. They can play important role starting from local to international level. The importance of empowering women may be pointed out as follows:

1. Development of women
2. Eradication of poverty
3. Education of children
4. Family planning
5. Improvement of health of family members
6. Decision making
7. Participation in cultural programme
8. Better housing
9. Participation in social work
10. Participation in politics

Table 9. Progress under microfinance-bank loans disbursed to self-help groups agency-wise position during 2015-16 (Amount in lakh)

Sr. No.	Name of the Agency	Loans Disbursed to SHGsby Banks During the Year		Out of Total-ExclusiveWomen SHGs		Out of Total-Under NRLM/SGSY		Out of Total-Under NULM/SJSRY	
		No. of SHGs	Loans Disbursed	No. of SHGs	Loans disbursed	No. of SHGs	Loans disbursed	No. of SHGs	Loans Disbursed
1	Commercial Banks	1132281	2518497.23	972524	2296692.09	511745	1137201.78	79117	193173.20
2	Regional Rural Banks	470399	916492.88	456352	900746.18	271423	482639.00	30299	65790.18
3	Cooperative Banks	229643	293699.98	199795	243703.67	32364	58737.52	1755	3059.09
	Total	1832323	3728690.09	1628671	3441141.94	815532	1678578.30	111171	262022.47

Source: Status of Microfinance in India, NABARD, 2016

11. Minimizing violence against women etc.

A recent World Bank report confirms that societies that discriminate on the basis of gender pay the cost of greater poverty, slower economic growth, weaker governance, and a lower living standard for all people. At a macro level, it is because 70 percent of the world's poor are women. Women have a higher unemployment rate than men in virtually every country and make up the majority of the informal sector of most economies. They constitute the bulk of those who need microfinance services. Giving women access to microcredit loans therefore generates a multiplier effect that increases the impact of a microfinance institution's activity benefiting multiple generations. Microfinance is promising as a commanding instrument for poverty alleviation in the new economy. Skill development is a vital tool for recovering the employability and increasing productivity of the working poor women and thereby reducing poverty and exclusion. Rural poor women typically face difficulties or discrimination in accessing good quality training. Keeping the above in view, NABARDcontinued with Micro Enterprise Development Programme (MEDP) to take care of the entrepreneurial talents of members of mature SHGs to set up and run micro enterprises as a livelihood option in farm or non-farm sector. Around 14352 number skill up gradation training programmes have been conducted under this initiative covering about 4.02 lakh members of advanced SHGs up to 31 March, 2016. In India, Microfinance scene in conquered by SHGs Bank linkage programme as a cost effective methods for providing financial services to the poor people, particularly poor and needy women and it has been successful not only in meeting financial needs of the rural poor women but also strengthen collective self help capacities of the poor leading to their empowerment. Rapid progress in SHGs formation has now turned into an empowerment of women in India. The SHG-Bank Linkage Programme started as an Action Research Project in 1989. In 1992, a Pilot Project was settled. The pilot project was planned as a partnership model between three agencies, viz., the SHGs, Banks and Non-Governmental Organizations (NGOs).The SHG Bank linkage Programme which started in 1992 has grown exponentially over two decades and around 1832323lakh SHGs are linked to different Banks up to March, 2016, of these nearly 65 per cent have direct credit link with bank. Out of these 1832323lakh SHGs,1628671 lakh are women.

From Table 9 it is observed that during the financial year 2015-16 a total of Rs.3728690.09 lakh loans were distributed by the all banks among 1832323 SHGs. Out of total 67.54% loans were distributed by the Commercial Banks among 61.79% SHGs, 24.58% loans were disbursed by Regional Rural Banks among 25.67% SHGs and 7.87% loans were distributed by Co-operative banks among 12.53% SHGs. Out of total 1832323 SHGs 88.88% SHGs are exclusively women SHGs. Commercial Banks alone distributed 66.74% loans to women SHGs and the balance 33.26% loans were distributed by regional Rural Banks and Co-operative Banks jointly. Out of total 45% loans were disbursed by the banks to 44.50% SHGs under NRLM / SGSY and 7.02% loans were distributed to 6.06% SHGs under NULM / SJSRY.

Table 10 represents the position of outstanding bank loans of the SHGs for the year 2015-16. Out of the total outstanding loan of Rs.5711923.47 lakh, Rs.3714562.48 lakh loans or 65.03% loans were distributed by the Commercial Banks among 2626364 SHGs, Rs.1610934.50 lakh or 28.20% loans were distributed by Regional Rural Banks (RRB) among 1445476 SHGs and Rs. 386426.49 lakh or 6.77% loans were disbursed by the Co-operative Banks among 600781SHGs.

The Table10 further shows that 2300521 SHGs out of 2626364 or 87.59% SHGs represent exclusively women SHGs which hold 89.36% outstanding loans of the Commercial Banks. Among 1445476 SHGs, 1272022 SHGs or 88.00% SHGs are exclusively for women of the RRB which hold 94.68% outstanding loans of the RRBs. In case of Co-operative Banks, the number of women SHGs is only 463683 out of the

Table 10. Progress under microfinance-bank loans outstanding to self help groups agency-wise position during 2015-16 (Amount in lakh)

Sr. No.	Name of the Agency	Total Outstanding Bank Loans against SHGs		Out of Total-Exclusive Women SHGs		Out of Total-Under NRLM/SGSY		Out of Total-Under NULM/SJSRY	
		No. of SHGs	Loans Outstan-ding	No. of SHGs	Loans Outstan-ding	No. of SHGs	Loans Outstan-ding	No. of SHGs	Loans Outstan-Ding
1	Commercial Banks	2626364	3714562.48	2300521	3319487.00	1275488	1767089.93	244007	286006.89
2	Regional Rural Banks	1445476	1610934.50	1272022	1525307.68	802776	804654.04	62152	106318.04
3	Co-operative Banks	600781	386426.49	463683	298095.96	112907	89271.57	6607	5650.25
	Total	4672621	5711923.47	4036225	5142890.64	2191171	2661015.54	312766	397975.18

Source: Status of Microfinance in India, NABARD, 2016

total of 600781 SHGs, which hold Rs.298095.96 lakh outstanding loans out of total of Rs.386426.49 lakh i.e. 77.14% outstanding loans belongs to 77.18% women SHGs. The Table 10 also shows that the number of SHGs under NRLM/SGSY of the three categories of banks is 2191171, which holds Rs.2661015.54 lakh outstanding loans jointly and the number of SHGs under NULM/SJSRY of the three categories of banks is only 312766, which holds Rs.397975.18 lakh outstanding loans together.

CONCLUSION AND POLICY SUGGESTIONS

In recent years Microfinance has turn out to be an important instrument for the development of Third World countries. Microfinance services play important role for socio-economic development of poor people. A wide range of services like, deposits, loans, insurance, savings, micro credit, payment services, money transfer etc. are provided by microfinance. In India, Microfinance institution is the most persistent features for poverty alleviation in rural areas, in addition microfinance programmes have an efficient contribution in development through empowering women. In India microfinance has been operating through the two models of Self Help Group and Microfinance Institutions. Both these delivery models have covered various regions of the country, but interestingly the Southern region has almost reached the maximum concentration of microfinance activities. While the North-Eastern region, which remains backward in terms of coverage by the microfinance sector. The success of microfinance activity in the future would be a function of the participatory approach of the MFIs, NGOs, SHGs, and banks. There is a great need for integration and linkage among these institutions for all types of resources including information sharing and delivery. Constitutional provision of equality and justice must be maintained by the general people and effort should be made to avoid gender discrimination while implementing developmental policy. The impact of microfinance on poverty alleviation is a keenly debated issue as we have seen, and it is generally accepted that it is not a silver bullet, it has not lived up in general to its expectation. However, when implemented and managed carefully, and when services are designed to meet the needs of clients, microfinance has had positive impacts, not just on clients, but on their families and on the wider community. There is however a need for greater assessment of these wider impacts if the true value of microfinance to development is to be understood. The microfinance services have attempted to bring out the poor (women in particular) from below poverty line and fight against the poverty through organizing the financial and non-financial services. Various skill improvement, trainings and awareness programmes, networking with various institutions, etc, will make the welfare path soften towards poor. The microfinance services not only uplifted the poor from income poverty but it also from the knowledge poverty. Hence, easily available and reasonable services should be provided to the helpless poor who are excluded socially and economically for a long period of time. MFIs therefore need to improve their depth and breadth of outreach. They must design appropriate products based on the needs of the poorest and they must ensure such products are delivered in a cost-effective manner.

REFERENCES

Biswas, M. P., & Rao, M. R. M. (2014). Role of NGO in Empowering Women through Microfinance: A Conceptual Study. *Journal of the Humanities and Social Sciences*, *19*(5).

Christabell, P.J., & Vimal, R. A. (2012). Financial Inclusion in Rural India: The role of Microfinance as a Tool. *Journal of the Humanities and Social Sciences*, *2*(5), 21–25.

Cheston, S., & Kuhn, L. (2001). *Empowering Women through Microfinance*. Academic Press.

Dasgupta, R. & Rao, K.D. (2003). Microfinance in India: Issues, Challenges and Policy Options. *Savings and Development, 2*(37).

Dhar, P. (2016). Microfinance Penetration in India: A State Wise Analysis. *International Journal of Interdisciplinary Research in Science Society and Culture*, *2*(2).

Karmakar, K. G. (2009). Emerging Trends in Microfinance. *Economic and Political Weekly*.

Mahanta, P., & Panda, G. (2012). Status of microfinance in India- A review. *International Journal of Marketing, Financial Services & Management Research, 1*(11).

Mayoux, L. (1997). *Micro-finance and the empowerment of women - A review of the key issues*. MFIN Micrometer.

NABARD. (2016). *Status of Microfinance in India 2015-16*. NABARD.

Nair, T. (2012). Financing of Indian microfinance evidence and implications. *Economic and Political Weekly*, *67*(25), 33–40.

Nasir, S. (2013). Microfinance in India: Contemporary Issues and Challenges *Middle East Journal of Scientific Research*, *15*(2), 191–199.

Sa-Dhan. (2015). *Bharat Microfinance Report-2015*. New Delhi: The Association of Community Development Finance Institutions.

Sa-Dhan. (2016). Microfinance Directory (2nd ed.). Sa-Dhan, The Association of Community Development Finance Institutions.

Sarumathi, S., & Mohan, K. (2001). Role of Microfinance in Women's Empowerment. *Journal of Management and Science, 1*(1).

Srinivasan, N. (2009). *Microfinance India, State of the Sector Report 2009*. New Delhi: Sage Publications.

Tiwari, A. (2012). Is microfinance working for what it is meant to be? A comparative study on Bangladesh and India. *International Journal of Multidisciplinary Research, 2*(3), 148-164.

Chapter 7
An Empirical Study on Economic Empowerment of Women Through Self-Help Group of Indian Sunderban Delta of North 24 Parganas of West Bengal, India

Amit Majumder
Bijoy Krishna Girls' College, India

ABSTRACT

Empowerment of women is a comprehensive issue and it is a dynamic, multi-dimensional process which enables women to realize their full distinctiveness and power in all spheres of life. In order to achieve it, mobilization and organization of women into self-reliant groups is indispensable for gaining solidarity and strength and inducing collective actions in right time. Against this backdrop, the chapter is conducted through a questionnaire-based survey on the members from a representative sample of the women-run SHGs under the aegis of Sandeshkhali Large-Sized Multipurpose Co-Operative Societies (LAMPS), West Bengal Tribal Development Co-operative Corporation Ltd. (WBTDCC) under Backward Classes Welfare Department, Government of West Bengal in the backward class-dominated, economically backward, and naturally disadvantageous 13 Mouzas in two Blocks of Sandeshkhali of the Sunderbans area. It is revealed from the survey that, since joining the SHG movement, the economic condition, decision-making power relating to expenditure, status within the family and the society has increased favorably for the women members.

INTRODUCTION

There is no chance of the welfare of the world unless the condition of women is improved. It is not possible for a bird to fly on one wing. (Swami Vivekananda as cited in Kanoria, 2012)

DOI: 10.4018/978-1-5225-5240-6.ch007

Empowerment of women is a comprehensive issue and it is a dynamic, multi-dimensional process, which enables women to realize their full distinctiveness and power in all spheres of life. It is also a socio-economic-political issue which embraces the degree of shift in the locus of the decision-making process in different entities. Women have been regarded as the nuclei of a nation and the builder and moulder of its destiny. The position and status of women in any society is an index of the socio-economic-cultural achievement of that society. According to the Census 2011 (Chandramouli, 2011), out of a total population of 1,21,01,93,422, females are 58,64,69,174. As per this, the Gender Ratio of India is 940. The gender ratio at the national level has risen by seven points since the last Census 2001. This is the highest since 1971. In the USA, Russian Federation, Brazil and Japan, females outnumbered males (United Nations, 2011).The development of a nation depends a lot on the status of women in that country, particularly when that nation aspires to achieve the target of holistic development and inclusive growth. Empowerment is a multi-faceted process, encompassing many aspects like enhancing awareness, increasing access to economic resources and increasing involvement in the economic, social and political fields. In order to achieve that, mobilization and organisation of women in the form of self-reliant groups is indispensable.

Even though the Self-help Group (SHG) movement has had a late start in the state of West Bengal, off late it has gained momentum. It was estimated there were more than seven lakh SHGs in the state, out of which nearly 2,00,000 SHGs had been formed under the Swarnajayanti Gram Swarojgar Yojana (SGSY), nearly 3,00,000 SHGs had been promoted by the NABARD, around 1,50,000 SHGs by the Primary Agricultural Cooperative Societies (PACS) and another 50,000 by the SIDBI. In the year 2011-12, the SHGs with outstanding loans dropped to `3,82,942 from `5,74,036 in 2011-12 (Puhazhendhi, 2012). Besides these, the West Bengal Tribal Development Cooperative Corporation (WBTDCC) Ltd., under the aegis of the Backward Classes Welfare (BCW) Department, Government of West Bengal, set up Large-Scale Multipurpose Cooperative Societies (LAMPS) [under the West Bengal Co-operative Societies Act, 1973 (now West Bengal Co-operative Societies Act, 1983)] in 1976 to operate at the block level as the primary co-operative societies in 15 districts of the state with a view to providing credit, non-credit and technical support to the tribal women in West Bengal, the objective being their holistic empowerment and inclusive development (Table 1). Each LAMPS is to have a minimum of 500 members in its operational area (not more than one from a family). By a subsequent decision, LAMPS in the hilly areas may be constituted with a minimum of 300 Scheduled Tribe (ST) members. In 2011-12 members of all the 155 LAMPS in West Bengal taken together were 3,06,263 families in the 16 districts of West Bengal. The pioneering scheme of the WBTDCC Ltd. is the Adivasi Mahila Swashaktikaran Yojana (AMSY)which is a micro-credit project for the empowerment of poor tribal women, offering loans as well as subsidy facilities on easy terms to the tribal women for poverty alleviation and self-employment. The maximum project cost is limited to 50,000 with the provision for subsidy up to 50%., subject to a maximum of 10,000. The loan is granted at an interest rate of only 3%. The AMSY covers schemes like sal-leaf plate-making, grocery, paddy-husking, goatery, piggery, house dairy, and various other schemes suitable and cost-effective for the tribals. Schemes under the AMSY have proved to be highly effective for economic upliftment of the poor tribals because the schemes are implemented entirely by the tribal women who, unlike their male counterpart, plan for the future. Technical trainings are also provided to facilitate proper implementation of the projects.

Besides implementing the AMSY, the LAMPS could be considered as instrumental towards upliftment of social, economic and political status of the tribal women in West Bengal by implementing various schemes like Procurement of Non-Timber Forest Produces (NTFP) Scheme, Lac Cultivation Scheme, Village Grain Bank Scheme (VGB), Minor Forest Produces (MFP) Scheme, Adivasi Sanchay-o-Dadan

Table 1.Performance of AMSY (2003-04 to 2010-11)

Districts	Beneficiaries (No.)	Loan (` in lac)	Subsidy (` in lac)	Total Outlay (` in lac)
Purulia	6168	735.51	748.63	1484.14
Bankura	4601	429.95	368.62	798.57
Paschim Medinipur	3106	290.29	291.66	581.95
Jalpaiguri & Darjeeling	1698	158.75	156.94	315.69
Maldah	2510	234.62	238.83	473.45
Birbhum	3086	288.22	294.16	582.38
Bardhaman & Hooghly	653	62.07	54.48	116.55
South Dinajpur	637	59.51	61.46	120.97
24 Pgs. (N) & 24 Pgs. (S)	1624	150.62	95.66	246.28
Purba Medinipur	62	5.82	6.20	12.02
Total	**24145**	**2415.36**	**2316.64**	**4732.00**

Source: Annual Administrative Report 2010-11, Backward Classes Welfare Department, Government of West Bengal, Kolkata

Ara (Mini-Banking) Scheme, Subsidised Credit Scheme (named as Disha), and Micro-Credit Scheme. The fact underlying all these major schemes is, in general, such finance is provided preferably to the SHGs run by women for a certain period during which they will not only get financial assistance but also technical support from the LAMPS. However, in the present study the Sandeshkhali LAMP under North Indian Sunderban Delta (ISD) had been covered.

Sunderbans area, with a population of over 4 million people, where a large part of the area does not have permanent human habitation, is suffering from increasing rural indebtedness, thus, resulting in growing pauperisation of the marginal people. The aquatic resources of the Sunderbans are an important component of its biodiversity and are important sources of food and income for the human population there. The forest provides raw materials for the wood-based industries. In addition to the traditional forest produces like timber, fuel wood, pulpwood, etc., non-wood forest products such as thatching materials, honey, bees-wax, fish and crustacean and mollusc resources are also available. The vegetated tidal lands of the Sunderbans also function as essential habitat, nutrient producer, water purifier, nutrient and sediment trap, storm barrier, shore stabilizer, energy storage and aesthetic attraction. Various non-timber forest produces and plantations help generate considerable employment and income opportunities for, at least, half-a-million poor coastal population. The area is inundated twice in a day during high tide. The salinity decreases along the coast from west towards east (and, of course, from the sea towards inland). The weather has a high seasonality with around 80% of the annual rainfall occurring during the monsoon (June-October). Cyclones hit the area occasionally (e.g., Aila) with storm surges of up to 7.5 metres. Severe oil spills have taken place over the years. The region consists of 102 islands out of which 54 are inhabited. The remoteness of the area is amply understood by the fact that, in 4500 sq. kms. of the inhabited areas, there is only 42 kms. of railway line and about 300 kms. of pucca road network. The only means of communication between the islands is the waterways which are poorly organized and people have to depend on the mechanized private boats.

Still the area is home to over 4 million people. Going by the Census 2001, the population density in the Sunderbans area is approximately 934 per sq. km. and the number of females per thousand males stands around 946 (Census of India, 2001). Nearly 36.5% of its population belongs to the SC/ST category compared to the state average of 25.6%. Typically, in this delta region, rain-fed single-crop agriculture and fishing are the two main sources of livelihood. Nearly 95% of the population primarily depend on agriculture. About 50% of the agriculturists are landless labourers. For the blocks bordering the reserve forest, during the agricultural lean season, a substantial part of the population depends on the forest and river resources. During April-May, some people enter the forests with permits for collection of honey and bees-wax, which is partly purchased by the Forest Department. Besides, some households entirely and some households partially engage in catching fish and crab in the rivers and the creeks. Both these operations are perceived to be considerably dangerous due to tigers in the forest and crocodiles in the rivers. It can be perceived that these people directly depend on the forest as a last resort for their livelihood and are always almost very poor with nil or unsustainable landholding. Income from these occupations is often supplemented by catching 'meen', the local term for shrimp seedlings. The seedlings of the tiger prawns, which are hatched in the saline waters, are much in demand by the inland prawn farms and fetch hard cash for the poor. A large section of women and children from the poor households catch these tiny prawn seedlings with fine nets and then sell those to the owners of the 'bheries' (i.e., water bodies for growing fish in brackish water). The estimated value of the shrimp trade from this delta region, including the exports, is worth over `100 crore. However, the real beneficiaries are mostly the middlemen and the exporters. Amidst the natural adversities, these 4 million odd people are fighting each day not only for their square meals but also for their holistic upliftment. Moreover, in order to protect this world-acclaimed rich natural bio-diversity, the creation and development of alternative occupations for the residents remains a sine qua non in this region.

All these facts make the Sunderbans area with a high potential for the activities of the SHGs and the Microfinance Institutions (MFIs). At the policy level, the effectiveness of microfinance in eradicating the malaise of rural poverty, largely through empowerment of rural women by creating different types of SHGs run by women, needs to be thoroughly enquired into with special reference to the Sunderbans area of West Bengal.

REVIEW OF LITERATURE

The term 'empowerment' has been used to represent a wide range of concepts and to describe a proliferation of outcomes. Several authors have argued that women's empowerment requires systemic transformation in not just in any institution but fundamentally in those supporting patriarchal structures (Kabeer, 2001; Bisnath & Elson, 1999; Sen & Grown, 1987; Batliwala, 1994). Feminist writings often promote empowerment of individuals and organizations of women (Sen & Grown, 1987; Jahan, 1995; Kumar, 1993) but those vary in the extent to which they conceptualize it or discuss how to identify it. Buvinic (1996) states that the most straightforward vehicle to 'empower' poor women is to increase their productivity in home and market production and the income they obtain from work. The ILO (2002), (in Kessides, 2005) has proposed various strategies to combat this problem, such as increasing women's access to land and other assets. However, the most comprehensive policy alternative for women empowerment has been recommended by Mayoux (2000). According to him, empowerment relates more directly with power as 'a multidimensional and interlinked process of change in power relations'. It consists of: (1) 'power within', enabling women to articulate their own aspirations and strategies for change, (2)'power to', enabling women to develop the necessary skills and access the necessary resources to achieve their aspirations, (3) 'power with', enabling women to examine and articulate their collective interests, to organize, to achieve them and to link with other women's and men's organizations for change and (4) 'power over', changing the underlying inequalities in power and resources that constrain women's aspirations and their ability to achieve them. These power relations operate in different spheres of life (e.g., social, economic, political) and at different levels (e.g., individual, household, community, market, institutional). Offering women a source of credit has been found to be a very successful strategy for alleviating poverty because it enhances the productivity of their own small enterprises and the income-generating activities in which they invest. Results include an increase in women's self-confidence and status within their families as well as income that can be used to improve their families' well-being through improved health and nutrition (Goetz & Gupta, 1996). Hashemi et al. (1996) also argue that credit programmes have been successful in providing a cost-effective means of transferring scarce resources to the poor through women. The most successful of these schemes – the Grameen Bank, the Bangladesh Rural Advancement Committee (BRAC) and the Self-Employed Women's Association (SEWA) in India–have served as models for other programmes worldwide. Nanda's (1999) study of rural microfinance projects in Bangladesh has revealed that improving women's access and control over resources can potentially alleviate their health problems and enhance their decision-making power within the household. Her study indicates that participation in economic activities is more valuable for empowering a woman than household income or socio-economic status. Rogers and Youssef (1988) also recognize the importance of group savings programmes and cooperatives as catalysts for empowering women. These programmes not only allow impoverished women to interact with one another but also help in creating a platform for exchanging of ideas and information, increase women's ability to earn a greater income and allow them to have a more flexible work environment where they can rely on other women for support on matters such as childcare.

Against this backdrop a quick review of literature in respect of implications of micro-credit-led SHG movement on economic empowerment of rural women in the developing economies like India in general and West Bengal in particular is made below.

Early studies on 'women's status' have often covered aspects of empowerment without explicitly labelling it as such. One of the earliest empirical studies in this area, for example, has used the more general term 'women's status' but located a nexus of gender-related power differentials in the household, noting how important the family unit is for understanding the operation of gender in a society (Acharya & Bennett, 1981, 1983). They have also highlighted the links between women's economic roles and their control over resources and life options.

Rajagopalan (1989) delineates the linkages between micro-credit and women's empowerment. The study looks at the space available to women and used by them in their individual capacity as a group engaged in savings-and credit-related activities in the larger socio-economic environment. The findings of the study are quite encouraging. Even the SHGs, which started just three years prior to the study, have a significant impact on women's empowerment. The major findings of the research show major changes in the lives of individual women because of micro-credit in terms of access to savings and credit, increase in income, acquiring new skills and mobility. Within their communities, the SHGs are respected, women are visible and sought after at the block-level and district-level meetings and are accepted as leaders.

Kalbagh (1991) has observed that the role of women in production and reproduction should be concerned as complementary and interactive in order to realize women's potential for complete participation in the productive and decision-making processes. Without economic independence, women cannot achieve equality. Therefore, measures to improve their economic status and provision of necessary infrastructure for them should be treated as important and integral parts of the development strategy.

Iyer (1991) has analysed the major constraints faced by women entrepreneurs and reflected upon the specific policies and programmes for women entrepreneurship development. Singh (1992) has made an attempt to construct the women entrepreneurs' profile and has identified their dominating entrepreneurial traits, forces motivating them and their performance, both quantitatively and qualitatively, and has tried to understand the nature of entrepreneurial development among women and highlight their existing status and contributions to the national economy.

A World Bank Policy Paper (1994), which has examined the actions that can help bring down inequitable situation, has come out with strong evidences particularly in five areas, viz., education, health, wage labour, agriculture and natural resource management, and financial services. It has also widened the 'Women in Development' approach in the context of the 'Gender and Development' strategy that takes into account the roles and responsibilities of women in the long run.

Sarangadharan and Raisa Begum (1995) have made an attempt to study the access of women enterprises to institutional support. The problems of women entrepreneurs at different stages in running the units have also been ascertained and incorporated in their study by holding interviews with selected owners of the women enterprises. Women's participation in the process of economic development calls for arrangements that would enlighten them more about economically-and socially-productive work. This calls for identification of opportunities for women and a conscious effort towards the development of women entrepreneurship. Lalitha (1996), in the context of making women entrepreneurs effective, has focused, inter alia, on the profits of the enterprises run by them, the strengths and opportunities of such enterprises, factors motivating them and their attitudes and achievement-orientation, apart from their ability to balance gainful employment and domestic responsibilities.

Mayoux's (1998) study has proposed a participatory approach for integrating women's empowerment concerns into the on-going programmes of learning, which itself would be a contribution to empowerment. Microfinance programmes for women are currently promoted not only as a strategy for poverty alleviation but also for women's empowerment. Sahay (1998) has argued that approaches and strategies for women empowerment should be developed by identifying first the mechanisms that still today influence women empowerment. Multi-dimensional decision-making process should be operationalised for women to help them realize their full identity and power in all walks of life. The one, who is educated, economically independent and has rights to decide about own spending; can be termed as 'empowered' in the real term. It is imperative to promote women's economic independence, including provision for employment and eradicate the persistent and increasing burden of poverty on women by addressing the structural causes of poverty through changes in economic structures, ensuring equal access for all women, including those in the rural areas, as vital development agents, to productive resources, opportunity, and public services for their empowerment.

Tzannatos (1999) has examined the level of, and changes in, female and male participation rates, employment stagnation and female wages relative to male wages across the world. Sufficient evidences have been found to support the view that labour markets in the developing countries are transformed relatively quickly in the sense that gender differentials in employment and pay are narrowing much faster in those countries than in the industrialized countries. The growth benefits women in general. Inequalities can have significantly adverse effect on welfare and market-based development.

It has been observed that investment in women has an incredibly high rate of return. Women in the developing areas are exceptional at savings, providing for their families and generating income (http://www.ekya.org/currentprojects.html?gclid=CL39753LgbYCFcV56wod3UkA3w).

Punitha, Sangeetha and Padmavathi (1999) have focused on the emergence of women as entrepreneurs in the labour market as a positive aspect of the process of economic development of a country, which increases the opportunities for demonstrating their skills and talents, thus, contributes to their empowerment. Most of the women entrepreneurs in the rural areas own manufacturing enterprises, while most of them in the urban areas are largely concentrated in the trading sector. Among the rural enterprises, the major problems that are faced by them are competition from better quality products, irregular work, and difficulty in getting loan.

Nagayya (2000) maintains that an informal arrangement for credit supply to the poor women through the SHGs is fast emerging as a promising tool for promoting the income-generating enterprises. He has reviewed the initiatives taken at the national level regarding institutional arrangements to support this programme for alleviation of poverty among the poor, with focus on women. He has observed that the NABARD and the SIDBI are playing a prominent role at various stages of operationalisation of the SHGs. There are also other national-level bodies supporting the NGOs/voluntary associations, e.g., Rastriya Mahila Kosh (RMK), Rashtriya Gramin Vikas Nidhi (RGVN), etc. He has called for an immediate need to enlarge the coverage of the SHGs in terms of advance portfolio of banks as part of their corporate strategy recognizing the perceived benefits of financing the SHGs in terms of reduced default risk and transaction costs.

Gaonkar (2001) has observed that the SHG movement can significantly contribute towards the reduction of poverty and unemployment in the rural sector of the economy and the SHGs can lead to social transformation in terms of economic development and social change. Sharma (2001), in his study on performance of the SHGs in Uttar Pradesh, has observed that women empowerment is taking place through the SHGs. Their participation in the economic activities and decision-making at the household level and the societal level is increasing and making the process of rural development participatory, democratic, sustainable and increasingly independent of subsidy, and, thus, micro financing through the SHGs is contributing to the development of rural people in a meaningful manner.

Puhazhendi and Satyasai (2002) have evaluated the SHGs in India and observed that about 59% of the sample households registered an increase in assets and 47.9% moved above the poverty line in the post-SHG situation in India, resulting in increased social empowerment in terms of improvements in members' confidence level, treatment within the family, communication skills and other behavioural aspects. Also, for the southern and western regions, the index for economic and social status of the poor rural women members of the SHGs was higher compared to the other two regions. Kabeer (2005), in a study, has observed that, while access to financial services can and does make important contributions to the economic productivity and social wellbeing of poor women and their households, it does not 'automatically' empower women. Rather, educations, political quotas, access to wage work and certain other interventions have also their significant contributions.

Ramachandran and Seilan (2005) have indentified the benefits of SHG, namely, development of savings habit among the poor women and access to better technology and various promotional assistances. The important indicators of empowerment are their ability to contribute towards the family income, skill up gradation, and understanding of the banking operations, improved standard of living, better leadership and communication skills, health awareness and decision-making ability at the household, community and village levels. Ramanjaneyulu (2006) has ventured into enquiring about the favourable circumstances for women to start business, the relevant motivational factors, and the socio-economic and managerial aspects vis-á-vis the tangible and intangible benefits of women's micro-enterprises.

Christen (2006) has examined the changing general perception of bankers, and observed that that the SHGs are profitable clients. The SHGs are the vehicles through which banks can most effectively reach out to the rural communities. It has been pointed out that long-term viability of microfinance through the SHGs requires a number of services and support functions such as provision for liquidity facility, staff training, standardization of product design and appropriate interventions. In this regard, experiences of other developing economies, like Peru, Mexico, Indonesia and Philippines, have been shared.

Naidu, Jayaraju and Dasartharamaiah (2006) have revealed that the annual income of the SHG members have increased considerably. Due to effective organization of the Development and Children in Rural Areas (DWCRA) programme, the man- days of employment among all the sections of the rural women have increased significantly. The self-employment programmes like dairying, poultry, farming, tailoring, running small shops and working as rural artisans are very much essential to create self-employment as well as wage employment among the rural women.

Pramod (2006) has indicated that the SHG-bank linkage programme has been acclaimed as the fastest growing and highly cost-effective microfinance initiative in the world as it has enabled millions of poor families to practise thrift and find access to financial services offered by the formal financial system. Over 90% of the SHGs have been set up by women, which help in ameliorating the adverse socio-economic conditions of their families and also help in bringing enormous social changes, thereby, empowering them. This study has also highlighted the important role of the NABARD in terms of various aspects of the programme.

Malik and Vani (2006), in their empirical study, have observed that the SHG-led micro-enterprises fulfil four objectives, namely, poverty reduction, employment generation, enterprise development and empowerment of women. The SHG-led micro-enterprises contribute in terms of increase in diversification of household economic activities, productive activities and economic security. The micro-enterprises have significant relevance in the empowerment of women. John (2008) has opined that membership in an SHG inculcates a great confidence among the majority of women to succeed in the day-to-day life. Positive change has found in the attitude of relatives and friends towards the women in the SHGs.

Lakshmi and Vadivalagan (2012) have conducted an empirical study on the performance of the SHGs and their impact on the women in the Dharmapuri District of Tamil Nadu and have observed that that the weighted average scores on empowerment after joining the SHG range from 2.762 to 4.293. They have measured the empowerment based on the indicators like economic independence, improvement in standard of living, leadership qualities,self-expression and decision-making power at the household, community and village levels, understanding of banking operations, knowledge on credit management, increased social participation, etc.

Suja (2012) has conducted an empirical study on 750 women SHG members of the Salem District of Tamil Nadu and has found that the Mean Percentage score of economic empowerment has improved from 64.57% in the Pre-SHG period to 83.49% in the post-SHG period. Moreover, the Mean Percentage Score of decision-making power has also improved by 29%. Likewise, a significant development has also been observed in the life of the women SHG members with respect to social empowerment, psychological empowerment, managerial qualities, personality development, leadership skills, legal awareness, social awareness and quality of work life, etc.

Wadhera and Koreth (2012) have conducted an empirical study on poor rural women micro-entrepreneurs in 18 villages in the Sewar block of the Bharatpur District of Rajasthan, using the Thematic

Appreciation Test (TAT) process, and has observed the presence of the 'inner need for achievement (N-ach)' among the women entrepreneurs. Moreover, women's micro-enterprises and the consequent social empowerment of women brought about a quiet and subtle change in the gender-balance equation in the family and the society without any social pressure or resistance. The economically-empowered women in the surveyed villages are now enjoying greater say in the decision-making process within the family, including on money matters, and have enhanced self-confidence.

Thapa (2012) has made a study on a sample of SHGs formed in Sikkim under the Swarnajyonti Gram Swarojgar Yojona (SGSY) scheme, monitored district-wise by the Sikkim Rural Development Agency (SRDA), and has found that the SHGs are pivotal in empowering women economically and also help the members in decision-making in the family regarding health, education and they are becoming self-reliant. Moreover, the SHGs have proved to be a great mechanism of enhancing skill and knowledge, applying technology, designing network, developing leadership quality, strengthening solidarity and ethnic-inter-mixing, ending social isolation, and making lives with dignity. Chettri (2012) has made a study on a sample of SHGs in Kalipmong under the Darjeeling District of West Bengal and has observed that self-confidence and self-respect of women members have increased significantly after joining the SHG movement. By joining the SHG movement female members feel that it has given them immense courage to fight against the evils within the family like alcoholism, polygamy, illicit relationship of their spouses and has also given them the confidence to voice their views on important matters in their family.

Bharali, Chiring and Konwar (2013) have made a study on a sample of SHGs formed in the Jorhat District of Assam under the SGSY scheme and has revealed that the SHGs have found as an effective tool for encouraging women in various income-generating activities, thereby, accelerating the growth in monthly income by 1.77 times and monthly savings by 2.44 times. However, the researchers could not find any significant association between the impact of the SHGs and the involvement of women in the key decision-making areas. Islam and Sarmah (2014) have made a survey on impact of empowering women through SHGs in two development blocks i.e. Juria and Batadrawa of Nagaon District of Assam by interviewing one member from each 152 functional SHGs and observed that SHGs lead to personal empowerment in terms of creating awareness on social issues and access to savings but unsuccessful to transform the endeavor into entrepreneurial or skill oriented income generation programme and mobilising members for community development issues.

Fernando and Azhagaiah (2015) have made a study economic empowerment of the SHG members through the SHGs in two blocks of Puducherry viz Puducherry and Oulgaret by conducting interview of 100 respondents, 50 each from the selected blocks. Paired t test was conducted inorder to find out the effect of becoming members in the SHG in respect of economic empowerment. The study revealed that the SHGs enabled the women to have a significant improvement in the economic empowerment.

Selvi and Shanmughun (2016) have made a study on empowerment of women through SHGs in Erode district of Tamil Nadu by interviewing the SHG members. It have been revealed that SHGs have been playing considerable role in training of Swarozgaris, infrastructure, development, marketing, technology support, communication level of members, self confidence among members, change in family violence, frequency of interaction with outsiders, change in the saving pattern of SHG members, change in the cumulative saving pattern of SHG members per month, involvement in politics, achieving social harmony, achieving social justice, involvement in community action, sustainable quality and accountability, equity within SHGs, defaults and recoveries, and sustainability -financial value etc.

Devi and Devi (2017) have made a fact-finding study on economic empowerment of rural women through SHGs with reference to Coimbatore district of Tamil Nadu and revealed that the members are economically benefited because of their membership in self-help group. Moreover, it was revealed that it is revealed that identified socio-economic factors played a significant role in enhancing the economic status of women on becoming the member in SHGs.

Many SHGs, especially in India, under the functioning under the NABARD's SHG-Bank-Linkage Programme, borrow from banks once they have a base of their own capital and have established a track record of regular repayments. By aggregating the individual savings of the members into a single deposit, the SHGs minimize the bank's transaction costs and generate an attractive volume of deposits. Through the SHGs, the bank can serve small rural depositors, while paying them a market rate of interest. The SHG-Bank-Linkage Programme since its beginning has been predominant in the southern region – Andhra Pradesh, Tamil Nadu, Kerala and Karnataka.

In West Bengal, the SHGs are reckoned as cooperatives within a cooperative. They are informal groups of 5-20 persons of the same low level economic condition, belonging to the same locality or hamlet. Open and voluntary membership, democratic control by the members, participation of the members in the economic activities of the group, autonomy and independence, education, training and information, cooperation amongst the different groups and concern for the community — all the seven cooperative principles are in application in the SHGs. The NABARD-sponsored SHG-Bank-Linkage Programme has acted as a booster and the SHGs in the cooperative sector in West Bengal have assumed the shape of a movement in the state. Group dynamism develops among the SHG members over time through periodical meetings, equal doses of savings at the end of every week/fortnight/ month, rotation of leadership and united fight against the evils in the family and the community, (http://coopwb.org/self-help-group.php).

SUNDERBANS AREA: AN OVERVIEW

Sundarbans area, formerly SUNDERBUNDS, is a vast tract of forest and salty water swamp, forming the lower part of the Gangetic Delta, extending about 160 miles (260 kms.) along the Bay of Bengal from the Hooghly River estuary in India to the Meghna River estuary in Bangladesh. The settlement history in the Sunderbans explains the presence of a relatively larger proportion of lower-caste people in this region (Hunter, 1875). The Indian Sunderbans (Latitude 21°32'-22°40'N, Longitude 88°22'- 89°0'E) in the north-east coast of India occupy 9630 sq.kms. and are bounded by the River Hooghly in the West, the River Raimangal in the East, the Bay of Bengal in the South and the Dampier Hodges Line in the North. There are 56 islands of various sizes and shapes in the Sunderbans area and these are separated from each other by a network of tidal channels, inlets and creeks, some of which act as pathways for both freshwater discharge from upland and to and fro movement of flood and ebb (DISHA, 2006). The Sunderbans area is a part of the world's largest delta formed by the Ganges, Brahmaputra and Meghna rivers. The Sunderbans area is the world's largest continuous mangrove area, covering some 10,000 kms. of land and water within the Gangetic Delta, with about 38% located in West Bengal, covering both the North 24 Parganas and South 24 Parganas Districts (Vyas, 2004). It was declared as a UNESCO World Heritage site in 1997. The Sunderbans area is also regarded as the largest biosphere reserve in the World. In order to protect its rich biodiversity, thinking in terms of alternative occupations for the inhabitants of Sunderbans area, especially for the marginalised sections of the population, through various mechanisms like SHG, is indispensable.

RESEARCH GAP

Studies relating to the economic empowerment of women are on the increase in the recent years. Moreover, researches are there on the role and functioning of the SHGs in India. However, the researcher has not come across any documented work on the role of the SHGs in economic empowerment of women particularly in the Sunderbans area of West Bengal which is unique in many respects including its adversities. This has prompted the researcher to take up an in-depth empirical study on the role of the SHGs in the Sunderbans area of the 24 Parganas (North) District in the economic empowerment of women.

OBJECTIVES OF THE STUDY

The Sunderbans area comes within the jurisdiction of both the 24 Parganas (South) and 24 Parganas (North) Districts of West Bengal. The operational area of the Sundarban Affairs Department, Government of West Bengal is spread over 19 Blocks in 5 Sub-Divisions of the 24 Parganas (South) and 24 Parganas (North) Districts.

Out of those, 19 Blocks, 6 Blocks (Hingalganj, Hasnabad, Sandeshkhali-I, Sandeshkhali-II, Haroa, Minakhan) are in one Sub-Division (Basirhat) under the 24 Parganas (North) District.

In order to make the study an intensive one, the researcher has covered 2 Blocks (i.e., Sandeshkhali-I and Sandeshkhali-II where LAMPS are functioning effectively) out of those 6 Blocks.

Like other part of the Sunderbans area, these blocks are also characterized by acute economic backwardness where people's survival is dependent on continuous battle against the very adverse nature. The marginalized people have no other option but to depend on nature. The major occupational activities are restricted to collecting forest produce and fishing, which are basically unorganized in nature. Due to lack of formal institutional arrangements in the job markets, the urgency of creation of job opportunities through formation of the SHGs, based on local resources, particularly among the women population, is essential in this region.

Against this backdrop, the present study has attempted to assess:

1. the present status of the women-run SHGs in the Sandeshkhali-I and Sandeshkhali-II Blocks of the Sunderbans area in the 24 Parganas (North) District of West Bengal, and
2. the impact of those women-run SHGs on economic empowerment of women in the Sandeshkhali-I and Sandeshkhali-II Blocks of the Sunderbans area in the 24 Parganas (North) District of West Bengal.

HYPOTHESES

Keeping the above objectives in mind, the hypotheses framed are stated below:

1. The surveyed women-run SHGs play a significant role in reducing the income equality among the women members of those SHGs in the Sandeshkhali-I and Sandeshkhali-II Blocks of the Sunderbans area in the 24 Parganas (North) District of West Bengal.

2. The income level of the women members of those SHGs in the Sandeshkhali-I and Sandeshkhali-II Blocks of the Sunderbans area in the 24 Parganas (North) District of West Bengal has increased after joining the SHG movement.
3. The expenditure level of the women members of those SHGs in the Sandeshkhali-I and Sandeshkhali-II Blocks of the Sunderbans area in the 24 Parganas (North) District of West Bengal has increased after joining the SHG movement.

METHODOLOGY

Sample Design

For the purpose of gathering relevant data regarding the contributions of the women-run SHGs towards economic empowerment of the women in Sandeshkhali Block-I and Sandeshkhali Block-II, a representative sample comprising 10% of the 390 women-run SHGs operating in 13 Mouzas in Sandeshkhali Block-I and Sandeshkhali Block-II have been chosen. 3 women-run SHGs have been randomly selected from each of the 11 Mouzas of Sandeskhali Block-I and from each of the 2 Mouzas of Sandeshkhali Block-II.

Data Collection

The present study is based both on primary and secondary data. A structured questionnaire has been administered for collecting the relevant primary data and such exercise has been supplemented by interviewing the knowledgeable persons. Secondary data have been gathered from relevant books, articles, reports and websites.

For the purpose of understanding better the profiles of the Blocks in the Sunderbans area chosen for this study, a relevant website (http://www.sadepartmentwb.org/Profile.htm) has been visited.

Analysis of Data

The relevant data collected have been tabulated, presented and then analysed with the help of appropriate statistical tools for the purpose of analysis. Based on such analysis, meaningful inferences have been drawn and an attempt has been made to come out with some policy prescriptions.

Firstly a Paired t-test is used to compare two population means in two samples in which observations in one sample can be paired with observations in the other sample with respect to before-and after-observations on the same subjects. Here, the paired t-test is used to understand the changes in the income level of the SHG members after joining the SHG movement.

Moreover, in order to measure the degree of income inequalities among the responding SHG members, the well-known economic measurement techniques like Lorenz Curve and Gini Coefficient have been used. The Lorenz Curve is used in economics and ecology to describe inequality in wealth or size. The Lorenz Curve is a function of the cumulative proportion of ordered individuals mapped on to the corresponding cumulative proportion of their size. If all individuals are of the same size, the Lorenz Curve is a straight diagonal line, called the Line of Equality. If there is any inequality in size, then the Lorenz Curve falls below the Line of Equality. The total amount of inequality can be summarized by the

Gini Coefficient (also called the Gini Ratio), which is the ratio between the area enclosed by the Line of Equality and the Lorenz Curve, and the total triangular area under the Line of Equality.

Finally, in order to test the variations of monthly average income across 13 Mouzas of 2 Blocks of Sandeshkhali of Sunderbans area Mann-Whitney U Test for 2 independent samples and Kruska-Wallis test for n independent samples have been used. The Mann-Whitney U test is used to compare differences between two independent groups when the dependent variable is either ordinal or continuous, but not normally distributed and the Kruskal-Wallis H test (sometimes also called the "one-way ANOVA on ranks") is a rank-based nonparametric test that can be used to determine if there are statistically significant differences between two or more groups of an independent variable on a continuous or ordinal dependent variable.

Study Period

The field survey was conducted during the period of June 2013 to December 2013.

SUMMARY OF FINDINGS

Block-Wise and Mouza-Wise Details of the Surveyed SHGs

In the present study, a 10% representative sample was chosen randomly, from all the 13 Mouzas of the 2 Blocks, out of the SHGs (390 in number) operating within the framework of the Sandeshkhali Large-Sized Multipurpose Co-operative Societies Ltd. (LAMPS). 3 SHGs run by women were selected randomly from 13 Mouzas of Sandeskhali Block-I (i.e. Najat, Boyermari, Dakhshin Akhratala, Khariat, Dekhanmari, Motbari, Sankardaho, Baunia, Petuadhanihati, Putimari and Bholakhali) and 3 SHGs run by women were selected randomly from 2 mouzas off the Sandeshkhail Block-II (Bermazur and Darikhjangal).

Organization Structure and Governance Practices of the Surveyed SHGs in the Sunderbans Area

1. **Size of the SHGs:** The average member-size of the surveyed 39 SHGs is 9. The maximum number of members in a single SHG is 15 and a minimum number of members in a single SHG is 6. It was observed that in a number of SHGs the size had increased significantly since their inception due to the effectiveness of their functioning and the attractiveness of enhanced economic powers of those SHGs over time.
2. **Meeting Procedure of the SHGs:** Participation of the members in meetings of the SHGs is a major determining factor for the smooth and effective functioning of the SHGs. It was observed that 88% of the SHGs showed a high level of attendance, i.e., in 80% to 100%. About 12% of the SHGs had attendance ranging from 60% to 80%. It was observed that the generally meetings are called by the secretaries when the members contact them for applying for fresh loans from the LAMPS. Apart from this, for discussing the general affairs and functioning of an SHG, meetings are called on fortnightly basis. The agenda of the meeting are determined by all the members of the SHG. The decisions of the meetings are taken by all the members through consensus and the resolution book of the meeting of the SHG is periodically sent to the LAMPS when any fresh application for loan is being made. The Accounts Officer of the Sandeshkhali LAMPS will then go through the

pass book and the loan ledger of the SHG along with the resolution book to check the eligibility of the SHG for the purpose of granting the amount of loan under the various schemes like AMSY, Disha, Micro-Credit, Village Grain Bank, Mini Bank, etc.

3. **Record Keeping of the SHGs:** Proper record keeping is very important for the efficient functioning of an SHG in order to avoid replication of the same functions, maintain the trust among the members, provide information about the attendance of the members in the meetings, know the status of the remittance of savings and know the status of the repayment of loans and assess the financial condition of the SHG. Moreover, it is essential, if the SHGs want to have linkages with financial institutions such as banks. It also ensures transparency in the functioning of the SHG. In case of the surveyed SHGs, it was observed that the membership register, attendance register, minutes book, weekly register, savings register, loan register, passbook and consolidated register are maintained. Almost all the SHGs kept the records like pass book, individual member's ledger, meeting attendance register and resolution book systematically and neatly with the proper help and able guidance of the officials in the Sandeshkhali LAMPS office.
4. **Leadership and Incentives:** Leadership of an SHG is a determining factor in the sustainability of the SHG. In the SHGs, comparatively the more educated women are elected as secretaries who are capable of managing the accounts properly, command respect from the other members and communicate well with the officials of the LAMPS and the Panchayat. It is insisted that the leadership must change once in two years. But problems, such as non-entry of the new leadership due to over-dominance of the old leadership and reluctance of the other members to take up responsibilities, are common in most of the SHGs. Usually, the secretary of an SHG keeps the registers and performs the functions on a voluntary and honorary basis. Laxity in the maintenance of records is often attributed to the pressure of work of the secretary. The secretary has to perform a number of functions (both organizational and financial). Absence of any incentive to perform such duties creates some degree of apathy on her part. It is the duty of the secretary of an SHG to continuously motivate her members and maintain their interest high in the activities, indeed a tiring job. So for effective management of the SHGs, it is desirable that the secretaries of the SHGs are given reasonable monetary incentives.

DEMOGRAPHIC STRUCTURE OF THE SURVEYED SHGS IN THE SUNDERBANS AREA

- **Age Group of the Members of the SHGs:** It was observed that 58% of the respondents from the different SHGs belong to the age group of '25-30', where 20% of the respondents belong to the age group of '20-25'. 13% of the respondents belong to the age group of '30-35' and the rest 9% of the respondents belong to the age group of '36 and above'. Findings from the survey are presented in Figure 1. So, it is quite clear from the survey that the younger generations are more inclined to form the SHGs for their mutual interest and economic benefits. The changes in the societal mindset and educational level and the growing awareness may be the reason that women are increasingly becoming ready to form the SHGs and free to interact with the government officials for the attainment of economic self-sustenance and holistic development.
- **Marital Status of the Members of the SHG**: Marital status of the members really matter. Factors like motivation from husband, family, friends and relatives are the influencing the women to large

extent to form and successfully operate the SHGs. It has been observed that majority of the respondents (62%) from the surveyed SHGs are married, whereas 14% of them are unmarried, 8% of them are widow and the rest 4% of them are divorcee. It was observed that 12% of the respondents have been destituted by their husbands and they get financial and mental support for herself and her children being an active member of an SHG. It is noteworthy to mention that a tribal widow member of an SHG at Najat has sent her only son to the Jadabpur University for studying M.Tech programme in Chemical Engineering. Finding from the survey is presented in Figure 2.

Source of Motivation Behind Joining the SHG

Motivation is one the major influencing factors vis-á-vis maximisation of the level of productive activity in the economy. Different avenues are available even for the women-run SHGs to start their own activity and develop self-reliance on the basis of their own capabilities. Out of the sample, married women have been found to be greatly influenced (78%) by their husbands to start their own SHGs, 12% women have joined the SHGs with self-motivation and 10% of them women have joined as a result of direct inspiration from the other members of the SHGs who happen to be either family members or neighbours.

Education Level of the Members of the SHGs

The education levels of the members of the surveyed SHGs in the Suderbans area are not really encouraging. It was observed that a few members (5 only) of the SHGs have reached the school-leaving level. The majority of the members (88%) can sign but a few of them have formal education up to class eight

Figure 1. Age Group of the Respondents
Source: *Field Survey*

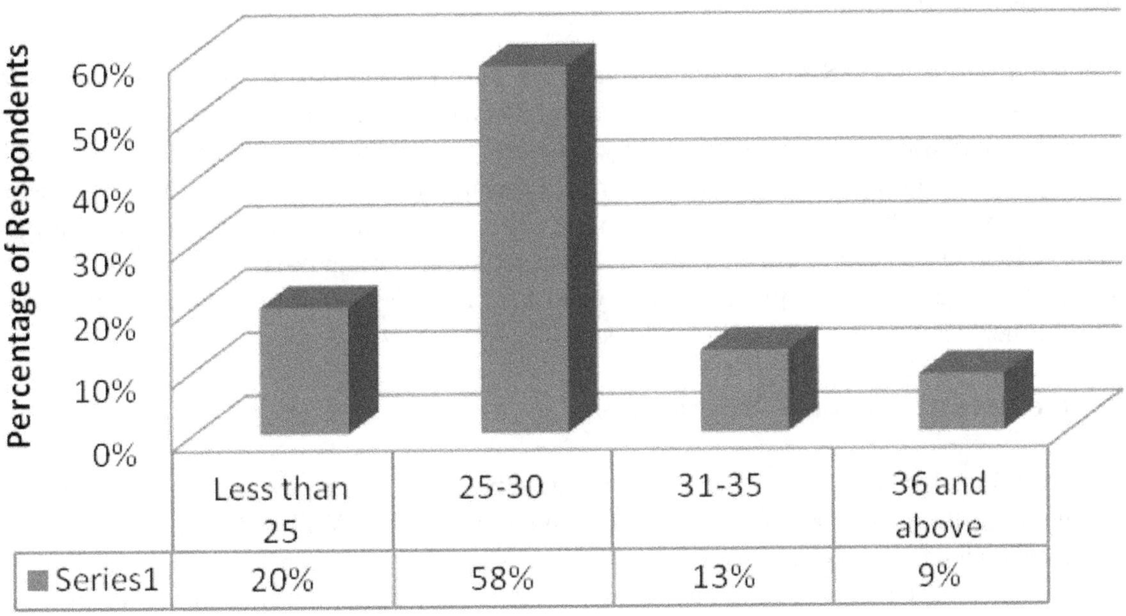

Figure 2. Marital Status of the members of the SHGs
Source: *Field Study*

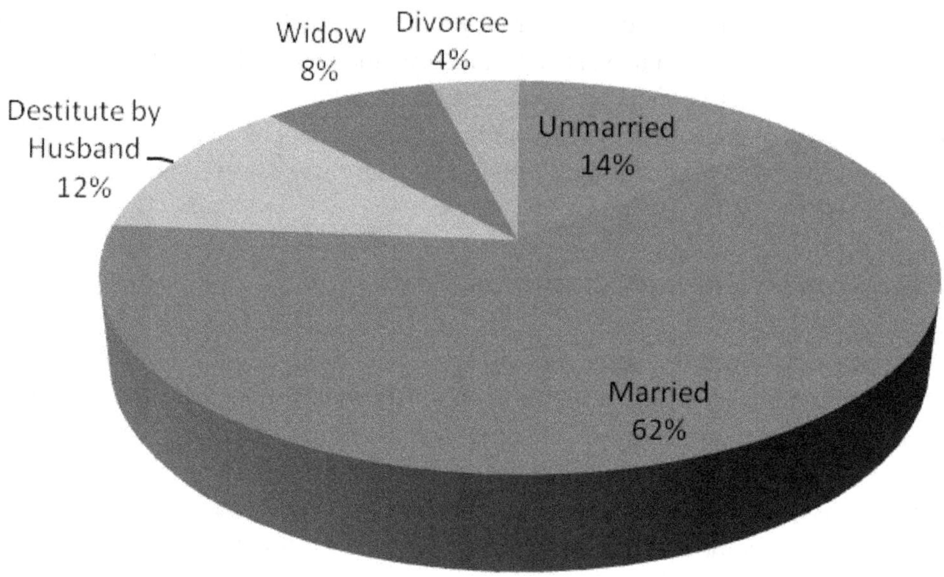

(20%). This may be due to low awareness about education, especially among the backward girl children as in different tribal-dominated parts of India. But the situation has drastically changed in recent times. It was observed that almost all the members of the SHGs are willing to provide the opportunity of basic as well as higher education to their children irrespective of the gender. A lot of members of the women-run SHG stated that they have sent their children for obtaining graduation and post-graduation degrees in colleges and universities.

Occupation of the Members of the SHGs

62% of the members of the SHGs are housewives. Generally, the members of the SHGs are involved in the activities like fishery, piggery, poultry farming, goatery, duckery, paddy husking and dairy farming. Income of about 88% of them is originated by catching 'meen', the local term for shrimp seedlings. The spawns of tiger prawn, which are hatched in these saline waters, are much in demand by the inland prawn farms, helping the poor to fetch hard cash. A large section of the women used to catch tiny prawn seedlings with fine nets, which are then sold to 'bheries' (brackish water bodies for growing fish). Apart from this, the occupations like piggery, goatery, duckery and poultry farming are also much popular among the members of the SHGs due to low recurring expenditure and good market.

Effectiveness of Training Programmes

For successful implementation of the different programmes and to empower the members of the SHGs in the true sense, the Sandeshkhali LAMPS, in collaboration with the WBTDCC Ltd., organized special technical training programmes for 960 from 125 women-run SHGs and imparted non-technical training to 280 members of the women-run SHG during 2010-11. The respondents unanimously agreed that such kind of training programmes is really beneficial for them to get new insights into their respective occupations and asked for more of such programmes to be organized by the LAMPS and the WBTDCC Ltd. at frequent intervals in the different Blocks.

Status of the Members Before Joining the SHGs

Generally, before joining the SHG, the respondents were confined to home or engaged as daily labourers in the agricultural land or fisheries or worked as maid servants. But, after joining in the SHGs, they are able to get financial support and now-a-days they are engaged in different independent activities to maintain the livelihood for themselves and their families like fishery, piggery, poultry farming, goatery, duckery, paddy husking and dairy farming. Thus, they are increasingly becoming economically self-sufficient and empowered in the true sense.

Family Income Level of the of Members of the SHGs

The income of the members of the surveyed SHGs has drastically increased after joining the SHGs. The women members of the SHGs responded that they are now reasonably independent to meet their personal expenditure, can save for the rainy season and contribute more to their household income. Many housewives did not earn anything before joining the SHGs but, after becoming members of the SHGs, they are also earning reasonably and contributing significantly to their family income. This is creating a positive impact on the other women and encouraged them to join the SHG movement and gain significantly.

It appears from the Table 2 that the monthly income of the members of the SHGs has increased significantly after joining the SHGs. While the percentage of the non-earning housewives has reduced from 34% to less than 1%, the income level in the higher tiers has increased significantly. While the percentage of the women with monthly income of less than 1000 has reduced significantly from 13% to 4% after joining SHGs, the percentage of women with monthly income of 5,001 and above has increased

Table 2.Monthly Incomes of the Members of the SHGs Before and After Joining the SHG Movement

Monthly Income ()	Before Joining SHGs		After Joining SHGs	
	No. of Respondents	Percentage	No. of Respondents	Percentage
Less than 1000	51	13.7837838	15	4.05405405
1,000-3,000	72	19.4594595	109	29.4594595
3,001-5,000	80	21.6216216	122	32.972973
5,001-7,000	19	5.13513514	59	15.9459459
7,001-9,000	10	2.7027027	31	8.37837838
9,001-11,000	8	2.16216216	22	5.94594595
Above Rs. 11,000	1	0.27027027	10	2.7027027
Non-earning members	129	34.8648649	2	0.54054054
Total	**370**	**100**	**370**	**100**

Source: Field Survey

Figure 3. Monthly income of members of the SHGs before and after joining the SHG movement
Source: Field Study

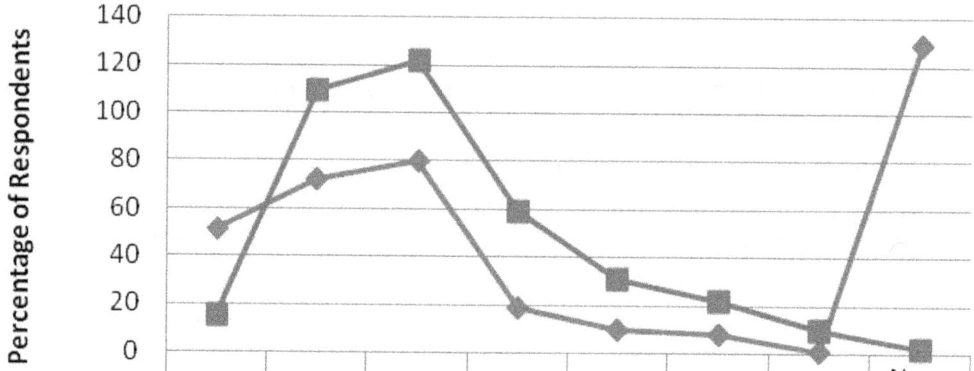

	Less than Rs.1,000	Rs. 1,000-3,000	Rs. 3,000-5,000	Rs. 5,000-7,000	Rs. 7,000-9,000	Rs. 9,000-11,000	Above Rs. 11,000	Non-earning Members
Before joining SHGs	51	72	80	19	10	8	1	129
After joining SHGs	15	109	122	59	31	22	10	2

from 10% to 33%. This finding reasserts the facts that the SHG movement has significantly contributed towards economic upliftment of the women in the surveyed Sunderbans area. By the scattered diagram of Figure 3 the monthly income of members of the SHGs before and after joining the SHG movement is presented.

In order to test the changes in the income level of the respondents after joining the SHG movement the Paired-t Test method has been used to test the null hypothesis that the income level of the respondents has not improved after joining the SHG movement against the alternative hypothesis that the income level of the respondents has improved after joining the SHG movement, i.e.,H_0: μ_d=0 against H_1:$\mu_d \neq 0$

Table 3. Paired samples statistics

		Mean	N	Std. Deviation	Std. Error Mean
Pair 1	Before Joining SHGs	100971.25	8	102809.534	36348.659
	After Joining SHGs	214546.25	8	171336.361	60576.551

Table 4. Paired samples correlations

		N	Correlation	Sig.
Pair 1	Before Joining SHGs & After Joining SHGs	8	.834	.010

Table 5. Paired Samples Test

		Paired Differences					t	df	Sig. (2-tailed)
		Mean	Std. Deviation	Std. Error Mean	95% Confidence Interval of the Difference				
					Lower	Upper			
Pair 1	Pair 1 Before Joining SHGs – After Joining SHGs	-113575.00	102728.004	36319.83	-199457.76	-27692.23	-3.127	7	.017

Source: Result computed by using IBM SPSS (version: 21)

at ∞=0.05 with d.f.=7. The output of statistical test results generated through IBM SPSS version 21 is presented in Table 3, 4 & 5.

It has been observed that since the observed modulus t value (3.127) is greater than tabulated value 2.37 or, in other words, since the p value is less than 0.05 (p=0.017), there is no statistical significance to accept the null hypothesis and it may be concluded that association with the SHG movement has helped the women of the Sandeshkhali Blocks of the Sunderbans area to improve their overall income level.

Measurement of Inequality of Income

In order to measure the pattern of inequality of income of the respondents before joining the SHGs and after joining the SHGs, the Lorenz Curve has been used. In the following Table 6 and Table 7 the measurement of inequality of income before and after joining SHGs are presented. Moreover, the Figure 4 reveals the movement towards reduction of inequality of income after joining the SHG movement with the help of widely accepted Lorenz Curve.

From the table it is clear that, before joining the SHG movement, more than 70% income was concentrated in the hands of around 11% respondents. But on the other hand, after joining SHG movement, the situation has drastically improved by inclusion of more respondents (around 65%) in the comparatively middle-to-higher income brackets.

Table 6. Measurement of inequality of income before joining SHGs

Monthly Income (`)	Before Joining the SHGs				
	%Population	% Income	Income/Population	C% Population	C% Income
Non-earning members	34.86486	0	0	34.86486	0
Less than 1000	13.78378	5.808584	0.421407	48.64865	5.808584
1,001-3,000	19.45946	18.27253	0.939005	68.10811	24.08111
3,001-5,000	21.62162	40.11043	1.855107	89.72973	64.19154
5,001-7,000	5.135135	14.34814	2.794112	94.86486	78.53968
7,001-9,000	2.702703	9.965708	3.687312	97.56757	88.50539
9,001-11,000	2.162162	10.00285	4.626317	99.72973	98.50824
Above Rs. 11,000	0.27027	1.491761	5.519517	100	100

Table 7. Measurement of inequality of income before joining SHGs

Monthly Income (`)	After Joining the SHGs				
	%Population	% Income	Income/Population	C% Population	C% Income
Non-earning members	0.540541	0	0	0.540541	0
Less than 1000	2.972973	0.589616	0.198326	3.513514	0.589616
1,000-3,000	29.18919	12.89932	0.441921	32.7027	13.48893
3,001-5,000	32.16216	28.07961	0.873064	64.86486	41.56854
5,001-7,000	17.83784	23.45648	1.314985	82.7027	65.02502
7,001-9,000	8.648649	15.00842	1.735348	91.35135	80.03344
9,001-11,000	5.945946	12.94593	2.177269	97.2973	92.97937
Above Rs. 11,000	2.702703	7.020631	2.597633	100	100

Source: Worked out by the researcher from the survey data

Figure 4. Measurement of inequality of income through Lorenz Curve
Source: *Worked out by the researcher from the survey data*

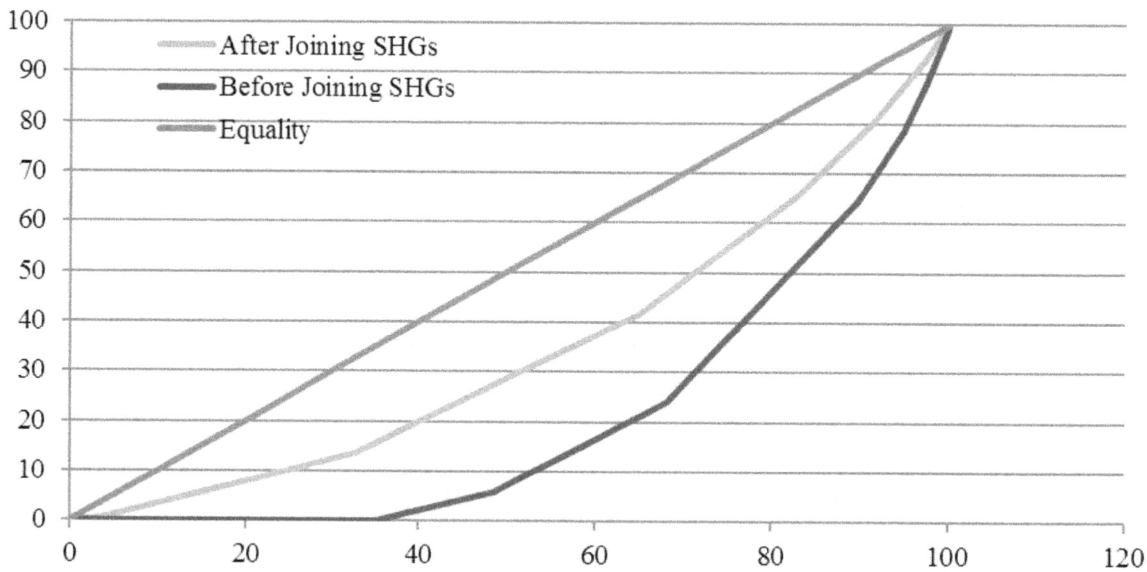

The same is also supported by the Lorenz Curve for measuring income inequalities. It has been observed that, after joining the SHG movement, the Lorenz Curve tends to move towards the equality curve. This is really an encouraging step towards reducing the income inequality among women by strengthening the SHG movement.

Moreover, the same can also be substantiated by the famous income inequality measurement indicator, known as Gini Co-efficient which is shown in the Table 8. It can be observed the Gini Co-efficient has been improved substantially by 46.29% among the women in the Sandeshkhali Blocks of the Sunderbans area after joining the SHG movement.

Table 8. Measurement of inequality through Gini Ratio

Before Joining the SHGs C% Population	C% Income	x(I)*y(i+1)	y(I)*x(i+1)	After Joining the SHGs C% Population	C% Income	x(I)*y(i+1)	y(I)*x(i+1)
34.86486	0	0.020	0.000	0.540541	0	0.000	0.000
48.64865	5.808584	0.117	0.040	3.513514	0.589616	0.005	0.002
68.10811	24.08111	0.437	0.216	32.7027	13.48893	0.136	0.087
89.72973	64.19154	0.705	0.609	64.86486	41.56854	0.422	0.344
94.86486	78.53968	0.840	0.766	82.7027	65.02502	0.662	0.594
97.56757	88.50539	0.961	0.883	91.35135	80.03344	0.849	0.779
99.72973	98.50824	0.997	0.985	97.2973	92.97937	0.973	0.930
100	100			100	100		
		4.077	3.499			3.047	2.736
Gini Co-efficient	**0.579**			**0.311**			

Source: Worked out by the researcher from the survey data

Moreover, in order to check the variations of average monthly income of the respondents across 13 Mouzas in 2 Blocks of Sandeshkhali in Sunderbans area statistical tests like Mann-Whitney U Test for 2 independent samples and Kruskal-Wallis Test for k independent samples have been used. In order to test variations of average monthly income of the members of SHGs between 2 Blocks of Sandeshkhali of Sunderbans area the Mann-Whitney U Test method has been used to test the null hypothesis that the average monthly income of the members of the SHGs between 2 Blocks are same against the alternative hypothesis that average monthly income of the members of the SHGs are different, i.e.,H_0: $\mu_{Sandeshkhali-I} = \mu_{Sandeshkhali-II}$ against H_1: $\mu_{Sandeshkhali-I} \neq \mu_{Sandeshkhali-II}$ at ∞=0.05 at 11 d.f. The summary of 1st Hypothesis test result is presented by the Table 9 followed by the Stem-Leaf plot of the statistical output in Figure 5.

It has been observed form the Table 9 and Figure 5 that since the 'p' value is less than 0.05 (p=0.026), there is no statistical significance to accept the null hypothesis and it may be concluded that there exists variations in average monthly income of the women of between 2 Blocks of Sandeshkhali in the Sunderbans area.

Finally, in order to check the variations of average monthly income of the women members of the SHGs across 13 Mouzas of 2 Blocks of Sandeshkhali of the Sunderbans area k independent samples Kruskal-Wallis Test has been used to test the null hypothesis that the average monthly income of the

Table 9. Summary of hypothesis #1 test result

Hypothesis Test Summary				
	Null Hypothesis	**Test**	**Sig.**	**Decision**
1	The distribution of Average Monthly Income is the same across categories of Respective Block.	Independent-Samples Mann-Whitney U Test	.026[1]	Reject the null hypothesis.

Asymptotic significances are displayed. The significance level is .05.

[1]Exact significance is displayed for this test.

Figure 5. Stem-Leaf plot of statistical test result
Source: *Result computed by using IBM SPSS (version: 21)*

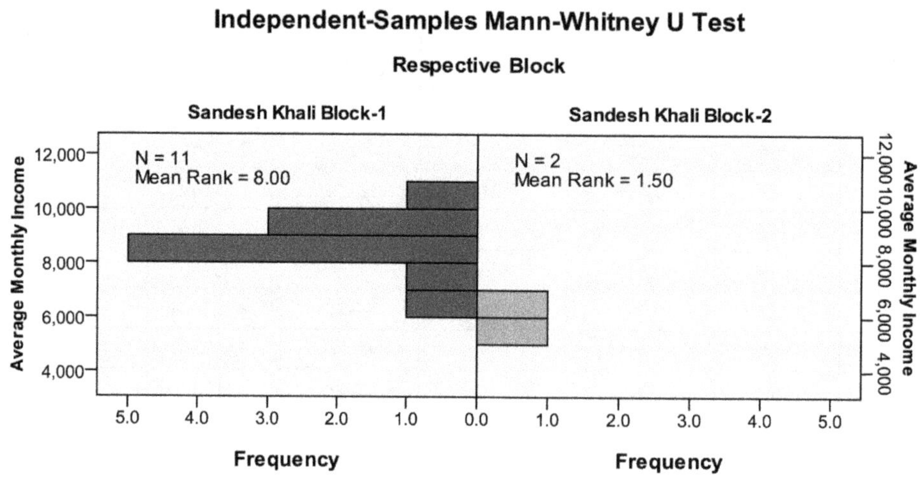

Total N	13
Mann-Whitney U	.000
Wilcoxon W	3.000
Test Statistic	.000
Standard Error	5.066
Standardized Test Statistic	-2.171
Asymptotic Sig. (2-sided test)	.030
Exact Sig. (2-sided test)	.026

members of the SHGs among 13 Mouzas of 2 Blocks of Sandeshkhali are same against the alternative hypothesis that average monthly income of the members of the SHGs among 13 Mouzas of 2 Blocks of Sandeshkhali are different, i.e.,H_0: $\mu_{Najat} = \mu_{Boyermari} = \mu_{DakhshinAkhratala} = \mu_{Khariat} = \mu_{Dekhanmari} = \mu_{Motbari} = \mu_{Sankardaho} = \mu_{Baunia} = \mu_{Petuadhanihati} = \mu_{Putimari} = \mu_{Bholakhali} = \mu_{Bermazur} = \mu_{Darikhjangal}$ against H_1: $\mu_{Najat} \neq \mu_{Boyermari} \neq \mu_{DakhshinAkhratala} \neq \mu_{Khariat} \neq \mu_{Dekhanmari} \neq \mu_{Motbari} \neq \mu_{Sankardaho} \neq \mu_{Baunia} \neq \mu_{Petuadhanihati} \neq \mu_{Putimari} \neq \mu_{Bholakhali} \neq \mu_{Bermazur} \neq \mu_{Darikhjangal}$ at ∞=0.05 at 12 d.f. The summary of 2nd Hypothesis test result is presented by the Table 10 followed by the Stem-Leaf plot of the statistical output in Figure 6.

It has been observed from the output of Table 10 and Figure 6 that since the p value is greater than 0.05 (p=0.446), there is no statistical significance to reject the null hypothesis and it may be concluded that there exists no variations in average monthly income of the women across 13 Mouzas in 2 Blocks of Sandeshkhali in the Sunderbans area.

Table 10. Summary of Hypothesis #2 test result

	Null Hypothesis	Test	Sig.	Decision
1	The distribution of Average Monthly Income is the same across categories of Respective Mouzas.	Independent-Samples Kruskal-Wallis Test	.446	Retain the null hypothesis.

Asymptotic significances are displayed. The significance level is .05.

Figure 6. Stem-Leaf plot of statistical test result
Source: *Result computed by using IBM SPSS (version: 21)*

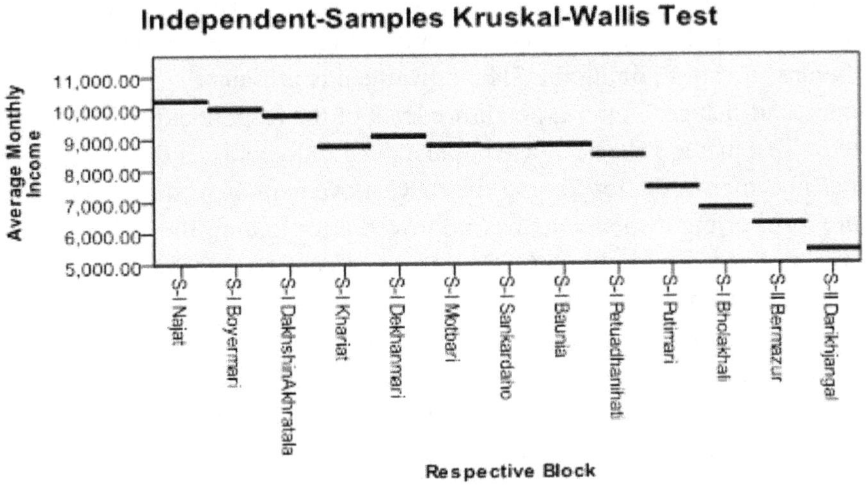

Total N	13
Test Statistic	12.000
Degrees of Freedom	12
Asymptotic Sig. (2-sided test)	.446

1. The test statistic is adjusted for ties.
2. Multiple comparisons are not performed because the overall test does not show significant differences across samples.

Family Expenditure Level of the Members of the SHGs and Their Decision-Making Authority

The family expenditure of the members of the surveyed SHG in the surveyed Sunderbans area has increased due to positive change in their income. The incremental income has not only enhanced the expenditure of the family but has also promoted the savings of the family after they have joined the SHG movement. Usually working women are being respected by the household members and the society and that fact has been reasserted through the responses of the members of the surveyed SHGs. It has also been revealed from the study that, although the husbands are primary motivational forces for the married women to join the SHGs, yet, at the time of spending the money they do not the sole authority to decide on the amount on spending. It emerges from the survey that the women have started taking the key decisions about spending in terms of household expenditure, educational expenditure for children and acquiring land or capital assets. Monthly expenditures of the members of the SHGs before and after joining the SHG movement is presented through the Table 11.

It was observed during the field survey that, being a part of an SHG, the spending capacity of the member, has increased significantly to a higher level. It was observed that the members' capacity to spend 2,000 per month and above has increased from 42% to 54% after joining the SHG. Even it was observed that after joining the SHG, the members' capacity to spend `6,501 per month and above has increased from 3% to 6%. By the scattered diagram of Figure 7 the monthly expenditures of members of the SHGs before and after joining the SHG movement is presented.

In order to test the changes in the expenditure level of the respondents after joining the SHG movement the Paired-t Test method has been used to test the null hypothesis that the expenditure level of the respondents has not improved after joining the SHG movement against the alternative hypothesis that the expenditure level of the respondents has improved after joining the SHG movement i.e. H_0: μ_d=0 against H_1:$\mu_d \neq 0$ at ∞=0.05 with d.f. = 6. The output of statistical test results generated through IBM SPSS version 21 is presented in Table 12, 13 & 14.

It has been observed that since the observed modulus t value (2.714) is greater than tabulated value 2.37 or, in other words, since the p value is less than 0.05 (p=0.035), there is no statistical significance to accept the null hypothesis and it may be concluded that association with the SHG movement has helped the women of the Sandeshkhali Blocks of the Sunderbans area to improve their overall expenditure level.

Loan Recovery Rate of SHGs

Maintaining the tradition of high rate of recovery of loan sanctioned especially to the women-run SHGs in different part of West Bengal, the surveyed SHGs in 13 Mouzas in 2 Blocks, operating within the framework of the Sandeshkhali LAMPS, have registered a nearly 100% loan recovery rate (99.13%) so far as the different schemes like AMSY, Disha, Micro-Credit, etc., are concerned. Moreover, it was observed during the survey that there is too much of peer pressure on the indebted members for repay-

Table 11. Monthly expenditures of the members of the SHGs before and after joining the SHG movement

Monthly Expenditures (`)	Before Joining the SHGs		After Joining the SHGs	
	No. of Respondents	Percentage	No. of Respondents	Percentage
Less than 500	93	25.1351351	23	6.21621622
501-2,000	122	32.972973	149	40.2702703
2,001-3,500	72	19.4594595	85	22.972973
3,501-5,000	59	15.9459459	72	19.4594595
5,001-6,500	13	3.51351351	20	5.40540541
6,501-8,000	8	2.16216216	12	3.24324324
Above Rs. 8,000	3	0.81081081	9	2.43243243
Total	**370**	**100**	**370**	**100**

Source: Field Survey

Figure 7. Monthly expenditure of members of the SHGs before and after joining the SHG movement
Source: *Field Study*

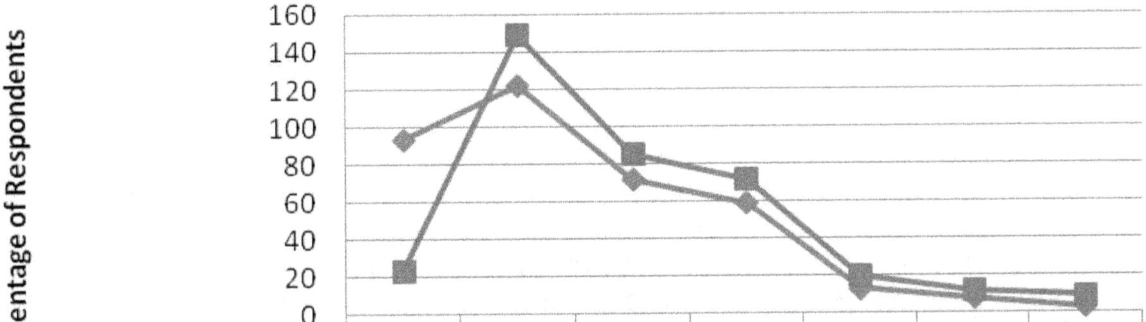

	Less than Rs.500	Rs. 500-2,000	Rs. 2,000-3,500	Rs. 3,500-5,000	Rs. 5,000-6,500	Rs. 6,500-8,000	Above Rs. 8,000
Before joining SHGs	93	122	72	59	13	8	3
After joining SHGs	23	149	85	72	20	12	9

Table 12. Paired samples statistics

		Mean	N	Std. Deviation	Std. Error Mean
Pair 1	Before Joining SHGs	116050.71	7	86859.011	32829.620
	After Joining SHGs	146491.43	7	102701.518	38817.525

Table 13. Paired samples correlations

		N	Correlation	Sig.
Pair 1	Before Joining SHGs & After Joining SHGs	7	.965	.000

Table 14. Paired samples test

		Paired Differences					t	df	Sig. (2-tailed)
		Mean	Std. Deviation	Std. Error Mean	95% Confidence Interval of the Difference				
					Lower	Upper			
Pair 1	Pair 1 Before Joining SHGs – After Joining SHGs	-30440.714	29675.123	11216.142	-57885.626	-2995.803	-2.714	6	.035

Source: Result computed by using the IBM SPSS (Version: 21)

ment of loan since fresh loan will not be issued to any member of the SHG unless the earlier loans are fully recovered. Moreover, the members, who find it difficult to repay the loan, may be given necessary technical support by the authorities and persuaded by the fellow members.

Social Empowerment

From the questionnaire-based survey, it was revealed that about 85% of the members have awareness about the various programmes/ activities relating to health (like immunization programme), education, water and sanitation, and legal rights. The members have adopted certain health-related practices like regular medical check-ups organized by the LAMPS office (82%), supplementary nutrition to children (54%) and family planning (57%). More than 94% of the members observed that they are sending their children to school. Overall, around 74% of the respondents have learnt to sign. When it comes to reading and numerical skills, only around 57% and 53% of the respondents respectively have acquired the skills. Regarding septic tank, latrine and hygienic toilet system, the members are far behind the desired level (only 12%). Regarding the dwelling house, the members use to stay in kachha house but, in a few cases, the members have built pucca house with asbestos. But, generally, the members said that they will definitely built pucca house with good sanitary system in future once they will be in a position to have a handsome savings in their kitty. The members of the SHGs were unanimous that, after joining the SHGs, their status in the family as well as in the community has improved a lot. The members, when asked, had given positive opinion on the issues like widow marriage, inter-caste and inter-religion marriage and strongly protested against child trafficking, child marriage, female foeticides, etc.

Political Empowerment

Almost all the members use to ceremoniously participate in the elections by casting their vote in the Parliament, Assembly and Panchayet elections. A few members had expressed their interest in filing nomination in the Panchayet election in West Bengal. However, a majority of the members are not quite aware about the three-tier panchayet system or issues like land reforms. Quite large number of members of the SHGs surveyed (72%) had expressed their concern regarding the functioning of the existing three-tier Panchayet system and issues like nepotism, corruption, political influence, exploitation and autocratic attitudes of some elected members in their localities and they had asked for certain changes in the systems immediately.

POLICY RECOMMENDATIONS

Even after six decades of Independence, almost 26% of the Indian population remains below the poverty line. The people in the higher echelons of the society are oblivious of the reality that a vast majority of people are deprived of the basics of life. An integrated effort from all the corners--the government (both at the central and state levels), private and individual initiatives--is the need of the day to eradicate the malice of poverty from the Indian society. The alleviation of poverty may largely possible be approached from three inter-related angles:

1. Creation of wide range of economic opportunities.
2. Sufficient provisions for the poor against intended and unintended financial sanctions.
3. Socio-economic-political Empowerment.

All these need to be taken up simultaneously as one reinforces the other. A new form of organization, namely, the SHG, has been designed to help in developing the sense of mutual help and self-employment, a different orientation to strengthen the human and capital base collectively and also to develop rural entrepreneurship. A lot of initiatives have already been undertaken both at the government and private levels to promote the formation of the SHGs especially for the women (since, out of 1.3 billion people living below the poverty line, 70% are women) for socio-economic-political empowerment. Generally, the SHGs in West Bengal are suffering from certain problems mentioned below.

1. Very low scale of production.
2. Deficient marketing mechanism.
3. Lack of active linkages.
4. Lack of proper training.
5. Absence of promotional incentives.

A new policy has to be evolved in order to raise the scale of production, ensure improved marketing mechanism, ensure streamlining of the linkages, arrange for the relevant training programmes and make provision for promotional incentives at the institutional level. In this connection, a set of suggestions has been offered and discussed below with a view to improving the productivity of the SHGs.

1. **Raising the Scale of Production:** In this age of modern and scientific processes of production, one needs to focus on the issues relating to the increasing impulses of diversification of business on a sufficient scale based on the understanding of the Business Development Planning (BDP). The BDP involves fairly a large number of exercises which may go a long way in sensitizing the group entrepreneurship in terms of new knowledge about resource plan, business input plan, strategic business plan, marketing plan, etc. Now, the SHG being a collective unit, should look beyond just the frontiers of production and income for the development of input and output markets and also appreciate the feasibility of tapping the available resources in and around the locality. Of course, one may experience some transitory problems since most of the members of the SHGs are less educated. Hence, there should be a launching pad initiated preferably at the governmental levels and/or at the private levels so that the members of an SHG can look beyond the horizon.
2. **Improving the Marketing Mechanism:** Market interaction is the key to any productive process. In fact, the advantage of division of labour and the large scale of production 'is limited by the extent of the market' (Adam Smith). The modern concept of globalization implies competitive expansion of the market beyond the geographical frontiers. The message is simple. As far as the market of the product is concerned, the whole world matters. It is necessary to produce standardized commodities and compete. Therefore, production is going to be driven and directed by the structure and extent of demand. It is the age of 'perform or perish'. In the face of steady inflow of competitive products in the market, it becomes a big question whether and how long the conventional commodities produced by the SHGs of West Bengal can have the ready market. Marketing assistance

should be extended to the SHGs both by the government and the big private organisations so that they can appreciate and measure the market requirements at the local, national and global levels and produce accordingly.

3. **Streamlining the Linkages:** According to Michael Porter's famous Value Chain Analysis, the competitive advantage of a firm depends on successful management of both forward and backward linkages. In the common parlance, they have to organize the available resources, procure the raw materials, manage the logistics and timely distribute the end products efficiently at the points of consumption. The quality of the backward linkages depends largely upon the quality of the forward linkages. In other words, the quantum, the rate, the timing and the type of inputs will largely determine the quality and quantity of the output. The two Iinkages must match with each other. The linkages, so far as the SHGs in West Bengal are concerned, at the moment are so weak that those become the source of 'fear of failure'. As far as the inter-SHG linkages are concerned, visibly there is lack of proper and competitive co-ordination. The experience of one SHG may be shared by another SHG. The inter-SHG linkage is bound to be an asset in the context of increasing competition along with the need for distributive justice. The latest information acquired by one SHG, being used by that SHG alone and not making that information being available to the other SHGs, is, perhaps, because of the lack organized institutions for that purpose. But it must be recalled that the producers have to act on the latest information available in the market. So the apex bodies of the SHGs, like the LAMPS, should initiate timely steps for effective information management, manpower development and credit management across the SHGs.
4. **Arranging for Proper Training:** Training programmes need to be arranged for the maximum benefit of the members, keeping in mind, their respective fields of work so that those may create more interest in the production and marketing aspects of functioning. Short-term training programmes for the women entrepreneurs need to be organized at regular intervals in order to improve their skills and capabilities. A system of training-cum- production centres and pilot workshops may go a long way in encouraging the use of improved techniques and designs. Moreover, proper education and training for the members will also be a positive step towards improvement in terms of building varied types of capacity and their effective integration.
5. **Providing Promotional Incentives:** There are institutional incentives which act as unpaid factors of production but which do stimulate and strengthen the long-run productivity of any concern. The institutional incentives may come from the government and the other local bodies in terms of providing better rural road, better transport, better power and water facilities etc. Secondly, the outstanding performance needs proper recognition and wider appreciation. This psychological effect is a driving force for the forward move of the SHG. The commercial temptation is to be stimulated by the proper recognition of every SHG. The human use of the human beings is going to be the major determinant of proper administration of the inputs. In order to stimulate and irrigate the minds of members, the 'Best SHG Award' may be instituted and the SHGs may also organize 'Industrial Visits' to the places where successful industrial units are located. Another area of concern is the lack of proper health care of the members of the SHGs. Most of the members of SHGs are functioning without proper health care and sanitation. Without good health of the lady workers, it is difficult to have higher productivity. The SHG-Health Programme, jointly sponsored by the LAMPS, for the different SHGs may be a rewarding area in the long run.

CONCLUSION

Economic empowerment of women is central to the consideration of their personal independence and self-esteem. To this end, employment and entrepreneurial opportunities would go a long way in making women really self-reliant. To end discrimination against women in the field of employment and to realize their right to work, women should be given the right to employment opportunities, the free choice of occupation, job security, and equal remuneration. The status of women in employment will never improve without taking care of these issues.

Empowerment is an active, multidimensional process, which enables women to realize their full identity and power in all spheres of life. The economic empowerment of women requires transfer of managerial skills and control of the economic activities to the women's groups over a period of time to enable women to feel confident and empowered. From the women's empowerment perspective, it is important to ensure that the women's economic activities are economically viable and the capacities and competencies of poor women, individually and collectively, are enhanced for organising and managing the economic activities. Empowerment, in the real sense, would be attained only when women are actively involved in the larger struggle for social change. Self-employment is a major sub-sector of employment where the poor women are concentrated. But, in most of the cases, the scale of operation is small and the consequent returns are miniscule. The women empowerment and, thereby, the community development through combined efforts of men folk and women folk require a holistic approach. As Sen (2001) has rightly observed 'there are no good reasons to abandon the understanding that the impact of women empowerment in enhancing the voice and influence of women does help to reduce gender inequality of many different kinds, and can also reduce the indirect penalty that men suffer from the subjugation of women.

Empowerment connotes a process through which the hitherto marginalized social categories of are able to successfully contest the dominant social, economic, political and cultural formations that perpetuate the dominant subordinate way of life. The change in power relationship, it is assumed, can be attained by providing the poor, especially the women, access/entitlement to credit. This credit, in turn, can be used to own and control assets and build capabilities. The economic approach underlying the micro-credit scheme, directed towards providing women's control over, and access to, small finance, will result in fulfilment of practical and strategic gender needs, and leading to their empowerment. Providing micro-credit to the self-employed groups of women will not only help them economically empower themselves but also help them contribute significantly towards the GDP of the nation. This statement has been reasserted by the findings of the study made on 39 SHGs functioning in 13 Mouzas of 2 Blocks within the framework of the Sandeshkhali LAMPS. It has been found, based on the analysis of the data collected through from the questionnaire-based survey, involving 370 members of those 39 SHGs, which, after joining the SHGs, the social status, economic power and political awareness of the members have enhanced significantly. However, the issues like the lack of awareness about health care and sanitation, the problems relating to the marketing of products, the problems associated with the conventional production facilities, the lack of rural infrastructure like electrification, road, etc., are the major areas of concern and both the central and state governments should initiate proper and timely measures to harness the latent potential of half of the population of the rural India in general and the rural West Bengal in particular. Moreover the justification for creating alternative occupation for the poor inhabitants in the Sunderbans area, in the form of functional SHGs, is very much there in the wider context of protecting the rich and unique bio-diversity, the Sunderbans area is endowed with, and a lot of initiatives need to be taken, particularly at the government levels.

LIMITATIONS OF THE STUDY

All the problems that are associated with any study based on data collected from a sample survey, are there in this study also. However, the major lacunae of this present survey are stated below:

1. The study is restricted to only the Indian part of the Sunderbans areaand specifically to northern part of the Indian Sunderbans area. The study will be more effective if one can cover both the Bangladesh part and entire Indian part of the Sunderbans area.
2. Out of the 6 Blocks in Basirhat Sub-Division which fall under the jurisdiction of the northern part of the Indian Sunderbans, only 2 Blocks have been covered based on concentration of the backward-class-dominated functional women-run SHGs. The study will be more comprehensive if one can have access to the topographically remote Blocks of the northern part of the Indian Sunderbans area (e.g. the Hingalganj, Minakhan Blocks, etc.).
3. Though the findings are relevant to the Sunderbans area, a unique region in the state, outcome of the survey, right now may not be fully relevant for the other districts of West Bengal.

In spite of these limitations, it is only expected that this study would bring out the pertinent issues regarding women empowerment through the SHGs in West Bengal over time.

SCOPE FOR FURTHER RESEARCH

1. A comparative study on the performance and role of the SHGs towards socio-economic-political empowerment of the women in the northern and southern parts of the Sunderbans area in West Bengal may be undertaken.
2. An inter-temporal analysis may be undertaken to explore the degree of improvement of socio-economic-political status of the women members of the SHGs before and after joining the SHG movement based on different parameters in different Mouzas in the Sunderbans area.
3. A comparative study of the degree of performance and role of SHGs under the patronage of different Governmental schemes/agencies like AMSY, SGSY, LAMPS, NABARD etc. may be envisaged in different Blocks of the Sunderbans area.
4. An impact study on the SHG-Bank-Linkage programme in a district-wise manner in West Bengal may be conducted.
5. A comparative analysis between performance, loan recovery rate, role towards upliftment of socio-economic-political status of the members of male-and female- run SHGs in West Bengal in a district-wise manner may be undertaken.

6. A study on role of the SHGs towards socio-economic-political empowerment of the tribal women in West Bengal may be undertaken.
7. A comparative analysis of performance and role of the government-sponsored SHGs (like LAMPS, PACS, etc.) and the private MFIs-backed SHGs (like Bandhan, Ujjivan, etc.) towards women empowerment may be undertaken.

REFERENCES

Acharya, M., & Bennett, L. (1981). Rural women of Nepal: An aggregate analysis & summary of 8 village studies. In The Status of Women in Nepal. Volume II, Part 9: Field Studies. Centre for Economic Development & Administration. Kathmu: Tribhuvan University.

Acharya, M., & Bennett, L. (1983). *Women and the subsistence sector: Economic participation and household decision-making in Nepal*. Working Paper Number 526. Washington, DC: World Bank.

Batliwala, S. (1994). The meaning of women's empowerment: new concepts from action. In Population Policies Reconsidered: Health, Empowerment & Rights. Cambridge, MA: Harvard University Press.

Bennett, L. (2002). *Using empowerment & social inclusion for pro-poor growth: A theory of social change. Working Draft of Background Paper for the Social Development Strategy Paper*. Washington, DC: World Bank.

Bharali, R. K., Chiring, A. J., & Konwar, D. (2013). Empowering women through self-help groups (SHGs). In Financial Inclusion, Self-help Groups (SHGs) & Women Empowerment. New Delhi: New Century Publications.

Bisnath, S., & Elson, D. (1999). *Women's empowerment revisited, Background paper, Progress of the World's Women*. UNIFEM. Retrieved from www.unifem.undp.org/progressww/empower.html

Buvinic, M., Gwin, C., & Bates, L. (1996). *Investing in women: Progress and prospect for the World Bank*. Washington, DC: World Bank.

Chambers, R. (1997a). Editorial: Responsible wellbeing: a personal agenda for development. *World Development*, *25*(11), 1743–1754. doi:10.1016/S0305-750X(97)10001-8

Chambers, R. (1997b). *Whose reality counts? Putting the first last*. London: Intermediated Technology Publications. doi:10.3362/9781780440453

Chandramouli, C. (2011). *India 2011 Census Data*. Office of the Registrar General & Census Commissioner, Ministry of Home Affairs, Govt. of India.

Cheston, S., & Kuhn, L. (2002). Empowering women through microfinance. In Pathways Out of Poverty: Innovations in Microfinance for the Poorest Families. Bloomfield, CT: Academic Press.

Chettri, D. (2012). Empowering women of rural Kalimpong through Self Help Group. In Microfinance & Self-Help Group: Policy & Practice. Kolkata: Readers Service.

Christen, R. P. (2006). Microfinance and sustainability: International experiences and lessons for India. In *Towards a sustainable Micorfinance outreach in India* (pp. 43–68). Mumbai: NABARD, GTZ & SDC.

Devi, R., & Devi, V. N. (2017). Economic empowerment of rural women throughSHGs with reference to Coimbatore district. *International Journal of Engineering Development & Research*, *5*(3), 1111–1113.

Everett, J. (1991). *The global empowerment of women*. Summary of the annual conference of the Association for Women in Development, Washington, DC.

Fernando, A. R. R., & Azhagaiah, R. (2015). Economic empowerment of women through self help groups. *Pacific Business Review International*, *8*(5), 91–98.

Friedmann, J. (1992). *Empowerment: The politics of alternative development*. Oxford, UK: Blackwell.

Gaonkar, R. R. (2001). Working and impact of Self-Help Groups in Goa. *Indian Journal of Agricultural Economics*, *56*(3), 471.

Goetz, A., & Sen Gupta, R. (1996). Who takes the credit? Gender, power and control over loan use in rural credit programs in Bangladesh. *World Development*, *24*(1), 45–63.

Goetz, A., & Sen Gupta, R. (1996). Who Takes the Credit? Gender, Power & Control Over Loan Use in Rural Credit Programs in Bangladesh. *World Development*, *24*(1).

Hashemi, S., Schuler, S., & Riley, A. (1996). Rural credit programs and women's empowerment in Bangladesh. *World Development*, *24*(4), 635–653. doi:10.1016/0305-750X(95)00159-A

Hazarika, G., & Guha-Khasnobis, B. (2008). *Household access to microcredit & children's food security in rural Malawi: A gender perspective*. Discussion Paper No. 3793. Institute for the Study of Labor.

Hulme, D., & Mosley, P. (1996). *Finance against poverty* (Vol. 1 & 2). London: Routledge.

Hunter, W. W. (1875). *A statistical account of Bengal*. London: Trübner & Co.

Islam, M., & Sarmah, J. K. (2014). Impact of self help groups in empowering women:A study of rural Assam. *Social Change & Development*, *11*(2), 90–98.

Iyer, L. (1991). *Women entrepreneurs challenges and strategies*. New Delhi: Federich, Ebert Stiftung.

Jahan, R. (1995). *The Elusive agenda: Mainstreaming women in development*. Zed Books Ltd.

John, G.M. (2008, March 1). Women empowerment through self help groups. *Southern Economist*, 234-54.

Kabeer, N. (1997). Women, wages & intra-household power relations in urban Bangladesh. *Development and Change*, *28*(2), 261–302. doi:10.1111/1467-7660.00043

Kabeer, N. (2005, October 29). Is micro finance a 'magic bullet' for women's empowerment? Analysis of findings from South Asia. *Economic and Political Weekly*, 4709–4718.

Kalbagh, C. (1991). *Women and development* (Vol. I). New Delhi: Delhi Discovery Publishing House.

Kanoria, H. P. (2012). *Swami Vivkananda's thoughts on women.* Retrieved from http://indiansrgr8.blogspot.com/2012/01/swami-vivekanandas-thoughts-on-women.html

Kessides, C. (2005). Contributions of urban development to economic growth and poverty reduction in Sub-Saharan Africa. Washington, DC: World Bank.

Kumar, R. (1993). *The History of doing: An illustrated account of movements for women's rights and feminism in India, 1800-1990.* New York: Verso.

Lakshmi, R., & Vadivalagan, G. (2012). Impact of self help groups on empowerment of women: A study in Dharmapuri district, Tamilnadu. *Journal of Management & Sciences, 1*(2), 43–55.

Lalita, R. (1996). Women entrepreneurs. New Delhi: A.P.H. Publishing Corporation.

Mahmud, S. (2003). Women and transformation of the domestic spaces for income generation in Dhaka bustees. *Cities (London, England), 20*(5), 321–329. doi:10.1016/S0264-2751(03)00049-0

Malhotra, A., Schuler, S. R., & Boender, C. (2002). *Measuring women's empowerment as a variable in international development.* Background paper for World Bank Workshop on Poverty & Gender: New Perspectives.

Malik, B.S., & Vani, S. (2006). Micro-enterprises for empowerment of women. *Kissan World, 33*(5).

Mayoux, L. (2000). *Microfinance and the empowerment of women: A review of the key issues.* Social Finance Unit Working Paper, 23. Geneva: ILO.

Morduch, J. (2000). The microfinance schism. *World Development, 28*(4), 617–629. doi:10.1016/S0305-750X(99)00151-5

Nagayya, D. (2000). Micro-finance for self help groups. *Kurukshetra, 48*(11), 10-15.

Naidu, M. C., Jayaraju, M., & Dasaatharamaiah, K. (2006). Women's empowerment through DWCRA – empirical study. *Social Welfare, 51*(12), 32–38.

Nanda, P. (1999). Women's participation in rural credit programs in Bangladesh and their demand for formal health care: Is there a positive impact? *Health Economics, 8*(5), 415–428. doi:10.1002/(SICI)1099-1050(199908)8:5<415::AID-HEC450>3.0.CO;2-L PMID:10470548

Narayan, D., Chambers, R., Meera, K., Shah, M. K., & Petesch, P. (2000a). *Voices of the Poor: Crying out for change.* Oxford, UK: Oxford University Press. doi:10.1596/0-1952-1602-4

Narayan, D., Patel, R., Schafft, K., Rademacher, A., & Koch-Schulte, S. (2000b). *Voices of the poor: Can anyone hear us?* Oxford, UK: Oxford University Press. doi:10.1596/0-1952-1601-6

Overseas Development Council Census of India. (2001). *2001 Data.* Office of the Registrar General & Census Commissioner, Ministry of Home Affairs, Govt. of India.

Pramod, B. (2006). SHG-Bank linkage programme: Future scenario. In *Towards a sustainable microfinance outreach in India - Experiences and perspectives* (pp. 69–82). Mumbai: NABARD, GTZ & SDC.

Puhazhendi, V., & Badatya, K. C. (2002). *SHG-Bank linkage programme for rural poor – An impact assessment.* Paper presented at the SHG-Bank Linkage Programme Seminar, New Delhi, India.

Punitha, M., Sangeetha, S., & Padmavathi, K. (1999). Women entrepreneurs: Their problems and constraints. *The Indian Journal of Labour Economics, 42*(4), 707–716.

Rajagopalan, T. (1989). *Farm credit in dry land areas: A study of credit needs & problems of small & marginal farmers in Chityal Mandal, AP, India* (Unpublished Thesis). Asian Institute of Technology, Bangkok, Thailand.

Ramachandran, T., & Seilan, A. (2005). Socio-economic empowerment and self help groups. *Social Welfare, 52*(6), 26.

Ramanajaneyulu, M. (2006). *Economic empowerment of women in India.* New Delhi: Anmol Publications Pvt. Ltd.

Ravallion, M., & Chen, S. (2001). *Measuring pro-poor growth, Policy Research Working Paper no. WPS2666.* Washington, DC: World Bank.

Report, A. A. (2012). *Backward Classes Welfare Department* (pp. 2010–2011). Kolkata: Government of West Bengal.

Rogers, B., & Youssef, N. (1988). The importance of women's involvement in economic activities in the improvement of child nutrition & health. *Food and Nutrition Bulletin*, 10.

Sahay, S. (1998). *Women and empowerment approaches and strategies.* New Delhi: Discovery Publishing House.

Sarangadharan, M., & Rasia Begum, S. (1995). *Women entrepreneurship.* New Delhi: Discovery Publishing House.

Selvi, R. R., & Shanmughun, R. (2016). A study on women empowerment through self-help groups in Erode district. *International Journal of Multidisciplinary Research & Modern Education, II*(I), 383–388.

Sen, A. (1973). *On economic inequality.* Delhi: Oxford University Press. doi:10.1093/0198281935.001.0001

Sen, G., & Grown, C. (1987). *Development, crises and alternative visions: Third world women's perspectives.* New York: Monthly Review Press.

Sharma, K. C. (2001). Micro financing through self help groups. *Journal of Agricultural Economics, 56*(3), 460–461.

Singh, K. (1992). Women entrepreneurs. Ashish Publishing House.

Suja, S. (2012). Women empowerment through self-help group – An evaluative study. *Sona Global Management Review, 6*(3), 68–83.

Thapa, S. (2012). Self-help group and women empowerment: Problems and prospects (A Study in Sikkim). In Microfinance and self-help group: Policy and practice. Kolkata: Readers Service.

Tzannatos, Z. (1999). Women and labour market changes in the global economy: Growth helps: Inequalities hurt and public policy matters. *World Development, 27*(3), 551–569. doi:10.1016/S0305-750X(98)00156-9

UN Division for the Advancement of Women (UNDAW). Department of Economic & Social Affairs. (2001). *Empowerment of women throughout the life cycle as a transformative strategy for poverty eradication*. Report of the Expert Group Meeting, New Delhi, India.

United Nation. (2011). *United Nation's Human Development Report 2011*. New York: United Nations Development Programme.

United Nations Children's Fund (UNICEF). (1999). *Human rights for children & women: How UNICEF helps make them a reality*. Retrieved from http://www.unicef.org/pubsgen/humanrights-children/index.html

Vyas, P. (2004). A Step towards joint tiger census with Bangladesh. West Bengal, India: Academic Press.

Wadhera, K., & George, K. (2012). *Empowering rural women: Micro enterprise through achievement Motivation, New-Delhi*. SAGE Publications.

White, S. (1991). *Evaluating the impact of NGOs in rural poverty alleviation: Bangladesh country study*. London: ODI.

World Bank Policy Paper (1994). *Enhancing women's participation in economic development*. No.13415. World Bank.

KEY TERMS AND DEFINITIONS

Economic Empowerment of Women: Economic empowerment deals with the issue which embraces the degree of shift in the locus of the financial decision-making process in different entities as well as creation of financial independence of the entities.

Empowerment: Empowerment is a comprehensive issue and it is a dynamic, multi-dimensional process, which enables the incumbent to realize their full distinctiveness and power in all spheres of life.

LAMPS: Large-scale multipurpose cooperative societies (LAMPS) are the block level primary co-operative societies in various districts of the state with a view to providing credit, non-credit and technical support to the tribal women in West Bengal, the objective being their holistic empowerment and inclusive development.

Sandeshkhali: Sandeshkhali I is a community development block that forms an administrative division in Basirhat subdivision of North 24 Parganas district in the Indian state of West Bengal.

SHGs: SHG is a holistic program of micro-enterprises covering all aspects of self-employment, organization of the rural poor into self Help groups and their capacity building, planning of activity clusters, infrastructure build up, technology, credit and marketing.

Sunderbans: Sundarbans area, formerly Sunderbunds, is a vast tract of forest and salty water swamp, forming the lower part of the Gangetic Delta, extending about 160 miles (260 kms.) along the Bay of Bengal from the Hooghly River estuary in India to the Meghna River estuary in Bangladesh. Sunderbans area is the world's largest continuous mangrove area, covering some 10,000 kms. of land and water within the Gangetic Delta Sunderbans was declared as a UNESCO World Heritage site in 1997. The Sunderbans area is also regarded as the largest biosphere reserve in the World.

WBTDCC: West Bengal Tribal Development Co-Operative Corporation Ltd. (WBTDCC) has been set up under the aegis of the Backward Classes Welfare (BCW) Department, Government of West Bengal with a view to providing all kinds of supports, financial, technical, marketing and others, to the tribal people of the state for their socio-economic development.

Chapter 8
Examining the Viability of Social Responsibility of Microfinance by the Bank Compartamos, Mexico

José G. Vargas-Hernández
University of Guadalajara, Mexico

María Alejandra Santos Huerta
University of Guadalajara, Mexico

Kinkini Bhattacharjee
Katwa College, India

ABSTRACT

Microfinance achieves financial inclusion to the poor population stimulating the creation of sources of income and employment. Banco Compartamos is an institution that has more market share and has more than 20 years providing financial services to their specific sector of the population. The chapter analyzes the viability of social responsibility of microfinancing by the Compartamos banco of Mexico for the period 2002-2015. The results show that microfinance working on social responsibility by the Compartamos Banco is not viable as there are the results of inverse correlation results. However, the banco served some social responsibility by means of pulling people out of poverty. It further concludes that these organizations fulfill their main objective, which is to benefit the people of the base of the pyramid in Mexico.

INTRODUCTION

Civil society has driven some forms of social organization and responsible participation to reverse the deterioration of the living conditions of the population. The social, economic and political model of Mexico for more than 60 years had shown the flexibility to incorporate and involve the entire popula-

DOI: 10.4018/978-1-5225-5240-6.ch008

tion in an efficient and productive capacity. There is a problem within Mexican companies regarding the adoption of social responsibility practices, which is not exclusive to the country, as this is a pattern that is repeated in developing countries (Azmat & Ha, 2013), a category to which Mexico still belongs, since it meets certain characteristics which makes it to be within this group. The main characteristics of this group are that they are countries with faster economies of expansion, as well as growing markets making them profitable to do business on the part of companies.

In addition, it is usually where the social environment and its crises are usually more sensitive than in other countries. For this environment of sensitivity is where factors such as globalization, economic growth, investment and business have greater impact either negative or positive. For this reason, it can be considered that this type of economy handles with different treatment the issue of social responsibility as opposed to the developed economies (Visser, 2008). According to Schmidheiny (2006), Latin American countries tend to be more concerned with social problems than with other problems regarding social responsibility, such as ethics, environment and stakeholders.

So the objective of this chapter is to publicize the importance of the use of these practices in Mexican companies, the benefits they have both in the community where they are executed, the social benefits, the reputation that is obtained and that can attract investment by interest groups and what is more important, in increasing their profits, since it is the main reason why companies start to take this type of measures (Lizarzabaru & Del Brio, 2016). Thus encourage the development of strategies that help implement social responsibility within firms. It is a question of further clarifying the weight of social responsibility through a case study, a Mexican micro finance company called Banco Compartamos, then presenting the results that are arrived at through the case study analysis and finally presenting the conclusions and recommendations that are made about the work developed.

This chapter hopes to demonstrate social responsibility that has had the financial institution "Banco Compartamos " with viability to execute the purpose to eradicate financial exclusion through microfinance, especially credit, savings, insurance, financial education and means of payment. Throughout its history with the civil society, it has been creating value for its customers, suppliers, shareholders, employees.

In this chapter it is first exposed the origin of microfinance, which is Banco Compartamos, its history, major products, and the reason for choosing such case. Second it is exposed the social responsibility actions of Compartamos Banco with feasibility of operations.

ORIGIN OF MICROFINANCE

Microcredit emerged as a mechanism to facilitate access to monetary resources at a lower cost and charges set by usurers and moneylenders. Microcredit occurs when groups of people establish funds and savings and loan cycles. Most microfinance arise from a solidarity work so unfolded as nongovernmental organizations (NGOs), which, in attempting to meet the needs of disadvantaged communities in the country, eventually became involved in the activities of credit unions.

The financial activity of NGOs involved the receipt of funds from savings of the general public is restricted and is necessarily subject to official supervision activity. At that time was not regulated. Microfinance is seen as an alternative financial inclusion or as a mechanism to provide the "seed capital" to carry out a productive initiative or as a mechanism for governmental financial support to low-income population. But not necessarily all the microcredits help to support and encourage micro business duly formalized. As the report National Microenterprise Financing Program (2014) says are definitely an alternative to detonate micro business or occupation means for segments of the population without access to traditional credit.

DEFINING THE PROBLEM

Knowing whether microfinance, taking the case of Compartamos Banco, apply to social responsibility to the population in general and its market. This research is based on the principle that these companies work with the poor population also called "bottom of the pyramid" and its heritage.

RESEARCH QUESTION AND ASSUMPTION

Do microfinance businesses apply social responsibility towards the population that benefit from their services? Or do so at the expense of the heritage of this population to whom they say they benefit?

Due to the increase in the number of people who are located at the base of the pyramid, benefits for this sector of the population would be profitable due to the much larger market to which they are targeted. However, it is imperative that the general public may have access to financial services nationwide and are not discriminated against. To this end microfinance is created, however, it may not have a social responsibility to their customers, which is critical because of the large number of people living in social, equity, and economic deprivation.

It is pretended to know what action takes Compartamos Banco as a model and when the microfinance more market share.

CONCEPTUAL AND THEORETICAL BACKGROUND SOCIAL RESPONSIBILITY

Definition of Social Responsibility

Corporate social responsibility, according to Peng (2012) is on matters beyond the economic, technical and legal requirements of the company to accomplish social benefits along with the traditional economic gains which the organization seeks. Social responsibility is exposed by Vallaeys (2012) as the responsibility for the social and environmental impacts of decisions and actions of the organization through transparent and ethical behavior that:

1. Contribute to sustainable development of society including health and welfare.
2. Take into account the expectations of stakeholders.
3. Comply with international law and standards.
4. It is integrated into the entire organization and implementation in all relationships.
5. (ISO 26000, 2010).

The Corporate Social Responsibility (CSR) is understood as the active and voluntary contribution to social, economic and environmental improvement by companies, with the objective of improving their competitiveness, and its added value, according to the Ministry of Economy (SE, 2016). For the International Labor Organization, the social responsibility of the company is the set of actions that companies take into account so that their activities have positive repercussions on society and affirm the principles and values by which they are governed, both in their own internal methods and processes as well as in their relationship with other actors (OIT, 2007, p.53).

The origin and evolution of the concept has six phases according to Bhaduri (2016):

- 1950-1960 - Period of introduction of CSR in the academic field and corporate philanthropy as CSR.
- 1970s-Period of rapid growth in the concept of CSR.
- 1980s-Period of stakeholder theory and business ethics.
- CSR of the 1990s.
- 2000 onwards - Empirical work period to investigate determinants and Consequences of CSR in corporate strategy.

The concept of CSR has been studied from the economic, social and environmental point of view. Within an economic approach there are two main aspects of study, productivity in relation to the CSR model based on indicators of productivity in workers and the second is profitability as marketing techniques for consumers. This point is studied in depth and validated. In this approach the economic benefit is taken as the most important variable of study. Social responsibility takes sustainability into consideration. Several authors agree, such as Haneke, Glosw, Hernand (1998) in a definition *ad literam* development that satisfies the needs of the present generation without compromising the ability of future generations to meet their own needs.

Within the social perspective, studies are justified by productivity indicators tending to economic issues. However, there are no studies that verify the truthfulness of improving the quality of life of workers in relation to the establishment of CSR practices in the company that they work, which in turn, can influence the productivity of the workers and therefore in a decrease welfare in the society that ends in economic repercussions for the Mexican economic environment. From an environmental point of view, there are economic, environmental, and an example, the Kuznets environmental curve (Correa, Vasco, Pérez, 2015) that directly affect the company as a structure, the viability of legal framework in Mexico and its incentives towards the company, which also tends to be conditioned by economic factors.

As pollution vs. economic growth is a debate within the environmental sciences and economics. In addition to the above, the concept has also been studied from the biological point of view, which focuses on minimizing pollution regardless of economic costs or viability within the current economic system, tends to be more utopian (Gudynas, 2009). Sustainable development has become more a discourse than a resource, a way and a method of reconfiguring society and preserving nature and life itself (Salinas, 2007). The technical problem of this is to obtain an acceptable estimate of the social cost and externalities to bring the tax (or subsidy) in line, which raised the need to carry out, in collaboration with other specialists, environmental impact assessments that would serve as a basis for the desired pecuniary estimates. Even though the obligatory partiality and arbitrariness of such assessments has served most often to provide benign estimates of the social costs that justify state authorization of damages (Cruz, 2006).

Although the issue of CSR is not new, the line that investigates the impact of the application of CSR practices on workers has little depth of theoretical and methodological research, since research on the subject focuses more, the profitability of the company and its effectiveness as a marketing theme. Certified models known in Mexico, Family Responsible Enterprise (EFR), Socially Responsible Enterprise (ESR), Including Company (DEI), the three above, are programs operated by the Federal Ministry of Labor and Social Prevention (STPS) (PROFEPA) and at the state level, exclusive of the state of Jalisco, the Voluntary Environmental Compliance Program (PCAV), in addition to ISO 26000 in Social Responsibility and ISO 14000 Focused on the environment, and lastly the A8000 certificate focused on the practices of corporate social development. Do these certifications actually work? What do they work for? An example is the Family Responsible Company model, 5 years after its implementation, what benefits have been achieved? Does the quality of life of the workers actually increase?

An example more attached, is the Family Business model, which was replicated in Mexico through the program of distinctions awarded by the Secretary of Labor and Social Prevention (STPS). This program was developed by the business school of the University of Navarra, Spain, where through assumptions and theories of competitiveness and productivity in workers, justify the importance and feasibility of its implementation.

However, there are no studies that demonstrate the evaluation of the model, once it has been implemented. The most attached to this is the IESE FAMILY-RESPONSIBLE EMPLOYER INDEX developed by the same University of Navarra and analyzes the level of implementation of the Responsibility Familiar Corporate and its impact on people and organization. However, their studies do not take into account Mexico, so there is a lack of information regarding the feasibility of implementing these practices in Mexico and creates doubts, whether or not true these practices work as they say on their website.

Conceptual Theoretical Review

In this section it is developed the theoretical concepts to be used within the work, as well as the set of ideas, background and theories that support the research in order to make clear each of the terms that are mentioned and can understand the perspective from where to leave. So far only the main theme has been referred to in a superficial way. It is up to here to define what has at first been described as social responsibility. From this point it is referred to this as corporate social responsibility (CSR).

In some companies (if not most) when referring to social responsibility practices they use the term socially responsible company, whereas in the scientific literature there does not seem to be a difference between CSR and socially responsible companies, rather than as an adjective on the part of the second to indicate that they make use of this type of measures. Therefore, both terms will be understood as equal.

In most of the concepts within the world of research there is a great debate to have a single definition that serves as a basis, and CSR has different (Azmat & Ha, 2013), although the study of this topic is not new since it has been developed for decades. It has not been possible to reach a consensual definition by the guild (McWilliams, Siegel & Wright, 2006). In this paper it is used as reference but not as absolute definitions, the ones supported by Ramasamy and Yeung (2009) and Mcguire (1963, p. 144). The idea of social responsibility means that the corporation not only has economic and legal obligations, but also certain responsibilities towards society that go beyond these obligations. In addition, Davis (1973, p. 313) goes further since it explains what should not be a socially responsible enterprise: Social responsibility begins where the law ends. A company is not socially responsible if it simply meets the minimum requirement of the law, because this is what any good citizen would do ... Social responsibility is a step forward. It is the acceptance of a company from a social obligation beyond the requirement of the law.

There are different theories of CSR, however Garriga and Melé (2004) find that they are focused on four main aspects: To reach the main objectives of the company using CSR; Maximizing shareholder value and gaining a competitive advantage based on the resources and capabilities for long-term benefits. In addition, using the power with which it counts as a company in a responsible manner, refers to implementing activities that help society through altruistic acts where the same company is taken as a citizen more involved in a community that has to support. Another aspect that Garage and Melé consider is that of integrating social demands is based on the way in which the company manages the social demands that it has mainly with the stakeholders. To take the CSR as a company policy that goes beyond the law is a measure adopted before a demand of the public opinion. Finally, the company must focus on doing good for a better society, that is, consider human rights, labor and care and respect for the environment, everything revolves around a more ethical approach.

Table 1 presents the work done by Lizarzaburu and Del Brio (2016) who were in charge of combining the approaches proposed by Garriga and Melé (2004), as well as the main points of each approach. They were also able to identify the main researchers who have developed CSR and locate them in some of the aspects that the model mentions. This is how RSC understands many terms and therefore it has not been easy to reach a consensus in its definition. Already with a clearer picture of what CSR is about, there are still some terms that need to be defined in order to continue with the development of ideas. Companies should take into account different perspectives according to their needs to take choosing appropriate strategies for it is necessary to know the different theories that help to understand the organization in its different edges. Mahoney (2012) talks about five blocks that make up the organizational economy, they are:

1. behavioral theory where the main variable at stake is uncertainty because the company is an organization composed of people and these are full of limitations. Although Adam Smith talks about the rational individual and his choices, trying to maximizing his own benefit, in practice it is not as simple as Simon (1957) says about limited rationality, which is given by limited resources available, asymmetric information, and different cognitive abilities. Although the individual is rational, sometimes the problems often exceed their abilities.
2. In addition, the theory of transaction costs where Coase (1937), Williamson (1979) and Arrow (1974), explain that there are certain mechanisms that allow a company to grow, one of which is the costs associated with the moment of realization. Some operations, either internally or externally, and opportunism plays a key role within this block, as long as greater opportunism can be generated, transaction costs will be greater (Vargas-Hernández, 2014).
3. The third block refers to the theory of property rights, Mahoney (2012) refers to this as an important point that should be obtained well-defined and correctly allocated rights to create wealth.
4. In block of agency theory, Peng (2012) is clear in saying the problems that can occur between the principal and agent because of the divergence of interests on the part of one and another, where transaction costs are generated, usually caused by the principal's interests to maximize the value of their long-term actions, while agents seek to maximize their own profit (Vargas-Hernández, 2014).
5. Finally, the theory based on resources and capabilities, where Penrose (1959) emphasizes the internal resources and management capabilities of the company in relation to its growth. Through the study by Mintzberg, Quinn and Voyer (1997) using the five forces developed by Porter is how they perform a company strategy analysis and thus improve their performance:

Table 1. Approaches to Corporate Social Responsibility

Investigation CSR	
1. Instrumental Theories (CSR as Instruments of Wealth)	
1.1 Maximizing shareholder value	Friedman, 1970; Jensen & Meckling, 1976; Ross, 1973; Jensen, 2000; Hartojo, 2015
1.2 Other competitive advantages	Husted & Allen, 2000; Goss & Roberts, 2011
1.3 Extend marketing effects	Varadarajan & Menon, 1998; Smith & Higgin, 2000
2. Political Theories (Power of the Company in Society)	
2.1 Corporate constitutionalism	Davis, 1960,1967)
2.2 Integral social contract	Donaldson, 1982; Donaldson & Dunfee, 1994, 1999, 2000
2.3 Corporative citizenship	Davis, 1973; Altman & Vidaver-Cohen, 2000; Matten et al., 2003
3. Integrative Theories (Response to Stakeholder Demand)	
3.1 Management approach	Sethi, 1975; Greening & Gray, 1994; Wartick & Rude, 1986
3.2 Business policies towards social direction	Preston, & Post (1975, 1981), Bouslah et al, 2013; Jizi et al, 2014; Bouslah et al, 2016
3.3 Decision-making effects on stakeholders	Rowley, 1997; Berman et al, 1999; Agle et al, 1999
3.4 Corporate Social Performance	Carrol, 1997; Wood, 1991
4. Ethical Theories (Ethical Responsibility with Society)	
4.1 Stakeholder Normative Theory	Freeman (1984)
4.2 Theory of universal rights	Cassel (2001); Giuliani, 2016
4.3 Theories of sustainable development	The World Business Council for Sustainable Development (2000)
4.4 Common Good Approach	

Source: Lizarzaburu & del Brio, 2016, p. 46.

Intensity in Rivalry Between Competitors

It seeks to measure the degree of concentration within an industry, the less competitors the less concentrated the industry will find.

Threat of Potential Entries

Companies seek to reach the market more and the less competitors will be better for them, since they can impose their conditions on many occasions, to protect themselves from new competition. They apply for entry barriers in this way, they increase transaction costs, which discourage the entry of new firms.

The Bargaining Power of Suppliers

It refers to its ability to raise prices and / or reduce the quality of goods and services. It has four conditions: The dominance of industry by companies, product differentiation, if the focal firm is not an important customer and whether suppliers can become suppliers and rivals (Peng, 2012).

The Bargaining Power of Buyers

Also considered are four conditions which are if there is a strong bargaining power on the part of the buyers, if there is an impact on the quality of life of the buyers, the consideration of buying branded products without considering brands and entering the focal industry by delayed integration (Vargas-Hernández, 2014).

Threat of Substitute Products

This is about new products that can be launched by the competition that seek to compete and relegate either through quality or are produced at low cost.

However, not only must take into account the aspects based on the company and the industry, since they influence in a great way other actors of a firm in the institutional, cultural, and ethical aspect. This theory is called institutional theory (Peng, 2012) which explains the influence that exists on the part of the State and the society when the strategies are presented within a company, the way in which the institutions affect to a great extent the moment of creation of a firm, expansion of the same or in the entry of new products, there are several aspects to be taken into account since there are regulations that must be complied with which are imposed by the government. However, the same measures implemented by one country may not be applied in another, that is why the interaction between institutions and organization is so important (Scott, 1995). Hofstede (1997) proposes five different dimensions of culture, encompassing the extreme parts that could be presented in any region or organization: The distance of power, that is, the inequality that exists in an organization or society, individualism and collectivism, masculinity and feminism, evasion of uncertainty and long-term orientation can be found in societies where more is planned for the future with better planning towards goals. While ethics refers to the norms, principles or standards that organizations have regarding their behavior and performance (Vargas-Hernández, 2014). For example, in organizations it tries to encourage companies with their participation in activities that society requires.

REVIEW OF THE EMPIRICAL LITERATURE

CSR is used to differentiate products within the competition, as explained by McWilliam, et al. (2006) since by means of a vertical differentiation one product is preferred to another, so it happens when the desired product which has characteristics of CSR is better than the other that does not have them. For example, the case of Honda, where many of its consumers prefer the hybrid Accord instead of the conventional model even though they have to pay much more for the first one, this because the characteristics that make up the hybrid is to be less polluting what is more valuable to the customer. In developed countries, CSR is increasingly a marketing strategy in order to gain trust and consumer loyalty, use different communication tools such as certificates, reports, everything to announce that they are doing internships of social responsibility (Azmat & Ha, 2013).

To date, most of the research carried out on Corporate Social Responsibility has been in developed countries. In the case of developing or emerging economies, the study of CSR is very useful. The justification for doing so, is that these economies represent a market in full expansion, which turns out to be a very lucrative business for companies. Where social and environmental crises are most accentuated. In addition, the impact on society of economic aspects such as globalization, investment and entrepreneurial activities have drastic repercussions, whether positive or negative.

The problems of developing countries with respect to CSR are very different from those in developed countries. The main aim is to improve living conditions through private sector participation (Jamali & Mirshak, 2007). This is why Visser (2008) proposes, based on Carroll's initial model of CSR, to make modifications and to exchange the priorities of each level of the pyramid as shown in Figure 1, in which economic responsibility remains the most important pillar within the emerging countries, because of the amounts of money that governments have for companies to set up in their territory, in addition to the jobs it generates, however, for the same reason of wanting to retain what governments have achieved. To overlook some ethical, environmental or social risks in order to retain companies.

The second block is the philanthropic responsibility where more than an act of good faith is a necessity and where companies need to improve the conditions of the community to operate in a good way. Legal responsibilities have a lower priority, as Peng (2012) explains. Usually, in the emerging countries there are weaker institutions which encourages companies to settle as there is less pressure from the government. For the developing countries, the lowest priority is ethical responsibility, says Visser (2008), as corruption still largely affects business activity, although there have been cases such as South Africa that with its CSR inclusion report managed to cover issues Social, ethics, security, among others, is still an exception to the rule.

In Latin American and Caribbean countries, the most associated problems are social and not environmental problems, as can happen in developed countries, because the emerging countries have more problems than developed countries, such as poverty, lack of medical care, housing problems and education, as governments fail to meet these needs, the societies of the population, civil societies pressure companies to cover government inefficiency (Schmidheiny, 2006). According to the Mexican Center for Philanthropy (Centro Mexicano para la Filantropía, Cemefi) (2017), there are several reasons to ap-

Figure 1. Carroll's Pyramid of the four classes of responsibilities modified by Visser
Source: Visser (2008), p. 489.

ply CSR to companies, because they have positive effects on them which can be measured by means of quantitative and qualitative information. Some of them extracted from the same portal (Cemefi):

1. Loyalty and less turnover of the stakeholder groups.
2. Improvement of relations with neighbors and authorities.
3. Contribution to the development of communities and the common good.
4. Increased visibility among the business community.
5. Access to capital by increasing the value of its investments and its long-term profitability.
6. Better informed business decisions.
7. Increased ability to receive financial support.
8. Improvement in financial performance, reducing operating costs by optimizing efforts and making resource use more efficient by focusing on sustainable development.
9. Improvement of the corporate image and strengthening of the reputation of the company and its brands.
10. Increase in sales, reinforce consumer loyalty
11. Increased productivity and quality.
12. Improvement in the skills to attract and retain employees creates loyalty and a sense of belonging among the staff.
13. Reduction of regulatory oversight.
14. Teamwork is promoted and made more efficient.

Some studies, such as the one by Vasal (2009) carried out in India, where they sought to analyze the relative performance of the equity portfolio of companies that execute social responsibility practices, finding that there is a positive but statistically non-significant return. This type of results has influence on the shareholders. While in other countries like Bangladesh (Azmat & Ha, 2013), it tries to explain the difficulties of the Asian country and how CSR with the government could help improve the supply chain.

CASE COMPARTAMOS BANK´S SUSTAINABILITY MODEL

Compartamos Banco called "Our Cause" education model which describes "the family as the seed of all change and social welfare." Since Gentera is interested to contribute to progress and access to educational opportunities for integral development of the person and since 2009 make a contribution towards social responsibility and potentiate the development of the individual and society. Social responsibility, individual and social development especially are linked to actions seeking the common good, solidarity and justice, to raise the quality of life, empowerment and community development, especially in education issues. In basic education, for example sustainability and entrepreneurship promotion are important duties (Compartamos, S.A.B, 2013).

The image given in Table 2 shows more clearly some of these actions:

Table 2. Family as seed of any change and social welfare

Final Objective of Social Action GENTERA	Strategic Approach	Vectors of Actions	Actions
Generate opportunities	Generate opportunities	EDUCATION AND HEALTH	
The family as the seed of any social change and welfare	Being better persons, forge better families and a better country	DEVELOPMENT FOR LIFE ENTREPRENEUR SHIP EDUCACIÓN FINANCIERA HEALTHY HABITS AND SPORTS	Human development I. Values: Honesty, trust, conscience, corresponsability, compromise, participation, hope, citizenship, coexistence II. Environmental education Formal /informal education for children, youngers and adults. Schooled education, literacy, job training and for teachers Training for business: To initiate activities or improve the performance of small business, through financial education, management, sales, marketing, personnel management, planning, and commercialization of product to generate income through productive projects. To foster the development of abilities, behavioral changes, competencies, knowledge, in the persons in themes of financial health such as savings, insurance, budgeting, credit, over debt, with the aim to foster the personal and family welfare. Food and nutrition Attention and prevention of diabetes and hypertension Programs of physical activity and healthy occupation of free time

Source: Own elaboration based on data from Compartamos, S.A.B (2013).

CONTEXTUAL FRAMEWORK

What Is Compartamos Banco?

Compartamos Banco has the aim to eradicate financial exclusion through microfinance using credit, savings, insurance, means of payment and financial education. Additionally, Gentera defines itself as a group of companies, which mainly includes Compartamos Banco in addition to other subsidiaries in different countries of Latin America. Gentera is the entity responsible for the management, expansion and communication of companies within the same group and the integration of the historical aspects and the philosophy of the group. This institution was chosen to be the financial institution because it has a greater influence in the market for microcredit to have a share of 44% based on the share of wallet and customer (Figure 2). It shows the market share of the top 20 microfinance institutions.

Main Objectives of Banco Compartamos

Its main objectives are seeking people to live gender equity in which women have field development and personal growth. Also, Banco Compartamos aims to generating values, bringing the social value to the most of people in the shortest possible time following the sustainable model and quality. To its colleagues, there is a need to know the importance of continuing to generate social, economic and human value in every person in Mexico and the rest of America. They are defined as "People always concentrates on Generate Value; committed to its roots, with the seed that defined our origin "(Compartamos SAB 2013).

Figure 2. Market share of microfinance companies
Source: Programa Nacional de Financiamiento al Microempresario (2014).

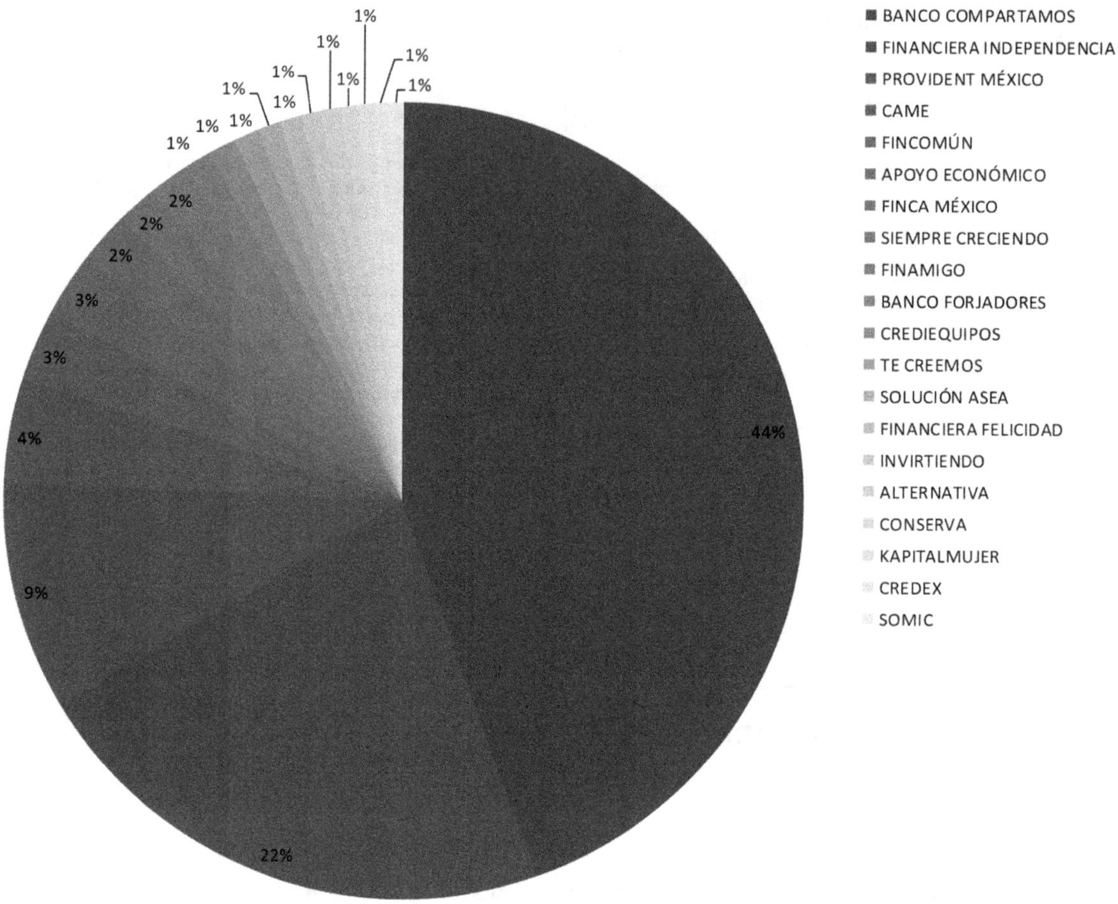

History and Development to Date of Compartamos Banco

Origin

Compartamos is the result of a project that a group of young entrepreneurs began over 20 years ago. In 1990 Compartamos Partnership Program, IAP was born, as a Non Governmental Organization (NGO) that was given the task of providing financial services aimed at the base of the pyramid. Initially, services were directed only to women, for them to be the mainstay of the family. Compartamos provide credit to micro entrepreneurs, mainly in the states of Oaxaca and Chiapas.

Once the model was tested successfully, the challenge was to make it reach to the most people in the shortest possible time, promoting economic development of families.

Evolution

1. In 1993 Compartamos Banco had already 5,000 customers and 3 offices.
2. Some staff visited microfinance institutions in Asia, where a vision of mass was obtained. In the same year the methodology Generating Income (GDI) consolidates and growth begins in Chiapas and Oaxaca.
3. In 1995, Compartamos Banco had 17,500 customers and 7 offices.
4. In Boulder, Colorado, the first meeting of experts from around the world was made to give training courses in micro finance. In this meeting of experts, it was included Banco Compartamos with the world of microfinance, and it obtained multiple contacts.
5. In 1997, Compartamos Banco had 37,254 customers and 10 offices.
6. Financial self-sufficiency is achieved. The level of profitability of Compartamos Banco supported a specific real possibility of expansion of the service in Mexico. Compartamos Barco starts preparing its transformation from NGOs (Non-Governmental Organization) into a Regulated Financial Intermediary.
7. In 2001 Compartamos Banco achieved 64,000 customers and 5 offices.
8. Compartamos Banco was formalized as Financiera Compartamos, SA de C.V. Sfol, which were able to access commercial funding sources. This action enabled Financiera Compartamos to realize the original vision of mass to serve more people.
9. In 2002, Compartamos Banco had 144,000 customers and 52 offices.
10. First issuance of stock certificates. Financiera Compartamos was the first institution in the microfinance sector worldwide, who manages to issue debt in the stock market with its own warranty.
11. In 2004, Financiera Compartamos achieved 617,000 customers and 188 branches.
12. A program for stock certificates was authorized, for an amount of $ 500,000 pesos, valid for three years and having the flexibility of having or not guaranteed.
13. In 2007, Financiera Compartamos achieved 40,000 customers and 253 branches.
14. Banco Compartamos participates in the Mexican Stock Exchange. .
15. In 2008, Financiera Compartamos achieved 1,000,000 customers and 314 offices.
16. There was change of image. It exemplified the way it works, a team formed by a bank of fish as it strives to reach its goal, simply, trust, honesty and transparency.
17. In 2009, Financiera Compartamos had 1,500,000 customers and 325offices.
18. 500,000 active insurance policies and 100 thousand Credits to Improve Your Home were reached. This is supporting customers to improve the quality of life for his family. These achievements are proof of the dedication of the employees and adherence to the methodology.
19. 2010
20. Compartamos Banco is First on the list of best companies to work for. Guided by a clear philosophy based on values, principles and ethics.
21. It was given the beginning of the process to form a group with several companies, all with the same sense of purpose and vision.

Current Situation

In 2011 Compartamos began operations in Central and South America, becoming Financial CREATE, Financiera Compartamos Today in Peru and constituting Compartamos SA in Guatemala. Also, it starts Yastás operations, company that offers a network of means of payment of all types through non-banking correspondents. In 2011 the Foundation was founded with the goal of being an efficient operator arm that adds solid strategy to social responsibility. Aterna started operations in 2012 as a specialist business in micro-enterprise. Thus, in 2013 it evolves into the group identity for all Gentera.

In its annual report 2013, Compartamos Banco poses a possible excess demand or excess supply in the markets where it competes. Since it has focused on addressing a new segment that was not subject to receive financial services. So that at the end of 2013, Compartamos Banco had 2,488,616 customers and its target market is constantly growing so does not consider the existence of services on offer.

Through Banco Compartamos, currently the Company provides services to over 2.5 million customers in Mexico offering credit products for working capital, savings and life insurance. However, there are new competitors that offer such services.

Gentera Fundation

Gentera Foundation defines itself as a foundation that generates social and human value. Gentera Foundation is committed to the person, creating opportunities for development in vulnerable segments. (Genetera Foundation, 2013). Its main goal is to be an efficient operator arm that adds solid strategy to social responsibility. In response to the pressing needs of the communities, Gentera has worked for more than 23 years ago. It is in 2011 when Gentera Foundation constitutes itself as a means to continue to generate social and human value. Through the Foundation are operated some projects that can offer opportunities for development in the field of education, health, basic needs and promoting volunteerism in various communities it operates (Genetera Foundation, 2013).

Major Products and Services Offered by Compartamos Banco

Products offered by Compartamos Banco to its customers are divided into 3 main categories:

1. Credit:
2. Credit to women.
3. Extra credit
4. Credit to improve and grow
5. Individual credit
6. Credit to traders

Out of which credit women is the main product of Compartamos Banco. This is a group loan offered to a group of between 10 and 50 women with independent activities located in rural or semi-urban areas.

1. Insurance offered to customers through Aterna, a company that is part of the same group.
2. Basic life insurance.
3. Integral life insurance.

4. Capture.
5. Personal Account Compartamos.
6. Basic Account Compartamos.

OPERATIONAL ANALYSIS OF BANCO COMPARTAMOS FOR THE PERIOD 2002-2015

We have considered the variables such as asset values, borrowings, operational cost, return on assets, per borrower borrowing, per officer borrowing, etc. and done basic statistical analysis to have some ideas on sustainability of operation of the banco. The data base has been borrowed from MIX Database. Figure 3 and 4 present the trends of asset values, borrowings, per borrower borrowing and

It is observed from Figure 3 that both the series of asset values and total borrowings are rising but the series for the latter takes downward direction from 2013 to 2014. The rate of increase for both the series is higher from 2011 to 2012.

It is again observed from Figure 4 that the trend for per borrower borrowing is upward sloping but that for the borrowers per staff member is downward sloping. The similarity between them is that they have fluctuations for the period 2008-2012 which may be due to the outbreak of financial crisis at the global level.

In our data set, there is a sharp rising trend among asset values, gross loan portfolio, No. of active borrowers and borrowings. For them mean value is lie between the years of 2008 to 2010. Now considering the measure of relative variations it has been observed that except Borrowers per staff members and

Figure 3. Borrowings and Asset Values over time

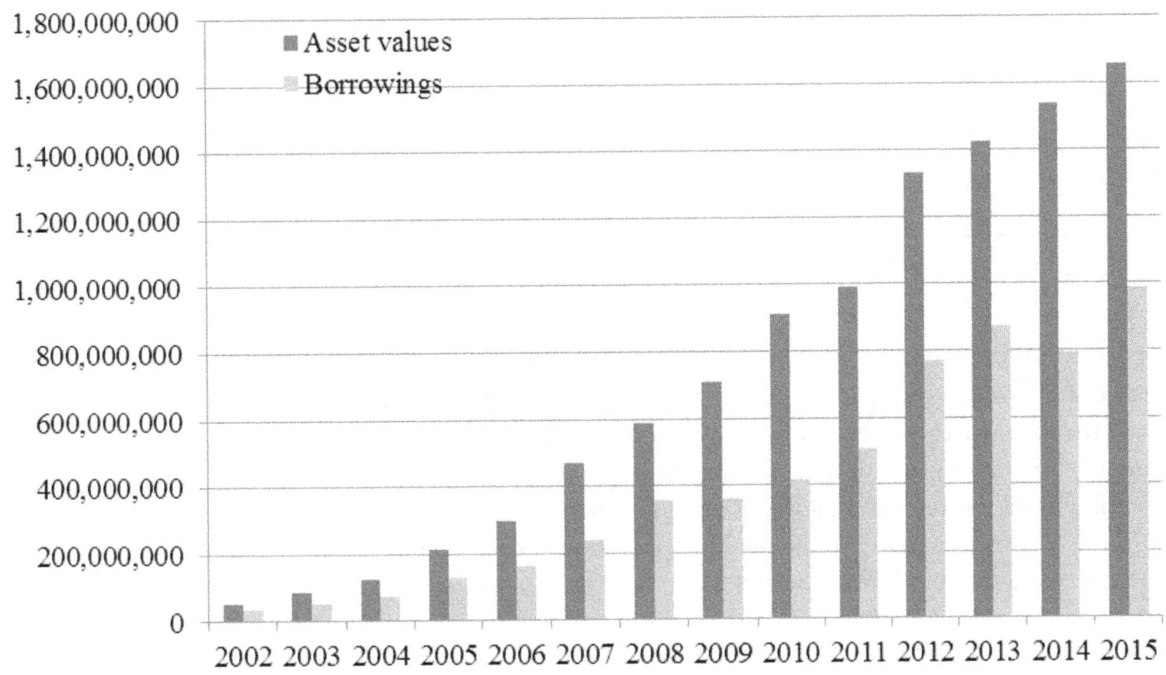

Figure 4. Trends of per borrower and per staff borrowing

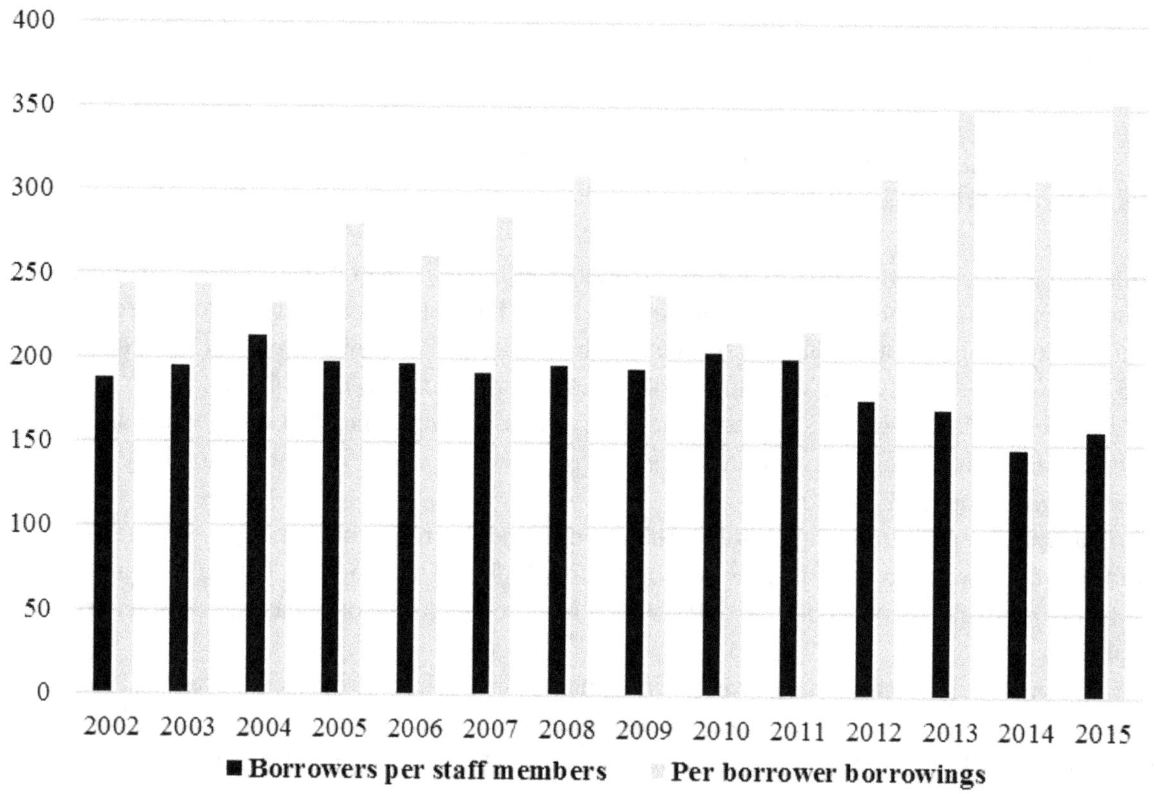

Table 3. Different micro financial aggregates of Banco Compartamos

	Asset Values	Gross Loan Portfolio	No. of Active Borrowers	Borrowings	Borrowers per Staff Members	Per Borrower Borrowings
Mean	742409471.57	615388529.64	1419960.93	410460869.14	187.86	274.67
SD	570751098.76	477996473.56	997541.84	327046286.86	18.42	46.41
CV	76.88	77.67	70.25	79.68	9.80	16.90

Source: Computed by the authors based on MIX database

per borrower borrowings CV is more than 70 percent. As obvious Borrowers per staff members and per borrower borrowings shows a fluctuating trend over the years and having a lower SD caused lower CV of 9.80 percent and 16.90 percent correspondingly (Table 3).

Figure 5 depicts the trends of operating expenses and return on assets where the former shows a mild increasing trend but the latter shows declining trend over time. The combinations of the trends do not justify the true sustainability of the banking operation. There is negative correlation between the two.

The formula for correlation coefficient is –

$$r = \text{cov}(x, y) \;/\; SDx.SDy$$

Figure 5. Operating expenses and Return on assets of Banco Compartamos

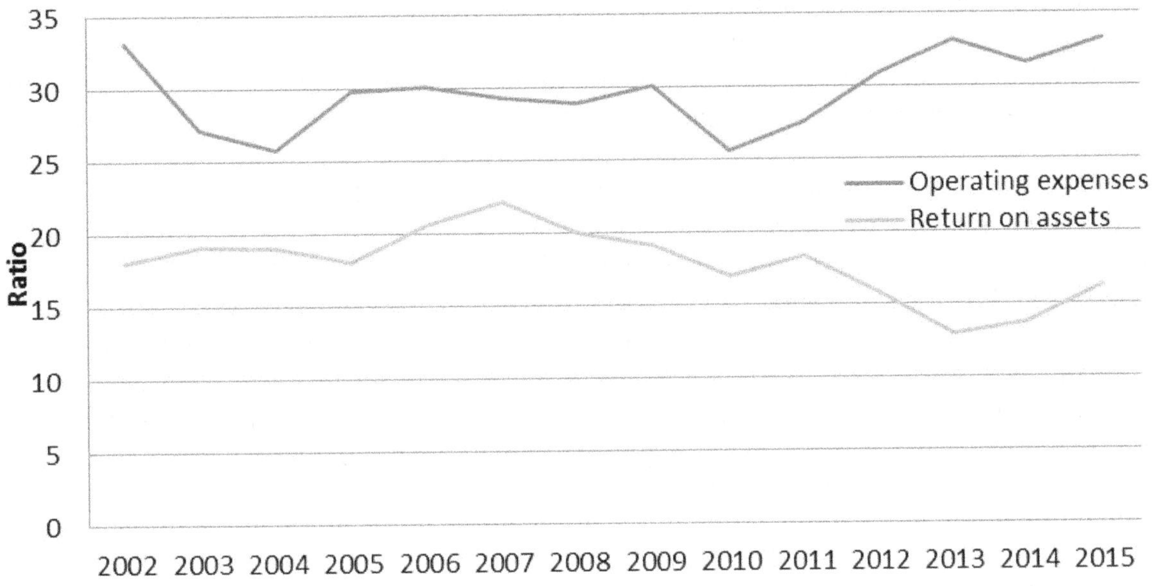

where 'r' stands for correlation coefficient, SDx for standard deviation of variable 'X' and SDy for standard deviation of variable 'Y'. Its significance has been tested by the following Student's 't' statistic which is-

$$t = r\sqrt{(n-2)} \; / \; \sqrt{(1-r^2)}$$

where (n-2) is the degrees of freedom. We have n = 14 (2015-2002) and so the degrees of freedom is 13.

By measuring correlation coefficient of borrowings, return on assets and operating expenses we can conclude about the strength and direction of a linear relationship between variables. The result shows that there is moderate downhill relationship between return on assets and operating expenses (r = -0.46) and significant at 9 percent level. But there is a moderate uphill relationship between borrowings and operating expenses (r = 0.50) which is significant at 7 percent level. And there is a strong downhill linear relationship between borrowings and return on assets (r = -0.74) with 0.2 per cent level. It thus justifies that there is inefficiency in the operational analysis of the bank.

POVERTY IN MEXICO

As the main goal of Compartamos Banco is to eradicate financial exclusion through microfinance in the less favored sectors of society, briefly it is analyzed the situation of poverty in Mexico and the world.

Globally, to eradicate poverty has been one of the main objectives of the Millennium Summit of the United Nations celebrated in September 2000, where the Millennium Development Goals (MDGs) were established to be achieved in 2015. The first of these is to eradicate poverty and hunger. 8 out of 10 people in the world are hungry, according to the United Nations in the report of the Summit (United

Nations, 2000). At this Summit, it was pointed out to measurably among other objectives to achieve full and productive employment and decent work for all.

According to the National Institute of Statistics, Geography and Informatics (Instituto Nacional de Estadística, Geografía e Informática (INEGI, 2012) in Mexico in 2012 there were 53.3 million people in poverty, equivalent to 45.5% of the total national population. The National Council for Evaluation of Social Development Policy (CONEVAL) (2012) defines poverty population as someone that has at least one of the six social deprivation such as lack of education, access to health services and public safety quality and living spaces, basic services in the home and access to food; besides insufficient income to acquire the goods and services required to meet their food and non-food needs.

That's why it is used an institution that seeks to reduce poverty through the development of the country. For Compartamos Banco a way to decrease the national poverty is through financial inclusion in the "bottom of the pyramid" through microfinance to generate economic, social and human value to people (Compartamos, S.A.B., 2013). For purposes of this article, it will be taken the economic value that Banco Compartamos aims to achieve building innovative, efficient and profitable business models from which everyone can benefit (Compartamos, S.A.B., 2013).

METHODS

The analytical method has been achieved through the analysis of the object of study, which allows a clear view of the important strategies for analyzing the impact of the number of customers of Compartamos Banco on national poverty population.

A linear regression model was performed in order to observe the variation of the population in poverty versus the number of customers of Banco Compartamos. Note that the representation of Compartamos Banco against the total population in poverty is very limited, especially considering that it's not a private and public institution and has limited scope as such with a population of approximately 50.6 million people.

ANALYSIS OF RESULTS

From the creation of Banco Compartamos, poverty has varied from 57% of the total population in 1992 to 47% in 2013. Taking only people with equity gaps in general has decreased though not in the same proportion as the Banco Compartamos growth, which in late 2013 had 2.3 million customers, representing 4.54% of the National Poverty Population.

As a result of the regression, it was observed that the number of people in patrimonial poverty without asset has decreased while at the same time has increased the number of customers of Compartamos Banco

CONCLUSION

It can be analyzed, since its inception that Banco Compartamos was born to offer development opportunities in communities, especially the poorest, acting according to the values set by its staff for Banco Compartamos, customers, suppliers, and others. Besides, Compartamos Banco is promoting and favoring development through the family as the seed of all change, social welfare and continuing education as a way to eradicate financial exclusion.

From the creation of Banco Compartamos, according to the National Institute of Statistics, Geography and Informatics (INEGI) based on the report submitted by the (CONEVAL, 2013), poverty has varied from 57% of the total population in 1992 to 47% in 2013. Taking only the population that lacks equity in general has decreased though not in the same proportion as the growth of Compartamos Banco, which in late 2013 had 2.3 million customers, representing 4.54% of the national population in.

Compartamos Banco as an alternative business has been very profitable. From the interest earned on loans has achieved utilities while continuing to benefit more people without being at the expense of their customers. Since being so important the number of customers the benefits from each credit is representative. In general, if the interest rate is higher than has other financial institutions such as commercial banks and less than that given by lenders such as loan sharks, because the transaction costs are higher for the size of the different types of loans to customers as well as ensuring to have for recovery of the amount borrowed.

It is observed that the operation of the banco is not efficient as the correlation between the concerned variables are not usual. However, social responsibility can be seen through the responsibility that has since its inception with the individuals at the bottom of the pyramid, especially women, through transparent and ethical behavior that contributes to sustainable development of these people. Sustainable development comes through financial inclusion, continuing education and the promotion of entrepreneurship. Besides, offering insurance to their clients for contingencies such as death. Clearly, Compartamos Banco is complying with applicable law to the National Banking and Securities Commission (CNBV), and other institutions that govern it as a financial institution.

REFERENCES

Arrow, K. (1974). The limits of organization. New York, NY: W.W. Norton and company.

Azmat, F., & Ha, H. (2013). Corporate social responsibility, customer trust, and loyalty-perspectives from a developing country. *Thunderbird International Business Review*, *55*(3), 253–270. doi:10.1002/tie.21542

Bhaduri, L. (2016). La importancia de la responsabilidad social empresarial, Evolucion del concepto. *Negocios y entorno, 32*(4), 7-17.

Centro Mexicano para la Filantropía (Cemefi). (2017). *CEMEFI, Servicios*. Recuperado de https://www.cemefi.org/

Coase, R. (1937). The nature of the firm. *Economica, 4*(16), 386–405. doi:10.1111/j.1468-0335.1937.tb00002.x

Compartamos, S. A. B. (2013a). Recuperado el 07 de mayo de 2014, de http://www.gentera.com.mx/wps/portal/Gentera/Acerca/QuienesSomos

Compartamos, S. A. B. (2013b). Recuperado el 2014 de mayo de 02, de http://www.gentera.com.mx/wps/portal/Gentera/Sustentabilidad/NuestraCausa

Compartamos, S. A. B. (2013c). Recuperado el 02 de mayo de 2014, de http://www.compartamos.com.mx/wps/portal/Banco/AcercaCompartamos/NuestroProposito

Compartamos Banco. (2013). *Reporte anual 2013.* Author.

CONEVAL. (2012a). *CONEVAL - Informe de pobreza y evaluacion en el Estado de Jalisco 2012.* Author.

CONEVAL. (2012b). *Informe de pobreza y evaluacion en el Estado de Jalisco 2012.* Author.

CONEVAL. (2013). *Informe sobre la pobreza y evaluación en México.* Author.

Correa, F. Vasco, A. & Pérez, C. (2005). La curva medioambiental de Kuznets: evidencia empírica para Colombia. *Semestre económico, 8*(15), 13-30.

Cruz, C. (2006). Valoración de bienes y recursos ambientales y naturales: El problema de la medición. *Registro Colombia, 21*(2), 11–17.

Davis, K. (1973). The Case for and against business assumption of social responsibilities. *Academy of Management Journal, 16*(2), 312–322. doi:10.2307/255331

Fundacion Genetera. (2013). *Informe de Actividades.* Fundación Gentera.

Garriga, E., & Melé, D. (2004). Corporate social responsibility theories: Mapping the territory. *Journal of Business Ethics, 53*(1/2), 51–71. doi:10.1023/B:BUSI.0000039399.90587.34

Gudynas, E. (2009). La ecología política de la crisis global y los límites del capitalismo benévolo. *Iconos de Ciencias Sociales, 6*(36), 53–67.

Haneke, D., Glosw, R., & Hernand, S. (1998). Medio Ambiente y desarrollor sustentable. *Revista sustentable LDC, 3*(2), 18-24.

Hofstede, G. (1997). *Cultures and organization: Software of the mind.* New York: McGraw Hill.

INEGI. (2012). *Encuesta poblacion y vivienda.* INEGI.

Jamali, D., & Mirshak, R. (2007). Corporate social responsibility (CSR): Theory and practice in a developing country context. *Journal of Business Ethics, 72*(3), 243-262. doi: 10.1007A10551-006-9168-4

Lizarzaburu, E., & Del Brio, J. (2016). Responsabilidad social corporativa y reputación corporativa en el sector financiero de países en desarrollo. *GCG: Revista De Globalización. Competitividad & Gobernabilidad, 10*(1), 42–65. doi:10.3232/GCG.2016.V10.N1.02

Mahoney, J. (2012). *The theoretical building blocks of organizational economics. Economic Foundation of Strategy.* SAGE.

McGuire, J. W. (1963). *Business and society.* New York: McGraw-Hill.

McWilliams, A., Siegel, D. S., & Wright, P. M. (2006). Guest editors introduction: Corporate social responsibility: Strategic implications. *Journal of Management Studies, 43*(1), 1–18. doi:10.1111/j.1467-6486.2006.00580.x

Mintzberg, H., Quinn, J., & Voyer, J. (1997). Capítulo 4: Análisis de estratega a nivel empresa. En el proceso estratégico. Pearson.

OIT. (2007). *Organización Internacional del Trabajo, ¿Quiénes somos?* Recuperado de http://www.ilo.org/inform/online-information-resources/research-guides/lang--es/index.htm

Peng, M. (2012). *Global strategy*. Cincinnati, OH: Thomson South Western.

Peng, M. (2012). *Estrategia Global*. Queretaro, Mexico: Cengage.

Penrose, E. (1959). *The theory of the growth of the firm. Nueva York, EstadosUnidos*. John Wiley and Sons.

Programa Nacional de Financiamiento al Microempresario. (2014). *Benchmarking de las finanzas en México 2012-2013*. Author.

Ramasamy, B., & Yeung, M. (2009). Chinese consumers' perception of corporate social responsibility (CSR). *Journal of Business Ethics, 88*(S1), 119-132. doi: 10.1 007/sl 055 1 -008-9825-x

Salinas, C. (2007). El desarrollo Sustentable. *Memorias del Segundo Congreso de In- vestigación sobre Sustentabilidad y Calidad de Vida, UAEM, 2*(2), 12-21.

Schmidheiny, S. (2006, Spring). A view of corporate citizenship in Latin America. *Journal of Corporate Citizenship, 2006*(21), 21–24. doi:10.9774/GLEAF.4700.2006.sp.00004

Scott, W. (2013). Chapter 3: Crafting an analytic framework 1, Three pillars of institutions. Institution and organization, ideas, interest, and identities. SAGE cuarta edición.

SE. (2017). *Definición de Responsabilidad Social Empresarial*. Recuperado de https://www.gob.mx/se/articulos/responsabilidad-social-empresarial-32705

Simon, H. A. (1957). *Models of Man*. John Wiley.

United Nations. (2000). *Millennium Development Goals (MDGs)*. Author.

Vallaeys, F. (2012). Observatorio Regional de Responsabilidad Socila para America Latina y el Caribe. In *Observatorio Regional de Responsabilidad Socila para America Latina y el Caribe* (p. 13). IESALC-UNESCO.

Vargas-Hernández, J. G. (2014). *Capítulo VIII. ¿Cómo los agentes y como los administradores confunden las cosas? Teoría de la agencia. Gestión estratégica de organizaciones*. Buenos Aires, Argentina: Elaleph.

Vasal, V. (2009). Corporate Social Responsibility & Shareholder Returns - Evidence from the Indian Capital Market. *Indian Journal of Industrial Relations, 44*(3), 376–385. Recuperado de http://www.jstor.org/stable/27768210

Visser, W. (2008). Corporate Social Responsibility in Developing Countries. In A. Crane, A. McWilliams, D. Matten, J. Moon & D. Siegel (Eds.), The Oxford Handbook of Corporate Social Responsibility (pp. 473-499), Oxford, UK: Oxford University Press.

Williamson, O. (1979). Transaction cost economics: The governance of contractual relations. *Journal of Economics, 22*(2), 233–261. Recuperado de http://www.jstor.org/stable/725118

KEY TERMS AND DEFINITIONS

Borrowings: This is the amount of loan people takes from the bank.

Compartamos Banco: It is the largest bank in Mexico providing micro financial facilities.

Mean: This is the middle most value in a series of observations used in central tendency of a statistical data.

Microfinance: It is the small financial transactions targeted generally to the poor and backward classes of a country.

Operating Expenses: It takes into account all forms of costs in operating banking business.

Returns on Assets: It measures the amount of earning against the banking assets used for lending purposes.

Social Responsibility: It refers to maintaining the overall status of the people in a society through ensuring better livelihoods.

Section 2

Microfinance: A Weapon to Combat Poverty and Inequality in Countries

Chapter 9
Reflections on Microfinance:
Poverty Nexus From India – An Empirical Inquest

Sovik Mukherjee
Shri Shikshayatan College, India

Ramesh Chandra Das
Katwa College, India

ABSTRACT

Microfinance has become the latest buzzword in the credit markets where it shoulders the responsibility of alleviating poverty coupled with socio-economic development. Dealing with microfinance coupled with the issue of poverty reduction, the first concern is to handle the twin objectives of poverty alleviation and achievement of financial self-sufficiency, which are often at loggerheads. To begin with, the present chapter constructs a five-dimensional human poverty index (HPI) in terms of the rate of unemployment, state wise illiteracy rate, state-wise infant mortality rate, state-wise percentage of population below the poverty line, and the percentage of population not having an access to electricity for the states across India. Thus, this will serve as an index for the extent of poverty. Consequently, a fall in the value of the index actually implies poverty alleviation. This empirical model does not justify the hypothesis that "microfinance reduces poverty" at the macro level using cross-state panel data for India.

INTRODUCTION

If you think creating a world without any poverty is impossible; let's do it. Because it is the right thing to do.

The only place where poverty should be is in museums.

(Muhammad Yunus, as cited by Yunus Centre, 2011)

DOI: 10.4018/978-1-5225-5240-6.ch009

But are these words of Professor Yunus relevant in the Indian context given every 1 in 5 Indian is poor? Can microfinance institutions solve the problem? So it boils down to "credit" playing a vital role in rural development and poverty alleviation (Pitt & Khandker, 1998). Although the banking system has experienced phenomenal growth in terms of its geographical proliferation, creation of deposits, etc. bank credit remains on the whole inaccessible for the poor. After more than six decades of independence, the formal financial institutions have not been able to ensure better and uniform distribution of credit. The reluctance shown by the Indian poor to engage themselves in formal banking sector has made the things even more worse. A continuous tryst with poverty and lack of adequate rural credit were one of the major constraints in the economic upliftment of rural households in the pre globalization era. As history of development economics reveals in the Indian context that not all poverty eradication programs have been successful in reaching the poorest of the poor. But the microfinance revolution has come out as one of those gifted programmes which not only requires less investment but can also serve a sizeable portion of the poor that conventional banking generally finds unprofitable (Aghion & Morduch, 2004). Some recent statistics suggest that post globalization, there is a lot of enthusiasm that has been building up about a set of remarkable financial institutions flourishing in every nook and corner of the country. These institutions having a collective common goal of driving financial inclusion have all come together under the banner of "microfinance". Microfinance institutions (MFIs) at present span across the 29 States, 4 Union Territories and 588 districts in India. The reported 166 MFIs have a branch network of with 12,221 employees and has reached 39 million clients having an outstanding loan portfolio of Rs. 63,853 crore in 2016. This number of clients is the highest till date. This includes a managed portfolio of Rs. 16,914 crore. The average loan outstanding per borrower stood at Rs. 11,425 and 94 per cent of loans were used for income generation purposes. Interestingly, women borrowers constitute 97 per cent of the total clientele of MFIs. In terms of outreach and reaching out to clients is concerned, it grew by 8 per cent with the Southern region continuing to be the best performer followed by the Eastern region. In addition, growth rates have improved in the Northeastern and Central regions. Does it mean that poverty has gone down?

The main idea of the paper is to emphasize the role played by the formal Self Help Group (SHG) – Bank Linkage model in its pathway of poverty eradication which commenced with a set of guidelines issued by NABARD in 1992. Given this, Self Help Group Bank Linkage Programme (SBLP) is a modest step in bringing the "unbanked" poor to the formal banking system and generating healthier livelihood opportunities by means of access to credit from these financial institutions. Figure 1 clearly illustrates that the total number of SHGs saving-linked with banks stands at 16.3 lakhs with the savings amount of the SHGs linked with banks is Rs. 27582 crore. Even the non-performing assets of these MFIs have declined by 0.59 per cent as compared to 2015 (Sa-Dhan, 2016). With such impressive numbers, by this time, poverty should have come down at its minimum but table 1 tells something else. Poverty is such a deep rooted problem in the Indian context, the key is to re-examine the relationship between microfinance and poverty.

In spite of such a remarkable performance, there is still some doubt regarding the liaison between microfinance and poverty and this paper provides some new empirical evidence on the poverty-reducing effects of MFIs across states in India. The existing studies in the context of Asia have shown great disparity in terms of impact of microfinance having a considerable positive impact in Bangladesh to almost no effect in case of Thailand (Cull et al., 2009). Given this backdrop, this paper argues that the future innovations in the microfinance sector will have an impact on the financial condition of the poor households. In a country like India, poverty as a social evil has been grabbing the eyeballs of policy makers

Figure 1. Historical trend in number of SHGs and total bank loan disbursed
Source: Compiled from Sa-Dhan Report (2016)

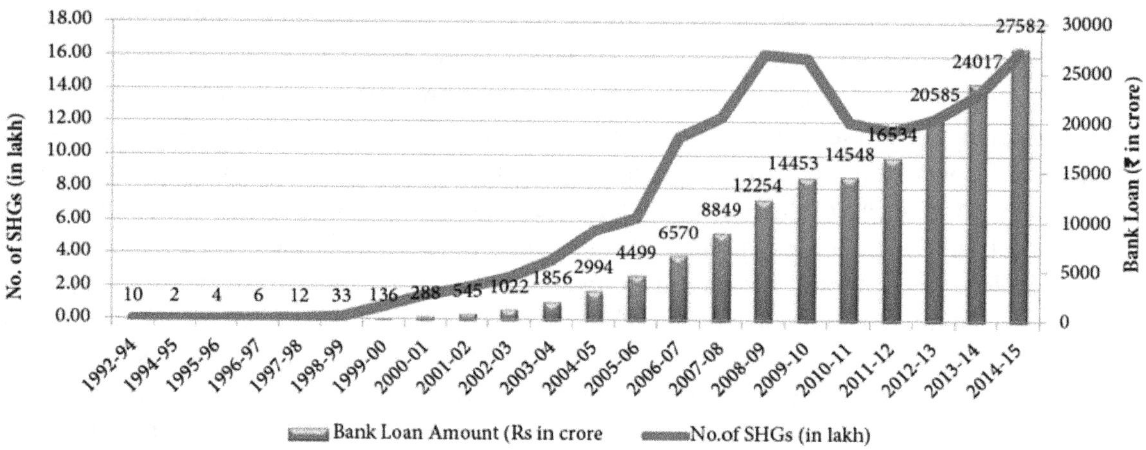

since independence. Talking about the incidence of poverty or for that matter severity does not matter much until and unless the multi-dimensional aspects get captured. To capture the multi-dimensional aspects of poverty, the authors here make use of five aspects, namely, the rate of unemployment, state wise illiteracy rate, state wise infant mortality rate, state wise percentage of population below the poverty line and percentage of population not having access to electricity for the states across India. In India, despite the surge in growth, the incidence of poverty in urban India is estimated at 14 per cent while it is 25 per cent in rural India with almost 80 per cent of India's poor living in the rural areas (Sa-Dhan, 2016). Going by the Planning Commission (2014) estimates, the proportion of persons below the poverty line has declined from around 36 per cent of the population in 1993-94 to 27.5 per cent in 2004-05 and to 21.92 per cent in 2012, India's foremost challenge in the 21st century is still poverty reduction. The World Bank's Global Monitoring Report (2015) even accredited India as the biggest contributor to the cause of poverty reduction between the years 2008 and 2011, with approximately 140 million people lifted out of absolute poverty.

Post globalization in the 1990s, the concept of MFIs on account of their better access to localities at the community level and the flexible use of peer group monitoring has made them to access the mass of populace with such ease. Also, the facts show that "micro-savings" have a special place for health and education of the kids of the depositors (Mosley & Arun, 2003). Given the figures reported in table 1, the authors have calculated the simple correlation i.e. 0.47 (although a crude measure) between the poverty head count ratio and the number of SHG members. This kind of reinforces the fact that indeed the focus variables of the paper are correlated to a certain extent. The maximum number of microfinance clients is found at Andhra Pradesh with a slightly more than 1.5 crore clients followed by Karnataka and West Bengal. While the lowest number of microfinance clients seen at Arunachal Pradesh. All Northeastern states have performed badly except Assam. But there is a wide range of variation in terms of performance across the states in India and this compels the authors to ask that whether microfinance reduces poverty across states in India and whether there exists a long run relation between the two. Interestingly, the empirical model used in this paper does not justify the hypothesis that "microfinance reduces poverty" at the macro level using cross-state panel data for India.

Table 1. Microfinance and poverty in India in 2012 as per Tendulkar methodology

States	Head Count Ratio (%)	No. of SHG members
Andhra Pradesh	9.20	10541557
Arunachal Pradesh	34.67	4004
Assam	31.98	1412034
Bihar	33.74	2461433
Chhattisgarh	39.93	1166945
Delhi*(Uninon Territory)	9.91	13377
Goa	5.09	39182
Gujarat	16.63	848016
Haryana	11.16	254553
Himachal Pradesh	8.06	240851
Jammu & Kashmir	10.35	29159
Jharkhand	36.96	751530
Karnataka	20.91	6889389
Kerala	7.05	1863654
Madhya Pradesh	31.65	1269073
Maharashtra	17.35	2632136
Manipur	36.89	34411
Meghalaya	11.87	24752
Mizoram	20.40	14820
Nagaland	18.88	18252
Odisha	32.59	3068546
Punjab	8.26	205985
Rajasthan	14.71	1554891
Sikkim	8.19	7917
Tamil Nadu	11.28	5552989
Tripura	14.05	83343
Uttar Pradesh	11.26	2914145
Uttaranchal	29.43	346645
West Bengal	19.98	7606508
All India	**21.92**	58086340

Source: Compiled from Planning Commission data book (2014) and NABARD's Sa-Dhan Report (2014)

The rest of the chapter has been organized as follows; The immediate next section presents an outline of the related literature, both theory and empirics. The following section looks at the derivation of the five dimensional Human Poverty Index in India in the present context. In the subsequent section, the empirical model coupled with the methodology and the results have been discussed thereof. The last section concludes the entire study.

A BRIEF REVIEW OF THE SELECT LITERATURE

The conflicting views regarding the assessment of microfinance projects on poverty eradication makes it even more interesting as an area of research. It is commonly asserted that MFIs are not reaching the poorest of the poor in the society. Nonetheless, despite some skepticist remarks made by researchers about the impact of microfinance on poverty reduction, studies have shown that microfinance has been successful in many situations. According to Littlefield et al. (2003), projects across countries like India, Indonesia, Zimbabwe, Bangladesh and Uganda show very positive effects of microfinance in reducing poverty. Contrary to this argument, Dichter (1999) in his paper shows that microfinance does not have any positive influence on poverty reduction. Hulme and Mosley (1996) in their study across the different levels of income across seven countries which include India, Bangladesh, Sri Lanka, Bolivia, Indonesia, Malawi and Kenya. They make a case that microfinance programmes can improve the income levels of the middle class and the poor and can move them out of poverty. So these credit schemes are influential in nature. In their book, Johnson and Rogaly (1997) in the context of Asian countries also refer to examples whereby savings and credit schemes were able to meet the needs of the poorest of the poor. They state that microfinance programmes are being designed in a way so that they improve the level of economic security rather than income generation. In the context of Bangladesh, Chowdhury and Bhuiya (2004) comment that — "Bangladesh Rural Advancement Committee (BRAC's) poverty alleviation programmes involved seven dimensions of "human well-being", *viz.,* provision of microfinance, training of clients on human rights, child survival rates, higher nutritional status, improvement in the basic level of education, and increased networking in the community." Their results stressed on the fact that "children of BRAC clients suffered from far less protein-energy malnutrition than children of non-members, and the educational performance of BRAC member's children was also higher than that of children in non-BRAC households.

From the cross country studies the authors now shift their focus on studies in the Indian context. Kamath et al., (2013) carried out a study on how the daily household cash flows for 90 poor households in Ramanagaram, Karnataka. The results make a comparison between the cash flows of households with MFI loans and without MFI loans. In the same spirit, Sarmah and Das (2012) attempt to analyze socio-economic upliftment of the poor people in the Lakhimpur District of Assam in the backdrop of the performance of Self-Help Groups (SHG). This study was based on a primary survey of 250 respondents and concluded that after joining the SHGs the income of the poor people has increased and hence a positive correlation. Mula (2012) made an attempt to relate economic growth and promotion of SHGs in the backdrop of the performance of financial institution in microfinance in Cooch Bihar District, West Bengal. Their study opined that in spite of showing slower growth the district took the second position among the other districts in West Bengal in terms of credit linkage. There is already a flourishing literature on the varied aspects of microfinance in the Indian context. The authors here will review only a few recent selected ones which are closely related in this context as it is not possible to report each and every single study. The research findings by Ranjani (2012) summarizes the need for conceptual framework for the regulation of MFI in India will not only do good to the customers but also the industry at large when they subject themselves to both "self and statuary regulations". To resolve poverty related issues and ensure the protection of the consumers Sane and Thomas (2013) concentrate on the modification of the micro-prudential regulations. Their results echo the one proposed by Ranjani (2012). Talking about the situation of microfinance in India, Nasir (2013) tries to outline the mechanism through which cost effectiveness can be achieved in credit delivery and reaching out to the poor. There are studies which have also given emphasis to improving the effectiveness of microfinancing and microinsurance in achieving the socio-economic goals of poverty alleviation, women empowerment and development of rural poor in India (Vichore & Deshpande, 2012; Vijender et al., 2012). Theoretically, Kundu (2011) makes use of a two stage game to study the impact of microfinance when principal's role is taken up by a commercial bank and government. Even studies have compared India's case with that of Bangladesh (the Mecca of microfinance). Tiwari (2012) made a comparative analysis between India and Bangladesh highlighting that social protection programs conducive to the political environment have a greater significance in reducing poverty in India as compared to Bangladesh. There are many more studies pertaining to microfinance and some have been cited in the additional readings section for further reference). Again going back to cross country studies in a different context, Barinaga (2013) describes the influence of microfinance as a tool to work with susceptible groups (lying at the bottom of the income pyramid) in Sweden and shows that mobilization of social capital through microfinance is actually possible. Banerjee et al., (2013) went on to study the first randomized evolution of the impact of introducing standard microcredit group-based lending product in Hyderabad, India. The results said something very contradictory as they did not notice any significant impact on the development outcomes on account of microfinance programmes including health, education, and women empowerment. This paper tries to develop a kind of multi-dimensional poverty index (five dimensions) and then tries to relate poverty reduction to the extent of members participating in the SHGs as a proxy for penetration and outreach of microfinance in a panel data setup. The novelty of this paper lies in the construction of a five dimensional human poverty index using Principal Component Analysis (PCA). This paper makes a modest attempt to construct such an index which has so far not figured in the existing literature and then apply panel causality and cointegrating techniques to relate the focus variables econometrically.

FIVE DIMENSIONAL HUMAN POVERTY INDEX (HPI): METHODOLOGY

Keeping in mind the importance of this issue, the research objective of this section is to estimate the human poverty index for the periods between 1993 to 2015 by compiling data across all the major states in India. The idea is to determine the position of the states in 2015 with respect to poverty in terms of the five dimensions discussed below. The data has been compiled from — www.indexmundi.com, www.indiastat.com, *Planning Commission database* and the Ministry of Statistics and Programme Implementation (MOSPI) site at http://www.mospi.gov.in/data, NSSO reports for various rounds and NABARD's reports for various years. For only some states the data were not available for every year particularly the state illiteracy rates and number of SHG members, thus it had to be accordingly interpolated using Newton's interpolation formula (Refer to key words definitions for details). This paper follows the linear interpolation techniques as used by Alimukhamedova (2014). The present article has collated the data for 28 states in India with respect to five parameters over a period of 23 years, *viz.*,

1. Rate of unemployment (G_1);
2. Illiteracy rate (G_2);
3. State wise infant mortality rate (G_3);
4. Percentage of population below the poverty line (G_4);
5. Percentage of population not having access to electricity for the states across India (G_5);

The authors wanted to construct a poverty index which not only takes into account deprivation in terms of income but also in terms of health, education and energy following the standard Senian methodology. This index should be in terms of deprivation and not attainment levels. Hence, Human Development Index style of formulation is not the methodology to be used. Also, this index is different from the standard human poverty index as it not only takes into account an additional component in terms of energy poverty but also moves away from equal weightage representation and endogenizes the weights. The issues related to the weighting scheme has been subsequently discussed. Since all these variables augment poverty levels, given the theoretical concepts, a unit rise in the value of any of these variables will lead to an increase in the overall value of this five dimensional poverty index.

Following the concept of Human Poverty Index formula, propounded by Anand and Sen (1997), the authors consider the following deprivation index function for a particular state,

$$DI_j(\alpha) = \left[\frac{\sum w_i G^\alpha{}_i}{\sum w_i}\right]^{\frac{1}{\alpha}} \tag{1}$$

where, $G_i = i^{th}$ source of deprivation in the jth state, α here stands for the order of the average, w_i be the weights attached to G_i parameter, $i = 1, 2, 3, 4, 5$ in the jth state. Equation (1) does follow some important properties of a good index but it needs to be mentioned that $DI(\alpha)$ suffers from the problems of overlapping dimensions and multi-collinearity (Roy & Haldar, 2010). To solve such a problem, employing Principal Component Analysis (PCA) is the best procedure. The weights attached to each of the deprivation parameters are not arbitrarily given; it is determined endogenously from the data matrix through PCA (Bhattacharya & Haldar, 2014). These weights are given by the eigen values equivalent to the principal components that have been extracted.

That is, $w_i = \dfrac{\lambda_i}{\sum \lambda_i}$

α can be termed as 'Benthamite – Rawlsian factor' which corresponds to 'average' rule where the five dimension human poverty is average deprivation across dimensions and with maximum, that is, $\alpha \rightarrow$ infinity, reduces to the 'Rawlsian rule' where the HPI index is identified with the dimension having the maximum deprivation. The authors make an assumption that the value of $\alpha = 2$. There is a justification for considering $\alpha = 2$ as it corresponds to Euclidean distance, i.e., common understanding of distance. In addition to this, it is justified on the ground that higher weight is attached to the more deprived dimension (Reddy & Nathan, 2011). Now, the question is how many PCAs to extract? In this article, the authors have extracted two PCs based on Scree Test criteria. The Scree-Plot criterion, proposed by Cattell (1966), plots the successive eigen values, which drop off sharply and then tend to level off and thus become flat (Dunteman, 1989). The elbow rule suggests retaining all the eigen values in the sharp descent before the first one on the line where they start to level off. This implies that the eigen values on the line before they start to level off explain a major proportion of the variability while the others explain only a negligible portion and are likely to be unimportant (Mukherjee, 2017). The results show that the first principal component explains 69 per cent of the total variance whereas the second principal component explains 28 per cent of the total variance and together they have explained almost 97 per cent of the total variance. In addition to the Scree Test criteria, the authors have employed

Table 2. Kaiser method results

Principal Component	Eigen Value
1	3.451
2	1.412
3	0.137

Source: Computed by the authors in SPSS 20

the Kaiser (1958) method of retaining those components having eigen values greater than one. So, table 2 shows results consistent with the Scree Plot criteria fact there should be precisely two principal components in this particular analysis. Therefore, it is possible to represent the states' deprivation position in a reduced space dimension with limited loss of information.

The five dimensional Human Poverty Index for the jth state has the form of –

$$DI_j(\alpha) = \left[\left(\frac{w_1}{w_1 + w_2} \right) \left\{ \left(PC_1 \right)_j \right\}^{\alpha} + \left(\frac{w_2}{w_1 + w_2} \right) \left\{ \left(PC_2 \right)_j \right\}^{\alpha} \right]^{\frac{1}{\alpha}} \qquad (2)$$

The states have been ranked on the basis of the five dimensional HPI to find out which state's performance is the best and which ones have lagged behind.

Findings

From the methodological framework discussed in the previous section, the results have been reported in table 3. It should be noted that the list excludes the union territories.

The next part of the analysis is mainly concerned with the liaison between the extent of poverty and the number of SHGs. For that first of all, the number of SHGs which is an absolute number had to be normalized using the following formula for comparison purpose,

$$X_{iN} = \frac{\left(X_i - X_{\min} \right)}{\left(X_{\max} - X_{\min} \right)}$$

X_{iN} is the normalized value, X_{min} is the minimum value observed across the 28 states considered for number of SHGs, X_{max} is the maximum value observed across the 28 states for number of SHGs and X_i is the value of number of SHGs for state i. Normalization yields a value for every parameter for every state which lies between 0 and 1. The value '0' depicts the worst case and '1' depicts the best case scenario. The more the value is the higher will be the merit ranking.

To explain the four quadrant diagram in figure 2, first, quadrant I stands for states having both HPI value and index of SHGs value greater than the average. Second, quadrant II shows states having index of SHGs value greater than the average but HPI value less the average. Reaching quadrant II is the desired goal for any state as this is the optimization quadrant. Quadrant IV is just the opposite of quadrant II and is never desirable. But quadrant III is also not desirable given that states having lower index of

Table 3. PGDI scores: A state level study for 2014-2015

State	HPI Score (2015)	Rank
Andhra Pradesh	0.56	25
Arunachal Pradesh	0.68	28
Assam	0.54	24
Bihar	0.67	27
Chhattisgarh	0.38	14
Goa	0.21	3
Gujarat	0.17	1
Haryana	0.32	11
Himachal Pradesh	0.61	26
Jammu & Kashmir	0.29	8
Jharkhand	0.41	18
Karnataka	0.23	5
Kerala	0.19	2
Madhya Pradesh	0.38	14
Maharashtra	0.44	21
Manipur	0.40	17
Meghalaya	0.33	12
Mizoram	0.42	19
Nagaland	0.31	10
Orissa	0.51	22
Punjab	0.26	7
Rajasthan	0.29	8
Sikkim	0.38	14
Tamil Nadu	0.25	6
Tripura	0.33	12
Uttar Pradesh	0.51	22
Uttarakhand	0.42	19
West Bengal	0.22	4

Source: Computed by the authors

SHGs values and also lower HPI values. Quadrant III is still preferable but quadrant IV is strictly sub-optimal. Coming to the results derived in this paper, Karnataka, Kerala, Tamil Nadu and West Bengal have lived up to their expectations. States like Arunachal Pradesh, Assam, Himachal Pradesh, Jharkhand, Manipur, Mizoram, Uttarakhand have poverty head count ratio on the lower side but in terms of rates of unemployment, illiteracy rates and access to electricity these have lost out. Chhattisgarh, Goa, Gujarat, Haryana, Jammu & Kashmir, Madhya Pradesh, Meghalaya, Nagaland, Punjab, Rajasthan, Sikkim, Tripura all lie in quadrant III. These states kind of provide a contradiction that one can reduce poverty but at the same time that poverty reduction drive is not driven by the influence of microfinance institutions.

Figure 2. The four quadrant diagram — where the states stand in terms of HPI and No. of SHG members_2014-15

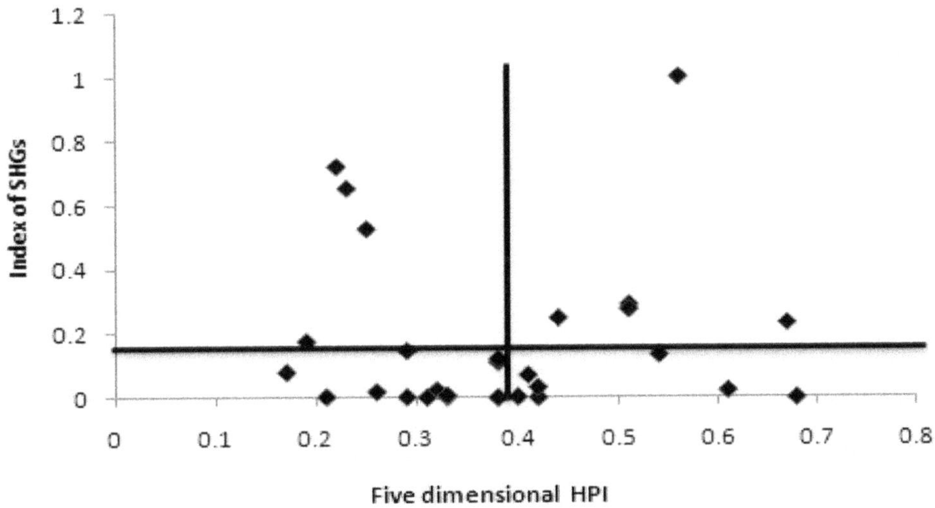

So, again the authors' ask this question that whether there exists any relation between poverty reduction and influence of microfinance institutions?

It is interesting to note that the results in table 3 show that Gujarat is the best state in terms of poverty reduction but with respect to proliferation of SHGs, it has not performed that well. States like Maharashtra and Andhra Pradesh have performed above expectations but in terms of the five dimensional poverty indices their scores are very high indicating a sub optimal performance. For Maharashtra, the unemployment rate per 1000 employable persons is 21 per cent which is low compared to other states but Maharashtra has lost out in terms of having access to electricity and infant mortality rate. It is indeed a

Table 4.

Quadrant I	*Quadrant II*	*Quadrant III*	*Quadrant IV*
Andhra Pradesh	Karnataka	Chhattisgarh	Arunachal Pradesh
Bihar	Kerala	Goa	Assam
Maharashtra	Tamil Nadu	Gujarat	Himachal Pradesh
Orissa	West Bengal	Haryana	Jharkhand
Uttar Pradesh		Jammu & Kashmir	Manipur
		Madhya Pradesh	Mizoram
		Meghalaya	Uttarakhand
		Nagaland	
		Punjab	
		Rajasthan	
		Sikkim	
		Tripura	

Source: Based on authors' calculations

Figure 3. Movement in the five-dimensional HPI between 2009-2015 (All India)
Source: Based on authors' calculations

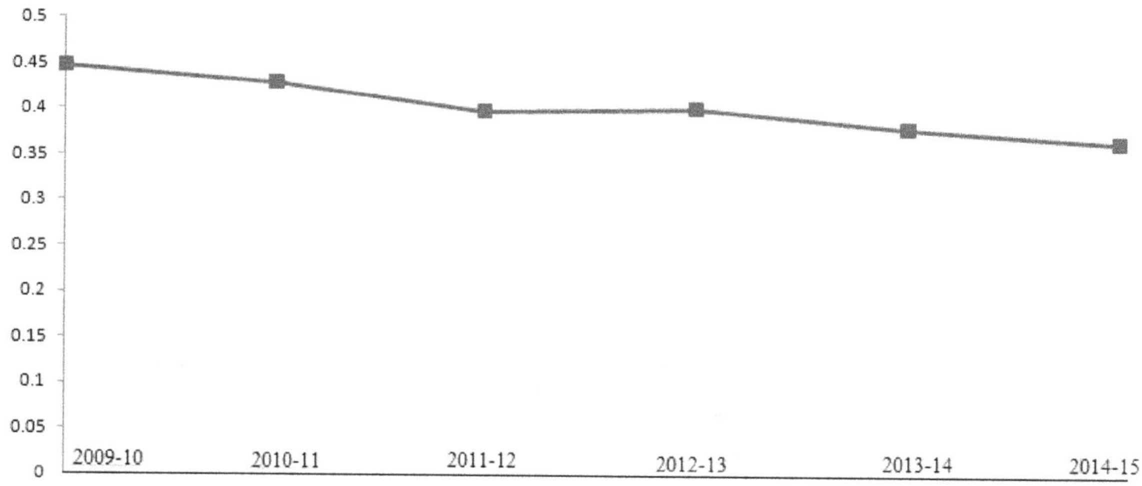

tough job for the policy makers to formulate policies which would not only reduce poverty but also bring in a role for microfinance. Given the variation in the results across the states in India, the model states can be Kerala, Karnataka, West Bengal and Tamil Nadu. Shifting focus to figure 3 it is obvious that the five dimensional HPI has over the years declined slightly and is mostly stagnant. The poverty figures have fallen indeed but have the multi-dimensional poverty figures gone down? The answer is a big no.

THE EMPIRICAL FRAMEWORK

Econometric Methodology

Before starting off with the panel unit root tests, the heteroskedasticity needs to be looked at. The Chi-Square value of 20.21 in table 5 is low and lies within the confidence limits and the results unquestionably endorse the nonexistence of heteroskedasticity as the null hypothesis of "constant variance in the model" holds good.

Levin, Lin and Chu (LLC) unit root tests have been used in this study. The test is based on their model given below:

$$\Delta y_{it} = \alpha_i y_{it-1} + \sum_{j=1}^{p_j} \beta_{ij} \Delta y_{it-j} + x_{it}' \delta + \varepsilon_{it}$$

Table 5. Heteroskedasticity results

Likelihood-Ratio Test		
H_0: Constant variance	LR Chi-Square value (χ^2)	Probability > Chi-Square (χ^2)
	20.21	0.95*

Notes: * denotes significance at 95 per cent level and calculation has been done by the authors in Stata 12

Here, α_i is the error correction term and consequently, the null hypothesis of non-stationarity is as follows:

Tests hypotheses:

H_0: $\alpha_i = 0$ for all the cross section units, so the series is non-stationary and has a unit root.

H_1: $\alpha_i < 0$ for at least one cross section unit, so the series is trend stationary.

When the probability value obtained from the test results is smaller than 0.05, H_0 is rejected and the stationarity of the series gets determined. LLC panel unit root test results that I have got are reported in table 5. As Levin, Lin and Chu (2002) have pointed out; this test-statistic performs well when N lies between 10 and 250 and when T lies between 5 and 250. To determine whether a cointegrating relationship exists or not, the methodology proposed by Pedroni (1999) has been employed. Fundamentally, it employs four panel statistics and three group panel statistics to test the null hypothesis of no cointegration against the alternative hypothesis of cointegration. The first set is the within-dimension approach comprising of four statistics that are: panel v-statistic, panel ρ-statistic, panel PP-statistic and the panel ADF-statistic (Pedroni, 1999).

The first set pools the autoregressive coefficients across various members for the unit root tests to be carried out on the estimated residuals. The second set of statistics, centered on the between-dimensional approach, includes three statistics that are respectively the group ρ-statistic, group PP-statistic and group ADF-statistic (Mukherjee, 2017). If the variables are not 'cointegrated' it means that the residuals are not I(0). These estimators are based on Monte Carlo simulations and the details for these calculations are given in the original paper (Refer to Pedroni, 1999). If the null hypothesis is rejected in the panel case, then the variables in question are cointegrated for all the 28 states considered. On the other hand, if the null is rejected in the group panel case, then cointegration among the relevant variables exists for at least one of the states.

The VECM framework used is given as follows.

$$\Delta MFIN_{i,t} = \alpha_{1,i} + \varphi_{1,i} ECT_{i,t} + \sum_{j=1}^{k} \beta_{1,j,i} \Delta HPI_{i,t-j} + \sum_{j=1}^{k} v_{1,j,i} \Delta MFIN_{i,t-j} + \varepsilon_{1,i,t}$$

$$\Delta HPI_{i,t} = \alpha_{2,i} + \varphi_{2,i} ECT_{i,t} + \sum_{j=1}^{k} \beta_{2,j,i} \Delta HPI_{i,t-j} + \sum_{j=1}^{k} v_{2,j,i} \Delta MFIN_{i,t-j} + \varepsilon_{2,i,t}$$

Where i ($i = 1,...N$) denotes the state, t ($t = 1,...T$) the period, j is the optimum lag considering the Akaike Information Criteria (AIC). ECT is the lagged error correction term derived from the long-run co-integrating relationship; the φ_1 and φ_2 are the adjustment coefficients; $\varepsilon_{1,i,t}$ and $\varepsilon_{2,i,t}$ are disturbance terms assumed to be white-noises and hence uncorrelated. The focus variables of this paper are the number of SHG members and the five dimensional HPI. The coefficients on ECTs represent how fast the deviations from the long-run equilibrium are eliminated pursuing a change in each of these variables.

If the ECT's coefficients are zero i.e. $\varphi_{1,i} = 0$ or $\varphi_{2,i} = 0$ for all $i \Rightarrow$ then there is no error correction and thus there exists no cointegration.

But if, $\varphi_{1,i} < 0$ or $\varphi_{2,i} < 0$ then there exists error correction and consequently cointegration.

Now, the authors move on to the causality issue in case of panel data. Given that, this analysis is being carried out across the 28 states in India over a period of 23 years, the assumptions that coefficients are different across cross-sections follows from Dumitrescu and Hurlin (2012), i.e.

$\beta_{1,i} \neq \beta_{1,j}, \ldots \beta_{p,i} \neq \beta_{p,j}$ & $\eta_{1,i} \neq \eta_{1,j}, \ldots \eta_{p,i} \neq \eta_{p,j}$ for all i and j.

Bivariate regressions in Dumitrescu and Hurlin (2012) take the form with k lags,

$$y_{i,t} = \alpha_{0,i} + \sum_{p=1}^{k} \alpha_{p,i} y_{i,t-p} + \sum_{p=1}^{k} \beta_{p,i} x_{i,t-p} + \varepsilon_{i,t}$$

$$x_{i,t} = \mu_{0,i} + \sum_{p=1}^{k} \mu_{p,i} x_{i,t-p} + \sum_{p=1}^{k} \eta_{p,i} y_{i,t-p} + e_{i,t} \text{ where,}$$

t denotes the time period dimension of the panel, and i denotes the cross-sectional dimension and k is the number of lags. This assumption is appropriate for the states in India contrary to the assumption where the panel gets treated as one large stacked data set. Therefore, the target is to perform Granger causality regressions for each and every individual cross-sectional ingredient. Subsequently, take the average of the Wald statistics derived from each cross section to get the *W-bar* statistic.

RESULTS AND DISCUSSION

Table 6 presents the results of the Levin, Lin, Chu (LLC) unit root tests. The results indicate that both variables are stationary after first differencing. In other word, both variables are integrated of order (1). Hence, we can apply the procedure of Pedroni (1999) to look into the cointegration possibility between the focus variables. In this study, given the AIC criteria, an optimum lag of 1 has been considered. The results in table 7 designate the existence of a cointegrated relationship between health spending and per-capita economic growth in the long run. Under the alternative hypothesis, the panel-v statistic diverges to positive infinity (∞^{+}), and the right-hand tail of the standard normal distribution has been used to reject the null hypothesis. However, all the other panel cointegration test statistics diverge to negative infinity (∞^{-}). Thus, the left-hand tail of the standard normal distribution is used to reject the null hypothesis (Mukherjee, 2017). Here, the authors have found a strong evidence of panel cointegration as the test statistic values lie in the critical region (be it right-hand tail or left-hand tail) and the null hypothesis of 'no cointegration' gets resoundingly rejected.

This tests that whether MFIN and HPI follows a unit root process or not. At the level value, the approximate p-value for MFIN and HPI is 0.55 and 0.21 respectively. So, the null hypothesis of existence of unit root cannot be rejected. This makes the authors to carry out the first of the data and the results

Table 6. LLC Unit Root Test Results

Variables	Level	Probability	1st Difference	Probability	Result
MFIN	0.44	0.55	-3.98	0.00*	Integrated of order 1
HPI	-0.75	0.21	-5.31	0.00*	Integrated of order 1

Notes: * denotes significance at 95 per cent level and calculation has been done by the authors in Eviews-7

Table 7. Panel cointegration test

Test Procedure	Test Statistic	Probability Value	Result
Panel v-statistic	2.28	0.00*	Cointegration
Panel rho-statistic	-3.11	0.00*	Cointegration
Panel PP-statistic	-4.08	0.00*	Cointegration
Panel ADF-statistic	-3.31	0.00*	Cointegration
Group rho-statistic	-4.56	0.00*	Cointegration
Group PP-statistic	-3.01	0.00*	Cointegration
Group ADF-statistic	-7.22	0.00*	Cointegration

Notes: * denotes significance at 95 per cent level and calculation has been done by the authors in Eviews-7

suggest that the both the MFIN and HPI series become stationary at first order. The p-value of 0.00 implies that the null hypothesis of presence of unit root gets rejected. But the presence of cointegration does not guarantee the existence of causality between the concerned variables in this section. The results of the test for causality are reported in table 8.

The authors have found only one cointegrating vector. The normalized cointegrating relation is given by —

$$MFIN = 1.01HPI + 0.04HPI_{-1} \tag{3}$$

This is justified because given the fact that if the five dimensional poverty index rises by 1 unit then approximately 1 new member joins the SHG programme. Surprisingly, the results in table 7 states that when new members join the SHG programme or in fact there is an increase in the penetration and out-reach of MFIs, there is no impact on poverty reduction. This result justifies the fact that why a majority of the states were located in quadrant III and I in figure 2. It is an indication of the fact that joining SHG

Table 8. Results of Panel Causality Test

Null Hypothesis	W-bar Statistic	Probability
MFIN does not Granger Cause HPI	1.17	0.12
HPI does not Granger Cause MFIN	5.60	0.00*

Notes: * denotes significance at 95 per cent level and calculation has been done by the authors in Eviews-7

programmes does not guarantee a fall in the poverty index value. Also, states like Andhra Pradesh, Bihar, Maharashtra, Orissa and Uttar Pradesh doing so well in terms of mobilizing microfinance participation can not reduce poverty. That means that it is not only income poverty that needs to be looked at but also human developmental parameters like literacy, unemployment rates, access to electricity, etc. have to be taken into consideration for poverty reduction. Therefore, the unilateral causality running from HPI to MFIN is justified.

CONCLUSION

To sum up, studies like Khadker (2005) and Gaiha et al. (2009) have powerfully stressed on the positive effects of microfinance on poverty reduction. But as per this analysis it can be said that the so called "magic" of microfinance is fizzling out. The findings of such negligible or almost no impact on poverty reduction is simply turning the tide against it. One can criticze the study on account of the lack of variables which may have been potential determinants of access to MFIs but one can always extend this model by either incorporating gross loan portfolio of MFIs. The authors could not consider gross loan portfolio of MFIs across states in India on account of the lack of availability of data from 1993 onwards. But for cross country studies gross loan portfolio can be an important factor and reexamining this liaison will be worth it. The paper talks about a five dimensional HPI which is something new in the Indian context. Again, the five dimension index can be extended by adding other variables like access to safe drinking water or for that matter per capita consumption expenditure along with poverty based tension (Kakwani & Son, 2016). The authors believe that reaching the poor without the use of proper ICT techniques is kind of baseless irrespective of what the number articulate. Moreover, poverty is not only income poverty *per se* but multi-dimensional in nature so targeting only the incomes of the poorest of the poor household won't mean much. In conclusion, microfinance is lacking the "magic" and has gone off the mark, if not largely mistaken.

REFERENCES

Alimukhamedova, N. (2014). *Measuring the Impact of Microfinance* (Doctoral dissertation). Retrieved from https://is.cuni.cz/webapps/zzp/download/140035583

Anand, S., & Sen, A. (1997). Concepts or Human Development and Poverty! A Multidimensional Perspective. *United Nations Development Programme, Poverty and human development: Human development papers*, 1-20.

Banerjee, A., Duflo, E., Glennerster, R., & Kinnan, C. (2015). The miracle of microfinance? Evidence from a randomized evaluation. *American Economic Journal. Applied Economics*, *7*(1), 22–53. doi:10.1257/app.20130533

Barinaga, E. (2013). Introducing micro-finance in Sweden. *Journal of the International Academy for Case Studies*, *19*(3), 33–44.

Bhattacharya, G., & Haldar, S. K. (2014). Trend, Differential and Determinants of Deprivation of Reproductive and Child Health in the Districts of West Bengal, India. *Journal of Health Management, 16*(1), 93–112. doi:10.1177/0972063413518686

Cattell, R. B. (1966). The scree test for the number of factors. *Multivariate Behavioral Research, 1*(2), 245–276. doi:10.120715327906mbr0102_10 PMID:26828106

Chowdhury, A. M. R., & Bhuiya, A. (2004). The wider impacts of BRAC poverty alleviation programme in Bangladesh. *Journal of International Development, 16*(3), 369–386. doi:10.1002/jid.1083

Cull, R., Demirgüç-Kunt, A., & Morduch, J. (2009). Microfinance meets the market. In *Moving Beyond Storytelling: Emerging Research in Microfinance* (pp. 1–30). Emerald Group Publishing Limited. doi:10.1108/S1569-3759(2009)0000092004

De Aghion, B. A., & Morduch, J. (2004). Microfinance: Where do we stand? In *Financial development and economic growth* (pp. 135–148). Palgrave Macmillan. doi:10.1057/9780230374270_5

Dichter, T. W. (1999). Globalization and its effects on NGOs: Efflorescence or a blurring of roles and relevance?. *Nonprofit and Voluntary Sector Quarterly, 28*(1_suppl), 38-58.

Dumitrescu, E. I., & Hurlin, C. (2012). Testing for Granger non-causality in heterogeneous panels. *Economic Modelling, 29*(4), 1450–1460. doi:10.1016/j.econmod.2012.02.014

Gaiha, R., Imai, K., & Nandhi, M. Adhi. (2009). Millennium development goal of halving poverty in Asia: Progress, prospects and priorities. *Journal of Asian and African Studies, 44*(2), 215–237. doi:10.1177/0021909608101411

Hulme, D., & Mosley, P. (1996). *Finance against poverty* (Vol. 2). Psychology Press.

Johnson, S., & Rogaly, B. (1997). *Microfinance and poverty reduction*. Oxfam. doi:10.3362/9780855988005

Kaiser, H. F. (1958). The varimax criterion for analytic rotation in factor analysis. *Psychometrika, 23*(3), 187–200. doi:10.1007/BF02289233

Kakwani, N., & Son, H. H. (2016). Measuring Social Tension. In *Social Welfare Functions and Development* (pp. 45–76). Palgrave Macmillan. doi:10.1057/978-1-137-58325-3_3

Kamath, R., Dattasharma, A., & Ramanathan, S. (2013). *MFI (Microfinance Institutes) Borrowers: Their loans and Repayments – A study in Ramanagaram, India.* Working Paper No. 397. Indian Institute of Management, Bangalore.

Khandker, S. R. (2005). Microfinance and poverty: Evidence using panel data from Bangladesh. *The World Bank Economic Review, 19*(2), 263–286. doi:10.1093/wber/lhi008

Kundu, A. (2011). Savings, lending rate and skill improvement in microfinance operating through public-private cooperation. *IUP Journal of Managerial Economics, 9*(4), 33–52.

Levin, A., Lin, C. F., & Chu, C. S. J. (2002). Unit root tests in panel data: Asymptotic and finite- sample properties. *Journal of Econometrics, 108*(1), 1–24. doi:10.1016/S0304-4076(01)00098-7

Littlefield, E., Morduch, J., & Hashemi, S. (2003). Is microfinance an effective strategy to reach the Millennium Development Goals? *Focus note, 24*(2003), 1-11.

Mosley, P., & Arun, T. (2003). *Improving access to rural finance in India: Supply side constraints.* Unpublished background paper to the economic and sector work study on access to finance. Washington, DC: World Bank, South Asia Finance and Private Sector Development Unit.

Mukherjee, S. (2017). Anatomy and Significance of Public Healthcare Expenditure and Economic Growth Nexus in India: Its Implications for Public Health Infrastructure Thereof. In *Social, Health, and Environmental Infrastructures for Economic Growth* (pp. 120–144). IGI Global. doi:10.4018/978-1-5225-2364-2.ch007

Mukherjee, S. (2017). India's Looming Power Crisis and the Way Forward: An Ode to Sustainability. *International Journal of Sustainable Economies Management, 6*(1), 64–81. doi:10.4018/ijsem.2017010104

Mula, G. (2012). Micro finance scenario of eastern part of India under SGSY. *ARPN Journal of Agricultural and Biological Science, 7*(3), 182–187.

NABARD. (n.d.). *Micro-Credit Innovation Department.* Retrieved from https://www.nabard.org/english/shgs.aspx

Nasir, S. (2013). Microfinance in India: Contemporary issues and challenges. *Middle East Journal of Scientific Research, 15*(2), 191–199.

Pedroni, P. (1999). Critical values for cointegration tests in heterogeneous panels with multiple regressors. *Oxford Bulletin of Economics and Statistics, 61*(S1), 653–670. doi:10.1111/1468-0084.61.s1.14

Pitt, M. M., & Khandker, S. R. (1998). The impact of group-based credit programs on poor households in Bangladesh: Does the gender of participants matter? *Journal of Political Economy, 106*(5), 958–996. doi:10.1086/250037

Planning Commission. (2014). *Data-book Compiled for Use of Planning Commission.* New Delhi: Planning Commission, Government of India.

Ranjani, K. S. (2012). Regulating Microfinance Institutions in India: A Conceptual Framework. *Synergy 10*(1), 51-62.

Reddy, B. S., & Nathan, H. S. K. (2011). *Emerging Energy Insecurity - The Indian Dimension.* Academic Press.

Roy, K., & Haldar, S. K. (2010). Measuring Poverty and Socio-Economic Deprivation Inequalities in India at Sub-National Level. *Asia-Pacific Social Science Review, 10*(1).

Sa-Dhan. (2014). *The Bharat microfinance report 2014.* Accessed at http://www.sa-dhan.net/Resources/Finale%20Report.pdf

Sa-Dhan. (2016). *The Bharat microfinance report 2016.* Accessed at https://www.microfinancegateway.org/ sites/ default/ files/ publication_files/ the_ bharat_microfinance_report_2016-min.pdf

Sane, R., & Thomas, S. (2013). Regulating microfinance institutions. *Economic and Political Weekly, 18*(5), 59–67.

Sarmah, G. N., & Das, D. K. (2012). Micro finance, self help groups (SHGS) and the Socio- Economic development of rural people (A case study with special reference to the Lakhimpur district of Assam). *Asian Journal of Research in Business Economics and Management, 2*(4), 145–159.

Tiwari, A. (2012). Is microfinance working for what it is meant to be? A comparative study on Bangladesh and India. *ZENITH International Journal of Multidisciplinary Research, 2*(3), 148–164.

Vichore, S., & Deshpande, S. (2012). Microfinance in India — A comprehensive analysis of the growth and performance MFIs. *Research Journal of Social Science and Management, 2*(1), 51–56.

Vijender, A., Rachna, A., & Parul, K. (2012). Micro finance and risk management for poor in India. *Research Journal of Recent Sciences, 1*(2), 104–107.

World Bank. (2015). *Global Monitoring Report 2015/16*. Accessed at http://www.worldbank.org/en/publication/global-monitoring-report

ADDITIONAL READING

Aghion, P., Howitt, P., & Murtin, F. (2010). *The relationship between health and growth: when Lucas meets Nelson-Phelps (No. w15813)*. National Bureau of Economic Research. doi:10.3386/w15813

Armendáriz, B., & Morduch, J. (2010). *The economics of microfinance*. USA: MIT Press.

Banerjee, A. V. (2013). Microcredit under the microscope: What have we learned in the past two decades, and what do we need to know? *Annual Review of Economics, 5*(1), 487–519. doi:10.1146/annurev-economics-082912-110220

Battilana, J., & Dorado, S. (2010). Building sustainable hybrid organizations: The case of commercial microfinance organizations. *Academy of Management Journal, 53*(6), 1419–1440. doi:10.5465/AMJ.2010.57318391

Chakrabarty, S., & Bass, A. E. (2014). Institutionalizing ethics in institutional voids: Building positive ethical strength to serve women microfinance borrowers in negative contexts. *Journal of Business Ethics, 119*(4), 529–542. doi:10.100710551-013-1833-9

Copestake, J. (2002). Inequality and the polarizing impact of microcredit: Evidence from Zambia's copperbelt. *Journal of International Development, 14*(6), 743–755. doi:10.1002/jid.921

Dasgupta, R. (2005). Microfinance in India: Empirical evidence, alternative models and policy imperatives. *Economic and Political Weekly*, 1229–1237.

Dutta, P. (2011). The Growth and Impact of NABARD's SHG-Bank Linkage Programme in India. *Indian Journal of Finance, 5*(12), 38–43.

Kundu, D. (2016). Microfinance delivery institutions in India-governance and management challenges. *Journal of Commerce and Management Thought*, *7*(2), 278. doi:10.5958/0976-478X.2016.00019.7

Manoharan, P., Ramachandran, R., & Devi, N. (2011). Microfinance institutions in India – A study on financial performance. *International Journal of Micro Finance*, *1*(1), 57–68.

Samuel, J., Kunnal, L. B., & Ashalatha, K. V. (2011). Impact of Microfinance on the upliftment of Rural Women-an Economic Analysis. *Journal of Rural Development*, *30*(2), 127–127.

Shetty, N. K. (2008). Microfinance for micro enterprise development: An inquiry for a new paradigm. *The IUP Journal of Financial Economics*, *6*(1), 88–98.

Yunus Centre. (2011). Quotes by Professor Yunus. Retrieved from http://www.muhammadyunus.org/index.php/news-media/quotes/453-quotes-by-professor-yunus

KEY TERMS AND DEFINITIONS

Cointegration: Cointegration is an econometric characteristic where a collection of time series variables ($X_1, X_2, X_3, ... X_k$) being integrated of the same order (greater than zero i.e. non- stationary) can be combined to generate a linear combination from this collection of variables which is integrated of order zero (i.e. a stationary trend). Then the time series variables $X_1, X_2, X_3, ... X_k$ are said to be cointegrated.

Granger Causality: Granger causality is a statistical hypothesis that asserts that a time series variable say X, is said to "Granger cause" another time series variable Y, if and only if the past values of X contain adequate information to predict Y.

Illiteracy Rates: The percentage of the total population in an area during a specific point of time aged seven years or above who can not read and write with understanding (i.e., 100 literacy rate is equal to the illiteracy rate).

Microfinance: Microfinance is defined as the art of providing micro loan to poorest of the poor i.e. those individuals who are not able to enter the formal banking sector and are considered unbankable. It not only provides financial resources for the poorest of the poor but also for small businesses lacking access to banking and other related services. These lending activities happen both at the individual and community level with peer-group monitoring being something very essential.

Newton's Interpolation Formula: Newton's forward and backward interpolation formula is used to interpolate the missing values and they look like, Newton's forward interpolation formula: $U_{a+rh} = U_a + r_{C_1}\Delta U_a + r_{C_2}\Delta^2 U_a + ...r_{C_n}\Delta^n U_a ; r = \frac{x - x_0}{h}$ where, h is the difference between two consecutive step values and x_0 is the initial value. Newton's backward interpolation formula: $U_{n+vh} = U_n + v\Delta U_{n-1} + \frac{v(v+1)}{1\times 2}\Delta^2 U_{n-2} + ... \frac{v(v+1)....(v+n-1)}{1\times 2\times ......\times n}\Delta^n U_a ; v = \frac{x - x_n}{h}$ where, h is the difference between consecutive step two values and x_n is the terminal value.

Panel Data: Also called longitudinal data, represents cross-sectional time series data i.e. data on multi-dimensional cross-sections (comprising of individuals, firms, and countries) over a period of time.

Poverty: In simple terms, one can define poverty as a situation where a person at the individual level or the community on the whole does not have the financial resources to enjoy a minimum standard of living that is considered to be acceptable in society. The poverty with which this paper talks about is in point of fact "multi-dimensional" in nature (refer to the text for details).

Vector Error Correction Mechanism (VECM): The VEC has cointegration relations built into the specification so that a series of partial short run dynamic adjustments allow for the correction in the deviation from long-run equilibrium. Consider a two-variable system with one cointegrating equation and no lagged difference terms. The cointegrating equation of two endogenous variables is given by, $y_{2,t} = \beta y_{1,t}$ The corresponding VEC model for y_1 and y_2 is, $\Delta y_{1,t} = \alpha_1(y_{2,t-1} - \beta y_{1,t-1}) + \varepsilon_{1,t}$ $\Delta y_{2,t} = \alpha_2(y_{2,t-1} - \beta y_{1,t-1}) + \varepsilon_{2,t}$ In this simple model, α_i measures the speed of adjustment of the ith endogenous variable towards the equilibrium. Nevertheless, if y_1 and y_2 tend to deviate from the long run equilibrium, the value of the error correction term will be non-zero and each variable will hence adjust partially to restore back the equilibrium relation.

Chapter 10
Effect of Microfinance on Poor Peri-Urban Female-Headed Households and the Vulnerability of Women to Poverty in Ghana

Bertha Z. Osei-Hwedie
Ghana Institute of Management and Public Administration, Ghana

Napoleon Kurantin
Ghana Institute of Management and Public Administration, Ghana

ABSTRACT

This chapter analyzes the impact of microfinance on poverty, in general, and female-headed households, in particular, for Ghana. The analysis shows that there are three types of microfinance institutions in Ghana, and successive governments have identified and upheld microfinance as the means to reduce national poverty rates and close the gender gap in the country. The analysis also demonstrates that microfinance has both positive and negative impacts on poverty and female-headed households. Microfinance has contributed to narrowing the poverty gap between the female and male gender, and improving the quality of their lives. However, on its own, it is not sufficient and necessary means to poverty reduction, growth, and development. The extent to which microfinance impacts on poverty is not conclusive. This necessitates remedial measures such as regulation and monitoring, proper balance between needs of clients and commercial interest of institutions, incentives to microfinance institutions, and capacitation of the poor and institutions.

INTRODUCTION

Poverty remains a pervasive problem throughout the world, more so in the developing countries, especially in Africa. In spite of improved annual growth rates in African countries in the 2000s, the continent is still the poorest region in the world. Poverty has a gendered face with the majority of the poor as females.

DOI: 10.4018/978-1-5225-5240-6.ch010

Women make up the largest number of the poor globally, regionally and at the national level. As the poorest and most vulnerable group in society, and with the substantive increase in the number of female headed households, women are the normal target of development projects, worldwide.

Governments, non-government organizations, and international donor agencies and organizations have, for years, strived to empower women to reduce or eliminate poverty in a bid to achieve gender equality. Unfortunately, efforts at the global level to tackle poverty have not yielded substantive reductions in poverty, generally and among females, in particular. Microfinance, since the 'success' of the Grameen Bank in Bangladesh, has been seen as the most effective tool, even a panacea, for empowering women economically and alleviation of their poverty. This is because poor women are 'unbankable', therefore, lack access to formal credit of financial or banking institutions. Lack of resources and opportunities contributes to the inequality gap between female and male in society. Yet poor women, if capacitated, are a very valuable resource that could contribute to buoyant economy. However, there are challenges that constrain maximization of the benefits associated with microfinance.

REVIEW OF RELATED LITERATURE

Two concepts of poverty and microfinance have to be clarified before delving into the impact of microfinance on poverty reduction. Poverty is universally defined as an economic and non-economic condition. Thus, poverty is a situation suffered by people who do not have money to buy the basic necessities of life in the marketplace and non-material needs through their own efforts. Therefore, it is both income poverty that results in lack of food, clean water, education, health and sanitation; and human poverty in terms of lack of human dignity, agency, opportunity and choices. The chapter relies on the conception of microfinance as small and short-term loans to poor entrepreneurs who are excluded from accessing start-up capital from formal financial institutions (Rudd, 2011, p. 1). This is complemented by a broadened definition of microfinance as the provision of financial services such as loans, savings, insurance, and transfer services to low income clients or the poor (Asiama & Osei, 2007, p. 3).

Literature has for a long time indicated that microfinance is critical to financially capacitating the poor in general and women in particular to start and expand micro businesses to generate income and stimulate growth and development in local communities (Rudd, 2011). This became more pronounced with the success of the Grameen Bank that provides female clients with small loans for business investment as a means to empower them. Bateman (2011, p. 1) acknowledges that for three decades, microfinance has been the major tool for poverty reduction and bottom-up local economic and social development. The United Nations (UN) (2013) emphasizes the importance of microfinance in offering women economic opportunities and resources as a means to alleviate poverty, and empowerment so that they are able to deal with their vulnerabilities.

The UN (2013) labelled 2005 as the International Year of Microcredit, in recognition of its ability to lift families out of poverty and achieve six of the eight millennium development goals (MDGs). Thus, it forms the core means for successful realization of the MDGs. In this respect, microfinance became a global strategy for poverty reduction, transforming and improving the quality of life of the poor and vulnerable groups, and empowering women. Indeed, classical theory posits that microfinance (loans) is expected to earn high returns, improve welfare and living conditions to break the stranglehold of poverty and reduce inequalities, unemployment and deprivation. The expectation is that the poor would achieve financial self-sustainability (Bateman, 2011; Rudd, 2011).

Microfinance is explained by theories of neo-liberalism and participatory development (Shepard, n.d) operating simultaneously and reinforcing each other. Specifically, the focus is on neo-liberalism, participatory development, and model of optimization of economic policy. Microfinance is viewed as a neo-liberal "bottom-up method of poverty alleviation" through formalization of the informal economy in so far as individuals are viewed as rational decision makers that maximize their life chances and improvement of the quality of life of the whole society through participation in the market. Microfinance, through neo-liberal prisms, sees borrowers as clients (Shepard, n.d). Neo-liberalism is supplemented by participatory development which views microfinance as the instrument through which local communities can participate to decide the best way to develop themselves for their own betterment, without constraints of the bureaucratic state. Thus, participatory development is geared towards achievement of sustainable livelihoods. In this respect, participatory development views borrowers of microfinance as beneficiaries (Shepard, n.d). As a corollary, economic theory posits that financial services, such as microfinance, lead to financial development which contributes to economic growth. This, in turn, helps to alleviate poverty (Barr, 2004). Therefore, financial services are an essential input that stimulates economic growth and development. Such an explanation stems from logical deduction: micro businesses financed through microfinance to the poor "will generate income and catalyze growth in developing communities" (Rudd, 2011, p. 1).

Participatory development is reinforced by the model of optimization in the theory of economic policy that assumes rationality, and that household decisions on enterprise and consumption allow for empirical evaluation of a relationship between household poverty and possession of assets. The model assumes that households as producers maximize benefits (asset-based welfare economics) subject to technological restrictions of the production function, and as consumers maximize their welfare by optimizing their consumption and work decisions subject to the gains. Therefore, a direct connection between possession of, and access to, assets and levels of spending by the household or individual in attempt to reduce poverty could be established, thereby promote social protection and economic development. The relationship between possessions and the condition of poverty can be either a poverty profile or an attempt to understand the determinants of poverty (Escobal, 2001). Based on the static model of optimization of household decisions on production and consumption, it is possible to derive a relationship between household poverty and possession of assets, which is susceptible to empirical evaluation. It should be noted that under the consumption model, assets and income are seen as alternative forms of economic resources available for consumption, the former as future consumption, and the later as current consumption. This means that household poverty is strongly determined by how readily a household can use assets for consumption when current income declines.

The utility of microfinance lies in its impacts on household and the community as a whole. Impacts of microfinance on livelihoods of beneficiary households are measured through four variables – economic, welfare, human capital, and social capital; and changes of these variables overtime. The emphasis is on the beneficial impacts of microfinance on poverty reduction, development, social relations, household, community and empowerment (Wrenn, 2005). Chowdhury (2009) puts stress on the impacts of microfinance on poverty reduction. When measuring effects impacts of microfinance on livelihoods of beneficiaries, Wrenn (2005) utilizes the sustainable livelihoods framework or security composed of: Level of impact on household and community; types of impact, economic and social; and three sets of impact variables – economic (income, household assets, housing and access to food), human capital (education, health, confidence, skills and empowerment), and social capital (social networks and social mobility). Impact is also measured in terms of welfare. Rudd (2011) measures welfare as savings, debts and consumption and the changes in these variables overtime. The World Bank (1990), on its part, highlights a two-pronged impact of microfinance on poverty alleviation, that of boosting the productivity and incomes of the poor. Improved productivity and incomes would, in turn, enable them to access social services such as health care, education, family planning and nutrition.

This means, therefore, that microfinance has two missions: one, social and the other commercial. These avail financial services to the poor; and aim to achieve financial sustainability, respectively. The basic assumptions are that such loans would be invested in productive activity that generates income and allow for repayment of loans. Such an income, in turn, would have multiplier effects on the quality of life of borrowers in terms of empowerment, increased education and nutritional standards. Therein lies the role of microfinance in development, measured in three major ways. First, it empowers women through facilitating their participation in the economy and contribution to economic growth, thereby promoting gender equity. Second, it assists the poor households, which are mostly female-headed; to satisfy their basic needs, thereby uplifting their quality of life. Third, it contributes to boosting household economic welfare and reducing poverty (Asiama & Osei, 2007).

In this chapter, the focus is on the developmental role of microfinance and its impacts on incomes, household assets, housing, food security, savings; and debt of, and vulnerability for, female-headed households in Ghana. Through these variables, the chapter assesses whether microfinance ensures sustainable enterprises of female clienteles in the informal sector, and analyzes these variables by relying on the data from the World Bank, Ministry of Finance of Ghana and other secondary sources.

MICROFINANCE AND POVERTY REDUCTION: THE DEBATE/CONTROVERSY

There is increased debate as to whether microfinance is given more credit than it deserves in relation to empowering the poor, including females, and alleviating their poverty situation. Whereas, microfinance has shown a positive relationship between microfinance and poverty alleviation, it has had some negative outcomes as well. It has been argued that microfinance led to reduction in poverty among the poor and improved quality of life due to increased incomes, and assets, access to health care and education, and reductions in vulnerability in Bangladesh, Ethiopia, India, Indonesia and Uganda (Boateng, Boateng & Bampoe, 2015). Similarly, microfinance is said to have produced positive outcomes in terms of increases in income, women empowerment, respect, and decision rights within the family and self-esteem in Ghana (Boateng et al., 2015). Evaluations of the impacts of microfinance show that it has serious negative consequences (Bateman, 2011; Rudd, 2011; UN, 2013). Rudd (2011), a fervent critique of microfinance, is forthright in his scepticism, backed by empirical evidence. Studies have shown both the positive and negative impacts of microfinance on poverty alleviation, worldwide. Empirical studies suggest that microfinance has brought about widespread poverty in Bangladesh, in spite of initial successes. Evidence from India shows that Indian farmers in Andra Pradesh have committed suicides due to inability to settle enormous debts owed to microfinance institutions (Biswas, 2010; Bateman, 2011; UN, 2013). Empirical evaluations of the impact of microfinance show negative consequences of poverty and debts. The UN (2013) argues, emphatically, that microfinance alone is insufficient as a solution to alleviate poverty and backfires on women clientele in the form of domestic abuse, huge debts, and unsustainability.

MICROFINANCE AND POVERTY ALLEVIATION IN GHANA

Ghana is well endowed with enormous natural resources ranging from cocoa, gold, diamonds, bauxite, manganese, timber and the newly found wealth in oil and gas, since 2007 (Cooke, Hague & McKay, 2016; Fosu, 2017). Ghana has been one of the fastest growing economies in the world in the 2000s (World Bank, 2015), yet the numbers of poor citizens has not diminished. This means that growth is not enough to reduce poverty and its wealth has not been distributed equitably, and has not benefited all citizens, respectively, leaving more than 28% and 24.2% of the population poor in 2006 and 2013, respectively (Boateng et al., 2015, p. 100; Cooke, Hague & McKay, 2016). Such high rates of poverty are unacceptable for a lower middle-income country such as Ghana. In this respect, Ghana can be characterized as a country with 'poverty amidst plenty or abundance'.

The country is dominated by the informal sector which accounts for more than 80% of the economy, from which the majority of the population derive their livelihoods. It is estimated that 88 to 91% of population are self-employed or employed in the informal sector, with no access to credit to start or grow their businesses. The majority of the poor in Ghana are found in the informal sector, are unskilled, have low levels of education, and are females (Boateng et al., 2015, p. 100; Baah-Boateng, 2017, p. 301). Most of the females in the informal sector are engaged in trade as the main source of income generation, and have mostly micro- and small- scale enterprises.

Successive governments of Ghana, together with international development agencies such as the World Bank and the International Monetary Fund, and donor agencies, such as USAID and through the Millennium Challenge Account, have undertaken a number of policies, measures and tools to deal with poverty in a bid to narrow the gender inequalities. One of these is microfinance, which has been viewed as a very significant tool of availing financial services to the poor, and for reducing poverty. Seddoh (2014) argues that microfinance is expected to reduce poverty, empower women and encourage family planning and practices. Whether this has been due to microfinance, this chapter aims to contribute to the analysis. It is important to acknowledge that over the years, there has a marked reduction in poverty rates in general and women's poverty in particular leading to narrowing of gender gaps. National poverty rates fell from 51.7% in 1992 to 28.6% in 2006 and 24.2% in 2013 (Cooke, Hague & McKay, 2016; McKay & Osei-Assibey, 2017, p. 287), with variations among regions in terms of poverty levels, with rural areas hit the hardest.

In general, the gender gap in poverty rates has been reduced because more females have attained high levels of education which have allowed them to be absorbed in the formal wage sector. This could explain the decline of females in self-employment and informal sector economic activities (Baah-Boateng 2017, pp. 305-6). Female-headed households, on average, registered lower poverty rates of 19.1% in 2013 relative to men-headed households at 25.9% (Cooke, Hague & McKay, 2016, p. 9). However, the gender of the head of household and economic activity presents a stark picture: females face more deprivation levels than men and have higher levels of income poverty than men. And, female-headed households dependent on agricultural activity for income generation and with high numbers of dependents fare worse than female-headed households in urban areas such as the peri-urban (McKay & Osei-Assibey, 2017, p. 287; Adjei, 2010, p. 94). Furthermore, while poverty rates have declined, a new problem has emerged that of increased inequality between the wealthiest and poorest in the country, thereby nullifying the positive effects of high annual growth rates on poverty (Cooke, Hague & McKay, 2016, p. 14).

The majority of the poor, including women, do not have access to credit, which has contributed to the growth of microfinance. This is primarily because women lack or have little assets. For example, due to patriarchal culture, women are constrained in owning or buying assets and properties. This is compounded by women's lack of or little economic power relative to men to buy assets such as land or businesses (Adjei, 2010). For example, in the Greater Accra Region, 3.4% of women own agricultural land than men with 7.8% ownership, and women own 55.2% of businesses compared to men with 39.4%. The only drawback is that women's businesses are much smaller than men's, and their portion of business wealth is much lower than that of men. These account for the gender gap in business incomes. Women are in micro and small-scale enterprises involving trade, cloth-making, tailoring, food, etc. Evidence also points to the fact that women are less likely to have savings accounts than men in formal financial institutions, and their predominance in the informal sector (Oduro & Ackah, 2017, p. 329). Yet savings are a very important source of investment or collateral for borrowing from established financial institutions or a readily available resource in case of emergency or crisis.

It should be noted that gender gaps discussed above have impacts on education, health, participation, legal rights, social protection, and general welfare (Adjei, 2010). These are good indicators of consumption of households, and present a good picture of poverty situation in Ghana. Also, there have been improvements in closing the gap between the poor and wealthy and urban and rural areas in terms of access to health facilities, nutrition and immunization (McKay & Osei-Assibey, 2017, p. 292). However, equity remains problematic as there is no parity between genders, groups, classes and regions, with female and the poorest being the hardest hit. The quality of life is still challenged by low doctor-patient ratio, vulnerability to diseases, live deaths as per Millennium Development Goals, low life expectancy of 57 years relative to 64 years at the world level, increase in numbers of handicapped peoples, inadequate access to health facilities, lack of affordable and quality health care, poor sanitation, and infant and mortality rates. On all these indicators, rural areas lag behind urban areas (McKay & Osei-Assibey, 2017, pp. 293-5; Adjei, 2010). Similarly, educational status of households, critical to well-being, has improved, save for pupil-teacher ratio, especially, at primary level which still needs improvement, as well as quality of education. However, the limited absorption capacity of the formal sector of employable human resources, undermines the desire to ameliorate the poverty situation of the poor through employment creation, and foster their upward mobility to improve their welfare and quality of life. Similarly, the fact that access to health, education and water is determined by public policies and institutions, households on their own cannot be held accountable for access to such services (Adjei, 2010, pp. 95-6). Adjei (2010, p. 66) cites the Freedom from Hunger's Credit with Educational programme on the Lower Pra Rural Bank in coastal Ghana as successful in terms of impact on incomes, savings, health, nutrition, empowerment of women and household food security.

Additionally, the government of Ghana, through the Ghana Shared Growth and Development Agenda 2010-13 (GSGDA 1) provided for uplifting women's quality of life by tackling poverty through improving women's access to credit and reviewing the regulatory systems of microfinance institutions to make them more accessible and beneficial to the female clientele (Oduro & Ackah, 2017, p. 324). In this way, governments in Ghana expect to narrow inequalities between genders, classes and groups, in both urban and rural areas.

Microfinance has had some import, how much exactly, is not easy to discern as studies show that microfinance has contributed to poverty reduction; others show that microfinance has not been important; yet other studies show both positive and negative relationships (Boateng et al., 2015, p. 100; Antwi, 2015, p. 22; Frimpong & Kalbersonn, 2014; Adjei, 2010). There is considerable literature on microfinance and poverty alleviation in Ghana, mostly focused on rural areas. This chapter focuses on female-headed households in the peri-urban area of Ghana.

Ghana has many microfinance institutions, which can be categorized into three types, namely, Rural Community Banks, Savings and Loan Companies, and non-governmental organizations (Adjei, 2010). However, microfinance faces numerous challenges in Ghana, including poor recovery rate; lack of capital for sustainable operations as financial institutions; inadequate credit delivery and management; difficulty of providing the services to the most vulnerable and marginalized; regulation, monitoring and supervision, and high turnover of staff (Boateng et al., 2015, p. 100; Antwi, 2015, p. 22; Adjei, 2010; Frimpong & Kalbersonn, 2014).

OBJECTIVES OF THE CHAPTER

The chapter analyzes the impact of microfinance on poor female headed households' incomes. It also measures household vulnerability to poverty after access to microfinance in peri-urban of the Greater Accra, Ghana. The focus of the chapter is on poor female headed households which have sourced financial services in the form of small loans from microfinance institutions in the Accra region of Ghana. The main objective is to analyze the impact of microfinance on household income as well as measure household vulnerability particularly of women to poverty after access to microfinance. Moreover, the objective is to discuss how microfinance works for poor female headed households; impacts on their living standards measured as income, savings, and assets; and improved access to health, education and housing. Ultimately, the chapter analyzes both the benefits and negatives to women in terms of improved livelihoods or welfare, and understand why there are variations in outcomes of clientele that borrow from microfinance institutions.

The specific objectives of the chapter therefore are to: examine the relationship between MFOs and client income on Human Development Index (HDI); gauge if there is any significant relationship between Microfinance Operations (MFOs) deposits (savings) and HDI; assess the impact of MFOs client indebtedness; discuss MFOs to Enterprise Development and HDI; analyse the impact of MFOs relative to client poverty levels to HDI; and, measure the impact of MFOs relative to real growth rate of Gross Domestic Product (GDP) to HDI.

Questions that are raised and answered in this chapter include: What is the impact of microfinance on living standards, empowerment and poverty alleviation of poor female households in Ghana? In other words, does microfinance benefit poor female headed households or leave them worse off?

DATA AND METHODOLOGY

The chapter relies on combined quantitative and qualitative methodologies to analyze the role of microfinance in poverty reduction, development, empowerment of female-headed households in Ghana's peri-urban area of the Greater Accra. Using secondary data-sets of selected nine variables (from the World Bank, UNDP, Ministry of Finance, etc.), our study integrates time series technique within quantitative methodology of design and approach such as regression analysis. In order to achieve the main goal of this chapter, which is to test and analyze the economic and social impacts of microfinance (MF) on development, measurements of income, savings, poverty, deposits, indebtedness, enterprise development, social capital (social networks and social mobility), human capital (skills and empowerment) and real GDP growth rate on livelihoods or welfare (HDI) are used. Although aggregated variables could suffer from the problem of deviation of the macro parameters from the average of the corresponding micro parameters, aggregation to a degree reduces such a problem as measurement errors at the micro level cancel each other (Aigner & Goldfeld, 1974). Moreover, the aggregated datasets used in this chapter allowed for smoother development and easier modelling in terms of forecasting relative to the disaggregated data sets at the local and/or micro level respectively (Ilmakunnas, 1990). Particularly, the chapter analyzes the impact of microfinance on poor female household incomes; it measures household vulnerability to poverty after access to microfinance loan and credit facilities in peri-urban communities within Ghana. The relationship between MFOs and HDI in Ghana includes data-sets between the periods of 1995 – 2015.

The best econometric approach for analysing the time series relationships, the Ordinary Least Square (OLS) method/technique, is employed. It is seen and, to a degree, regarded as superior to all other estimation techniques because of the 'BLUE' (Best, Linear, Unbiased, and Efficiency) property it possess and, underpinning its iterations (Admola & Arogundade, 2014). The standard regression technique/method rely on the key assumption that the regression errors are either independent, identically distributed (i.i.d.), or at least being uncorrelated having the same variance; this latter property is called homoscedasticity. The Generalized Least Squares (GLS) estimator is Best Linear Unbiased Estimator (BLUE) but its computation depends on the structure of the underlying heteroscedasticity. Typically, this structure is unknown, and the GLS estimator is intractable; in this case, practitioners encouraged to use the traditional OLS estimator which will still be valid that is, unbiased and consistent, under general conditions (Politis & Poulis, 2014).

Within its key assumption that the error variance is unknown, it is possible to give an approximation to the GLS estimator. For instance, Caroll (1982) is able to show that it is possible to construct estimates of regression parameters that are asymptotically equivalent to the weighted least squares estimates. In a seminal presentation, White (1980), employed the application of the OLS residuals in order to get an estimate of the standard error of the OLS estimator that is valid, that is, consistent, under an unknown structure of the underlying heteroscedasticity. OLS regression technique could be applied to both single and/or multiple explanatory variables as well as categorical explanatory variables (Tranmer & Elliot, 2008).

Alexopoulos (2010), maintains that the goal in any data analysis is to extract from raw information the accurate estimation; one of the most important and common question concerning if there is the statistical relationship between a response variable (***Y***) and explanatory variables (X_i). An option to answer this question is to employ regression analysis in order to model its relationship. There are various types of regression analysis. The type of the regression model depends on the type of the distribution of ***Y***; if it is continuous and approximately normal we use linear regression model; if dichotomous we use logistic regression; if Poisson or multinomial we use log-linear analysis; if time-to-event data in the presence of censored cases we use Cox regression as a method for modelling. Normally, the questions of interest are how to predict ***Y*** on the basis of the ***X's*** and what is the respective "independent" influence of an ***X*** variable on ***Y***? These questions can in principle be answered by multiple linear regression analysis. In the multiple linear regression models, ***Y*** has normal distribution with mean:

$$Y = \beta_0 + \beta_1 X_1 + \ldots + \beta p X p + \sigma(Y),\ sd(Y) = \sigma \text{ (independent of } X\text{'s)}$$

The model parameters $\beta_0 + \beta_1 + \ldots + \beta p$ and σ must be estimated from the data.

β_0 = intercept

$\beta_1 \ldots \beta\rho$ = regression coefficients

$\sigma = \sigma_{res}$ = residual standard deviation

Interpretation of Regression Coefficients

In the equation $Y = \beta_0 + \beta_1 X_1 + \ldots + \beta\rho X\rho$

β_1 equals the mean increase in Y per unit increase in X_i, while other $X_{i's}$ are kept fixed. In other words β_i is influence of X_i corrected (adjusted) for the other X's. The estimation method follows the least squares criterion (Shedecor & Cochran, 1989; Draper & Smith, 1998).

If $b_0, b_1 \ldots b\rho$ are the estimates of $\beta_0, \beta_1, \ldots, \beta\rho$ then the "fitted" value of Y is

$$Y_{fit} = b_0 + b_1 X_1 + \ldots + b\rho X\rho$$

The $b_0, b_1, \ldots, b\rho$ are computed such that $\Sigma(Y-Y_{fit})^2$ to be minimal. Since $Y - Y_{fit}$ is called the residual; one can also say that the sum of squared residuals is thus minimized (Alexopoulos, 2010).

In relation to poor female household incomes and economic development in Ghana within the peri-urban areas, measurements used include income, savings, poverty, indebtedness, enterprise development, social capital (social networks and social mobility), human capital (skills and empowerment), real GDP growth rate on livelihoods or welfare (HDI). Relationships among variables are captured in the multi-variate regression model specified below:

$$HDI = \beta_o + \beta_1 GDP_1 + \beta_2 Inc_2 + \beta_3 Sav_3 + \beta_4 Pov_4 + \beta_5 Ind_5 + \beta_6 EntDev_6 + \beta_7 SocCap_7 + \beta_8 HumCap_8 + \beta_9 Dep_9 + \mu \quad (1)$$

where:

$$HDI = HumanDevelopment^1$$
$$GDP = \text{Re}al\ Gross\ Domestic\ \text{Pr}oduct$$
$$Inc = Income$$
$$Sav = Savings$$
$$Pov = Poverty$$
$$Ind = Indebtedness$$
$$EntDev = Enterprise\ Development$$
$$SocCap = Social\ Capital$$
$$HumCap = Human\ Capital$$
$$Dep = Deposits$$
$$\beta_0 = intercept$$

$\beta_1\beta_2\beta_3\beta_4\beta_5\beta_6\beta_7\beta_8\beta_9 = parameters$
$\mu = error\ term$

[1] HDI = Human Development Index; a proxy for economic development in this stance, human welfare.

Hypotheses (Null Forms)

$$(\beta_1 > 0, \beta_2 > 0, \beta_3 > 0, \beta_4 > 0, \beta_5 > 0, \beta_6 > 0, \beta_7 > 0, \beta_8 > 0, (\beta_1 > 0, \beta_2 > 0, \beta_3 > 0, \beta_4 > 0, \beta_5 > 0, \beta_6 > 0, \beta_7 > 0, \beta_8 > 0, \beta_9 > 0,)\beta_9 > 0,) \quad (2)$$

The prior expectation and results is that the parameters in the form of equation (1) coefficients are positive and therefore greater than zero as in equation (2). To estimate the multiple regression model as depicted in equation 1 above, annual data on the specified variables were sourced from the Bank of Ghana (BoG), Ghana Association of Bankers, Ghana Statistical Service, Ghana Microfinance Institutions Network (Ghamfin), Ghana Association of Microfinance Companies (GAMC), Micro-Credit Association of Ghana (MCAG) formerly Money Lenders Association, World Bank (Global Findex Database), and the Ministry of Finance (Ghana). The chapter adapted secondary data-sets based on five per-urban communities at different stages of incorporation into the general fabric within the Greater Accra Metropolitan Region of Ghana. Peri-urban communities include: La Bawaleshie located very close to the centre of the capital city of Accra mostly surrounded by urban and modern processes of development; Pantag, hitherto located beyond the physical limit of the Greater Accra Metropolitan centre; and Ashale Botwe, Agbogba and Gbawe all located between the peripheries of the capital city and the Eastern Region of Ghana, an area experiencing the most rapid land-use change (Gough & Yankson, 2000).

Qualitative methodology provides tools for researchers to study complex phenomena within their contexts as it facilitates the exploration of a phenomenon using a variety of data sources. This ensures issues to be investigated through a variety of lenses which allows for multiple facets of the phenomena to be revealed and to, a degree, comprehensively understood. Henceforth, it allows for analysis of individuals or organizations, complex interventions, relationships, communities, or programme (Yin, 2003) and supports the deconstruction and the subsequent reconstruction of various phenomena.

RESULTS AND DISCUSSION

The study indicates both positive and negative impacts of microfinance on female borrowers, depending on their enterprise and consumption decisions. In this section of the chapter the results of the data analysis are presented. The data were collected and then processed in response to the goal and objectives as presented in preceding sections. Two fundamental goals drove the collection of the data-sets and the subsequent data analysis. Those goals were to investigate, test and analyze the economic and social impacts of MF on development using varied measurements of income, savings, poverty, deposits, indebtedness, enterprise development, social capital (social networks and social mobility), human capital (skills and empowerment) and real GDP growth rate on livelihoods or welfare (HDI). Second, the chapter analyzes the impact of microfinance on poor female household incomes; it measures household vulnerability to poverty after access to microfinance loan and credit facilities in peri-urban communities within Ghana and to determine if current perception and utilization are consistent with the basic goals or principles of microfinance as a conduct through which poverty can be alleviated. Table 1 presents summary of the descriptive statistics.

Table 1 shows that the highest amount disbursed to microfinance clients (customers) per annum during the period under review is 18 million Ghana Cedis. The minimum and maximum deposits for the same time period were 111 million Ghana Cedis and 297 million respectively; thus, variability in deposit is evidenced from the wider standard deviation of 80011.0. Low levels of microfinance registry and bank deposits are in accord with Nyantakyi and Sy (2015) findings.

To compare the two types of correlation matrices, a matrix of differences can be displayed. This enables and allows for the determination of which pairs of variables require further investigation. Table 2 presents a correlation matrix of deposit relative to microfinance indebtedness by its customers' and clients. It allows for the specification of set of partial variables; provides a statistical adjustment to the remaining variables using multiple regression (NCSS Statistical Software, 2017). In regression analysis, the purpose of examining these correlations is two-fold: to find outliers and to identify collinearity.

Although not a perfect relationship in terms of collinearity; table 2 depicts strong correlation between microfinance deposits (DEP) and indebtedness (IND).

The savings variable used in this chapter is formulated on the basis of the ideas of Friedman's (1957) Permanent Income Hypothesis (PIH) and Modigliani and Brumberg's (1954) Life Cycle Hypothesis (LCH). In explaining the LCH, Ando and Modigliani (1963) emphasized that individuals accumulate wealth during their working years and make provisions for old age when they will no longer be able to earn income. Specifically, during young age, individuals earn low income relative to their consumption, and borrow to finance their consumption needs. An important assumption of the PIH is that permanent changes in income exert more influence on consumption than temporary changes in income. An important determinant of permanent income is individuals' assets categorized into both human (such as

Table 1. Descriptive Statistics

	HDI	GDP	INC	SAV	POV	IND	DEP	ENTDev	SocDep	HumCap
Mean	0.344400	5.842857	61625.87	8.979287	35.8666	7.64795	95621.0	20.7546	16.4000	0.518714
Median	0.340400	40786.80	57542.74	7.443261	36.3333	6.45551	76654.1	20.6435	15.3000	0.51
Maximum	0.403000	84044.47	110676.5	19.33516	40.1111	18.0818	29701.7	30.0012	16.5100	0.579
Minimum	0.310000	15340.10	23006.60	1.997004	33.0000	1.00011	11100.1	30.0111	16.1000	0.473
Std. Dev.	0.017214	15280.06	1866.7.76	4.867196	1.93192	6.12063	80011.0	1.82110	5.62222	0.03937
Skewness	0.653324	0.143800	0.250372	0.598936	0.07445	0.39472	0.49814	0.06334	5.55555	0.324479
Kurtosis	1.357635	1.701521	1.776616	0.484144	0.48156	1.40559	1.65412	0.37145	4.32333	1.58249
Jarque-Bera	1.081428	0.516321	0.624100	0.373133	0.27045	1.30448	1.54241	0.16034	0.22333	0.14351
Probability	0468288	0.630616	0.581664	0.262123	0.15134	1.20337	1.43121	0.14133	0.21121	0.13341
Sum	3.444000	418063.1	616258.7	516257.7	753.222	160.607	18183.1	643.110	16.6752	10.893
Sum Sq. Dev.	0.006110	5.16E+08	6.87E+08	8.8E+07	3.5E+08	7.6E+09	9.5E+05	2.7E+05	1.6E+04	5.1E+8
Observations	31	31	31	31	31	31	31	31	31	31

Source: Authors' Compilation, (2017)

Table 2. Correlation matrix: deposit and indebtedness

	HDI	IND	DEP	FTR
HDI	1.000000	0.534765	0.550460	-0.160044
IND	0.53773	1.000000	0.877167	0.047144
SAV	0.630630	0.876166	1.000000	-0.034656
FTR	-0.160024	0.037133	-0.033646	1.000000

Source: Authors' Compilation, (2017).

education) and non-human assets (for example, bonds, property __ housing, etc.). Both the LCH and PIH apparently are identical in many aspects because they assume that forward-looking (rational) consumers plan for their future consumption by making an attempt to smooth-out consumption as much as they can due to variations in their income streams (Jappelli, 2005; Pistaferri, 2009; Rao & Sharma, 2007). Thus, savings by which MFI sees borrowers as clients is a variable instead of loans. Loans are at the heart of microfinance, which do not merely serve as a conduit to mobilize resources and hence, sustain MFOs, but also enhance poor people's survival and therefore, uplift the poor from poverty. Table 3 below brings to the fore the result of the chapter's regression model and analysis; microfinance phenomenon – savings mobilization and credit disbursement in the form of indebtedness.

The equation from the above regression model is:

$$HDI = 0.350701 - 0.000471\text{Ind} + 0.00550\text{Sav}$$

The equation shows a situation whereby the saving (Sav) variable is indeed significant with a positive (+) sign showing and/or meaning that funds mobilized from peri-urban communities have a positive influence on HDI and hence, by extension, the processes of socio-economic growth and development in Ghana. Thus, a unit increase in d savings thus, results in a 0.00550 unit increase in HDI __ a population-based index.

Based on the static model of optimization of household decisions on production and consumption, it is possible to derive a relationship between household poverty and possession of assets, which is susceptible to empirical evaluation. It should be noted that under the consumption model, assets and 'income' are seen as alternative forms of economic resources available for consumption, the former as future consumption, and the later as current consumption. This means that household poverty is strongly determined by how readily a household can use assets for consumption when current income declines.

Table 3. Multiple regression analysis

Variable	Coefficient	*T-Test*	*P-value*	Remarks
C	0.350701	11.4718	0.0000	Significant
Ind	-0.000471	-2.1114	0.0615	Significant **
Sav	0.00550	2.5605	0.0358	Significant *
F – statistics			5.621406	Significant *
R^2 = 61.5%	***Adjusted R^2*** = 53%	Durbin-Watson Stat -2.5		

Source: Authors' Compilation, (2017).

Table 3 gives credence to optimization as savings which may help to build a cushion to confront future shocks as experienced by poor and vulnerable women in peri-urban communities and therefore, alleviate poverty.

Contrary to the above positive impact of MFOs, the impact of microfinance on poor female household incomes; the vulnerability to poverty after access to microfinance facilities in peri-urban communities within Ghana is demonstrated through the loan (indebtedness) variable as the parameter as it is negatively (-) correlated and is insignificant at 5% level. In other words, indebtedness resulting from loans granted by MFIs within the period under review contributed negatively to socio-economic development.

Schicks' (2010, p. 140) analysis applies to our study of female-headed households in peri-urban area of the Greater Accra region: "A microfinance customer is over-indebted if he/ she is continuously struggling to meet repayment deadlines and structurally has to make unduly high sacrifices related to his/her loan obligations". The model regressors were able to explain 62% of the variation in the HDI which makes the model a good fit __ it is seen and, to a degree 'BLUE' (Best, Linear, Unbiased, and Efficiency). The F-statistic which is significant at 5% level confirms the overarching influence of savings variable within the models specifications; the adjusted ***R*** squared of 53% is fair for its purposes of influences. The 38.5% unexplained variation is due to other variables not captured by the chapters' regression model; these may include, insurance, business start-up advisory services, fund transfer services and fees, transaction cost, interest charges, culture and customs peculiar to rural societies as found in peri-urban communities in Ghana.

The Durbin-Watson figure may suggest the presence of autocorrelation and henceforth, the case of a spurious regression model and results cannot be used for analysis and policy making, and thus are ruled out. The R^2 of 53% < than the DW of 2.5 rules out the case of a spurious regression model in this chapter. Essentially, auto-correlation and multi-collinearity are core data-set challenges and indebtedness resulting from loans could not be divorced and dissociated from saving which form the bulk of banking theory including microfinance operations.

Elder and Kennedy (2001) argue that a unit root test tests whether a time series variable is non-stationary and possesses a unit root. The null hypothesis is generally defined as the presence of a unit root and the alternative hypothesis is stationarity, trend stationarity or explosive root depending on the test applied. Moreover, Mohamed (2008) explains that the Augmented Dickey–Fuller test (ADF), tests the null hypothesis that a unit root is present in a time series sample. The alternative hypothesis is different depending on which version of the test is used, but is usually stationarity or trend-stationarity. Test for co-integration could not be undertaken as data-set is relatively small. However, an ADF test confirms that both indebtedness (Ind) and deposit (Dep) variables are stationary at first differencing and therefore, integrated at order 1 while at the same time the regress and HDI is stationary at level that is order zero (see Table 4).

Table 4. Unit Root test results

Variable	Critical Values	ADF *t-test*	Order
HDI		-3.121541	1(0)
Ind	1%: -3.471537	-5.817055	1(1)
Dep	5%: -2.20858 10%: -2.731718	-3.702212	1(1)

Source: Authors' Compilation, (2017)

The estimated result presents indebtedness as inverse relationship with HDI which contrary to a priori expectation the P-value of 0.0615 although not statistically significant at 5% level is significant at 10%. The null hypothesis of no significant relationship is not rejected although one is cautioned since the alternative hypothesis could be accepted at a 10% level of significance and for its socio-economic significance. The deposit (Dep) variable has a positive relationship with HDI which is in accord with the chapter's priori expectation with a coefficient of 0.00550 and a *P-value* of 0.0358 which is very significant. Therefore, the null hypothesis is rejected and, accepts the alternative which states that there is a significant relationship between microfinance savings relative to HDI in peri-urban communities and hence, Ghana.

The Granger test determines the direction of causality between microfinance operations and socio-economic development; it could be unidirectional or bidirectional (Granger, 1969). The null hypothesis tests the independence of the variables; it may be necessary to establish linkages and the impact of one variable on another. It is applied in the test of short run direction of causality between variables X and Y. The test is based on the estimation of the bi-variate regression as below:

$$y_t = \sum_{i=1}^{u} \alpha Xt +^{n-k} \tag{3}$$

The results of Granger (Pair-wise) tests are presented below:

Table 5 shows that savings mobilized from microfinance clients particularly, women granger causes HDI since the P-value is highly statistically significant. It is unidirectional causality stemming from deposit to HDI. Causality equally results from deposits to HDI, however, there exists a degree of independence between saving and deposits variables respectively.

CONCLUSION AND POLICY SUGGESTIONS

This chapter focuses on the peri-urban area, and the female-headed households' access to credit facilities as extended by microfinance institutions in terms of financial intermediation, inclusion and intervention roles as part of the effort at poverty alleviation policies and projects. The research is on the developmental role of microfinance and its impacts on incomes, household assets, housing, food security, savings, debt of, and vulnerability for, female-headed households peri-urban area of Ghana. Through these variables, the chapter assesses whether microfinance ensures sustainable enterprises of female clienteles in the

Table 5. Granger Causality test results

Null Hypothesis	Obs	F-*Statistic*	Prob.
Indebtedness does not Granger Cause HDI HDI does not Granger Cause Indebtedness	31	20.2111 1.35631	0.0158 0.2483
Deposit does not Granger Cause HDI HDI does not Granger Cause Deposit	31	16.2723 1.35463	0.0113 0.2486
Saving does not Granger Cause Indebtedness Indebtedness not Granger Cause Savings	31	2.01161 5.12767	0.1810 0.0761

Source: Authors' Compilation, (2017)

informal sector, and analyzes these variables by relying on the data from the World Bank, Ministry of Finance of Ghana and other secondary data-sets. The chapter presents a mixed picture of the importance and relevance of microfinance operations.

Given the important of microfinance to the poverty alleviation agenda and the predominance of the informal economy in Ghana, the suggestion to the government is to regulate it in such a way as to balance the demands of development by communities and the need for financial sustainability of microfinance institutions. Further, the government has to regulate microfinance institutions to prevent negative impacts on the clientele. If possible, the government should capacitate microfinance institutions, both financially and expertise-wise, to improve their service provision and management of their services. Moreover, it is recommended that the government should institute and implement a national identification policy that could allow peri-urban rural dwellers possess an identity to enable an enhanced access to microfinance credit. The government is also encouraged to provide an incentive package including tax reduction and lower property tax rates to microfinance institutions that locate their services in peri-urban areas instead of the capital city of Ghana. Moreover, there is a need for targeted credit facility for poor peri-urban women, which would enhance socio-economic development of the country.

REFERENCES

Ademola, A. E., & Arogundade, K. (2014). The Impact of Microfinance on Economic Growth in Nigeria. *Journal of Emerging Trends in Economics and Management Science*, *5*(5), 397–405.

Adjei, J. K (2010). *Microfinance and Poverty Reduction: The Experience of Ghana.* Accra Central:Bold Communications Limited.

Aigner, D. J., & Goldfeld, S. M. (1974). Estimation and Prediction from Aggregate Data When Aggregates Are Measured More Accurately Than Their Components. *Econometrica*, *42*(1), 113–134. doi:10.2307/1913689

Alexopoulos, E. C. (2010). Introduction To Multivariate Regression Analysis. *Hippokratia*, *14*(1), 23–28. PMID:21487487

Ando, A. & Modigliani, F. (1963, March). The 'Life Cycle' Hypothesis of Saving: Aggregate Implications and Tests. *American Economic Review*.

Antwi, B. D. (2015). *Microfinance and Poverty Reduction in Ghana: Evidence from the Dormaa Area Teachers Co-operative Credit Union in Dormaa Municiplaity-Brong Ahafo* (Master Thesis). Norwegian University of Life Sciences, Faculty of Social Science, School of Economics and Business.

Asiama, J. P., & Osei, V. (2007). *Microfinance in Ghana: An Overview*. Research Department, Bank of Ghana.

Baah-Boateng, W. (2017). Employment and Labour Market. In E. Aryeeetey & R. Kanbur (Eds.), *The Economy of Ghana Sixty Years after Independence* (pp. 137–154). Oxford, UK: Oxford University Press. doi:10.1093/acprof:oso/9780198753438.003.0018

Barr, M. S. (2004). Microfinance and Financial Development. *Michigan Journal of International Law*, *26*(2), 271–296.

Bateman, M. (2011). *Microfinance as a Development and Poverty Reduction Policy: Is It Everything It's Cracked Up To Be?* Background Note, Overseas Development Institute. Retrieved from https://www.odi.org/resources/docs/6291.pdf

Biswas, S. (2010). *India's Micro-finance Suicide Epidemic*. BBC News.

Boateng, G. O., Boateng, A. A., & Bampoe, H. S. (2015). Microfinance and Poverty Reduction in Ghana: Evidence From Policy Beneficiaries. *Review of Business and Finance Studies*, *6*(1), 99–107.

Carol, J. R. (1982). Adapting for Heteroscedasticity in Linear Models. *Annals of Statistics*, *10*(14), 1224–1233. doi:10.1214/aos/1176345987

Chowdhury, A. (2009). *Microfinance as aPoverty Reduction Tool – A Critical Assessment*. Retrieved June 20, 2017 from www.un.org/esa/desa/papers/2009/wp89_2009.pdf

Cooke, E., Hague, S & McKay A. (2016). *The Ghana Poverty and In equality Report: The 6th Ghana Living Standards Survey*. Academic Press.

Draper, N. R., & Smith, H. (1998). *Applied Regression Analysis*. Wiley Series in Probability and Statistics. doi:10.1002/9781118625590

Elder, J., & Kennedy, P. E. (2001). *Testing for Unit Roots: What Should Students Be Taught?* Retrieved from http://citeseerx.ist.psu.edu/viewdoc/download?doi=10.1.1.140.8811&rep=rep1&type=pdf

Escobal, J. (2001). The Determinants of Non-farm Income Diversification in Rural Peru. *World Development*, *29*(3), 497–508. doi:10.1016/S0305-750X(00)00104-2

Fosu, A. K. (2017). Oil and Ghana's Economy. In E. Aryeeetey & R. Kanbur (Eds.), *The Economy of Ghana Sixty Years after Independence* (pp. 137–154). Oxford, UK: Oxford University Press. doi:10.1093/acprof:oso/9780198753438.003.0009

Friedman, M. (1957). *A Theory of Consumption Function*. Princeton, NJ: Princeton University Press.

Frimpong, D.K & Kalbersonn, N.J (2014). Assessing the Contribution of Microfinance Institutions to Poverty Reduction in Ghana: A Case Study of the Christian Rural Aid Network (CRAN), Hohoe, Ghana. *International Journal of ICT and Management.*

Gough, K. V., & Yankson, W. K. P. (2000). Land Markets in African Cities: The Case of Peri-urban Accra, Ghana. *Urban Studies (Edinburgh, Scotland)*, *37*(13), 2485–2500. doi:10.1080/00420980020080651

Granger, C. W. J. (1969). Investigating Causal Relations By Econometric Models and Cross-spectral Methods. *Econometrica*, *37*(3), 424–438. doi:10.2307/1912791

Ilmakunnas, P. (1990). Aggregation versus disaggregation in forecasting construction activity. In T. Barker & M. H. Pesaran (Eds.), *Disaggregation in Econometric Modelling*. London: Routledge.

Jappelli, T. (2005). *The Life-cycle Hypothesis, Fiscal Policy, and Social Security*. CSEF Working Paper 140.

McKay, A., & Osei-Assibey, E. (2017). Inequality and Poverty in Ghana. In E. Aryeeetey & R. Kanbur (Eds.), *The Economy of Ghana Sixty Years after Independence* (pp. 317–331). Oxford, UK: Oxford University Press. doi:10.1093/acprof:oso/9780198753438.003.0017

Modigliani, F., & Brumberg, R. H. (1954). Utility Analysis and the Consumption Function: An Interpretation of Cross-section Data in Post-Keynesian Economics. Rutgers University Press.

Mohamed, I. E. (2008). *The Augmented Dickey – Fuller (ADF) Test*. Retrieved from: http://www.lex-jansen.com/nesug/nesug08/po/po05.pdf

NCSS Statistical Software. (2017). *Statistical, Graphics, and Sample Size Software*. Retrieved from: https://www.ncss.com/

Nyantakyi, E., & Sy, M. (2015). The Banking System in Africa. *Main Facts and Challenges, AEB*, *6*(5), 28–29.

Oduro, A. D., & Ackah, C. G. (2017). Closing the Gender Gaps in Ghana. In E. Aryeeetey & R. Kanbur (Eds.), *The Economy of Ghana Sixty Years after Independence* (pp. 317–331). Oxford, UK: Oxford University Press. doi:10.1093/acprof:oso/9780198753438.003.0019

Pistaferri, L. (2009). The Life-cycle Hypothesis: An Assessment of Some Recent Evidence. *Rivista di Politica Economica*, 35–65.

Politis, D.N. & Poulis, S. (2014). *Heteroskedastic Liner Regression: Steps Towards Adaptivity, Efficiency, and Robustness*. Retrieved from: file:///G:/PhD_Quantative%20Research%20Methods%20and%20Computer%20Applications/Heteroskedasticity%20linear%20regression__%20steps%20towards%20adaptivity,%20efficiency,%20and%20robustness%20__%2001+.pdf

Rao, B. B. & Sharma, K. L. (2007). *Testing the Permanent Income Hypothesis in the Developing and Developed Countries: A Comparison between Fiji and Australia*. MPRA Paper 2725.

Rudd, A. (2011). *Microfinance as a Poverty Alleviant: Have We Given it Too Much Credit? An Analysis of Variance in Welfare Outcomes*. Retrieved from econweb.ucsd.edu/.../MICROFINANCE%20AS%20POVERTY%2

Schicks, J. (2011). *Over-Indebtedness of Micro-Borrowers in Ghana: An Empirical Study from a Customer Protection Perspective*. Retrieved from: https://centerforfinancialinclusionblog.files.wordpress.com/2011/11/111108_cfi_over-indebtedness-in-ghana_jessica-schicks_en_final.pdf

Seddoh, J. (2014). The Impact of Plan Ghana's Microfinance Scheme on Poverty Reduction Among Women in Lower Manya Krobo. *Journal of African Studies and Development*, *6*(8), 132–139. doi:10.5897/JASD2014.0285

Shedecor, G. W., & Cochran, W. G. (1989). Statistical Methods. Iowa State University Press.

Shepard, E. (n.d.). *Situating Micro-Finance on a Theoretical Spectrum: The Case of Bolivia*. Retrieved from https://atlismta.org/online-journals/0607-journal-development

Tranmer, M., & Elliot, M. (2008). *Multiple Linear Regression.* Retrieved from: http://www.ccsr.ac.uk/publications/teaching/mlr.pdf

United Nations (2013). *Microfinance in Africa: Overview of Suggestions for Action by Stakeholders.* Office of Special Adviser on Africa. Author.

White, H. (1980). A Heteroskedasticity-consistent Covariance Matrix Estimator and a Direct Test for Heteroskedasticity. *Econometrica, 48*(4), 817–838. doi:10.2307/1912934

World Bank. (1990). *World Development Report 1990: Poverty.* New York: Oxford University Press.

World Bank. (2015). *GDP Growth (annual %).* Data - World Bank Data. [Online], Available Data.worldbank.org/indicator/NY.GDP.MKTP.KD.ZG

Wrenn, E. (2005).Microfinance: Literature Review. www.dochas.ie/Shared/Files/2/MicroFinance_literature_review.pdf. Retrieved 8 July 2017.

Yin, R. K. (2003). *Case Study Research: Design and methods* (3rd ed.). Thousand Oaks, CA: Sage.

KEY TERMS AND DEFINITIONS

Enterprise Development: Refers to the use of microfinance as tool and means of financing the needs of micro and medium size enterprises geared towards women empowerment.

Female-Headed Household: Refers to a household whose head is a female due to no husband or father figure.

Human Capital: Refers to the use of microfiance towards the development of entrepreneurial start-ups especially by female headed households within the informal economy.

Human Development Index (HDI): Human development index; a proxy for economic development in this stance, human welfare.

Microfinance: Is the provision of financial services to the "unbankable" poor, such as small loans, to enable them to start small businesses in a bid to promote their socio-economic development.

Poverty: Refers to lack of, or inadequate income to purchase basic necessities of life including food, clothing, housing that are critical to living a good and happy life.

Poverty Reduction: Is the amelioration of the poor conditions within which the majority of the population live through a public policy, project, instruments or service.

Social Capital: Refers to the social interactions of women groups particularly in the informal sector related to microfinance operations.

Chapter 11
An Analysis of Poverty and Inequality Among the Members of SHGs in West Bengal, India

Santanu Bisai
Syamaprasad College, India

Debashis Mazumdar
The Heritage College, India

ABSTRACT

Economic development in the truest sense remains far from the development targets and millennium development goals in many less developed and developing countries of the world particularly because of the perennial problems of poverty and inequality in the distribution of income and wealth. The trajectory of planned economic development of India has also experienced the said problem. One of the escape routes for the poverty trap particularly in the rural areas of India has been the formation of self-help groups (SHGs) and the provision of microfinance to the SHGs. The present study tries to analyze the intensity of poverty and inequality among the rural households of some of the backward regions of West Bengal. This study indicates that the incidence of poverty remains less among the SHG members in comparison with the non-SHG households in both drought prone and non-drought prone areas of rural West Bengal. Further, the inequalities in the distribution of income and expenditure among the SHG members are also found to be more prominent in non-drought prone areas compared to drought prone areas.

INTRODUCTION

Poverty is more pervasive and intense in rural areas than in their urban counterparts particularly in the less developed and developing countries of the world. The World Development Report (1990) rightly observed, "poverty as measured by low income tends to be at its worst in rural areas, even allowing for the often substantial differential in cost of living between town and countryside". The problems of malnutrition, lack of education, low life expectancy and substandard housing are also, as a rule, more severe in rural areas. The importance of rural poverty is not understood partly because the urban poor

DOI: 10.4018/978-1-5225-5240-6.ch011

are more visible and more vocal than their rural counterparts. If these people are to raise level of life's sustenance, human dignity and freedom, when there is absence of any rapid expansion in the urban and industrial sectors, income has to be generated in rural areas.

Formation of Self-Help Groups (SHG) by the rural poor and their access to micro credit can contribute to a long-lasting increase in their income opportunities by means of a rise in investments of weaker sections of the society in income generating activities and to a possible diversification of source of income, to an accumulation of their assets and can contribute to better education, health and housing of the rural poor.

LITERATURE REVIEW

Hulme and Mosley (1996) conducted a comprehensive study based on the effect of microfinance on poverty. This study indicated that well-designed programmes could improve the income of the poor and could move them out of the clutches of poverty. When these poverty-stricken people are encouraged to save, they would become less vulnerable to poverty in future. The financial services to the poor, through the fulfillment of some social objectives, can become more inclusive and can contribute to poverty reduction (Chowdhury et al., 2004). Some related studies in this field indicated that the microfinance programme enabled the poor borrowers to spend greater part of their increased income on children's health and education (Montgomery, 2005). A study made by Sivaramakrishnan (2003) mentioned that organization of the rural poor into Self-Help Groups (SHGs) was one of the ways to reduce the incidence of poverty. The SHG-bank linkage and the role of Regional Rural Banks (Thorat, 2005) in combating poverty through microfinance in Indian context was the focal of point of some research studies. Pattenden (2010) noted the prominence of SHGs within current anti-poverty policy framework of India, and analysed the impacts of government and NGO-backed SHGs upon poverty alleviation in rural areas of North Karnataka. This study also indicated that the SHGs represented a partial neo-liberalisation of civil society in that they addressed poverty through low-cost methods that did not challenge the existing distribution of power and resources between the dominant class and the labouring class of poor. A study undertaken by Puhazhendhi and Satyasai (2000) covered 560 sample households from 223 SHGs spread over 11 states across India, and this study indicated a 33 per cent rise in average annual income of the households through group activities, and a decline in BPL (below poverty line) families by about 20 per cent after the formation of SHGs.

Many micro finance schemes had a clear focus on women. The vast majority of microfinance clients are women, particularly the poor women. Research studies show that women borrowers, even from the poorer sections, are more regular in repaying their debt obligations with the banks. Moreover, women use a more substantial part of their income for health and education of their children (Pitt & Khandker, 1998). Thus women play an important role in reducing the incidence of poverty within households.

However, there are also doubts as to whether micro credit can contribute to a substantial reduction in poverty, particularly of the 'core poor'. Firstly, these extremely poor people often decide not to participate in micro finance programmes since they lack confidence or they value the loans to be too risky (Hulme & Mosley, 1996; Marr, 2004). Several studies indicate that it is the 'better off poor' rather than the 'core poor' who stand to benefit most from the microfinance programme. Secondly, staff members of microfinance institutions may prefer to exclude the core poor since lending to them is seen to be an extremely risky proposition (Hulme & Mosley, 1996). Finally, the ways in which the programmes of microfinance institutions are organized and set up, may often lead to the exclusion of the core poor.

Such exclusions might be the results of the norms followed by the micro-finance institutions, say, the requirement to save before a loan can be granted, the minimum amount of loan that needs to be accepted and the requirement that an organization has to be registered before the loan is sanctioned (Kirpatrick & Maimbo, 2002; Mosley, 2001).Hence, many poor households were excluded from the formal credit network which had negatively affected the role of microfinance and SHGs in poverty alleviation (SU, 2007).

That income inequality among the SHG members can be reduced significantly through the formation of SHGs and flow of micro finance from institutional sources has been analyzed in a regional study (Vachya et al., 2009) based on some selected villages in Andhra Pradesh. It is felt that this initiative directly involves the promoting institution and the poor in the process of poverty alleviation and ultimately benefits the poor people in attaining better standard of living.

The rural poor now feel that they can also be the partners in the process of rural development by joining in the SHG movement. This perception has been reflected in some research works (Mehta, Mishra & Singh, 2011) which suggest that SHG-Bank Linkage Programme in Jammu (India) has significantly improved the access to financial services for the rural poor and has considerable positive impact on the socioeconomic conditions and the reduction of poverty among the SHG members and their households. A similar study (Chitagubbi et al., 2011) on Karnataka (India) has dealt with the usefulness of SHG membership to women for economic and social empowerment.

However, another regional study (Suprabha, 2014) based on Karnataka (India) related to this issue points out that micro finance can be an effective strategic instrument for poverty alleviation only if it is used for income generating microenterprise development. Although the micro finance clients, viz., the SHG members face several obstacles in the process of transition from such clients to microenterprise investors and run those microenterprises on a viable and sustainable basis, this problem can be minimized to a large extent through empowering the SHG members both in terms of finance and education.

In fact, many studies have indicated that the SHGs formed by the poor people can act as a catalyst for poverty reduction and women empowerment in several parts of India. One such study (Vasantha, 2015) has clearly shown that both consumption and employment indicators (measured in terms of Improvement in food security, Improvement in food intake, Increases in duration of work per week/month, greater income opportunities etc.) have improved among the SHG members in Tamil Nadu (India). Based on a survey conducted in the city of Chennai, another research paper (Nithyanandhana et al., 2015) tests the effect of SHGs in reducing poverty levels by comparing the level of incomes of the respondents before and after three years of programme intervention. The findings revealed significant improvements in the level of poverty among the respondents, viz., the poor women members of the SHGs. In this development process, the women belonging to the lowest strata had been given a chance to interact with many groups like banks, NGOs and officials from the government and they were exposed to public institutions. Normally the women have been found to spend most of their income on their household expenses. Therefore, wherever women are helped to increase their incomes, the welfare of the whole family improves. That this SHG programme can ensure a reduction in gender based inequality in a country like India was also revealed in some study (Chhipa et al., 2014) that hinted upon the problems associated with gender inequality in the demographic composition of Rajasthan (India) and the potentiality of microfinance institutions in reducing the intensity of gender inequality and ensuring women empowerment.

The SHG has been found to be an important tool which helps the rural women to acquire power for their self-supportive life. A regional study (Saravanan, 2016) on this issue shows that the SHG Programme clearly plays a central role in raising the living standard of the poor, particularly the poor women in rural areas of Tamil Nadu (India). Empowering women is not just for meeting their economic needs but also more holistic social development. The food security was higher among the SHG members and this had also led to more self-confidence among the SHG members. This often generates a more lasting achievement in social and economic fronts.

A recent study (Maity & Sarania, 2017) on the role of SHG for poverty alleviation in Assam (India) has shown that the SHG-bank linkage programme creates a positive and statistically significant impact on the monthly income, employment days, and financial inclusion level of participants of the SHG programme compared to a control group of non-participants.

However, the existing literature on this theme is clearly deficient at the regional and sub-regional level, particularly in the Drought-Prone (DP) region of West Bengal. Hence, the present study aims at filling some of those gaps in the existing studies.

OBJECTIVE OF THE STUDY

The impact of group formation, particularly by the women, has important bearing upon poverty and inequality. The basic objectives of the present study are: (i) To estimate the depth and severity of poverty among the households who are engaged in SHG activities;(ii) To estimate the incidence of poverty difference between the SHG and non-SHG households; (iii) To identify the factors responsible for poverty among the households involved in SHG activities both in drought prone and non-drought prone areas of rural West Bengal; (iv) To estimate the inequality in the distribution of expenditure and income among the members of SHGs and the differences in this distribution between the drought prone and non-drought prone areas of rural West Bengal.

This chapter is divided into three parts. In section 1 we examine the impact of the group formation on poverty and section 2 does soon inequality among the SHG members. Section 3 does give the summary of this chapter.

DATABASE AND METHODOLOGY

This work is based on primary data. 2011-12 constitutes the year for which necessary primary data (cross section) have been collected from the sample households. In the present study the primary data have been collected from extensive field surveys. Paschim Medinipur and Bankura districts of West Bengal have been chosen purposively for this sample survey. A multistage random sampling method has been used to collect primary data from these two districts. The blocks of these sample districts are treated as first stage sample units, the village (*gram*) panchayetsas the second stage units, the SHGs as the third stage sample units, and the households as the ultimate stage units. We have randomly selected eight droughts prone (DP) blocks (Binpur II, Gopibhallavpur II, Jhargram, Jambani, Chhatna, Khatra, Indpur and Saltora) and seven non-DP blocks (Kharagpur II, Salboni, Binpur I, Debra, Bishnupur, Kotolpur and Indus). Within a block all Gram Panchayets are not equally important in respect of socio-economic characteristics. In view of this, the sample gram panchayets have been randomly chosen from the DP and non-DP blocks. Thus, 24 sample gram panchayets from the sample DP blocks and 21 sample gram panchayets from the sample non-DP blocks were selected. From each sample gram panchayet, two sample SHGs have been randomly selected. We have thus selected 48 sample SHGs in DP areas (DPAs) and 42 sample SHGs in non-DPAs. All the member households of the sample SHGs have been studied. We have also collected data from persons other than the members of SHGs from five DP blocks (Binpur II, Gopibhallavpur II, Jhargram, Jambani, and Indpur) of Paschim Medinipur and Bankura districts as the control group so to help us analyzing the impacts of SHG formation on its members.

Methods of Data Analysis

Simple statistical techniques like mean, standard deviation, and regression have been used to analyze the data (Sarkhel et al., 2007). In order to examine the impact of the SHG formation on poverty, the notions of poverty gap and square poverty gap have been used, and a Probit model has been used to identify the significance of some factors in the incidence of poverty. We have also examined the inequality among the members of SHGs by using Gini coefficient and Lorenz curve. A comparison has also been made in this respect between the members of SHGs and non-SHG persons (viz. the control group) to examine the impact of group formation.

Measurement of Status of Poverty

The status of poverty is measured by using the methodology of Foster, Greer and Therbecke (1984) as

$$P_{\alpha} = \frac{1}{N}\sum_{i=1}^{q}\left(\frac{Z - Ei}{Z}\right); \alpha = 0, 1 \text{ and } 2$$

Where Z denotes poverty line, E_i is the expenditure of the i-th household, N represents the total number of individuals in the population, q denotes the number of poor individuals having income less than Z and α is a measure of sensitivity such that

For $\alpha = 0$, P0 implies the incidence of poverty, i.e,. head-count ratio (HCR)

For $\alpha = 1$, P1 (= poverty gap (PGP)) implies the depth of poverty and

For $\alpha = 2$, P2 (= square poverty gap (SPGP)) implies the severity of poverty

The formula of this method is expressed as

$$PGi = \frac{1}{N}\sum_{i=1}^{N}\frac{I - E_i}{I}$$

Square Poverty Gap

This notion has been used to compare the severity of poverty among the members of SHGs. This is a strictly convex function, a desirable property of a welfare function. The formula of this method is noted below:

$$SPG = \frac{1}{N}\sum_{i=1}^{N}\left(\frac{I - E_i}{I}\right)^{\alpha}$$

Lorenz Curve and Gini Concentration

The Lorenz curve and Gini concentration have been used to measure the inter-regional disparities in inequality of per capita income, per capita food expenditure, per capita non-food expenditure and per capita total expenditure. The greater is the departure of the Lorenz curve from the egalitarian line, the greater will be the degree of inequality. Lorenz curve lies between zero and unity (both inclusive).

Let F(x) and φ (x) denote respectively the per cent cumulative frequency of income earners and per cent cumulative total of income (*x*) upto the value *x*.

Thus, $F(x) = \frac{100\sum_{x_i \le x} f_i}{\sum_i f_i}$ and $\varphi\,(x) = \frac{100\sum_{x_i \le x} f_i x_i}{\sum_i f_i x_i}$

Naturally, both of them vary from 0 to 100. The curve obtained by putting φ (*x*) against F(*x*) for different values of *x*is known as Lorenz curve. In case, φ (x) = F(x) for all values of *x*, there remains no concentration in the distribution of *x*, and we get the *egalitarian line* or the line of equal distribution. If, on the other hand, φ (*x*) < F(*x*), there remains a concentration in the distribution of *x*.

The area between the line of equal distribution and the Lorenz curve is called as the area of concentration. It is the indicator of the degree of concentration of income distribution. Twice this area is called as *Gini coefficient*. It is denoted by

$$G = \frac{\Delta_1}{2\bar{x}} \text{ where } \Delta_1 = \frac{1}{N^2}\sum_{i,j=1}^{n} f_i f_j \left|x_i - x_j\right|, \text{ and } N = \sum_{i=1}^{n} f_i$$

The area of concentration lies between 0 to $\frac{1}{2}$, and therefore, G lies between 0 to 1. If G=0, it implies 'no inequality', while G=1 implies 'complete inequality'.

Probit Model

To analyze the performance of SHGs in DPAs and to analyze poverty we have been used Probit estimates.

The steps involved in the estimation of the probit model have been as follows:

1. From the grouped data, the probability that an event will occur, i.e, P_i is estimated. This P_i is estimated by $\frac{n_i}{N_i}$, where n_i is observed frequency and N_i is the total frequency.
2. 2. Given the estimated $P_{i,}$ the normal equivalent deviate (n.e.d) (= I_i) is obtained from the standard normal cumulative distribution function (CDF). That is

$$I_i = F^{-1}\left(P_i\right) = \beta_1 + \beta_2 x_i$$

3. The estimated normal equivalent deviate so obtained is used as the dependent variable in the regression, i.e. $I_i = \beta_1 + \beta_2 x_i + U_i$
4. If required, we add 5 to the estimated *n.e.d* to convert it into probit and use the probits thus obtained (probit = n.e.d +5) as the dependent variable in the above regression equation.
5. One can conduct hypothesis testing in the usual fashion, keeping in mind that the conclusions drawn will hold true asymptotically, that is, in the large samples.
6. R^2. is considered as a measure of goodness of fit; however, it is not particularly well-suited for the dichotomous dependent variable models, and therefore, one suggested alternative is the χ^2. test (Das, 2010).

Result Analysis: Poverty

We measured poverty gap and square poverty gap of the households of the members of SHGs and non-SHG households to examine the depth and severity of poverty. It has been observed that in DPAs of the sample districts, the poverty gap (as a proportion of deficit in expenditure to the poverty line estimate) of the member-households of SHGs was 0.198 whereas it was 0.375 for non-SHG households. Similarly, the square poverty gaps of the SHG households and non-SHG households are estimated to be 0.180 and 0.196 respectively (Table 1). Thus, in both the cases, the non-SHG households are seen to be poorer than the SHG households. So, it seems that SHGs have played an important role in the alleviation of rural poverty in West Bengal.

While following Probit estimates, the dependant variable, viz., whether the household is lying below poverty level or not, is represented by a dummy variable(where '1' is put for poor and '0' for non-poor). On the other hand, four independent variables are: the amount of credit (Rs) the members received, the amount of land holding of the members of SHGs, level of education of the members of SHGs, and the number of days they were engaged in MG-NREGA (income generating activities under Mahatma Gandhi National Rural Employment Guarantee Act) activities.

Mean, Standard Deviation and the notations used for the variables are shown in Table 2. The factors which are supposed to influence the dummy variable have been grouped into three categories: institutional, cultural, and economic.

The equation of the Probit model is shown below.Here we have considered 4 independent variables that affect the level of poverty and the necessary information regarding these variables have been collected from 447 members of sample SHG. The necessary information and results in the Probit model are shown in Table 3

Table 1. Poverty gap and square poverty gap of SHG and non-SHG households in DPAs

Measure of Poverty	Among Members of SHGs in DPAs	Among non-SHG Households in DPAs
Poverty Gap	0.19833	0.374749
Square Poverty gap	0.180043	0.195502

Source: Author's calculation fromField Survey (2011-12)

Table 2. Notation, specification, mean and standard deviation of variables used in Probit estimation

Nature of Variables	Notation	Specification	Mean	Standard Deviation
Dependent Variable	DPOV (Y .)	Whether the members are poor or not if poor '1, otherwise '0'	0.71	0.454
Institutional factors	Credit (X_1)	Amount of credit (Rs.) the members received	7738.06 (Rs.)	8459.08 (Rs.)
Cultural factor	EDU(X_3 .)	Level of education (years) (δ)	1.98 years	3.462 years
Economic Factors	LAND(X_2 .)	Having land holding	17.55 dec.	24.077 dec.
	NREGA(X_4 .)	Number of days they are engaged in NREGA	6 days	8.1 days

Notes:DPOV indicates the dummy variable having the value '1' for the poor and '0' otherwise,EDU = Education, δ '0'for illiterate, '1' for primary level, '2' for upper Primary level, '3'for secondarylevel, '4' for higher secondary Leland '5'under graduate level

Table 3. Probit estimates onpoverty of the members of SHGs in drought-prone areas of West Bengal

Variables	Coefficients	Z-Values	P > Z
Intercept	1.058007	8.15** 0.000	
Credit	– 0.000014	–1.86#0.063	
Land	– 0.0143808	–5.54**0.000	Prob. >chi2 = 0.000
Education	– 0.025832	–1.430.151	Pseudo R^2 =0.0651
NREGA	– 0.0138247	– 0.175#	0.080

Notes: **Significant at the 0.01 level, #Significant at the 0.10 level

Source: Author's calculation from Field Survey (2011-12)

The equation of Probit model:

$$Y = \beta_0 + \beta_1 X_1 + \beta_2 X_2 + \beta_3 X_3 + \beta_4 X_4 + U_i$$

Where Y= the dummy variable representingpoor(if Yes, Y=1, and if No, Y= 0).

x_1 =credit they have received,

x_2 = land holding of the members of SHGs..

x_3 =. Level of educationof the members of SHGs,

$x_4 =$. How many days they are engaged in NREGA activities and in income generating activities.

$U_i =$ Error terms.

The Probit estimate is shown in Table 3.

Table 3 reveals that the variation in poverty of the members of SHGs in DPAs is significantly explained by credit, land and involvement in MG-NREGA activities. The result implies that the incidence of poverty among the SHG members can be reduced significantly with an increase in credit flow, bigger land holding and greater employment and income opportunities from MG-NREGA activities. The second and the third factors, however, are not determined by the activities of the SHGs.

We have also analyzedthe factors which explain the severity of poverty among the members of SHGs operating in both DP and non-DP areas of West Bengal.Here also the dependent variable is considered to be the Dummy variable indicating whether poor or not ('1' is put for poor and '0' for non-poor); the independent variables include: a Dummy variable indicating whether SHGs formed in DPAs or not ('0' is put for SHGs formed in DPAs and '1' is put for SHGs formed in non-DPAs), aDummy variable for Grade-II passed SHGs('1' is put for having Grade II and '0' for not having Grade II), the amount of land holding of the members of SHGs, and the level of education of the members of SHGs.For this purpose, we considered 4 variables from 902 members in DPAs and non-DPAs.

It is important to note in this connection that the SHGs are to undergo periodic assessment on the basis of some various performance parameters by the local self-government body (viz. panchayat) and the bank to be rated as Grade I or Grade II. A group is accorded Grade I if the members are active after groups are formed and meet every month, regularly deposit money with their savings account and a Grade I group is eligible to receive the revolving fund from the bank. A Grade I group is escalated to Grade II rating if it performs satisfactorily in the front of deposit accumulation in the six months post the entitlement to the revolving fund and thereby becomes eligible to get the facility of credit linkage scheme. In case of credit linkage, there is a sizeable part of subsidy given to the groups.

T necessary information and results in the Probit model are shown in Table 5.

The equation of this Probit model is noted below:

$$Y = \beta_0 + \beta_1 X_1 + \beta_2 X_2 + \beta_3 X_3 + \beta_4 X_4 + U_i$$

Where Y= the dummy variable representing poor (if Yes, Y=1, and if No, Y= 0. ummy variable for SHGs formed in DPAs. Yes=0, No= 1

$x_2 =$. the groups qualified for Grade II. We take dummy variable for Grade II passed.

Does group qualify for Grade II? Yes=1, No=0 $x_3 = \text{land holding of the members of SHGs}$.

$x_4 =$ vel of educationof the members of SHGs, or terms.

Table 4. Notation, specification, mean and standard deviation of variables used in Probit estimation

Nature of Variables	Notation	Specification	Mean	Standard Deviation
Dependent Variable	DPOV (Y .)	Whether the members are poor or not if poor '1, otherwise '0'	0.86	0.35
Regional factor	DDPA (X_1)	Whether the SHGs formed in DPAs or non-DPAs. Yes=0, No= 1	0.50	0.50
Institutional factor	DGII (X_2 .)	Whether the groups qualified for Grade II or not. Yes=1, No= 0	0.65	0.48
Economic Factor	LAND(X_3 .)	Having land holding	1.26 Dec.	1.6 Dec.
Cultural factor	EDU(X_4 .)	Level of education (years)δ	1.43 Years	.99 Years

Notes:DPOV indicates the dummy variable having the value '1' for the poor and '0' otherwise,EDU = Education,
δ0'for illiterate, '1' for primary level, '2' for upper Primary level, '3'for secondarylevel, '4' for higher secondary leveland '5'under graduate level
Source:Author's calculation fromField Survey (2011-12).

It is revealed from Table 5 that the variation in poverty of the members of SHGs in DPAs and non-DPAs are significantly explained by dummy variable for SHGs formed in DPAs, dummy variable for Grade II passed and the landholding of the members. Contrary to the common perception, it is observed that the incidence of poverty has been less among the members of the SHGs that operate in DPAs rather than non-DPAs. Again, it is observed that the incidence of poverty is less among the members of SHGs which have attained Grade-II independent of their area of operation.

Inequality

Some earlier studies clearly indicated that (Banerjee,2009) the average income of the members of SHGs improved but the inequality of distribution of income remained high among the group members relative to the non-group members. There still remains an inequality in the distribution of expenditure and income among the members of SHGs, i.e., while some of the members are nearer to the poverty line, some other members remain much below the poverty line. In this section we shall analyze the pattern of inequality in the distribution of income and expenditure among the members of sample SHGs in our

Table 5. Probit estimates on poverty of the members of SHGs in drought-prone and non- drought-prone areas of West Bengal

Variables	Coefficients	Z-Values	P > Z
Intercept	1.98841	2.21	0.000 LR chi 2(4) = 67.37
Ddpa	– 0.7368	–6.36**	0.000 log likelihood = -329.26
G II	– 0.2422	–2.00*	0.045 Prob. > chi2 = 0.000
Land	– 0.158	– 4.92**	0.000 Pseudo R^2 =.0928
Education	– 0.0550	-1.00	0,317

Notes: **Significant at the 0.01 level, *Significant at the 0.05 level

study area. Table 6 shows that such inequality (measured by Gini coefficients) in terms of Per Capita Monthly Total Expenditure (PCMTE) remains slightly higher in non-DPAs compared to that of DPAs. This might be due to the existence of relatively high percentage of SHG members with higher Per Capita Monthly Income (PCMY) in non-DPAs. However, the inequality in the distribution of PCMY is found to be marginally higher in DPAs. We have also measured this inequality in terms of the distribution of Per Capita Monthly Food Expenditure (PCMFE) and Per Capita Monthly Non-food Expenditure (PC-MNFE) among the SHG members. Here, higher incidence of inequality is observed in terms of PCMFE in non-DPAs compared to that in DPAs.

It is observed that there remain inter-block variations in inequality in the distribution of PCMTE among the members of sample SHGs within the DP blocks. The Gini coefficients, measuring such inequalities for DP blocks, are found to remain higher for sample DP blocks like Jhargram, Indpur, Jamboni and Khatra while these values are found to remain lower in DP blocks like, Binpur II, Gopibhllavpur II, Chhatna and Saltora. Similar such inter-block variations are also observed in the distribution of PCMFE (Table 7).

In most cases, the inequality in the distribution of PCMNFE is higher than that in PCMFE. The possible explanation for such higher inequality regarding the distribution of PCMNFE might be the fact that after group formation, the members, mostly the women, became more conscious regarding the health and educational attainments of their children. Hence, within each block, some of the sample groups have been found to spend relatively high share of their expenditure on such non-food items, while most of the sample groups used to spend greater part of their income on food items. This leads to greater inequality in the distribution of PCMNFE within a sample block.

Again this may also happen due to the presence of relatively high percentage of APL(above-poverty line) members in the total number of SHG members in any particular block since it is expected that for APL families, percentage of non-food expenditure in total expenditure would be higher compared to BPL (below poverty line) families.

Here, an inter-block comparison in the distribution of PCMFE, PCMY and PCMNFE has been made on the basis of the minimum and maximum values of Gini coefficients in respect of PCMFE, PCMY and PCMNFE among the sample DP blocks. The Lorenz curves clearly reflect such inter-block disparities regarding the distribution of PCMTE (Figure 1), PCMNFE (Figure 2) and PCMY (Figure 3) among the members of sample SHGs within DPAs.

The variation in Gini in respect of PCMY is significantly explained by the variation in percentage of SHGs passed Grade II and the PCC (per capita credit) received from the banking institutions across the sample DP blocks (Table 8).

The coefficient of percentage of SHGs passed Grade- II is seen to be negative and significant at 1% level. It implies thatif higher percentages of SHGs are qualified for Grade- II then the poor members

Table 6. Inequalities among the members of sample SHGs in DPAs and non-DPAs

Indicators Block	PCMFEGini	PCMNFE Gini	PCMTE Gini	PCMY Gini
DPAs	0.20	0.17	0.20	0.24
Non-DPAs	0.24	0.17	0.22	0.23

Note: PCMFE = per capita monthly food expenditure, PCMNFE = per capita monthly non-food expenditure, PCMTE = per capita monthly total expenditure, PCMY = per capita monthly income

Source: Author's calculation from field Survey (2011-12)

Table 7. Inequalities of members of sample SHGs in DPAs and non-DPAs among the blocks

	PCMFE Gini	PCMNFE Gini	PCMTE Gini	PCMY Gini
		DP block		
Binpur-II	0.2229	0.2505	0.1697	0.2202
Gopiballabpur- II	0.2017	0.2805	0.1914	0.2233
Indpur	0.2548	0.2980	0.2492	0.2789
Saltora	0.2269	0.2562	0.2293	0.2251
Chhatna	0.2464	0.2386	0.1922	0.2406
Jhargram	0.2241	0.2875	0.2662	0.2628
Khatra	0.2576	0.3164	0.2400	0.3818
Jamboni	0.2833	0.2145	0.2469	0.3371
		Non-DP block		
Kharagpur- II	0.2718	0.3254	0.2474	0.4028
Bishnupur	0.2294	0.2977	0.1934	0.2164
Kotolpur	0.2463	0.2647	0.1923	0.2437
Debra	0.2358	0.2757	0.1890	0.2744
Salboni	0.2094	0.2077	0.1615	0.1861
Binpur I	0.2360	0.3102	0.1915	0.2577
Indus	0.1864	0.2908	0.1636	0.2050

Note: PCMFE = per capita monthly food expenditure, PCMNFE = per capita monthly non-food expenditure,
PCMTE = per capita monthly total expenditure, PCMY = per capita monthly income
Source: Author's calculation fromField Survey (2011-12)

will earn higher income and thus inequality will diminish. The coefficient of PCC is seen to be positive and significant at 5% level. Thus,if per capita credit rises for the relatively non-poor SHG members and that credit is used productively then the income disparity between the poor and non-poor will increase.

Again, the variation in Gini in respect of PCMTE is significantly explained by the variation in percentage of SHGs passed Grade II and the educational level across the sample DP blocks to the extent of 44.1%. (Table 9).

This result also signifies that if higher percentages of illiterate members of SHGs become literate, they will have improved capability and, hence, they can earn more leading possibly to a fall in the inequality in income and expenditure.

Table 8.Regression equation concerning Gini PCMY in DPAs

Regression Equation	Adjusted R-Square	F
Gini PCMY $_{DPAs}$ = 0.469 - 0.003**Grade II + 3.689*e-7 PCC (-6.73) (2.63)	0.479	4.218*

Notes: PCMY = per capita monthly income, PCC = per capita credit,
**Significant at the 0.01 level, *Significant at the 0.05 level
Source: Author's calculation fromField Survey (2011-12)

Table 9. Regression equation concerning Gini PCMTE in DPAs

Regression Equation	Adjusted R-Square	F
Gini PCMTE $_{DPAs}$ = 0.432 - 0.002**Grade II - 0.027*Education (-5.021) (-2.737)	0.441	3.763*

Notes: PCMY = per capita monthly income, **Significant at the 0.01 level,*Significant at the 0.05 level
Source: Author's calculation fromField Survey (2011-12)

The variation in Gini in respect of PCMFE is significantly explained by the variation in percentage of SHGs passed Grade II and the year of functioning across the sample DP blocks to the extent of 49.3%(Table 10). It seems that the period of operation of any SHG has also a significant bearingupon the level of inequality in the distribution of per capita monthly expenditure on food items by the SHG members in DPAs. Thus, the vintage value of the SHG can help in reducing this inequality. This might be due to the functioning of the experienced members in more productive activities over time.

Inter-block differences in inequalities in the distribution of PCMFE, PCMNFE and PCMTE are also observed within non-DP blocks. Here inequalities in respect of PCMTE are found to be higher in non-DP blocks like Kharagpur II, Bishnupur and Kotollpur. Just like the DP blocks, here also we observe higher inequality in the distribution of PCMNFE in most of the blocks compared to that in PCMFE (Table 7). Here also the Lorenz curves represent inter-block differences in the distribution of PCMTE (Figure 1), PCMNFE (Figure 2) and PCMY (Figure 3) among the members of sample SHGs within non-DPAs.

In fact, in case of PCMNFE, the priority of such expenses is expected to differ from group to group in accordance with their level of consciousness after group formation and percentage of APL members in the group. Again, this happens due to the fact that though most of the group members in non-DPAs are

Figure 1. Inter-block difference in the distribution of PCMTE in DP and non-DP blocks

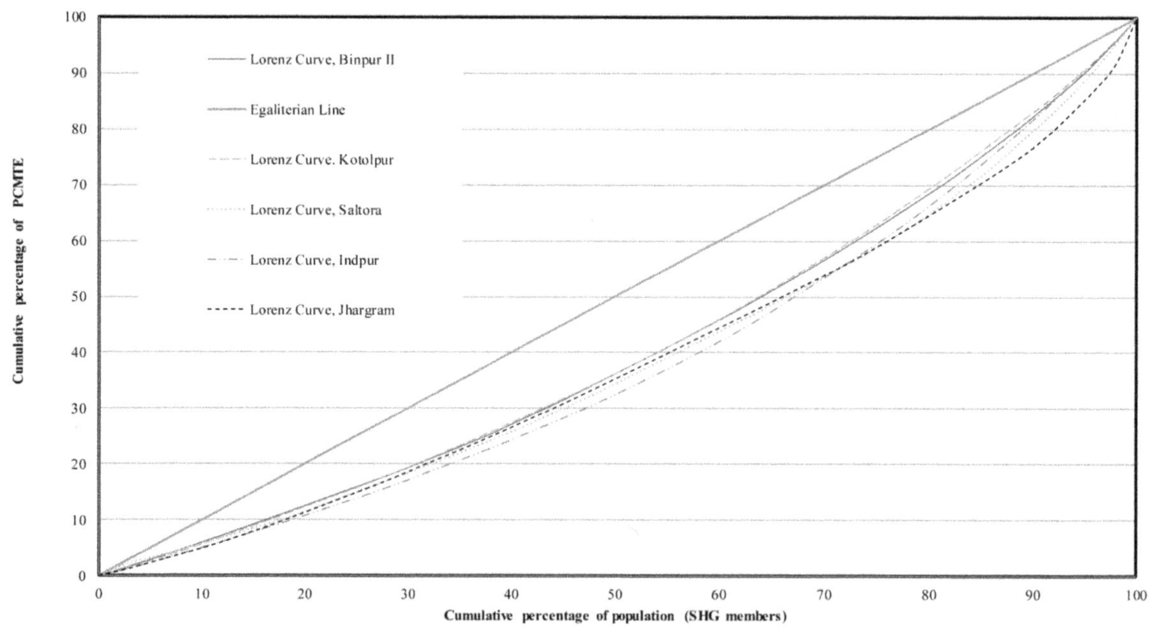

Figure 2. Inter-block difference in the distribution of PCMNFE in DP and non-DP blocks

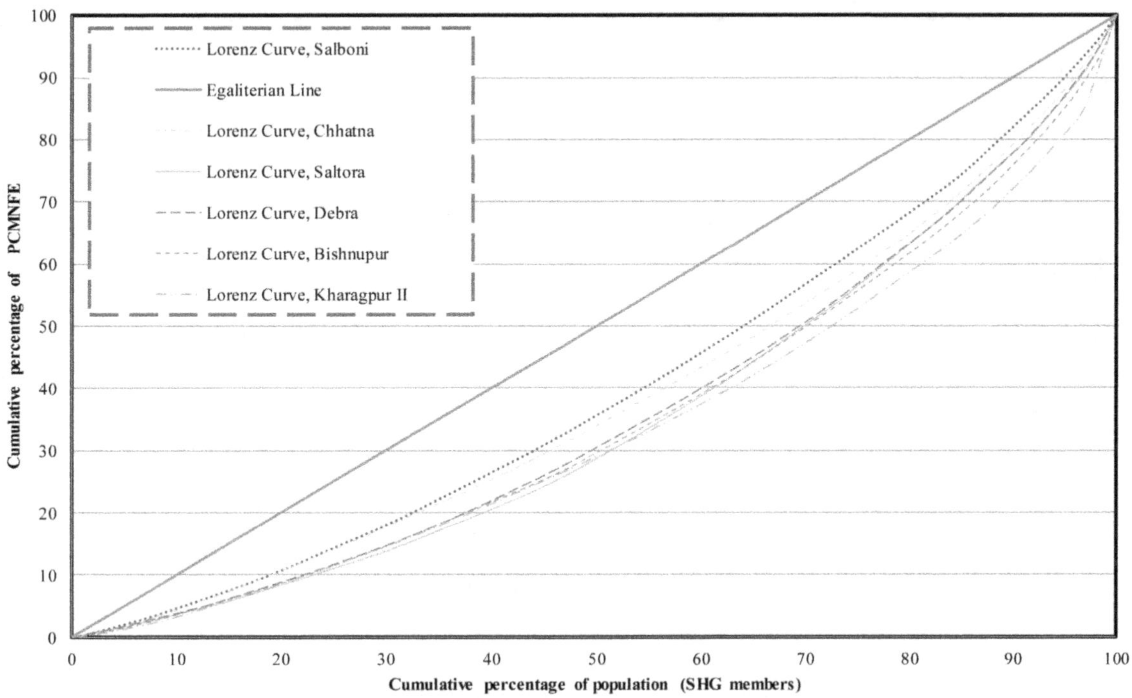

Table 10. Regression equation concerning Gini PCMFE in DPAs

Regression Equation	Adjusted R-Square	F
Gini PCMFE $_{DPAs}$ = 0.372 - 0.001**GR II - 0.009*YOF (6.944) (-2.297)	0.493	4.403*

Notes: **Significant at the 0.01 level, *Significant at the 0.05 level
Source: Author's calculation from Field Survey (2011-12).

below the poverty line but amongst them some of the group members have been found to remain closer to poverty line whereas some other members are found to remain far below the poverty line. Thus, the group members who are closer to the poverty line are expected to spend relatively greater share of their income on non-food items compared to those who remain much below the poverty line.

Inter-block differences in inequalities in the distribution of PCMFE and PCMNFE are also observed among the other non-SHG household members within DP blocks (we have taken 5 sample DP blocks for such non-SHG household members). Here inequalities in respect of PCMFE are found to be higher in DP blocks like Binpur- II and Gopibhallavpur- II.

Just like PCMFE, here also we observe higher inequality in the distribution of PCMNFE in most of the blocks. Here also the Lorenz curves represent inter-block differences in the distribution of PCMFE (Figure 4) and PCMNFE (Figure 5) among the non-SHGs households within DPAs. However,in the absence of any significant difference in respect of PCMTE and PCMY for the non-SHG household members (Table 11), the Lorenz curves representing inter-block differences in the distribution of PCMTE and PCMY in respect of non-SHGs households have not been derived.

Figure 3. Inter-block difference in the distribution of PCMY in DP and non-DP blocks

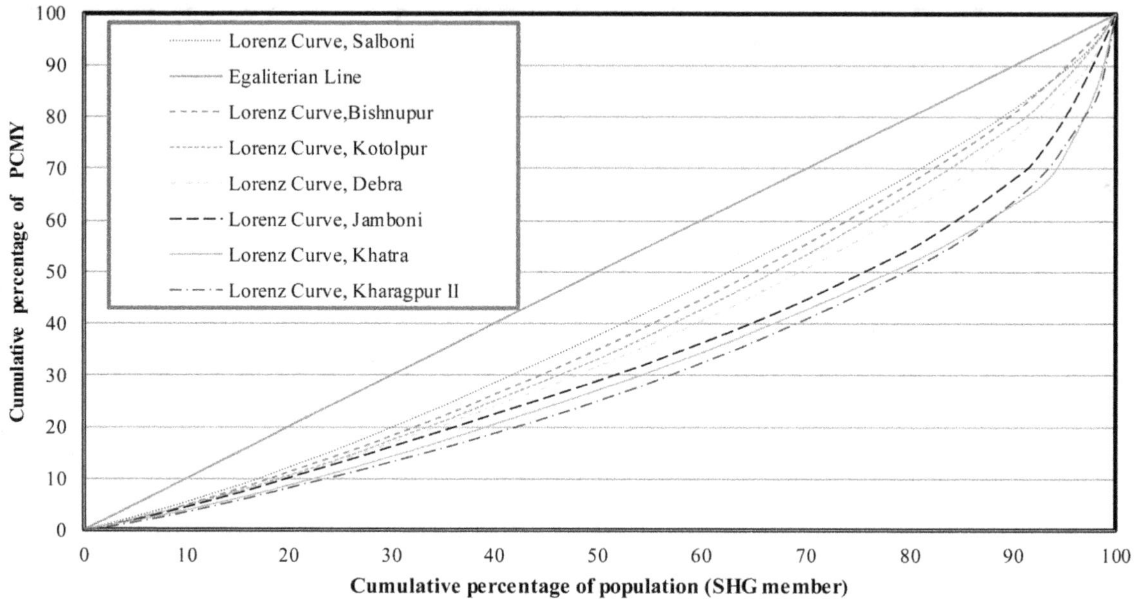

Table 11.Inequalities among the sample non-SHG household within DP blocks

Indicators NDP Block	PCMFE Gini	PCMNFE Gini	PCMTE Gini	PCMY Gini
Indpur	0.1869	0.2281	0.1831	0.1777
JAMBONI	0.1784	0.2413	0.1727	0.1668
BINPUR-II	0.2026	0.2111	0.1906	0.1872
JHARGRAM	0.1849	0.2585	0.1872	0.1838
GOPIBHALLAVPUR-II	0.2060	0.2619	0.1873	0.1735

Note: PCMFE = per capita monthly food expenditure, PCMNFE = per capita monthly non-food expenditure, PCMTE = percapita monthly total expenditure, PCMY = per capita monthly income
Source: Author's calculation fromField Survey (2011-12).

From this study it becomes clear that though most of the members of the SHGs in both DPAs and non-DPAs remain below the poverty line, there remains an inequality in the distribution of PCMTE and PCMY among them. There remain both inter-regional and intra-regional disparities in this distribution pattern. It is also observed that inequality in the distribution of PCMY isrelatively high in DPAs compared to that in non-DPAs.Hence, effective steps should be taken by the government to minimize this inequality in the distribution of income through the formation of more SHGs in DPAs as well as by making the existing SHGs more efficient and productive.

Figure 4. Inter-block difference in the distribution of PCMFE of non-SHG households in DPAs

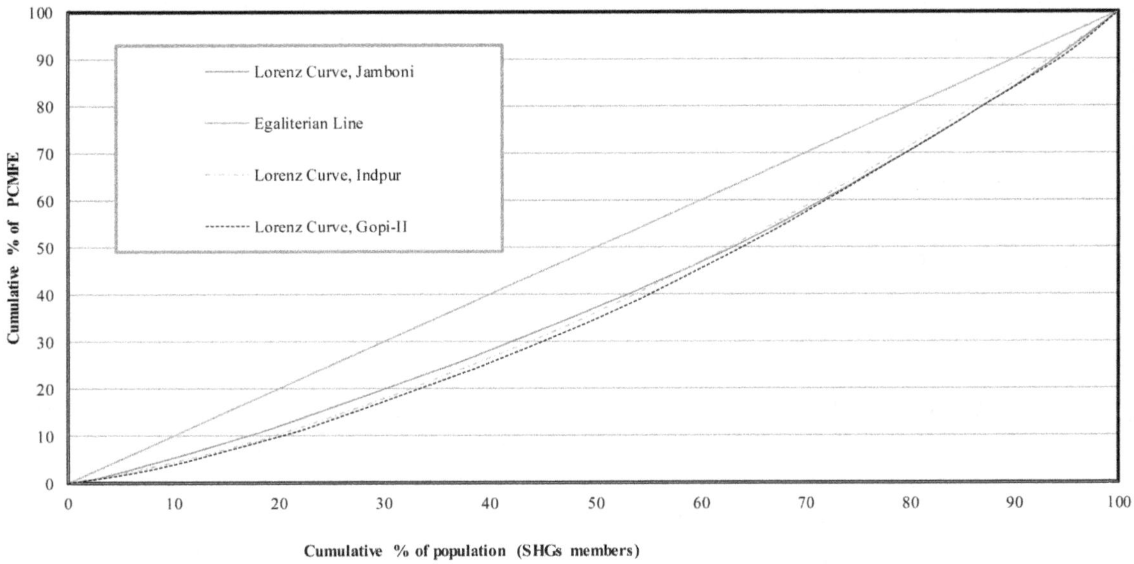

Figure5. Inter-block difference in the distribution of PCMNFE of non-SHG households in DPAs

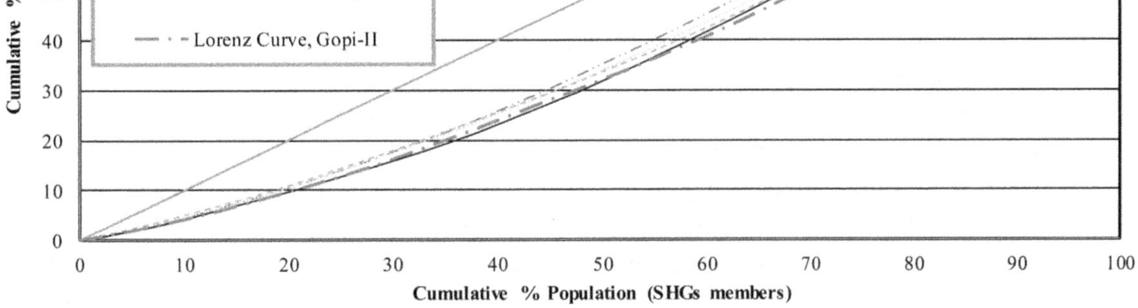

POLICY SHIFT: FROM SGSY TO NRLM

The Ministry of Rural Development, Government of India, has launched National Rural Livelihood Mission (NRLM) by restructuring Swarnajayanti Gram Swarozgar Yojana (SGSY) replacing the existing SGSY scheme since April 1, 2013.

Since the present study was undertaken during 2011-12, and meanwhile there has been a policy shift, so it is necessary to throw some light upon the new policy parameter and its difference with the old one, viz. SGSY and the implication of such policy shift for the incidence of poverty and income inequality among the members of SHGs.

The NRLM is the flagship program of Government of India for the alleviation of poverty through the creation of strong institutions of the poor, particularly women, and enabling these institutions to access a range of financial and livelihoods services.

Principal Features of NRLM

Some of the key features of the NRLM are as follows:

1. **Universal Social Mobilization:** The NRLM would ensure that at least one member from each identified rural poor household, preferably a woman, is brought under the SHG network within a target time period.
2. **Participatory Identification of Poor:** The experience from the earlier SGSY scheme suggests that the current BPL (Below poverty Line) list has large inclusion and exclusion errors. Hence, for widening the target groups beyond the BPL list and to include all the needy poor, NRLM will undertake community based process, i.e., participation of the poor people in the whole process to identify its target group. Over the years, the participatory method of identifying the poor have been developed and applied successfully in different states of India such as Andhra Pradesh, Kerala, Tamil Nadu and Odisha. Similar process can also be adopted in West Bengal.
3. **Promotion of Institutions of the Poor:** Strong institutions of the poor such as SHGs and the village level and higher level federations of these SHG members are necessary to provide space, voice and resources for the poor and for reducing their dependence on external agencies. It is hope that such collective action would enable the poor to optimize their limited resources.
4. **Strengthening all Existing SHGs and Federations of the Poor:** The NRLM would strengthen all existing institutions of the poor in a partnership mode. These institutions include the SHGs as well as several other NGOs (Non-Government Organizations) who work for the benefit of poor and under-privileged people in the society. All SHGs in a village would come together to form a federation at the village level. Such village federation is supposed to be a very important support structure for the members and their SHGs. At the next stage, there will be a cluster federation consisting of a group of villages within a block. The exact configuration will vary from State to State, but typically a cluster consists of 25 – 40 villages.
5. **Emphasis on Training, Capacity Building and Skill Formation:** The NRLM would ensure that the poor are provided with the requisite skills for managing their institutions, linking up with markets, managing their existing livelihoods, enhancing their credit absorption capacity and credit worthiness, etc. A multi-pronged approach is envisaged for continuous capacity building of the targeted families, SHGs, their federations, government functionaries, bankers, NGOs and other key stakeholders.
6. **Revolving Fund and Community Investment Support Fund:** A Revolving Fund would be provided to eligible SHGs as an incentive to inculcate the habit of thrift and accumulate their own funds towards meeting their credit needs in the long-run as well as to fulfill immediate consumption needs in the short-run. The Community Investment Support Fund (CIF) would be a corpus

and it would be used for meeting the members' credit needs directly and as catalytic capital for leveraging repeat bank finance. The CIF would be routed to the SHGs through the Federations.

7. **Universal Financial Inclusion:** The NRLM would work towards achieving universal financial inclusion, beyond basic banking services to all the poor households, SHGs and their federations. Both demand and supply sides of Financial Inclusion would be taken care of by the NRLM. On the demand side, it would promote financial literacy among the poor and provide catalytic capital to the SHGs and their federations. On the supply side, it would coordinate with the financial sector and encourage the use of modern ICT-based financial technologies, business correspondents and community facilitators like '*Bank Mitras*'(the agents or representatives of different commercial banks would help the SHGs in accessing several facilities from the banking institutions). It would also work towards universal coverage of rural poor against loss of life, health and assets. Further, it would work on remittances, especially in areas where migration is endemic.
8. **Provision of Interest Subvention:** The rural poor also need credit at low rates of interest and in multiple doses to make their ventures economically viable. In order to ensure affordable credit, the NRLM has a provision for subvention on interest rate above 7% per annum for all eligible SHGs, who have availed loans from mainstream financial institutions.
9. **Funding Pattern:** The NRLM is a Centrally Sponsored Scheme and the financing of the programme would be shared between the Centre and the States in the ratio of 75:25 (90:10 in case of North Eastern States including Sikkim; and completely from the Centre in case of Union Territories). The Central allocation earmarked for the States would broadly be distributed in accordance with the incidence of poverty in the States.
10. **Phased Implementation:** Social capital of the poor consists of the institutions of the poor, their leaders, community professionals and more importantly community resource persons (say, the poor women whose lives have been transformed through the support of their institutions). The NRLM aimed at improving this social capital in a phased manner in all the districts of India within March, 2017.

Now, if we review the basic features of SGSY and NRLM, we can identify some of the difference between NRLM and SGSY:

The NRLM, in its structure, has shown a major shift from purely 'allocation based' strategy to a 'demand driven' strategy wherein states have the flexibility to develop their own plans for capacity building of women SHGs and Federations, infrastructure and marketing, and can frame required policy for financial assistance to the SHGs. Further, the NRLM will promote the formation of women SHGs on the basis of affinity and not on the basis of a common activity, as it used to be under SGSY. The NRLM will also provide continuous hand-holding support to SHGs, and their federations. This was missing in SGSY. The NRLM would encourage public sector banks to set up Rural Self Employment Training Institutes (RSETIs) in all districts of the country. So the scope of NRLM is much broader than that of SGSY. Hence, it is hoped that this policy shift would help in reducing the poverty and income inequality among rural poor in general and among the SHG members in particular.

CONCLUSION

The present study clearly shows that the participation in SHGs by the poor people, particularly the socially backward and economically poor women, resulted in some positive impacts in terms of a reduction in the incidence of poverty in rural West Bengal.Among the factors which determine the intensity of poverty among the members of SHGs,credit received from financial institutions, quantity of landholding by the members, involvement in MG-NREGA scheme, and regional differences (in terms of proneness to drought conditions) are found to be statistically significant. However, among theexplanatory variables stated, area of operation and the landholdings of the members have been observed to be more significantinexplaining the incidence of poverty. In other words, qualifying for Grade II and the vintage value of any SHG have minimum effect on the incidence of poverty among the members of SHGs. Rather, theflow of micro credit to the SHGs seems to carry more importance in this respect.

The Gini coefficients measuring inequalities in the distribution of income among the members of the SHGs are found to remain higher for sample DP blocks on an average than thesample non-DP blocks. However, in terms of the distribution of total expenditure, inequalities are found to remain lower in DPAs than those in non-DPAs. This might be due to greater benefit provided by the government to BPL families in making consumption expenditure in DPAs and the presence of a few APL households in DPAs who might not get this facility in consumption expenditure. So far as the inequality in the distribution of per capita monthly non-food expenditure is concerned, though there are inter- block variations in both DP and non-DP blocks, there remains no such inter-regional difference on an average. This might be particularly due the increased consciousness among the women members of the SHGs regarding the health and education of their children in both DPAs and non-DPAs.

It appears that state intervention in the form of the creation of proper marketing infrastructure and promotion of research and development facilities for product innovation might result in added benefit to these poor people engaged in SHG activities in the backward regions of West Bengal and would result in an effective and sustained poverty alleviation process.

REFERENCES

Banerjee, A. (2009). Globalization and inequality: A review of evidences. *Artha Beekshan, 18*(2).

Chippa, M. L., Sharma, S., & Dubey, R. K. (2014). Impact of Microfinance on Women Empowerment, Poverty Alleviation and Employment Security in Rural Areas of Rajasthan. *International Journal of Innovative Research in Science Engineering and Technology, 3*(2), 9073–9080.

Chitagubbi, G., Shivalli, R., & Devendrappa, S. (2011). A study on the usefulness of Self Help Group membership to women for empowerment. *Journal of Farm Sciences, 1*(1), 112–119.

Chowdhury, M., & Simanowitz, A. (2004). The Social impact of Microfinance. *Journal of International Development, 16*(3), 30.

Das, P. (2010). *Rural Non-Farm Employment in India-Pattern of Growth and determinants*. Firma KLM Private limited.

Foster J, Greer J & Thorbeke E (1984). A class of decomposable poverty measure. *Econometrica, Journal of Econometric Socity*, 761-763.

Kirkpatrick, C., & Maimbo, S. (2002). The implications of the evolving microfinance agendafor regulatory and supervisory policy. *Development Policy Review*, *20*(3), 293–304. doi:10.1111/1467-7679.00172

Maity, S., & Sarania, R. (2017). Does microfinance alleviate poverty and inequality? Studying self-help groups in Bodoland, Assam. *Development in Practice*, *27*(7), 1006–1019. doi:10.1080/09614524.2017.1355353

Marr, A. (2004). A challenge to the orthodoxy concerning microfinance and poverty reduction. *Journal of Microfinance*, *5*(2).

Mehta, S. K., Mishra, H. G., & Singh, A. (2011). Role of Self-Help Groups in Socio-Economic Change of Vulnerable Poor of Jammu Region. *International Conference on Economics and Finance Research IPEDR*, 4, 519-523.

Mosley, P. (2001). Microfinance and Poverty in Bolivia. *The Journal of Development Studies*, *37*(4), 101–132. doi:10.1080/00220380412331322061

Nithyanandhana, S. H., Mansorb, N., & Nairc, S. (2015). Self Help Groups as Modalities for Poverty Alleviation for Women in India. *Institutions, Etc.*, *7*(3), 67–94.

Pitt, M. M., & Khandker, S. (1998). The impact of group-based credit programs on poor households in Bangladesh: Does the gender of participants' matter? *Journal of Political Economy*, 2.

Puhazhendhi, V., & Satyasai, K. J. S. (2000). Micro Finance for Rural People: An impact Evaluation. Microcredit Innovations Department, National Bank for Agriculture and Rural Development.

Saravanan, M. (2016). The Impact of Self-Help Groups on the Socio-Economic Development of Rural Household Women in Tamil Nadu- A Study. *International Journal of Research – Granthaalayah*, *4*(7), 22-31.

Sarkhel, J., & Dutta, S. (2010). *An insight into statistics. Book syndicate PVT.* LTD.

Scully, N. (2004). *Microcredit: 'No panacea for the poor women.* Washington, DC: Global DevelopmentResearch Centre.

Simanowitz, A. (2002). *Microfinance for the poorest: A review of issues and ideas for contribution of Imp-Act.* An action Research Programme.

Sivaramakrisnan, K. (2003). Poverty alleviation through Self Help Groups. *Cooperation*, *3*(5).

SU. (2007). From marginal tinkering to major changes: Microfinance and poverty alleviation. *Economic and Political Weekly*, *42*(5), 3.

Suprabha, K. R. (2014). Empowerment of Self-Help Groups (SHGs) towards Microenterprise Development. *Procedia Economics and Finance*, *11*, 410–422. doi:10.1016/S2212-5671(14)00208-1

Thorat. Y.S.P. (2005). Microfinance in India: Sectoral issuses and challenges. *High level policy conference on Microfinance in India.*

Vachya, L., Pesala, B., & Nagarjuna, B. (2009). Impact of Micro Finance Inequality Among the SHG Women: Selected Villages in Andhra Pradesh. *Small Enterprises Development, Management & Extension (Sedme) Journal, 36*(4). Retrieved from http://ojs.nimsme.org/)

Vasantha. (2015). Microfinance through self-help group as catalyst for poverty reduction and women empowerment. *Asian Journal of managerial Research, 6*(2), 243-257.

KEY TERMS AND DEFINITIONS

Gini Concentration: The area between the line of equal distribution and the Lorenz curve is called as the area of concentration. It is the indicator of the degree of concentration of income distribution. Twice this area is called as Gini *concentration* or Gini coefficient (G). This notion has been used to estimate the inequality in the distribution of monthly per capital consumption expenditure of SHG members across the Drought Prone and Non-Drought Prone Sample Blocks in this study. The area of concentration lies between 0 to1/2, and therefore, G lies between 0 to 1. If G=0, it implies "no inequality," while G=1 implies "complete inequality."

Inequality: It shows inter class or inter group differences in any economic, social or natural indicators.

Lorenz Ratio: It is a diagrammatic presentation of economic inequality in a box framework. The diagonal of the box shows absolute equality and the magnitude of inequality gets larger if the curve moves away from diagonal towards the right.

Poverty Gap: The poverty gap signifies the gap between the cut off line of monthly per capita consumption expenditure needed to maintain the minimum standard of living of a person in the rural West Bengal and the actual monthly per capita consumption expenditure of the sample SHG members.

Self-Help Groups (SHG): Self-help groups (SHGs) are organizations of rural people consisting of 10-20 members. The members of SHGs have common perception of their need and the importance of collective action. The members of SHGs should have the same social and financial background. The members of SHGs help one another to solve their problems. The groups promote savings among members and use the pooled resources to meet the emergent needs of their members, including the consumption needs. The major objectives of SHGs are as follows: a) to create a habit of savings; b) to mobilize the resources of the individual members for their collective economic development; c) to develop leadership qualities; d) to build up team work; e) to pay interest on organizing training for skill development; f) to assist the members financially at the time of need; g) to identify, analyze, and find solutions of the problems in the group; h) to avail of loan from the common fund of the group; i) to create confidence and capabilities of the members; j) to help the members by collective decision making.

Square Poverty Gap: This notion has been used to compare the severity of poverty among the members of SHGs. It simply implies the square of the ratio of average income or extra consumption needed to get all the poor members in the SHG up to the poverty line. This is a strictly convex function, a desirable property of a welfare function.

Chapter 12
A Tri-Variate Nexus of Microfinance-Growth-Inequality: The South-Asian Experience

Sovik Mukherjee
Shri Shikshayatan College, India

Asim Kumar Karmakar
Jadavpur University, India

ABSTRACT

Policymakers throughout the world have actively been in pursuit of improvements of financial markets in the developing regions, but often with disappointing results. In this background, this chapter claims that microfinance can play a significant role in financial development, and that by concentrating on microfinance, development policy can consolidate the links between financial development, growth, and thus inequality reduction. The inequality computation used is based on the generalized entropy index (standard assumption of weight equal to 2 is applicable). Panel cointegration and panel causality are the techniques that have been applied in a vector error correction mechanism (VECM) set-up using panel data for fifteen years across seven South-Asian nations (i.e., Bhutan, India, Afghanistan, Bangladesh, Nepal, Pakistan, and Sri Lanka). The findings validate the existence of a cointegrated relation coupled with a tri-variate causality linking the focus variables in this model in the way that microfinance initiatives, their outreach is beneficial for the reduction of inequality but that inequality reduction does not promote economic growth per se.

INTRODUCTION

...Strikingly, 30 years into the microfinance movement we have little solid evidence that it improves the lives of clients in measurable ways. (Roadman & Morduch, 2014)

DOI: 10.4018/978-1-5225-5240-6.ch012

Microfinance, the indispensable multiplier. Money to pay for a cow. Fresh milk and something wondrous called 'income'. The cow became a diary, then a milk distribution business. (The Award Committee awarding the 2008 Hilton Humanitarian Prize to BRAC as cited in Bateman, 2010)

How is inequality generated and does it impact growth? In this regard, can financial inclusion be of any significance? In fact, there is ambiguity to a certain extent on the impact of microfinance on growth across countries. But if one can bring in inequality then the story becomes interesting. Numerous researchers have tried to answer the first question over the years but examining this trivariate nexus has remained subservient. In the beginning, economists paid attention to factors that determine income inequality. To start off, Kuznets (1955) in his study analyzed the extent of influence of the distribution of income on economic growth. Empirically, in a panel set-up, Kuznets (1963) found an inverted U-shaped relation between income inequality and GNP per capita. This historical result highlighted the role that the distribution of income has on the transition of an economy from an agrarian based one to an industrialized one. The reason often cited for this "inverted U" relation is the sectoral shift that takes place in an economy i.e. the share of the industrial sector in GDP increases in comparison to the primary sector. However, there has been a lot of debate regarding the measure of capturing inequality. That is to say, can any one voice forth: should it be wealth, income or land inequality? There exist arguments in the literature for and against the relevance of this general relation proposed by Kuznets (1955) (see, for example, Ferreira, 1999; Arjona et al., 2003). Delving deep into the recent literature, Ravallion (2004) in his empirical analysis surprisingly gets zero correlation between the change in inequality and economic growth. In contrast to Ravallion (2004), this paper shows that for South Asian countries economic growth has been accompanied by a reduction in inequality over a span of 15 years from 2002 onwards. Interestingly, neither does this result lend support to the Kuznets relationship nor does it validate the idea of zero correlation.

Studies have looked also at inequality and growth in South Asia but till date studies looking at these two variables in the presence of the outreach of microfinance programmes have not come into existence. This has motivated the authors to drop in this third variable and examine the tri-variate nexus. Going back to some historical evidence especially in the context of Bangladesh, Pakistan, India and Nepal), while the informal sector financing can be traced back to the era of Kautilya in the fourth century B.C.E. (Rangarajan, 1992), the modern microfinance took shape after passing of Cooperative Credit Societies Act in 1904. The cooperative movement was aimed at providing agricultural credit rather than non-agricultural credit. Nepal saw the cooperative movement being formalized into a cooperative legislation in the year 1911 and by the year 1950 formal credit services could be accessed by only a small number of clients in the whole of Nepal. Eventually, the cooperatives failed to cater to the needs of the farmers, artisans and persons having limited earnings which led to the nationalization of commercial banks in the seventies in the region giving rise to the launch of microfinance in Nepal. Shifting focus on the origin of modern microfinance in Bangladesh, the legendary Dr. Mohammed Yunus started experimenting with the rural poor by providing small loans to them. One of the studies by the World Bank in 2005 found that 86 per cent of the 14.3 million active borrowers in Bangladesh at that time were served by NGO-MFIs including pioneers like the Grameen bank and the Bangladesh Rural Agricultural Cooperatives (BRAC) in Bangladesh. The Grameen Bank alone has 29 per cent share in micro lending with BRAC, Association for Social Advancement (ASA), and Proshika, making up for the rest. For Sri Lanka, the same survey made a comment that 65 per cent of the micro credit is provided by the government with the Samurdhi Development Programme since 1995 (under the purview of the Department of Cooperative Development (DCD)) being the largest of such initiatives aimed at poverty reduction. In Pakistan, microfinance banks, rural support programmes and specialised MFIs like — Akhuwat, Asasah, Kashf Foundation, Taraqee Foundation, Helping Hand for Relief and Development (HHRD), The Pakistan Microfinance Network (PMN), The Jinnah Welfare Society (JWS), Sindh Agricultural and Forestry Workers Coordinating Organization, are the key players in the microfinance sector. Coming to figures for Afghanistan as reported by Hussein (2009), 12 MFIs have opened around 128 branches covering half of the provinces across 120 districts having 120,000 active loan clients of which 80 per cent clients are women. Some of the major microfinance institutions in Afghanistan include the Microfinance Investment Support Facility for Afghanistan (MISFA) is an apex group funded by the World Bank's Afghanistan Reconstruction Trust Fund (ARTF). These include the likes of IIFC Group, OXUS-AFG group Mutahid, Afghanistan Microfinance Association (AMA), etc. Given the inadequacy of data, the authors have decided to leave out Maldives and carry out the analysis with the other South Asian countries. Moving to Bhutan, we have the Bhutan Development Finance Corporation (BDFC) and the Bhutan Development Bank Limited (BDBL) — the two organizations in the country engaged in the field of providing agricultural credit to marginal farmers and microfinance. The products that they offer are mostly similar. These include, small individual loans (SIL, loans less than Nu.100000 having a rate of 12-14 per cent against a collateral having at least 1:1 ratio of loan amount is a must),commercial agricultural loans (CAL, only for commercial farmers with a loan size of greater than Nu.100000 and interest rate ranging between 13-15 per cent with the ratio remaining same), group guarantee lending scheme (GGLS, is an adaptation of the Grameen model where no collateral is required and the maximum loan size is Nu.50000)(Hussein, 2009).The recent microfinance data for Bhutan retrieved from www.themix.org/mixmarket/profiles/bdbl shows that in Trashigang and Mongar districts almost 68 per cent of the loans have been disbursed for rural housing and 20 per cent for the purpose of agriculture. However, due to the lack of adequate infrastructure along with low literacy rates the growth of such institutions has got hampered.

To sum up the introductory observations, over the last thirty years microfinance has become one of the most important international development policy interventions in the field of inequality reduction, poverty alleviation and development. The basic idea of microfinance is that if poor people are provided access to financial assistance, including credit, they may be able to start or expand a micro enterprise that will allow them to come out from the quagmire of poverty. Microfinance: a set of financial practices designed to serve the unbanked poor — is seen by some as a magic wand against inequality and poverty that is supposed to solve it all. For others, microfinance practiced nowadays is nothing more than an innovative wave of usurious practices reframed and glorified. This extreme view, to a certain extent, gets validated by believable stylized facts, case studies, and, in some instances by meticulous academic empirical research.

From the authors' standpoint, however, the reality is to be found in nuances and perspectives. Most recent estimates suggest that microfinance has reached more than one hundred and fifty million individuals worldwide. The number of the unbanked poor estimated by some authors is very large— more than two and a half billion. The recent estimates by the World Bank suggest that about 2.5 billion people, or one-third of humanity, live on incomes of $2 a day or less. These numbers are indeed something to reckon with. But, a severe criticism of microfinance, however, is that it has been around for over 30 years now, and numerous critics are vociferous over the question — "Why is it that a renowned and well-funded innovation such as microfinance letting so many of the unbanked poor down?" Bereft of these, the authors believe that microfinance is exactly what the poor want and need, directly helps the very poorest of the poor, working in favour of generating additional income and employment for the most marginalized and 'at-risk' of the poor in the community. This kind of sets the tone for this empirical research in the context of South Asian countries.

Given the meteoric rise in the number of microfinance clients and credit requirement between a span of six years as reported in table 1, the authors believe that microfinance can indeed resolve the issue of inequality to a certain extent and hence this leads to the investigation of the trivariate nexus.

The rest of the chapter has been organized as follows; Section 2 presents an outline of the related literature, both theory and empirics. Section 3 looks at the microfinance scenario in India in the present context. In Section 4, the empirical model coupled with the methodological issues and the empirical results thereof have been discussed. To conclude, section 5 summarizes the results and gives recommendations for further studies in this area.

A BRIEF REVIEW OF THE SELECT LITERATURE

Research on the study of the liaison between income inequality and growth has always held an important place in the sphere of economics of developing economies. But there are contradicting viewpoints. Some economists suggest that the unequal distribution of income motivates growth, while others have articulated that income inequality hampers growth and contributes to increase in poverty. Bourguignon (2003) argue that reducing inequality causes the reduction of poverty. Deininger and Squire (1996) in their study call for the reduction of poverty and they empirically show that it actually promotes growth. But on a cautious note, their belief is that it is necessary for public authorities to strengthen their efforts towards an equal distribution of income. In this context, Piketty and Saez (2003) kind of reinforce the results that countries with a large number of poor and unequal distributions of income cannot reap the benefits from growth. In contrast, countries on the other side of the pole that are characterized by an equal distribution of income are at an advantageous position to reap such benefits. The question that automatically arises in this context is the importance of income distribution. Atkinson (2002) explains the importance of income distribution for two reasons. He articulates that countries having a more equal income distribution experience growth over an extended period of time. As already mentioned, Kuznets (1955), known by the famous Inverted-U, connects the national income per capita and the level of inequality. This hypothesis hypothesizes that an increase in inequality during the first period is followed by a decline in the subsequent periods since the late nineteenth or early twentieth century. Kuznets (1955) was

Table 1. Microfinance in South Asia: what the numbers say?

Countries	Microfinance Clients (Millions)_2006	Credit Requirement (Aggregate in Millions)_2006	#Predicted Microfinance Clients (Millions)_2012	#Predicted Credit Requirement (Aggregate in Millions) _2012
Afghanistan	0.12	400	0.50	455
Bangladesh	16.00	1733	22.00	1810
India	15.00	10909	19.67	11000
Nepal	0.50	213	0.73	250
Pakistan	0.58	1700	0.81	1756
Sri Lanka	2.50	200	2.52	221

Source: Computed by the authors based on World Bank (2006) using simple linear trend forecasting

however silent regarding the role of income distribution and severe criticism was raised from Deininger and Squire (1996) (Banerjee & Duflo, 2003).

Another strand of literature including Norton (2002) and Galor and Zeira (1996), believes that it is actually growth that leads to the creation of employment opportunities which acts on the wage differentials to reduce inequality. In this paper, the authors have commented that it is actually a unidirectional causality from growth towards inequality. Consequently, the results support this aspect of literature contrary to the bidirectional causal relations proposed by the likes of Bertola (1991), Alesina and Perotti (1994), Perotti (1994), etc. Using panel data analysis, Barro (2000) concluded that the effect of income inequality on growth can be positive or negative depending on the level of economic development of the country. Income inequality in poor countries retards economic growth, while income inequality in rich countries stimulates growth. The two opposing schools of thought in point of fact exist because the relation between inequality and economic growth is country specific and hence contradicting results arise. Among economists that showed a positive relationship between income inequality and growth are—Bourguignon (2003), Aghion and Howitt (1996), Forbes (2000). The results derived in this paper stands in sharp contrast to these predictions. The pioneering works related to a negative relation are carried out by Perotti (1994), Alesina and Perotti (1996). There is also a role for the initial level of inequality, that is, if initial inequality is low it can accelerate growth and this contributes to the slow down of poverty (Alesina & Rodrik, 1994). Empirical studies by Pitt and Khandker (1998),Roodman and Morduch(2014) in the context of Bangladesh deliberate about the impact of microfinance on the poor but inequality and growth have remained silent in their writings. Some have evaluated the impact of joint lending in the context of microfinance (Gine & Karlan,2009) and women empowerment Kabeer (2001). Studies concerned with different aspects of microfinance are many in number but only few are insightful in this regard. Bringing in the trivariate nexus among microfinance-growth-inequality in the South Asian context is thus the beginning of the modern story, as till date, there is nothing like the tri-variate nexus that exists in the literature.

MICROFINANCE IN INDIA: A BRIEF RECAPITULATION

The origin of modern day microfinance in India happened during the latter half of the 20th century especially during the seventies. Government's initiative to reduce poverty by improving access to financial services to poor started since independence and the All India Rural Credit Survey was one such step in that direction. This gave rise to the notion of 'social banking' which led to the nationalization of commercial banks, adoption of direct lending programmes to rural areas and development of credit institutions such as Regional Rural Banks (RRBs) and National Bank for Agriculture and Rural Development (NABARD). The emergence of the microfinance sector has its roots in the efforts of various non-governmental organizations and the breakdown of existing structures to deliver financial services to the needy and the poor. One can refer to figure 1 for the different channels for microfinance services in the country but first of all one needs to clearly understand what figure 1 exhibits. The "Access Points" derived by MIX (Microfinance Information exchange), a global web platform on microfinance, uses the number of entry/access points to financial institutions per 10000 adults at the national level and segmented state-wise. To understand this, in figure 1, the top 12 states in terms of providing financial services across the whole of India have been reported. Interestingly, the number of microfinance institu-

Figure 1. Cross state presence of Microfinance Institutions in 2016
Source: Compiled by the authors from http://finclusionlab.org/market-insights/india

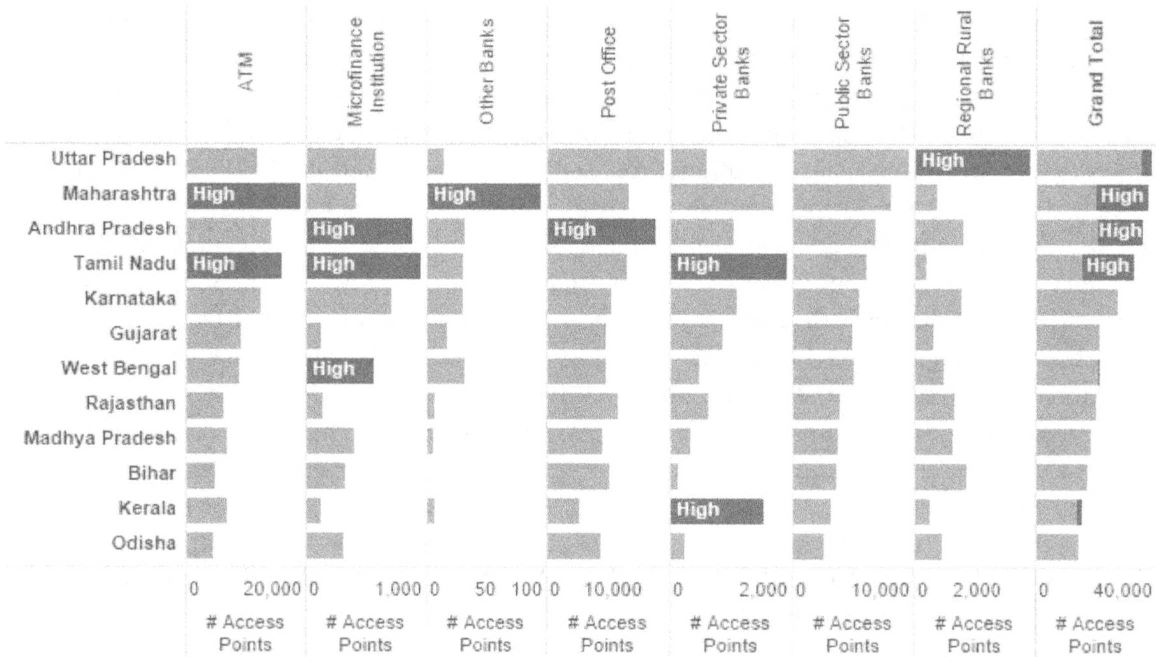

tions across these states is much less compared to public sector banks, regional rural banks or for that matter post office. Reportedly, states like Andhra Pradesh, Tamil Nadu and West Bengal have a higher number of such institutes relative to the other states.

Efforts from NABARD helped in the materialization of SHG (Self Help Group)-Bank Linkage Channel (SBLC) in the early nineties. Back then, it was one of its kinds but with the passage of time, many Non-Governmental Organizations (NGOs), Community Based Organizations (CBOs) and Self Help Groups has started micro finance delivery systems successfully in rural areas. The second medium of Microfinance institutions (MFIs) began in 1974 with the Self Employed Women's Association (SEWA) Bank in Ahmedabad, Gujarat. The expedition at first began with hiccups as formal financial institutions were reluctant to be involved with the MFIs on account of their commercial viability. Since then innovative partnership models have been developed between the banks and the MFIs and consequently enabled the MFIs to boost up their scale and outreach. In a survey conducted by the Microfinance Information Exchange (MIX) among 78 countries in 2005 saw the largest per-MFI percentage increase in active borrowers between 2000 and 2005 as compared to any other country. The microfinance sector report in 2009 officially reported that the number of registered microfinance institutions came up to 149, a rise of roughly 13 percent. Of these, about 11 per cent of the large micro finance companies controlled for 82 percent of the clients.

As figure 1 and 2 points out, the concentration of MFIs is on the South Eastern coast with nearly 30,000 cooperative organizations and NGOs are engaged in 105 microfinance activities only in Andhra Pradesh itself. There are more than 2000 NGOs involved in the NABARD SHG-Bank linkage programme. Of these, approximately 800 NGOs are involved in some form of financial intermediation (Rangarajan,

Figure 2. The geographic concentration of MFIs across states in India in 2016

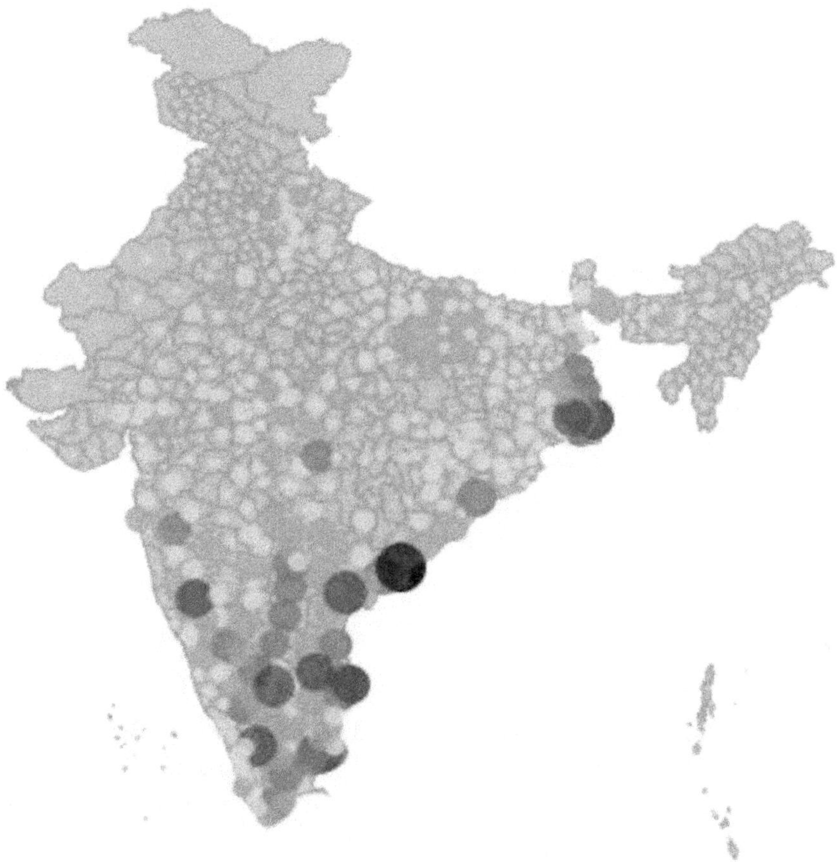

2008). At the moment, in terms of branch network, Bandhan bank has the highest number of branches standing at 2022 considerably higher than 1273 branches of SKS Microfinance that comes in a distant second. Only 4 MFI's in India have a branch network that is greater than 500 and the other two in this list are — Spandana Sphoorty Financial Limited and Share Microfin Limited.

THE EMPIRICAL FRAMEWORK

The discussions in the preceding section will motivate the empirical structure developed in this section. Preferably, one should consider a simultaneous equation framework that facilitates the measurement of feedback effects and hence establishes the interdependence between inequality, economic growth, and financial development i.e. the extent of financial inclusion proxied by the gross loan portfolio in PPP$. This has been shown using a schematic diagram in figure 3.

Figure 3. The Causal Nexus

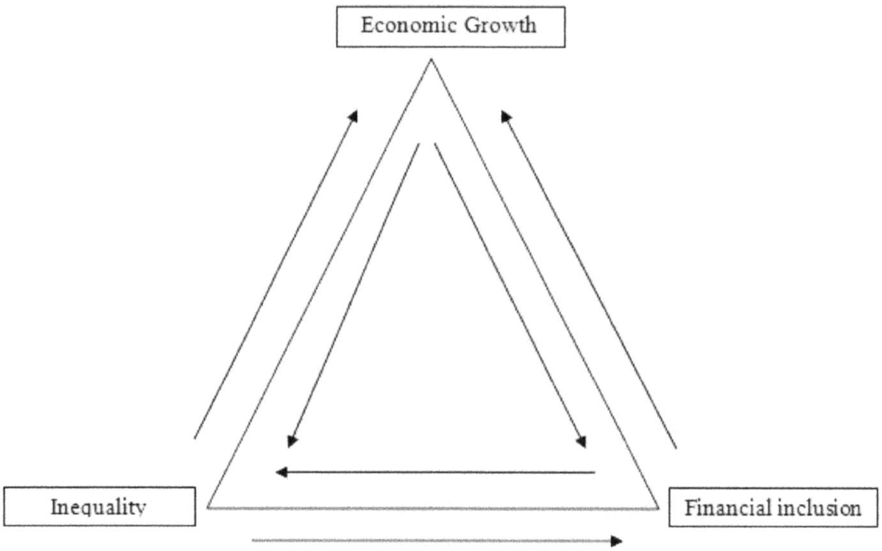

Data Description

Given the methodological constraints of which variable to be used to measure the extent or the outreach of microfinance in the microfinance cross-country literature and the availability of data, the most plausible alternative is to utilize the one which is widely used. The microfinance cross-country and panel data studies are limited by the availability of suitable data. This is based on the data generated by the Microfinance Information Exchange (2016) or MIX and the World Bank database. The data for every country and for every year was not readily available and so had to interpolated accordingly as per Newton's forward and backward interpolation formula and then data for every country was converted in terms of the corresponding PPP$ for that particular year available at https://data.oecd.org/conversion/purchasing-power-parities-ppp.htm.The derivation of the inequality data i.e. generalized entropy measure value has been discussed in the following sub-section. The data on per capita economic growth for the 15 years have been compiled from https://tradingeconomics.com/gdp-per-capita and from the world bank database retrieved from http://data.worldbank.org/indicator/NY.GDP.PCAP.KD. *ZG* for the countries concerned.

Calculating the GE(2) Measure of Inequality

The calculation of the Generalized Entropy measure entailed a lot of complicated stuff. The data availability became a serious constraint. The formal definition of GE(2) as reported in keywords definitions section necessitates an estimate of a ratio between the income of the ith class and the average income. But unfortunately, this data is not available so the authors have slightly kind of modified the GE(2) index and instead of that ratio this paper takes into account the ratio of 1st decile income to 5th decile income and the ratio of 5th decile income to 9th decile income. This happens for all the South Asian countries under consideration. Here, 5th decile kind of acts as the mean decile. The data has been accessed from OECD database at: h*ttps://stats.oecd.org/Index.aspx?DataSetCode=DEC_I*

Given the definition of the Generalized Entropy measure in the keywords definitions section, the purpose of taking the weight equal to 2 comes from the fact that for lower values of weights, a measure from the GE class is sensitive to the lower end of the distribution. As this paper deals with countries which are mostly developing in nature, the focus remains more on the lower tail of the distribution and as a result, $\alpha = 2$ is taken into consideration.

To remove the units and derive at the final GE(2) index in terms of deprivation i.e. the extent of inequality over and above the minimum, each indicator value of GE(2) has been normalized by –

$$X_{iN} = \frac{\left(X_i - X_{\min}\right)}{\left(X_{\max} - X_{\min}\right)} \text{ where,}$$

X_{iN} is the normalized value, X_{min} is the minimum value i.e. 0 and X_{max} is the maximum value i.e. 1. Normalization yields a value for every parameter for every state which lies between 0 and 1. The value '0' depicts the best case and '1' depicts the worst-case scenario in terms of merit. The values have been computed from 2002 but the authors have reported only for 2015 as a specimen. The values stress on the fact that Sri Lanka and India have a more unequal income distribution as compared to the other South Asian countries in 2015 in table 2.

Econometric Methodology

Before starting off with the panel unit root tests, the heteroskedasticity needs to be looked at. The Chi-Square value of 11.22 in table 3 is low and lies within the confidence limits and the results unquestionably establish the "absence of heteroskedasticity" as the null hypothesis of "constant variance in the model" gets

Table 2. Computation of Generalized Entropy (GE) measure of inequality for 2015_weight = 2

Countries	GE(2) Index Values
Afghanistan	0.278
Bangladesh	0.363
Bhutan	0.383
India	0.401
Nepal	0.328
Pakistan	0.345
Sri Lanka	0.443

Source: Computed by the authors

Table 3. Heteroskedasticity results

	Likelihood-Ratio Test	
H_0: Constant variance	**LR Chi-Square value (χ^2)**	**Probability > Chi-Square (χ^2)**
	11.22	0.96*

Notes: * denotes insignificance at 95 per cent level and calculation has been done by the authors in Stata 12

accepted. The foremost difference lies in the fact that in case of a panel data study, it is required to take into account the asymptotic behaviour of the time-series dimension T and cross-sectional dimension N.

To motivate the empirical structure and the estimation procedure related to Granger causality and cointegration, first one should focus on the basic structure of a two variable primitive First Order Auto-Regressive

$$\begin{pmatrix} 1 & b_{12} \\ b_{21} & 1 \end{pmatrix}\begin{pmatrix} Y_t \\ Z_t \end{pmatrix} = \begin{pmatrix} b_{10} \\ b_{20} \end{pmatrix} + \begin{pmatrix} \gamma_{11} & \gamma_{12} \\ \gamma_{21} & \gamma_{22} \end{pmatrix}\begin{pmatrix} Y_{t-1} \\ Z_{t-1} \end{pmatrix} + \begin{pmatrix} \varepsilon_{Yt} \\ \varepsilon_{Zt} \end{pmatrix},$$

There is a simultaneous impact of x on y and y on x so both the variables are endogenous and this is the starting point of VAR analysis. To give a brief idea about the econometric tools, let's start with the issue of Granger causality. It is used to test whether the lagged values of one variable enter into the equation of another variable. Extending the two variable case to a n variable VAR model with 1 lag, one can write it as,

$$\begin{pmatrix} x_{1t} \\ x_{2t} \\ \vdots \\ x_{nt} \end{pmatrix} = \begin{pmatrix} A_{10} \\ A_{20} \\ \vdots \\ A_{n0} \end{pmatrix} + \begin{pmatrix} A_{11}(L) & A_{12}(L)\cdots & A_{1n}(L) \\ A_{21}(L) & A_{22}(L)\cdots & A_{2n}(L) \\ \vdots & \vdots & \vdots \\ A_{n1}L) & A_{n2}(L) & A_{nn}(L) \end{pmatrix}\begin{pmatrix} x_{1t-1} \\ x_{2t-1} \\ \vdots \\ x_{nt-1} \end{pmatrix} + \begin{pmatrix} \varepsilon_{1t} \\ \varepsilon_{2t} \\ \vdots \\ \varepsilon_{nt} \end{pmatrix}$$

One can comment that x_{jt} does not Granger cause x_{it} *$(i \neq j)$ if and only if $A_{ij}(L) = 0$*. The null hypothesis (H_0) under Granger Causality (Granger, 1969) is:

H_0= no granger causality and,

H_1(alternative hypothesis) = there exists granger causality.

Before moving to the cointegration issue using the Vector Error Correction mechanism (VECM), Levin, Lin and Chu (LLC) panel unit root tests have been used in this study. The test is based on their model given below:

$$\Delta y_{it} = \alpha_i y_{it-1} + \sum_{j=1}^{p_j} \beta_{ij} \Delta y_{it-j} + x_{it}'\delta + \varepsilon_{it}$$

Here, α_1 is the error correction term and consequently, Δ is the first difference operator. The null hypothesis of non-stationarity is as follows:

Tests hypotheses:

H_0: $\alpha_i = 0$ for all the cross section units, so the series is non-stationary and has a unit root.

H_1: $\alpha_i < 0$ for at least one cross section unit, so the series is trend stationary.

When the probability value obtained from the test results is smaller than 0.05, H_0 is rejected and the stationarity of the series gets determined. LLC panel unit root results that have been derived are reported in table 4. As pointed out by Levin, Lin and Chu (2002), this test-statistic performs well when N lies between 10 and 250 and when T lies between 5 and 250. To determine whether a cointegrating relationship exists or not, the methodology proposed by Pedroni (1999) has been employed. Fundamentally, it employs four panel statistics and three group panel statistics to test the null hypothesis of no cointegration against the alternative hypothesis of cointegration exists. The first group is the within-dimension approach comprising four statistics that are — panel v-statistic, panel ρ-statistic, panel PP-statistic and the panel ADF-statistic (Pedroni, 1999). This set pools the autoregressive coefficients across various members for the unit root tests to be carried out on the estimated residuals. The second set of statistics, centered on the between-dimensional approach, includes three statistics that are respectively the group ρ-statistic, group PP-statistic and group ADF-statistic. If the variables are not cointegrated it implies that the residuals are not I(0). These estimators are based on Monte Carlo simulations and the details for these calculations are given in the original paper (Refer to Pedroni, 1999). If the null hypothesis is rejected in the panel case, then variables in question are cointegrated for all South Asian countries considered. On the other hand, if the null is rejected in the case of group panels, then cointegration among the relevant variables exists for at least one of the countries concerned. The VECM framework used is given as follows,

$$\Delta GDPgr_{i,t} =$$
$$\alpha_{1,i} + \varphi_{1,i} ECT_{i,t} + \sum_{j=1}^{k} \beta_{1,j,i} \Delta INQ_{i,t-j} + \sum_{j=1}^{k} \delta_{1,j,i} \Delta GLMFI_{i,t-j} + \sum_{j=1}^{k} v_{1,j,i} \Delta GDPgr_{i,t-j} + \varepsilon_{1,i,t}$$

$$\Delta INQ_{i,t} =$$
$$\alpha_{2,i} + \varphi_{2,i} ECT_{i,t} + \sum_{j=1}^{k} \beta_{2,j,i} \Delta INQ_{i,t-j} + \sum_{j=1}^{k} \delta_{2,j,i} \Delta GLMFI_{i,t-j} + \sum_{j=1}^{k} v_{2,j,i} \Delta GDPgr_{i,t-j} + \varepsilon_{2,i,t}$$

$$\Delta GLMFI_{i,t} =$$
$$\alpha_{3,i} + \varphi_{3,i} ECT_{i,t} + \sum_{j=1}^{k} \beta_{3,j,i} \Delta INQ_{i,t-j} + \sum_{j=1}^{k} \delta_{3,j,i} \Delta GLMFI_{i,t-j} + \sum_{j=1}^{k} v_{3,j,i} \Delta GDPgr_{i,t-j} + \varepsilon_{3,i,t}$$

Table 4. Levin-Lin-Chu (LLC) Unit Root test results

Variables	Level	Probability	1st Difference	Probability	Result
GDPgr	0.21	0.50	-3.88	0.00*	I(1)
INQ	-0.86	0.31	-5.68	0.00*	I(1)
GLMFI	0.43	0.67	-6.33	0.00*	I(1)

Notes:* denotes significance at 95 per cent level and calculation has been done by the authors in Eviews-7

Where $i(i = 1,...N)$ denotes the state, t $(t = 1,...T)$ the period, j is the optimum lag considering the Akaike Information Criteria (AIC). ECT is the lagged error correction term derived from the long-run co-integrating relationship; the φ_1 and φ_2 are the adjustment coefficients; $\varepsilon_{1,i,t}$ and $\varepsilon_{2,i,t}$ are disturbance terms assumed to be white-noises and hence uncorrelated.

The coefficients on ECTs represent how fast the deviations from the long-run equilibrium are eliminated pursuing a change in each of these variables. If the ECT's coefficients are zero i.e. $\varphi_{1,i} = 0$ or $\varphi_{2,i} = 0$ for all i, then there is no error correction and thus there exists no cointegration. But if, $\varphi_{1,i} < 0$ or $\varphi_{2,i} < 0$ then there exists error correction and consequently cointegration.

This paper looks at the nexus between GDP growth rate, inequality and extent of microfinance outreach by taking advantage of the heterogeneous panel cointegration framework developed by Pedroni (1999) across eight South Asian countries. It should be noted that the first four statistics fits with the 'within-dimension' based jargon of panel data and the rest are 'between-dimension' based statistics. Now, the authors move on to the causality issue in case of panel data. Given that, this analysis is being carried out across the eight South Asian countries, the assumption that the coefficients are different across the cross-sections follows from Dumitrescu and Hurlin (2012), i.e.

$\alpha_{0,i} \neq \alpha_{0,j}, \alpha_{1,i} \neq \alpha_{1,j}, \ldots \alpha_{p,i} \neq \alpha_{p,j}, \mu_{0,i} \neq \mu_{0,j}, \mu_{1,i} \neq \mu_{1,j}, \ldots \mu_{p,i} \neq \mu_{p,j}$ and

$\beta_{1,i} \neq \beta_{1,j}, \ldots \beta_{p,i} \neq \beta_{p,j}$ & $\eta_{1,i} \neq \eta_{1,j}, \ldots \eta_{p,i} \neq \eta_{p,j}$ for all i and j.

Bivariate regressions in Dumitrescu and Hurlin (2012) take the form,

$$y_{i,t} = \alpha_{0,i} + \sum_{p=1}^{k} \alpha_{p,i} y_{i,t-p} + \sum_{p=1}^{k} \beta_{p,i} x_{i,t-p} + \varepsilon_{i,t}$$

$$x_{i,t} = \mu_{0,i} + \sum_{p=1}^{k} \mu_{p,i} x_{i,t-p} + \sum_{p=1}^{k} \eta_{p,i} y_{i,t-p} + e_{i,t} \text{ where,}$$

t denotes the time period dimension of the panel, and i denotes the cross-sectional dimension and k is the number of lags. This assumption is applicable for South Asia contrary to the assumption where the panel gets treated as one large stacked data set. The intention is to perform Granger causality regressions for each and every individual cross-sectional element. Subsequently, take the average of the Wald statistics derived from each cross section to get the *W-bar* statistic.

RESULTS AND DISCUSSION

Table 4 presents the results of the Levin, Lin, Chu (2002) unit root tests. The results indicate that all the three variables are stationary after first differencing i.e. integrated of order (1). Hence, we can apply the procedure of Pedroni (1999) to look into the cointegration possibility between the focus variables. Here, given the AIC norm, an optimum lag of 1 has been taken into account. The results in table 5 designate the existence of a cointegrated relationship between inequality as measured by GE(2), economic growth and gross loan portfolio [(PPP$) as a measure of financial inclusion] in the long run. Under the alternative hypothesis as discussed, the panel-v statistic diverges to positive infinity (∞^{+}), and the right-hand tail of the standard normal distribution has been used to reject the null hypothesis. On the other hand, all the other panel cointegration test statistics diverge to negative infinity (∞^{-}). Therefore, the left-hand tail of the standard normal distribution is used to reject the null hypothesis. There is a strong evidence of panel cointegration as the test statistic values lie in the critical region (in both the cases i.e. on the left tail and on the right tail respectively) and the null hypothesis of 'no cointegration' gets resoundingly rejected.

This LLC unit root test tests that whether GDPgr, INQ and GLMFI follows a unit root process or not. At their level value, the approximate p-value for GDPgr, INQ and GLMFI is 0.50,0.31 and 0.67 respectively. So, the null hypothesis of existence of unit root cannot be rejected. The next step is to carry out the first order differencing of the data and the results suggest that all the variables become stationary at the first order. The p-value of 0.00 implies that the null hypothesis of presence of unit root gets rejected. However, the presence of a cointegrating liaison in table 5, where GLMFI reduces inequality and GLMFI promotes growth as expected. But this does not give any clear idea regarding the causality between the concerned variables in this section. The results of the test for causality are reported in table 6.

The authors have found two cointegrating vectors. The normalized cointegrating relationships are given by:

$$INQ = -0.81GDPgr - 0.52GDPgr_{-1} - 0.59GLMFI - 0.004GLMFI_{-1} \tag{1}$$

$$GLMFI = 0.63GDPgr + 0.06GDPgr_{-1} - 0.01INQ - 0.0008INQ_{-1} \tag{2}$$

In this model, a lag value of one seems to be appropriate. From the theoretical understanding, the results seem to be consistent. This is justified because a rise in the amount of gross loan portfolio can act as a stimulant in reducing inequality (refer to equation 2) which is bound to produce a repercussion effect on income growth in the long run. But the results in this paper (refer to table 6) say that the repercussion

Table 5. Panel cointegration test

Test Procedure	Test Statistic	Probability Value	Result
Panel v-statistic	3.19	0.00*	Cointegration
Panel rho-statistic	-2.35	0.00*	Cointegration
Panel PP-statistic	-3.08	0.00*	Cointegration
Panel ADF-statistic	-2.90	0.00*	Cointegration
Group rho-statistic	-4.72	0.00*	Cointegration
Group PP-statistic	-2.77	0.00*	Cointegration
Group ADF-statistic	-8.11	0.00*	Cointegration

Notes: * denotes significance at 95 per cent level and calculation has been done by the authors in Eviews-7

Table 6. Results of Dumitrescu and Hurlin Panel causality test

Null Hypothesis	W-Bar Statistic	Probability
I. Between INQ &GDPgr		
INQ does not cause GDPgr	0.89	0.37
GDPgr does not cause INQ	8.55	0.00*
II. Between INQ & GLMFI		
INQ does not cause GLMFI	8.52	0.00*
GLMFI does not cause INQ	3.64	0.00*
III. Between GLMFI &GDPgr		
GLMFI does not cause GDPgr	3.85	0.00*
GDPgr does not cause GLMFI	3.60	0.00*

Notes: * denotes significance at 95 per cent level and calculation has been done by the authors in Eviews-7

effects of inequality reduction on growth does not take place. As a result, the policy formulations at the centralized level should take into account this liaison but what happens to this relation at the state level across these countries has been left for further research and is very much worth exploring.

The W-bar statistic for every possible case as suggested by the p-value, the null hypothesis gets rejected except the case where 'INQ does not cause GDPgr'. Therefore, there exists a bilateral causal relation running between GDPgr and GLMFI and also INQ and GLMFI. This means that microfinance actually has solved the problem of inequality in the South Asian countries taken in this exercise, if not wholly but definitely to a certain extent. Moreover, the bidirectional causality between economic growth (GDPgr) and gross loan portfolio (GLMFI)complement the results of cointegration derived. Interestingly, the results, however, show that a rise in inequality does not affect growth rate but growth rates does affect inequality as expected. However, the authors have found evidence for the falling part of the existence of the 'inverted U' hypothesis. Also, Kuznets' (1955) idea that growth reduces inequality is justified in the light of the Kuznets curve. Recent studies on the income distribution based inequality and endogenous growth theory by Bertola (1991), Alesina and Perotti (1996), Perotti (1994), etc. talk about the two way causation contrary to what this paper says. Social welfare schemes, several redistribution schemes and inequality-reducing measures might have had little impact on the growth rates of these countries so this brings us to the next question that if not inequality, then does it mean that one should go for the nexus between poverty, growth and microfinance? This has been left for further research.

CONCLUSION

As discussed in the preceding section, looking at the poverty-growth-microfinance nexus in a panel data set-up will be indeed novel. Moreover, comparing the two nexuses can give an idea regarding the kind of policy intervention required at the macro level. Also, carrying out the same exercise across different countries may be for different regions like Africa, Latin America, other parts of Asia, New Zealand and Australia, Europe by putting in dummies for each region and doing the difference estimator to tackle the fixed effects. Countries have been caught up in the celebratory atmosphere surrounding microfinance and its ability to 'help the poor', microfinance initiatives have taken center stage. Summing up, these results tell something very interesting, that is, microfinance initiatives, their outreach is beneficial for the reduction of inequality but that inequality reduction does not promote economic growth *per se*. Possibly, from the authors' point of view, in the development paradigm, microfinance has evolved as a need–based policy and programme to cater to the neglected groups of society in any economy. But for the improvement of microfinance what is needed is the necessity to adopt a 'system perspective', a strategic management framework and good governance above all.

REFERENCES

Aghion, P., & Howitt, P. (1996). Research and development in the growth process. *Journal of Economic Growth*, *1*(1), 49–73. doi:10.1007/BF00163342

Alesina, A., & Perotti, R. (1996). Income distribution, political instability, and investment. *European Economic Review*, *40*(6), 1203–1228. doi:10.1016/0014-2921(95)00030-5

Alesina, A., & Perotti, R. (1994). The political economy of growth: A critical survey of the recent literature. *The World Bank Economic Review*, *8*(3), 351–371. doi:10.1093/wber/8.3.351

Alesina, A., & Rodrik, D. (1994). Distributive politics and economic growth. *The Quarterly Journal of Economics*, *109*(2), 465–490. doi:10.2307/2118470

Arjona, R., Ladaique, M., & Pearson, M. (2003). Growth, inequality and social protection. *Canadian Public Policy*, *29*, S119–S139. doi:10.2307/3552279

Banerjee, A. V., & Duflo, E. (2003). Inequality and growth: What can the data say? *Journal of Economic Growth*, *8*(3), 267–299. doi:10.1023/A:1026205114860

Barro, R. J. (2000). Inequality and Growth in a Panel of Countries. *Journal of Economic Growth*, *5*(1), 5–32. doi:10.1023/A:1009850119329

Bateman, M. (2010). *Why Doesn't Microfinance Work?: The Destructive Rise of Local Neoliberalism*. London: Zed Books Ltd.

Bertola, G. (1991). *Factor shares and savings in endogenous growth (No. w3851)*. National Bureau of Economic Research. doi:10.3386/w3851

Bourguignon, F. (2003). The growth elasticity of poverty reduction: explaining heterogeneity across countries and time periods. *Inequality and Growth: Theory and policy implications, 1*(1).

Decile ratios of gross earnings. (n.d.). *OECD Statistics*. Retrieved from https://stats.oecd.org/Index.aspx?DataSetCode=DEC_Ioecd.org/Index.aspx?DataSetCode=DEC_I

Deininger, K., & Squire, L. (1996). A new data set measuring income inequality. *The World Bank Economic Review*, *10*(3), 565–591. doi:10.1093/wber/10.3.565

Dumitrescu, E. I., & Hurlin, C. (2012). Testing for Granger non-causality in heterogeneous panels. *Economic Modelling*, *29*(4), 1450–1460. doi:10.1016/j.econmod.2012.02.014

Ferreira, F. H. (1999). *Inequality and economic performance: a brief overview to theories of growth and distribution*. World Bank.

Forbes, K. J. (2000). A Reassessment of the Relationship between Inequality and Growth. *The American Economic Review*, *90*(4), 869–887. doi:10.1257/aer.90.4.869

Galor, O., & Zeira, J. (1993). Income distribution and macroeconomics. *The Review of Economic Studies*, *60*(1), 35–52. doi:10.2307/2297811

GDP per capita economic growth. (n.d.). Retrieved from https://tradingeconomics.com/gdp-per-capita

Giné, X., & Karlan, D. S. (2009). *Group versus individual liability: Long term evidence from Philippine microcredit lending groups*. Academic Press.

Hussein, M. H. (2009). *State of Microfinance in Afghanistan*. Dhaka, Bangladesh: Institute of Microfinance.

Hussein, M. H. (2009). *State of microfinance in Bhutan*. Prepared for Institute of Microfinance (InM) as part of the project on State of Microfinance in SAARC Countries.

Kabeer, N. (2001). Conflicts over credit: Re-evaluating the empowerment potential of loans to women in rural Bangladesh. *World Development*, *29*(1), 63–84. doi:10.1016/S0305-750X(00)00081-4

Kuznets, S. (1955). Economic growth and income inequality. *The American Economic Review*, *45*(1), 1–28.

Kuznets, S. (1963). Quantitative aspects of the economic growth of nations: VIII. Distribution of income by size. *Economic Development and Cultural Change*, *11*(2), 1–80. doi:10.1086/450006

Levin, A., Lin, C. F., & Chu, C. S. J. (2002). Unit root tests in panel data: Asymptotic and finite- sample properties. *Journal of Econometrics*, *108*(1), 1–24. doi:10.1016/S0304-4076(01)00098-7

Market Insights. (n.d.). Retrieved from http://finclusionlab.org/market-insights/india

Microfinance Information Exchange. (n.d.). Retrieved from https://www.themix.org

Norton, S. W. (2002). Economic growth and poverty: In search of trickle-down. *The Cato Journal*, *22*, 263.

Pedroni, P. (1999). Critical values for cointegration tests in heterogeneous panels with multiple regressors. *Oxford Bulletin of Economics and Statistics*, *61*(S1), 653–670. doi:10.1111/1468-0084.61.s1.14

Perotti, R. (1994). Income distribution and investment. *European Economic Review*, *38*(3), 827–835. doi:10.1016/0014-2921(94)90119-8

Piketty, T., & Saez, E. (2003). Income inequality in the United States, 1913–1998. *The Quarterly Journal of Economics*, *118*(1), 1–41. doi:10.1162/00335530360535135

Pitt, M. M., & Khandker, S. R. (1998). The impact of group-based credit programs on poor households in Bangladesh: Does the gender of participantsmatter? *Journal of Political Economy*, *106*(5), 958–996. doi:10.1086/250037

Purchasing power parities (PPP). (n.d.). Retrieved from https://data.oecd.org/conversion/purchasing-power-parities-ppp.htm

Rangarajan, L. N. (Ed.). (1992). *The Arthashastra*. Penguin Books India.

Ravallion, M. (2004). *Pro-poor growth: A primer*. Academic Press.

Roodman, D., & Morduch, J. (2014). The impact of microcredit on the poor in Bangladesh: Revisiting the evidence. *The Journal of Development Studies*, *50*(4), 583–604. doi:10.1080/00220388.2013.858122

World Bank. (2006). *World development indicators database*. Author.

World Bank. (2011). *World development indicators database*. Author.

ADDITIONAL READING

Armendáriz, B., & Morduch, J. (2010). *The economics of microfinance*. USA: MIT press.

Aghion, P., Howitt, P., & Murtin, F. (2010). *The relationship between health and growth: when Lucas meets Nelson-Phelps (No. w15813)*. National Bureau of Economic Research. doi:10.3386/w15813

Banuri, S. (2006). *Impact of microfinance on poverty, income inequality and entrepreneurship. A Term Paper Submitted to School of Economic*. Richardson, Texas, USA: Political and Policy Sciences Political Economy and Public Policy.

Chakrabarty, S., & Bass, A. E. (2014). Institutionalizing ethics in institutional voids: Building positive ethical strength to serve women microfinance borrowers in negative contexts. *Journal of Business Ethics*, *119*(4), 529–542. doi:10.100710551-013-1833-9

Copestake, J. (2002). Inequality and the polarizing impact of microcredit: Evidence from Zambia's copperbelt. *Journal of International Development*, *14*(6), 743–755. doi:10.1002/jid.921

Dasgupta, R. (2005). Microfinance in India: Empirical evidence, alternative models and policy imperatives. *Economic and Political Weekly*, 1229–1237.

Devlin, N., & Hansen, P. (2001). Health care spending and economic output: Granger causality. *Applied Economics Letters*, *8*(8), 561–564. doi:10.1080/13504850010017357

Erdil, E., & Yetkiner, I. H. (2009). The Granger-causality between health care expenditure and output: A panel data approach. *Applied Economics*, *41*(4), 511–518. doi:10.1080/00036840601019083

Hermes, N. (2014). Does microfinance affect income inequality? *Applied Economics*, *46*(9), 1021–1034. doi:10.1080/00036846.2013.864039

Inoue, T., & Hamori, S. (2013). Financial permeation as a role of microfinance: Has microfinance actually been a viable financial intermediary for helping the poor? *Applied Financial Economics*, *23*(20), 1567–1578. doi:10.1080/09603107.2013.839859

Jauch, S., & Watzka, S. (2016). Financial development and income inequality: A panel data approach. *Empirical Economics*, *51*(1), 291–314. doi:10.100700181-015-1008-x

Rankin, K. N. (2002). Social capital, microfinance, and the politics of development. *Feminist Economics*, *8*(1), 1–24. doi:10.1080/13545700210125167

Kim, J. C., Watts, C. H., Hargreaves, J. R., Ndhlovu, L. X., Phetla, G., Morison, L. A., & Pronyk, P. (2007). Understanding the impact of a microfinance-based intervention on women's empowerment and the reduction of intimate partner violence in South Africa. *American Journal of Public Health*, *97*(10), 1794–1802. doi:10.2105/AJPH.2006.095521 PMID:17761566

Nair, T. S. (2001). Institutionalising microfinance in India: An overview of strategic issues. *Economic and Political Weekly*, 399–404.

O'Gorman, M. (2010). Microfinance in India. *Canadian Journal of Development Studies/Revue canadienned'études du développement, 31*(1-2), 225-227.

Risso, W. A., & Carrera, E. J. S. (2010). *Inequality and Economic Growth in China: Pre-and Post-reform Periods*. Università di Siena.

Reddy, C. S., & Manak, S. (2005). Self-help groups: A keystone of microfinance in India- women empowerment and social security. Andhra Pradesh Mahila Abhivruddhi Society (APMAS). India: Hyderabad.

Tchouassi, G. (2011). Microfinance, inequality and vulnerability: Empirical analysis from Central African countries. *Journal of Development and Agricultural Economics*, *3*(3), 150–156.

Wagner, C. (2012). From boom to bust: How different has microfinance been from traditional banking? *Development Policy Review*, *30*(2), 187–210. doi:10.1111/j.1467-7679.2012.00571.x

KEY TERMS AND DEFINITIONS

Cointegration: Cointegration is an econometric characteristic where a collection of time series variables (X_1, X_2, X_3, ...X_k) being integrated of the same order (greater than zero i.e. non- stationary) can be combined to generate a linear combination from this collection of variables which is integrated of order zero (i.e. a stationary trend). Then the time series variables X_1, X_2, X_3, ...X_k are said to be cointegrated.

Economic Growth: It can be defined as the increase in the capability of an economy to produce goods and services from one period to another. It can be measured either in nominal terms or in inflation adjusted real terms. Typically, GDP or GNP is taken as a measure of economic growth. In notational terms, GDP growth rate, g_t, $g_t = \frac{GDP_t - GDP_{t-1}}{GDP_{t-1}} \times 100$ where, *t* indicates the particular time point; Here, economic growth actually means per capita economic growth (i.e., growth rates adjusted for population levels).

Generalized Entropy Index: The generalized entropy (GE) index derived from information theory has been proposed as a measure of income inequality in a population satisfying all the five desired properties, *viz., mean independence, population size independence, symmetry, Pigou-Dalton transfer sensitivity and decomposability*. The formula for GE (2) is given by, $GE(2) = \frac{1}{2N}\sum_{i=1}^{N}\left[\left(\frac{y_i}{\bar{y}}\right)^2 - 1\right]$ where,

N is the number of cases (e.g., households or families), y_i is the income for case i and, $\alpha = 2$ is the weight assigned to the distances between incomes at different parts of the income distribution.

Newton's Interpolation Formula: Newton's forward and backward interpolation formula is used to interpolate the missing values and they look like, Newton's forward interpolation formula: $U_{a+rh} = U_a + r_{C_1} \Delta U_a + r_{C_2} \Delta^2 U_a + ...r_{C_n} \Delta^n U_a; r = \frac{x - x_0}{h}$ where, h is the difference between two consecutive step values and x_0 is the initial value. Newton's backward interpolation formula: $U_{n+vh} = U_n + v\Delta U_{n-1} + \frac{v(v+1)}{1\times 2}\Delta^2 U_{n-2} + ...\frac{v(v+1)....(v+n-1)}{1\times 2\times ......\times n}\Delta^n U_a; v = \frac{x - x_n}{h}$ where, h is the difference between consecutive step two values and x_n is the terminal value.

Panel Data: Also called longitudinal data, represents cross-sectional time series data (i.e., data on multi-dimensional cross-sections [comprising of individuals, firms and countries] over a period of time).

South Asia: The term Southern Asia encompasses the southern region of the Asian continent (i.e., the sub-Himalayan SAARC countries and, for some authorities, adjoining countries to the west and the east). Topographically, South Asia is bounded on the south by the Indian Ocean and shares its geographical boundaries with West Asia, Central Asia, East Asia, and Southeast Asia. The countries on which this paper carries out its analysis include—Bhutan, India, Afghanistan, Bangladesh, Nepal, Pakistan and Sri Lanka.

Vector Error Correction Mechanism (VECM): The VEC has cointegration relations built into the specification so that a series of partial short run dynamic adjustments allow for the correction in the deviation from long-run equilibrium. Consider a two-variable system with one cointegrating equation and no lagged difference terms. The cointegrating equation of two endogenous variables is given by, $y_{2,t} = \beta y_{1,t}$ The corresponding VEC model for y_1 and y_2 is, $\Delta y_{1,t} = \alpha_1(y_{2,t-1} - \beta y_{1,t-1}) + \varepsilon_{1,t}$

$\Delta y_{2,t} = \alpha_2(y_{2,t-1} - \beta y_{1,t-1}) + \varepsilon_{2,t}$ **In this simple model:** α_i measures the speed of adjustment of the ith endogenous variable towards the equilibrium. Nevertheless, if y_1 and y_2 tend to deviate from the long run equilibrium, the value of the error correction term will be non-zero and each variable will hence adjust partially to restore back the equilibrium relation.

Chapter 13
The Quest for Financial Inclusion and Microfinance Institutions in India

Amir Manzoor
Bahria University, Pakistan

ABSTRACT

Financial inclusion refers to providing unconditional and affordable access to financial services in an effective and efficient manner for all needy people. Microfinance institutions (MFIs) play an important role in financial inclusion and societal development. One important part of the financial inclusion strategy is to provide access to finance to those people belonging to remote and disadvantaged areas. The aim of this chapter is to study the concept of microfinance and microfinance institutions and its impact on financial inclusion in India. This study provides recommendations to grow and sustain microfinance institutions to achieve greater financial inclusion.

INTRODUCTION

Financial Inclusion is delivering banking services at affordable prices to that section of society which has low income and low opportunities of availabilities of different economic and social services. Financial Inclusion lists out various measures and initiatives by the Government of India and the central bank of the country, Reserve Bank of India (RBI) towards socio-economic growth. India has been divided into three categories on a state wise index mainly high, medium, and low-income groups. Sadly, a large section of our society is facing the problem of financial exclusion. It is mainly due to lack of socio-economic financial literacy and infrastructure. At a global level, many countries have adopted the concept of financial inclusion including US, France, UK (Mehta, Jindal & Singh, 2015; Ahmad, 2012).

DOI: 10.4018/978-1-5225-5240-6.ch013

Meaning of Financial Inclusion

Financial inclusion refers to delivery of financial services at an affordable cost in a fair, transparent terms and conditions to vast sections of disadvantages, weaker, low-income groups' including household enterprise, small medium enterprise, and trade INR (Mehta, Jindal & Singh, 2015).

Financial Inclusion is:

NFA + Banks+ OFIs+ MFI+ IT = Financial Inclusion.

Where,

- **NFA:** No frills bank account
- **OFIs:** Financial Institutions
- **MFI:** Micro Financial Institutions
- **IT:** Information Technology.

FINANCIAL INCLUSION IN INDIA

In India, the apex bank Reserve Bank of India (RBI) along with some commercial banks has undertaken the initiative to promote financial inclusion. Many projects have been launched like mobile banking; micro financial institutions etc. (Mehta, Jindal & Singh, 2015). During the recent past, banks have played an important role in making people meet their needs. Many studies have been carried out to know about the role of banks in financial inclusion for sustainable development. Many regional rural banks (RRBs) and commercial banks have joined hands for the development of nation. Choubey (1983) has evaluated that commercial banks have failed to fill serious gaps and deficiencies in farm credit which the RRBs can manage to do. He emphasized on the fact that National Bank for Agriculture and Rural Development (NABARD) would be required to pay special attention to depoliticisation of agricultural credit and Government credit agencies. He suggested that NABARD might help in raising agriculture and rural sector productivity at a faster rate. Husain (1987) analyzed the development of commercial banks in India and shed light on reorientation of credit policy and resource mobilization for regional development. Financial inclusion is the key determinant to sustainable and inclusive growth, which will unlock the vast hidden potential of savings, consumption, and investment propensities of the poorer sections of society. It will help to transact the national forum for financial inclusion in which all people have access to appropriate and have defined products and services in order to manage their money effectively. It is achieved by both financial literacy and financial capability on the part of consumer. It also helps in the financial access of product and services (Mehta, Jindal & Singh, 2015).

Sendhilvelan and Karthikeyan (2006) concluded with a view to ensure financial inclusion of everyone by publicizing the facility of "no frills" account in both rural and urban banks and shifting from the conceptof 'anytime, anywhere banking' to 'anytime, anywhere and to everyone banking'. Mitra (2007) stressed on the fact that instead of being confined to the four walls, bank policies should touch the doorsteps of the common person having more inclusive capitalist growth strategy bordering theprinciples of laissez faire. The relevance of allying the policies with masses to transform them into reality has been highlighted. Ghorude(2009) indicated that the problem of poverty could not be solvedby distributing loans to some people since India is suffering fromhuge and diverse problems of micro financing. Social, political, andeconomic inclusion also needs to be done to obtain inclusive growth. This can be strengthened by developing a micro entrepreneurship with organizational and community support (Mehta, Jindal & Singh, 2015; Thorat, 2006).

Manoharan and Muthiah(2010) stated thata major constraint to the growth of financial services like loans,insurance is due to limited access to the vast majority of the populationin the rural area and unorganized sector studied that were ten villages of Vadipatti panchayat of Madurai District. Many villagers were nothappy using these financial services mainly due to language differences, documentation, and other conditions. Dhiraj and Sumanjeet (2012) highlighted that financial inclusion is beneficial to reduce the poverty line. They emphasized on opening of bank accounts and active participation for financial inclusion. Credit Counseling centers and literacy center are the initiatives for the same. Roy (2012) emphasized that The Government of India hastaken many initiatives for the banks to serve the poor hassle-free andthe pros and cons of financial inclusion in India. Many branches havebeen set up in rural areas to bring a large segment of the society under the umbrella of financial inclusion (Mehta, Jindal & Singh, 2015; Sriram, 2010; Sriram & Upadhyayula, 2002).

Purvi and Medha (2015) discussed about the importance of good quality financial services for rural areas, as their funding will lead to economic growth. They have also thrown light on the initiatives taken by Government and Reserve Bank of India for strengthening financial inclusion in the country. No frills accounts should be publicized and technology should be brought in to make transactions more users friendly (Mehta, Jindal & Singh, 2015).

Measuring Financial Inclusion

Financial Inclusion Index is one of the measures to see the level of financial inclusion. This index is based on three basic dimensions of an inclusive financial system–banking penetration, availability of the banking services and usage of the banking system. Banking penetration is definitely the most critical parameter for measuring the depth of financial inclusion and is measured as a ratio of bank accounts to the total population (Shetty, 2009; Sinha, 2005; Srinivasan, 2010).

FINANCIAL INCLUSION ISSUES AND CHALLENGES

Financial inclusion is a long-term strategy, but to achieve its objectives we need to keep in mind the key areas it should address:

1. It should provide access to basic financial services like banking.
2. The usage of financial services should address the needs of the poor.
3. The financial products should be affordable.
4. Quality of product and services must be enhanced.

Defining Technology, Financial Inclusion and Security Market

Recent developments show that technology plays an important role in improving financial inclusion because of the following reasons:

1. It helps to reduce cost of the product.
2. Reduces transaction cost.
3. Improves quality of the product.
4. Helps in increasing choices and flexibility to customer.

Various benefits to the clients have also been identified like easy access to banking services, faster loan processing, reduced transaction costs, improved quality of information, increased outreach, reduction in operational costs, and increase in customer satisfaction.

ICT has been used to create ——branchless banks through mobile banking, automated teller machines (ATM), point-of-sale (PoS) networks, and so on, where clients can access various financial services. According to Beck, Levine and Kunt (2007), the use of ICT can be used to cut down the costs of coordination, communication, and information processing, and to enable efficient service provision at lower costs. ICT is a strategic tool that enables users to be efficient and effective. It promotes the dual objectives of microfinance sustainability and outreaching the poor. Although ICT can help MFIs to reduce transactional costs, expand their market and provide affordable and flexible services to customers, many of them continue to rely on inefficient manual data processing systems that can create ambiguity (Mehta, Jindal & Singh, 2015).

Importance of Financial Inclusion

In remote, hilly, and sparsely populated areas with poor infrastructure, physical access itself acts as a deterrent against development. Based on Demand, Lack of awareness, low incomes/assets, social exclusion, and illiteracy also act as barrier. From supply side, distance from branch, branch timings, cumbersome documentation and procedures, unsuitable products, language, staff attitudes are the common reasons for exclusion. On the other hand, the ease of availability of informal credit sources makes these popular even if it costs more.

The importance can be verified by the fact that if poor are not connected to our formal financial system, their growth and improvement will not take place even as top line growth prevails. There can be fraud money saving schemes and lack awareness of investing. That is the reason why financial inclusion is important for any country for its growth. However, if a customer is well educated financially, he can make better choices regarding various products that can fulfill his individual needs. This will result in overall growth of the country, as access to financial services at affordable cost will improve life of the poor (Mehta, Jindal & Singh, 2015; Patil & Karjat, 2011; Rao, 2008; Reddy & Manak, 2005).

FINANCIAL EXCLUSION

Financial Exclusion signifies inability of access by certain segments of society to low cost, fair, and safe financial products and services. It is mainly a denial or inaccessibility to some basic financial services due to various factors like social and economic position, financial literacy, distance in traveling, hours of operation, etc. (Nasir, 2013; O'Gorman, 2010; Panwar & Carmody, 2011).

Consequences of Financial Exclusion

Consequences of financial exclusion vary depending on the nature and extent of services denied. It may lead to increased travel requirements, higher incidence of crime, general decline in investment, difficulties in gaining access to credit or getting credit from informal sources at exorbitant rates, and increased unemployment, etc. The small business houses may suffer due to loss of access to middle class and higher-income consumers, higher cash handling costs, delays in remittances of money. Thus, the above barriers should be overcome and reaching out to the people lying at the bottom of the pyramid has become the order of the day (Mehta, Jindal & Singh, 2015; Mahajan & Ramola, 2003; Mahanta & Panda, 2012; Nair, 2001).

Financial Exclusion in India

As per the report by World Bank, In India, only 35.2 percent adults above the age of 15 years have an account at formal financial institutions. More than 50% of population has deposit accounts and only 9 percent population have credit accounts with formal financial institutions. Report shows that there is only one bank branch per 14,000 persons. Just 18% are debit cardholders and less than 2 percent are credit cards holders. There is only one bank branch over the 12.5 villages. The most common reason for not having a bank account is lack of enough money and hours based wage system (Mehta, Jindal & Singh, 2015).

Product-Based Approach

Reserve bank of India has been liberal and supportive while designing policies to enable financial institutions to come up with innovative products for enabling a common person to benefit out of the financial inclusion plan. Some products developed for fulfillment of this approach are No-Frills Account (NFA'S), Kisaan Credit Card, General Purpose Credit Cards, etc.

Bank-Led Approach

The bank provides the framework, accounting services and support to the group to manage their deposits and lending. This model follows the approach of savings first, lending later. The banks do not have a risk in such lendings as the borrower's reputation and peer pressure in the group would reduce the risk of bad loans considerably. However, the model has some issues that affect the program like inadequate outreach in many regions, Delays in opening of SHG accounts and disbursement of loans, impounding of savings by banks as collateral, Non-approval of repeat loans by banks even when the first loan was repaid and multiple memberships.

Regulatory approach includes simplified KYC Norms, simplified bank saving account opening and Bank branch authorization. Technology based approach includesMobile banking, ATM based banking, Branchless banking.

Government Initiatives

The Government has taken various initiatives indirectly through the regulators, Government promoted schemes through its various ministries like:

1. Induction of SHG-2: The original SHG as initialized by NABARD had certain limitations. This led to NABARD preparing a strategy to revitalize the SHG movement leading with the induction of SHG-2 model.
2. Women SHGs Development Fund: The Union Budget 2011-2012 proposed a "Women's SHG's Development Fund" with a corpus of INR 5 billion. The Government created this fund to empower women and promote their SHGs. The responsibility of managing the fund is of NABARD. It managed the same through two of its major microfinance funds, namely Financial Inclusion Fund (FIF) and the Financial Inclusion Technology Fund (FITF).
3. Swarnjayanti Gram Swarozgar Yojana (SGSY): It is a centrally sponsored scheme that follows the mechanism of forming SHGs of rural poor households, providing capacity building training and linking groups to banks. SGSY is primarily designed to promote self-employment oriented income generating activities for the Below Poverty Level (BPL) households in rural areas (Mehta, Jindal & Singh, 2015).

MICROFINANCE

Microfinance is buzzword that describes financing for micro entrepreneurs. This concept was emerged to empower under-privileged classes of society, women, and poor. The principles of Microfinance are founded on the philosophy of cooperation and its central values of equality, equity, and mutual self-help. At the heart of these principles are the concept of human development through people working together to achieve a better life for themselves and their family. Micro credit is the most common product offering. Micro-finance in India is synonymous with micro credit. The motherland for Indian Microfinance is Andhra Pradesh, mainly because of the state government's critical efforts in the late 1980s in building SHG-bank linkage models with loans from NABARD (National Bank of Agriculture and Rural Development) which built up a strong Micro-finance portfolio (Verma & Aggarwal, 2014; Kline & Sadhu, 2012; Mader, 2013; Mahajan & Nagasri, 2000).

Microfinance Institution (MFI)

A MFI is an organization that acts as an interface between the formal credit delivery institutions and credit seekers, with an aim to assist for the socio-economic development of poor and marginalized people. MFIs are essential to encourage micro enterprises and empower local people including women. The geographical distribution of MFIs is very much concentrated in the Southern India where the rural branch network of formal bank is excellent (Verma& Aggarwal, 2014; Ghosh, 2005; Jayadev, 2016; Kaladhar, 1997; Karmakar,2008).

Types of MFI

Depending on their legal structures, MFIs may be classified as follows:

Not -for-Profit MFIs

These include societies (e.g. Bandhan, Gram Utthan), Public trusts (e.g. Shri Khetra Dharmasthala Rural Development Project), and Non-profit companies (e.g. Indian Association for savings and credit).

Mutual Benefit MFIs

These include Co-operatives registered under state or National Acts (e.g. sakh Sahkari) and Mutually-aided Co-operative societies (e.g. Sewa Mutually Aided Co-operative Thrift Societies Federation Ltd.).

For–Profit MFIs

These include Non-banking financial Companies (e.g. Bharatiya Samruddhi Finance Ltd), Producer Companies (e.g. Sri VijayaVisakha Milk Producers Co. Ltd.) and Local area banks (e.g. Krishna Bhima Samruddhi Local Area Bank.).

Working of Microfinance Institutions

The Microfinance Institutions (MFIs) take little or no collateral security for the credit extended. The clients of MFIs are generally those people who cannot avail loans from conventional banks due to the lack of collateral against loans. MFIs provide small individual loans but the total amount of loans disbursed by MFIs is substantial when the entire financial year is considered. Banks unable to extend loans to the poor because of high default risk. Here the question arises as to how the MFIs are able to thrive and perhaps record a staggering growth rate over the years with almost no default risk. The clients of MFIs are divided into groups headed by a leader chosen from group members. The amount to be repaid by every individual member is guaranteed by the remaining members of the group. About five groups from one particular are combined to form a batch. Again, this batch is headed by a leader chosen from members of the batch. A field officer is appointed by MFI who oversee the collection of payments done by the batch (Verma & Aggarwal, 2014; Dasgupta, 2005; Devaraja, 2011; Ghate, 2007). The default risk is further reduced by applying more conditions such as gradually increasing the size of loan.

Microfinance in India

In India, Microfinance Revolution began in the 1980s with the formation of pockets of informal Self Help Groups (SHG). These SHGs were engaged inmicro activities financed by Microfinance. India's first Microfinance Institution 'Shri Mahila SEWA Sahkari Bank was set up asan urban co-operative bank, by the Self Employed Women's Association (SEWA). The idea of Microfinance was developed as a survival strategy for the poor. Ela Bhatt in India and Professor Muhammad Yunus of Bangladesh are the pioneers in this field. Ela Bhatt founded Self Employed Women's Association (SEWA) in1972. The aim of this association was to bring poor women together and give them ways to fight for their rights and earn better livings. Over the past few decades, this innovative scheme has attracted a range of nongovernmental and state-sponsored institutions. Some of the leading financial institutions include Small Industries Development Bank of India (SIDBI), the National Bank for Agriculture and Rural Development (NABARD) and the Rashtriya Mahila Kosh (RMK). A few NGOssuch as PRADAN, ICECD, MYRADA, and SEWA have played a significant role in promoting micro-credit. With micro-credit becoming financially viable, even commercial banks like ICICI Bank, ABNAMRO, HDFC Bank, UTI Bank and international banks like Citibank have also entered the field. Non-banking corporate is participating as well (Verma & Aggarwal, 2014).

Presently, MFIs are operating in 517 districts in India spread across 27 states.The total MFI client outreach as of March 2011 was 3.17 crore while the total microcredit outstanding was Rs. 2500 crore-which have been scrutinized to banks.During 2010-11, the microfinance through MFI channel had grown 18.75 percent in terms of client outreach and13.15 percent in terms of credit portfolio.MFIs collectively disbursed Rs. 33730 crore as loans to clients during 2010-11 and the average loan per client was Rs. 5706, which was less than that of Rs.9766 in 2010.

In India, the MFI sector has grown remarkably during past two decades, spreading across the country and surviving the 2010 Andhra Pradesh microfinance crisis. As on 31 March 2016, they reached out to 40 million clients with an outstanding credit of 63,853 crore5 . There was a steady growth in the average credit outstanding per client, by 76% from r7481 in 2011 to r13162 in 2015. Interestingly, in the recent past MFIs are growing fast in the states like Punjab, Haryana, Gujarat, Himachal Pradesh, and Uttar Pradesh, which are left uncovered by SHG-BLP. Though MFIs provided loans for both consumption and productive purposes, a major part of the credit flow, 94% in 2016, is channelized for income generating activities. Agriculture, Animal husbandry, and small trading are the major income generating activities that account for 79% of the micro credit provided by MFIs in 2016. Non-income generating loans are mostly used for consumption, housing, and education of children. MFIs played a significant role in bridging the gap between the formal financial institutions and the rural poor. However, of late, their increasing urban orientation and providing pure credit products without the capacity building component have been criticized, for the situation in rural areas is not of credit shortage alone. It is more of shortage of entrepreneurial capabilities and lack of technical skills. These aspects need attention (NABARD, 2017).

Role of MFIs in Financial Inclusion in India

Microfinance is increasingly being considered as one of the most effective tools of reducing poverty. Microfinance has a significant role in bridging the gap between the formal financial institutions and the rural poor. The Microfinance Institutions (MFIs) obtain financial resources from the banks and other mainstream financial institutions, provide financial, and support services to the poor.

MFIs could play a significant role in facilitating inclusion, as they are uniquely positioned in reaching out to the rural poor. Many of them operate in a limited geographical area, have a greater understanding of the issues specific to the rural poor, enjoy greater acceptability amongst the rural poor, and have flexibility in operations providing a level of comfort to their clientele (Verma & Aggarwal, 2014). In India, more than 350 million people are below the poverty level and for them the Microfinance is more than the life. By providing small loans to these people, Microfinance helps in reducing thepoverty. For MFIs, thereis a huge demand and network of people and for borrower there are many small and medium size MFIs are available in even remote areas (Verma & Aggarwal, 2014).

In India,rules and regulation of MFIs are not developed properly. In this situation, there would be high case of credit risk and defaults.According to a report of World Bank, report 80% of the Indian poor cannot access to formal sources of finance and therefore they depend on the informal sources for their borrowing. However, these informal sources charges very high interest rates ranging from 40 to 120%p.a. India is considered as the second fastest developing country after China, with GDP over8.5% from the past 5 years. However, if we look at the GDP per capita, situation is not encouraging. India's 70% of the population lives in rural area, and that population is not fully involved in the national economy (Verma & Aggarwal, 2014; Bi & Pandey, 2011; Chakrabarti & Ravi; 2011).

In India, only few MFIs are serving a very large number of poor people.There is huge opportunity for the MFIs to serve the poor people and increase their living standard. The annual demand of Micro loans is nearly Rs. 60,000 crore and only 5456 crore are disbursed to the borrower. Microfinance helps the poor people by providing them with loan, helping them in their business, educating them and their children etc. Therefore, in this way Microfinance is helping to increase the employment opportunity for poor and for the society. India's total population is more than 1000 million. Out of this population, 350 million is living below poverty line. Therefore, there is a huge opportunity for the MFIs to meet the demand of that untapped market.

Still, MFIs face the threat of high level of competition as more players come in themarket. MFIs face high transaction cost and after entrant of new players these transaction cost will increase further (Verma& Aggarwal, 2014; Ananth, 2005; Banerjee, Duflo, & Hornbeck, 2014).

Microfinance and Women Empowerment

MFIs in India, through its major channels, are serving large number of women clients. Empowerment is a social action process that promotes participation of people, organization, and communities in gaining control over their lives in their community. There is urgent need of rural women empowerment. The formation of SHGs and MFIs will enhance their socioeconomic position in the society. Small loans can help rural women start small businesses. Women can gain a lot from micro-finance because it gives them an independent means of generating wealth and becoming self-reliant in a society that does not offer much entrepreneurship opportunity for them. Since women are the ones who run the household, a higher standard of living for women means better governance and a healthier and more prosperous future for their children and the nation. One of the major reason for success of micro credit initiatives is their focus on empowering women and encouraging them to generate their own means of income. Various case studies show that there is a positive correlation between credit availability and women's empowerment. Women in rural India lived in virtual isolation, unable to access even the most basic services. However, with the formation of Women's SHGs, these women are now achieving social and physical mobility. It is recognized that while the empowerment of women is a process that will not happen automatically, SHG isa suitable means for the empowerment of women. The impacts of SHGs on socio-economic status of women are significant (Verma & Aggarwal, 2014).

SOLUTIONS AND RECOMMENDATIONS

In this section, we provide specific, detailed recommendations for establishing an enabling environment to promote sustainable MFIs in India.For supporting MFIs operating in the markets of developing world, including India, to overcome the hurdles and challenges facing them, many options are available (Alshebami & Rangarajan, 2017).

The MFIs in India should have an immediate linkage with other financial institutions and commercial banks in the formal sector so that they can benefit from the facilities available for them such as the branches network spread in different governorates following uniformity in the financial norms and identification of target groups.The Indian government and other official bodies should support the existing MFIs to convert from their existing NGOs status into professional microfinance banks with diversified financial services. The reason is to allow them find new funding sources for their operations or at least support them financially and technically to expand their network operationby opening new branches in the un-served rural areas.

A clear distinction should be made to differentiate between the different categorization of units in the SMEs sector i.e. the micro, small, medium enterprises including the micro ones so that the MFIs clients target inclusion is clearer.The Indian government should provide the required necessary financial and physical infrastructures in the market so that MFIs can be supported in their operation and their delinquency risks can be reduced to the last extent.The Indian government should encourage the commercial banks to invest in the microfinance sector rather than investing in the treasury bills of the Reserve Bank of India. It should also provide all the necessary regulatory facilities for effective functioning in rural areas.

MFIs should introduce the concept of integrated microfinance so that microfinance could usher in a positive outcome in the demand side in terms of enhanced reduction of the potential risk attached with the borrowers' businesses and eventually buoyant in the standard of living of the poor people.

The Indian government in cooperation with some donors should work on a guarantee system to support the poor people who cannot provide any collateral for their loans, besides promoting social mobilization of the poor in the form of Self Help Group (SHG) system. With the likely large number of MFIs in the sector, self-regulation and supervision would be required. RBI may carry out supervision through recognized self-regulatory organizations. MFIs with large business volumes should be regulated as per the normal regulatory framework, except for entry-level capital, which should be smaller and capital adequacy, which should be higher. Such MFIs should be supervised by the normal supervision agencies.

In India, 237 million people do not have access to electricity and around 841 million still use dirty biomass for cooking. Microfinance and energy access seem like natural companions. Access to clean energy needs finance and MFIs already have a customer base that may be deprived of clean energy sources either for lighting or for cooking. Another aspect that draws companies into the business of promoting products and services that enhance access to clean energy is the fact that the MFIs have already established trust and a level of engagement with the consumers. However, the MFIs are essentially banks offering financial products. For an optimal solution, a MFI should collaborate with an energy service provider, which has certified and tested products with an established service infrastructure. The provider should add value to the business of the MFIs, instead of just depending on their customer database. Microfinance should support the aspirational needs of people seeking energy access. On the same lines, their partner's energy service should be supporting the people climbing the energy ladder—starting from meeting the lighting and mobile charging needs, increasing product portfolio to include devices like fan and TV and electrifying the house for them to use in any way they deem fit (Kumarankandath, 2017).

India is the largest emerging market for microfinance. However, the demand needs to be organized and converted into effective demand. The need for credit by the poor should be backed by willingness to pay the price for the financial services. Only then, demand is sustainable. MFIs should offer sustainable financial services and reach a stage of high access and high sustainability, which is the desired level. There is emerging price competition from mainstream banks as they are able to cross-subsidize their micro-credit operations and charge interest rates below cost. MFIs should be regulated but regulation should not hamper financial sustainability. The key to MFI financial sustainability is controlling costs and bad debts, increasing volumes and by offering savings and insurance services. The ownership pattern and governance of an MFI are crucial to its sustainability. Irrespective of the mode of ownership, professional management is key. While all human resources are the key to the long run sustainability of any organization, there is a serious shortage of microfinance entrepreneurs. There is a need of changes in various laws and regulations in India and for changing the guidelines to apex financial institutions, such as NABARD, to provide a supportive environment for MFIs to emerge and become sustainable.

Apart from promotion of SHGs in priority states, identification of livelihoods, skill development and capacity building, taking forward the programme of SHG members as agents/BC/Bank Sakhi and collaboration with new partners for strengthening/ deepening the SHG movement at Pan India level may be the future direction for SHG-BLP. Some RRBs have started using the services of our partner SHPIs as agents/ BF for credit linkage of SHGs and recovery of dues from them on the lines of ICICI bank model. While SHG-BLP has grown strong on the pillars of financial inclusion and social capital, the recent addition of technology as the third pillar has shown immense potential to strengthen its base. The Eshakti initiative in select 25 districts during last two years has shown the way. It needs to be expanded to cover all the SHGs in the country. Support of every stakeholder in this endeavor is essential. SHG Federations may emerge to be useful institutions in the SHG eco-system through both financial and non-financial supports. There is, however, lack of proper legal form to suit the structure and other issues impacting viability. There is need to search for suitable solution to the issues impacting the structure (NABARD, 2017).

CONCLUSION

Micro-finance is one of the ways of building the capacities of the poor and graduating them to sustainable self-employment activities by providing them financial services like credit, savings, and insurance. To provide micro-finance and other support services, MFIs should be able to sustain themselves for a long period. MFIs deal with a vulnerable segment of the society that gets affected quickly by any internal or external factors that might disturb the area of operation. Inaddition to that, the surrounding environment where MFIs exist might not provide a suitable platform for these MFIs to operate. MFIs might be engulfed with many challenges such as the continuous negative foreign invasions, the politician's interventions, the absence of the required physical and financial infrastructures, and the lack for qualified human resources to run these institutions and most importantly the unwillingness of the commercial bank to take part in investing and supporting the microfinance industry and MFIs operating there.

From the perspective of future development of poor through micro credit, there is an imperative need for a comprehensive study on structure of various financial institutions and their products and services in India. This chapter would facilitate to work out strategies for making prudential institutional linkages and designing integrated pro-poor microfinancial products and services. Further, this kind of integrated products would helpintensive financial inclusion of the hither too excluded poor. This will also ensures cooperation between MFIs and other financial players in the market so that microfinance can meet its target and fulfill the financial needs of the poor people who have been denied financial access from the commercial banks and other formal financial Institutions. This will facilitate the process of reduction in unemployment and poverty in India.

The Indian economy at present is at a crucial juncture. On one hand, the optimists are talking of India being among the top five economies of the world by 2050. On the other hand, there is presence of 260 million poor forming 26% of the total population. The enormity of the task can be gauged from the above numbers. If India is to stand among the comity of developed nations, there is no doubt that poverty alleviation & reduction of income inequalities has to be the top most priority (Verma & Aggarwal, 2014).

The important challenge facing the banking sector is to extend financial services to all sections of society. Like others, the poor need arange of financial services that are convenient, flexible, and affordable and not just loans. Financial inclusion can serve the interests of both society and the banking system. As a complementary to this, micro-finance can serve as a powerful tool to fight poverty and become the effective approach of financial inclusion. With the new philosophy and policies pertaining to micro credit, Microfinance institutions (MFIs) such as SHGs have emerged and they now have a strong footing in India. Microfinance still plays a modest role in India. At national level, less than 5 per cent of poor rural households have access to Microfinance (as compared to 65 per cent in Bangladesh) with significant variation exist across the states. The key factors that can drive success for MFIs are robust systems, and processes and efficiency and productivity levels, maintaining asset quality, prevention of credit losses and capital erosion and remaining adequately capitalized to fund growth plans.

REFERENCES

Ahmad, R. (2012). *Microfinance in India*. Mittal Publications.

Alshebami, A. S., & Rengarajan, V. (2017). Microfinance Institutions in Yemen "Hurdles and Remedies.". *International Journal of Social Work*, *4*(1), 10. doi:10.5296/ijsw.v4i1.10695

Ananth, B. (2005). Financing microfinance–the ICICI Bank partnership model. *Small Enterprise Development*, *16*(1), 57–65. doi:10.3362/0957-1329.2005.009

Banerjee, A., Duflo, E., & Hornbeck, R. (2014). Bundling health insurance and microfinance in India: There cannot be adverse selection if there is no demand. *The American Economic Review*, *104*(5), 291–297. doi:10.1257/aer.104.5.291 PMID:25214652

Beck, T., Demirgüç-Kunt, A., & Levine, R. (2007). Finance, inequality and the poor. *Journal of Economic Growth*, *12*(1), 27–49. doi:10.100710887-007-9010-6

Bi, Z., & Pandey, S. L. D. (2011). Comparison of performance of microfinance institutions with commercial banks in India. *Australian Journal of Business and Management Research*, *1*(6), 110.

Chakrabarti, R., & Ravi, S. (2011). *At the crossroads: Microfinance in India*. Academic Press.

Choubey, B. N. (1983). *Agricultural banking in India*. National.

Dasgupta, R. (2005). Microfinance in India: Empirical evidence, alternative models and policy imperatives. *Economic and Political Weekly*, 1229–1237.

Devaraja, T. S. (2011). *Microfinance in India-A tool for poverty reduction.* Mysore: University Grants Commission of India.

Financial Inclusion in India. (n.d.). *A road map towards future growth | sumanjeetkaur - Academia.edu.* Retrieved December 16, 2017, from https://www.academia.edu/4018810/Financial_Inclusion_in_India_A_road_map_towards_future_growth

Ghate, P. (2007). *Microfinance in India: A State of the Sector Report.* Retrieved from https://www.microfinancegateway.org/sites/default/files/mfg-en-paper-microfinance-in-india-a-state-of-the-sector-report-2007-2007.pdf

Ghorude, K. N. (2009). Microfinance for Financial Inclusion and Sustainable Rural Development. *Southern Economist*, *48*(1), 47–50.

Ghosh, R. (2005). *Microfinance in India: A critique*. Retrieved from http://unpan1.un.org/intradoc/groups/public/documents/APCITY/UNPAN024232.pdf

Guruprasad, L. (n.d.). *Sustainability & growth of Microfinancing in India*. Retrieved from http://www.academia.edu/4364486/Sustainability_and_growth_of_Microfinancing_in_India

Hussain, F. D. (1987). *Public Sector Commercial Banking in India-Development-Constraints-Recent trends*. New Delhi: Deep & Deep Publications.

Jayadev, M. (2016). Microfinance in India. *Changing Contours of Microfinance in India*, 8.

Kaladhar, K. (1997). Microfinance in India: Design, structure and governance. *Economic and Political Weekly*, 2687–2706.

Karmakar, K. G. (2008). *Microfinance in India*. SAGE Publications India.

Kline, K., & Sadhu, S. (2012). *Microfinance in India: A new regulatory structure*. Centre for Microfinance.

Kumarankandath, A. (2017, April 28). *Microfinance and energy access*. Retrieved December 16, 2017, from http://www.downtoearth.org.in/blog/microfinance-and-energy-access-57720

Mader, P. (2013). Rise and fall of microfinance in India: The Andhra Pradesh crisis in perspective. *Strategic Change*, *22*(1-2), 47–66. doi:10.1002/jsc.1921

Mahajan, V., & Nagasri, G. (2000). *Building sustainable microfinance institutions in India*. Internal Document.

Mahajan, V., & Ramola, B. G. (2003). *Microfinance in India: Banyan Tree and Bonsai. Background Paper Prepared for the World Bank*. Washington, DC: World Bank.

Mahanta, P., & Panda, G. (2012). Sreekumar (2012). Status of microfinance in India: A review. *International Journal of Marketing. Financial Services & Management Research, 1*(11), 142–155.

Mehta, L., Jindal, S., & Singh, K. (2015). Financial Inclusion in India: Shifting the Base towards Crowning Glory. *Arabian Journal of Business and Management Review, 5*(6). Retrieved from https://www.omicsonline.org/open-access/financial-inclusion-in-india-shifting-the-base-towards-crowning-glory-2223-5833-1000158.php?aid=61775

Muthiah, M. P., & Muthiah, K. (2010). Financial Inclusion in the Indian Rural Area Context–A Micro Level Study. *Research Highlights, 20*(2), 71–74.

NABARD. (2017, March 31). *Status of Microfinance in India 2016-17*. Retrieved from http://www.nabard.org/auth/writereaddata/Flipbook/2017/Publication/Nabard-17-Status-of-Microfinance-in-India-2016-17/files/assets/basic-html/page6.html

Nair, T. S. (2001). Institutionalising microfinance in India: An overview of strategic issues. *Economic and Political Weekly*, 399–404.

Nasir, S. (2013). Microfinance in India: Contemporary issues and challenges. *Middle East Journal of Scientific Research, 15*(2), 191–199.

O'Gorman, M. (2010). Microfinance in India. *Canadian Journal of Development Studies/Revue Canadienned'études Du Développement, 31*(1–2), 225–227.

Panwar, J. S., &Carmody, L. (2011). *Microfinance in India*. Academic Press.

Patil, V. G., & Karjat, Y. (2011). Microfinance in India. *Golden Resrach Thoughts, 1*, 1–4.

Rao, K. M. (2008). MFIs in India: An overview. *Microfinance in India*, 57–66.

Reddy, C. S., & Manak, S. (2005). Self-help groups: A keystone of microfinance in India-women empowerment and social security. Andhra Pradesh MahilaAbhivruddhi Society (APMAS). India: Hyderabad.

Rona, M. (2006, April). Financial Inclusion: Meeting The Challenge. *People's Democracy,* 22.

Roy, S. K. (2012). Financial inclusion in India: An overview. *Asian Journal of Multidimensional Research, 1*(5), 136–138.

Sendhilvelan, M., & Karthikeyan, K. (2006). No Frills Account: A basic drive for financial inclusion. *Southern Economist, 45*(3), 13–14.

Shah, P., & Dubhashi, M. (2015). Review Paper on Financial Inclusion-The Means of Inclusive Growth. *Chanakya International Journal of Business Research, 1*(1), 37–48. doi:10.15410/cijbr/2015/v1i1/61403

Shetty, N. K. (2009). The microfinance promises in financial inclusion: Evidence from India. *IUP Journal of Applied Economics, 8*(5/6), 174.

Sinha, F. (2005). Access, use and contribution of microfinance in India: Findings from a national study. *Economic and Political Weekly*, 1714–1719.

Srinivasan, N. (2010). *Microfinance India: state of the sector report 2009*. SAGE Publications India.

Sriram, M. S. (2010). Commercialisation of Microfinance in India: A Discussion of the Emperor's Apparel. *Economic and Political Weekly*, 65–73.

Sriram, M. S., & Upadhyayula, R. (2002). *The transformation of microfinance in India: Experiences, options and future*. Indian Institute of Management Ahmedabad, Research and Publication Department.

Sujatha, B. (2007). *Financial Inclusion: Concepts and Strategies*. ICFAI University Press.

Thorat, Y. S. P. (2006). Microfinance in India; Sectoral issues and challenges. *Towards a Sustainable Microfinance Outreach in India*, 27–42.

Verma, S., & Aggarwal, K. (2014). Financial Inclusion through Microfinance Institutions in India. *International Journal of Innovative Research and Development*, *3*(1). Retrieved from http://www.ijird.com/index.php/ijird/article/view/46389

KEY TERMS AND DEFINITIONS

Financial Exclusion: Financial exclusion is the inability of individuals, households or groups to access financial services in an appropriate form. Financial exclusion is either a cause or a consequence of social exclusion, or both.

Financial Inclusion: Financial inclusion means that individuals and businesses have access to useful and affordable financial products and services that meet their needs—transactions, payments, savings, credit, and insurance—delivered in a responsible and sustainable way.

Financial Stability: Financial stability is a state in which the financial system (i.e., the key financial markets and the financial institutional system) is resistant to economic shocks and is fit to smoothly fulfil its basic functions: the intermediation of financial funds, management of risks and the arrangement of payments.

Financial Sustainability: An organization is financially sustainable if its core work will not collapse, even if external donor funding is withdrawn.

Microfinance: Also called microcredit, it is a type of banking service that is provided to unemployed or low-income individuals or groups who otherwise have no other access to financial services.

Microfinance Institution (MFI): A microfinance institution is an organization that offers financial services to low income populations. Almost all give loans to their members, and many offer insurance, deposit, and other services.

Operational Efficiency: Operational efficiency is the capability of an enterprise to deliver products or services to its customers in the most cost-effective manner possible while still ensuring the high quality of its products, service, and support.

Chapter 14
Reducing Inequality in Developing Countries Through Microfinance:
Any Correlation So Far?

Richardson Kojo Edeme
University of Nigeria, Nigeria

Chigozie Nelson Nkalu
University of Nigeria, Nigeria

ABSTRACT

Even though microfinance is expected to significantly affect macro variables such as inequality, poverty, and human development, there has not been enough empirical study on the impact analysis at the macro level, such as the effect of microfinance on inequality, especially in developing countries of Africa. This chapter, therefore, provides a detailed empirical analysis of the correlation between microfinance and inequality in West Africa sub-region. The correlation coefficient shows that although there is a positive linear connection between the possibilities of microfinance to reduce inequality; it has not contributed significantly to poverty reduction with the independent variables. The findings further suggest that the most robust explanatory variables for inequality reduction are GDP per capita and democracy which are invariably significant with positive sign. Taken together, these findings reinforce the intuition that greater democracy and provision and expansion of financial infrastructures especially in backward countries of the region are necessary for microfinance to thrive and contribute abundantly to inequality reduction.

INTRODUCTION

The positive impact of financial deepening in poverty-inequality reduction, human development, consumption smoothening, gender equality and economic growth across countries or regions has been emphasized in the literature (World Bank, 2001; Ahlin & Jiang, 2008; Swain & Floro, 2008; Kai & Hamori, 2009; Bird, Hattel, Sasaki & Attapich, 2011; Tchouassi, 2011;Kazi & Leonard, 2012;Leikem, 2012; Kasali,

DOI: 10.4018/978-1-5225-5240-6.ch014

Ahmed & Lim, 2015, *inter-alia*). Microfinance as a veritable tool to delivering financial services to rural dwellers plays an important role in making financial market meet its obligation of bridging the financial bank between urban and rural dwellers. Since the 1990s, there is enough evidence suggesting that the number of microfinance has been on the rise. From 2006-2007, Microfinance in the continent experienced a 25 percent rapid increase in the number borrowers and 31 percent in savers. Although it is expected that such increase in the number of microfinance would improve human development through reduction in inequality in the region, there has not been enough empirical research on the impact, such as the correlation between microfinanceand inequality reduction in West Africa sub-region.

The establishment of Microfinance is predicated on economic development paradigm that aims at poverty reduction through financial services to the poor, low income earners and micro-entrepreneurs that cannot access similar services from the formal financial market (Ashraf & Ibrahim 2014). It is therefore a means of advancing small loans to the poor with to enable them finance small and medium scale businesses that would provide them adequate income to take care of their needs. The institutions were originally designed to assist the poor households and advance credits to entrepreneurs, provide services like savings, rural credit, consumer credit and other financial services (Duku, 2002). In this regard, the provision of microfinance institutions connotes the procedure of making available very small range of financial services to the poor with the purpose of making them take up new opportunities which the development process offers. It is a development tool that makes the rendering of services like money transfers, savings opportunities, and credit and insurance services possible. It is therefore an economic phenomenon that enhances the potentials of low income group in the society (Basir, Amin & Naeem, 2010; Muller & Bibi, 2010). It is an essential aid to increase productivity of the poor and essential ingredient for economic development. Microfinance came to beïng because of the need to enhance the latent capacity of the poor for entrepreneurship by providing microfinance services to enable them engage in economic activities and be more self-reliant, increase employment opportunities, enhance household income and create wealth (CBN, Microfinance Policy, 2005). Hence, microfinance can be described as poverty alleviation interventions which enable banks to lend small credit to the poor, to offer them opportunity to take part in economic activities. The poor are thus helped to escape the poverty trap.

In principle, a better microfinance can help overcome economic barriers, and thereby increase growth and reduce inequality. Indeed, a more developed and deeper financial sector has been shown to aid economic growth. But it should be noted that financial reform will only reduce inequality if it improves access for more individuals with growth opportunities. Microfinance enables poor women to engage in income-generating activities that help them become financially independent, strengthening their decision-making power within the household and society.

Meanwhile, a study by International Finance Corporation (IFC) (2014) highlighted that one of the largest constraints to private sector development in Africa is lack of access to financial services. This is particularly severe in Sub-Saharan Africa, where only between 5 percent and 25 percent of households have a formal relationship with a financial institution. UNDP (2013) notes that most African countries are undertaking economic reforms, including the establishment of sound macroeconomic conditions, market-based economic policies and improvements of the business environment all of which support growth of microfinance. The report highlights various ways in which the economic environment for microfinance has improved, including through strengthened regional arrangements and benefit from bilateral trade preferences, as well as the rise of emerging markets as fertile ground for entrepreneurs. However, microfinance in Africa still faces challenges, which dampens the strengths and opportunities and thus inhibited its capacity to unleash its potential to better contribute to the fight against poverty and income inequality.

Financial deepening has recently been analyzed from both theoretical and empirical fronts. But empirical studies have not reached a common front and have been controversial with some arguing that financial deepening leads to efficient credit allocation and reduction in risk through the diversified investment and information production of financial intermediaries, which stimulates economic development and lowers inequality and poverty reduction (Jalilian & Kirkpatrick, 2002;Goel & Rishi, 2012). Others opine that financial deepening only benefits the richsince the poor depend mainly on informal finance. Li, Squire and Zou (1998) indicate that financial deepening lowers inequality, a more detailed analysis on the correlation that exist between them is requiredbecause the impact of overall financial deepening on inequality seems to be obscure.Although, the equalizing effect of microfinance can be explained theoretically, there is no sufficient empirical study exposing the correlation so far. What mainly exist are impact analyses at the household level, such as analyses of the effect of microfinance on household income or consumption. Khandker, (1998), Pitt and Khandker (1998),Morduch (1999), Parker and Nagarajan, (2001) and Zaman, (2001), Chowdhury (2009), Kalirajanand Singh (2009), Yang, Jialali and Wei (2011) shows that microfinance decreases the consumption volatility of households and improve consumption smoothing, an impact analyses such as the effect of microfinance on income or poverty reduction are controversial, provide different results for different subjects and difficult to generalize.

It has also been established in both theoretical and empirical literature that financial development is generally good for growth and human development. It entails the wider use of existing financial instruments as well as the creation and adoption of new ones for intermediating funds and managing risk. However, for African countries, with external demand and financing conditions significantly worsening, and a much less favorable growth outlook, identifying untapped or underutilized sources of growth and reducing the volatility of that growth have become even more urgent (Mlachala, Jidoud, Newiak, Radzewicz-Bak, Takebe,Ye & Zhang, 2016). Financial development positively affects growth through several channels. First, it helps catalyze savings into more usable forms, and supports efficient allocation of capital and enhancement of total factor productivity. Second, it supports diversification and management of risk. Third, it reduces information asymmetries, and transaction and monitoring costs. Fourth, it can reduce volatility of the economy by providing a variety of instruments and information to help households and firms cope with adverse shocks through consumption and investment smoothing (Sahay,Cihak, N'Diaye & Barajas, 2015a). Levine (2005), in a comprehensive review of the literature was able to establish the robust linkage between financial development and growth.Microfinance could well be one of the tools to address the issue of inequality. Without being the panacea to fight poverty, microfinance can be one way to spur more human development in rural areas and promote growth (Beck & Maimbo 2013).

For the past five years, available statistics revealed that some developing countries have experienced growth; such growth hasnot shown significant trickle-down or equalizing effect (Ostry, Berg & Tsangaride, 2014). Accordingly, these countries need to focus more on the equalizing effect through microfinance. It has been opine that the high inequality in developing countries is largely attributable to credit constraints on the poor or to financial market failure, which largely benefit the rich. Microfinance can effectively do this by providing loans to the poor with a high repayment rate using its unique technique which is expected to ease the credit constraints on the poor and hence lower inequality. Microfinance also allows the poor not only to obtain loans but also to increase their productivity through borrowing activity with appropriate training. Thus, microfinance copes with market failure in order to promote well-balanced financial development, leading to economic growth and improvement of social welfare (Dabla-Norris, Ji, Townsend & Unsal, 2015).

Although majority of countries of Africa are witnessing the strongest growth in the number of microfinance, but despite being one of the largest markets in Sub-Saharan Africa, its impact in poverty-inequality reduction remains very low in comparison to its potential. Furthermore, microfinance activities are largely concentrated in urban areas, where there is actually a risk of over-indebtedness, whereas rural areas are still poorly covered (Sahay, Cihak, N'Diaye, Barajas, Bi, Ayala, Gao, Kyobe, Nguyen, Saborowski, Svirydzenka &Yousefi, 2015b).While debates have revolved around whether microfinancial institution is an engine for inequality reduction or just a lubricant in developing countries of Africa, any financial institution that can significantly ameliorate income equality prospects for the region is worth examining in detail.This clearly underpins the necessity to expose the correlation that exists between microfinance and inequality reduction in ECOWAS sub-region, which is the concern of this chapter.

Following from the introduction above, other sections of the chapter is structured as socio-economic profile of ECOWAS and penetration of Microfinance in the sub-region, review of relevant literature, methodology, results and discussion. The chapter is rounded off with conclusion and policy suggestions.

SOCIO-ECONOMIC PROFILE OF ECOWAS AND OUTREACH OF MICROFINANCE PROGRAMME IN THE SUB-REGION

The Economic Community of West African States (ECOWAS) is a regional economic union established in 1975. It consists of two sub-regional blocs: The West African Economic and Monetary Union (UEMOA) made up of French-speaking countries within ECOWAS established in 1994 and the West African Monetary Zone (WAMZ) established in 2000 and comprise mainly of six English-speaking countries of the region. In all, it is made up of fifteen countries and collectively, these countries cover an area of 5,114,162 km^2 (1,974,589 sq mi), and had an estimated population of over 349 million in 2015. The agricultural sector which employs about 60 percent of the working population in the region is still suffering from low productivity and over reliance on the weather, although in 2014, the sector recorded growth in some countries like Nigeria and Cote d'Ivoire. With regard to the secondary sector, the share of the manufacturing sector, estimated at about 9 percent of GDP in 2013 remained modest, leading to a marginal expansion in labour intensive and high value addition subsector ECOWAS (2015). For the past five years, economic growth in the region has followed a positive trend. For instance, between 2010 and 2014, economic growth was 6.3 percent as against 5.6 percent growth experienced between 2000 and 2009. This situation stemmed from an accelerated economic growth experienced. Among the countries, Côte d'Ivoire experienced 9.5 per cent growth, the Gambia (7 per cent), Senegal (5.4 per cent), Guinea Bissau (4.7 per cent) and Burkina Faso (4.4per cent), Togo (5.8 per cent) and Benin (5.2 per cent) recorded a slight downturn in economic growth, and to a lesser extent, Mali (4.9 per cent) and Niger (4.4 per cent), which experienced relatively solid growth for the period. For Nigeria, growth rate fell to 4 per cent in 2015, down from 6.3 per cent in 2014. For Ghana, subdued economic activity led to a 0.5 percent decline to 3.5 per cent. Inspite of the growth recorded, the level of youth unemployment in the region is still high with an average of 65 percent (IMF, 2014). ECA/SRO-WA, (2015) estimate that the youth unemployment rate in the region is generally 1.9 times higher than that of adults.

Meanwhile, money supply in the ECOWAS region expanded between in 2013 and 2015 by 4.7 percent as against 15 percent recorded between 2010 and 2012. This expansion mainly stem from the 12.3

percent increase in outstanding domestic credit for the countries. In 2013, the region recorded an overall deficit balance of 0.4 percent of GDP against a surplus of 2.7 percent in 2012. The level of inflation reduced from 7.42 percent in 2014 compared to of 7.6 percentlevel in 2013. However, the average inflation rate increased slightly from 8.3 percent in 2015 to 8.4 per cent in 2016. The lowest level of inflation was observed in the Monetary Union area where the average inflation rate at 1.63 per cent partly due to the drop in oil prices. According to UN-DESA (2015), the overall fiscal balance excluding grants as a percentage of GDP for ECOWAS improved from -4 percent in 2013 to -2.9 percent in 2014. In terms of human development, with an average development index of 0.450, most of the countries in the region fall within the category of countries with low human development, except Cape Verde and Ghana are in the category of countries with average human development.

In West Africa, Microfinance has some decades of history and since the last 5-7 years, there has been a clear acceleration of the outreach, both in number of clients served and in the volume of transactions. In 1997, a total number of 188 microfinance institutions have been established, serving about 1440, 000 clients, representing 2% of total population in the region. A microfinance portfolio report by Consultative Group to Assist the Poor (CGAP) (2009) reveals that the commitments for the period, 1995-1998 stood at 300 million USD, representing 21.5 percent of the total loan, and ranked the first among all regions in the world. West Africa sub-region represented 35.6 percent, the highest in Africa. The phenomenon growth in microfinance in West Africa is due to two reasons. First is a dominant situation on the microfinance market, like FECECAM in Benin, which holds 56 percent of the clients and where the banking sector is totally absent. In this case, the rapid growth is fully demand driven. Second, is the existence of a highly competitive situation, where usually two MFIs of equal (or comparable) strength and growth is the result of a strategy to occupy the territory and become the notable. These are obviously more supply driven, with a strong impulse from donors who always give precedence to the more visible institution in a country (Ouattara, 2005; CGAP, 2009). Apart the issue of growth, there is also the organizational strategy chosen by the microfinance institutions that can influence the outcome. A greater number the leading microfinance have opted for a rather centralized form of organization, considering that it will provide economy of scale and assure better control. Along the same line, the leadership and management culture in West Africa, appear to be more adapted for small and medium size institutions, than large nation-wide entities. After some years of initial struggle, the microfinance institution in West Africa is now focused on issues such as outreach and sustainability. Another feature for the West African microfinance institutions is the rural focus. There may be many small initiatives in the bigger cities, but majority of the microfinance institutions are located in the rural areas and serve in large proportion rural micro entrepreneurs. As a result of this, they are faced with some constraints such as low density of the rural communities, poor infrastructures, illiteracy and the small size of the markets (Honohan & Beck, 2007).

The dynamics and the potential profitability of the microfinance institutions in ECOWAS sub-region have however attracted new promoters coming from the private sector. For instance, some commercial banks are creating microfinance windows, such as the experience of CCEI in Cameroon, with the MC2, or professionals coming from commercial banking background who get together and promote a credit union using bank management skills, as Taïmako in Niger. There are young unemployed graduates in urban areas, who consider that creating a microfinance business is rapidly profitable, without necessitating initial capital investment. What they share in common is total independence from donors influence and funding at the embryonic stage. Those who have been more visible or successful are now exposed to the aid mode of thinking and operating, as many donors have contacted them to subcontract credit operations through them. In recent times, many of the new promoters are turning to donors for start-up grants. A new generation of microfinance institutions, tallying with the new promoters or not, is emerging and challenging the leading microfinance institutions with their commercially more aggressive behaviours (Meagher, 2002).

In the classification of microfinance organizations, the Africa Development Bank (ADB) (2006) adopted a pragmatic typology which comprises of the following: the savings and credit institutions, including the classical credit unions (inspired by Raffeisen & Desjardins) and the more recent experiences of caissesvillageoisesautogérées (CIDR type), the microcredit organizations with lending as a unique or major activity, inspired by the Grameen Bank experience and those with a credit component where credit is a marginal activity. But it is now well admitted in West Africa, among practitioners and microfinance experts that the different typologies tend to merge, giving rise to institutions that are all, more or less borrowing the best and the most efficient practices from each other.One notable way of doing this is linking rural development with entrepreneur skills. It has been shown that empowering entrepreneurial activities has a way of reducing inequality. Khanna (2000) exposed the critical role played by new entrepreneurs in determining the relative economic success across a sample of transition countries while Fisman and Tarun (1998) provide evidence that a large formal small and medium enterprise (SME) sector is a major ingredient of successful economies. Apart from driving growth, the overall competitiveness of the business environment fosters growth, development and poverty alleviation. There are other macro and micro evidence that links microfinance, even in the face of other barriers, and rural development (Clarke, Xu & Zou, 2003). Even though a deeper financial system may be associated with improvement in income across all levels, perhaps very few households have benefited from such. The resulting benefit may then be of lower quality, as it fails to renew the set of productive rural dwellers as it spurs inequality further (Bourguignon & Thierry 2000b; Morck, Wolfenzon & Yeung, 2004).In other words, strong financial reform has a way of influencing inequality. In his regard, reforms need to broaden, not just deepen finance but also other financial system in the economy thus lending support for the establishment of microfinance, especially in the rural areas (Cemoglu, Johnson, Robinson, & Thaicharoen 2002; Acemoglu, 2003).The last 30 years have shown that microfinance is a proven development tool capable of providing a vast number of the poor, particularly women, with sustainable tailored financial services that enhance their welfare.

Although microfinance still has low penetration rates in ECOWAS region compared to other region of Africa, it is growing rapidly, but differences remain in rates of penetration of services rendered. Available statistics indicates that West Africa shows the highest, with 5 out of the 10 countries with the highest penetration rates for both savers and borrowers, with North Africa having the lowest. Towards standardizing products and practices of microfinance in the region, the Central Bank of West Africa States came up with regulations to enable them play their role in a sector that has grown considerably in the 1990s (Mees, 2015). According to Microcredit Summit Campaign Report (2015), 3,098 microfinance institutions had reached over 211 million clients by 2013, 114 million (54 percent) of whom were living in extreme poverty and of these poorest clients, 83 percent were women.

REVIEW OF RELEVANT LITERATURE

A number of studies have attempted to measure the impact of microfinance on poverty reduction. In 2008, Ahlin and Jiang adopted a model in which microfinance is described as a financial development variable to estimate the impact of microfinance on poverty reduction and found that microfinance decreases inequality. Results had it that microfinance lowers inequality by increasing the income of the poor and lowering the income of the wealthy. Bird, Hattel, Sasaki and Attapich (2011) argue that such improvement in the financial access of the poor can directly enhance poverty reduction, since an imperfect financial market, which excludes the poor, is an important factor that affects poverty. Based on the experience of selected countries (Benin, Ghana, Guinea-Bissau and Tanzania), Basu, Rodolphe and Yulet (2004) displayed a critical presentation of the development of the microfinance in Africa to support the view that microfinance institutions, especially those engaged in full financial intermediation complement effectively the banking sector in extending financial services to the poor drawn heavily on the rich experience of community-based development and preexisting informal methods of financial intermediation. This has been made possible by the growing linkages between microfinance institutions and the banking system and the dissemination of good practices by non-government organizations, supported by regulation and supervision by local authorities. Asghar (2012) affirms that microfinance can serve as a strong tool to increase the income of the poor and education of the household. In essence, income generated from the credit of microfinance will reduce poverty and increase both economic and social well beings.

In a major study, Kai and Shigeyuki (2009) used cross-sectional data from 61 developing countries to illustrate that microfinance plays an important role in creating a financial system endowed with the equalizing effect. The study finds that microfinance can lower inequality and that poorer countries need to focus more on the equalizing effects of microfinance. The empirical results confirm that microfinance lowers inequality, and that it can be used as an effective tool for income redistribution. The study also find that economic development lowers inequality after a country's income reaches a certain level while economic growth increases inequality up to a certain level of economic development, such as occurs in developing countries.

On the role of microfinance on poverty reduction, Yunus (1999) opine that microfinance could correct the market failure by opening access to credit to the poor. Credit in turn creates economic power that would generate into social power, lifting the poor out of poverty. But Chowdhury (2009) argues that while microfinance has developed some innovative management and business strategies, its impact on poverty reduction is doubtful. To Leikem (2012), microfinance has offered important contributions to development by providing savings that are vital and perhaps more important to the poor and the poorest. In another study for Bagladesh, Mahjabeen (2008) used the general equilibrium model to show that microfinance lowers inequality but there was no sufficient empirical romance on the effect of microfinance on inequality in developing countries of Africa.

In a study on the poverty, income inequality and microfinance linkage in Thailand, Bird, Hattel, Sasaki and Attapich (2011) came to conclusion that financial exclusion of the lower income households also explains persistence of high rates of household income inequality in Thailand. According to their research, while government programs have expanded microcredit, low-income families still have limited access to financial services, including savings products, transfer payments products, insurance, and pension programs, among others. Providing cross-country empirical evidence from 11 developing countries in Central Africa, Tchouassi, (2011)examined the inter-link among microfinance, inequality and vulnerability and results indicate that the number of microfinance institutions has a negative impact on the Gini index. Implied is that when the microfinance institutions in the country become dense, inequality decreases. Kazi and Leonard (2012) however contend that Microfinance has the potency to reduce poverty and improve youth employment when properly applied. This is because high unemployment has direct relationship with poverty in any measure (Emeka, 2011).

While microfinance is widely recognized as a strategy to fight poverty, it has long been considered as having its roots in the women gender equality movements. While this is true for the evolution and development of microfinance in many countries over the years, Arunachalam (2007) notes that it has more of finance and less of gender in its overall programme. Yet, a significant proportion of the poor throughout the world who still lack access to financial services are women, and any attempt to tackle poverty must focus on them. It is therefore critical that microfinance addresses gender challenges as it moves forward in its journey of empowering the poor, especially women to achieve not only of sustainability and inclusive outreach but also of livelihood security and gender impact. Owusu-Danso (2015) seeks to investigate whether increased access to microfinance by poor households affects intra-household gender inequality and gender asset gap between male-headed households and female-headed households using micro-economic data from Ghana. Employing beta regression and the Oaxaca decomposition models, a comparative analysis shows that on the average female-headed households receiving micro-credit tend to spend equally on male and female children at the primary and secondary school levels whereas education expenditure is skewed in favor of male children relative to female children in the case of female-headed households without micro-credit which translates to higher years of schooling for children in female-headed households On average, females in households receiving micro-credit have a higher share of household assets relative to females in households without micro-credit. The results suggest that microfinance helps to reduce intra-household gender inequality and gender asset gaps between male-headed and female-headed households.

Zhang and Posso (2017) provided further insight on how microfinance reduces women inequality in developing countries, although there was evidence of a negative relationship between women's participation in microfinance and gender inequality. Implied is that gender inequality will potentially decrease when women's participation increases. On the average, an increase in microfinance by around 15 percent is associated with a decline in gender inequality by about half. It was also found that cultural characteristics such as cooking and rearing of children can potentially limit women's ability to fully adopt employment opportunities through microfinance-generated investments. Given these findings, governments in developing countries should continue to promote microcredit institutions to indirectly empower women. Since cultural factors play a key role in determining how microfinance interacts with gender inequality, they should be considered when assessing the impact of microcredit. Vong et al. (2013) in a study of formal financial access to rural women micro-entrepreneurs in Indonesia find that women micro entrepreneurs face multiple forms of constraints arising from an underlying gender inequality in the country. They suggested that while working around this short coming, the opportunity for women micro entrepreneurs can be addressed by micro financiers. However, the gender inequality issues should be the focus during the design stage of successful microfinance programmes. Hermes (2014) study addresses the question whether participation of the poor in microfinance contributes to reducing a country's level of income inequality. Using data from 70 developing countries, he showed that higher levels of microfinance participation are indeed associated with a reduction of the income gap between rich and poor, however, the effects of microfinance on reducing income inequality are relatively small. This study is a modes contribution to the discussion on the impact of microfinance on poverty by showing that, although access to microfinance does seem to improve the relative income position of the poor, this improvement is modest due probably to the use of microfinance that is relatively small as compared to the size of the economy of the countries in used for the study.

The theoretical thesis that microfinance is an effective tool for reducing poverty at the macro level was tested by Zang (2017) using cross-country panel data from 106 countries developed and developing countries for the period, 1998-2013, taking into cognizance the potential problem of sample selection bias and endogeneity. The results which are robust to the choice of microfinance measures and poverty indicators show that microfinance has a negative effect on poverty, especially in developing and emerging economies. The study encourages the establishment of more Microfinance institutions and more funds from development agencies channeled into Microfinance institutions to enable them reduce poverty in these countries. In a review of synchronization between microfinance and poverty reduction at the macro-level, Miled and Rejeb (2015) confirm the role of microfinance in poverty reduction. Using cross-sectional data covering 596 microfinance institutions for 2011 supplemented by a two-period (2005 and 2011) panel data of 1132 microfinance institutions in 57 developing countries and taking into account of the endogeneity associated with microfinance loan, it was shown that a country with higher microfinance gross loan portfolio per capita tends to posses lower levels of poverty reduction. Other factors found to contribute to poverty reduction are GDP per capita, financial development, international openness and inflation.

Corsi, Botti, Rondinella and Zacchia (2006), from their research on the impact of micro-finance on women empowerment in Mediterranean countries assert that empowerment through finance seem more effective than programs that are specifically targeted at reducing gender discrimination. Several other studies such as Rankin (2002), Beatriz and Jonathan (2005) have also pointed out that the provision of credit alone is insufficient in empowering women. Gaiha and Kulkarni (2013) contend that even though the magic of microfinance in empowering the vulnerable in the society has been eroded with financial sustainability overriding social goals, there exist ample evidence for optimism about resolving this trade-off. Not withstanding the mixed evidence, microfinance reduces poverty, vulnerability to health shocks and hastens recovery after a natural disaster. Also, there are heterogeneous impacts in terms of women's empowerment across households that vary with gender defined social norms. Although Microfinance are celebrated as saviors in economic systems with few formal jobs, since they provide individuals with access to capital and thereby a means to survive in the informal sector, Kellett (2011) study on microfinance programs in the rural highlands of Peru illustrates how theycan undermine the financial security of borrowers, increase economic inequality and decrease food security. Research findings suggest that microfinance programs are unable to address the needs of women in the informal sector. For this reason, it is necessary to evaluate the effects of microfinance programs beyond that of the individual borrower. Drawing from research on the Zambia's copperbelt, Copestake (2002) show how impact on income distribution is influenced by who obtains loans, who graduates to larger loans, who exits and group dynamics.

Microfinance has also been used severally to reduce poverty, especially in rural areas because it is seen as an important aid that can improve the economic performance of the rural poor. According to Kasali, Ahmad and Lim (2015), microfinance loan is one of the efforts towards alleviating poverty in rural Nigeria, but in spite of this, poverty still remains pervasive and widespread in the country especially in the rural areas. The study revealed that microfinance loan have made significant impact on the loan beneficiaries in South-West Nigeria which lead to poverty reduction, the study suggests that government should provide more enabling environment to make Microfinance operations more effective in the reduction of poverty in the rural areas. In furtherance, Makarfi and Olukosi (2011) measured the performances and challenges of microfinance as financiers of poor entrepreneur farmers and other low resource-based individuals in Kano State, Nigeria. Levels of savings of members, microloans packaged and delivered, women participation, and profits generated as well as returns to investments and to assets were measured. The results showed that three categories of microfinance: formal finance institutions (FFIs), semi-formal finance institutions (SFFIs), and informal finance institutions (IFFIs) that operate in the area each are faced with its unique features and mode of operations and share common problems such as low level of member which renders its potency to reduce poverty. In his part, Doçi (2016) find that macroeconomic variables such as household final consumption expenditure, gross domestic product, gross loan portfolio of microfinance and the number of active borrowers of microfinance loan has a role to play in the ability of Microfinance to reduce poverty. It was found that an increase in final consumption expenditure, gross domestic product, and gross loan portfolio mitigates poverty while an increase in number of active borrowers fuels poverty. The study by Rout, Das, Ranasingh and Behera (2015) provides strong evidence of the positive effect of microfinance programs on the income of the households participating in microfinance programs, but the microfinance interventions did not have a significant impact on income distribution equality.

On the impact of microfinance on women empowerment, Herath, Guneratne and Sanderatne (2015) investigates the impact of microfinance on poverty and socio-economic vulnerability of women and the ability to form social capital through group-based micro loans. The study uses four criteria: access, creation and control over private resources; freedom of decision making at home; self-confidence on socio-economic activities and status in community and family to examine the impact of microfinance on poverty and vulnerability of women borrowers. Using three logistic regression models and a women's empowerment index, the results revealed that the household income level before taking microcredit, age of the household head and market availability for products are significant in affecting women's empowerment and reducing vulnerability. The disaggregated and overall Women Empowerment Indices (WEIs) clearly illustrate a considerable development after joining the microfinance institutions.

Going beyond the economics of gender inequalities in microfinance, Voola (2014) compared how gender inequalities were problematic in the policy and practice of microfinance in India and Australia. Despite differences in historical background, socio-cultural norms and geo-political configurations between the countries, the study reveals certain similarities in the normative structuring of gender inequalities. The association between gender inequalities and microfinance were problematic in relation to accessing finance, market work and business opportunities, expansion of formal and informal support networks, accessing educational experiences, maintaining the care economy and securing personal safety. The study suggests that microfinance policy and practice can promote gender equality by intentionally seeking out economic and beyond economic outcomes. Wry (2015) took a cursory look at how poverty rooted in gender or other forms of systematic discrimination affect the disparity between social outreach and financial performance of microfinance organizations. An interesting finding is that level at which the social and financial performances have become compatible and systematically affected not only by the quality of market institutions in the country but also the nature of poverty. When poverty was decomposed based on gender or other forms of inequality, the transaction costs were found to be higher for the organizations in terms of outreach, and this makes it more expensive to tackle poverty in a sustainable way.

From the list of studies reviewed, no study has examineddirectly the correlation between microfinance and inequality reduction in a cross-section of developing countries of Africa, especially West Africa sub-region. This identified gap is the main contribution of this chapter.

OBJECTIVE OF THE STUDY

The objective of this chapter is to analyze the correlation between microfinance and determine itsequalizing effect on inequality reduction so far in West Africa sub-region for the period, 2003-2014.

DATA AND METHODOLOGY

The data employed are obtained from World Development Indicators. Two set of data were used for regression: the 2010 cross-sectional data, with the number of microfinance as the measure of microfinance intensity and the 2003-2014 pooled data, using the number of borrowers in a country as the measure of microfinance intensity. The income Gini measure of inequality generated from the World Bank database was also utilized. Since the World Bank publishes inequality data almost every five years and its year of publication differs for various countries, the data employed ranges from 1992-2012. The data on the number of microfinance in each country is obtained from the Microfinance Industry Report and the democracy index employed is Institutionalized Democracy, obtained from Marshall and Jaggers (2015).

The empirical analysis is that microfinance has a role to play in reducing inequality.To investigate primarily the impact of microfinance on inequality, panel dataset comprising of 15 countries of West Africa sub-region from 2009-2014 is used. To match with the dependent variable, six-year average of our data was taken on other explanatory and control variables.To be more specific in carrying out econometric estimation, several models were estimated to achieve our objectives. The first as well as the base model is of the following form:

$$IQ_{it} = a + \beta_1 MF_{it} + \beta_2 C_{it} + \varepsilon_{it} \tag{1}$$

In equation (1), *i*and *t* indicate country and year respectively, *IQ* stands for inequality measure, *MF* is the degree of microfinance intensity (measured by the number of microfinance and the number of borrowers in a particular country). C_{it} .s the vector of all control variables, namely per capita GDP, inflation, degree of openness (measured by ratio of export-import to GDP) and democracy index.In the above equation, $\varepsilon .t$ is the disturbance error term whichcomprises both time-invariant unobserved country-specific effects (fixed effects) e_i . and a time-variant unobserved component, v_{it} .

From equation (1), the equalizing effect of microfinance can be determined. To be consistent with previous studies, we specify an equa5ion in which the logarithm of the intensity of microfinance is employed as:

$$IQ_{it} = \alpha + \beta_1 l\_MF_{it} + \beta_2 C_{it} + \varepsilon_{it} \tag{2}$$

It is assumed that a higher income level increases inequality, but its effect declines after a certain point. We therefore include the logarithm of GDP per capita and its square terms in the model.

Since panel data is used, the estimation technique is based on panel data analysis. Traditionally, as a starting point for panel data analysis, the estimation begins by applying pooled ordinary least square

(OLS) methods to the above specifications. The advantage of using pooled OLS is that it employs more information by combining both cross-sectional and time series observations to generate more reliable estimates compared to cross-sectional OLS. Besides, it provides unbiased and consistent estimates as long as the composite error term u_{it} .s uncorrelated with X_{it}. However, the presence of unobserved time-invariant country-specific feature or fixed effects e_i .n the composite error term u_{it} .akes it likely to be correlated with the explanatory variables. To overcome this problem,the fixed-effect method can be employed, which removes the unobserved country-specific heterogeneity by within-transformation effects. However, the fixed-effect model does not allow estimating the effect of time-invariant independent variables. Alternatively, the random effects specification can be employed, although its application lies on a basic assumption that the unobserved country-specific effect e_i .s random and independent of v_{it}. that is, country-specific unobserved heterogeneity is uncorrelated with independent variables. Although the random-effect model provides better efficiency and allows coefficients of time-invariant covariates to be estimated, the assumption of e_i .eing uncorrelated with X_{it} .s often violated. For this reason, it is more likely that random-effect estimates suffer from omitted variable bias. For the appropriateness of these specifications, the Hausman test can be used to test the null hypothesis of individual effects uncorrelated with any of the regressors as:

$$\hat{H} = \dot{m} - \dot{n} \tag{3}$$

Assuming the null hypothesis, Hausman test shows that:

$$w(d) = w\left(\dot{m}\right) - w\left(\dot{n}\right) \tag{4}$$

where ω .s variance. Taking $\omega .\dot{m})$ to be consistent estimator of $\omega .\dot{n})$,Hausman test provides that the test statistic $d^1 [\omega .d)]^{-1} d$ is asymptotically distributed as Y^2 .with n def; where *n* is the number of *Y* variables involved in the regression. Insignificance of the test statistic will support the null hypothesis that the *X* and ϵ .variables are independent in the model given by:

$$X = Y_m + \varepsilon \tag{5}$$

Rejection of the null hypothesis in the former test, and the acceptance of the null hypothesis in the latter, indicate that the random-effect model is more appropriate. We employ panel data instrumental variables methods to address endogeneity problems and control for the relevant covariates and carry out robustness checks on the results.

RESULTS AND DISCUSSION

Table 1 contains the summary statistics of the variables used for analysis.

From the data shown in Table 1, inequality for the region averaged 43.76 with a standard deviation of 5.66. The mean number of microfinance and borrowers is 65600 and 1440000 with standard deviation of 8095 and 358900 respectively. With respect to the inflationary rate observed, the average figure stands at 12.38 across the region with a standard deviation of 10.80. The average democracy for the sub-region stands at 2.80 within the periods under investigation and the standard deviation of that value is 0.50.

The presentation of the regression results is based on the findings of the baseline model in equations (1) and (2). Although we report results for both fixed-effect (FE) and random effect (RE) models, our preferred approach is fixed-effect (FE) in each Tables 2 and 3 based the outcome of the Hausman specification test. Table 1 contains the empirical result of the regression using the number of microfinance as the degree of microfinance intensity. Model 1 contains the results of model 1 which employs the number of microfinance as the degree of microfinance intensity while Model 2 present the result which employs the logarithm of the number of microfinance as the degree of microfinance intensity.

The empirical results show that microfinance intensity is negatively and statistically associated with inequality at 5 percent level of significance, an indication that microfinance lowers inequality. But the estimated coefficient logarithm of GDP per capita is positive while its square term is negative.We also examine the effect of inflation on inequality. The coefficient of the inflation rate is positive and statistically significant at the 1 percent level. Thus, an increase in the inflation rate may increase and at the same time worsen inequality. Furthermore, the result indicates that while microfinance is positively related to inequality in some countries, it is natively related to some other countries within the sub-region, though not statistically significant at 10 percent. The implication of this is that increase in the number of microfinance is the region has not accentuated inequality reduction.We can therefore infer that the equalizing effect is low. In all, the value of coefficient of determination (R^2) of 0.354 indicates that 35.4 percent of the general variation (percentage of microfinance to alleviate inequality) is explained by the cause variation of two variables in the specified models. The correlation coefficient is 0.595, which shows there is a positive linear connection between the possibilities of microfinance to reduce inequality with the independent variables.

We went further to use the number of borrowers in the country as the degree of Microfinance intensity and the result is presented in Table 3. Model 1 contains the result of the number of microfinance as

Table 1. Summary statistics

Variable	Mean	Standard Deviation
Inequality	43.76	5.66
Number of Microfinance	65600	8095
Number of Borrowers	1440000	358900
L_GDP per capita	3.12	1.54
Openness	28.22	19.09
Inflation rate	12.38	10.80
Democracy index	2.80	0.50

Source: Authors' calculation based on panel dataset

Table 2. Regression results using the number of microfinance as the degree of microfinance intensity

Variable	Model 1		Model 2	
	RE	FE	RE	FE
Constant	-27.546 (-1.007)	-27.773 (-2.205)	-23.232 (-0.724)	-21.245 (-1.819)
Number of Microfinance	-0.076** (-1.301)	-0.055** (-0.608)	-0.108** (-0.786)	-0.521** (-0.523)
l_ of Microfinance	-0.049* (-0.066)	-0.080* (-0.101)	-0.414* (-0.049)	-0.002 (-0.041)
l_ GDP per capita	0.009 (0.001)	0.108 (0.000)	0.005 (0.005)	0.001 (0.002)
Square of l_GDP per capita	-0.065 (0.064)	-0.066 (-0.049)	-0.009 (-0.002)	-0.008 (-0.034)
Openness	-0.065 (0.064)	-0.066 (-0.049)	-0.009 (-0.002)	-0.008 (-0.034)
Inflation rate	1.113 (-0.233)	1.302 (-0.322)	0.609 (-1.901)	1.401 (-1.647)
Democracy	0.167** (0.054)	0.167** (0.084)	0.105** (0.025)	0.128** (0.058)
Benin	-0.092 (0.021)	-0.082 (0.022)	-0.019 (0.025)	-0.012 (0.020)
Burkina Faso	0.032 (0.002)	0.033 (0.002)	0.034 (0.001)	0.029 (0.001)
Cape Verde	0.112 (0.022)	0.115 (0.022)	0.110 (0.023)	0.111 (0.024)
Cote d'Ivore	0.009 (0.000)	0.009 (0.000)	0.008 (0.000)	0.008 (0.000)
Gambia	0.005 (0.001)	0.007 (0.001)	0.006 (0.001)	0.005 (0.001)
Ghana	0.010 (0.054)	0.015 (0.084)	0.011 (0.025)	0.011 (0.028)
Guinea	-0.009 (-0.023)	-0.007 (-0.033)	-0.008 (-0.034)	-0.007 (0.033)
Guinea Bissau	0.005 (0.108)	0.005 (0.107)	0.004 (0.106)	0.003 (0.105)
Liberia	0.002 (0.090)	0.002 (0.084)	0.001 (0.086)	0.001 (0.085)
Mali	-0.102 (0.000)	-0.101 (0.001)	-0.100 (0.000)	-0.101 (0.001)
Niger	-0.200 (0.005)	-0.199 (0.005)	-0.197 (0.004)	-0.196 (0.005)
Nigeria	-0.009 (0.008)	-0.008 (0.008)	-0.007 (0.007)	-0.007 (0.007)
Senegal	0.001 (0.001)	0.001 (0.001)	0.001 (0.000)	0.001 (0.000)
Sau Tome & Principe	0.005 (0.092)	0.005 (0.090)	0.004 (0.091)	0.004 (0.090)
Togo	-0.100 (-0.022)	-0.100 (-0.020)	-0.099 (-0.020)	-0.098 (-0.020)
R^2 (Overall)	0.354			
P value	0.007	0.000	0.000	0.007
Hausman test statistic	0.432	0.290	0.144	0.119
R (Correlation Coefficient)				

Source: Authors' calculation based on panel dataset

Note: Figures in parenthesis are the t-values; *Variables are significant at 1 percent level; **Variables are significant at 5 percent level; Variables are significant at 10 percent level

the degree of microfinance intensity while Model 2 is for the logarithm of the number of microfinance as the degree of microfinance intensity. Most importantly, democracy and GDP per capita continues to retain positive coefficient.

The results in Table 3 clearly show that the coefficient on the number of borrowers and the coefficient on the logarithm of the number of borrowers are negative in both specifications, with estimated coefficient of -0.000019 and -0.000015 respectively. Thus, microfinance leads to a decline in inequality, its impact in doing this is not statistically significant, indicating that the equalizing effect of microfinance is low. The coefficient for GDP per capita shows that is positive and its square term is estimated to be significantly negative at 5 percent level of significance. With a correlation coefficient of 0.688, it implies although there is positive linear connection between the possibilities of microfinance to reduce inequality, it has not contributed significantly in doing so, with the independent variables.

CONCLUSION AND POLICY SUGGESTIONS

In this chapter, attempt has been made to ascertain the correlation between microfinance and inequality reduction in a cross-section of developing countries of West Africa sub-region. Our results suggest that the most robust explanatory variables for inequality reduction are GDP per capita and democracy which are invariably significant with a positive sign. In all, the correlation coefficient of 0.595 shows there is a positive linear connection between the possibilities of microfinance to reduce inequality with the independent variables. Taken together, these findings reinforce the intuition that greater democracy promotes the enabling environment for microfinance to contribute to inequality reduction. Inflation and openness retards microfinance ability to reduce inequality. As far as the policy implications are concerned, efforts for microfinance to promote greater inequality reduction in the region should aim at improving income per capita.Greater democracy in conjunction with provision and expansion of financial infrastructure such as establishment of a common specific financial framework that encourages microfinance institutions in rural areas,improve financial to the rural poor,especially in the backward states in the region,promotes this. Apart from alleviating absolute and grinding poverty, microfinance can help to redress the harmful effects of inequality, especially inequality of opportunity, which is arguably the great reason for establishing microfinance institutions. The regional microfinance associations should therefore enhance client protection, support other retail providers and interface with policymakers and regulators. This could help identify gaps at the institutional and national levels. Otherwise, all efforts by microfinance in the direction of accentuating inequality reduction with increased prosperity for the majority of the citizens in the region, especially the poor, will be fruitless.

Table 3. Regression Results using the number of borrowers in the country as the degree of Microfinance intensity

Variable	Model 1		Model 2	
	RE	FE	RE	FE
Constant	-18.009 (-3.900)	-18.000 (-3.809)	-20.580 (-3.800)	-20.009 (-3.009)
Number of borrowers	-0.000021 (-2.090)**	-0.000019 (-2.089)**	-0.000018 (-2.079)**	-0.000015 (-2.077)**
L_ of Number of borrowers	-0.01100 (-3.000)**	-0.01000 (-3.000)**	-0.01000 (-2.079)**	-0.01000 (-2.057)**
l_GDP per capita	20.169 (3.509)**	19.309 (3.500)**	20.554 (2.558)**	20.100 (2.550)**
Square of l_GDP per capita	-1.890 (0.005)	-1.772 (0.002)	-1.560 (0.002)	-1.402 (0.001)
Openness	-0.0041 (0.000)	-0.0056 (0.000)	-0.0061 (0.000)	-0.0059 (0.000)
Inflation rate	-2.100 (0.001)	-2.001 (0.001)	-2.009 (0.001)	-2.005 (0.001)
Democracy	0.0090 (0.003)	0.0076 (0.034)*	0.0055 (0.025)	0.0044 (0.022)
Benin	-0.092 (0.021)	-0.082 (0.022)	-0.019 (0.025)	-0.012 (0.020)
Burkina Faso	0.032 (0.002)	0.033 (0.002)	0.034 (0.001)	0.029 (0.001)
Cape Verde	0.112 (0.022)	0.115 (0.022)	0.110 (0.023)	0.111 (0.024)
Cote d'Ivore	0.009 (0.000)	0.009 (0.000)	0.008 (0.000)	0.008 (0.000)
Gambia	0.005 (0.001)	0.007 (0.001)	0.006 (0.001)	0.005 (0.001)
Ghana	0.010 (0.054)	0.015 (0.084)	0.011 (0.025)	0.011 (0.028)
Guinea	-0.009 (-0.023)	-0.007 (-0.033)	-0.008 (-0.034)	-0.007 (0.033)
Guinea Bissau	0.005 (0.108)	0.005 (0.107)	0.004 (0.106)	0.003 (0.105)
Liberia	0.002 (0.090)	0.002 (0.084)	0.001 (0.086)	0.001 (0.085)
Mali	-0.102 (0.000)	-0.101 (0.001)	-0.100 (0.000)	-0.101 (0.001)
Niger	-0.200 (0.005)	-0.199 (0.005)	-0.197 (0.004)	-0.196 (0.005)
Nigeria	-0.009 (0.008)	-0.008 (0.008)	-0.007 (0.007)	-0.007 (0.007)
Senegal	0.001 (0.001)	0.001 (0.001)	0.001 (0.000)	0.001 (0.000)
Sau Tome & Principe	0.005 (0.092)	0.005 (0.090)	0.004 (0.091)	0.004 (0.090)
Togo	-0.009 (0.000)	-0.009 (0.000)	-0.009 (0.000)	-0.008 (0.000)
R^2	0.473			
Hausman test statistic	0.0908	0.005	0.100	0.009
P value	0.109	0.100	0.233	0.190
R (Correlation coefficient)	$\sqrt{0.473} = 0.688$			

Source: Authors' calculation based on panel dataset

Note: Figures in parenthesis are the t-values; *Variables are significant at 1 percent level; **Variables are significant at 5 percent level; Variables are significant at 10 percent level.

REFERENCES

Acemoglu, D., Johnson, S., Robinson, J., & Thaicharoen, Y. (2002). Institutional causes, macroeconomic symptoms: Volatility, crises, and growth. *Journal of Monetary Economics*, *50*(1), 49–123. doi:10.1016/S0304-3932(02)00208-8

Acemoglu, D. (2003). *The form of property rights: Oligarchic vs. Democratic societies, Mimeo*. MIT. doi:10.3386/w10037

Ahlin, C., & Jiang, N. (2008). Can micro-credit bring development? *Journal of Development Economics*, *86*(1), 1–21. doi:10.1016/j.jdeveco.2007.08.002

African Development Bank (ADB) (2006). *Microfinance-Policy and Strategy*. ADB.e

Arunachalam, R. S. (2007). *Microfinance and innovative financing for Gender Equality: Approaches, challenges and strategies. Background paper prepared for the Commonwealth Secretariat*. Chennai, India: Independent Consultant.

Asghar, N. (2012). Microfinancing for poverty reduction: An empirical study of rural areas of Tehsil Gujrat-Pakistan. *International Journal of Advances in Management &Economics*, *1*(4), 14–19. Retrieved from http://www.managementjournal.info

Ashraf, M. A., & Ibrahim, Y. B. (2014). Poverty alleviation and identifying the barriers to the rural poor participation in MFIs: A case study in Bangladesh. *Journal of Economic Cooperation & Development*, *35*(3), 99–132.

Basir, M. K., Amin, A., & Naeem, M. K. (2010). Micro-credit and poverty alleviation in Pakistan. *World Applied Sciences Journal*, *8*(11), 1381–1386.

Basu, A., Rodolphe, B., & Yulet, M. (2004). *Microfinance in Africa: Experience and lessons from selected African countries*. International Monetary Fund Working Paper, WP/04/176.

Beatriz, A., & Jonathan, M. (2005). *The Economics of microfinance*. MIT Press.

Beck, T., & Maimbo, S. M. (Eds.). (2013). *Financial sector development in Africa: Opportunities and challenges*. Washington, DC: World Bank.

Beck, T., Demirgüç-Kunt, A., & Levine, R. (2004). *Finance, inequality and poverty: Cross-country evidence*. NBER working paper 10979.

Bird, K., Hattel, K. E., Sasaki, & Attapich, L. (2011). *Poverty, income inequality and Microfinance in Thailand.* ADB Southeast Asia Working Paper Series, 6.

Bourguignon, F., & Thierry, V. (2000b). Oligarchy, Democracy, Inequality and Growth. *Journal of Development Economics*, *62*(2), 285–313. doi:10.1016/S0304-3878(00)00086-9

Central Bank of Nigeria (CBN). (2005). *Microfinance policy regulatory and supervisory framework for Microfinance*. Abuja, Nigeria: Author.

Chowdhury, A. (2009). *Microfinance as a poverty reduction tool-A critical assessment*. DESA Working Paper No. 89ST/ESA/2009/DWP/89.

Clarke, G. L. C., Xu, & Zou, H. (2003). *Finance and income inequality: Test of alternative Theories*. Washington, DC: World Bank Policy Research Working Paper, 2984.

Consultative Group to Assist the Poor (CGAP). (2009). *Financial Access Report*. CGAP. Accessed from www.cgap.org/publications/financial-access-2009

Consultative Group to Assist the Poor (CGAP). (2009). *What do we know about the impact of Microfinance*. Accessed from www.cgap.org/p/site/c/template.rc/1.26.1306/

Copestake, J. (2002). Inequality and the polarizing impact of microcredit: Evidence from Zambia's copperbelt. *Journal of International Development*, *14*(6), 743–755. doi:10.1002/jid.921

Corsi, M., Botti, F., Rondinella, T., & Zacchia, G. (2006). Women and Microfinance in Mediterranean Countries. *Development*, *49*(2), 67–74. doi:10.1057/palgrave.development.1100247

Cuong, N. V., Bigman, D., Van den Berg, M., & Thieu, V. (2007). Impact of micro-credit on poverty and inequality: The case of the Vietnam Bank for Social Policies. Paper submitted to Microfinance: What Do We Know? Groningen, Netherlands.

Doçi, E. (2016). Microfinance and the interaction of Macroeconomic factors in poverty reduction. *Academic Journal of Interdisciplinary Studies*, *5*(2), 209–218. doi:10.5901/ajis.2016.v5n2p209

Duku, O. P. (2002). A critical assessment of Jamaica's national poverty eradication programme. *Journal of International Development*, *14*(6), 773–788. doi:10.1002/jid.923

ECA/SRO-WA. (2015). *West Africa Regional Integration Report, Inclusive green growth to accelerate socio-economic development in West Africa*. Author.

ECOWAS. (2015). *Rapport Annuel 2015: La CEDEAO après 40 années: réalisations, défis et perspectives*. CommunautéÉconomique des États de l'Afrique de l'Ouest.

Emeka, E. O. (2011). Youth unemployment and implications for stability of democracy in Nigeria. *Journal of Sustainable Development in Africa, 13*(1).

EPA. (2014). *African Economic Outlook: West Africa*. EPA.

Fisman, R., & Tarun, K. (1998). *Facilitating Development: The role of Business Groups*. HBS, Working Paper.

Gaiha, R., & Kulkarni, V. S. (2013). *Credit, Microfinance and empowerment, invited contribution to expert group meeting on policies and strategies to promote empowerment of people in achieving poverty eradication, social integration and full employment and decent work for all, September 10 -11*. New York: United Nations Secretariat Building.

Green, C. J., Kirkpatrick, C. H., & Murinde, V. (2006). Finance for small enterprise growth and poverty reduction in developing countries. *Journal of International Development*, *18*(7), 1017–1030. doi:10.1002/jid.1334

Greenwood, J., & Jovanovic, B. (1990). Financial development, growth, and the distribution of income. *Journal of Political Economy*, *98*(5), 1076–1107. doi:10.1086/261720

Herath, H. M., Guneratne, L. H., & Sanderatne, N. (2015). Impact of microfinance on women's empowerment: A case study on two microfinance institutions in Sri Lanka. *Sri Lanka Journal of Social Sciences, 38*(1), 51–61. doi:10.4038ljss.v38i1.7385

Hermes, N. (2014). Does microfinance affect income inequality? *Applied Economics, 46*(9), 1021–1034. doi:10.1080/00036846.2013.864039

Honohan, P., & Beck, T. (2007). *Making Finance Work for Africa*. Washington, DC: World Bank.

International Monetary Fund (IMF). (2014). *Regional Economic Outlook: Sub-Saharan Africa*. Author.

International Finance Corporation (IFC). (2014). *Microfinance in Africa banking for the smallest Businesses inclusion and their impact on GDP and inequality*. IMF Working Paper 15/22. International Monetary Fund.

Jalilian, H., & Kirkpatrick, C. (2002). Financial development and poverty reduction in developing countries. *International Journal of Finance & Economics, 7*(2), 97–108. doi:10.1002/ijfe.179

Kai, H., & Hamori, S. (2009). Globalization, financial depth, and inequality in Sub-Saharan Africa. *Economic Bulletin, 29*(3), 2025–2037.

Kalirajan, K., & Singh, K. (2009). The pace of poverty reduction across the globe: An exploratory analysis. *International Journal of Social Economics, 36*(6), 692–705. doi:10.1108/03068290910956921

Kasali, T. A., Ahmad, S. A., & Lim, H. E. (2015). The role of Microfinance in poverty alleviation: Empirical evidence from South-West Nigeria. *Asian Social Science, 11*(21). doi:10.5539/ass.v11n21p183

Kazi, M. H., & Leonard, J. E. (2012). Microfinance, poverty and youth unemployment of Nigeria: A Review. *Global Journal of Human Social Science, Sociology, Economics & Political Science (Wellington, N.Z.), 12*(13), 45–59.

Kellett, N. C. (2011). Microfinance and economic inequality in the Peruvian highlands. *Ethnology, 50*(3), 59–78.

Khandker, S. R. (1998). *Fighting poverty with microcredit: Experience in Bangladesh*. New York: Oxford University Press.

Khanna, T. (2000). Business groups and Social welfare in emerging markets: Existing evidence and unanswered questions. *European Economic Review, 444*(6), 748–761. doi:10.1016/S0014-2921(99)00059-8

Leikem, K. (2012). *Microfinance: A tool for poverty reduction?* A Project submitted to University of Rhode Island.

Levine, R. (2005). Finance and Growth-Theory and Evidence. In P. Aghion & ... (Eds.), *Handbook of Economic Growth*. Elsevier North Holland.

Makarfi, A. M., & Olukosi, J. O. (2011). Microfinance institutions as vehicles for sustainable credit access by the poor in Kano state, Nigeria. *European Journal of Finance & Banking Research, 4*(4), 34–48.

Mahjabeen, R. (2008). Microfinancing in Bangladesh: Impact on households, consumption and welfare. *Journal of Policy Modeling, 30*(6), 1083–1092. doi:10.1016/j.jpolmod.2007.12.007

Meagher P. (2002). *Microfinance regulation in Developing Countries: A comparative review of current practice.* IRIS Center, University of Maryland.

Mees, M, (2015). The effects of regulation on microfinance in West Africa. *Zoom Microfinance, 43.*

MicrocreditS. C. R. (2015). Accessed from www.mfw4a.org/access-to-finance/microfinance.html

Miled, K. B. M., & Rejeb, J. B. (2015). Microfinance and poverty reduction: A review and synthesis of empirical evidence. *Procedia: Social and Behavioral Sciences, 195*(3), 705–712. doi:10.1016/j.sbspro.2015.06.339

Mlachala, M., Cui, L., Jidoud, A., Newiak, M., Radzewicz-Bak, B., Takebe, M., . . . Zhang, J. (2016). Financial Development in Sub-Saharan Africa: Promoting inclusive and sustainable growth. International Monetary Fund, 61.

Morck, Wolfenzon, & Yeung. (2004). *Corporate governance, economic entrenchment and Growth.* NBER, Working Paper 10692.

Muller, C., & Bibi, S. (2010). Refining targeting against poverty. Evidence from Tunisia. *Oxford Bulletin of Economics and Statistics, 72*(3), 381–410. doi:10.1111/j.1468-0084.2010.00583.x

Ostry, J. D., Berg, A., & Tsangaride, C. (2014). *Redistribution, inequality, and Growth, IMF Staff Discussion Note 14/02.* Washington, DC: International Monetary Fund.

Owusu-Danso, T. (2015). *Implications of Microfinance for gender inequality in Ghana.* Accessed from https://www.aeaweb.org/conference/2015/retrieve.php?pdfid=983

Ouattara, K. (2005). *Microfinance regulation in Benin-Implications of the PARMEC Law for Development and performance of the industry. Africa Region Working Series.* Washington, DC: World Bank.

Rankin, K. N. (2002). Social capital, microfinance and the politics of development. *Feminist Economics, 8*(1), 1–24. doi:10.1080/13545700210125167

Responsibility. (2016). *Microfinance market outlook: Development, forecasts and trend.* Accessed from https://www.microfinancegateway.org/.../microfinance-market-outlook-2016-develop

Rout, R. K., Das, L. K., Ranasingh, N., & Behera, S. (2015). Impact of Microfinance on household income: Evidence from village level study in Orissa. *International Journal of Management &Economics Invention, 1*(10), 436–441.

Sahay, R., Cihak, M., N'Diaye, P., & Barajas, A. (2015a). *Financial inclusion: Can it meet multiple macroeconomic goals? IMF Staff Discussion Note 15/17.* Washington, DC: International Monetary Fund.

Sahay, R., Cihak, M., N'Diaye, P., Barajas, A., Bi, R., Ayala, D., ... Yousefi, S. R. (2015b). *Rethinking Financial deepening: Stability and growth in emerging markets, IMF Staff Discussion Note 15/08.* Washington, DC: International Monetary Fund.

Tchouassi, G. (2011). Microfinance, inequality and vulnerability: Empirical analysis from Central African countries. *Journal of Development and Agricultural Economics, 3*(4), 150–156.

Tressel, T. (2003). Dual financial systems and inequalities in economic development. *Journal of Economic Growth, 8*(2), 223–257. doi:10.1023/A:1024464506029

UN-DESA. (2015). *World Economic Situation and Prospects*. Author.

UNDP. (2013). *Microfinance in Africa: Overview and suggestions for action by stakeholders*. Author.

Voola, A. (2014). *Beyond the economics of gender inequalities in microfinance: Comparing problem representations in India and Australia* (PhD thesis). Sydney School of Education and Social Work.

Vong, J. (2013). Impact of microfinance on gender inequality in Indonesia. In *Proceeding of the International Conference on Managing the Asian Century*. Springer. doi:10.1007/978-981-4560-61-0_23

World Bank. (2001). *World Development Report 2000/2001*. New York: Oxford University Press.

Wry, T. (2015). *What impact does microfinance have on inequality?* Accessed from https://www.weforum.org/.../12/what-impact-does-microfinance-have-on-inequality

Yang, B., Jialali, P., & Wei, X. (2011). Microfinance in China's poor area and its impact to loan type-evidence from Xinjiang Uygur autonomous region. *Fourth International Conference on BusinessIntelligence and Financial Engineering*, 486-490, 10.1109/BIFE.2011.82

Yunus, M. (1999). *Banker to the Poor*. New York, NY: Public Affairs.

Zaman, H. (2001). *Assessing the poverty and vulnerability impact of micro-credit in Bangladesh, A case study of BRAC*. Background paper for the WDR 2000/2001.

Zang, Q. (2017). Does microfinance reduce poverty? Some international evidence. *The B.E. Journal of Macroeconomics, 17*(2). doi:10.1515/bejm-2016-0011

Zhang, Q., & Posso, A. (2017). *How Microfinance reduces gender inequality in developing countries*. Accessed from www.huffingtonpost.com/.../how-microfinance-reduces-gender-inequality-in-develop

KEY TERMS AND DEFINITIONS

Correlation: Degree of associations between two variables that exist.

Developing Countries of Africa: These are countries within West Africa sub-region.

ECOWAS Sub-Region: The region of fifteen countries African countries lying in the west of north-south axis of Africa.

Human Development: This is a process of improving human welfare through advancement in knowledge, sustainable environment and expression of freedom to live longer and healthier and creative life.

Inequality: Economic difference between the rich and the poor.

Microfinance: It is the financial services such as savings and loans provided to poor and low-income clients to enable them improve their access to income.

Panel Data Set: Data from 15 countries of West Africa sub-region from 2009-2014.

Poverty Reduction: Improving the poor access to economic opportunities.

Chapter 15
Microfinance and Gender Discrimination:
Measurement of Vulnerability of the Group Members in the Context of West Bengal, India

Avijit Brahmachary
Kandi Raj College, India

ABSTRACT

Gender bias retards economic growth. In India women face gender discrimination, specifically male bias, both within the household and in the workplace. It is widely assumed that microfinance will have a positive impact on women's income, employment, self-worth through self-help group. Further, it has a strong positive effect on women empowerment and thereby reduces gender discrimination prevailing in the society. In this chapter, the extent of vulnerability between male and female SHG members have examined using vulnerability index, which is constructed considering different quantitative and subjective issues. For this, the micro level data have been collected from the state of West Bengal (India). The index value in the study shows that female is 56% more vulnerable than male even after joining in SHG and, therefore, requires large policy attention and intervention from different agencies to minimize such discrimination.

INTRODUCTION

It is clear that in spite of rapid advancement, gender disparities continue throughout the world. In various nations women need autonomous access to land and other family resources. They have very limited command over the family property and cannot conduct business or other income earning activities without their husband's/households' male member's consent. They can't move outside the village without male members' approval and usually suffer from severe financial crisis which contributes varied health hazards within the household. It is evident that in the labour market women are less represented than

DOI: 10.4018/978-1-5225-5240-6.ch015

the male even when they have the same education and work experience as men. Additionally, they are significantly under-represented in different household decision making and village level politics (King & Mason, 2001). According to different scholars and researchers, women in India are facing the following problems in general with varied magnitudes and dimensions (Sen & Kumar, 2001; Meenai, 2003):

1. Nutritional Discrimination,
2. Little control over own fertility and reproductive health,
3. Zero or very low literacy with higher dropout rates,
4. Participates largely in undervalued and unorganized sector in the labour market,
5. Earn lower wages than male for the same work,
6. Face physical and mental violence inside and outside family throughout their lives, and
7. Highly under-represented in governance and decision making.

It is seen that gender inequality impedes economic growth and development. To minimize gender inequality as prevailing everywhere in the society, distinctive policies have been implemented throughout the world. Apart from women's exclusive programmes, the gender perspective has been incorporated in almost all development programmes. Since independence, Government of India has introduced different policies to reduce gender disparity and empower the deprived women. Development for Women and Children in Rural Areas (DWCRA), Integrated Rural Development Programme (IRDP), Swarnajayanti Gram Swarojgar Yojana (SGSY), National Rural Livelihood Mission (NRLM) etc. are the example of few flagship programme in India introduced by the government to empower the women in India.

Microfinance through SHGs has come to be seen as an important development policy to reduce poverty, vulnerability and inequality in the society since 1990s. According to Tchouassi (2011), if vulnerable poor people receive more microcredit, inequality, poverty and vulnerability will be reduced. But, such straightforward conclusions are highly challenging due to lack of reliable data, methodological and measurement controversy and because impact studies are highly region and subject specific. Thus various doubts and questions regarding the impact of microfinance on different economic (income, savings, consumption, etc.) and social indicators (self-worth, voice representation, etc.) have risen by many researchers in many times. Despite some positive income studies conducted by various scholars, still the welfare effect of microfinance programme is under doubt.

REVIEW OF LITERATURE

One of the fundamental goals of microfinance programme around the world is to empower the rural poor, especially women, through their socio-economic improvements. It is broadly assumed that group based microfinance programme have a strong positive impact on women's livelihood by (a) raising their income, (b) increasing women's employment, and (c) enhancing their self-confidence and status within the family (Dichter, 1999; NABARD, 2000). However, Beek et al. (2004) points out that, since poor and vulnerable populations depends mainly on informal source of finance namely, friends, relatives, etc. the development of formal financial sector is beneficial only to the wealthier section. Ahlin and Jiang (2008) found in their study that microfinance decreases inequality. According to them microfinance lowers inequality by increasing the income of the poor. Green et al. (2006) argues that improvement in the financial access of the poor and vulnerable populations can directly enhance poverty reduction in the society. It is believed that microfinance decreases the consumption volatility within households and leads to increased production (Zaman, 1999; Cuong et. al, 2007; Tchouassi, 2011).

The impact of microfinance on poverty and voice representation of the participating members have analyzed vividly by various authors in the context of a number of countries have revealed that microfinance intervention can play an important role in reducing vulnerability through a number of channels. In international lexicon, the impact study of microfinance on poverty and vulnerability of the members have been analyzed by Zaman (1999) considering 547 members of BRAC, Bangladesh. Using a multivariate analysis, the study concluded that micro credit interventions can play an important role in reducing vulnerability through a number of channels. Vulnerability is reduced by smoothening consumption, building physical assets, providing emergency assistance and contributing to female empowerment improving some social indicators such as self-worth, voice representation, decision making, etc. More access to financial resources in small amount enhances the female control over some assets. In India, Holvet (2005) carried out a study about the impact on decision making by the members in the context on Tamil Nadu and found a strong positive impact of credit on women's decision making in the households. Similarly, Hashemi, Schuler and Riley (1996) in their study on the measurement of women empowerment have also found that participation in credit programmes has a very strong positive effect. On the issue of some social indicators such as domestic violence among women the impact study of NABARD (2000, 2016) clearly suggest that women are absolutely better placed in the household in the post-SHG period as compared to pre-SHG situation.

However, some researchers have expressed their doubt about the effectiveness of microfinance programme to empower the poor women as stated above. They have brought up issues on the naivety of the assumption that economic empowerment is a straight forward process, and facilitating women's entrance to credit or financial markets will translate their control over its use without any other interventions or hazards. As indicated by various researchers that (Mayoux, 1997; Goetz, Marie & Sengupta,1996) impact on empowerment can't be conjectured from the use of financial services or repayment levels by the members specifically, for women. In a number of case it is well found that women repay the husband's loan liability taking advances somewhere else and increases the probability to fall into serious debt in future. Furthermore, women take frequent loan for the husband or household business or to set-up an enterprise over which they have very little or zero control. In few cases they have been employed as unpaid family workers with little or no benefits at all (Brahmachary, 2013).

A study conducted by Bhatt and Bhatt (2016) on the women empowerment of a microfinance institution namely Light Microfinance Private Limited reveals that the loans were granted to the members for the purpose of economic activities only. The loan repayment performance of these members was good and satisfactory. Most of the loan receiver agreed that the micro loans had helped them to finance their business and reported an increase of their income. However, their findings revealed that an improvement is still required in matters related to purchase of household assets or decision in the household which requires high volume of cash flow. Basically the decision regarding different activities which requires high volume cash flow such as set-up of new business, asset purchase, building renovation, etc. are usually taken by the male members of the family and female has very limited role in this regard. However, in case of child education they found that the decision is taken jointly by the parents and there is no discrimination in between male and female child. Thus, as like Mayoux (2006), Galab and Rao (2003), and Rajendran-Raya (2010) the findings of the study reveal that microfinance through SHGs improved women's access to and control over their savings, credit and income. But, such control does not ensure their enhanced self-worth within the household. Even though they meet every week for group meeting but there was no exchange of information resulting zero or very limited awareness about legal and political knowledge of them.

Another study conducted by Borah (2014) on women empowerment through Self-Help-Groups in Nagaon District of Assam showed that women SHG plays very crucial role in eradication of poverty for the BPL families. From the study it is found majority of women SHG members have taken loan for various economic activities such as handloom works, animal husbandry, agriculture, food processing, etc. The loan that women receive is used mainly for earning activities and they have good control on their own earnings from such activities. Though, such control on own earning does not ensure the women empowerment but there is no doubt that such improvement of women's status ensures income security of the women. Income security is one of the pillars of women empowerment which these members achieved successfully at a micro level.

All these studies, however, tell that women empowerment is not a straight forward process. Though microfinance through SHG have ensured the income security among the members to some extent the social and voice representation security of the members especially women members are far behind than the threshold level. As a result, the overall livelihood security of the SHG members is still in challenging situation. The situation is more severe for women member who's social and voice representation in our country is in very tardy situation and makes them a vulnerable section within the society even after joining in SHG for better livelihood (Brahmachary, 2014).

STATUS OF MICROFINANCE IN INDIA

Microfinance has evolved as a major flagship pro poor programme in India since 1999-2000. To provide financial assistance among the poor people in India the usual microfinance programme operates through two main channels (NABARD, 2016) –

1. Banking system through the SHGs under SHG-Bank Linkage (SBL) programme, and,
2. Through Microfinance Institutions (Individual and Group Approach).

Both the Banking system approach and Microfinance Institution (MFI) approach are growing rapidly in India and NABARD provides different financial assistance to the implementing agencies for accelerating such programmes. The overall progress under SHG-Bank linkage programme (the most popular microfinance approach in India) has shown in Table 1 and 2.

From Table 1, it is clear that as on March, 2016 out of total number of SHGs (79.03 Lakhs), 67.63 Lakhs are exclusively women SHGs. That is, 85.58% of total SHGs are women which mobilized the 88% of total amounts. In 2015-16, about 18.32 Lakh SHGs were credit linked with banks out of which 88.92% (16.29 Lakhs) were exclusive women SHGs. The total estimated number of families covered under SHG-Bank linkage programme up to March, 2016 is 1010 Lakhs. About the support from NABARD the table shows that during 2015-16 near about 3906 Lakh capacity building programme were organized during 2015-16 where total number of participants trained was 1.21 Lakhs. During 2015-16, NABARD have extended Rs 6906 crore financial assistance to banks (Refinance support) and the total cumulative refinance released to banks as on March, 2016 was 37663.60 crore. The overall progress of SHG-Bank Linkage programme in India under NABARD support in the last 3 years (2013-2016) has shown in Table 2.

Table 1. Status of SHG-Bank Linkage Programme in India, 2015-2016

SL	Particulars	Achievements	
		Physical (No. in Lakh)	Financial (Rs. In Crore)
1	Total number of SHGs savings linked with banks	79.03	13691.39
	Out of total Savings linked SHGs, exclusive women SHGs	67.63	12035.78
2	Total number of SHGs credit linked with banks 2015-2016	18.32	37286.90
	Out of total credit linked SHGs, exclusive women SHGs	16.29	34411.42
3	Total number of SHGs having loans outstanding as on March 2016	46.73	57119.23
	Out of total SHGs, exclusive women SHGs	40.36	51428.91
4	Estimated number of families covered up to March 2016	1010	-
5	Support from NABARD		
a) Number of Capacity Building Programmes 2015-2016 b) Number of participants covered during 2015-2016 c) Cumulative number of participants trained 2015-2016		3906 1.21 34.02	- - -
6	Refinance Support from NABARD		
a) Refinance to banks 2015-2016 b) Cumulative refinance released up to March, 2016		- -	6906.03 37663.60
7	Revolving Fund Assistance (RFA) and Capital support to MFIs		
a) RFA outstanding as on March, 2016 b) Capital support outstanding as on March, 2016 c) Refinance disbursed to NBFCs and MFIs 2015-2016		- - -	7.25 4.42 2300.00

Source: Status of microfinance in India 2015-16, NABARD, 2016

Table 2. Overall progress under SHG-Bank Linkage Programme - 2013-2016

Particulars		2013-14		2014-15		2015-16	
		No. of SHGs (Lakh)	Amount (Rs. Crore)	No. of SHGs (Lakh)	Amount (Rs. Crore)	No. of SHGs (Lakh)	Amount (Rs. Crore)
SHGs Savings with Banks as on March, 2016	Total SHGs	74.30	9897.42	76.97	11059.84	79.03	13691.39
	Women SHGs	62.52	8012.89	66.51	9264.33	67.63	12035.78
	% of Women Gr.	84.15	80.96	86.41	83.77	85.58	87.91
Loans Disbursed to SHGs 2015-2016	Total SHGs extended Loans	13.66	24017.36	16.26	27582.31	18.32	37286.90
	Exclusive Women SHGs	11.52	2103.97	14.48	24419.75	16.29	34411.42
	% of Women Gr.	84.3	87.6	89.05	83.53	88.92	92.29
Loans Outstanding against SHGs as on March 2016	Total SHGs Linked	41.97	42927.52	44.68	51545.46	46.73	57119.23
	No. of Women SHGs Linked	34.06	36151.58	38.58	45901.95	40.36	51428.91
	% of Women SHGs	81.2	84.2	86.35	89.05	86.37	90.04

Source: Status of microfinance in India 2015-16, NABARD, 2016

However, the overall progress of SBL programme in India does not reflect the outreach of such programme in different parts of the country. Specifically, in some geographical location the outreach of the programme is too high, and in some other parts of the country it is quite negligible. Therefore, to understand the true picture of the country in respect of SBL programme the region-wise distribution has shown in Table 3 & Figure 1.

According to Table 3, the outreach of microfinance programme concentrated mainly in the Southern states of the country (namely, Andhra Pradesh, Karnataka, Kerala, etc.) followed by Eastern (West Bengal, Orissa, Jharkhand, Bihar, etc.), Western (Gujarat, Maharashtra, etc.), Central (Madhya Pradesh, Chhattisgarh, Uttarakhand, etc.), North-East (Assam, Tripura, Sikkim, Meghalaya, etc.) and Northern Region (Himachal Pradesh, Rajasthan, Haryana, New Delhi, etc.). However, in 2015-16 the progress of the programme slightly decreased in the southern region and witnessed a mild increase in Eastern Region. As on March 2016, the regional distribution of savings linked SHGs in India (%) has shown in Figure 1.

The savings outstanding of SHGs as on March, 2016 is Rs. 13691 crore. The average savings outstanding per SHG increased by 21% during the year 2015-16 to Rs. 17324 crore from Rs. 14368 crore a year back. The average savings outstanding was heighest is Southern region and lowest in North-East region (Figure 2) in absolute term. However, in percentage term the increase in total savings outstanding

Table 3. Region wise distribution of SHGs (%)

Year	Southern Region	Eastern Region	Western Region	Central Region	Northern Region	North-Eastern Region
2013-14	49.75	19.77	12.07	9.23	4.92	4.26
2014-15	48.32	19.81	12.23	10.62	4.69	4.34
2015-16	44.87	21.51	12.88	10.32	4.98	5.44

Source: NABARD, 2016

Figure 1. Region wise distribution of Savings Linked SHGs (%)

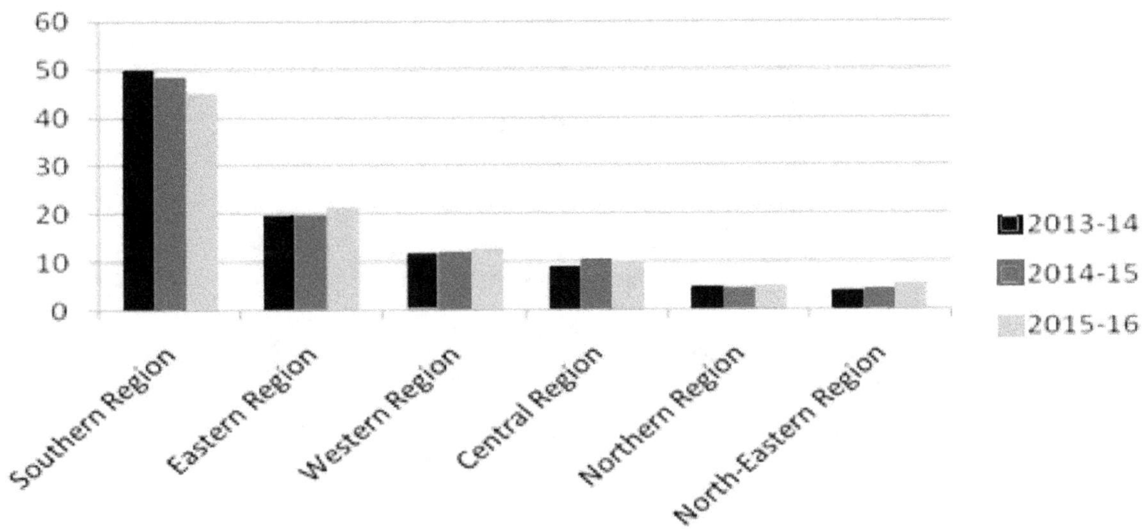

was witnesed by North (88%), followed by North-East (46%), and Southern region (3%). Region wise average savings outstanding during 2015-16 has shown in figure 2.

Credit disbursement is the main engine of the microfinance programme. During 2015-16, near about 23.2% of total SHGs (18.32 Lakhs) have received loans from different banks as compared to 21.1% of total SHGs (16.26 Lakhs) during the previous year (2014-15). In terms of credit disbursement during 2015-16, the Southern region again received the heighest loans (Rs. 258966) followed by Western (Rs. 167636), Central (Rs. 141272), Northern (Rs. 126746), Eastern (Rs. 84709) and North-Eastern (Rs. 84375) regions. The overall bank loan disbursement increased by 35% in 2015-16 from the previous year, taking it to Rs. 37287 crore from Rs. 27582 crore. The average loan disbursement per group during 2015-16 was Rs. 2.03 Lakh which showed an increase of 20% from Rs. 1.69 Lakh during 2014-15. The region wise average loan disbursement during 2015-16 has shown in figure 3.

METHODOLOGY OF THE STUDY

Against these backdrops, in this paper, however, we would like to concentrate on the gender issues of microfinance programme in India context. For this purpose here we have tried to construct a 'Vulnerability Index' which can reflect an indicative picture of male and female SHG members depending on some quantitative (say, income, education, etc.) and subjective or qualitative parameters (say, decision making power, relation with officials, etc.).

The construction of 'vulnerability index' involves one's subjective views on a range of issues (Dabir-Alai 2004). In the absence of any predetermined methodology available in constructing a 'vulnerability index' we have been led by our own insights in this exercise. It is a straight-forward binary composite approach ascribing the value of zero or one to a series of nine parameters. The full list of parameters used, with their respective binary codes and justification is shown in table 4.

Figure 2. Region wise average savings outstanding, 2015-16 (In Rs. per SHG)

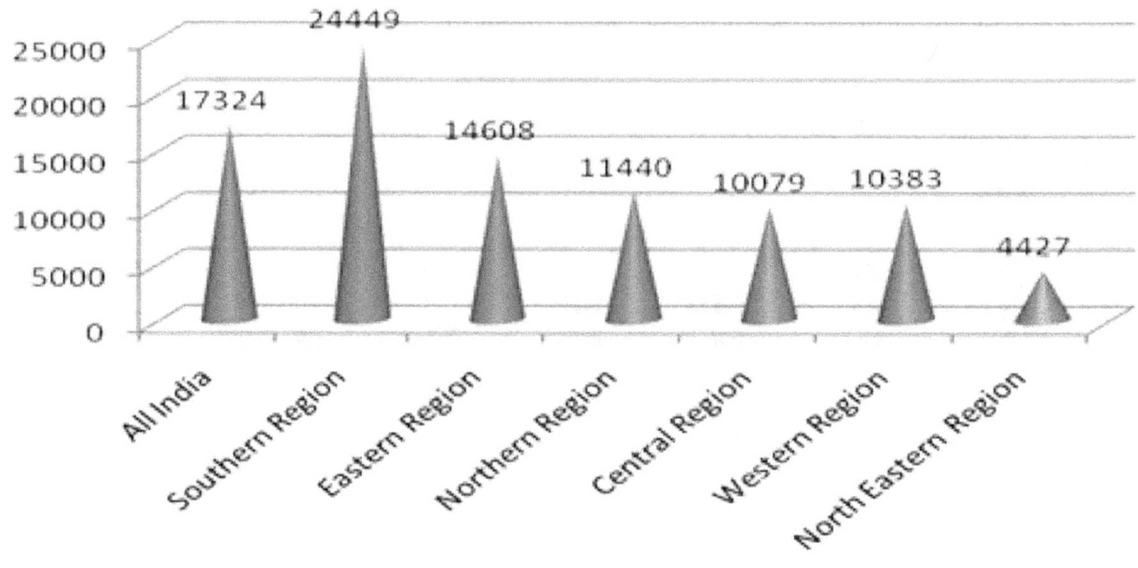

Figure 3. Region wise average loan disbursement per SHG, 2015-16 (In Rs.)

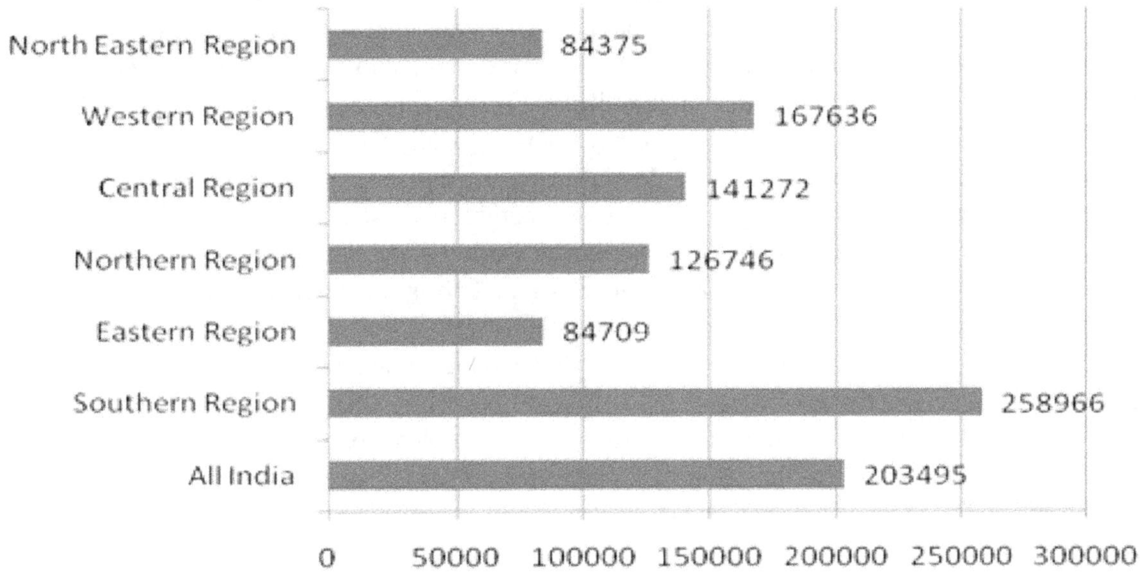

Table 4. List of parameters used in the vulnerability index

Parameters	Binary Value = 0	Justification	Binary Value = 1	Justification
Income of the member	Higher than sample average	Higher than average income ensures that such a member enjoys some kind of income security and lower vulnerability than others	Lower than or equal to sample average	More vulnerable in terms of income than others
Education of the member	Assign 0 if the members has at least some basic education (Class IV)	Greater ability to use economic and other opportunities	If the members have no formal education	Lower ability to use different opportunities
Relation with neighbors	Assign 0 if they report good relation	Village level group activities highly depends on the co-operation of neighbors and good cooperation ensures better performance and low vulnerability	If they have no friendly relation	Group performance worsen which in turn generates more vulnerability both in the household as well as in the village level
Relation with bank/ NGO officials	Good relation	Good relation with financial institutions and NGOs makes the group based credit programme viable and useful for the poor and reduces vulnerability among the members	No more good relation	Challenges programme sustainability and makes the member more vulnerable than others
Power to take decision in major events in the household (such as decision about business, child education, asset purchase, etc.)	Assign zero if they have some degree of power	Indicates that the members are better placed in the household and are able to take different activities according to his/ her own choice	Assign 1 if they have no power	Members are remain vulnerable in the household
Help from family members in loan repayment	Assign zero if help persist	It indicates that the loan repayment scheduled have been treated as the household liabilities instead of individual liabilities which ensures higher value of the member to the household	Assign 1 if there is no help	Indicates that the status of the members remain unfair in the household
Total hours spent in earning activities per month	Lower than sample average	Suggests a better hourly earning than others	Higher than sample average	More vulnerable than others in terms of hourly earning
Mobility outside the village	If yes	Ensures member's capability to go outside the village usually for business or household wellbeing	No	Members have no capability and therefore, more vulnerable than others
Power to control over own income	Assign zero if the member enjoys some power	Indicates member's self-worth and decision making power in the household	Assign 1 if the members have no power	Members who have no power on its own earning are extremely vulnerable in the household

After assigning the binary code to each parameter according to the responses of each member we have constructed the 'vulnerability index', just taking the simple average of all these parameters. Here, we have given equal weight to each parameter, though such an index can be constructed by giving different weights to the different parameters according to the researcher's choices. Here it is noted that though some researchers advocate for an index giving different weights on the parameters instead of the equal weight as mentioned here, but such emphasis may not be logically valid for all analysis. The method of weight selection and the construction of index in that case may generate large questions since a large number of parameters under the study are subjective in nature. In these circumstances the simple average equal weight index is widely accepted throughout the world by the policymakers whereas there is no predetermined methodology of index construction assigning different weights on parameters. Therefore, without loss of any generality of the study we can carry forward our analysis in this chapter considering the equal weight vulnerability index as mentioned above to highlight an indicative result on the issue of microfinance and gender discrimination.

In this framework, therefore, an index of zero suggests complete absence of any real sense of vulnerability felt by the members. On the other hand, an index of 1 suggests the most acute form of vulnerability possible. The index value scoring between zero and 1 experience commonly escalating levels of vulnerability as captured by the set of descriptors as given in Table 5.

Considering the above methodological approach however, in this paper we have tried to examine the extent of vulnerability between male and female members using the relevant micro level data.

SAMPLE SELECTION AND SALIENT FEATURES OF STUDY AREAS

West Bengal is an Indian state situated in Eastern India on the Bay of Bengal. It is the fourth most crowded state in India, with more than 90 million inhabitants (as per 2011 census). The total area of the state is 88,752 km2 (34,267 sq mi). West Bengal shares the boundaries of five Indian states - Odisha, Jharkhand, Bihar, Sikkim, and Assam. The capital of the state is Kolkata (Calcutta). Kolkata is the seventh-biggest city in India. Concerning geology, the state West Bengal incorporates the Darjeeling Himalayan slope district, the Ganges delta, the Rarh area, and the seaside Sundarbans. The major ethnic groups in the state are the Bengalis. West Bengal is mainly agriculture based and occupies the 6th position in terms of contribution to India's net domestic product. The state has a strong cultural and religious background. The two Nobel Laureate scholars Rabindra Nath Tagore and Amartya Sen, religious reformers such as Mahaprabhu Sree Chaityanya, Ramakrishna, Swami Vivekananda, etc. are the pride of the state and enlightened the country in the world. Kolkata is known as the social capital of India.

Table 5. Categories of vulnerability index according to descriptors

Descriptor	Vulnerability Index Value
Weakly Vulnerable	0.00 – 0.20
Vulnerable	0.21 – 0.40
Quite Vulnerable	0.41 – 0.60
Extremely/ Strongly Vulnerable	0.61 – 0.80
Acutely Vulnerable	0.81 – 1.00

Keeping in mind the gender issues related with group-based microfinance programme here we have collected the relevant micro-level data from the state of West Bengal (India) through field survey to develop a concrete understanding about the extent of vulnerability among the participating members. In India microfinance programme has rapidly accelerated officially from 1999 (with the introduction of Swarnayanti Gram Swarozgar Yojana which remodeled to NRLM or National Rural Livelihood Mission in 2011) and presently considered as an important and effective tool of poverty alleviation and empowerment of the deserving section, especially women. West Bengal is one of the important states of India where microfinance programme is growing very rapidly as a poverty alleviation tool and empower the poor especially, women.

There are 23 districts in West Bengal. Among these we have selected two districts purposively for our field study – Nadia and Murshidabad. The area of Nadia is arranged in the core of the Bengal delta held inside the arms of the waterway Ganga, including the Bhagirathi on the west and the Padma on the east circumscribing Bangladesh. The district Nadia shares boundary on the north and north-west by the district of Murshidabad. On the south-east and east it is bounded by the Republic of Bangladesh. The district is around 46ft. over the mean ocean level and the tropic of cancer partitions the region into two sections. The district has a rich historical background. The religious reformer Sree Chaitanya was born in this district and started the famous spiritual movement (Bhakti movement) from here. The main occupation of the district people is agriculture. It is also enriched with the presence of huge number of cottage and small scale industries, among which hand woven textile industries are more visible.

The other district of our study is Murshidabad which is the neighbor district of Nadia. Murshidabad district also have strong historical background. The geological range of Murshidabad region can be extensively separated into two sections: the eastern part and the western part. The eastern piece of the locale which lays the east part of the river Bhagirathi is known as Bagri and the western piece of the area which lies the west of Bhagirathi is known as Radh. During the 5th century AD some portion of the modern Murshidabad district belonged to the territory of Gupta Empire. In the 7th century AD King Sasanka ruled over the whole of Radh including some portions of 'Vanga' like Bagri. The capital city of King Sasanka's empire Karnasubarna is now connected through Karnasubarna (formerly Chiruti) railway station which is the part of Kandi Sub-Division of the Murshidabad district. The main occupation of the district is agricultural activities. Besides, local tobacco manufacturing industries (Bidi industry) contribute a large scale employment within the district. Murshidabd silk is very popular throughout the country and generates good employment opportunities in the cotton and textile sector in the district.

However, the two districts chosen for this study from the State of West Bengal are Nadia and Murshidabad. Here we have selected these two districts purposively due to the following reasons: (i) All models of SHG-Bank linkage are present here and (ii) Nadia and Murshidabad are the two neighbor districts of West Bengal where the SHG-Bank linkage programme is growing rapidly as a pro-poor programme under the aegis of the government due to the backwardness of some development indicators of these two districts.

Some development indicators (such as literacy rate, employment structure, population composition, etc.) of these two districts and the state as a whole have shown in Table 6.

We randomly selected a total of six villages from these two districts - 3 from each districts. From these six villages we randomly selected 315 SHG member households who belong to those SHGs which are in operation for at least 3 years or more and collected required data from these households through questionnaire based survey method. Besides, 104 non-member households were also selected randomly from these sample villages as a control group and requisite information was gathered from them. Thus

Table 6. Some development indicators of the sample districts and West Bengal (India)

	Nadia	Murshidabad	West Bengal	India
1. (a) Total Population (No.)	5167600	7103807	91276115	1210854977
(b) Male (%)	51.34	51.07	51.28	51.50
(c) Female (%)	48.66	48.93	48.71	48.49
(d) Rural Pop. (%)	72.16	80.28	68.13	68.84
(e) Urban Pop. (%)	27.84	19.72	31.87	31.16
(f) Rural Male Pop. (%)	51.52	51.16	51.21	51.40
(g) Rural Female Pop. (%)	48.48	48.84	48.79	48.60
(h) Urban Male Pop. (%)	50.92	50.67	51.44	52.60
(i) Urban Female Pop. (%)	49.08	49.33	48.56	47.40
2. Sex Ratio				
(a) Total	947	958	950	943
(b) Rural	941	955	953	947
(c) Urban	964	974	944	926
3. Literacy Rate				
(a) Total	74.97	66.59	76.26	74.04
(b) Male	78.75	69.95	81.69	82.14
(c) Female	70.98	63.09	70.54	65.46
(d) Rural Male	54.43	53.66	78.44	78.57
(e) Rural Female	45.57	48.84	65.51	58.75
(f) Urban Male	53.04	50.67	88.37	89.67
(g) Urban Female	46.96	49.33	80.98	79.92

(Source: MOSPI, 2011)

we carried out our study considering 419 sample households - 315 member households and 104 non-member households. It may be noted that all the member and non-member households belong to the same socio-economic class and geographic location. The sample design for this study is shown in Table 7.

The socio-economic characteristics of the sample households (Table 8) show that the average household size of the member household is 5.11 persons as against 4.76 persons for non-member households. Among the sample members 66.03 percent are female and 33.97 percent are male. In case of household head 33.34 percent are female and 66.66 percent are male. Therefore, it is clear that though the microfinance programme in our sample villages have included female members more significantly than the males, most of these members belong to the male headed households. It is believed that mF programmes yield better results if it can be spread among the female poor who belong to the female headed households. However, in our sample, though respondents report that they faced some obstacles from the male household head at the time of joining the groups, eventually their participation has been accepted by the male members. Interestingly, at present, senior men members of the household have become strong advocates for participation of women as a group member in such programmes.

Table 7. Sample design

Village	Districts	Group Promoting Agency	Group Financed by	No. of Groups >3 years	Total Members (No.)	Group Surveyed (No.)	Members Surveyed (No.)
Ruppur	Nadia	Nadia Gramin Bank (NGB)/Bangiya Grameen Bikash Bank (BGB)	NGB/BGB	20	280	12	51
Rabonbor	Nadia	Nadia District Central Co-operative Bank Ltd.	Nadia District Central Co-operative Bank Ltd.	17	233	11	48
Kulgachi	Nadia	Sreema Mahila Samity (SMS)	NGB/BGB	25	341	16	71
Gokarna	Murshidabad	United Bank of India/ Block Office	United Bank of India	17	231	11	47
Jashahari	Murshidabad	United Bank of India/ Block Office	United Bank of India	21	294	12	50
Purandarpur	Murshidabad	United Bank of India/ Block Office	United Bank of India	17	245	10	48
Total				117	1624	72	315

Source: Survey Data

Table 8. Socio-Economic characteristics of the sample households

Characteristics	Members	Non-Members
Sample Size	315	104
Household Size (Avg.)	5.11	4.76
Sex of the respondents		
Male (%)	33.97	32.69
Female (%)	66.03	67.31
Sex of the household head		
Male (%)	66.66	69.23
Female (%)	33.34	30.77
Years of Schooling of the respondents (Average)	5.42	5.04
Years of Schooling of the household head (Average)	3.07	3.01
Agricultural land holding of the households (avg.)	5.16*	8.15*
Avg. Income of the Respondent (Rs. Monthly)	1419.00	1678.00
Avg. Income of the household (Rs. Monthly)	2838.00	3516.00
Principal economic activity of the households (%)		
Farm Production	22.53	28.85
Non-Farm Prod.	03.81	08.65
Farm Labour	16.19	11.53
Non-Farm Labour	17.77	14.42
Petty Trader, Vendors, Hawker, etc.	23.49	18.49
Others (such as Livestock rearing, fishery, etc.)	16.21	18.26

* Here agricultural land holding is measured by the unit "Katha", where 20 Katha= 0.33 acre.

Source: Survey Data

A MEASURE OF VULNERABILITY FOR WOMEN AND MEN

In order to gain insight into the issue of gender discrimination I have constructed a vulnerability index for female and male members. Before presenting the estimated result of the vulnerability index as obtained from our sample data let us consider briefly the issue of women's empowerment in terms of some broad indicators such as occurrence of physical violence, wife beating in the household, control over household economic resources, etc. We have compared the responses of female members on these events between pre- and post-SHG period to identify the extent of improvement in the status of women, if any, after joining in SHG.

It is clear according to the responses obtained from female SHG members, that the position of women in the household as well as in the society have improved significantly from pre- to post-SHG period (Table 9). Whereas in the pre-SHG situation nearly 60 percent of women faced strong resistance from their spouses or other members of the households about their joining in income earning activities outside the village, the protests, however, have been brought down to about 37 percent in the post-SHG period. Similarly, significant improvements have been observed in cases of physical torture of women in the household. While about 69 percent of the female members reported that they experienced different kinds of physical torture from their spouses/ household members, in the pre-SHG situation, post-SHG, these incidents seem to have declined significantly (32%). The control over own and household economic resources by the female members have also improved from pre- to post-SHG situation. Though the power enjoyed by women in taking decisions in the household with regard to marriage, new business, land purchase, etc., have not registered a significant improvement from pre- to post-SHG situation, a significant proportion of female members (46%) have reported that they are enjoying better respect (and self-worth) from the other household members after joining in the SHG.

The table 9 clearly indicates that the socio-economic status of women has improved significantly from pre- to post-SHG situation. Though the concept 'empowerment' is multidimensional, in a narrow sense we can say that the improvement in women's status from pre- to post-SHG situation indicates a positive jump by the members from an underpowered to the empowered state.

Table 9. Behavior of women members (%) under the following situations (N=208)

Situation/ Fact	Before		After	
	Yes	No	Yes	No
Strong resistance from the household to participation in income earning activities outside village	60.09	39.91	37.50	62.50
Physical violence in the household	69.24	30.76	32.21	67.79
Control over own earnings	28.36	71.64	36.06	63.94
Control over household economic resources	27.88	72.11	39.42	60.58
Power to take decision about children's education	31.73	68.26	40.38	59.61
Power to take decision in major events (such as marriage, business, land purchase, etc.) in the household	31.73	68.26	45.19	54.81
Increased self worth and respect from household members	28.84	71.15	46.15	53.85

Source: Survey Data

However, although women have attained a better position than earlier after joining the SHGs (Table 10), they still remain more vulnerable than men. An examination of the extent of vulnerability between male and female members as prevailing in our sample shows that the extent of vulnerability (Table 10 and Figure 4) is more severe for female than for male members. The index value for female (0.5817) is about 56 percent higher than that for male (0.3738), suggesting that even after joining the SHGs women remain the most vulnerable individuals in the society and the extent of vulnerability as compared to male members is not negligible.

The frequency distribution of members according to the vulnerability index classes (Table 8) indicates that the pattern of distribution of women and men members is, with a few exceptions, exactly opposite to each other. While more than half (53%) the women suffer from either extreme or acute form of vulnerability, for men, the majority of them (52%) exhibit only lowest degrees of vulnerability. Moreover, just 2.5 percent of total male members are "acutely vulnerable" against as much as a sixth of all women.

On the other hand, in the classes with lower degree of vulnerability and male members seem to outnumber their female counterparts. The frequency distribution of members according to index values, therefore, suggests that the magnitude of vulnerability (as measured by the nine components) is more

Table 10. Value of Gender-wise Vulnerability Index for SHG members

Category	Index Value (Mean)
Female (N=208)	0.5817
Male (N=107)	0.3738
Total	0.5111

Source: Computed from survey data

Figure 4. Gender-wise mean vulnerability index values

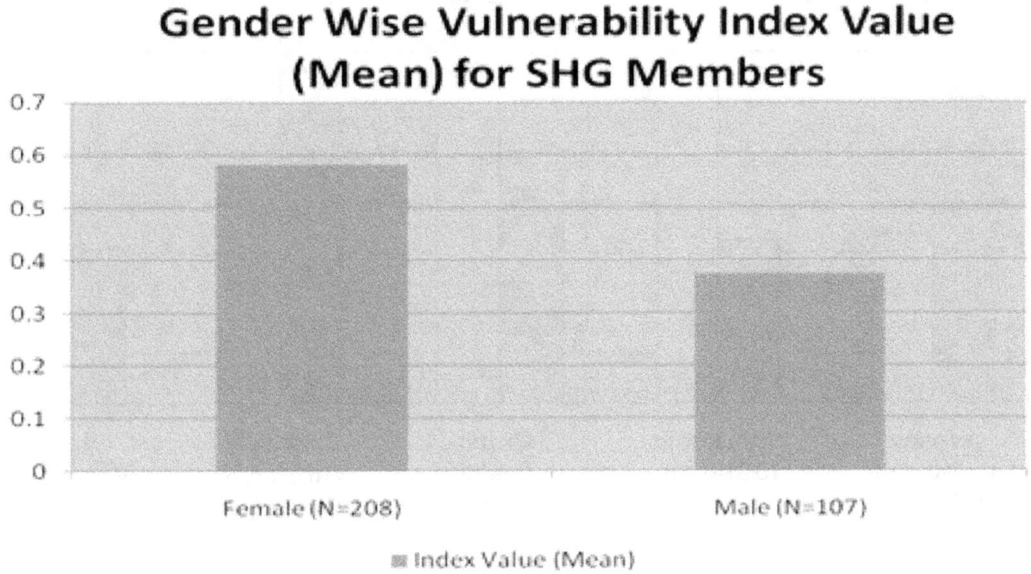

severe for the female than the male. The distribution of members according to different index classes is shown in Figure 5.

Thus, the study clearly shows that gender discrimination is a serious issue in the society even after the introduction of group based microfinance programme in the society. Since the proponents of group based microfinance programme advocates about the economic and social empowerment of the rural poor especially women poor through the microfinance programme therefore, such discrimination should minimize as soon as possible to achieve the basic goal of the group based financial programme. The study crudely indicates that to reduce such discrimination / gap among women members, government agencies and microfinance providers should join hands to concentrate on high value components of the vulnerability index. In our study some of these high value components for female members are ‘income’, ‘relation with bank /NGO officials’, ‘help from family/counterpart in loan repayment’, ‘power to control on own income’, ‘mobility outside village’, etc. Income of an individual is a crucial determinant about

Table 11. Distribution of members (%) according to the value of vulnerability index

Index Value	Female (N=208)	Male (N=107)
0.00-0.20	9.21	17.28
0.21-0.40	16.09	34.57
0.41-0.60	21.26	33.33
0.61-0.80	37.93	12.35
0.81-1.00	15.51	2.47
Total	100.00	100.00

Source: Survey data

Figure 5. Distribution of members according to the extent of vulnerability (% of members)

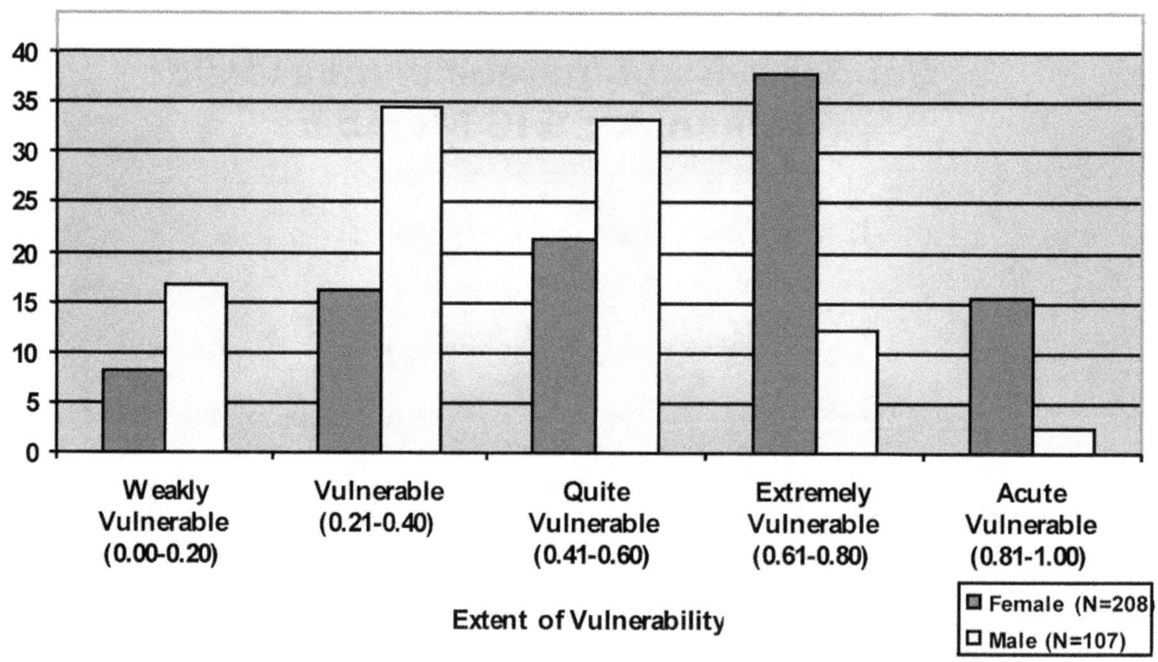

his/her power and influence in the family as well as in the society. Unfortunately, in microfinance sector the income earned by the most women SHG member is very negligible and therefore, have very limited or zero influence in the household. Usually, the female SHG members are often engaged in low remunerative jobs due to lack of proper skill development and therefore, receive very low wages from such activities as compared to male. Most of these jobs are in unorganized sector where government employment acts / rules are not applicable. Furthermore, the income which they earn from such activities have very limited or zero control and mostly compelled to surrender their whole earning to their counterparts / male members of the family for different expenditures.

It is noted that though the SHG members under our study is better placed as compare to the non-members still they are suffering from different disadvantages due to male dominance in the household and thereby restrict themselves to move outside the village to find for better remunerative jobs. This is one of the fundamental reason that why female SHG members are frequently less remunerative, or purely unemployed at all. Besides, such members don't get any help from their counterparts / male members of the family to repay their outstanding loans taken from the group. But, it is the fact that in most cases they take such loans for the need of the households as a whole. The benefit of such loan if any, utilize by all the members of the family but in time of loan repayment very limited are co-operate the loan receiver. As a result, the said member compels to find any kind of earning activities to repay the loan.

The relation of the group members with concerned bank / NGO officials is also an important determinant for the smooth and successful functioning of the group activities. It has been observed that though theoretically group lending activities in India has considered as a priority sector lending by the formal financial institutions such as banks and other institutions, still they have very limited time and scope to accelerate such programme in every part of the country. Most of the bank officials (Except very few cases) are not interested about microfinance and SHG lending activities due to very small volume of financial transaction. Here group members should take frequent initiative with the help of NGO / Local Government such as Panchayet / Club, etc. for continuous association with the banks for different group financial transactions. Unfortunately, in rural West Bengal (India) all such initiative from the part of Women SHG members is not possible always due to their limited mobility outside the village and lower knowledge to cope with the bank officials for different financial transactions. As a result, some intermediary person (usually male) do the necessary official activities with the concerned banks and other institutions on behalf of the group and thereby the self representation of the women members remains absent even though they have the legal right for banking activities. Occasionally, they visit the bank branch when emergency need arises and therefore, their relation with the bank officials remains very poor. Thus, women's representation in the society even after joining in SHG has not improved significantly. Usually, such problem is not observed among the male group members and therefore, they try to reap the full benefit of group financial activities through SHG based microfinance mechanism.

Thus, the above components contribute a high value for the women members and thereby makes a high vulnerability index value for the women as compare to the male members in our study and require a number of policy attentions to combat the issues.

However, the gender wise 'Vulnerability Index' for non-members also depicts a very disappointed picture in our study (Table 12). The table shows that in case of non-members female vulnerability index value (0.6061) is about 64.5% higher than the male index value (0.3684) which witnessed that female non members are more vulnerable as compare to the female SHG members in the society.

Table 12. Gender wise vulnerability index (mean) for non-members

Category	Index Value (Mean)
Female (N=66)	0.6061
Male (N=38)	0.3684
Total	0.5193

Source: Computed from survey data

CONCLUSION

One of the basic hypotheses of the proponents of microfinance programme is that the extent of vulnerability among the poor would diminish over time due to socio-economic impact of the programme on members. It is assumed that the gender discrimination among the poor (as prevailing both in the household as well as in the society) would decline after joining SHGs. But unfortunately, our findings show that even after joining in SHG the extent of disparity for female members are highly severe which makes them the most vulnerable section in the society. Though the findings indicate that the position of women both in the household as well as in the society have improved significantly from pre-to post-SHG period, still they continue to suffer different kinds of discriminations from different parts of the society.

It is the fact that in India, a large portion of rural women workers are unskilled and 90 percent of them work in the informal/ unorganized sectors. Most of the rural women receive 30-50 percent less wage than male and generally work as casual labour where the incidence of poverty is higher (Meenai, 2003; Chakraborty & Chakraborty, 2009; Brahmachary, 2015). In our sample most of the women members are unskilled and work mostly in the informal unorganized sector which is less remunerative and requires hard work at low wages. This is the actual picture of women employment in India. Chakraborty and Chakraborty (2009) argued that increasing female participation in work force through different channels definitely a good indicator for the society but we should be cautious about such straight forward conclusion. Sometimes female participation in employment activities (self or remunerative) increases the entry in unorganized sector rapidly and also reports a high school drop-out rates. Undoubtedly, such employment retards the progress of the female and the society as a whole even though they witness some improvement in social indicators due to join in so called microfinance programme. Furthermore, the obstacles posed by families prohibiting women from moving outside the village for better employment is another reason of income insecurity of women SHG members as compare to their male counterparts.

Besides, the treatment that women experience within their households is also not as fair as we would generally think. It appears that women have little power to take major decisions in the household (21% of total female members) even after joining in SHG and about 30 percent of the female have no control over their own earnings. Only 40% of the female members have reported that they have the power to take decisions about their children's education. In case of loan repayment also such gender discrimination prevails in the households. Whereas in case of husband's group loan repayment his spouse plays an important role through different kind of help (such as thrift, part time income, etc.), but in case of female's group loan repayment most husbands are not willing to accept any liability to timely repay that loan. In most cases female members take group loans for husband's/ household's business or for household consumption needs. But they have no claim on the profit of the business where her loans have been invested. Moreover, they have no choice of accepting any production or other income earning activities according to her expertise and in this respect they are compelled to abide by the husband's/ household head's decision.

All these together contribute to a gender gap among the group members. To reduce such discrimination / gap among women members, government agencies and microfinance providers should join hands to concentrate on high value components of the vulnerability index. In our study some of these high value components for female members are 'income', 'relation with bank/NGO officials', 'help from family/ counterpart in loan repayment', 'power to control on own income', 'mobility outside village', etc. A close attention and sincere effort is needed on the part of the microfinance providers on these components of the index as much as possible. Simultaneously, appropriate policy mix from the government is also essential to support and strengthen such multi-dimensional activities. Though it is true that women empowerment (through the reduction of vulnerability) is not a straight forward process like increase in income, savings, or other tangible assets, and microfinance programme is not a panacea of the all social ills, the present study clearly indicates that such programme do have some considerable potential to minimize the gender gap through socio-economic improvement of the women members and thereby help them in their journey from an underpowered to an empowered state.

REFERENCES

Ahlin, C., & Jiang, N. (2008). Can microcredit bring development? *Journal of Development Economics*, *86*(1), 1–21. doi:10.1016/j.jdeveco.2007.08.002

Beck, T., Demirguc-Kunt, A., & Levine, R. (2004). *Finance, Inequality and Poverty: Cross country evidence*. NBER working paper, 10979.

Bhatt, A., & Bhatt, S. (2016). *Microfinance Institutions: Do they Empower Women? A Case Study of Light Microfinance Pvt. Ltd. NMIMS Management Review, 28.*

Borah, A. (2014). Women empowerment through Self Help Groups-A case study of Barhampur Development Block in Nagaon District of Assam. *IOSR Journal of Economics and Finance, 4*(3), 56-62. Retrieved from www.iosrjournals.org

Brahmachary, A. (2015). Female Work Force Participation in India: Present Trends and Underlying Processes. *Look East, 5*(1).

Brahmachary, A. (2014). *For a Better World: Livelihood Security Measurement of the SHG Members. In Microfinance, Risk-taking Behaviour and Rural Livelihood*. Springer.

Brahmachary, A. (2013). Gender Discrimination: A Decomposition Analysis of Income Gap between Male and Female SHG Members. In *Proceedings of Women Empowerment And Rural Development: Role of Microfinance*. Berhampore Girls College.

Chakraborty, I., & Chakraborty, A. (2009). *Female Work participation and Gender Differential in Earning in West Bengal*. Occasional Paper, No. 18. Institute of Development Studies.

Cuong, N. V., Bigman, D., Van den Berg, M., & Thieu, V. (2007). *Impact of micro-credit on poverty and inequality: The case of the Vietnam Bank for Social Policies*. Paper submitted to Microfinance: What Do We Know? Groningen, Netherlands.

Dabir-Alai, P. (2004). The Economics of Street-Vending: An Empirical Framework for Measuring Vulnerability in Delhi in the Late 1990s. Paper presented in EGDI and UNU – WIDER Conference, Helsinki, Finland.

Dichter, T. (1999). *Non-Governmental Organizations (NGOs) In Microfinance: Past, Present and Future–An Essay, Case Studies in Microfinance.* Retrieved from www.esd. worldbank.org/ sbp/ end/ ngo.htm

Galab, S., & Rao, N. C. (2003). Women's Self-Help Groups, Poverty Alleviation and Empowerment. *Economic and Political Weekly, 38*(12/13), 1274–1283.

Goetz, A. M., & Sen Gupta, R. (1996). Who takes the Credit? Gender, Power and Control over Loan Use in Rural Credit Programmes in Bangladesh. *World Development, 24*(1), 45–63. doi:10.1016/0305-750X(95)00124-U

Green, C. J., Kirkpatric, C. H., & Murinde, V. (2006). Finance for small enterprise growth and poverty reduction in developing countries. *Journal of International Development, 18*(7), 1017–1030. doi:10.1002/jid.1334

Hashemi, S., Schuler, R. S., & Riley, I. (1996). Rural Credit Programmes and Women's Empowerment in Bangladesh. *World Development, 24*(4), 635–653. doi:10.1016/0305-750X(95)00159-A

Holvoet, N. (2005). The Impact of Microfinance on Decision-making Agency: Evidence from South India. *Development and Change, 36*(1), 75–102. doi:10.1111/j.0012-155X.2005.00403.x

King, E. M., & Mason, D. A. (2001). Engendering Development Through Gender Equality. Development Outreach, 3(2).

Mayoux, L. (2006, February). *Women's Empowerment through Sustainable Micro-finance: Rethinking Best Practice.* Retrieved from http://lindaswebs.org.uk

Mayoux, L. (1997). *The Magic Ingredient? Microfinance and Women's Empowerment.* Paper for Micro Credit Summit. Retrieved from www.gdrc.org

Meenai, Z. (2003). *Empowering Rural Women: An Approach to Empowering Women Through Credit –Based, Self- Help Groups, Aakar.* Delhi: Books.

NABARD. (2000). NABARD and microfinance. National Bank for Agricultural and Rural Development.

NABARD. (2016). *Status of Microfinance in India 2015-16.* National Bank for Agricultural and Rural Development. Retrieved from https://www.microfinancegateway.org/sites/default/files/publication_files/smfi_2015-16.pdf

Rajendran, K., & Raya, R. (2010). *Impact of Micro Finance - An empirical Study on the Attitude of SHG Leaders in Vellore District.* Tamil Nadu, India: Global Journal of Finance and Management.

Sen, K. M., & Kumar, A. K. S. (2001). Women. In *India, How Free? How Equal?* New Delhi: Office of the United Nations Resident Coordination in India.

Tchouassi, G. (2011). Microfinance, inequality and vulnerability: Empirical analysis from Central American countries. *Journal of Development and Agricultural Economics, 3*(4), 150-156.

Zaman, H. (1999). *Assessing the Impact of Micro-credit on Poverty and Vulnerability in Bangladesh.* Policy Research Working Paper 2145. World Bank.

Ministry of Statistics and Programme Implementation (MOSPI). (2011). *Census of India.* Retrieved from www.mospi.gov.in

KEY TERMS AND DEFINITIONS

India: The Republic of India is a country in South Asia. It is the seventh largest country in terms of area and the second populous country in the world. India is the most populous democracy in the world. New Delhi is the capital city of India. As per 2017 estimates India is the sixth largest economy in terms of nominal GDP (gross domestic product). The main occupation of India is agriculture. In terms of employment in the country, agriculture occupies the first position followed by service and manufacturing sector. Indian cultural history spans near about 5000 years. The country is famous for its religious diversity where Hinduism, Buddhism, Sikhism, Jainism, Islam, Christianity, etc. are well practiced by the inhabitants within the country without any hazard and conflict. In the field of Literature, Art and Culture India is highly enriched from the ancient age. Hindi, Bengali, Telugu, Marathi, Urdu, Gujarati, Kannada, Malayalam, etc. are the major language spoken group/families in India. The official language of the country is Hindi and English.

Microfinance: Microfinance is a provision to offer different financial services such as savings, credit, insurance, etc. to the poor unemployed or low-income individuals or groups who otherwise have very limited or zero access to any formal financial services. This is nothing but a banking practice of the poor unbanked people in the society through different formal financial institutions. If only the savings and credit components are associated in this mechanism it is popularly known as microcredit instead of microfinance.

MFI: Microfinance finance institutions.

NABARD: National Bank for Agriculture and Rural Development.

SBL: Savings bank linkage.

Self-Help Group (SHG): A self-help group (SHG) is a formal group usually composed of 10–20 local poor members especially women for the practice of banking and financial activities with the help of formal financial institutions. Usually, all the members of the group belong to same gender and come from homogeneous economic background. Heterogeneous groups are not allowed to form for microfinance activities for smooth functioning. For the delivery of microfinance or microcredit to the collateral less unbanked poor Self-help group mechanism has considered as the most effective mechanism throughout the world.

Vulnerability Index: The dictionary meaning of Vulnerability indicates a situation or state where someone is staying without protection and is in weak condition so that they are easily hurt by others physically or emotionally. In Indian society since most of the female inhabitants are suffer from different kinds of discrimination both in the household as well as in the society therefore, they are frequently referred as the vulnerable section in the country. One of the basic hypotheses of the proponents of SHG based microfinance program is that it can eases the degree of vulnerability prevailing among the poor women. Vulnerability Index is used here by the researchers to measure the degree or extent of vulnerability among the focused group quantitatively considering a number of subjective and quantitative issues/parameters.

West Bengal: West Bengal is an Indian state situated in Eastern India on the Bay of Bengal. It is the fourth most crowded state in India, with more than 90 million inhabitants (as per 2011 census). The total area of the state is 88,752 km2 (34,267 sq mi). The capital of the state is Kolkata (Calcutta) which is the seventh-biggest city in India. The major ethnic groups in the state are the Bengalis. West Bengal is mainly agriculture based and occupies the 6th position in terms of contribution to India's net domestic product. The state has a strong cultural and religious background. The two Nobel Laureate scholars Rabindra Nath Tagore and Amartya Sen, religious reformers such as Mahaprabhu Sree Chaityanya, Ramakrishna, Swami Vivekananda, etc. are the pride of the state and enlightened the country in the world. Kolkata is known as the social capital of India.

Women Empowerment: Women empowerment refers to an environment where equal right of women in terms of economic, social, political and legal aspect can be ensured and they can make decision of their own and confident to claim their rights and justice in the society. The meaning of the term is very wide. Along with the livelihood security it also refers the social, legal and voice representation security of the women with equal right like men. For every developed society ensure of women empowerment is a prerequisite condition.

Chapter 16
The Effect of Microfinance on Inequality and Household Shocks Easing in Nigeria

Ezebuilo R. Ukwueze
University of Nigeria, Nigeria

Henry T. Asogwa
University of Nigeria, Nigeria

Augustine C. Odoh
Godfrey Okoye University, Nigeria

ABSTRACT

The chapter aims at finding the microfinance effect on households' shocks easing of Nigerians, and estimating the inequality in the use of MFIs' services under the backdrop that rural farmers do not have access to credits to boost productivity and this affects their income and widens inequality. Based upon the World Bank microdata on financial inclusion survey for 2014 (the Global Fundex survey data set), the study employed the Heckman selection model and concentration index. The results show that households in urban areas have more access to MFIs services than rural households in terms of mobile money accounts, emergency funds, and receiving remittances to smooth their consumption shocks. The results also show wide disparities in deprivation of owning accounts, in loans for apartment, in trend of saving habits, in capacity to participate in MFIs services between the rich and the poor. The study, therefore, recommends that more MFIs can be established in rural areas and more awareness campaign be carried to reach out to the targeted households.

INTRODUCTION

Generally, microfinance programmes are basically meant to provide financial services to the poor especially those that are under-served by mainstream financial service providers. These services include microcredit, micro-savings, micro-leasing, and micro-insurance and payment transfer (Babajide, 2011).

DOI: 10.4018/978-1-5225-5240-6.ch016

Microfinance impact analysis is the process by which one determines the outcomes (effects) of microfinance as an intervention (Ledgerwood, 1999). Microfinance Institutions (MFIs) do the provision of financial services to low-income individuals, and also the self-employed. The services include credit, savings, insurance and payment. However, Koveos and Randhawa (2004) argued that the main idea behind microfinance is to reduce and ultimately eliminate poverty by providing credit to individuals who are too poor to access fund from the formal financial institutions. Microfinance has come to replace or reduce the activities of private money lending activities with their high interest-charging capacities which are mostly usurious, and other illicit activities beclouding it.

It should be noted that it is not only the very poor that benefit from the microfinance credits; the "working poor" also patronize the MFIs. The working poor are those who are working but have little earned income or those whose earned income cannot meet their household needs. They cannot also borrow from the formal financial institutions, due to their inability to provide collaterals. The links between microfinance development and improvement in lives and welfare of households have come to focus in empirical studies, especially as this plays veritable role in reducing inequality in the areas of consumption smoothening. Developing countries are characterized by disparities: income gaps, inequality, poverty, vulnerability and welfare levels. Greater households depend on subsistence income accrued from rural faming and other related economic activities. These rural farmers do not have access to credits to boost productivity and this affects their income and widens inequality.

Providing effective financial services to low-income households often requires social intermediation, the process of creating social capital as a support to sustainable financial intermediation with poor and disadvantaged groups or individuals (Bennett, 1997). Also, some MFIs provide enterprise development services such as skills training and basic business training (including bookkeeping, marketing, and production) or social services such as health care, education, and literacy training. These services can improve the ability of low-income households to operate microenterprises either directly or indirectly. It should be noted that the type of services rendered by the MFIs depend on the MFI's objectives, the demands of the target market, the existence of other service providers, and an accurate calculation of the costs and feasibility of delivering additional services (Ledgerwood, 1999).

According to Ledgerwood (1999), there are four cardinal services which may be provided to microfinance clients and include: first, financial intermediation, or the provision of financial products and services such as savings, credit, insurance, credit cards, and payment systems. Second, social intermediation is the process of building the human and social capital required by sustainable financial intermediation for the poor. Third, they provide enterprise development services or non-financial services that assist micro-entrepreneurs. They include business training, marketing and technology services, skills development, and subsector analysis. Fourth, social services or non-financial services that focuses on improving the well-being of micro-entrepreneurs. They include health, nutrition, education, and literacy training.

Since microfinance is believed to ease the microcredit constraints on the poor, it is expected to have equalizing effects on income disparity and by extension has the capability of cushioning the effects of shocks on poor households' consumption. Shock easing effect of microfinance is easily manifested in the consumption smoothening potential of the microfinance institution (Dunford, 2013). The ability of households to smoothen consumption portrays an important dimension of wellbeing as it shows people's capability to satisfy their basic needs despite the occurrence of shocks (Sugiyanto, Kusumastuti & Donna, 2012). According to Hashemi and Rosenberg (2006:1), microfinance enables poor people to use loans, deposits, and other financial services to reduce their vulnerability, seize opportunities, and increase their earnings, hence alleviating their poverty.

Microfinance has also some safety nets built in it. According to Padró (2004:1) "a social safety net is there to meet the needs of those who need assistance in one form or another." This implies that although welfare does form a part of social safety nets, these programmes also concern other factors such as education, labour welfare and workplace conditions, health care, quality of life, amongst others (Padró, 2004). However, the World Bank (2010) also refers to the fact that some people see social safety nets as welfare programmes or as providing social assistance. This is far from that, but when thinking about the introduction of safety nets in a country or region, there is the need to carefully access the needs of the people living there. This is because each kind of safety net has certain attributes and covers some aspects better than other programmes (Vella, 2011). Following from this, Grosh et al. (2008) said, "A good safety net system is more than a collection of well-designed and well-implemented programmes." They went on to argue that safety net systems are linked to one another by complementing both other safety net programmes and social policies within the country.

Government of Nigeria has at one time or the other implemented many poverty reduction strategies/policies through the establishment of what seemed like microfinance and which eventually metamorphosed into microfinance institutions (MFIs). These include: Agricultural Credit Guarantee Scheme (ACGS); Nigerian Agricultural and Co-operative Bank (NACB) and the National Directorate of Employment (NDE), Nigerian Agricultural Insurance Corporation, National Poverty Eradication Programmes, and the Family Economic Advancement Programme. These were modified into Peoples Bank, (1990-2002), Community Banks and now to full blown microfinance institutions in 2005. This study, from literature search, extends the research beyond the relationship between microfinance and poverty to the effect of microfinance on inequality and household shocks easing.

REVIEW OF RELATED LITERATURE

Conceptual Framework

Generally, microfinance programmes are basically meant to provide financial services to the poor and the vulnerable, especially those that are under-served by mainstream financial service providers. These services include microcredit, micro-savings, micro-leasing, and micro-insurance and payment transfer (Babajide, 2011). The vulnerable are most affected by the lack of or insufficient access to these services. Who are the vulnerable?

Vulnerability is a concept that has been viewed differently by researchers and thus has been given varied definitions and measures. Prowse (2003: 9) sees vulnerability as a condition which can cause poverty or hinder people from escaping poverty. Some other researchers who support that poor people are generally more vulnerable are Cannon and Rowell (2003), and Feldbrügge and von Braun (2002). It is observed that this view opines that vulnerability is the cause of poverty. However, the other group of researchers views vulnerability as stemming from poverty: they view this concept as being caused by poverty (Cardona, 2004). Calvo (2008) treats vulnerability as a dimension of poverty itself and define it as a threat of suffering any form of poverty in the future.

In Calvo and Dercon's (2005) analysis, vulnerability is seen as a combination of poverty (failure to reach a minimum outcome) and risk (dispersion over states of the world) that translates into a threat of being poor in the next period. The notion of vulnerability is found upon the probability of outcomes failing to reach the minimal standard as well as on the uncertainty (risk of falling into poverty) about how far households may fall below that threshold. This uncertainty is a source of distress and impinges directly on well-being (Swain & Floro, 2012).

Ligon and Schechter (2003) took a utilitarian approach in defining vulnerability, arguing that it depends not only on the mean of household consumption but also on variation in consumption in the context of a risky environment. The risk faced by the household, according to them, is decomposed into aggregate and idiosyncratic risk. Researchers have used various measures and/or proxies for vulnerability. Some have used household panel data, while others have used the extent of consumption fluctuations over time as households' experience income fluctuations (Morduch, 2005; Kamanou & Morduch, 2005). Still, others have examined the impact of various forms of shocks on households' consumption (Ligon & Schechter, 2003; Carter et al., 2007), or other aspects of household well-being, such as health (Dercon & Hoddinott, 2005). These measures have been used to estimate the effects of shocks on households' variations in income and thus be able to determine how microfinance has been able to mitigate the harsh effects on the poor households.

The intervention can come in the form of the services provided by the microfinance institutions (MFIs). As noted above, these services include micro credits, savings, insurance and transfer of funds. Microcredit refers to the ratio of loan amount to average per capita income (which differs across country but lies within 60-150% of the GDP per capita ratio) while micro-savings refers to savings account with a balance of less than 20% of the average annual income per capita (USAID, 2004). This shows that in 2016, loans of up to N290,000 was regarded as micro-loan in Nigeria while micro-savings with a balance less than N59,300 was regarded as micro-savings. Since microfinance is believed to ease the microcredit constraints on the poor, it is expected to have equalizing effects on income disparity and by extension has the capability of cushioning the effects of shocks on poor households' consumption.

Shock easing effect of microfinance is easily manifested in the consumption smoothening potential of the microfinance institution (Dunford, 2013). The ability of households to smoothen consumption portrays an important dimension of wellbeing as it shows people's capability to satisfy their basic needs despite the occurrence of shocks (Sugiyanto, Kusumastuti & Donna, 2012).

Household can employ either ex ante or ex post strategies consumption smoothing and it involves any or combination of these: employing additional income generation activities, sourcing for credit/ loans, or seeking transfers (Aryeetey, 2004). The ex-ante uncertainty about shocks enables households to have reserves of money through additional income generation activities and as well engage in ex post activities such as sales of assets, credit or insurance claims when ex-ante income turns out to be lower than the minimum level of disposable income required to satisfy the needs for food and other basic necessities (Zeller, 1999). Udry (1994) noted that ex ante strategy is used by household to reduce variance in income while ex post enables household to stabilize consumption in the case of volatility of income. This is similar to income smoothing or risk-management and consumption smoothing or risk-coping strategies as identified by Berg and Schrader (2009) which refers to income diversification by households and dealing with the effect of shocks respectively. Three different consumption smoothing mechanisms that have been identified in the literature to help reduce poverty and inequality include assets liquidation, adjustment in the investment in human capital and the use of external credit. Among these, it has been argued that access to external credit has been given least attention (Murdoch & Roodman, 2009). In line with Murdoch and Roodman, (2009), Zeller (2001) further argued that microfinance can smooth income and consumption in two different ways: (1) by raising the expected income and consumption and future investment assets and, (2) by decreasing the downward semi-variances of income and consumption.

The economics literature on the consumption smoothing behaviours follows two fundamental models: the first one models household behaviour based on the permanent income hypothesis and focuses on the aggregate consumption smoothing versus income (Deaton, 1992). The second, on the other hand, pays closer attention mostly on specific group of households. This study is basically on the effect of microfinance on the households and therefore hinges on the second model. In other words, the concern of this study is more on idiosyncratic shocks than covariate shocks. The idiosyncratic shocks include economic shocks, crime shocks, health shocks and familial shocks (Laws, 2016).

EMPIRICAL LITERATURE

Effect of Microfinance on Consumption Smoothing in Nigeria

Theoretically, microfinance is meant to reduce inequality, poverty, cope with shocks especially by smoothing income and generally improving the welfare of household, however in Nigeria, few evidence exist. Below, the study presented few empirical evidence. Findings by Carlos, Dabla-Norris, Saito and Shi (2015) for Nigeria revealed that household that have access to finance have more smooth consumption than those without. Specifically, the study found that those households that have access to finance and experienced negative shocks will have their consumption fall by 15 percentage point less than those with no access to finance. The study pointed out that the result is more robust for household that have more access to informal finance than those with access to formal financing. Microfinance access has also been found to have impacted positively on the rural farmers in Akwa-ibom through increasing their consumption, increase in their income and better nutrition for their children (Okon, Etim & Offiong, 2012). However, a contrary result was arrived at by Adebayo, Sanni and Baiyegunhi (2012) who investigated the impact of UNDP microcredit scheme on food security in Kaduna State. The study used Propensity Score Matching (PSM) and found that crop production by farmers who benefitted from the credit scheme was lower than those that never benefited from it. Those that benefited from the programme were also found to eat less calories of food than those that did not benefit. The implication is that the credit scheme negatively impacted on the beneficiaries and this cast doubt on the scheme in ensuring stability in consumption behaviour. Nyiatahger, Umeh and Ocholi (2015) worked on the mechanisms that households adopt in smoothing their consumption in adjustment to health shocks. A multi-stage sampling was applied to select 600 households that formed the sample. Evidence from the study indicated that the one of the adjustment strategies adopted by households in smoothing their consumption was micro-credit which played significant role in the short-run. Urdy (1990) found that in the Northern Nigeria, household shocks are mitigated through state-contingent loan contract entered by households within the same village. According to him, such loan provides a repayment procedure targeted to take care of the production and consumption shocks that affect both the borrower and the lender. In the event of shocks, the loan contract provides for renegotiation, especially if there is common knowledge about the shocks or their probability of occurring. This type of loan arrangement provides the opportunity to easily absorb either the production shock or the consumption shocks. Based on the 198 households that were used, it was found that about 42 percent of the households were affected by idiosyncratic shocks while 58 percent was hit by both the village shocks and other village related shocks. Ikpe (2016) considered various issues, which include sources of accessing microcredit, factors that determine access, the amount of credit, frequency of credit and the effect of microcredit on food security. The study found that 87.76 percent of the households are food secured while the remaining are not and that about 45.57 percent considered to be food secured achieved that through microcredit facilities. Microcredit was found to have a coefficient of 0.749 which explained most changes in food security compared to every other factor that affects food security. Similarly, Aideyan (2009) analyzed the effect of Lift Above Poverty Organization(LAPO) and Nigeria Agricultural Cooperative and Rural Development Bank(NACRDB) programmes on the households and the comparison households. The study concentrated on the impact of the two programs on the households' nutritional welfare by considering regularity of food, frequency of special food and the average weekly spending on food. For the LAPO program, it was found that only 12.4 percent of the program group (treated) have food deficit while up to 51.4 percent of the comparison group (control group) have food deficit. In case of NACRDB, 33.3 percent of the control group have food deficit while only 8.6 percent of the treated group have food deficit. For the frequency of special food, LAPO program shows 18 percent for treated group and 7 percent for the control group and for NACRDB, the treated group and the control group were 9.7 percent and 3.7 percent respectively. The weekly expenditure on food for both programs appeared to be higher for the treated group than the control group.

Furthermore, for the two programs, the study showed a significant difference between program households and the comparison with respect to average weekly expenditure and the regularity of daily feeding. This is evidence that the two microcredit programs helped in the smoothing of the household consumption. The United Nations Capital Development Fund (UNCDF) (2004) report based on the UNCDF-supported microfinance institution (MFIs) loan for Nigeria, Malawi, Haiti and Kenya showed that households divert programme loans meant for investment enterprise to smoothen their consumption. Evidence showed that for Nigeria, Malawi, Haiti and Kenya a positive association existed between the consumption smoothing (food security) and participation in the UNCDF-supported MFIs programme. For the four countries, higher food security was common among the household that are in the treatment group compared to the control and the difference was found to be significant at 6 per cent level of significance.

Effect of Microfinance on Consumption Smoothing in Other Countries

Islam and Maitra (2012) looked into the role of micro finance in absorbing the effect of health shocks in the consumption behaviours of households in rural Bangladesh. In their study, they identified that households either sell productive assets such as livestock or borrow from microfinance to cushion the effects of health shocks on consumption. The study also revealed that households that have access to microcredit do not need to sell as much livestock as those household that do not have access to in order to smoothen their consumption against health shocks. The implication of this study is that household can maintain stable consumption pattern despite shocks as far as they have access to microfinance. Pitt and Khander (1998) used quasi-experimental survey design in their study found that access to microcredit increases significantly consumption of poor households in Bangladesh. Berg and Emran(2011) found for Bangladesh that households that have access to microfinance have better chance for survival in the famine (Monga) period and that microfinance increases the probability that household will have three meals a day but reduces the probability that household will survive on one meal a day during Monga. This implies that microfinance can help household smoothen food consumption despite seasonal famine. Similarly, evidence from Khan, Khalily and Scheyvens, (2015) for North-Western Bangladesh is that households adopt various coping strategies against Monga, such as advance labour sale, asset sale, informal borrowing and migration and that all depend on the household ex-ante access to microfinance. For instance, it was found that for those with ex-ante access to microfinance, the number of days sold in advance was 3.52 days lower compared to a case without ex-ante access to microfinance and this was found to be significant at 1 percent. Further finding from the work is that an ex-ante access to microfinance brought about household selling of 20,967 days overlaboring advance, which is an average of nine days per household. However, when switching regression technique was used for analysis, it was revealed that about 73,803 more labour days were sold in advance for household with no ex-ante access to microfinance. This implies that having ex-ante access to microfinance reduces the labour days sold in advance. Ex-ante access to microfinance also reduces the dependence on selling of assets, informal borrowing and lowers the probability of migrating to another place to cope with Monga. Therefore microfinance reduces the choice of household using counterproductive coping strategies during Monga. For the same Bangladesh, Muhumed (2016) used a household survey data generated by the Bangladesh Bureau of Statistics (BBS) and applied various techniques which include direct OLS, direct 2SLS, probit OLS, probit 2SLS and marginal treatment effect (MTE) to check for the effects of microfinance on the food consumption and non-food consumption between borrowers and non-borrowers of microcredit. The result from the direct OLS showed that borrowers of microcredit have higher food and non-food consumption compared to non-borrowers. This was evidence that borrowing positively correlate with food and non-food consumption and by extension implies that microcredit can be used to smoothen consumption. To avoid the bias from direct OLS due to potential endogeneity problem in the dummy variable borrowed, other techniques, direct 2SLS, probit OLS, probit 2SLS and marginal treatment effect (MTE) were used and their estimates indicted no difference in both the food consumption and non-food consumption of borrowers and non-borrowers of microcredit. Furthermore, the result of direct OLS was later adopted after the endogeneity test using Hausman proved that the variable borrowed is truly exogenous. The study concluded based on direct OLS that microcredit borrowers have approximately 122 Taka higher weekly food consumption than non-borrowers, and about 34 Taka higher non-food consumption than non-borrowers. Evidence from Santos,Sharif, Rahman, and Zaman, (2011) is similar to that by Romero and Nagarajan, (2011) in that the result shows that Bangladesh poor are affected more by shocks than the non-poor which according to the study is because the poor tend to use the copping strategy that affect them negatively unlike the non-poor. The result from the study identified that microfinance impact significantly on the coping ability of the households. In a very recent work, Berg and Emran (2017) investigated the effect of microfinance on seasonal famine in Bangladeshusing a number of techniques which include Minimum Biased Inverse probability (MB-IPW) estimator, instrumental variable based onLocal Biprobit (LBiprobit) which provide for average treatment effect on treated(ATET) and Local Two-stage least squares(L2SLS) which provide local average treatment effect(LATE). Based on the MB-IPW, microfinance increases the probability of 3 meals by 1 per cent and decreases the probability of one meal by 5 per cent. It also increases the probability of not selling labour in advance by 2 per cent and increases the probability of migration by 2 per cent. The results from the L2SLS shows that households that are member of microcredit are more likely to have 3 meals in a day but reduces the likelihood of starving with only one meal a day. Evidence from the L2SLS however shows that microcredit membership does not have any effect on the propensity of household selling labour in advance as a coping mechanism but was significant in reducing the chance that household will migrate in a short term to avoid starvation during Monga. The estimate of the LBiprobit model were in line with the L2SLS that microfinance membership improves food security during the Monga period, and that microfinance does not have any significant effect on the probability that household will sell labour in advance to ensure resilience during Monga. Moreover, it was also revealed based on LBiprobit that microfinance reduces the probability that household will migrate in short term to cope with hunger.

It was also found forIndonesia that households that live closer to financial institution are able to insure consumption against health shocks than households that a relatively farer. Specifically, it was revealed by the study that for communities with Bank Rakyat Indonesia (BRI) branch, health shocks do not have significant impact on consumption but for areas not served by BRI health shocks lower consumption by 2 to 3 percent (Gertler, Levine & Moretti, 2003). Another study byGertler, Levine and Moretti, (2003) for Indonesia, shows that in the event of shocks, especially health shocks, microfinance provides an efficient way of insuring a smooth consumption and that the closer a household to financial institution the more the household can save to ensure consumption smoothing. Still for Indonesia, Deloach and Lamanna (2009) found that consumption smoothing in response to income shock is one of the channels through which microfinance can affect health of a child.

For Malawi using randomized encouragement trial design it was found that access to mobile banking, Opportunity International bank of Malawi (OIBM) was more effective for household with high level of wealth to cope with shocks than the household with low level of wealth as the low income households use sub-optimal coping strategies (Romero and Nagarajan, 2011).

The Self-Help microfinance groups(SHG) in India was found to have helped members of household in coping with shock through increasing household earnings, training, provision of consumption and providing support for women (Bali & Floro, 2010). Bergand Schrader (2009) found a significant evidence of microfinance contribution to shock easing in Ecuador. However, the study pointed out that it could only help to cushion the effect of shock when the household has an established relation with the institution before shocks, but for the first-timer, the probability of receiving credit in the event of the shock is low and thus will not help in cushioning the effects of the shocks. Janzen and Carter (2013) analysis of the impact of microinsurance (drought-induced insurance) on household consumption smoothing behaviours for Kenya revealed that household that holds such insurance is 36 percent point less tendency of selling asset in order to cope with shocks and 25 percent point less that the meal formula will be adjusted downwards. It was also explained that micro insurance reduces food security by reducing malnourishment and undernourishment especially during drought. The study further revealed that at some threshold level of asset holding, households that are not holder of such insurance are likely to sell their asset to cope, but about 64 percent point less likely when they are holder of such insurance policy.

The impact of microcredit for Ethiopia based on the study by Siyoum, Hilhorst and Pankhurst (2012) depend on the income level or group, that is whether a household is poor or not. Generally, they believe that credit is meant to be used by poor households to develop their potential that will move them out of poverty, but most of them (poor households) use it to as a means to smoothen their consumption within a short period. Thus, microcredit does not provide for food security of the poor in the long term since they use it for immediate consumption smoothing rather than in productive resources that guarantees long term food security.

Yasuharu, and LaStarria-CorNhieL (2015) investigated the impact of credit programme on consumption in Malawi using propensity score matching and the treatment effect model. In the preliminary results it was found that Malawi Rural Finance Company(MRFC) clients with in the programme village have a total mean consumption of 9252 MK(Malawi Kwacha) while non MRFC clients has a total mean of 9060MK. However, test of significance revealed no difference in the consumption between the MRFC clients and non-clients. The result from the propensity score matching and treatment effect model appear similar with respect of the impact of the programme in which none showed any significant improvement on food consumption and expenditure consumption due to the programme. Furthermore, both the propensity score matching and treatment effect model showed evidence non-food expenditure grew by

47.6 and 47.2 respectively at 1 per cent significant level due to the programme. For the total food expenditure, the propensity score matching indicated that total food expenditure grew by 16.6 percent as a result of the programme while the treatment effect model on the contrary revealed that MRFC agricultural scheme did not have any significant effect on the total food consumption. Banerjee, Duflo Glennerster and Kinnan (2015) found for Hyderabad India that household suffered different shocks which include shock resulting for illness, job loss and death of household member. Using a randomized evaluation, it was found that household borrowed from Spandana to cushion the effect of these shocks, though it seemed no significant difference was found between the treated group and control group because of other sources of borrowing aside Spandana. However, treatment group was found to be more likely to borrow from the Spandana to cushion the effects of shocks. Based on the randomized field experiments Attanasio, Augsburg, Haas, Fitzsimons and Harmgart, (2014) found evidence for Mongolia that access to group loans impact positively and significantly on food consumption especially items such as fruits and vegetable, and entrepreneurship while for individual lending, no evidence of significant increase in the food consumption. The positive and significant impact as evidenced for the group loan implies that microfinance can be used to cushion the effects of shocks.

OBJECTIVES OF STUDY

The broad objective of this study is to estimate the effect of microfinance of households' welfare. However, the specific objectives of the chapter are stated as follows:

1. To estimate find the effect of microfinance on households' shocks easing of Nigerians.
2. To estimate the inequality among households who benefit from the services of microfinance in Nigeria.

DATA AND METHODOLOGY

Analytical Framework

To ideally consolidate on policies and effort of government in Africa that is targeted at reducing inequality gap and poverty among households, there is an urgent need on improving mechanisms that improve on household per capita income which must be gender inclusive. Hence, to articulate a framework that could possibly develop a links between microfinance development and improvement in lives and welfare of households. This is expected to estimate the microfinance effect on households' shocks easing of Nigerians.

Therefore, the Heckman Selection Model is adopted for this study. And, this is because the Heckman's sample selection model is among the more significant work in 20th-century program evaluation. The sample selection model triggered both a rich theoretical discussion on modeling selection bias and the development of new statistical procedures that address the problem of selection bias. Heckman's key contributions to program evaluation include: (a) he provided a theoretical framework that emphasized the importance of modeling the dummy endogenous variable; (b) his model was the first attempt that estimated the probability (i.e., the propensity score) of a participant being in one of the two conditions indicated by an endogenous dummy variable, and then used the estimated propensity score model to estimate coefficients of the regression model; (c) he treated the unobserved selection factors as a problem of specification error or a problem of omitted variables, and corrected for bias in the estimation of the outcome equation by explicitly using information gained from the model of sample selection; and (d) he developed a creative two-step procedure by using the simple least squares algorithm.

A sample selection model always involves two equations: (1) the selection equation, considering a portion of the sample whose outcome is observed and mechanisms determining the selection process; and (2) the outcome equation considering mechanisms determining the outcome variable (Heckman, 1978, 1979). The model is expressed in two equations as follows:

$$z_j Y + u_{1j} > 0 \tag{1}$$

$$y_j = X_j \beta + u_{2j} \tag{2}$$

Where: y_j is the observed outcome of the jth household; X_j are factors determining y and uj are the error term. Given that equation 1 and 2 are the selection and outcome equations, respectively.

Model Specification

Having reviewed the Heckman's model first becauseit not only offers theoretical framework for modeling sample selection but is also based on what was at the time pioneering approach to correcting selection bias. More so, that the Heckman's model lays the groundwork for understanding the treatment effect model therefore, in other to estimate objective one of the study which is to analyze the factors that determine households' shocks easing in Nigeria.

Therefore, suppose we assume that households in rural areas are most likely not to have access to credits to boost productivity and this affects their income and widens inequality as given in the data set such that the probability of households' shocks easing is function of mobile money account (account mob), payments online using internet (online payment q16), emergency fund, domestic remittances, government transfer, savings, borrowing abilities and so on hence, to express the model, the researcher write two equations, the regression equation of indicators that determine households' shocks easing and the selection equation of indicators that determine households' shocks easing as represented on model 3.

$$hhshocks = \beta_0 + \beta_1 actmob + \beta_2 onlpa + \beta_3 emfun + \beta_4 remt + \beta_5 tran + \beta_6 savins + \beta_7 borr + \tag{3}$$

Thus, households' shocks easing are observed if;

$$hhshocks = \beta_0 + \beta_1 actmob + \beta_2 onlpa + \beta_3 emfun + \beta_4 remt + \beta_5 tran + \beta_6 savins + \beta_7 borr + U_2 > 0 \tag{4}$$

where equation three (3) is the regression equation and equation four (4) is the selection model. However, for this study selection equation indicates that households shocks easing is observedonly for those households whose households shocks easing were greater than0.

To estimate objective two this is the effect of microfinance on inequality among household shocks easing in Nigeria. The study employ concentration index as a measure of socioeconomic-related inequality among households in quintile. Thus the concentration index (c) can be computed very simply by making use of the convenient covariance:

$$C = 2\,\mathrm{cov}(y, R_i) \,/\, \mu \tag{5}$$

where y_i is the category variable, whose disparity is being measured, μ is its mean, R_i is the ith individual's fractional rank among household distribution (that is, in this case the household's wealth distribution factor as covered in the data set), and *cov(.,.)* is the covariance.

Justification of the Model

In most theoretical studies, Health sector variables are seldom continuous and fully observed. For example, they can be discrete (e.g., death), censored (e.g., health care expenditure), integer counts (e.g., visits to doctor), or durational (e.g., time to death). Multivariate analysis of such dependent variables requires nonlinear estimation.In this study, we consider the main (parametric) nonlinear estimators that are of relevance to the analysis of household shocks easing.Therefore, the study employs the 'Heckman two step' selection model to control for sample selection bias as the only standard measure to capture the objective of the study.

DATA AND SOURCES

The study employs cross sectional secondary data from the World Bank micro data on financial inclusion survey for 2014 (the Global Fundex Survey Data set) set to attain its objectives. The Global Fundex database provides in-depth data on how individuals save, borrow, make payments, and manage risks. It is the world's most comprehensive database on financial inclusion that consistently measures people's use of financial services across countries and over time. The 2014 Global Findex consists of over 100 indicators, also shown by gender, income, and age hence, was instrumental to this study.

RESULTS AND DISCUSSION

To achieve objective one, a Heckman estimation selection model was employed. Table 1 shows results from the Heckman Selection model and explains that households in urban areas are more likely to participate in microfinance services considering the indicators that determine households' shocks easing than households in rural areas. The results show that households in urban areas are open to mobile money account targeted to smooth shocks by 0.1414967 indexes when compared to rural households by 0.0650428 indexes despite that the outcome is not significant at 5% level. Similarly, households in

Table 1. Results of Heckman's estimation

	Household shocks	Coefficient	Standard error	z-statistics	P>(z)
Regression	**Rural**				
	Account_mob	0.0650428	0.26759650.240.808		
	Online payment	-0.1886112	0.1978283-0.950.340		
Emergency fund(q24)		0.2233616	0.04113575.430.000		
	Remittance(q28)	0.1364558	0.08559651.590.111		
	Transfer received (q39)	0.17252380.14408041.200.231			
	Savings	-0.1527843	0.1077207-1.420.156		
	Borrowed abilities	-0.1281957	0.0943206-1.360.174		
_cons	4.327151	0.63122416.860.000			
Selection Urban					
	Account_mob	0.1414967	0.39161820.360.718		
	Online payments(q16)	-0.3366953	0.3416145-0.990.324		
	Emergency fund(q24)	0.4638246	0.08926855.200.000		
	Remittance(q28)	0.2302115	0.13145531.750.080		
	Transfer received (q39)	0.1838265	0.23301680.790.430		
	Savings	-0.22150050.1557572-1.420.155			
	Borrowed abilities	-0.18984350.1363709-1.390.164			
	_cons	3.8336350.324664411.810.000			
MillsLambda	277.82	40.92		3.080.000	
Rho = 0.00000	Wald chi2(7) =57.18	Prob> chi2 =	0.0000Lambda = 277.16Sigma = 1.4102085		
No of obs = 1000Censored obs =423	Uncensored obs = 577				

Source: authors' computation, 2017

urban areas are more likely to access emergency fund on the average of ₦0.4638246than households in rural areas that spend on the average ₦0.2233616. However, this indicator (emergency funds) is shown to be statistically significant at 5% level.

However, the results also show that other indicators that determine that households shock easing is domestic remittances. Householdsin urban areas receive on the average of 0.2302115 indexesas remittances when compared to households in rural areas which receive as much as0.1364558indexes. All the indicators are statistically significant at 5% level except indicators like household online payments, transfer received, savings and borrowing abilities that were not statistically significant at 5% level, possibly due to the age variations and other households' characteristics like level of education, awareness of households of the existence and benefits of microfinance.

The results also show that the absolute rho value to be less than 1 indicate that the Heckman model was appropriate for the analysis. Outof the 1000 households sampled 423 were censored (not included in the analysis) while the remaining 577 households who are residents in rural areas were uncensored. And given the test Wald chi-square statistics of 57.18, which has a probability value of 0.000, implies that the results of this model is statistically significant at 5% level.

The second objective of the study which is to estimate the inequality among households, who have benefited from microfinance in Nigeria, was estimated using the Concentration index. The results of the estimation are shown in table 2.

Table 2. Concentration index model:using convenient covariance

	CIF	CISEF	Mean	Variance
Category variable				
Fin account disparity	-0.0088749	0.00642429	1.463	0.2488799
Loan disparity	0.00732252	0.00261597	1.948	0.0853814
Savings with informal club	0.0327806	0.00422694	1.832	0.197974
Mobile money	0.00206094	0.00148138	1.97	0.0291291
Savings disparity	0.00803114	0.00678472	1.298	0.2094054
Borrowing disparity	0.0191026	0.00580451	1.557	0.246998

The table shows the estimates from the concentration index.
CIF: concentration index using formula/covariance method
CISEF: standard errors of the concentration index using formula/ regression method

The results on Table 2 above indicate that microfinance accesses have created huge disparities among households in Nigeria and these have affected shocks easing as well. This is clearly displayed in table 5.2 as the CIF coefficients that the proportion of households who are more deprived of not having account with MFIs are more concentrated among the poor given by the concentration index of-0.0088749, and this is considered to present a reasonably high level of disparity. The results further show that among household levels, the disparity stillexistswith regard to loan from microfinance institutions for house, apartment or land given the concentration index of 0.00732252 across different households. This is also a reasonably high level of disparity.

Similarly, the results indicate weak disparity level between the poor and the rich households that inculcate savings attitude with informal club and some microfinance establishment by an index of 0.0327806. The results also show that among poor and rich household members that operate a mobile money account, clear disparity exists among them as shown by the index 0.00206094. While the index of 0.00803114 show the level of disparity that exist among poor and rich household members with trend of savings habits in microfinance institutions, which appear to favour more among rich household members. And, then the index of 0.0191026 showing the level of disparity among household members that borrowed from microfinance institutions to smoothen consumption shocks, implying that inequality is less between poor and rich households.

This indicates that households with more wealth capacity and higher per capita expenditure pattern have the potential to participate in financial services provided by microfinance institutions as compared to households with low wealth capacity and lower per capita expenditure pattern as shown by the disparity indexes that households in the highest quintile level have higher participation in financial goods as compared to households in the lower quintile level.

CONCLUSION AND POLICY SUGGESTIONS

So far, we have been able to showcase the Heckman's selection model the households' shocks easing in term of their expenditures. The urban householders benefit more from mobile money account targeted to smooth shocks than the rural dwellers. Also, urban households benefit more from access to emergency funds which place them better to smooth the consumption and/or expenditures. Similarly, households in urban areas receive more remittances to smooth the expenditures/consumption (shocks easing) than those in rural areas.

It has also been shown that the proportions of households who are more deprived of not having account with MFIs are more concentrated among the poor; they tend to have a higher concentration index. There also appeared a higher disparity among the households in their access to loans for land, houses and apartment. In the same vein, the level of disparity that exists among poor and rich household members with trend of savings habits in microfinance institutions, which appear to favour more among rich household members; this results show credence to the dictum that the rich have a higher propensity and capacity to save. Finally, households with more wealth capacity and higher per capita expenditure pattern have the potential to participate in financial services provided by microfinance institutions as compared to households with low wealth capacity and lower expenditure per capita. We therefore recommend that more microfinance banks/institutions be established in rural areas and more awareness campaign be carried out so that those households in these areas will participate more actively in the services of the MFIs, and their welfare improved.

REFERENCES

Adebayo, C. O., Sanni, S.A., & Baiyegunhi, L.J.S. (2012). Microcredit Scheme Impact and Food Security Status of Beneficiaries in Kaduna State, Nigeria: A Propensity Score Matching Approach. *African Journal of Agricultural Research, 7*(37), 5191-5197.

Aideyan, O. (2009). Microfinance and Poverty Reduction in Rural Nigeria. *Savings and Development*, 293-317.

Aryeetey, E. (2004). *Household Asset Choice among the Rural Poor in Ghana*. Paper Presented at the Authors' *Workshop for the Project on Understanding Poverty in Ghana, Organized by the Institute of Statistical, Social and Economic Research*, University of Ghana and Cornell University.

Attanasio, O., Augsburg, B., De Haas, R., Fitzsimons, E., & Harmgart, H. (2014). *Group Lending or Individual Lending? Evidence from A Randomized Field Experiment in Mongolia* (No. SP II 2014-303). WZB Discussion Paper.

Babajide, A. (2011). Impact Analysis of Microfinance in Nigeria. *International Journal of Economics and Finance*, *3*(4).

Bali, S. R., & Floro, M. (2010). *Reducing Vulnerability through Microfinance: Evidence from Indian Self-Help Group Program.* Working Paper 2010:23.

Banerjee, A., Duflo, E., Glennerster, R., & Kinnan, C. (2015). The miracle of microfinance? Evidence from a randomized evaluation. *American Economic Journal. Applied Economics*, *7*(1), 22–53. doi:10.1257/app.20130533

Bennett, L. (1997). *A Systems Approach to Social and Financial Intermediation with the Poor*. Paper presented at the Banking with the Poor Network/World Bank Asia Regional Conference on Sustainable Banking with the Poor, Bangkok, Thailand.

Berg, G., & Schrader, J. (2009). *Can Microcredit help to cope with Aggregate Shocks? Evidence from Ecuador.* First European Research Conference on Microfinance, Brussels, Belgium.

Berg, C., & Emran, M. S. (2015). *Does Microfinance help the Ultra-Poor cope with Seasonal Shocks? Evidence from Seasonal Famine (Monga) in Bangladesh.* Working Paper.

Calvo, C. (2008). Vulnerability to Multidimensional Poverty: Peru, 1998-2002. *World Development, 36*(6), 1011–1020. doi:10.1016/j.worlddev.2007.10.001

Calvo, C., & Dercon, S. (2005). *Measuring Individual Vulnerability.* Department of Economics Working Paper Series, 229. Oxford, UK: Oxford University.

Cannon, T. T., & Rowell, J. (2003). Social Vulnerability, Sustainable Livelihoods and Disasters. Report to DFID. Conflict and Humanitarian Assistance Department (CHAD) and Sustainable Livelihoods Office.

Cardona, O. D. (2004). The Need for Rethinking the Concepts of Vulnerability and Risk from a Holistic Perspective: a Necessary Review and Criticism for Effective Risk Management. In G. Bankoff, G. Frerks, & D. Hilhorst (Eds.), *Mapping Vulnerability: Disasters, Development and People* (pp. 37–51). London: Earthscan publications.

Carlosn, S., Dabla-Norris, E., Saito, M., & Shi, Y. (2015). *Household Financial Access and RiskSharing in Nigeria.* IMF Working Paper. WP/15/169

Carter, M., Little, P., Mogues, T., & Negatu, W. (2007). Poverty Traps and the Long term consequences of Natural Disasters in Ethiopia and Honduras. *World Development, 35*(5), 835–856. doi:10.1016/j.worlddev.2006.09.010

Deaton, A. (1992). *Understanding Consumption.* New York: Oxford University Press. doi:10.1093/0198288247.001.0001

Deloach, S. B., & Lamanna, E. (2009). *Measuring the Impact of Microfinance on Child Health Outcomes in Indonesia Revision 3.* Department of Economics Elon Univerity Working Paper Series, 2009-02r3.

Dercon, S., & Hoddinott, J. (2005). *Health, Shocks and Poverty Persistence.* Oxford, UK: Oxford University Press.

Dunford, C. (2013). *Evidence that Shocks are Managed Better with the Help of Microfinance.* Retrieved from http://microfinanceandworldhunger.org/2013/01/evidence-that-shocks-are-managed-better-with-the-help-of-microfinance-the-recent-rcts/

Feldbrügge, T., & von Braun, J. (2002). *Is the World Becoming A More Risky Place? Trends in Disasters and Vulnerability to Them. Discussion Papers on Development Policy No.46.* Bonn: Center for Development Research.

Gertler, P., Levine, D. I., & Moretti, E. (2003). *Do Microfinance Programs help Families insure Consumption against Illness?* Centre for International and Development Economics Research.

Grosh, M., del Ninno, C., Tesliuc, E., & Ouerghi, A. (2008). *For Protection and Promotion: The Design and Implementation of Effective Safety Nets.* Washington, DC: The International Bank for Reconstruction and Development /The World Bank. doi:10.1596/978-0-8213-7581-5

Hashemi, S., & Rosenberg, R. (2006). *Graduating the Poorest into Microfinance: Linking Safety and Financial Service, CGAP*. Washington, DC: World Bank.

Heckman, J. (1978). Dummy Endogenous Variables in A Simultaneous Equations System. *Econometrica, 46*(4), 931–961. doi:10.2307/1909757

Heckman, J. J. (1979). Sample Selection Bias as A Specification Error. *Econometrica, 47*(1), 153–161. doi:10.2307/1912352

Ikpe, O. U. (2017). *Effects of Access to Microcredit on the Food Security Status of Crop Farm Households in Niger Delta, Nigeria* (Doctoral dissertation).

Islam, A., & Maitra, P. (2008). *Health Shocks and Consumption Smoothing in Rural Households: Does Microcredit have a Role to Play?* Department of Economics, Monash University Discussion paper 22/08.

Janzen, S. A., & Carter, M. R. (2013). *The impact of microinsurance on consumption smoothing and Asset Protection: Evidence from A Drought in Kenya*. Selected paper prepared for presentation at the Agricultural & Applied Economics Association's 2013 AAEA & CAES Joint Annual Meeting, Washington, DC.

Kamanou, G., & Morduch, J. (2005). *Measuring Vunerability to Poverty in: Stefan Dercon* (I. A. Poverty, Ed.). Oxford, UK: Oxford University Press.

Khan, Khalily, & Scheyvens. (2015). *Impact of Ex-Ante Access to Microfinanceon the Coping Strategies to cope with Monga of Poor Households in North-Western Bangladesh*. Institute of Microfinance (InM) Working Paper. No 43.

Koveos, P., & Randhawa, D. (2004). Financial Services for the Poor: Assessing Microfinance Institutions. *Managerial Finance, 30*(9), 70–95. doi:10.1108/03074350410769281

Laws, E. (2016). *Social Assistance and Idiosyncratic Shocks*. GSDRC Helpdesk Research Report, 1383.

Ledgerwood, J. (1999). *Microfinance Handbook: An Institutional and Financial Perspective*. Washington, DC: The World Bank.

Ligon, E., & Schechter, L. (2003). Measuring Vulnerability. *Economic Journal (London), 113*(486), 95–102. doi:10.1111/1468-0297.00117

Morduch, J. (2005). *Consumption Smoothing Across Space: Testing Theories of Risk-Sharing in the ICRISAT Study Region of South India*. Oxford, UK: Oxford University Press.

Muhumed, M. M. (2016). The impact of microfinance on consumption in Bangladesh. *Journal of Economics and Sustainable Development, 7*(12).

Murdoch, J., & Roodman, D. (2009). *The Impact of Microcredit on the Poor in Bangladesh: Revisiting the Evidence*. Working paper 174, 2009 (June).

Nyiatahger, Z.T., Umeh, J.C., & Ocholi, A. (2015). Socio-Economic Effects of Malaria on Households' Consumption in North-Central Nigeria. *Journal of Agriculture and Veterinary Science, 8*(7), 65-72.

Okon, D.P., Etim, N., & Offiong, A.A.A. (2012). Impact of Micro Credit Scheme on Rural Farmers in Akwa-Ibom State, Nigeria. *Journal of Agriculture & Social Sciences, 8*(2).

Padró, F. (2004). *Statistical Handbook on the Social Safety Net*. London: Greenwood Press.

Pitt, M. M., & Khandker, S. R. (1998). The Impact of Group-Based Credit Programs on Poor Households in Bangladesh: Does the Gender of Participants Matter? *Journal of Political Economy*, *106*(5), 958–996. doi:10.1086/250037

Prowse, M. (2003). *Towards a Clearer Understanding of 'Vulnerability' in Relation to Chronic Poverty*. CPRC Working Paper No 24, University of Manchester.

Romero, J. M., & Nagarajan, G. (2011). *Impact of Micro-Savings on Shock Coping Strategies in Rural Malawi*. Retrieved from http://www.fsassessment.umd.edu/

Santos, I., Sharif, I., Rahman, H. Z., & Zaman, H. (2011). *How do the Poor cope with Shocks in Bangladesh? Evidence from Survey Data?* Policy Research Working Paper 5810.

Siyoum, A. D., Hilhorst, D. J. M., & Pankhurst, A. S. A. (2012). The Differential Impact of Microcredit on Rural Livelihoods: Case Study from Ethiopia. *International Journal of Development and Sustainability*, *1*(3), 1–19.

Sugiyanto, S., Kusumastuti, Y. S., & Donna, D. R. (2012). *Managing Risks: How do Poor Households Smooth their Income and Consumption? An Examination of Poor Households in Yogyakarta, Indonesia*. IMTFI Working Paper.

Swain, R. B., & Floro, M. (2012). Assessing the Effect of Microfinance on Vulnerability and Poverty among Low Income Households. Journal of Development Studies.

Udry, C. (1990). Credit Markets in Northern Nigeria: Credit as Insurance in A Rural Economy. *The World Bank Economic Review*, *4*(3), 251–269. doi:10.1093/wber/4.3.251

Udry, C. (1994). Risk and Insurance in a Rural Credit Market: An Empirical Investigation in Northern Nigeria. *The Review of Economic Studies, 61*(3), 495-526.

USAID. (2004). *Assessment of the Micro, Small and Medium Enterprises Sector in Nigeria: PRISMS: Promoting Improved Sustainable Microfinance Services*. Retrieved from http://www.usaid.gov/ng/downloads/reforms/ assessmentofthemsmesectorinnigeria.pdf

Vella, S. (2011). *The Link between Microfinance and Social Safety Net Programmes* (Bachelor's dissertation). University of Malta.

World Bank (2014). *Micro Data on Financial Inclusion Survey for 2014 (the Global Fundex Survey Data Set)*. Author.

Yasuharu, S., & LaStarria-CorNhieL, S. (2015). Agricultural Microcredit and Household Vulnerability in Rural Malawi. *Journal of International Cooperation Studies*, *22*(2), 3.

Zeller, M. (1999). *The Role of Micro-Finance for Income and Consumption Smoothing*. Paper presented at the Inter-American Development Bank Conference on Social Protection and Poverty, Washington, DC.

Zeller, M. (2001). The Safety Net Role of Microfinance for Income and Consumption Smoothing. *Shielding the Poor: Social Protection in the Developing World*, 217-238.

KEY TERMS AND DEFINITIONS

Consumption Smoothing: Consumption smoothing is a process that seeks to achieve a between the desire for a and the need to accumulate sufficient for a secure by "smoothing" out behavior during the years. Consumption smoothing means balancing out spending and saving to maintain the highest possible standard of living over the course of one's life. The big reason in favor of consumption smoothing is that it in theory balances between the two extremes. On one end, over-spending means that you consistently spend more than you earn, while over-saving means that you consistently spend less than you earn. Consumption smoothing is the process of managing your spending so that you feel like you always have roughly the same level of disposable income, even if your income is unsteady.

Income Variation: People's incomes do not remain constant. As one starts work, one's continues to rise as one gets promoted. His income continues rising until he gets to the peak of his career, beyond which it declines. The poor does not experience this continuous rise in income; his income dwindles always. He experiences income variation at all time most of his life. He cannot predict his income and is always vulnerable to vagaries of his environment. The poor cannot guarantee the next period he will earn the same or more income. In this case, his income is always varying.

Microfinance Institutions: Microfinance is often defined as financial services for poor and low-income clients offered by different types of service providers. The term is often used more narrowly to refer to loans and other services from providers that identify themselves as "microfinance institutions" (MFIs). A microfinance institution is an organization that offers financial services to low income populations. Almost all give loans to their members, and many offer insurance, deposit and other services. These institutions commonly tend to use new methods developed over the last 30 years to deliver very small loans to unsalaried borrowers, taking little or no collateral. These methods include group lending and liability, pre-loan savings requirements, gradually increasing loan sizes, and an implicit guarantee of ready access to future loans if present loans are repaid fully and promptly.

Policy Intervention: Due to the conditions and/or the circumstances of the poor, policies are designed to mitigate the harsh conditions for the poor's wellbeing to improve. Microfinance institutions (MFIs) are part of the policies which are designed for alleviation of the harsh conditions of the poor. Through this policy, the poor can borrow from the MFIs and establish small and medium scale enterprises (SMEs) at little or no collaterals; they can save to pay school fees of their children, etc. In fact, they can have access to all the services which the formal banks render to their customers, which, hitherto, have been difficult for them. These types of policies which are made to mitigate or palliate the sufferings of the poor are called policy intervention. The government has used policies to intervene to reduce hardships which the poor and masses suffer.

Sample Selection Bias: In a linear regression model, sample selection bias occurs when data on the dependent variable are missing non-randomly, conditional on the independent variables. A sample that is restricted on the dependent variable is effectively selected on the error of the regression equation; at any value of X, observations with sufficiently large positive errors are eliminated from the sample. As we know, the independent variable increases, the expected value of the error becomes increasingly negative, making these two elements negatively correlated.

Vulnerability: Vulnerability describes the characteristics and circumstances of a community, system or asset that make it susceptible to the damaging effects of a hazard. Vulnerability in this context relates to susceptibility to the shackles of poverty and related conditions. Some experts say that poverty is the cause of vulnerability, while others view vulnerability as stemming from poverty. Yet, some others are of the view that poverty and vulnerability are mutually related and are inseparable.

Chapter 17
Impact of Self-Help Group (SHG) Membership on Income and Income Inequality:
A Case Study of Birbhum District in West Bengal

Maniklal Adhikary
The University of Burdwan, India

Sumanta Kumar Das
The University of Burdwan, India

ABSTRACT

The microfinance program has now been recognized as an effective tool to empower economically the rural women folk. The earning is the most important direct outcome of micro finance participation unlike acquiring empowerment. Participation in the program helps women to inculcate their saving habit. It gives access to the formal credit to them. All these have direct impact on their economic condition. This study explores the impact of microfinance program on the income of the program participants of Birbhum District in West Bengal in India. The study also focuses on how participation helps in reducing inequality in income of the participants. The major finding of the study is that women self-help group (SHG) members have the higher level of income compared to that of non-SHG members. The study also shows that SHG participation also helps them in reducing inequalities in their income. Gini coefficient and Lorenz curve technique has been used to assess the income distribution of the respondents.

INTRODUCTION

The biggest economic problem in India over the decades has been the poverty on a mass scale. Solution of the problem is employment and income generation; but the poor people to that end lack the financial resources. The supply of financial resources could therefore be one nice solution to reduce the vulner-

DOI: 10.4018/978-1-5225-5240-6.ch017

ability of the rural poor. Nobody will deny that the supply of rural credit to its desirable extent and at amicable conditions by private financial institution is not possible. The banks were therefore nationalized and rural financial institutions were established with a friendly approach to provide credit to the poor people. The nationalized banking sector had accepted the challenges of supply of cheap, adequate and timely rural credit. In spite of forty years' effort of Indian banking sector, a large section of rural people has remained exiled in the of financial inclusion. Using the 59th round NSSO data, the committee of financial inclusion reports that 459 Lakh out of 893 Lakh, that is, 51.4% of farmer households are financially excluded from both the formal and informal sources. Of the total farmer households, only 27% had access in formal sources of credit. One third of them also borrow from non-formal sources. Of the total farmer households, 66% are the marginal farmer households. Only 45% of the marginal farmer households had access to formal or informal sources of credit. Among the non-cultivator households nearly 80% do not have access to credit from any sources. Only 36% of ST and 51% of SC and OBC farmer households are indebted mostly to informal sources. Owing to the region-wise NSSO data, it is evident that financial exclusion is most acute in Central, Eastern and North Eastern region. There was 64% of all financially excluded farmer households' concentration in these regions. Overall indebtedness to formal sources of finance alone is only 19.66% in these three regions (4.09% for North Eastern region, 18.74% for Eastern region and 22.45% for Central region). Analysis of the data provided by the Basic Statistical Returns (BRS) of scheduled commercial banks reveals that critical exclusion in terms of credit manifest in 256 districts, spread across seventeen states and one union territory with a credit gap of 95% and above. This is in respect of commercial banks and RRBs. Credit coverage by cooperatives is also on a relatively low level as nearly 62% of its members are non-borrowing members (Kapoor, 2011).

Former financial institutions were scared of providing rural credit due to their pre-conception that serving the rural poor is both costly and risky. This is primarily because of scattered nature of agricultural borrowers with the demand for credit in low volume. The expenditure on credit per transaction is remaining same, whatever the loan size. Expenditure on transaction on a large amount of loan is therefore relatively low compared to the small size loans. ICICI Bank in a study has shown that for a loan size of Rs. 25000/- the transaction cost comes to 8.62% for a bank, whereas for a loan of Rs. 10000/- it becomes 21.56% (Kapoor, 2011). The borrowers also involve transaction cost in terms of loss of valuable time, travel cost and other non-interest costs in getting and repaying loans. Providers may have the risks in the form of loan default, price risk due to unexpected change in interest rate and risk due to information asymmetries because the borrowers have more information about their project than do the lenders. Finally, the financial system developed in India is naive in serving financially the rural poor. India's policy has been largely supply and target driven. Emphasis has been given to credit rather than financial services. Credit largely directed for priority sector lending. Significant government subsidies have been channeled through the financial intermediaries. Rural finance was taken with a perspective of social obligation but not potential business opportunity. Further the formal financial sector failed to recognize the mismatch between the hierarchy of credit needs and credit availability, resulting in adverse usage of credit.

The conventional way of serving the poor by providing cheap credit therefore had come to an end with failure. Microfinance particularly the group based microfinance activity in this situation has emerged out as one of the solutions in serving the poor. Solidarity group approach inculcates the saving habits of the poor and thereby it is possible to mobilize rural savings. In microfinance lending collaterals are almost not required. However collective liability of the group can be considered as one kind of social collaterals. Microfinance activity also helps to reduce the transaction cost of the financial institutions. If the group members are properly trained they can maintain transaction records of the group and can communicate with the bank. Group members also have not maintained complex procedure involved in getting loans. Besides maintaining thrift fund and rotating loans, microfinance program also provides various kind of financial and non-financial services such as insurance, remittance, guidance, skill development training and motivation to start income generating activities. Thus microfinance program has emerged as a powerful instrument in reducing vulnerability of the poor. Poor women are greatly benefited as the program helps them to get economic confidence as well as their socio-economic development and empowerment.

REVIEW OF RELEVANT LITERATURE

Before going to analyze the impact of Self Help Group (SHG) membership on the income and income inequality of the rural women in the district of Birbhum in West Bengal, let us discuss the relevant and novel literatures on the issue of microfinance and its impact.

Hossain (1988) in his paper compared Grameen Bank members with the eligible non-participants in Grameen villages and with non-participants in non-Grameen Bank villages. The objective of the study is to assess the impact of credit provided by the Grameen Bank on poverty alleviation in rural Bangladesh. Hossain (1988) found that poverty rate is higher among the non-participants compared to that of Grameen Bank members. There was 61 percent moderately poor among the Grameen Bank members whereas there were 83.7 percent and 80.4 percent of moderately poor among the eligible non-participants and non-participants in comparison villages. 48 percent of Grameen Bank members were extremely poor but 76 percent of eligible non-participants in Grameen villages and 74.4 percent of non-participants in comparison villages were extremely poor. However, Hossain (1988) reported that impact assessment would be likely overstated as Grameen Bank members were younger and better educated while non-members more likely to be landless. Average household income of Grameen Bank members are 43 percent higher than that of non-participants in comparison villages and 28 percent higher than the eligible non-participants in Grameen villages. Grameen Bank members spent 8 percent more per capita on food and 13 percent more on clothing than the non-members in comparison villages. Grameen Bank members spent six times more on housing investment than the non-participants in comparison villages and three times more than the non-participants in Grameen villages.

Pitt and Khandker (1998) measured the impact of micro-credit on labour supply, schooling of children, household expenditure and assets on both male and female borrowers in Bangladesh. The study is based on quasi-experimental survey design. The reason is to correct biasedness from unobserved individual and village level heterogeneity. The chapter is pioneer in the assessment of microfinance impact on its borrowers all over the world. The study was based on the data collected by the World Bank and Bangladesh Institute of Development Studies (BIDS). Survey was conducted in 1991-92. Total 1798 households were surveyed who are either the members of Grameen Bank, BRAC or RD-12, a program of Bangladesh Rural Development Board and non-member households from comparison villages. Needless to say that it is very difficult to select the non-members from comparison villages and at the same time it is not possible to guess correctly whether the non-members are in better off position or not than the program participants. The authors (Pitt & Khandker, 1998) therefore modeled the demand for credits on various variables like education, land holding etc. to improve upon the standard comparison group. Pitt and Khandker (1998) chose the people from the comparison villages who would have joined the program if they are offered membership or the persons who are statistically more likely to have participated if given the choice. Pitt and Khandker (1998) employed very complicated model called "weighted exogenous sampling maximum likelihood-limited information maximum likelihood-fixed effects." Since Pitt and Khandker (1998) had cross sectional data, they used instrumental variables regression to increase the accuracy of the estimates. The Grameen Bank, BARC and RD-12 had a common feature that they generally target the households who had less than one acre of land. Therefore, participation in program to some extent is exogenously determined. It allowed Pitt and Khandker (1998) to correct selection bias problem and triangulate data.

Pitt and Khandker (1998) found that credit has greater impact on poor woman than a male borrower. Credit leads a woman to increase her household consumption expenditure to eighteen percent whereas for a male borrower the increment is only eleven percent. It is found that women borrowers have significant impact on the outcome variables namely labour supply, schooling of children, household expenditure whereas male borrowers have significant impact only on labour supply and schooling of boys. There was equality of men's and women's credit effects in only two cases, women's labour supply and women's non-land assets. Pitt and Khandker (1998) have shown that one percent increase in credit to Grameen Bank women has increased the probability of girls schooling enrolment by 1.86 percent. A ten percent increase in credit to women increased the arm circumference of girls by six percent. A one percent increase in credit to a woman increased the height-for-age of both boys by 1.42 percent and girls by 1.16 percent.

The chapter was severely criticized by Morduch and he responded with a paper "Does Microfinance Really Help the Poor? New Evidence from Flagship Programs in Bangladesh" (1998). Morduch (1998) revealed the fact to the readers that actually 20 to 30 percent of program participants had the land more than half an acre. It is therefore inappropriate to compare those with less than half acre to those with more than half acre of land as this rule was strictly enforced for comparison group. Morduch (1998) criticized that method to correct selection bias actually exacerbates the bias. Morduch (1998) used rather simpler model and showed that the impact was not as larger as shown by them. But Morduch (1998) agreed that program participation had improved the households' consumption level. Morduch (1998) showed that access to credit reduced the variability of consumption by 47 percent for eligible Grameen Bank households, 54 percent for eligible BRAC households and 51 percent for eligible BRDB households.

Coleman (1999), an economist of Asian Development Bank examined the impact of microfinance in northeast Thailand in a different way. Activity of two microfinance institutes Rural Friends Association and the Foundation for Integrated Agricultural Management was considered for the study. Coleman (1999) used different method to avoid sample selection bias problem. Coleman (1999) selected only those people in comparison villages who were in the waiting list of the village banks for loan. In other words, these are the people who had same "entrepreneurial spirit" but not yet offered loan. Coleman (1999) was able to compare the results what would have been without correction naively and estimates after correction. Coleman (1999) found that in the absence of corrections credit had positive impact especially on women's land holdings but with correction it was astonishingly found that credit had no impact on savings, physical assets, sales and school expenditure. The effect of households' medical expenditure is negative. The borrowing from village money lenders by the female borrowers also increases probably in order to repay the debt of village banks. The reason for weak impact is that richer individuals opted for self-selection in village banks and relatively small size of loans might be used for consumption purpose.

Chen and Donald (2001) conducted their study among the clients of SEWA Bank of Gujarat. Chen and Donald (2001) compared among the clients who borrow from the bank for self-employment, the clients who saved with the bank but did not borrow and non-clients who were chosen randomly where the bank was based. The study was conducted for the periods 1997 and 1999. Chen and Donald (2001) therefore compared credit-led and saving-led approach which rarely can be seen in literatures. The impact described in Chen and Donald (2001) has been briefed as follows

In round one it was seen that borrowers were in better position than savers who in turn were in better position than non-members. In the second round of impact assessment the borrowers were observed in better off position than savers and non-members. Borrowers' income remained 25 percent higher than that of savers and 56 percent higher than that of the non-members. Savers' income was 24 percent higher than that of non-members. But the annual growth rate of income of savers was higher in contrast to that of the borrowers and non-members. Poverty rate of borrowers in both the rounds were lower than the poverty rate of both the comparison groups; but there was reduction in poverty of both the savers and non-members. On the contrary, there was 1.9 percent increase in the poverty among the borrowers. It reflects greater variability in borrowers' income. From the study it is observed that repeated borrowing matters compared to single borrowing. Repeated borrowers had greater impact on food expenditure, consumer durables and household improvements and more likely on girls' enrolment in primary education.

Todd (2001) evaluated the impact of SHARE microfinance limited on its clients in the state of Andhra Pradesh of India. She compared among the 125 SHARE members who participated in the program for at least three years and 104 new clients who had not yet received any exposure to the program. Todd (2001) created a poverty index which comprises four indicators: source of income, productive assets, housing quality and household dependency burden. She measured the housing quality by constructing SML house index which was adapted by SHARE from CASHPOR house index. As SHARE keeps records of each incoming member regarding their occupation, assets etc., it helped Todd (2001) to observe the extent to which clients have moved out of poverty. The result shows that 76.8 percent of total clients experienced a reduction in poverty and 38.4 percent of total clients had shifted from very poor to moderate poor category. It was observed that 17.6 percent clients had shifted from very poor to non-poor category and 20.8 percent clients had shifted from moderately poor to non-poor category. Further, 21.6 percent of clients reported that they feel no change of their poverty situation. There are other broader aspects of the study also. Mature clients were more likely to send their sick family members in health centre compared to that of new clients. However, the effect of microfinance on the children education was not found very impressive. It was noted that 61 percent of boys from mature client families had completed their class appropriate for their age where as 49 percent from new client families had completed their class appropriate for their age and 37 percent of girls had completed school for their age grade and nearly half of girls had no schooling at all. There was no relation found between poverty status and school attendance for boys but the same relationship for girls is negative. Poor clients were more likely to send their girls to school.

Shirazi (2002) analyze the impact of micro credit on poverty alleviation in Pakistan. The study used secondary data and employs the difference of the difference approach to measure the net effect of microfinance on poverty. Shirazi (2002) found that impact of microfinance on poverty is marginal. The net effect of microfinance on household durables for poor non-borrowers is marginal while for poor borrower it is positive. Poor borrowers primarily borrow to meet their consumption need. The expenditure on familial and social matter was found to be very small.

Anand (2004), in her article seeks to explore the performance of selected SHGs and its impact on poverty alleviation. The study first tries to identify the factors which led to the successful functioning and sustainability of SHGs, second to assess the superiority of this participatory approach over the earlier poverty eradication strategies and finally to explore the impact of SHGs on poverty eradication and on women empowerment. The study was conducted in Malappuram district of Kerala, one of the poorest and educationally backward and densely populated districts with women outnumbering men of the state.

The study reveals that participation of women in SHGs make a change in their living standards "through regular savings, improved level of family earnings, expanded assets, better socio-political access thereby reducing vulnerability and poverty contributing to a wide range of development goals (Anand, 2004)." Their participation also helps them to change their social outlook and attitudes. Women SHG members have been able to overcome the feeling of low esteem and lack of confidence. At the same time, the study pointed to the illiteracy or low level of education, ignorance, adherence to the traditional values etc. which reduce the pace of development of women. So the study laid emphasis on informal education, and organizing programs for women to make them aware and to enhance their skill through the government and non-governmental agencies. The study also pointed to the threat of involvement of political and communal elements which now entered in SHGs activities. Because of vast potential of SHGs in mobilizing people, political parties and communal organizations "have been encouraging its members to penetrate into SHGs with parochial agenda hereby creating dangerous trend in the field." These may create serious repercussions in the long run which hinder the pace of SHGs role in alleviating poverty and women empowerment.

Kabeer and Noponen (2004) investigated the impact of a leading NGO and Microfinance Institution of India-PRADAN's SHG micro-finance and livelihood promotion program on the social and economic position of their members. PRADAN is a large rural livelihood development NGO in India. The study is conducted in three districts of Jharkhand, namely, Dumka, Godda and Banka. The study tried to explore the impact of membership on their capacity to meet basic needs, livelihood base, asset position, savings and debt position, women's voice and agency. Two comparisons are being made in this study. It compares between members and non–members of PRADAN and between PRADAN SHG members and SHG members who simultaneously participate in income generating program. This particular NGO generally started their poverty alleviation program from the poorest person of the poverty stricken areas. It is therefore possible that the new members may be economically in better off position than the old one. The comparison between old and new would have produced no or negative result. The researchers therefore compared members of more than three years against non-members. Greater care was taken in sampling non-members. The samples were collected from an area where PRADAN just started their program. A wealth index was constructed to choose the poor non-members. From this study it can be seen that PRADAN membership had a significant impact in reducing the level of overall poverty. However, the study also pointed to the very little basic need satisfaction of the people in the surveyed area. PRADAN members experienced less shortage of foods than the non-members. Their per week consumption of nutritious food were higher than that of the non-members. They had more favourable food situation in terms of adequacy and diversity of food, better access to safe drinking water and improved housing. Children attendance in schools and gender equity in school attendance were found in favour of PRADAN members. Due to interventions of PRADAN they had "more land and livestock asset more diversified cropping patterns, higher value of crops, more harvest and better agricultural practices" (Kabeeret al. 2004). The indebtedness of the members to the money lenders had been reduced. The impact of the program on the women skill and agency shows mixed results. However, the researchers had doubt about the endogeneity of program participation. It according to them may be possible that empowered women opt to participate in the income generation program. Kabeer and Noponen (2004) suggested a panel data study of the surveyed persons.

Khandker later in his paper "Micro-finance and poverty: Evidence Using Panel Data from Bangladesh" published in 2005 acknowledged the sensitiveness of the instruments used in their previous study. He used the panel data collected by the World Bank and BIDS in1998-99 and measured the impact of microfinance over the period from 1991-92. So he basically used the data with two or more time periods. Now he employed simpler model with few assumptions to evaluate the impact of microfinance. As per Goldberg (2005) this is the most reliable attempt to evaluate the impact of microfinance till date. Khandker (2005) found that each additional 100 taka of loan to a woman increased total amount of her household expenditures by more than 20 takas. There were 11.3-taka increase in food expenditure and 9.2-taka increase in non-food expenditure. This impact is greater than his previous study. Khandker (2005) found that there was diminishing return of borrowing over time. Actually earlier loans had the greater impact than the current loans. Of 20-taka increase in consumption expenditure from each 100 taka of loan, 4.2 taka was from current borrowing and 16.3 taka was from past borrowing that is during the year of 1991-92. Pitt and Khandker in their previous study in 1998 found that impact of credit on women borrowers was higher than that on men borrowers; but here they did not find any returns to men borrowers. Khandker (2005) found that there was reduction in overall moderate poverty by 17 percent. The reduction in poverty to the extent of 18 percent and 13 percent respectively can be seen in program area and non-program area. Among the program participants there was 20 percent decline in the poverty over the period from 1991-92 to 1998-99 and the annual declining rate is about 3 percent per year. The impact of microfinance is higher for extreme poverty than moderate one. There was a 2.23 percent reduction of extreme poverty per year whereas only 1.6 percent decline per year for moderate poverty.

Thakur and Tiwari (2005) opined that the impact of SHGs on rural poverty eradication and long term sustainability is limited. The reason they provided lies in the lack of proper understanding of the potential of SHG in removing poverty and implementing this strategy as minimalist approach. All these restricted SHGs to promote micro enterprise. Thakur and Tiwari (2005) also argued that some factors are important for long term sustainability and these factors are: (i) establishing proper process of SHG, (ii) financial viability, (iii) involvement in community based activities, (iv) convergence of other schemes saturation of SHGs and (v) there should be critical mass of SHG. Thakur and Tiwari (2005) conducted study in Patan district of Gujarat and found that none of the programs follows the said factors mentioned above.

Nirmala (2006) shows that human capabilities development in terms of education, experience, training and skill development have influence on the return of SHG credit. Considering the income of the SHG members, her findings show that average income in the pre-SHG situation was Rs. 17580.77. Average income in the post-SHG situation was Rs. 22850.70/- which is significantly higher than that in pre-SHG situation. But the increase in income fail to raise them above the poverty line minimum Rs 24000/- per annum stipulated by DRDR. It was found that 58 percent of respondents were engaged in non-farm activities but these activities were basically petty business type and therefore less remunerative. However, SHG participation increases the number of working days of the members. Days of employment per annum (281.73) in post-SHG situation are significantly higher than that in the pre-SHG situation (158). Productivity of credit was 70.63 percent. SHG participation increases the involvement of members in social services and organized action. Participation helps in gaining better social status and decision making position. Nirmala (2006) has pointed out that the wrong timing of the credit delivery, low rate of profit, and competition from mechanized products, marketing problems are some serious issues hindering the productive efficiency of SHG credit.

Asian Development Bank (ADB) in 2007 published a paper where the impact of its microfinance operation in three countries e.g. Bangladesh, Philippines and Uzbekistan has been examined. The objective of the study was to explore the extent to which ADB microfinance project is able to reduce the poverty of rural poor households. The study also investigated the impact on socio-economic status of the women in the said countries. Five projects e.g. Rural Microenterprise Finance Project in Philippines, Participatory

Livestock Development Project in Bangladesh, Second Participatory Livestock Development Project in Bangladesh, Rural Livelihood Project in Bangladesh and Small and Microfinance Development Project in Uzbekistan were selected for in-depth review.

Rural Microenterprise Finance Project in Philippines used quantitative tools to explore the impact of microfinance. Surveyors of the Project surveyed 2274 households from 116 villages and 28 microfinance institutions. Comparatively smaller samples were collected by the ongoing projects in the rest of the two countries. Bangladesh and Uzbekistan relied on the qualitative data to measure the socio-economic impact. The study compared households that receive micro-credit loans to the household that did not receive any loans but eligible to join the program.

The finding of the study shows that in Philippines access to credit had positive and mildly significant impact on the per capita income of the clients. Access to credit had also mild positive impact on per capita total expenditure and per capita food expenditure. However, the impact on per capita income and expenditure was found to be regressive. As shown in the study that impact was negative for the households having per capita income less than 34428 Peso and become positive only for the households with per capita income greater than 56200 Peso. Low income group people both in Bangladesh and Uzbekistan tended to be in better off position than the poor. It has suggested that targeting microfinance to the poorest households may not be appropriate in alleviating their poverty. Loans to the poorest were not able to generate sufficient profit to increase households' income. The dependence of the borrowers on local money lenders has been reduced. Significant impact found has been on the micro enterprises and the workers employed in there. It reflects that the program was designed to cater to the entrepreneurs' needs.

Swain and Floro (2008) in their paper have shown the effect of microfinance on the vulnerability of the rural poor. The study was based on panel data for the year 2000 and 2003 with 1025 rural household samples from ten representative districts, two each in five states used for the study. To avoid the selection bias non-SHG members were selected from non-SHG villages which were similar with the SHG villages in terms of economic, social, cultural and political condition and infrastructural facilities. As per Swain and Floro (2008) when an individual has the ability to deal with risks, shocks and proneness to food security and hence there is change in attitude towards undertaking risks, his vulnerability reduces. Three identified attributes e.g. 1) income-based poverty, 2) aggregate risks (drought, flood, market fluctuation etc.) and 3) idiosyncratic risks (severe illness, death etc.) and unexplained risks (due to variation in unobserved characteristics as well as measurement errors) were attributed to the vulnerability of the poor. Swain and Floro (2008) found that vulnerability in terms of welfare loss is lower for the SHG members compared to that for non-SHG members. SHG households have the 17 percent probability to have variation in their food consumption while the non-SHG members have the 22 percent probability. The finding shows that poverty is the largest source of vulnerability. Non-SHG households have the higher level of vulnerability due to poverty than the SHG members. It reflects that microfinance has the impact in reducing vulnerability via greater access to credit, productive training and employability etc. It has been found that the higher level of education has the significant impact in reducing vulnerability. Educated family has the higher expected income and higher possibility to deal with all kind of risks. Landholding of the respondents has no significant impact in reducing vulnerability as very small piece of land is used for subsistence purpose. Finally, respondents from southern part of India e.g. Andhra Pradesh, Tamil Nadu are more likely to come up with the risks than the other backward states like Orissa.

Adhikary (2010) conducted a study in Burdwan district of West Bengal to find the impact of SHG membership on the economic conditions of the rural poor in the said district. The study first attempted to see whether the membership in SHGs provide them an easy access to formal credit and whether SHG membership reduces their cost of borrowing compared to other sources of loans. It found that the assumptions he made earlier is true; that is, membership in SHG increase their accessibility to the formal credit and it also reduces their cost of borrowing. From these results it was concluded that "if the membership of SHG accelerates the accessibility to formal credit and reduces the cost of borrowing, it is natural to believe that the poor people should aspire after the membership of SHG." In other words, the study established the logic behind getting SHG membership. The author was very much concerned about the selection of bias problem. It might be possible that getting SHG membership was influenced by some other unmeasured attributes of the persons; it might also be possible that persons who belonged to the better off position joined the SHG to manage loans by using their influences in soft terms and conditions. To avoid this type of problem, the study conducted endogeneity test of the variable SHG membership status. In order to test the endogeneity it computed the predicted SHG membership status of the respondents. It is nothing but the probability of a person to join SHG. A logistic regression was also run to explore the factors responsible for SHG membership. From the test of endogeneity it has been found that the predicted SHG membership status is insignificant. Finally, the impact of SHG membership on the economic condition in terms of change in monthly expenditure on food and nutrition, fuel and energy, health care and education were measured. Data on the said monthly consumption expenditures for the three consecutive years were taken to feel the change. It has been found that the changes in all the items of monthly expenditures are significant at one percent level of significance. The results clearly show that SHG member households have been able to increase their average monthly expenditures on food and nutrition, fuel and energy, health care and education. In other words, SHG improves the economic condition of the rural poor of Burdwan.

Dhanya and Shivkumar (2010) have investigated the impact of microfinance on participants' economic empowerment in Kerala. Three Kudumbsree units in Thiruvananthapuram district were considered to conduct the survey. Dhanya and Shivkumar (2010) found that the level of income of the participants' family increases with respect to their pre-SHG situation but the contribution of the participants in their family was only marginal. The study considered only the impact on income ignoring other aspect of economic empowerment.

Appiah (2011) in Ghana found that micro finance activities to some extent helped women to improve their economic situation. They now have better standard of living condition. However high rate of interests, inflexible repayment schedule, lack of awareness act as obstacles for getting benefit from micro finance. Amutha (2011) in Tutikorin district found that main reasons to join SHGs by women is to supplement their family income, improve their standard, standard of living and provide better health and education to their children. SHGs help them to inculcate their saving habit. They now enjoy greater decision making power in their family and more recognition in society. Capacity building programs help them to improve their professional and entrepreneurial skill.

Dhabamani (2011) has focused on the financial activities of the women SHG members in the Sattur district of Karnataka. He found that the level of income and savings of the members increases with respect to their pre-SHG situation. They now have got significantly higher amount of loan from both the internal and revolving fund. They mainly demand for loans to spend for their children's education followed by investing in their business. Bhuiya et al. (2015) investigated the impact of microfinance on household income and consumption in Bangladesh. They compared client households of the microfinance program with non-clients of similar characteristics. The quasi experimental design of the survey helps to mitigate the self-selection issue of ongoing microfinance program; but still there would be some unobserved heterogeneity in the treatment variable. So the study used village fixed effect estimators.

Hausman test helped them to prefer fixed effect estimator in spite of its limitation. The finding of the study shows that clients of microfinance program tended to be poorer than the non-clients. It reflects that microfinance institutions gave priority to serve the poor. Another finding is that one percent increase in duration of membership helped the participants to increase their income by 0.19 percent and consumption by 0.16 percent and reduced the probability of being poor by 7 percent. The highly significant impact on consumption indicates that loans could be used for consumption purposes rather than investment in productive capacity. Man headed households were more likely to have higher level of income than the women headed households. Shocks like adverse environmental situation, illness, death etc. increase the vulnerability of the poor significantly.

Going through various literatures it can be seen that microfinance affects the economic condition of its clients though the impacts are not always enough to reduce the vulnerability of the rural poor. Further there is dearth of research papers on whether the credit programs are able to reduce the inequality in their income distribution or not.

OBJECTIVE OF THE CHAPTER

The first objective of the study is to explore the impact of SHG membership on their income along with some socio-economic and demographic characteristics of Birbhum District in West Bengal in India. We divide all the socio-economic and demographic characteristics into two broad categories that are individual/household characteristics and community characteristics. The individual/household characteristics include SHG membership status, duration of membership, age, level of education, employment, access to formal credit, training, social status and agricultural holding. The community characteristics include religion and caste status of the respondents.

The second objective is to investigate the income distribution pattern of the respondents. If it is found that due to participation in SHGs income of the respondents' increases, we further investigate whether the participation helps them to reduce inequality in their income over time and with respect to non-SHG members.

METHODOLOGY

Four stages stratified mixed sampling procedure has been adopted for the purpose of this chapter. The study has been carried out in the district of Birbhum in West Bengal. It is one of the backward districts in the state as well as the country; that is why, it receives grant from GRGF. The district is urbanized to a very little extent. According to census data 2011, 91.2 percent people live in rural areas. 49.09 percent of total population is below the poverty line (P&RD, 2005) and 75 percent of the working population is engaged in agricultural and farming activities. The lives of women in the district are extremely vulnerable. Their literacy rate is lower than that that of the male. The workforce participation of male is 57.5 percent that of female is 17.64 percent. In rural areas women's workforce participation rate is 20.07 percent whereas it is only 2.19 percent in urban areas. Number of women cultivators in the district decreases over time and that of female agricultural labourers increases during the same time. This clearly indicates that women are forced to participate in the low quality work due to their economic obligation.

Against this background the district has the immense possibility in improving in the quality of life of the rural poor by using SHG participation as a tool of improvement. A large number of SHGs in the district is operating in the rural areas. So, there is a scope to explore how the SHG system improves the quality of lives of the women in terms of their economic condition and empowerment.

There are 19 blocks in the district. These are Murari-I, Murari-II, Nalhati-I, Nalhati-II, Rampurhat-I, Rampurhat-II, Mayureswar-I, Mayureswar-II, Md. Bazar, Sainthia, Suri-I, Suri-II, Rajnagar, Dubrajpur, Khayrasole, Ilambazar, Bolpur, Labpur, and Nanur. From these 19 blocks two blocks namely Rajnagar and Suri-I have been selected purposively for the study. Since there is no heterogeneity in the population distribution of the said blocks, we have selected randomly four grampanchayats from each of the blocks. The selected grampanchayats from the Rajnagar block are Tantipara, Joypur, Chandrapur and Madhaipur and from Suri-I are Nagari, Chora, Karidhya and Patadanga. The survey was conducted in the month of January and February of 2016. For the survey a structured questionnaire was prepared. Four hundred women were interviewed. Among them 53.1 percent are SHG members and remaining are non-SHG members. To explore the impact of SHG membership, we have used multiple linear regression and Gini Coefficient and Lorenz curve technique. Statistical software Eviews has been used to estimate coefficients of linear regression equation and MS-Excel for calculation of Gini coefficients.

As mentioned in the previous section, in order to examine the impact of SHG membership status on earning of the rural women of Birbhum district, the following Model has been proposed.

Model: Linear Regression Model for Earning

ERNG=f (SHG membership status, individual/household characteristics, community characteristics, random disturbance term)

The specified model is:

$$ERNG = \alpha + \beta_1 SHGMS + \beta_2 DURSHGM + \beta_3 AGE + \beta_4 EDULVL + \beta_5 ROCAGRI + \beta_6 ROCNFSE$$
$$+\beta_7 ACTOCRDT + \beta_8 TRNG + \beta_9 AGRILAND + \beta_{10} RELIGN + \beta_{11} SC + \beta_{12} ST + \beta_{13} OBC$$

where the variables are defined as follows.

Earning (*ERNG*): It is monthly income of the respondents measured in terms of money.

SHG membership Status (*SHGMS*): It is a dummy variable such that *SHGMS* = 1, if a woman holds SHG membership and *SHGMS* = 0, if she does not hold membership.

Duration of *SHG* membership (*DURSHGM*): The duration of SHG membership is the period of time a woman acts as a SHG member. It is counted by years.

Age (*AGE*): Age is simply physical age of a woman counted by years.

Level of Education (*EDULVL*): It is the formal education that a woman acquires by attending school, college and university etc. It is generally counted by years a woman involved in formal education. Here we have considered as an ordered variable. *EDULVL*=0, if a woman is illiterate; *EDULVL*=1, if she has only primary level of education; *EDULVL*=2, if she has completed upper primary level; *EDULVL*=3, if she has completed the secondary level of education; and *EDULVL*=4, if she has completed the Higher Secondary level of education.

Occupational Status of the respondents: Occupational status is the economic activity in which women under study are involved to earn their livelihood. To segregate the impact of different occupation, woman is divided into four categories; namely, agricultural activities, nonfarm self-employment (e.g. handicraft and artisan, poultry farming, petty business, livestock rearing and fattening, fishery, nursery, bee-keeping, tailoring and weaving etc.) and wage employment (e.g. daily labor, maid serving, rice husking). These variables are taken as the categorical variables indicating whether a woman belongs to a specific occupation. Specifically, *ROCAGRI* = 1, if a woman is involved in agricultural activities and 0 otherwise. *ROCNFSE* = 1, if a woman is involved nonfarm self-employment and 0 otherwise.

Training (*TRNG*): Training enhances the quality/efficiency of a person to increase productivity leading to increase in income. *TRNG* = 1, if a woman has training which helps in enhancement of her productive skill and 0 otherwise.

Accessibility to Formal Credit (*ACTOCRDT*): It is a dummy variable such that *ACTOCRDT* = 1, if a woman has access to formal credit and 0, otherwise.

Religion (*RELIGN*): *RELIGN* = 1, if a woman belongs to Hindu religion and 0 otherwise.

Caste Status: Caste of a woman in this study has been considered as categorical variable. As per rule of Indian Government we have considered four categories of caste structure which are General Caste (*GEN*), Schedule Caste (*SC*), Schedule Tribe (*ST*) and Other Backward Caste (*OBC*). Thus, *GEN* =1, if a woman belongs to general caste category and 0 otherwise; *SC* = 1, if a woman belongs to *SC* category and 0 otherwise.*ST* = 1, if a woman belongs to *ST* category and 0 otherwise.*OBC* = 1, if a woman belongs to *OBC* category and 0 otherwise.

RESULTS AND DISCUSSION

We have divided all the socio-economic and demographic data into two groups as quantitative data and qualitative data. Table 1 depicts descriptive statistics of the quantitative variables and table 2 depicts percentage distribution of the Categorical variables. From the table 1 it can be seen earning of the respondents ranges from zero to four thousand. Average earning of the respondents is eighteen hundred rupees. The SHG members under study have at least two years of participations where as there are some members who have association with the SHG for fifteen years. The average participation rate of SHG members is 3.12 years. The age of the respondents ranges from 19 years to 71 years, however the average

Table 1. Descriptive statistics of quantitative variables

	ERNG	DURSHGM	AGE	AGRILAND	ESHGV
Mean	1648.50	3.122195	38.25	1.232	10.6
Median	1800.00	2	38	0	11
Maximum	4000.00	15	71	14	15
Minimum	0	0	19	0	6
Std. Dev.	1030.345	3.98	9.19	2.18	3.27
Skewness	-0.186778	1.05	0.364	2.61	-0.362
Kurtosis	2.004072	2.73	3.09	11.02	1.53
Jarque-Bera	18.90409	74.88	8.97	1529.48	44.8
Prob.	0.000	0.000	0.001	0.000	0.000

Source: Authors' own calculation based on primary data

age of the respondents is 38.25 years. That is most of the women are of middle age. The average land holding of the respondent's household is 1.23 bigha. There are some households who have no agricultural land. The maximum land holding of the respondent's household is fourteen bigha. The sample villages are such that they have the SHG program for at least six years. However, there are some villages where there is existence of such program for more than fifteen years.

Table 2 shows the percentage distribution of the categorical variables. Among the sample women 53.1 percent are SHG members where as 46.9 percent are non-SHG members. It has been found that 76.63 percent of the sample women are engaged in some income generating activities but 23.7 percent of sample women have no any sources of income. Almost 8 percent of total respondents are engaged in agricultural activities. Approximately 21 percent of the respondents are engaged in non-farm self-employment. The wage employee is 45 percent of the sample women. Only 29.7 percent of sample women have the access to formal credit. This implies that still now a considerable portion of women in the surveyed areas do not have access to formal credit. Out of the sample observations collected, 33.4 percent of the respondents are trained; that is, they have possessed productive capacity building training. Only 14.5 percent of sample women have higher social position in terms of leaders or assistant leaders in SHGs. Majority of the women are by religion Hindu. Out of total sample 30.9 percent belong to Schedule Caste, 17.5 percent to Schedule Tribe, 37.4 percent to Other Backward Caste and 8.47 percent to General Caste category. It is to be noted that we include all the Muslim women under OBC category.

Table 3 depicts the results of the test of sample proportion of categorical variables. The value of Z statistic for the difference of the sample proportion in the population under the group of SHG members and non-SHG members is 1.24 which is smaller than the critical value 1.96 obtained from the standard normal distribution table at 5 percent level of significance. It can therefore be confirmed that there is no bias in the selection of sample from both the groups. However, the sample proportion of employed and not employed, trained and not trained, possessing social position and not possessing, Hindu and non-Hindu, General and not General, SC and non-SC, ST and non ST and OBC and non OBC in the surveyed areas differ significantly.

Table 2. Percentage distribution of categorical variables

Categorical Variables	% of Sample Observations Having Values		
	0 (=No)	1 (Yes)	Total
SHG membership Status (SHGMS) (1=Yes)	46.9	53.1	100
Employment (EMPL) (1=Yes)	23.7	76.63	100
Access to Credit (ACTCRDT) (1=Yes)	70.3	29.7	100
Training (TRNG) (1=Yes)	66.6	33.4	100
Social Status (SSTS) (1=Yes)	85.5	14.5	100
Religion (RELIGN) (1=Hindu)	8.5	91.5	100
Schedule Caste (SC) (1=SC)	69.1	30.9	100
Schedule Tribe (ST) (1=ST)	82.5	17.5	100
Other Backward Caste (OBC) (1=OBC)	62.6	37.4	100

Source: Authors' own calculation based on primary data

Table 3. Test of sample proportion of categorical variables

Categorical Variables	Observations	Sample Proportion	Empirical Value of Test Statistics
SHG membership Status (SHGMS) (1=Yes)	0	0.469	1.24
	1	0.531	
Employment (EMPL) (1=Yes)	0	0.237	10.52*
	1	0.766	
Access to Credit (ACTCRDT) (1=Yes)	0	0.703	8.12*
	1	0.297	
Training (TRNG) (1=Yes)	0	0.666	-6.63*
	1	0.334	
Social Status (SSTS) (1=Yes)	0	0.855	-14.21*
	1	0.145	
Religion (RELIGN) (1=Hindu)	0	0.85	16.6*
	1	0.915	
Schedule Caste (SC) (1=SC)	0	0.691	-7.63*
	1	0.309	
Schedule Tribe (ST) (1=ST)	0	0.825	-13.01*
	1	0.175	
Other Backward Caste (OBC) (1=OBC)	0	0.626	5.04*
	1	0.374	

Source: Authors' own calculation based on primary data

EMPIRICAL ESTIMATION OF THE ECONOMETRIC MODEL

The coefficient of the variable SHG membership status is 663.37 and it is statistically significant at 1 percent level. It implies that the SHG members earn more on an average of Rs 663.37/- than the non-SHG members. Participation in SHGs therefore helps women to earn more than others. It is to be noted that any individual has to continue at least six months in order to be eligible for loan. During this phase she has to maintain regular savings in the group. They have to abide by all the rules and regulations of the group. All these help them to develop sound economic habit. It also helps them to build the confidence for access to formal financial institutions. After getting loans they can use it collectively to develop any enterprise of their choice or use the loan individually for production and consumption purposes. The participation therefore results higher level of income for the SHG members.

The coefficient of duration of SHG membership is 43.23 and the result is statistically significant at 1 percent level. It implies that with the increase in the association with the SHGs by one year, the income of the members would increase by Rs. 43.23. That is, the long term participation in SHGs affects the income of the members. Longer association with the SHGs increases the accessibility to formal credit. It helps the borrowers to get larger amount of loans. Longer participation also reduces their dependence on the informal sector for getting loan. It helps them to generate larger amount of saving in their account. They become more experienced in operating the group. She now knows how to continue their economic activity in better way. As a group they grow self-dependent and confident enough to tackle all the odds that come adversely against them.

The coefficient of age is positive. This means that with the increase in age earning of the surveyed women also increases but the result is statistically insignificant. The coefficient of level of education is positive, but the result is statistically insignificant. The majority of sample women, that is, 59.1 percent have only primary level of education, and 13.5 percent are illiterate. Only 6.2 percent and 1.7 percent have passed matriculation and higher secondary respectively. This minimum level of formal education is not sufficient to affect their productive efficiency. Further, they belong to poor and needy families; they had no scope to cultivate their knowledge which they acquire from the formal educational system of the state. So, the impact of their minimum level of education decayed over time.

Women who are engaged in agricultural activities have the income higher than the wage employees. The coefficient of occupation agriculture is 514.8 which is statistically significant at 1 percent. This means that incomes of the women in cultivation are on average Rs. 515 higher than that of the wage earners. Similarly, the women who are engaged in non-farm self-employment have the higher level of income of Rs. 232 on an average than that of the wage earners. The coefficient of nonfarm self-employment is statistically significant at 5 percent level. We, therefore, conclude that women engaged in agriculture have the higher level of income than that of all other employment category.

Table 4. Regression estimates of earning

Dependent Variable: Monthly Income (*ERNG*) Method: Least Squares Sample: 1 401; Included observation: 400				
Variable	**Coefficient**	**Std. Error**	**t-Statistic**	**Prob.**
C	689.04	256.3	2.68	0.007
SHGMS	663.37	123.91	5.35*	0
DURSHGM	43.24	15.06	2.87*	0.004
AGE	2.74	4.46	0.61	0.538
EDULVL	11.45	56.24	0.2	0.838
ROCAGRI	514.8	154.08	3.34*	0.001
ROCNFSE	231.97	107.78	2.15**	0.032
ACTFCRDT	185.97	98.02	1.90***	0.058
TRNG	504.31	108.28	4.66*	0
AGRILAND	35.09	18.53	1.89***	0.059
RELIGN	-16.57	150.92	-0.11	0.913
SC	-118.77	132.33	-0.89	0.37
ST	473.98	154.12	3.08*	0.002
OBC	-90.01	124.82	-0.72	0.471
		Diagnostic Statistics		
Log likelihood: -3217.96				
R-squared: 0.46	Adjusted R-squared: 0.44	F-statistic: 25.48	Prob(F-statistic): 0.000	Durbin-Watson stat:1.938

Source: Authors' own calculation based on primary data; * stands for significant at 1% level; ** at 5% level and *** at 10% level

The coefficient of access to formal credit is positive and statistically significant at 10 percent level which means that the women who have the access to formal credit have higher level of income than the women who have not access to formal credit. The main problem with the rural poor is that they lack the financial resources and unable to get rid of poverty. Access to informal financial sector for the resources lead them to debt trap. Access to formal financial sector through the SHGs help them to get cheap, adequate and timely credit for their purposes of economic and financial activity. The access to formal credit therefore leads them to generate higher level of income.

The impact of training on the earning of the women is statistically significant. The value of the coefficient is 504.3. This implies that the women who have the training earn on an average of Rs. 504/- more than the women who have not any training. These types of training help women to acquire better skill and technical knowledge. Training also helps them to continue their entrepreneurial and/or other activities in a better and much more profitable way.

The coefficient of agricultural land holding of the respondent's households is statistically significant at 10 percent level. This implies that with a one-unit increase in the land holding income of the respondent increases by Rs. 35. The survey areas are adjacent to the Chhotanagpur plateau. The rainfall in these areas is less than the other fertile areas of the state. There are no irrigation facilities here. The agricultural activities heavily depend on the rain water. Therefore, a large section of the farmers in these areas is engaged in production of vegetables, fruits and nursery which help them to generate higher level of income.

The coefficient of religion is negative which implies that women other than Hindu religion earn more than Hindu women, but the result is statistically insignificant. So, we conclude that religion has no significant impact on their earnings.

The coefficient of caste dummy SC is negative. It implies that women who belong to general caste category have the higher level of income; but the result is statistically insignificant. The coefficient of caste dummy ST is positive and it is statistically significant at 5 percent level. It implies that women who belong to ST category have the higher level of income than the women who belong to general caste category. As stated earlier the survey areas are close to the state of Jharkhand, where there are a considerable number of tribal habitats. There are various projects of state as well as centre and NGOs that are functioning in these areas for the upliftment of the tribal people. The impact of these ongoing projects may have reflection on the income of the rural tribal women in the district of Birbhum in West Bengal.

The coefficient of OBC dummy is negative. It implies that the incomes of the OBC women are lower than the general caste category but the result is insignificant.

Income Distribution Prior and Posterior to SHG Membership

Let us now explore the income distribution pattern of the sample women in the two blocks of the district under study. We have used Lorenz curve and Gini coefficient technique to observe the inequality level in the income distribution of the respondents. We have compared the Gini coefficients of incomes among the three groups of women SHG members corresponding to the year 2016 (current year of our data collection), 2015 and 2010. These Gini coefficients have been contrasted with the Gini coefficient of the non-SHG members in the year 2016. This exercise will help us to know among the non-SHG members and SHG members the degree of inequality associated with their income. We, therefore, have considered two hypotheses to check whether there is improvement in the distribution pattern of income in Birbhum.

Hypothesis 1

Income distribution in favour of SHG members is more equal than that of the non-SHG members. That is, SHG members have the smaller degree of inequality associated with their income compared to that of the non-SHG members.

Hypothesis 2

Membership in SHGs helps women members to improve their income distribution position over time. That is, income inequality associated with the income of the SHG members have been reduced compared to income inequality in the previous years.

Refer to the figure 1 as presented above. We have divided the SHG members and non-SHG members into ten income groups – each group having the same income range of Rs 400. The distribution of SHG members corresponding to the years 2016, 2015 and 2010 and that of non-SHG members for the year 2016 have been depicted in figure 1. We observe that the number of non-SHG members is steadily declining over the higher income groups. This implies that women being attracted at the success of SHG movement are now eager to participate in the group. The trend of SHG members in the years 2015 and 2016 over different ranges of income looks closely similar. There is a tendency in the distribution of the SHG members in the year 2015 and 2016 to have small number of respondents for the lower and higher income ranges. This is also true for the SHG members of the year 2010. This actually indicates the success of microfinance program through SHG. That is, loans from microfinance program of SHG brought economic independence to them. Thus, being economically independent through SHG in the district of Birbhum, the women are no longer dependent on the financial help from SHG.

Figure 1. Distribution of female SHG and non-SHG members
Source: Authors own calculation based on primary data collected from the Field Survey 2016

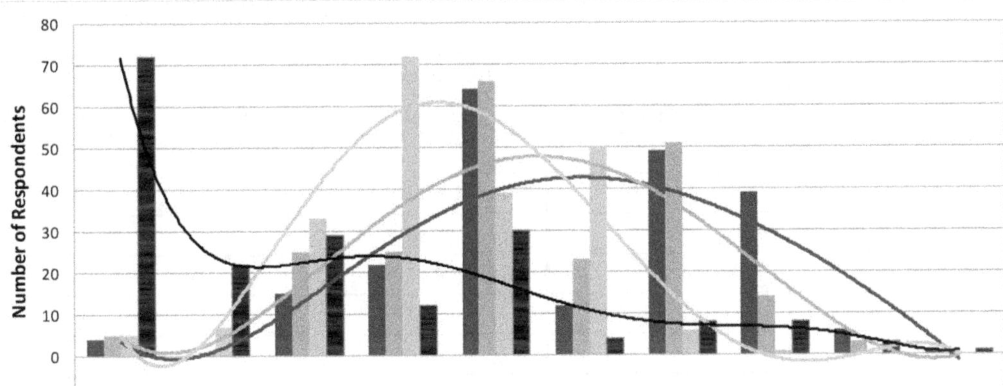

	Below Rs 400	Between Rs 400 and Rs 800	Between Rs 800 and Rs 1200	Between Rs 1200 and Rs 1600	Between Rs 1600 and Rs 2000	Between Rs 2000 and Rs 2400	Between Rs 2400 and Rs 2800	Between Rs 2800 and Rs 3200	Between Rs 3200 and Rs 3600	Between Rs 3600 and Rs 4000
SHG Members_2016	4	0	15	22	64	12	49	39	6	1
SHG Members_2015	5	1	25	25	66	23	51	14	3	0
SHG Members_2010	5	7	33	72	39	50	6	1	0	0
Non-SHG Members_2016	72	22	29	12	30	4	8	8	3	1

Refer to Table 5 which shows the percentage share of income for the SHG members in the year 2016, 2015 and 2010 and that for the non-SHG members in the year 2016. This percentage share of income has been considered for the deciles of income. Bottom ten percent of the SHG members have only 3 percent (but less than 4%) share of income which is slightly higher than their share of income in 2010. Similarly, in the deciles position second, third, fourth, and fifth, SHG members have the higher share of income compared to their previous year (2010) positions. On the contrary SHG members have the smaller share of income in 2016 in the sixth, seventh, eighth and ninth deciles position compared to their previous year (2010) share of income. The situation is reversed in 2010 and 2016 for the SHG members.

Let us now consider the percentage share position of the non-SHG members in the year 2016 in contrast to the percentage share position of the SHG members. In the first two deciles position, the non-SHG members have no share of income. Since a considerable number of non-SHG members are home makers, they have no any regular income. From the decile position third to fifth percentage share of income of the non-SHG members are sufficiently smaller than the respective deciles position of the SHG members. From the sixth decile position percentage share of income of non-SHG members are considerably higher than the respective decile position of the SHG members. The top 10 percent of non-SHG members have the 26.57 percent share of income. It can be seen that top 20 percent of non-SHG members have almost 48 percent share of income. It points to the higher degree of inequality associated in the income share of them.

The Lorenz curve is a graphical line. Its coordinates represent cumulative proportions of income/earning with respect to cumulative proportions of population/respondents. The straight line passing through the origin represents the line of perfect equality which indicates if there is equal income for all the respondents is called the egalitarian line. The curve that indicates actual income distribution of the population is known as Lorenz curve. The gap between line of perfect equality and Lorenz curve represents the degree of inequality in income distribution.

Table 5. Distribution of income

Deciles	Percentage Share of Income			
	SHG Members			Non-SHG Members
	Period (2016)	Period (2015)	Period (2010)	Period (2016)
First	3.01	3.83	2.63	0.00
Second	4.65	6.30	3.51	0.00
Third	7.00	7.86	4.39	0.70
Fourth	8.91	8.77	5.26	3.10
Fifth	8.93	8.27	5.26	5.73
Sixth	11.29	11.07	11.40	11.00
Seventh	11.27	11.04	14.91	14.02
Eighth	12.33	12.52	16.67	17.77
Ninth	13.35	11.67	17.54	21.10
Tenth	19.26	18.67	18.42	26.58

Source: Authors' own calculation based on primary data

Refer to the figure 2 which presents the Lorenz curves for SHG members in the years 2016, 2015 and 2010. The same for the year 2016 of the non-SHG members has also been drawn in figure 2. It is to note that the Lorenz curves for the SHG members are farther from the egalitarian line as we move back from the year 2016. The Lorenz curves for 2015 and 2016 are closely adjacent; but that for the year 2010 is farthest for the SHG members. If we look at the Lorenz curve for the non-SHG members in the year 2016, it takes the position far below the line of perfect equality and also lies below the Lorenz curves for the SHG members. Since with the distance of the Lorenz curves from the egalitarian the degree of inequality increases, it is obvious the income inequality declines due to participation in the SHG and also the degree of inequality varies inversely with the duration of SHG membership. The degree of inequality can be directly assessed from the Gini coefficients.

Gini coefficient is the ratio of area under the Lorenz curve and that under the line of equality. The value of Gini coefficient lies between zero and one. The closer the value of Gini coefficient to one, the more is the degree of inequality in income distribution whereas the value closer to zero indicates more equal distribution.

Figure 3 shows the value of Gini coefficients before and after the membership in self-help group movement. The Gini coefficient of the current year (2016) of the SHG members is 0.3505 which is smaller than the Gini coefficients of income of the previous years 2010 and 2015. The Gini coefficient of non-SHG members is comparatively higher than the coefficients of the SHG members' income. It is as high as 0.7561. The result therefore indicates that the distribution of non-SHG members' income is more unequal than that of the SHG members and there is also improvement in the distributional posi-

Figure 2. Lorenz Curves for SHG and Non_SHG members
Source: Field Survey 2016

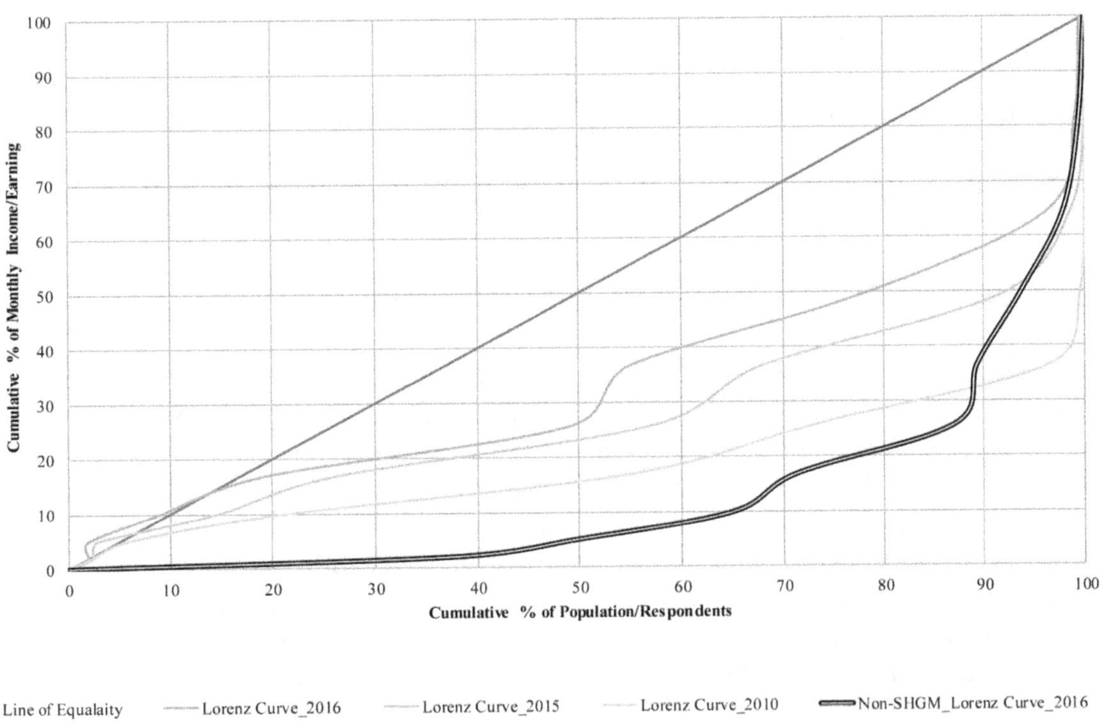

Figure 3. Gini Coefficients over time
Source: Authors own calculation based on primary data collected from Field Survey 2016

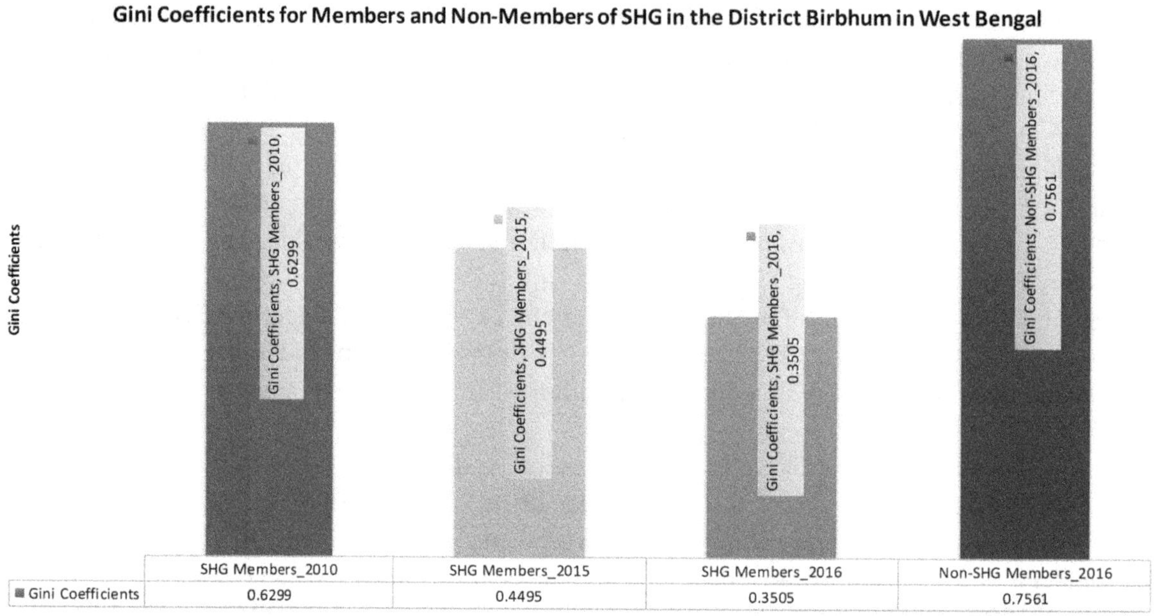

tion of the SHG members compared to their previous year position. The Lorenz Curves in figure 2 also supports the results. Thus, microfinance may be considered as an instrument in reducing the inequality in the distribution of income.

Refer to figure 4 where we have calculated the Gini coefficients for each income group (ten groups) of SHG members of the year 2016, 2015 and 2010 and also of the non-SHG members of the year 2016. We note that for each income group the Gini coefficients of the SHG members are declining over the time. Further, if we compare between the Gini coefficients of the SHG members and that of the non-SHG members, the former is much smaller than that of the latter. Hence, there is no doubt that the microfinance has reduced income inequality amongst women in the district of Birbhum in West Bengal over time.

CONCLUSION AND POLICY RECOMMENDATIONS

This empirical study has measured the impact of SHG membership along with other demographic and socio-economic characteristics on the earning of the women and income distribution pattern of the rural women of Birbhum. The results of the study show that due to participation in SHGs, earnings of the rural women increased. It also helps to reduce the inequality in income distribution of the SHG members. The findings of the study enable us to recommend some suggestions to help the service providers as well as beneficiaries of the SHG microfinance to carry on the microfinance operation in a better way.

Employment, productive training and access to formal credit have the important role in enhancing the earning ability of the individuals. The government, service providers and local administration should take steps toward more employment generation, diversification of employment opportunities in Birbhum.

Figure 4. Gini Coefficients over the income groups and over time
Source: Authors own calculation based on primary data from the Field Survey 2016

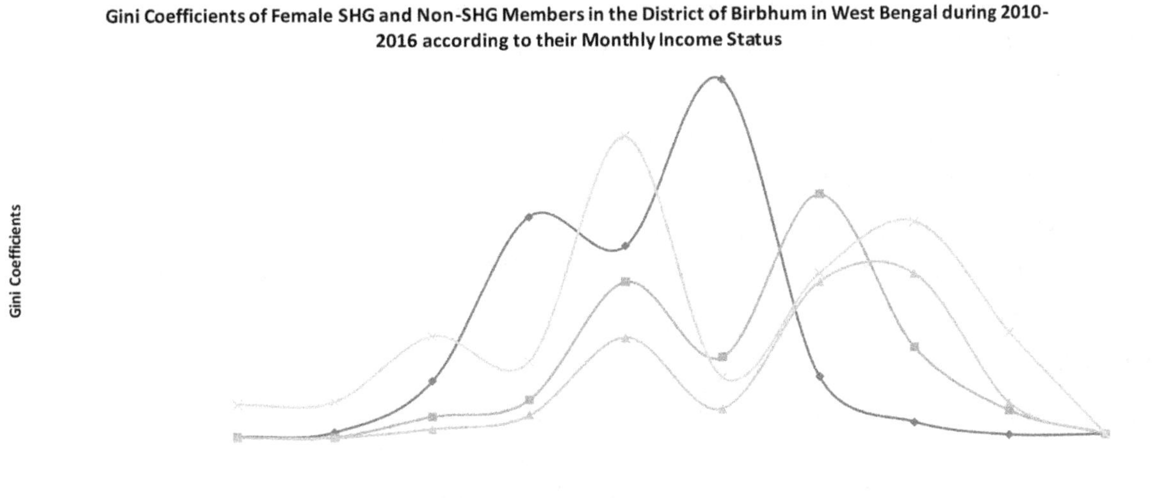

	Below Rs. 400	Between Rs. 400 and Rs. 800	Between Rs. 800 and Rs. 1200	Between Rs. 1200 and Rs. 1600	Between Rs. 1600 and Rs. 2000	Between Rs. 2000 and Rs. 2400	Between Rs. 2400 and Rs. 2800	Between Rs. 2800 and Rs. 3200	Between Rs. 3200 and Rs. 3600	Between Rs. 3600 and Rs. 4000
SHG Members_2010	0.00079	0.00388	0.03916	0.15380	0.13267	0.24921	0.04130	0.00910	0.00000	0.00000
SHG Members_2015	0.00038	0.00027	0.01424	0.02562	0.10774	0.05501	0.16844	0.06112	0.01674	0.00000
SHG Members_2016	0.00020	0.00000	0.00565	0.01491	0.06908	0.01899	0.10700	0.11258	0.02214	0.00000
Non-SHG Members_2016	0.02338	0.02501	0.07064	0.05261	0.20948	0.04092	0.11302	0.14940	0.07161	0.00000

Care should be taken to provide sufficient loans with cheap interest to the SHG members who have the plan to invest the loan amount in some income generating activity in Birbhum.

Capacity building training also helps the beneficiaries in increasing their productive capacity. The local administration and service providers should take care to extend capacity building training to make SHG programs more successful in the district of Birbhum.

SHG based microfinance should be implemented more intensively and extensively in the Birbhum district to avoid the problem of social exclusion of disadvantaged section of the society.

In the study area in the district of Birbhum in West Bengal, it has been found that along with SHG program there are some other microfinance programs like cooperative SHG program, microfinance under NGOs operating simultaneously. These programs maintain an atmosphere of competition which creates some misconception amongst the SHG members. A proper coordination and co-operation not the competition among these schemes need to be navigated in order for the microfinance program through SHG to be cent percent successful.

It has been seen in our study area that the non-farm self-employed persons are in the trap of middle man. So to get rid of them a scheme is needed which helps them in supplying raw materials and purchasing final product at a fair price from them.

Good communication, industrialization, diversification and commercialization of agriculture, which are lacking and lagging in the district of Birbhum in West Bengal, are also urgently needed in generating earning opportunities in the villagers of the district.

REFERENCES

Adhikary, M. L. (2010). *Self-Help Group Movement- An Engine of Rural Development: A Case Study in the District of Burdwan*. Retrieved from www.cdedse.org/ws2010/WS2010_PAPERS/MANIKLAL%20 ADHIKARY.pdf

Anand, J. S. (2004). *Addressing Poverty through Self-Help Groups: A Case Study*. Retrieved from www. img.kerala.gov.in/docs/papers/jsa1.pdf

Asian Development Bank (2007). *Effect of Microfinance Operations on Poor Rural Household and the Status of Women*. ADB, Special Evaluation Study, Sep. 2007, Ref No. SST:REG 2007-19.

Bansal, D. (2011). *Impact of Microfinance on Women Empowerment*. Retrieved from http:/hdl.handle. net/10603/3031

Bhuiya, M. M., Khanam, R., Rahman, M. M., & Nghiem, H. S. (2016). Impact of Microfinance on Household Income and Consumption in Bangladesh: Empirical Evidence from a Quasi-Experimental Survey. *Journal of Developing Areas*, *50*(3), 305–318. doi:10.1353/jda.2016.0111

Bhusal, M. (2010). *Does Microfinance Really Empower? A study on the contribution of microfinance in empowering the poor women of northern Bangladesh*. Retrieved from www.theseus.fi/bitstream/ handle/.../.202010.pdf

Chen, M. A., & Donald, S. (2001). *Managing Resources, Activities, and Risk in Urban India: The Impact of SEWA Bank*. Washington, DC: AIMS.

Coleman, B. (1999). The Impact of Group Lending in Northeast Thailand. *Journal of Development Economics*, *60*(1), 105–142. doi:10.1016/S0304-3878(99)00038-3

Das, S. K. (2012). Socio-Economic Empowerment of Women through SHG-Banking Linkage Programme: A Boon for Development. *International Journal of Management and Business Studies*, *2*(1).

Dhanya, M. B., & Sivakumar, P. (2010). *Women Empowerment and Microfinance: Case Study from Kerala*. Retrieved from http://mpra.ub.uni-muenchen.de/25337/1/MPRA_paper_25337.pdf

Dhavamani, P. (2010). Empowerment of Rural Women through Self Help Groups in Sattur Taluk of Virudhunagar District. *Journal of Bloomers of Research*, *2*(2).

Goldberg, N. (2005). *Measuring the Impact of Microfinance: Taking Stock of What We Know*. Grameen Foundation. Retrieved from www.gfusa.org

Hossain, M. (1988). *Credit for the Alleviation of Rural Poverty: The Grameen Bank in Bangladesh*. Washington, DC: IFPRI, Research Report No. 65 1988.

Kabeer, N., & Noponen, H. (2004). *Social and Economic Impacts of PRADAN's Self-Help Group Microfinance and Livelihoods Promotion Programme: Analysis from Jharkhand, India*. Imp-Act Working Paper No. 11, IDS, Brighton. Retrieved from www.ids.ac.uk/impact/publications/working_papers.html

Kaliranjan, K., & Singh, K. (2012). *Self Help Group-Banking-Poverty Reduction Nexus: A Case Study of Uttrakhand State, India*. ASARC Working Paper, 2012/2.

Kapoor, S. (2011). *Management Development Programme on Microfinance, Reading Material.* IIM Lucknow.

Khandaker, S. R. (2005). Micro-Finance and Poverty: Evidence Using Panel Data from Bangladesh. *The World Bank Economic Review*, *19*(2), 263–286. doi:10.1093/wber/lhi008

Kundu, A. (2009). *Joint versus Individual Liability in Microfinance-A Comparative Impact Evalutation Through Natural Experiment.* Retrieved from http://mpra.ub.uni-muechen.de/32695.pdf

Morduch, J. (1998). *Does Microfinance Really Help the Poor? New Evidence from Flagship Programs in Bangladesh.* Princeton University Working Paper 1998.

NABARD. (1999). *Microfinance Scenario in the country.* NABARD. Retrieved from www.nabard.org

NABARD. (2016). *Status of microfinance in India report 2014-15.* Author.

Pitt, M. M., & Khandker, S. R. (1998). The Impact of Group-Based Credit Programs on Poor Households in Bangladesh: Does the Gender of Participants Matter? *Journal of Political Economy*, *106*(5), 958–996. doi:10.1086/250037

Pitt, M. M., Khandker, S. R., & Cartwright, J. (2003). D*oes Micro-Credit Empower Women? Evidence from Bangladesh.* Policy Research Working Paper 2998, World Bank. Retrieved from http://econ.worldbank.org

Rangarajan, C. (2008). *Report of the Committee on Financial Inclusion.* Retrieved from www.sidbi.in

Sahu, A. B., & Das, S. R. (2006). *Women Empowerment Through Self Help Groups- A Case Study.* Retrieved from www.isical.ac.in

Swain, R. B., & Floro, M. (2015). *Effect of Microfinance on Vulnerability, Poverty and Risk in Low Income Households.* American University.

Todd, H. (2001). *Paths out of Poverty: The Impact of SHARE Microfin Limited in Andhra Pradesh, India.* Unpublished Imp-Act Report 2001.

KEY TERMS AND DEFINITIONS

Financial Inclusion: Financial inclusion can be defined as providing access of various kinds of financial services like savings, credit, payments and insurance etc. to the poor people who are hither to deny by the formal financial sectors. The first step towards the financial inclusion is providing access to a transaction account as it allows rural poor people to save, receive and send money.

Income: In this chapter income of the respondents is considered as the monthly earnings of them measured in terms of money.

Income Inequality: Income inequality arises due to the unequal distribution of income and wealth among the individuals or households. Lorenz Curve and Gini coefficient techniques are generally used to measure inequality in income distribution. These types of techniques measure the degree of inequality associated with the income distribution.

Microfinance: Microfinance is the provision of thrift, credit and other financial provisions like micro insurance. Remittance etc. to the rural poor to improve their living standards.

Rural Women: Rural women in context of this chapter are those women who reside in the Gram Panchayat areas with their families. We consider only those women as respondents who have the Voter Identity card indicating that they are residents of a particular sample village.

SHG: Self-help group or SHG is a group of ten to twenty people preferably belong to same economic strata who are organized either by the NGOs, nationalized banks, microfinance institutions, etc. for the purpose of microfinance.

Women Empowerment: Women empowerment is a psychological concept. It involves various dimensions like economic, social, political legal, inter-personal etc. and various levels like individual, community level etc. It is a continuous process of gaining more decision-making abilities in both within and outside the family.

Chapter 18
Poverty and Inequality of SHG-Member Households:
Evidence From Villages in North Andaman Island

Supravat Bagli
Presidency University, India

Ratan Dey
ICICI Bank – Port Blair, India

ABSTRACT

This chapter explores the penetration of SHGs and assesses socio-economic status and its inequality for the SHG-member households in North Andaman Island in the union territory Andaman and Nicobar Islands of India. The authors have used the Gini coefficients for computing inequalities and log-linear model for estimating the impact of borrowing on food and non-food expenditure. It is revealed that the incidence and intensity of poverty of the sample households is not so serious. Majority of the sample women under SHG schemes actively participate in group activities and have obtained micro credit. Inequality in household income is lower than the inequality in per capita income. Moreover, inequality for health expenditure is higher compared to the inequality in food expenditure. Borrowing through SHGs accelerates non-food expenditures not investment in income generating activities. However, SHGs inculcates empowerment of the participations.

INTRODUCTION

Group centric microfinance has a long history. In the late nineteen century there were many group-centric microfinance institutions in Asia. Credit union and Fisherman group in Indonesia, Totines or Hui in Vietnam, Bishimandal and Nidhis in India, particularly in southern part, were popular group-centric microfinance institutions in that time. The main characteristic of these groups was that members' periodic contribution pooled into one fund which was used to extend loan to the credit worthy member. Because

DOI: 10.4018/978-1-5225-5240-6.ch018

of no or negligible information gap between lender and borrowers there was low or negligible transaction cost for loan. However, these microfinance institutions were absolutely informal in nature and suffered from paucity of fund. These group-based microfinance institutions mainly provided business loan to the members. Actually, these groups were of the small business men. They had no role in poverty alleviation and inculcation of empowerment of the members and non-members in the service area. After penetration of the strong formal banking system these informal groups lost its function. But poor and vulnerable section in India remained outskirt of the banking system due to lack of appropriate banking counselling and collateral to the poor people. Throughout the last century cooperatives in India went in ups and down for accelerating rural development. Early time of the last quarter of the last century it was identified that poor people specially women found very little utility from the strong banking system in India and abroad. Different studies like Jain (1989), Narayanaswamy et al. (2003) have mentioned the limitations of the cooperatives for alleviating poverty in India. To bring up the economic and social conditions of the poor through financial inclusion, the SHG-bank linkage scheme in India has been coined in mid 1980s. The program initially promotes the savings habit of the SHG members and gradually provides loans to the members for income generating purposes or for meeting the emergencies. The SHG model in India, which is our prime interest, is a large model of group-based microfinance launched in 1992, but it is implemented far later in North Andaman Island. The model started under the supervision of NABARD. In this model, 5 to 20 poor people voluntarily form a group under a financial institution or a governmental/ non-governmental agency. After formation, each member of the group starts savings equally per week/month. Promoted agency introduces the group with a formal financial institution and group opens an account and deposits its pooled savings regularly. Usually after six months, the formal financial institution starts lending to the group and subsequently increases the amount depending on its pooled savings. Obtaining the loan the group extends the loan to the members in accordance with its own rules and regulations. In India banks charge 12% interest per year from the group and the group charges an interest rate of 24% to 36% per year from the SHG members (Adhikary & Bagli, 2012,). Most of the beneficiaries of the model are rural poor women. Loans are extended based on the pooled saving and policy of the financial institutions. Repayment schedule of these loan are flexible in between six months to thirty-six months. Theoretically, the participation in SHG is voluntary but in India some governmental or non-government organizations encourage potential poor persons to form group.

LITERATURE REVIEW AND OBJECTIVES

There have been many studies on the working of SHGs conducted in different parts of world including India. In India most of the empirical studies have covered the SHGs working in the States of Orissa, Andhra Pradesh, Maharashtra, Tamil Nadu West Bengal and Uttar Pradesh (Deshmukh-Randive, 2004; Kumar & Anand, 2007; Bali Swain & Varghese, 2009, Adhikary & Bagli, 2012). Most of the studies have discussed mainly various socio-economic parameters of SHGs members related to the situation during pre-SHG and post-SHG periods. They have found that participation in SHG ensures the financial inclusion for the rural unbanked people in general and women in particular. Participation and duration of involvement in SHG reduces borrowing cost. Borrowings from SHG smooth the expenditure on food, health and children education for the people. Other studies (Nair, 2005; Moyle et al., 2006; Chakrabarti, 2004) assessed more specific type of issues such as role of SHG federations in providing sustainability of SHGs, economic and personal empowerment of women and role of microfinance in poverty eradication.

The study of Moyle et al. (2006) on women empowerment found that a high proportion of women SHG members reported significant development of their self-confidence and work efficiency. The study also reported that most of the women experience pressure, challenges and stress due to extra work and more responsibilities. A study by NABARD covering 560 SHG member households from 223 SHGs across 11 states, showed many positive results of the impact of participation of rural poor in the SHGs (NABARD, 2002). It explores that SHG based microfinance is suitable for poverty alleviation and entrepreneurship development. However, Mukherjee and Kundu (2011) have examined the impact of participation in SHG under SGSY scheme in India on health, education and on women's empowerment across Socio Religious Communities (SRCs) in the district of Murshidabad, West Bengal. They have considered borrowed fund as a measure of participation. Removing household specific unobserved heterogeneity applying first difference regression this study has revealed that the programme has insignificant impact on health, education and women empowerment irrespective of SRCs.

The empirical study of Harika et al. (2015) shows the effectiveness of women SHGs in the promotion of the development of social capital through entrepreneurship development and on income variations of SHG households. Based on the primary survey of 400 member households in Visakhapatnam district of Andhra Pradesh they have found significant contribution of the SHGs in improvement in incomes and reduction of inequality in income distribution of the SHG member households. Field, et.al (2013) based on an experimental study in India establish that due to staring of repayment immediately after getting loan poor women borrowers are reluctant to undertake illiquid risky invest. Thus they argue that current SHG centric model with early repayment compulsion is not suitable for gauging the impact of SHGs on entrepreneurship development. We thus find mixed results of the impact of SHGs on socio-economic development indicators of the participants. However, the study on the SHGs in Andaman and Nicobar Islands focusing on a wide range of socio-economic issues, including the poverty and inequality aspects of SHGs households is really uncommon in the existing literature. The present study attempts to examine the socio-economic characteristics of the member households. Who are the participants of the SHGs in the union territory of Andaman and Nicobar Islands? Are they really poor? What is the nature of income distribution of the member households? We assess the social and economic impact of group formation in North and Middle Andaman district, which has not been covered in the literature. It is expected that poor women will participate and obtain loan for their livelihood promotion. Therefore, access micro credit should have a positive impact on income generation activities and thereby on poverty alleviation. If it happens, then question is that is the participation in SHG reduces income inequality or not. The planning commission, the Government of India did not calculate poverty line income of the union Territory of Andaman and Nicobar Islands. However, in accordance with the Indian poverty line income only one percent of population in this UT lives below poverty line income in 2011-12 (Planning Commission, 2014). Against this backdrop we would like to examine the extent of poverty and income inequality of the SHG-member households in Andaman and Nicobar Islands, India. We also like to examine the impact of participation measured by current borrowed fund on food and non-food expenditure of the SHG member households.

In this study we have set four objectives as follows:

1. Initially, we give an outline picture of SHGs and relating factors in Andaman and Nicobar Islands during 2012 to 2014.
2. Second, we explore the socio-economic condition of the SHG members residing in North Andaman Island of North and middle Andaman district.

3. Third, an attempt has been taken to measure the income poverty and inequality for the sample SHG member households.
4. Finally, the relation between borrowing form SHGs and food and non-food expenditure for the sample households has been assessed.

STUDY AREA, DATA, AND METHODOLOGY

Andaman and Nicobar Islands became a part of India in 1950. It is a Union Territory of India since 1956. It is a rural and remote part of India. Almost 95% of land in this Union Territory is covered by forest. It is a string of many small islands which is extended from North to South with an extent of more than 800 km. The Andaman and Nicobar Islands are divided by 10 Degree Channel. The climatic feature of these islands is tropical and warm. Over the year the temperature varies from 18°C to 35°C. The average annual rainfall ranges from 300 to 350 cm and humidity varies from 66 to 85 percent. Many times it has experienced rains during the entire year. These islands are prone to cyclone and earthquake. It is well known that a devastating Tsunami struck these islands on 26th December 2004 following a severe earthquake. Since pre-historic times, these Islands are the native land of aboriginal tribes namely, the Great Andamanese, Jarawa, Onge and Sentineles, all of Negrito Origin, in the Andaman group of Islands, while the tribes in the Nicobar Islands are Nicobarese and the Shompen, both of Mongoloid Stock. Currently it is the home of about 0.4 million people, among them only 7.5 percent are tribal. Major portion of the population is of settler from the mainland India. Majority of the population in this union territory earn their livelihood from nature, particularly from fishing, forestry and agriculture.

Andaman and Nicobar Islands was a single district until 31st July 1974. Now-a-days Andaman and Nicobar Islands has three districts viz. Nicobars, North & Middle Andaman and South Andaman. Port Blair town located in South Andaman is the Capital of this union territory. Each district has three Tehsils and three Development Blocks which are almost coterminous of the Tehasils. There is three-tier Panchayati Raj system in the Union Territory. There is a Municipal Council for the Port Blair town. Port Blair is the only statutory town in these Islands. It is important to note that seven tribal councils and 52 tribal village councils are functioning in tribal villages. This union territory has one Parliamentary Constituency.

In order to explore the socio-economic conditions of the SHG-member households and to estimate poverty and inequality of the same households this empirical study purposively conducted in Diglipur Tehasil/Community Development block in North & Middle Andaman district. Diglipur Tehsil is located at the northern most part of this territory. It has 72 inhabited villages which are spread over in seven inhabited islands viz., Narcondam, East, Land Fall, North Andaman, Smith, Curlew and Stewart Islands. We have randomly selected two villages namely Radha Nagar and Rabindrapalli from North Andaman Island. The socio-economic descriptions of the study are presented in table 1.

It is observed that two selected villages are not so large. Sex ratio of the Radha Nagar village and the sample block and that for the sample district is lower than the Indian average (940). In Rabindrapalli sex ratio is greater than the Indian average. In all respect literacy rates for the sample area are higher than that for India as a whole. In Andaman and Nicobar islands only 7% are tribal people. In North and Middle Andaman district less than one percent people are tribal. Actually our sample villages are the resident of non-tribal people. In this union territory dependency ratio is commendably high. In the sample villages 70% population are dependent member in their households.

Table 1. Demographic features of the study area

Area	No. of Households	Sex Ratio	Literacy rate (%)	Male literacy (%)	Female literacy (%)	ST Population (%)	Worker population ratio (%)
North and Middle Andaman (District)	26199	924.81	83.91	88.37	79.06	0.72	36.53
Diglipur (CD block)	10702	910.84	82.24	87.36	76.58	0.29	37.94
Radha Nagar (Village)	219	894.95	80.74	87.95	72.63	0.00	31.04
Rabindrapalli (Village)	72	981.25	81.85	86.11	77.37	0.00	29.34

Source: Census, 2011

The Census report 2011, reports that 4.2 percent of the households reside in dilapidated residency. It is observed from table 2 that no one of the sample villagers live in dilapidated residence. But 31.1% (8.6%) of the households in Rabindrapally (Radha Nagar) village have one room residence. In terms of asset holding poverty of the households is not serious at all. However, in the sample villages a large section of population drinks water from river or ponds. More than half of the households in Radha Nagar village, and 21% of Rabindrapalli village don't have access to improved power for lighting. A large section of population has no latrine facility within premises. Majority of the households uses dirty fuel for cooking. In 2011 more than 90% of the households in the sample villages are financially included. Therefore, in accordance with the report of population census average socio-economic condition of the population in the remote union territory is not poor at all. We are interested to examine what is the role of SHGs in financial inclusion for the sample persons particularly for women.

If we compare the statistics of the sample district of the union territory as a whole and the survey villages it is observed that tha combined sample villages are good representative of the sample district and Andaman and Nicobar union territory. Finally, relevant data have been collected from 75 SHG member households 55 from Radha Nagar village and 20 from Rabindrapalli village following random sampling process during the month of April, 2016.

The study also presents the fact-sheet of SHGs in Andaman and Nicobar Islands based on several reports of NABARD. Trend lines have been fitted to understand the performance of the stakeholders of SHGs. We have used several statistical tools and different graphical presentation to analyse the primary and secondary data.

Table 2. Access to basic improved amenities by the households in North and Middle Andaman District

Area	Dilapidated Residence	One Room Residence	No Safe Drinking Water	No Improved Power for Lighting	No Latrine Facility	Dirty Fuel for Cooking	Availing Banking Services	No Census Asset
North & Middle Andaman (District)	2.8	22.2	22.5	28.8	51.7	77.6	89.6	16.3
Diglipur (CD Block)	4.2	27.7	35.9	39.4	53.9	81.8	88.5	20.5
Radha Nagar (Village)	0	8.6	73.7	56	68.4	96.2	95.7	22.5
Rabindrapalli (Village)	0	31.1	33.8	21.6	62.2	82.4	91.9	14.9

Source: Census, 2011

There are several measures of poverty in literature. This study has applied Foster, Greer and Thorbecke (1984) measure of income poverty as specified below.

$$P_{\alpha} = \frac{1}{n}\sum_{y_i<z}\left(\frac{z-y_i}{z}\right)^{\alpha}$$

where, n stands for total number of population/households under study, z is poverty line income and y_i is the actual income of the poor. α is the distributional sensitivity parameter. It is a general measure of income poverty and highly distributional sensitive. When α =0 then we get poverty head count ratio. For α=1 we have poverty gap ratio. As the value of α increases larger poverty gap begins to acquire greater weight and the measure become increasing sensitive to these gaps. In our study we have considered α =2 for measuring income poverty of the SHG-member households in North Andaman Islands. Because, when α =2 the measure captures the effect of inequality in income and satisfy the transfer principle as well as transfer sensitivity.

In order to measure the inequality in income of the individual SHG members and for their households we have calculated Gini coefficient. Several methods were proposed in the literature for estimation of the Gini coefficient. In this study we have planned to apply the formula proposed by Sen (1973). It is specified as follows.

$$G = \frac{n+1}{n} - \frac{2}{\mu n^2}\sum(n+1-i)y_{|i|}$$

In this formula n denotes the total number of population/households in the society under consideration. μ denotes the mean income of the households under study. $y_{|i|}$ measures the income of the household of order i. In order to consider the all possible pairs in absolute income difference the Gini coefficient is normalised by n^2.

Finally, our objective is to investigate the impact of participation in SHG on expenditure pattern of the member households. The amount of current borrowing through SHG is the variable that has been considered as a measure of participation in SHG program. We have divided the monthly household expenditure in to two parts – food expenditure and non-food expenditure. Food expenditure of households is the market value of all non-cooked food items like rice, wheat, pulse, meat, fish, vegetables spices etc. consumed during the last month of the survey time. In this study food expenditure does not include expenditure for fuel and opportunity cost of the home makers as food expenditure. We have calculated the monthly expenditure for food of the households then calculated the per capita monthly food expenditure. In non-food expenditure we have taken the market value of all goods and services, including durable products such as cycles, scooter, TV, personal car, and computers, purchased during the last year. It also includes annual expenditure for health and hygiene, education of children and for fuel and energy. In case of non-food expenditure first calculating annual expenditure we have calculated the per capita monthly non-food expenditure for the sample households. Households' food and non-food expenditure is made out of the disposable income. Disposable income is the main determinant of food and non-food expenditure besides the level of physical and financial assets. The availability of easy loan may increase the food and non-food expenditure of the households. On the other hand, per capita monthly household income is the sum of annual income from all sources divided by family size. The current borrowed fund means the amount of loan that has been last time disbursed by the SHG to the member and did not repay. We have fitted log-linear model for estimating the impact of current borrowed fund from SHGs on rate of change of per capita expenditure on food and non-food items for the sample households. As income is the main determinant of the pattern of expenditure in addition to the current borrowed fund we have taken per capita household income as an explanatory variable of the model. Ordinary Least Squares method with all classical assumption of regression model has been used for estimation of the model.

SHGS IN ANDAMAN AND NICOBAR ISLANDS

This section discusses about the SHG bank-linkage programs in the Union territory of Andaman and Nicobar Islands. NABARD with the active collaboration of National Co-operative Union of India (NCUI) started SHG bank linkage program in this Union territory in 1992. The main objectives of this program were poverty alleviation and enhancement of women's empowerment through extending micro credit at an affordable borrowing cost. The data available in Status of Microfinance in India, during 2011-12, to 2016-17 published by NABARD reveal that number of savings linked SHGs is 4874 covering more than 64864 members as on 31st March, 2017. During the last six years no of SHGs grow at 32 percent rate per year in the union territory. Majority of the SHGs have been formed under the cooperative banks. The growth rate of SHG for the cooperative bank is 36% while it is 15% for the commercial banks. The details of savings linked SHGs in Andaman and Nicobar Islands have been presented in table 3. It is an important point to note that the regional banks have no role in promoting SHGs in this Union Territory.

In 2017 the SHG members have saved Rs. 8.72 crore in the banks. Therefore, the contribution of SHGs in formation of savings is no doubt commendable in the territory of Andaman and Nicobar Islands. The amount of savings reduces from Rs. 1.45 crore in 2013 to Rs.1.15 crore in 2015 which currently reach to Rs.8.72 crore in 2017. It may happen due to low performance of the commercial banks in the area of SHG formulation. The significant growth of number of SHGs and their savings volume under cooperative banks proves that the cooperative banks have been performing well in the field of microfinance in Andaman and Nicobar Islands. Perhaps as a result of the good performance of the cooperative banks savings again picked up to 872.82 crore in 2017. From the statistics of the amount of savings it is calculated that volume of savings of the SHG members' increases at a rate of 52%. The savings of the SHG members under cooperative banks grow at the rate of 61%, whereas the savings of the Group under commercial banks grows at the rate of 25%. Here we have considered only the principal amount of the savings that have been once deposited in formal financial institution. It is not included the interest and subtracted withdrawal during the period.

It is well known that SHGs are organized in two ways a) SHGs are formed by the banks directly or formed by NGOs and connected with banks. b) SHGs formed under the Governmental Schemes like NRLM, SGSY and others government sponsored schemes and linked with the banks. The cooperative banks have both types of SHGs. In table 4 we present the distribution of SHGs under the central cooperative bank in Andaman and Nicobar Islands of different types. Andaman and Nicobar Islands State Co-operative Banks (ANSCB) have played a key role in mobilizing SHG-Bank linkages activities especially among women folks of the Islands who are marginalized group in the society. In the financial year 2013-2014, the Co-operative Bank has successfully linked 4530 SHGs covering 54360 persons in the Islands. The total savings amounts to Rs. 92.44 lakhs. In 2014-15 the cooperative bank have introduced

Table 3. Details of savings linked SHGs in Andaman and Nicobar Islands

Institution	Indicator	2012	2013	2014	2015	2016	2017	Growth rate
Commercial Banks	No. of SHGs	1699	925	294	295	341	432	15%
	Cumulative No. of SHG	1699	2624	2918	3213	3554	3986	
	Savings Amount (lakh)	50.21	64.68	23.14	20.1	25.76	34.28	25%
	Cumulative Savings (lakh)	50.21	114.89	138.03	158.13	183.89	218.17	
Cooperative Banks	No. of SHGs	3822	4292	4530	4703	4134	4442	36%
	Cumulative No. of SHG	3822	8114	12644	17347	21481	25923	
	Savings Amount (lakh)	81.07	81.06	92.44	105.17	634.73	838.54	61%
	Cumulative Savings (lakh)	81.07	162.13	254.57	359.74	994.47	1833.01	
Total	No. of SHGs	5521	5217	4824	4998	4475	4874	32%
	Cumulative No. of SHG	5521	10738	15562	20560	25035	29909	
	Savings Amount (lakh)	131.28	145.74	115.58	125.27	660.49	872.82	52%
	Cumulative Savings (lakh)	131.28	277.02	392.6	517.87	1178.36	2051.18	

(Source: NABARD, 2012, 2013, 2014, 2015, 2016)

Table 4. Distribution of SHGs linked with the cooperative banks in Andaman and Nicobar Islands (Rs. in lakh)

Year	Details of SHGs Savings Linked With Banks			Out of Total-Under NRLM/SGSY & Other Govt. Sponsored Prog.			Out of Total SHGs –Exclusives Women SHGs		
	No. of SHG	No. of SHG member	Savings amount (Re.)	No. of SHG	No. Of SHG members	Savings amount	No. of SHG	No. Of SHG members	Savings amount (Re.)
2011-12	3822	45864	81.07	231	2772	44.50	3630	43570	77.01
2012-13	4292	51504	81.06	248	2480	25.12	4077	48924	77.00
2013-14	4530	54360	92.44	266	3192	6.38	4307	51684	51.68
2014-15	4703	56436	105.17	240	1440	1.45	4374	51921	97.80
2015-16	4134	49608	634.73	0	0	0	3803	45639	584.00
2016-17	4442	53304	838.54	0	0	0	4086	-	788.23

(Source: NABARD, 2012, 2013, 2014, 2015, 2016)

4703 SHGs with savings amount 1.05 crore. A small percentage of SHGs under the cooperative banks comes through the government sponsored schemes. In 2014-15, among the total SHGs under cooperative banks, 240 SHGs bringing 1440 persons comes from the SGSY or other schemes. It is fact that up to 2014-15 each year 92 to 95 percent of the SHGs are formed by women under cooperative banks. Thus the SHG-bank linkage program in Andaman and Nicobar Islands become successful to make financial inclusion for women. This financial inclusion explores the hidden savings habit of the women folk of a region that can take an important role to accelerate savings fund of a country. The volume of savings of the SHGs formed by women has increased 10 times during the last six years in the district of North and Middle Andaman. However, surprisingly since 2015-16 cooperative banks stop making financial inclusion of the SHGs under the government sponsored programs.

Let us now discuss the performance of different banks in terms of loan disbursement. Table-5 shows the performance of the commercial banks and co-operative banks in the field of microfinance in the union territory of Andaman and Nicobar Islands. Initially the commercial banks started lending to the SHGs but over time the intensity of lending by the commercial banks to the SHGs has been reduced. During 2014-15 the commercial banks lends only 20 SHGs the amount of which was Rs. 11.38 lakhs. Not only the total amount of loan disbursement reduced during 2012-2015, amount of lending per group has decreased significantly. It is Rs. 0.56 lakhs in the year 2014-15 which was Rs. 0.94 lakhs in the year 2011-12. In the year the loan intensity of the commercial bank is improved to 1.6 lakhs. Thus in terms of the loan expansion the performance of scheduled commercial banks is not noticeable in the Islands of Andaman and Nicobar. RRBs do not open any activities in this field. The cooperatives banks are actively disbursing loan to the SHG during the period. In average cooperative banks extend loan to 385 SHGs. Amount of loan disbursed increased 1.32 times during the period under study.

The details of loan disbursement scenarios of the cooperative banks are depicted in table 6. During 2011-12, the cooperative banks had extended credit facilities to the 596 SHGs. Among them 231 SHGs were formed under the government sponsored schemes and 271 were formed by women folk of the Islands. The total amount of loan extended to the groups was Rs. 461.75 lakhs of which Rs. 209.96 lakhs was extended to 219 women groups. During 2012-13, the cooperative banks had extended credit

Table 5. Disbursement of loan towards SHG by the banks (Rs. in lakh)

Financial Year	Commercial Banks		Cooperative Banks		TOTAL	
	No. of SHGs	Loans Disbursed Amount (Rs.)	No. of SHGs	Loans Disbursed Amount (Rs.)	No. of SHGs	Loans Disbursed Amount(Rs.)
2011-12	114	108.25	596	461.75	710	570.00
2012-13	82	109.90	333	427.94	415	537.84
2013-14	57	98.14	198	104.82	255	202.96
2014-15	20	11.38	244	345.94	264	357.32
2015-16	29	41.45	223	359.47	252	400.92
2016-17	124	198.55	307	612.70	431	811.25

(Source: NABARD, 2012, 2013, 2014, 2015, 2016)

Table 6. Disbursement of loan towards SHG by the Cooperative Banks in Andaman Nicobar Islands

Financial Year	Total Loans Disbursed During the Year		Out of Total-Under NRLM/SGSY & other Govt. Sponsored Prog.		Out of Total- Loan Disbursed Exclusive to Women SHGs	
	No. of SHG	Loan Disbursed	No. of SHG	Loan Disbursed	No. of SHG	Loan Disbursed
2011-12	596	461.75	231	108.63	271	209.96
2012-13	333	427.94	56	37.47	316	410.82
2013-14	198	104.82	35	22.22	145	74.34
2014-15	244	345.94	0	0	205	302.34
2015-16	223	359.47	0	0	211	337.90
2016-17	307	612.70	0	0	237	563.68

(Source: NABARD, 2012, 2013, 2014, 2015, 2016)

facilities to the 333 SHGs sanctioning Rs. 427.54 lakhs among them only 56 SHGs were formed under the government sponsored schemes while 316 groups were exclusively formed by the women. The total amount of loan extended among 216 groups of women was Rs. 410.82 lakhs. However, it is shocking that in the year 2013-14, the cooperative banks had extended credit facilities to 198 SHGs of women. Among them only 35 SHGs formed under the government sponsored schemes have got loan. In the year of 2016-17 the co-operative banks sanction total loan amount Rs. 563 lakhs to the 237 SHGs of women in the Islands. Thus overall performance of the cooperative banks in terms of loan disbursement during the last three years is in progress but highly dispersed.

It is interesting to note that the cooperatives banks provided Rs. 0.77 lakhs loan per SHG during 2011-12, whereas during 2013-14 per group loan disbursement of the cooperative banks reduces to Rs. 0.51 lakhs. Therefore, cooperative banks have wider coverage in terms of microfinance business in these Islands. Intensity of loan disbursement i.e loan per group is greater than that of commercial banks because the cooperative banks are relatively more dedicated in the field of micro finance business.

In addition to the banks in this Islands NGOs are playing a vital role to promote microfinance business and women's empowerment. The governments of India extend several non-monetary and monetary facilities to the NGOs in these Islands. Table 7 depicts that during the period 2012-2014, the government has sanctioned Rs. 346.48 lakhs to thirty four NGOs for extending microfinance business in this territory. However, the benefited NGOs have got Rs. 74.46 lakhs which is only 21% of the sanction grant. Using this 21% of sanction grant the NGOs organised 28% of targeted number. It is reported that during the three years under study the NGOs promoted 2766 SHGs; of them 2696 SHGs save regularly with financial institutions. Moreover, during the period 1506 SHGs have got loan through NGOs. Thus the NGOs in the union territory are functioning at the moderate level. We feel that if the government release the sanction fund to the NGOs the performance could be better.

Table 8 is devoted to focus the loan outstanding to the SHGs. Number of default SHGs has been declined in 2013-14 compared to 2012-13 but it is further increasing. But volume of outstanding has been increased. If we look only the volume of loan outstanding of commercial banks, it is declining compared to previous years. It should be noted that volume of loan outstanding is a serious problem in this Islands. It may happen due to lack of income generating activities of the SHG members. From the report of the Status of Microfinance in India we did not find any initiatives taken under the government sponsored microfinance scheme for entrepreneurial capacity development of the women members of

Table 7. NGOs in microfinance business in Andaman and Nicobar islands

Year	No. of Beneficiary NGOs	No. of Proposals	Grant sanctioned	Grant Released	No. of SHGs Proposed to Promote	No. of SHGs Promoted	No. of SHGs Saving Linked	No. of SHGs Credit Linked
2011-12	6	7	134.22	12.063	4850	471	459	182
2012-13	15	16	135.88	27.56	3050	1153	1095	585
2013-14	13	16	76.38	35.14	1700	1142	1142	735
2014-15	13	17	79.38	37.82	1800	1216	1181	796
2015-16	17	22	95.38	43.58	1960	1286	1251	901
2016-17	20	25	105.38	47.66	2060	1591	1556	1043

(Source: NABARD, 2012, 2013, 2014, 2015, 2016)

Table 8. Description of loan outstanding of the SHGs across the banks

Region/ State	Commercial Banks		Cooperative Banks		Total	
	No. of SHGs	Outstanding Amount	No. of SHGs	Outstanding Amount	No. of SHGs	Outstanding Amount
A & N (UT) (2011-12)	176	104.45	1173	505.77	1349	610.52
A & N (UT) (2012-13)	171	119.47	1328	592.75	1499	712.22
A & N (UT) (2013-14)	150	109.20	1028	797.97	1178	907.17
A & N (UT) (2014-15)	107	75.67	913	519.04	1020	594.71
A & N (UT) (2015-16)	87	55.47	536	495.10	623	550.57
A & N (UT) (2016-17)	851	565.71	871	766.67	1722	1332.38

(Source: NABARD, 2012, 2013, 2014, 2015, 2016)

SHGs in Andaman and Nicobar Island. Commercial banks including cooperative banks had also no program for skill development or training program for the women members. If this trend continues the microfinance business of the banking sector will be breakdown in near future in this Islands.

Thorough discussion of the secondary data relating to SHGs in Andaman and Nicobar Islands highlights the following major points in this field.

1. First, SHGs-bank linkage program in Andaman and Nicobar Island started in 1992 by the NABARD.
2. Second, the commercial banks in these Islands started the microfinance business through SHGs with a good speed but recently they have become reluctant to do this business.
3. Third, the cooperative banks play major role in the promotion of SHGs in these Islands.
4. Fourth, it is reported that the cooperative banks have wide coverage and greater per group loan disbursement than that of commercial banks.
5. Fifth, the government sponsored programs like SGSY have moderate performance in the field of microfinance in this Union Territory. Recently cooperative banks do not extend loan to the SHGs under the government schemes.
6. Sixth, like other states and UT in Andaman and Nicobar Island major numbers of SHGs are of women.
7. Seventh, a few number NGOs have been facilitated by the government, but due to paucity of fund they are functioning in a moderate level.
8. Eighth, the loan outstanding with the SHGs is a serious problem in this part of India.
9. Nine, there is no formal training and skill development program taken by the stakeholders of microfinance schemes for inculcating inspiring women to undertake income generating activities of the their own.

The SHG movement for social-economic development of the people of Andaman and Nicobar Islands is thus in the critical position and thereby it is the right time to assess the activities of the groups and their members for livelihood promotion because the program was launched to alleviate poverty through facilitating loan in livelihood promotion.

SOCIO-ECONOMIC CONDITIONS OF THE SAMPLE SHG-MEMBER HOUSEHOLDS

This section is devoted to exploring the socio-economic status of the SHG-member households in the district of North and Middle Andaman under the Union territory of Andaman and Nicobar Islands. The study is based on the primary survey of 75 SHG member households. It covers 30 SHGs among them majority of the groups are under cooperative banks. Only 4 groups are formed by the NGOs. All the sample members are female in gender. Thus like the other states and UTs in India, SHG-bank linkage program in Andaman and Nicobar Islands is successful to include women in the main stream development process through financial inclusion. Table 9 shows that three fourth of the sample women are homemakers. It is reported that 14 percent of the sample women are engaged in formal and informal services like cook in Mid-day meal program in school, health worker, teacher in private primary school etc. Although farming and fishing is the main occupation of the households of Andaman Islands, no one of the sample women is engaged in this occupation. Seven percent of the sample women earn from self-employed activities like tailoring, vegetable vendor. Only four percent of the women under study keep up their livelihood from selling labour. It is reported that majority of the sample SHG-members, who are member of SHGs for last five years, cannot change their occupation through participation and getting loan from banks. Thus SHGs in Andaman Island fail to help the member in occupational mobility.

Table 10 refers to the descriptive statistics of the SHG members in North Andaman Island. We see that average family size of the sample households is less than four. The majority of the sample households have family size of four members. Average age of the sample women is 30 years with median

Table 9. Occupation distribution of the sample SHG members (N=75)

Name of Occupation	Number of Persons	Percentage
Homemakers	56	74.66
Self-Employment	8	6.66
Service	11	14.66
Farming and Fishing	0	0
Labor	3	4
Total	75	100

Source: Field survey, 2016

Table 10. Descriptive statistics of the SHG members in North Andaman District (N=75)

Variable	Mean	Median	Mode	CV	Max	Min
Family size (Number)	3.48	4	4	28.264	5	1
Age (year)	29.62	28	26	34.323	58	20
Education (year)	9.6	10	12	47.002	16	0
Landholding (Bigha)	9.56	2.5	30	115.583	30	0
Worker Population Ratio (%)	36.93	33.33	25	52.02	100	20

Source: Field survey, 2016

28 years. The sample survey tells us majority of the sample women have secondary level education. It is informed that the landholding status of the sample households is not so poor. But there is strong disparity among the sample households. The area of landholding varies from 0 to 30 bighas. Majority of the sample households holds 2.5 bighas of land for cultivation. Average worker population ratio is 36.93 percent. It indicates that the dependency ratio of the household of SHG members is very high. In other word, the women belonging to high dependency ratio are more likely to participate in SHG in the district of North and Middle Andaman. The socio-economic status of the SHG-members confirms that SHG-based microfinance program in the Island serve young educated women from landed households.

Socio-economic attributes of the SHG members in North Andaman District have been depicted in Table 11. Among the sample women 92 percent are ever married women. Thus unmarried women are less likely to participate in SHG. It is interesting to note that only 15 percent of the sample women are belonging to poor family in accordance to having BPL card. Although the SHG-Bank linkage program was formulated basically for poor people, it includes poor and mainly non-poor households in the area under study. The field survey has found that forward castes and backward caste women are equally likely to participate in SHG in the district of North Andaman. We see that 51 percent women in our sample are belonging to forward caste community. It is reported that 85 percent women in our sample are belonging to Hindu religion. Only 4 percent are Muslim and 11 percent are Christian.

Almost half of the sample women reside in house made by mud and non-concrete material. Not only that a good number of the households has one room residence. We are happy to note that 80 percent households in our sample villages have access to safe drinking water. Another good indicator of rural infrastructure in North Andaman District is that sample villages are totally electrified. Thus the government has done well for infrastructure development in rural zones of the Andaman and Nicobar

Table 11. Socio-economic attributes of the SHG members (N=75)

Attributes	Yes (per cent)	No (per cent)
Marital status(married)	92	8
Having BPL Card	15	85
General Caste	51	49
Religion (Hindu)	85	15
Religion (Muslim)	4	96
Religion (Christian)	11	89
Having Concrete House	52	48
Access to Safe Drinking Water	80	20
Access to improved Sanitation	66	34
Household electrification	100	0
Having LPG connection	74	26
Holding more than three Census Assets	76	24
Having Bank Account of the SHG member	96	4
Access to bank loan	77	23
Having any kind of Insurance of the SHG member	18	82

Source: Field survey, 2016

Islands during last five years. The households can have access to all electronics goods if they demand. Three-fourth of the sample households uses LPG for cooking. It is indicative that access to improved energy (access to electricity and LPG) is at a commendable level for the households in North Andaman Island. In other words, the study district is not energy poor at all. However, only two third of the sample households have access to improved sanitation. Thus the households in North Andaman Island are not health and hygiene conscious. It is reported that 74% of the sample households have at least one census asset like bi-cycle, Television, radio, motor cycle, Refrigerator etc. So we can say that households are not asset poor too. Almost all the sample SHG-member households have at least one savings bank account. It establishes that SHG-bank linkage program is successful to make financial inclusion of the women in the district of North and Middle Andaman of the study Union Territory. However, being a SHG member still 23 percent women do not have access to formal credit. Only 18 percent of the sample women have any kind of insurance policy (Health Insurance, Life Insurance, Asset insurance, etc.). It is conclusive that households in the district of North and Middle Andaman are not so much financially literate.

Table 12 represents the group related statistics of the SHG members in North Andaman District. We find average group size 16, which ranges from 9 to 18 under the SHG bank linkage program. The SHG members save in average Rs. 337/- per month which varies from Rs.100/- to Rs. 500/-. In average our sample women have been participating for 4.6 years. The variation of the duration is not so high. We have already mentioned that 23% SHG members did not have access to formal credit. So far, in average the sample women have got Rs. 24000/- as loan through SHGs. There is, however, wide variation in amount access to formal credit. During the field survey we find that a large number of women have taken loan for non-food consumption. A number of women have taken loan for repaying past loan or borrow for meeting expenses in festivals. It is reported that average interest rate for borrowed fund is 30% per annum. It varies from group to group from 24% to 36%. We observe that the borrowers of SHG do not repay loan regularly. Only 15 percent of the borrowers repay loan seriously following proper schedule. No one of the sample women reported that she has taken income generating project with the help of loan from SHGs. A large number of member of women reported that they don't have any idea to undertake an income generating project of their own. There is no household level problem to the member women but lack of entrepreneurial knowledge and skill they fail to invest in income generating project. A handful of women tell us about the small amount of loan and recurrent repayment schedule immediately after the disbursement of loan are not suitable for entrepreneurship development. Actually, fund of SHGs is used as an emergency fund for the households of the group members. In the course of field survey we

Table 12. Group related statistics of the SHG members (N=75)

Variable	Mean	Median	Mode	CV	Max	Min
Group Size (number)	16.28	15	15	9.55	18	9
Savings Amount (Rs)	337.34	300	200	32.15	500	100
SHGs Duration (Month)	55.45	55.5	71	31.71	98	16
Loan Amount (Rs)	24000	19000	0	99.14	95000	0
Interest rate (%)	30	24	24	57.92	36	24
Repayment Status (%)	15.10	13	0	35.56	60	0

Source: Field survey, 2016

come to know that among the sample women a section borrow from other money lenders. They sometimes borrow from informal money lenders in the villages. It is also reported that one percent of sample women took loan from bank before joining the SHG.

INCOME POVERTY AND INEQUALITY OF THE SAMPLE HOUSEHOLDS

In the last section we have discussed socio-economic condition of the SHG members and their households in North Andaman Island. In this section we present the nature of income poverty and inequality of the sample SHG member households. In order to measure income poverty we apply Foster, Greer and Thorbecke (1984) methodology. We have considered Rs. 816/- as poverty line per capita income which is rural poverty line income for India as a whole (Planning Commission, 2014) because the Planning commission did not provide and separate poverty line income for rural Andaman and Nicobar Islands and instantly it is very difficult to estimate the poverty line income for the region. The results of estimated income poverty for the sample household are cited in table 13. It refers that poverty head count ratio is 0.2. It implies that only 20 percent of the sample households are income poor. This measure gives the incidence of income poverty. This result shows that incidence of income poverty in North Andaman Island is lower than the incidence of income poverty for India as a whole. It is also surprising that that SHG-centric program mainly serves the non-poor households in the district of North and Middle Andaman particularly in North Andaman Island.

In order to measure the intensity of poverty we have measured Poverty gap ratio and Foster, Greer and Thorbecke (FGT) measure. The figure of poverty gap ratio indicate that extent of income poverty is not so serious in the area under study. Even FGT measure point out that the value of the intensity of income poverty is also low when we have considered inequality adjusted figure. Thus finally we conclude that income poverty is not a serious problem for the SHG member households in the Island of North Andaman. From any readymade report we have no idea regarding income inequality of the district of North and Middle Andaman. Thus, this study has investigated the nature of income inequality in addition to the estimation of the extent of poverty for the Island of North Andaman.

Table 14 represents the analysis of income and expenditure inequality for the sample SHGs member households. It is reported that average monthly personal income of the sample SHG members is Rs. 6252/- during the year 2015-16. The value of median tells us majority of the sample SHG women earn rupees five hundred. The inequality in personal income is very high among the sample women. Average annual per capita household income is Rs. 51050/- . The Gini coefficient for per capita annual income is 0.54. Thus we can say that although the poverty is not so serious, income inequality is a serious problem in the area under study. Usually the policymakers advocate about SHG based microfinance programme for

Table 13. Estimates of income poverty of the sample women (N=75)

Poverty Measures	Value
Poverty Head Count Ratio ($\alpha=0$)	0.200
Poverty Gap Ratio ($\alpha=1$)	0.060
Foster, Greer and Thorbecke ($\alpha=2$)	0.025

Source: Field survey, 2016

Table 14. Intensity and inequality of income and expenditure of SHG households

Variables (Rs.)	Mean	Median	SD	CV	Gini Coefficient
Monthly Personal Income	6252	500	12361.15	1.977	0.792
Annual Per capita household income	51050.87	27750	62143.82	1.217	0.545
Annual Household Income	153360	9500	6284.304	0.570	0.283
Monthly Per capita food expenditure	2124.444	2000	990.515	0.466	0.263
Monthly Per capita health expenditure	404.666	0	1326.399	3.277	0.891
Monthly Per capita total expenditure	3306.344	3000	1820.694	0.550	0.288
Total Household Expenditure	11011.73	98000	155273.8	1.0124	0.493

Source: Field survey, 2016

poverty reduction and socio-economic up-liftmen of the poor women. Thus our findings show the failure of the program implementation to reach the target group. Not only the failure, rather has it proved the existence of the problem of self selection or endogeneity in the participation. It means that rich women are organised in SHG with their own interest and unobserved attributes towards getting loan. Actually credit worthy women formed the group and take advantage of easy access to microcredit. However, inequality in total household income is lower than the inequality in per capita income. In this study we also estimated the mean and dispersion of per capita expenditure for food, and health. The result shows that inequality for health expenditure is highest compared to the inequality in total expenditure, food expenditure, per capita income etc.

BORROWING FROM SHGS AND FOOD AND NON-FOOD EXPENDITURE OF THE HOUSEHOLDS

Above discussion establishes that SHGs in the north and middle Andaman district mainly serve the non-poor households. No one of the SHG member undertake income generating activities taking loan from SHGs. Thus borrowed fund mainly used in consumption purpose. In this section we have tried to estimate the impact of participation in SHG on per capita food and non-food expenditure of the SHG-member households in North Andaman Island. The current borrowed fund is the variable for measuring the extent of participation in SHG. The impact of income and borrower fund on food and non-food expenditure we have estimated a log-lin model. The estimated results are depicted in table 15 and in table 16. The model summary confirms that models are good fitted. There are no problems of multicollinearity, autocorrelation in both the models. Heteroskedasticity is not a problem in model for food expenditure but it is present in the model of non-food expenditure. To address the heteroskedaticity problem we have provided White heteroskedasticity-consistent standard errors and covariance for the model of non-food expenditure.

The coefficient of monthly per capita household income is positive and statistically significant at one percent level. The value of coefficient is 0.039 which means that other things remaining unchanged per capita food expenditure grow at 4 percent with extra one thousand per capita monthly incomes. On the other hand, the growth rate of per capita food expenditure is 3.7 percent with increase in borrowed fund. However, the impact of borrowed fund on per capita food expenditure is not statistically significant.

Table 15. Estimates of the Impact of borrowing on Food expenditure for the Sample Households

<table>
<tr><td colspan="7">Dependent Variable: log (Per capita Monthly Food Expenditure)
Method: Ordinary Least Squares
Observations: 1-75</td></tr>
<tr><th rowspan="2">Variable</th><th rowspan="2">Coefficients</th><th rowspan="2">Std. Error</th><th rowspan="2">t-stat</th><th rowspan="2">Sig.</th><th colspan="2">Collinearity Statistics</th></tr>
<tr><th>Tolerance</th><th>VIF</th></tr>
<tr><td>(Constant)</td><td>7.233</td><td>.099</td><td>73.410</td><td>.000</td><td></td><td></td></tr>
<tr><td>Amount of current borrowed fund (Rs. '000)</td><td>0.037</td><td>.000</td><td>1.505</td><td>.137</td><td>0.999</td><td>1.001</td></tr>
<tr><td>Per capita monthly household income (Rs. '000)</td><td>0.039</td><td>.000</td><td>4.151</td><td>.000</td><td>0.999</td><td>1.001</td></tr>
<tr><th colspan="7">Model Summary</th></tr>
</table>

R Square	Adjusted R Square	Std. Error of the Estimate	Durbin-Watson	Heteroskedasticity Test: White (Chi-square)	Condition Index
0.210	0.188	0.512	2.11	6.04 (.30)	3.064

Source: Field survey, 2016

Table 16. Estimates of the impact of borrowing on non-food expenditure for the sample households

<table>
<tr><td colspan="7">Dependent Variable: log (Per capita Monthly Non-food Expenditure)
Method: Ordinary Least Squares
Observations: 1-75
White heteroskedasticity-consistent standard errors & covariance</td></tr>
<tr><th rowspan="2">Variable</th><th rowspan="2">Coefficients</th><th rowspan="2">Std. Error</th><th rowspan="2">t-stat</th><th rowspan="2">Sig.</th><th colspan="2">Collinearity Statistics</th></tr>
<tr><th>Tolerance</th><th>VIF</th></tr>
<tr><td>(Constant)</td><td>6.301</td><td>.114</td><td>55.335</td><td>0.000</td><td></td><td></td></tr>
<tr><td>Amount of current borrowed fund (Rs. '000)</td><td>0.0628</td><td>.000</td><td>2.170</td><td>0.033</td><td>0.999</td><td>1.001</td></tr>
<tr><td>Per capita monthly household income (Rs. '000)</td><td>0.0624</td><td>.000</td><td>5.627</td><td>0.000</td><td>0.999</td><td>1.001</td></tr>
<tr><th colspan="7">Model Summary</th></tr>
</table>

R Square	Adjusted R Square	Std. Error of the Estimate	Durbin-Watson	Heteroskedasticity Test: White (Chi-square)	Condition Index
0.331	0.313	0.592	1.800	36.91 (0.000)	3.064

Source: Field survey, 2016

Therefore, participation in SHG does not certainly influence the change of food consumption expenditure of the member households.

In table 16 it is seen that coefficient of borrowed fund and the coefficient of per capita monthly income are positive and statistically significant at 3 percent level. It refers that other factors remaining unchanged per capita non-food monthly expenditure grow at 6 percent rate with borrowed fund and at the same rate with per capita monthly income. Therefore, borrowing through SHG has some favourable impact on per capita non food expenditure. It indicates that the participation in SHG only accelerate the growth of non-food consumption expenditure of the member households in North Andaman Island. It proves that SHG helps the participants to meet the unforeseen health expenditure and expenditure for education of their children. Sometimes with the loan amount they purchase households durables like TV, scooters, LPG connections etc. This study could not separate the impact of participation on health expenditure, expenditure for children education and on expenditure for household durables etc. due to small pool of data for each.

CONCLUSION

The empirical study based on secondary and primary data we can conclude that SHG bank linkage model for women development is relatively new phenomenon in the area under study. Among the financial institutions the cooperative banks play major role in the promotion of SHGs in this Union territory. The government sponsored programs like SGSY have moderate performance in the field of microfinance in the Islands of territory of Andaman and Nicobars Islands. Moreover, savings volume and credit worthy of the women borrowers proves the importance of the program for financial inclusion of women.

The analysis of primary data collected from two villages in North Andaman Island of North and Middle Andaman district we have observed that the incidence and intensity of poverty is not so serious in the area under study. In terms of education, asset and energy the sample women are not poor at all. The level of financial inclusion is moderate. Only access to improved sanitation is relatively poor for the sample households. But income inequality is a prominent problem in north Andaman Island. This study confirms that borrowing from SHG significantly accelerate the non-food expenditure of the households in North Andaman Island. The participation in SHG does not encourage the members in income generating activities rather inspire to spend on non-food consumption expenditure which is unproductive. The consequence of this behaviour makes the problem of non-repayment of loan. Thus the program cannot be sustainable in near future. Contraction of the microfinance business of the commercial banks put a big question on the sustainability of the program in this region. The direct observation of the data analysis tells us that SHG centric microfinance programs in north Andaman Island have no impact on women entrepreneurship, but cannot remain silent to explain the impact of the programs in women empowerment. There are at least four channels by which the participation in SHG and access to micro savings and credit are enhancing empowerment of the member women. (a) Accumulation of savings in women's bank account builds the self-confidence, economic security and feeling of holding financial assets which directly connected with economic empowerment. (b) Access to formal credit at an affordable cost establishes women's eligibility and dignity in terms of economic power within the household which inculcates self-esteem, economic decision making power which are the vital element of empowerment. (c) Establishment of social network through group activities with peer women which accelerates the social capital of the member women improving social connectedness, association, social awareness. (d) Institutional relation through institutional borrowing member women creates an institutional relation with bank or NGO which improve the knowledge of the member women regarding the values of the financial institutions to they life, make an identity which play a vital role in enhancing empowerment at national/ international level. Thus social and institutional experience and learning and improved dignity of the women definitely inculcate the overall empowerment of the member women in north Andaman Island.

The study has identified that women member of SHGs in Andaman and Nicobar Island fails to undertake income generating activities through borrowing from SHGs. It may be due to lack opportunity of getting entrepreneurship training and consultancy services from the lenders agencies. Therefore, the study suggest for launching capacity building program for potential women entrepreneurs in North Andaman Island. In addition to the Government sponsored programs, cooperative banks and NGOs should take part to arrange entrepreneurship development program.

Finally, the SHGs in North Andaman Island bypass the poor women who actually need the financial services from micro finance institutions. It is thus urgent to identify the real poor households and the programs of microfinance institutions are to be designed for the women in poor households. One hand, poor women could not save recurrently a desirable amount that determines the volume of loan. That is why often banks or NGOs bypass the poor women for high average transaction cost. On the other hand, due to small loan with immediate repayment schedule poor women bypass the participation in SHGs. In order to break this situation, we need to reformulate the policy of the cooperative banks. They initially should offer training to undertake income generating project for the targeted groups of poor women and then extend joint loan to those who really get education from training and willing to undertake suitable income generating activities jointly.

However, this study has some limitations. The study is based on relatively small sample. Sample is not stratified. We have only collected sample only from SHG members. We are not in position to inform the actual situation of the non-members of SHG in North Andaman Island.

REFERENCES

Adhikary, M. L., & Bagli, S. (2012). Self-Help Groups and Borrowing Cost: An Empirical Study Addressing Endogeneity Problems. *Microfinance Review*, *9*(1), 69–85.

Bali Swain, R., & Varghese, A. (2009). Does Self Help Group Participation Lead to Asset Creation? *World Development*, *37*(10), 1674–1682. doi:10.1016/j.worlddev.2009.03.006

Chakrabarti, R. (2004). The India Microfinance Experience – Accomplishments and Challenges. In Integrating the Rural Poor into Markets. Academic Foundation.

Dasgupta, R. (2005). Microfinance in India - Empirical Evidence, Alternative Models and Policy Imperatives. *Economic and Political Weekly*, *40*(12), 1229–1237.

Deaton, A. (1997). *The Analysis of Household Survey: A Microeconomic Approach to Development Policy*. Baltimore, MD: Johns Hopkins Press for the World Bank. doi:10.1596/0-8018-5254-4

Deshmukh-Randive, J. (2004). *Women's self-help groups in Andhra Pradesh: participatory poverty alleviation in action*. Washington, DC: World Bank. Retrieved from http://document.worldbank.org/curated/en/402521468752429977/women's-self-help-groups-in-Andhra-Pradesh-participatory-poverty-alleviation-in-action

Field, E., Pande, R., Papp, J., & Rigol, N. (2013). Does the Classic Microfinance Model Discourage Entrepreneurship Among the Poor? Experimental Evidence from India. *The American Economic Review*, *103*(6), 2196–2206. doi:10.1257/aer.103.6.2196

Foster, J., Greer, J., & Thorbecke, E. (1984). A Class of Decomposable Poverty Measures. *Econometrica*, *52*(3), 761–766. doi:10.2307/1913475

Government of India. (2011). *Population Census Report, 2011, Registrar General & Census Commissioner*. Ministry of Home Affairs.

Harika, K., Chiranjeevi, Ch., & Reddy, S. M. (2015). Income Inequalities of SHG Households: An Empirical Analysis. *Economic Affairs*, *60*(3), 467–471. doi:10.5958/0976-4666.2015.00066.2

Jain, D. (1989). Letting the Worm Turn: A Comment on Innovative Poverty Alleviation. In Assessing Participatory Development: rhetoric versus Reality. Westview Press.

Kumar, S. & Anand, S. (2007). Journey of Rural Credit in India over the Past Sixty Year. *Kurukshetra, 55*(12), 52-54

Kumaran, P. K. (2002). Role of Self-Help Groups in Promoting Micro-enterprises Through Micro Credit: An Empirical Study. *Journal of Rural Development, 21*(2), 231–250.

Morduch, J. (1999, December). The Microfinance Promise. *Journal of Economic Literature, 37*(4), 1569–1614. doi:10.1257/jel.37.4.1569

Moyle, T. L., Dollard, M., & Biswas, S. N. (2006). Personal and Economic Empowerment in Rural Indian Women A Self-help Group Approach. *International Journal of Rural Management, 2*(2), 245–266. doi:10.1177/097300520600200207

Mukherjee, A. K., & Kundu, A. (2011). Impact of Swarna Jayanti Gram Swarojgar Yojona (SGSY) on Health, Education and Women's Empowerment. *Microfinance Review, 3*(1), 36–52.

NABARD. (2002). *NABARD & microfinance 2001-2002: Ten Years of SHG-Banking Linkage*. Retrieved from https://www.microfinancegateway.org/sites/default/files/mfg-en-paper-nabard-and-microfinance-2002.pdf

NABARD. (2013). *Status of Microfinance in India 2012-13*. Retrieved from http://indiamicrofinance.com/status-microfinance-india-2012-2013-pdf-report-nabard.html

NABARD. (2014). *Status of Microfinance in India 2013-14*. Retrieved from www.nabard.org

NABARD. (2015). *Status of Microfinance in India 2014-15*. Retrieved from www.nabard.org

NABARD. (2016). *Status of Microfinance in India 2015-16*. Retrieved from https://www.microfinancegateway.org/sites/default/files/publication_files/smfi_2015-16.pdf

NABARD. (2017). *Status of Microfinance in India 2016-17*. Retrieved from https://www.nabard.org/auth/writereaddata/tender/1307174808Status%20of%20Microfinance%20in%20India%202016-17.pdf

Nair, A. (2005). Sustainability of micro finance self help groups in India; would federation help. *World Bank Policy Research Working Paper, 3516*. doi:10.1596/1813-9450-3516

Namboodiri, N. V., & Shiyani, R. L. (2001). Potential Role of Self-Help Groups in Rural Financial Deepening. *Indian Journal of Agricultural Economics, 56*(3), 401–409.

Narayanasamy, N., Manivel, S., & Bhaskar, B. (2003). Networking SHGs and Co-operatives—An Analysis of Strengths and Weaknesses. *Journal of Rural Development, 22*(3), 333–343.

Planning Commission. (2014). *Government of India, Report of The Expert Group to Review The Methodology for Measurement of Poverty*. Retrieved from http//www.planning commission.

Reddy, G. N. (2002). Empowering Women Through Self-Help Groups and Micro-Credit: The Case of NIRD Action Research Projects. *Journal of Rural Development, 21*(4), 511–535.

Sen, A. K. (1973). *On Economic Inequality*. Oxford Clarendon Press. doi:10.1093/0198281935.001.0001

KEY TERMS AND DEFINITIONS

Food Expenditure: Food expenditure of households is the market value of all food items like rice, wheat, pulse, meat, fish, vegetables spices etc. consumed during the last month of the survey time. In this study food expenditure does not include expenditure for fuel and opportunity cost of the home makers as food expenditure. We have calculated the monthly expenditure for food of the households then calculated the per capita monthly food expenditure.

Non-Food Expenditure: Non-food expenditure is the market value of all goods and services, including durable products such as cycles, scooter, TV, personal car, and computers, purchased during the last year. It also includes annual expenditure for health and hygiene, education of children and for fuel and energy. In case of non-food expenditure first annual expenditure has been computed and then calculated the per capita monthly non-food expenditure for the sample households.

Gini Coefficient: It is a statistical measure of inequality in a distribution. Greater value of Gini coefficient indicates the greater inequality in the distribution.

Measures of Poverty: It refers to the measure of quantitative deprivation like income of households, or region. Poverty line income is the primary measure of income poverty. Poverty line income is the income supposed to be just sufficient to avoid inadequate consumption. This measure fails to indicate the extent of poverty. In order to capture the extent and inequality in distribution in poverty measure FGT class of measures of poverty are considered for measuring poverty.

North Andaman Island: Andaman and Nicobar Islands a rural and remote Union Territory of India. It has three districts viz. Nicobars, North and Middle Andaman and South Andaman. North Andaman Island belongs to the North and Middle Andaman district. Since pre-historic times, these Islands are the native land of aboriginal tribes namely, the Great Andamanese, Jarawa, Onge and Sentineles, all of Negrito Origin, in the Andaman group of Islands. Currently it is the home of about 0.1 million people, among them less than one percent are tribal. Common people earn their livelihood from nature, particularly from fishing, forestry and agriculture.

Self-Help Group: Self-help group (SHG) is a voluntary group of 5-15 persons, particularly, poor women with common economic interest. Although the participation in SHGs is voluntary by nature, some governmental or non-government organizations encourage potential persons to form group. Members save money recurrently and arrange monthly meeting under the headship of one member. After the continuation of savings for six months the group starts lending to its members for consumption needs or undertaking petty business. If the working fund is not adequate to meet credit needs of the members the group approaches the bank for group loan. Peer pressure at the group level is main collateral for the bank to do business with the poorer, illiterates and informal groups. SHGs in India are of mainly two types - models under non-governmental organizations (NGOs) and models under governmental organization (GOs) respectively.

Chapter 19
Poverty and Microfinance in Char Areas of Dhubri District in Assam

Shahjahan Ali Sheikh
Ratnapith College, India

Kanchan Datta
North Bengal University, India

ABSTRACT

In India, 70% of population lives in rural area and 60% of population earn their livelihood from agriculture which implies a high rate of underemployment and poverty. The root cause of poverty is the low access to credit facilities. Micro finance in this respect can play a vital role in providing financial services to the poor. In India Micro finance is dominated by self-help groups (SHGs), bank linkage programs aimed at providing a cost effective mechanism for providing financial services to unreached poor to fight against poverty. The chapter, thus, aims at identifying the current status, role, and performance of microfinance in Char areas of Assam in India. The chapter is concluded with the stress that more and more number of SHGs should be encouraged to form among the poor household in the study area to avail the benefit and cross poverty line.

INTRODUCTION

According to Gandhiji, named after M. K. Gandhi, the father of nation, India lives in villages. It was said because 70 percent of the population of the country live in rural areas. Most of the population live in rural areas are depend upon the agriculture and allied sectors. Rural areas are witnessed a high percentage of poor people and 67 percentage of the rural people are found Below Poverty Line. The root cause of poverty is the low access to credit facilities. The traditional financial institutions like banks are not interested to provide financial services to the poor living in rural areas. Again requirements of formali-

DOI: 10.4018/978-1-5225-5240-6.ch019

ties of the formal banking sector are out of reach for the poor and deprived people. Micro finance in this respect can play a vital role in providing financial services to the poor.

Microfinance, also known as microcredit, is a financial service that offers loans, savings and insurance to entrepreneurs and small business owners who don't have access to traditional sources of capital, like banks. These days, microfinance has become an important institution and mechanism of credit delivery, particularly for the poor and the deprived. There have been a number of studies undertaken in India and other developing countries that have brought out the success of various micro finance programmes in alleviating rural poverty, promoting holistic development of individuals, communities and developing small enterprises. The ultimate recognition of the viability, suitability and efficiency of microfinance as an agent and institution of development has recently come about, because of the pioneering work undertaken by Prof. Yunus of Bangladesh. Microfinance and more specifically the credit element in it, is basically undertaken and promoted by various Microfinance Promoting Institutions (MFPIs). These institutions can be Non Government Organizations (NGOs), Self Help Group (SHGs) and other social groups. The importance of the microfinance programmes and the success of the MFPIs in various developing countries, get prominence, because of persistent market and government failures in the sphere of rural development in general and rural credit in particular. This very success also negates the age-old perception and belief of most of the formal sector financial institutions that the "poor are not bankable". The proposed Microfinance Services Regulation Bill of India defines microfinance services as "providing financial assistance to an individual or an eligible client, either directly or through a group mechanism for:

- An amount, not exceeding rupees fifty thousand in aggregate per individual, for small and tiny enterprise, agriculture, allied activities (including for consumption purposes of such individual).
- An amount not exceeding rupees one lakh fifty thousand in aggregate per individual for housing purposes.
- Such other amounts, for any of the purposes mentioned at items (i) and (ii) above or other purposes, as may be prescribed."

The bill further defines Micro Finance Institution as "an organization or association of individuals including the following if it is established for the purpose of carrying on the business of extending microfinance services:

- A society registered under the Societies Registration Act, 1860.
- A trust created under the Indian Trust Act, 1880 or public trust registered under any State enactment governing trust or public, religious or charitable purposes.
- A cooperative society / mutual benefit society / mutually aided society registered under any State enactment relating to such societies or any multistate cooperative society registered under the Multi State Cooperative Societies Act, 2002 but not including a cooperative bank as defined in clause (cci) of section 5 of the Banking Regulation Act, 1949 or a cooperative society engaged in agricultural operations or industrial activity or purchase or sale of any goods and services.

Microfinance institutions have witnessed enormous growth during the last couple of decades. The spread of the SHG-microfinance linkage programme in Assam is recent. In this study we want to explain the expansion of this programme in the Char areas of Assam and analyse how it compares with the other parts of the state. To put it straight, the specific objectives of the study are:

- To find out the current status and growth of micro finance in char areas of Assam.
- To have inter-regional comparison in the progress of this linkage programme.
- To find out the future prospects of microfinance in char areas in Assam.

POLICY ON RURAL DEVELOPMENT

Developing countries like India has been adopting rural development through various public policies since independence and the Policy makers have been emphasizing upon the need of rural development ever since the advent of planning process in the country. The ultimate objective of rural development was the eradication of poverty and improving the quality of masses. In formulating rural development policy, the whole approach has been fundamental and has been targeted at removal of poverty of rural people, which has been perpetuated over the ages. The concept of rural development has undergone many changes depending upon the requirements and social transformation of Indian democratic system. The Government of India was committed to formulate plan policies on rural development in its Five Year Plans.

After the independence, the Community Development Programme was launched in year 1952 with 55 pilot projects on experimental basis. By early 1960's, the programme was extended to almost all the 5011 Community Development blocks of the country. It was emerged that the developmental process would allow benefits to the lowest level of the society. It failed to achieve the desired results mainly because of the lack of functional responsibility and coordination of the part of administration. The food shortage in 1960's led to the policy shift and more emphasis was laid on production-oriented programmes like IADP and IAAP. This was followed by the adoption of a new strategy of agricultural development based on high yielding varieties of crops in the late 1960's. During 1970 Area Based Programmes were introduced like SFDA, DPAP, MFAL etc. 1980's emphasized on strengthening socio-economic infra-structure in rural areas, alienating disparities under Integrated Rural Development Programmes, creating new employment opportunities etc. 1990's era witnessed the policy shift and decentralized, people's centred and human face development approach and strategy was adopted.

REVIEW OF LITERATURE

Various studies have been conducted since the nationalization of commercial banks in 1969, highlighting the importance and use of credit particularly in rural areas. These studies look into the problems of over dues and the causes for poor recovery. Interestingly, several studies have been conducted by social scientists, financial institutions and agencies, which highlight the positive trends and impact of Self Help Groups on empowerment, credit accessibility and the social change. Some of the available relevant studies, particularly case studies, workshops, seminars and symposia, have been critically reviewed.

Nagayya (2000) maintains that an informal arrangement for credit supply to the poor through SHG's is fast emerging as a promising tool for promoting income-generating enterprises. He has reviewed the initiatives taken at the national level with a view of institutional arrangements to support this programme for alleviation of poverty among the poor, with focus on women. He called for an imperative need to enlarge the coverage of SHG's in advance portfolio of banks as part of their corporate strategy, to recognize perceived benefits of SHG's financing in terms of reduced default risk and transaction costs.

Ahmad (1999) through a case study on Thrift Groups in Assam highlighted that women are coming to the administration directly for their just rights and to address their grievances boldly. It proved that Self Help Groups are successful in North East India even in the midst of insurgency. Similarly, Gurumoorthy (2000) maintained that SHG is a viable alternative to achieve the objectives of rural development and to get community participation in all rural development programmes. SHG is a viable organizational setup to disburse micro credit to the rural women for the purpose of making them entrepreneur and encouraging them to enter into entrepreneurial activities. Credit needs of the rural women can be fulfilled wholesomely through the SHG's. The women led SHG's have successfully demonstrated how to mobilize and manage thrift, appraise credit needs, maintain linkages with the banks and enforce financial self-discipline. SHG's enhance the equality of status of women as participants, decision-makers and beneficiaries in the democratic, economic and social and cultural spheres of life. They encourage women to take active part in the socio-economic progress of the society.

Bhatia and Bhatia (2000) through few case studies highlighted that recovery of SHG's is higher than other credit extended to borrowers. Moreover, involvement of SHG's had helped the bank branches in recovery of old dues. They observed that there has been a perceptible change in the living standards of the SHG's members, in terms of ownership of assets, increase in savings and borrowing capacity, income generating activities and income levels as well. Rao (2002) maintain that a review of the genesis and development of SHG's in India reveals that the existing formal financial institutions have failed to provide finances to landless, marginalized and disadvantaged groups. The origin of SHG's could be treated to mutual aid in Indian village community. SHG's encourage savings and promote income generating activities through small loans. Rakesh Malhotra (2000) in his study of 174 women beneficiaries, in Rae Bareilly of the state of Uttar Pradesh, drawn and covered randomly from four formal agencies of credit i.e. CB's, RRB's, PACS, and ARDB's revealed that less than half a per cent of female population against 3.5 per cent of male population in the study area were clients of the banks. Furthermore, only 7.64 per cent of the total number of cases financed and only 6.96 percent of the total quantum of credit extended by RFI's have gone to women. It was observed that 83 per cent of loan cases availed by women; male members were primarily responsible for the end use of credit.

Dasgupta (2000) in his paper on informal journey through Self Help Groups observed that microfinancing through informal group approach has effected quite a few benefits viz.: savings mobilized by the poor, access to the required amount of appropriate credit by the poor, matching the demand and supply of credit structure and opening new market for FI's, reduction in transaction cost for both lenders and borrowers, tremendous improvement in recovery, heralding a new realization of subsidy less and corruption less credit and remarkable empowerment of poor women. He stressed that SHG's should be considered as one of the best means to counter social and financial citizenship not as an end in itself. In another study, Datta and Raman (2000) highlighted that SHG's are characterized by heterogeneity in terms of social and economic indicators. The success of SHG's in terms of high repayment is mostly related to the exploitation of prevailing social ties and cohesion found among women members. Social cohesiveness among members spring not only from their diverse background of knowledge base, skills occupations and income levels, but also due to the dynamic incentive system of progressive lending to the groups on the successful completion of loan repayment. However, SHG's are heavily dependent on external financial agencies for their lending operations.

In their study, Barbara and Mahanta (2001) maintained that the SHG's have helped to set up a number of micro-enterprises for income generation. Rastriya Gramin Vikas Nidhi's credit and saving programme in Assam has been found successful as its focus is exclusively on the rural poor. It adopted a credit delivery system designed especially for them with the support of a specially trained staff and a supportive policy with no political intervention at any stage in the implementation of the programme. Puhazhendhi, and Satyasai (2001) in their paper attempted to evaluate the performance of SHG's with special reference to social and economic empowerment. The study revealed that the SHG's as institutional arrangement could positively contribute to the economic and social empowerment of rural poor and the impact on the later was more pronounced than on the former. Though there was no specific pattern in the performance of SHG's among different regions, the southern region could edge out other regions. The SHG's programme has been found more popular in the southern region and its progress in other regions is quite low, thus signifying an uneven achievement among the regions. Older groups had relatively more positive features like better performance than younger groups. Manimekalai and Rajeshwari (2001), in their study, highlighted that the provision of micro-finance by the NGO's to women SHG's has helped the groups to achieve a measure of economic and social empowerment. It has developed a sense of leadership, organizational skill, management of various activities of a business, right from acquiring finance, identifying raw material, market and suitable diversification and modernization. Similarly, Sharma (2001) maintained that through SHG's women empowerment is taking place. Their participation in the economic activities and decision-making at the household and society level is increasing and making the process of rural development participatory, democratic, sustainable and independent of subsidy, thus, macro-financing through SHG's is contributing to the development of rural people in a meaningful manner. Interestingly, Singh (2001) in his study in Uttar Pradesh highlighted that the SHG's is now functioning in the place of moneylenders because loan could be taken at any time as and when needed for any purpose. There are no formalities involved and the transaction cost is low.

The above studies simply demonstrate that SHG's are playing a vital role in extending macro-finance to the rural poor. The functioning of SHG's has been based on participatory mechanism and therefore the impacts of SHG's on its members in terms of empowerment, accessibility to credit, socio-economic change etc. has been found positive. Though there are a number of studies which are related to functioning and micro-finance but only a few studies have been taken so far to assess the impact of Self Help Groups on the socioeconomic empowerment of the poor and deprived people living char area which is most backward and peculiar geographic area in Assam. In this context, the present study is important to assess the impact of Self Help Groups on its members in terms of socio-economic empowerment in char areas of Assam. The study findings may be useful for policy imperatives and smooth functioning of SHG's. More benefits of SHG's may be obtained through proper functioning of these groups and extending of micro-finance to develop and promote micro-enterprises.

RATIONALE FOR THE STUDY

Poverty alleviation is one of the primary objectives of any planning in a national economy. Therefore, it becomes imperative to formulate situation specific poverty alleviation policies and programmes for generation of a minimum level of income for rural poor, which form the substantial percentage of national population in developing societies. One initiative is credit infusion in the rural sector. Increased involvement of banks in rural credit in post nationalization in India was considered as integral part of socio-economic development efforts for the rural areas. However, despite a vast network of commercial, cooperative and rural banks and other financial institutions no significant impact could be made on the grim poverty situation prevailing in rural India. Knowing that the success of any credit programme for the rural areas hinges on its high out-reach and people friendly approach, the governmental and other institutional players stepped in to provide favourable environment to the poor to develop their organizations. The decade of 1990's witnessed growth of various people's organizations. In this context the role of Self-help groups (SHG's), especially of women has assumed a critical challenge. Self-help groups approach is the key element of social mobilization. Linked with micro-finance, the SHG approach and movement has now been accepted as an effective intervention strategy for poverty alleviation. India has nearly 400 million people, living below or just above the poverty line. About 75 million households therefore need micro-finance. Of these, nearly 60 million households are in rural India and remaining 15 million are urban slums. The current annual credit usage by these households was estimated in 1998 to be Rs. 465,000 million. It is estimated that the number of small loans accounts from banks covered some 40 million households in 2000. The remaining 35 million households are perhaps meeting their credit needs from the informal sector (Fisher et al., 2002). Statistics, available from NABARD (2003), suggest that more than 8.67 lakh SHG's in India made successful functioning, while NABARD's target of ensuring bank loans are extended to 1 million SHG's by 2008 with an average membership of 17, this would mean bank's outreach to some 17 million members, the vast majority of whom will be women, with an average size of Rs. 1766 per family, Banks loans were made available to 11.6 million families in 2002-03: Beside the big donor agencies like NABARD, SIDBI etc. there are 2800 partner NGO's working extensively in this field. Two specific programmes viz. Swayam Sidha and Sivashakti which envisage formation, stabilization and bank linkages of women's self help groups are quite important. Southern region accounts for lion's show i.e. 64 percent in SHG bank linkage while Central India (11 percent), Eastern India (13 percent), Western India (6 percent) and Northern India (5 percent) account for nominal share. North-eastern region has negligible share i.e. 1 percent in total bank linked SHG's.

The government of India as well as the state governments has initiated a number of projects and programmes for socio-economic empowerment of the poor. The microfinance project intervention in terms of formation and stabilization of SHG for extending credit support and promotion of thrift to promote viable economic activities in the backward areas has resulted empowerment. However, there is scarcity of resource literature regarding the impact of SHG's on their socio-economic empowerment. Against this background, present study has been carried out in Char areas of Dhubri district in Assam to assess the impact of micro-finance or SHG on socio-economic conditions and eradication of poverty of the people.

MAJOR MODELS OF MICROFINANCE INITIATIVES

The literature on microfinance listed 12 various models of microfinance institutions working in different countries. This classification is on the basis of regulatory structure and operational methods. Few models are not common in international level and few others are complimentary. NGOs and self help groups are example. Most of the Self Help Groups have a promoter NGO. At the same time many NGOs have direct microfinance chains. Like that commercial banks are implementing microfinance operations through its SHGs. In these cases two models are working together to serve poor. Some models are working in the informal sector only. Major models are Grameen bank, Village bank; Credit union, Cooperatives, Self Help Groups, Commercial banks, NBFCs, Association of persons, *Nidhi* model, Community banking, NGOs and ROSCAs.

There are different organizations engaged in programmes of microfinance. In India this programme is predominantly undertaken and has been made successful by another institution popularly known as

SHGs. P Satish (2005), has defined SHG as a voluntary group valuing personal interactions and mutual aid as a means of altering the problems perceived as alterable, pressing and personal by most of its participants. These groups are voluntary associations of people formed to attain certain collective goals that could be economic, social or both. These days it is being increasingly realized that, the best strategy of ensuring simultaneously growth and human development, is by promoting the growth of SHGs. Hence both in development theory and development practice, microfinance and SHGs have become important institutions.

Microfinance has become one of the most discussed subjects in the last two decades all over the world. While one group advocates that it has significant impacts in reducing poverty (Prof Yunus Mohammed of Grameen Bank is an ardent promoter of this idea and has recently been awarded Nobel Peace prize for this endeavour); others caution against such optimism and point to negative impacts. There are still others who follow the middle path and argue that while micro finance does increase access of capital for the poor, in order to reduce poverty other non-financial services must be added on. Whatever may be the case, today microfinance programmes and institutions have become increasingly important components of strategies to reduce poverty or promote micro and small enterprise development in many of the developing countries.

Microfinance means the provision of thrift, credit and other financial services and products of very small amounts to the poor in rural, semi urban or urban areas for enabling them to raise their income levels and improve their living standards. Usually, the loan size would be below Rs 50,000 or so. Thus microfinance does not mean only the size. It means a change in the approach and philosophy to a demand led financial services and products for all of those who have been left out of the formal banking sector.

DATA SOURCE AND METHODOLOGY

The present study is both descriptive and empirical. This is based on group discussion among the beneficiaries with the help of well-structured questionnaires and supplemented by secondary data whenever necessary. The relevant secondary data have been collected from books, journals, research paper, newspaper, Government Reports and related websites. The present survey has been carried out in char villages of the district of Dhubri. Considering the availability of data, State level, District level and Block level information has been used for stratification purpose. A multi-stage sampling procedure was adopted for the investigation.

EMERGENCE AND NATURE OF CHAR LAND

The mighty Brahmaputra is the mainstream of the state of Assam. In the dynamics of erosion and accretion in the rivers, the sandbars emerging as islands within the river channel, or as attached land to the riverbanks, often create new opportunities to establish settlements. Once vegetated, such lands are commonly called '*chars*' in Assam. These are of two types:

- Areas created with sand of river within the bed as disjoint island (i.e. Chars) and
- Areas on the bank of river attached to the mainland (i.e. Chapori).

That sandy land area which is surrounded by river is known as *'Char' and 'Chapori'* is that land which is located on the bank of river. When a river changes its direction, a large number of *'chapori'* go into the heart of the river as eroded land and after a few years, it grows as a new *'Char'* and time taken in this process is usually ten to twenty years. In this sense high sandy land surrounded by river in different districts in Assam are termed as 'Char Areas' including *'Majuli'*, the greatest river island in the world.

According to longevity, the char areas can be divided into three categories viz. Temporary, Semi-permanent and Permanent. The char which exists less than 15 years categorised as temporary. The char having life span between 15 to 30 years are categorised as semi-permanent and the rest are termed as the permanent char. But it should be noted that no char is permanent in the sense that they everlasting after their emergence. Most of the temporary char areas are not inhabited. They are generally cultivated as they are naturally fertile. Of course some people build temporary cottage and used them as farm house. Needless to say that these houses are washed away by the river during flood and people build new cottage every year. The size and nature of char areas seriously affected by flood and erosion occurred every year which in turn influence on the socio-economic condition of the people living in char areas.

PROFILE OF THE CHAR AREAS

As per survey of the Government of Assam, there are 2251 numbers of char villages scattered in 23 sub divisions of 14 districts in Assam (Table 1). Total area under char is 3,60,927 acres of which cultivable land is only 2,42,277 acres and remaining 1,18,650 acres of land is not cultivable at all. That is 67.13% of land in char areas is used for agricultural purposes and 32.87% of land either used for residential purpose or waste land.

HISTORY OF MICROFINANCE

While the concept has been used globally for centuries, Bangladesh's Muhammad Yunus is the pioneer of the modern version of microfinance, according to Kiva, a crowd funding-based micro lending organization inspired by Yunus' work. While working at Chittagong University in the 1970s, Yunus began offering small loans to destitute basket weavers. Yunus carried on this mission for nearly a decade before forming the Grameen Bank in 1983 to reach a much wider audience.

Joseph Blatchford, former head of the Peace Corps and a UC Berkeley law student, is also credited with building up the modern-day micro financing efforts. Blatchford founded nonprofit Action as a volunteer project in 1961, and in 1973, the organization began offering small loans to entrepreneurs in

Table1. Profile of Char areas

Total *Char* Villages	2251
Total Areas (in acres)	3,60,927 acres
Cultivable Land (in acres)	2,42,277 acres
Non-Cultivable Land (in acres)	1,18,650 acres
Population	24,90,097

Brazil to see if a one-time influx of money could help lift them out of poverty. The operation was a success: 885 loans helped create or stabilize 1,386 new jobs. Action expanded the model to 14 other Latin American countries over the next decade.

GROWTH OF MICROFINANCE IN ASSAM

The economy of Assam is agricultural in nature. Most of the people are rural and relatively poor. Despite the large size and depth of the Indian financial system and thousands of bank branches across the country, Assam is still lagging behind in terms of financial inclusion. The people of Assam have very little access to formal finance. They have little access to other financial services such as savings accounts, life, health and crop insurance. To meet their short term and long term credit needs these rural poor have to depend on money lenders, friends and relatives and shopkeepers rather than on formal credit institutions. This is due to the fact that they do not have any collateral to offer. Despite very high rate of interest rate and other hazards, the absence of formalities scores over them and attract a large number of clientele to the fold of unorganised sector. In this context we can mention the importance of the alternative credit delivery mechanism like the SHG based microfinance programme in providing essential, financial services to poor.

The SHG group formation in the state started with a very slow footing. From the year 1988 some groups were formed but actual progress was after 1990-91 with the initiative taken by many NGOs. The microfinance movement in Assam started only around 1996-97 with a strong thrust by NABARD. However, prior to that SIDBI, with its earlier avatar of Micro Credit Scheme did start up with funding some NGOs. It is only in 1996-97 that they ventured in a slightly large fashion with Rastriya Gramin Vikas Nidhi (RGVN) under the Credit and Saving Programme (CSP) in Assam. Thus we can say that microfinance movement started in Assam around 1996-97. Introduction of SHG-bank Linkage Programme (SBLP) in 1996, further geared many NGOs, banks and government agencies to promote group formation and their subsequent linkages. In 2000 another programme called Swanajoyanti Gram Swarojgar Yojona (SGSY) was introduced as anti poverty programme. The SGSY and the SBLP are the two main programmes under which the formation of SHGs is undertaken for providing credit to members.

STATUS OF MICROFINANCE IN ASSAM

Both the models of micro finance i.e., SHG-Bank Linkage Model and MFI Bank Linkage Model which are operational in India are also operational in the State of Assam. But the micro finance programme in the State of Assam has not progressed in the same manner as it has progressed in other parts of the country up to 1999-2000. This was mainly because of the lack of awareness and exposure among the various stakeholders. However, there has been visible progress under SHG-Bank Linkage Programme from the year 2000-01 onwards. The cumulative number of SHGs having savings account with the banking agencies stood at 245120 SHGs up to 31st March, 2011. On the other hand, as on 31st March, 2011, the number of groups having bank loan outstanding stood at 111589 SHGs (Table 2).

NABARD through it Regional Office in the state headquarter is playing an active role in the promotion of micro finance movement in the state. Under its Self Help Promoting Institutions (SHPIs) Programme, NABARD has been providing grant assistance to NGOs and RRBs for promotion and nurturing of SHGs

Table 2. Progress of SHG-Bank Linkage Programme in Assam

Year	No of SHG Credit Linked	No of SHG Refinance Linked
1998-99	14	1
1999-00	53	46
2000-01	209	120
2001-02	748	528
2002-03	2453	1225
2003-04	7229	3309
2004-05	20528	3076
2005-06	25215	859
2006-07	25005	3167
2007-08	20318	5871
2008-09	26448	1779
2009-10	39058	3133
2010-11	29094	3030

Source: NABARD

so that they could become a viable group. In this regard, NABARD has sanctioned a grant assistance of Rs. 416.06 lakh to NGOs and Rs. 10.95 lakh to RRBs for promotion and credit linkage of 16,409 and 1300 SHGs respectively. NABARD has also sanctioned a grant assistance of Rs. 135.18 lakh to utilise the services of 751 Individual Rural Volunteers (IRVs) in 25 districts for promotion and credit linkage of 7,510 SHGs with the banking system. Till date, 2288 SHGs have been promoted through 126 IRVs and so far, 1141 SHGs have been credit linked.

The NABARD Regional Office, with a view to increasing the flow of credit particularly to the small borrowers, is also working to popularise the concept of Joint Liability Group (JLG) financing in the state. It is a group of 5 to 10 members having limited or no collateral to offer, come together voluntarily to avail bank loans. Borrowers are individually and jointly liable for repayment. To achieve this JLG financing, NABARD Regional Office has sanctioned Rs. 45.86 lakh, Rs. 40.60 lakh and Rs. 1.80 lakh respectively to Assam Gramin Vikash Bank (AGVB), Langpi Dehangi Rural Bank (LDRB) and UCO Bank for formation and credit linkage of 2,293, 2030 and 90 JLGs over a period of three years. NABARD is also supporting various NGOs across the state for organising Micro Enterprise Development Programme (MEDPs) to enable the mature SHG members to strengthen existing economic activities/ take up new activities.

The progress under SHG-Bank Linkage Programme in the State of Assam since inception is given in Table below. It is observed from the table that during 1998- 99, only 14 SHGs were provided with bank loan which has increased to 29094 SHGs during 2010-11. On the other hand, the number of refinance linked SHGs had increased from only one SHG during 1998-99 to 3030 SHGs during 2010-11.

GROWTH OF MICROFINANCE IN DHUBRI AND ITS CHAR AREAS

Informal credit delivery system assumes importance in the present rural economic scenario. Though formal banking structure has a wide network of branches in rural areas, the rural poor still continue to be in the clutches of money lenders mainly due to reluctance of banks in meeting the credit needs of the small farmers. In this context, Self Help Groups formed on the basis of mutual interest have proved to be an effective alternative credit delivery mechanism to reach the unreached poor. Although, SHG bank linkage programme was launched in the year 1992, a beginning of formation of SHGs was made in the district by *Chilarai Krishi Vikash Samiti* in the year 1999. It needs no mention that when SHG Bank Linkage programme was picking up in the country, Government of India had announced SGSY programme with a component of subsidy. As a result, Government Machineries, PRI, NGOs started to propagate formation of SHGs with the objective to get benefit of subsidy under SGSY. More particularly, bank officials had also shown much interest to help SHGs under SGSY. But, due to various reasons, subsidy did not reach smoothly to SHGs. Practically most of the SHGs, so formed did not get any benefit in the form of bank loan or subsidy till 2002-03. However, the situation has improved subsequently. The SHG-Bank Linkage Programme is being implemented in all the 13 development blocks of the district through Assam Gramin Vikash Bank, Commercial Banks like UCO Bank, United Bank, SBI etc. Further, NGOs and Farmers Clubs are also involved in promotion and linkage of SHGs in the district.

PROGRESS OF SHG-BANK LINKAGE PROGRAMME IN DHUBRI DISTRICT

The highlight of SHG-Bank Linkage Programme in the district is given in Table 3. It is observed from the table that as on 31st March 2011, a total of 4,885 SHGs were formed under the SHG-Bank linkage programme in the Dhubri district of Assam which is only 3 percent of total SHGs formed in the state under the same programme. On the other hand, the number of credit linked SHGs in the district is 2,157 and Rs. 343.9 lakh was disbursed to these SHGs as bank loan. Almost 67 percent of the total SHGs formed in the district is exclusively for women. Further the average loan per SHG during 2010-11 in the district is Rs. 85,766 which is more than the state's figure of Rs. 58,000 but lower than the all India per SHG bank loan of Rs. 90,000.

Dhubri is one of the most backward districts in Assam both economically and socially. The slogan of inclusive development and financial inclusive is lagging in the district. The mahajan, money lender, kabuliwala, marowaris are main source of micro credit of the poor. The formal banking sector always keeps a distance with poor people and farmers. It was between 1998 and 2004, micro finance taking place in the district with the initiative of some NGO like *Chilarai Krishi Vikash Samiti* under Swanojayanti

Table 3. Status of SHG-BLP of Dhubri district (As on 31st March, 2011)

	Total no of SHG	Total Amount (Rs)	Amount Per SHG (Rs)
Savings performance of SHG	4885	116.7 Lakhs	2390
Bank loan disbursed	401	343.9 lakhs	85,766
Bank loan outstanding	2432	834.7 lakhs	32,969

Source: NABARD Regional Office, Guwahati.

Swarojgar Yojona (SJSY). Due to lack of availability of banking facilities, the char areas of the district are far lagging behind. People of char areas become to learn about SHG only after 2000-01.

The economy of char areas is depending upon the agriculture which is basically traditional. Most of the people in char areas earn their livelihood from agriculture. As the productivity of agriculture per head or per unit of land is low, majority of the farmers are fails to fulfil their basic need and hence live below poverty line. The ownership of land is in the hand of few rich farmers known as *Matabar.* They hold 90% of the land and other farmers work as agricultural labour, marginal farmer etc. The formal banking sector is maintaining a far distance from these poor farmers. Actually speaking there is no any branch of any nationalised or regional bank in char areas of Assam particularly in the district of Dhubri. Very few people are maintaining their saving account in the bank which is located at towns and bazaars.

The poor performance in the progress of micro finance is mainly due to the sparse population in this region, lacked of experienced NGOs for formation and nurturing of SHGs and lack of homogeneity in Groups in the respective States.

INTERPRETATION OF THE RESULT AND FINDINGS

The Dhubri district is includes highest number of char villages i.e. 480 numbers of char villages are in the district. Population is near about 5 lakhs i.e. nearly 40% of the population of the district live in char areas. But due to several factors growth and extension of financial institutions either formal or non-formal sector to provide financial services to the poor and deprived people are found as not satisfactory. Following are the main findings (or challenges) of the study.

- Most of the SHGs found in char areas are formed and established during 2001 and 2005. SHGs formed after 2005 in char areas were unable to open an account in the branch of bank. This inability of the SHGs to have an account in the bank discourages the interest of the youth in involving with SHGs.
- There are 2157 (in 2005) and 4885 (in 2011) numbers of SHG found in the district having banking linkage. But the char areas of the district have only 664 such banking linkage SHGs which is much less than any average either state or national level.
- Among 664 SHG having banking linkage of char areas, only 104 have received a loan of Rs 2.0 (two) lakhs only. Other have received only a revolving fund of Rs. 10.0 (ten) thousands. Members reported that they become tired following different level of official.
- Absence of bank branch in char areas is another bottleneck for the proper functioning of the SHGs. It is found that most of the char villages are located at far distance from town and bazaars where to be found any branch of bank.
- Town based branches of nationalised bank and regional bank are always reluctant to open account to the poor people living in char areas. Middle class bank official, as reported by the SHGs, given no interest to the poor members of SHGs of char areas.
- Another important finding of the study is that of the shortage of staffs in the existing banks. Due to shortage of staff and imposition of responsibilities from the government side in respect of job card account, old age pension account etc, and banks denied opening any account to SHGs.

- Most of the women in char areas are indifferent about formation, benefit etc of SHG and other related matters. This indifferent attitude is due to the illiteracy, lack of information and social restrictions.
- Ignorance about micro credit or SHGs is acute and it is found to be 85% of the respondents were totally ignorant about micro finance and financial services.
- Nonexistence of the local guiding institutions is found to be another hindrance of the growth of micro credit in char areas. Most of the NGOs working in formation and guidance of SHGs are found to be town base and their workers shows little interest to work with the people of char areas.
- The district suffers lack of bank branch. Only a few banks are operating in the district which is very few and not sufficient to serve public.
- Most of the respondents report of loss of working day in the name of depositing monthly collection money at bank branches. As there are no bank branch in char areas and located at the far distant, poor people are loss their working day at bank.
- No Customer Service Point (CSP) is found in the entire char areas of the district. Though few such CSP are allotted area wise they are working by sitting at town. They place their argument as no electricity facilities are available in char areas.
- Religious and social restriction, conservation and illiteracy at mass level among the people in char areas is another main factor for lagging behind in financial education and empowerment.
- Fear about non-payment of bank loan by the people in char areas is another main factor of financial exclusion. As divesting flood occurs recurrently every year, heavy loss of assets and livestock taken place. But banks show indifferent attitude about such natural calamities. So illiterate people have always a fear about bank loan.

POLICY IMPLICATIONS

Majority of the beneficiaries obtained microfinance for dairy farm. Many more other activities like goat farm, fishery etc to be included to start their unit and financial support is to be extended by the banks.

In case of dairy farm one cow was not sufficient to raise income and employment level. To earn income and generate employment throughout the year few more cows should be provided for the beneficiaries by extending micro finance required based on the performance.

The micro finance was extended to only few poor rural women in the study area. Financial assistance is to be extended to more and more youth both male and female in different activities as per their interest in order to create an environment of work and to provide opportunities to earn income.

Poultry, Duck farming, goat farming are feasible enterprise and very much suitable for women in char areas to practice and empower them economically and socially. So the financial institutions and NGO's should come forward to extend financial support and guidance through Self Help Groups to take up such enterprise as an income generating activity.

Government and rural development department should focus on various programmes and schemes on rural development in every village through Panchayat institutions, NGOs and other stakeholders. Government may take initiative to establish more branches of banks either nationalised or regional rural banks particularly to serve the people of char areas which is most backward in every respect.

To overcome the problem of illiteracy and ignorance among mass people Adult education scheme may introduce in order to make awareness programme easy.

Extension of training services among the young male and female people in char areas must be strengthened in order to make the char areas people more efficient in terms of skill, capacities to work and enhance productivity and net returns.

CONCLUSION

Self Help Group or Microfinance is an important tool for upliftment of living standard of a poor. It can help a person or group of persons to have all kinds of financial services like saving, credit, insurance and so on. The movement of SHGs could not serve the poor of the country as it ought to be. Particularly, the state of Assam is lagging behind the country in this regard. Again, the district of Dhubri which is one of the most backward districts in the state and its *Char areas* are found to be at bottom of the list. Formal financial institution like banks shows their reluctant attitude to the poor of the char areas and hence SHG movement could not help them to get financial services.

Based on the results, it is suggested that SHG members be given a better understanding on financial services- such as opening of savings account in formal institutions, participation in fixed/recurring deposit scheme, and availing of life insurance for the entire family. NGOs and other agencies need to increase the awareness by providing proper information and training to reach the currently un-reached segments of population and should motivate members to take up more productive activities to enhance the income of the household in order to avail these facilities. The chapter is concluded with the stress that more and more number of SHGs should be encouraged to form among the poor household in the study area to avail the benefit and cross poverty line.

REFERENCES

Anjuman, M., & Alugumoni, T. (2001). Impact of Microfinance through SHG-A Case Study. *Indian Journal of Agricultural Economics*, *56*(3).

Bhuyan, S. (2008). *Micro finance and Self Help Groups; A case study of Assam* (Unpublished M.Phil dissertation). NEHU.

Caramela, S. (2017). *Microfinance: What it is and why it matters*. Retrieved on November 27, 2017 from http//www.businessnewsdaily.com/4286-microfinance.html

Census. (2001). *Primary Census Abstract*. Census of India, Office of the Registrar General, India.

Das, D. (2006). *SHG-Bank Linkage Programme in NER with special reference to Assam- an Evaluative Study* (Unpublished Project Report). Deptt. of Commerce, Gauhati University.

Dasgupta, R. (2001). An Informal Journey through Self Help Groups. *Indian Journal of Agricultural Economics*, *56*(3).

Government of Assam. (2003). Socio-Economic Survey Report of Char Areas of Assam 2002-2003. Directorate of Char Area Development of Assam, Guwahati.

Govt of Assam. (2011). Assam: District Census Handbook, Director of Census.

Govt of Assam. (2012). *Statistical Handbook.* Deputy Director of Economics and Statistics, Dhubri.

Khandker, S. R. (1998). *Fighting Poverty with Microcredit: Experience in Bangladesh.* New York: Oxford University Press.

Kumar, I., & Kondeti, S. (2014). Impact of micro finance on dairy enterprise women – A case study in Rayalaseema region of Andhra Pradesh. *Economic Affairs, 59*(4), 489. doi:10.5958/0976-4666.2014.00017.5

Pati, A. P. (2006). Financial Sustainability of Micro Lending Through SHG-Bank Linkage Programme. ICSSR.

Saha, G. (2015). Microfinance sector towards rural Development in North East. *International Journal of Recent Scientific Research, 6*(6).

Sarma, A. (2006). Microfinance: Hope for the Poor. *Yojona, 50.*

Satish, P. (2005). Mainstreaming of Indian Microfinance. *Economic and Political Weekly, 40*(17).

Umdor, S. (2006). An Assessment of the Self Help Groups Credit Programme in Meghalaya (Unpublished Ph.D. Thesis). Deptt. of Economics, North Eastern Hill University, Shillong.

Yunus, M., & Jolis, A. (1998). Banker to the poor: the autobiography of Muhammad Yunus, founder of the Grameen Bank. Aurum. Official Records of NABARD Regional Office, Guwahati.

KEY TERMS AND DEFINITIONS

Char Area: The extremely braided channels of the river along with its unique gradient, suspended particles and bed load combine together during floods to give rise to 'almond' shaped alluvial formations known as chars. The mid-channel bars (locally referred as char) are an integral part of the fluvial regime of the river Brahmaputra and its tributaries in Assam.

Living Standards: Standard of living generally refers to the level of wealth, comfort, material goods and necessities available to a certain socioeconomic class, in a certain geographic area. An evaluation of standard of living commonly includes the following factors: income, quality and availability of employment.

Micro Finance Institutions: Micro finance institutions, also known as MFIs, a microfinance institution is an organization that offers financial services to low income populations. Almost all give loans to their members, and many offer insurance, deposit, and other services.

Microfinance: Microfinance, also known as microcredit, is a financial service that offers loans, savings and insurance to entrepreneurs and small business owners who don't have access to traditional sources of capital, like banks.

Poverty: Poverty means not having enough money for basic needs such as food, drinking water, shelter, or toilets. Many people in different countries live in poverty, especially in developing countries.

SHG: Self-help group (SHG) is a small voluntary association of poor people, preferably from the same socio-economic background. They come together for the purpose of solving their common problems through self-help or mutual help. The SHG promotes small savings among its members. The savings are kept with a bank. This common fund is in the name of the SHG. A SHG has specific number of members like 15 or 20.

Women Empowerment: Women empowerment refers to the creation of an environment for women where they can make decisions of their own for their personal benefits as well as for the society. It refers to increasing and improving the social, economic, political and legal strength of the women, to ensure equal rights to women, and to make them confident enough to claim their rights.

Compilation of References

Abdulkadir, F. I., Umar, S., Garba, B. I., & Ibrahim, S. H. (2012). The Impact of Micro-finance Banks on Women Entrepreneurial Development in Metropolis. *Scientific and Academic Publishing.*, *1*(3), 28–38.

Acemoglu, D. (2003). *The form of property rights: Oligarchic vs. Democratic societies, Mimeo.* MIT. doi:10.3386/w10037

Acemoglu, D., Johnson, S., Robinson, J., & Thaicharoen, Y. (2002). Institutional causes, macroeconomic symptoms: Volatility, crises, and growth. *Journal of Monetary Economics*, *50*(1), 49–123. doi:10.1016/S0304-3932(02)00208-8

Acha, I. A. (2012). Microfinance Banking in Nigeria: Problems and Prospects. *International Journal of Finance and Accounting*, *1*(5), 106–111.

Acharya, M., & Bennett, L. (1981). Rural women of Nepal: An aggregate analysis & summary of 8 village studies. In The Status of Women in Nepal. Volume II, Part 9: Field Studies. Centre for Economic Development & Administration. Kathmu: Tribhuvan University.

Acharya, M., & Bennett, L. (1983). *Women and the subsistence sector: Economic participation and household decision-making in Nepal.* Working Paper Number 526. Washington, DC: World Bank.

Ackerly, B. A. (1995). Testing the Tools of Development: Credit Programmes, Loan Involvement and Women's Empowerment. In *Getting Institutions Right for Women in Development.* IDS. doi:10.1111/j.1759-5436.1995.mp26003007.x

Adebayo, C. O., Sanni, S.A., & Baiyegunhi, L.J.S. (2012). Microcredit Scheme Impact and Food Security Status of Beneficiaries in Kaduna State, Nigeria: A Propensity Score Matching Approach. *African Journal of Agricultural Research, 7*(37), 5191-5197.

Ademola, A. E., & Arogundade, K. (2014). The Impact of Microfinance on Economic Growth in Nigeria. *Journal of Emerging Trends in Economics and Management Science*, *5*(5), 397–405.

Adhikary, M. L. (2010). *Self-Help Group Movement- An Engine of Rural Development: A Case Study in the District of Burdwan.* Retrieved from www.cdedse.org/ws2010/WS2010_PAPERS/MANIKLAL%20ADHIKARY.pdf

Adhikary, M. L., & Bagli, S. (2012). Self-Help Groups and Borrowing Cost: An Empirical Study Addressing Endogeneity Problems. *Microfinance Review*, *9*(1), 69–85.

Adjei, J. K (2010). *Microfinance and Poverty Reduction: The Experience of Ghana.* Accra Central:Bold Communications Limited.

African Development Bank (ADB) (2006). *Microfinance-Policy and Strategy.* ADB.e

Aghion, P., & Howitt, P. (1996). Research and development in the growth process. *Journal of Economic Growth, 1*(1), 49–73. doi:10.1007/BF00163342

Ahlin, C., & Jiang, N. (2008). Can micro-credit bring development? *Journal of Development Economics*, *86*(1), 1–21. doi:10.1016/j.jdeveco.2007.08.002

Ahmad, R. (2012). *Microfinance in India*. Mittal Publications.

Aideyan, O. (2009). Microfinance and Poverty Reduction in Rural Nigeria. *Savings and Development*, 293-317.

Aigner, D. J., & Goldfeld, S. M. (1974). Estimation and Prediction from Aggregate Data When Aggregates Are Measured More Accurately Than Their Components. *Econometrica*, *42*(1), 113–134. doi:10.2307/1913689

Akanji, O. O. (2006). Microfinance as A Strategy for Poverty Reduction, *Central Bank of Nigeria Economic and Financial Review*, *39*(4).

Akinsanmi, A. (2005). Working under Constraint: Women, Poverty and Productivity. *Women and Environments International*, *66/67*, 17–18.

Akintoye, I. R., & Owojori, K. (2009), Microfinance Banking System: A Counsel to the Nigerian Populace. *Paper presented at the 6th African Finance Journal Conference*, Cape Town, South Africa. July 16-17.

Albee, A. (1994). Support to Women's Productive and Income Generating Activities. UNICEF Evaluation and Research.

Alesina, A., & Perotti, R. (1994). The political economy of growth: A critical survey of the recent literature. *The World Bank Economic Review*, *8*(3), 351–371. doi:10.1093/wber/8.3.351

Alesina, A., & Perotti, R. (1996). Income distribution, political instability, and investment. *European Economic Review*, *40*(6), 1203–1228. doi:10.1016/0014-2921(95)00030-5

Alesina, A., & Rodrik, D. (1994). Distributive politics and economic growth. *The Quarterly Journal of Economics*, *109*(2), 465–490. doi:10.2307/2118470

Alexopoulos, E. C. (2010). Introduction To Multivariate Regression Analysis. *Hippokratia*, *14*(1), 23–28. PMID:21487487

Alila, P. O. (1993). Informed credit and Rural Enterprise Sector Development.

Alimukhamedova, N. (2014). *Measuring the Impact of Microfinance* (Doctoral dissertation). Retrieved from https://is.cuni.cz/webapps/zzp/download/140035583

Alshebami, A. S., & Rengarajan, V. (2017). Microfinance Institutions in Yemen "Hurdles and Remedies.". *International Journal of Social Work*, *4*(1), 10. doi:10.5296/ijsw.v4i1.10695

Amatucci, F. M., & Crawley, D. C. (2011). Financial self-efficacy among women entrepreneurs. *International Journal of Gender and Entrepreneurship*, *3*(1), 23–37. doi:10.1108/17566261111114962

American Association of Family and Consumer Sciences. (2004). *A brief history of AAFCS*. Retrieved May 10, 2004, from http://www.aafcs.org/about/history.html

Anand, J. S. (2004). *Addressing Poverty through Self-Help Groups: A Case Study*. Retrieved from www.img.kerala.gov.in/docs/papers/jsa1.pdf

Anand, S., & Sen, A. (1997). Concepts or Human Development and Poverty! A Multidimensional Perspective. *United Nations Development Programme, Poverty and human development: Human development papers*, 1-20.

Ananth, B. (2005). Financing microfinance–the ICICI Bank partnership model. *Small Enterprise Development*, *16*(1), 57–65. doi:10.3362/0957-1329.2005.009

Ando, A. & Modigliani, F. (1963, March). The 'Life Cycle' Hypothesis of Saving: Aggregate Implications and Tests. *American Economic Review*.

Anjugam, M., & Alagumani, T. (2001). Impact of Micro Finance through Self Help Groups: A Case Study. *Indian Journal of Agricultural Economics*, *56*(3), 458.

Anjuman, M., & Alugumoni, T. (2001). Impact of Microfinance through SHG-A Case Study. *Indian Journal of Agricultural Economics*, *56*(3).

Antwi, B. D. (2015). *Microfinance and Poverty Reduction in Ghana: Evidence from the Dormaa Area Teachers Co-operative Credit Union in Dormaa Municiplaity-Brong Ahafo* (Master Thesis). Norwegian University of Life Sciences, Faculty of Social Science, School of Economics and Business.

Arjona, R., Ladaique, M., & Pearson, M. (2003). Growth, inequality and social protection. *Canadian Public Policy*, *29*, S119–S139. doi:10.2307/3552279

Armendáriz, B., & Roome, N. (2008). Gender Empowerment in Microfinance. In *Microfinance: Emerging Trends and Challenges, edited by Sundaresan* (p. 108). New York: Edward Elgar Publishing. doi:10.4337/9781848445178.00011

Arrow, K. (1974). The limits of organization. New York, NY: W.W. Norton and company.

Arunachalam, R. S. (2007). *Microfinance and innovative financing for Gender Equality: Approaches, challenges and strategies. Background paper prepared for the Commonwealth Secretariat*. Chennai, India: Independent Consultant.

Aryeetey, E. (2004). *Household Asset Choice among the Rural Poor in Ghana*. Paper Presented at the Authors' *Workshop for the Project on Understanding Poverty in Ghana, Organized by the Institute of Statistical, Social and Economic Research*, University of Ghana and Cornell University.

Asemelash, B. (2002). The Impact of Microfinance in Ethiopia: The case of DCSI in Ganta Afeshum Woreda of Eastern Tigray. Unpublished MA thesis, Addis Ababa University, Ethiopia.

Asghar, N. (2012). Microfinancing for poverty reduction: An empirical study of rural areas of Tehsil Gujrat-Pakistan. *International Journal of Advances in Management &Economics*, *1*(4), 14–19. Retrieved from http://www.management-journal.info

Ashraf, M. A., & Ibrahim, Y. B. (2014). Poverty alleviation and identifying the barriers to the rural poor participation in MFIs: A case study in Bangladesh. *Journal of Economic Cooperation & Development*, *35*(3), 99–132.

Ashraf, N., Karlan, D., & Yin, W. (2010). Female Empowerment: Impact of a Commitment Savings Product in the Philippines. *World Development*, *38*(3), 333–344. doi:10.1016/j.worlddev.2009.05.010

Asiama, J. P., & Osei, V. (2007). *Microfinance in Ghana: An Overview*. Research Department, Bank of Ghana.

Asian Development Bank (2007). *Effect of Microfinance Operations on Poor Rural Household and the Status of Women*. ADB, Special Evaluation Study, Sep. 2007, Ref No. SST:REG 2007-19.

Attanasio, O., Augsburg, B., De Haas, R., Fitzsimons, E., & Harmgart, H. (2014). *Group Lending or Individual Lending? Evidence from A Randomized Field Experiment in Mongolia* (No. SP II 2014-303). WZB Discussion Paper.

Awojobi, N. O. (2013). Microfinance as a Strategy for Poverty Reduction: The Nigerian Experience [Master Thesis]. Berlin School of Economics and Law, Berlin, Germany.

Awojobi, N. O. (2014). Empowering women through Micro-finance: Evidence from Nigeria. *Australian Journal of Business and Management Research*, *4*(1), 17–26.

Azmat, F., & Ha, H. (2013). Corporate social responsibility, customer trust, and loyalty-perspectives from a developing country. *Thunderbird International Business Review*, *55*(3), 253–270. doi:10.1002/tie.21542

Baah-Boateng, W. (2017). Employment and Labour Market. In E. Aryeeetey & R. Kanbur (Eds.), *The Economy of Ghana Sixty Years after Independence* (pp. 137–154). Oxford, UK: Oxford University Press. doi:10.1093/acprof:oso/9780198753438.003.0018

Babajide, A. (2011). Impact Analysis of Microfinance in Nigeria. *International Journal of Economics and Finance*, *3*(4).

Baden, J. A. (2006). Social Entrepreneurship and Quality of Life. *Posted on June 07, 2006FREE Insights. Topics in Cognitive Science.*

Bali Swain, R., & Varghese, A. (2009). Does Self Help Group Participation Lead to Asset Creation? *World Development*, *37*(10), 1674–1682. doi:10.1016/j.worlddev.2009.03.006

Bali, S. R., & Floro, M. (2010). *Reducing Vulnerability through Microfinance: Evidence from Indian Self-Help Group Program.* Working Paper 2010:23.

Banerjee, A. (2009). Globalization and inequality: A review of evidences. *Artha Beekshan*, *18*(2).

Banerjee, A. V., & Duflo, E. (2003). Inequality and growth: What can the data say? *Journal of Economic Growth*, *8*(3), 267–299. doi:10.1023/A:1026205114860

Banerjee, A., Chandrasekhar, A. G., Duflo, E., & Jackson, M. O. (2013). The Diffusion of Microfinance. *Science*, *341*(6144), 6144. doi:10.1126cience.1236498 PMID:23888042

Banerjee, A., Duflo, E., Glennerster, R., & Kinnan, C. (2015). The miracle of microfinance? Evidence from a randomized evaluation. *American Economic Journal. Applied Economics*, *7*(1), 22–53. doi:10.1257/app.20130533

Banerjee, A., Duflo, E., & Hornbeck, R. (2014). Bundling health insurance and microfinance in India: There cannot be adverse selection if there is no demand. *The American Economic Review*, *104*(5), 291–297. doi:10.1257/aer.104.5.291 PMID:25214652

Bansal, D. (2011). *Impact of Microfinance on Women Empowerment.* Retrieved from http:/hdl.handle.net/10603/3031

Barinaga, E. (2013). Introducing micro-finance in Sweden. *Journal of the International Academy for Case Studies*, *19*(3), 33–44.

Barrett, M. (1980). *Women's Oppression Today*. London: Verso.

Barr, M. S. (2004). Microfinance and Financial Development. *Michigan Journal of International Law*, *26*(2), 271–296.

Barro, R. J. (2000). Inequality and Growth in a Panel of Countries. *Journal of Economic Growth*, *5*(1), 5–32. doi:10.1023/A:1009850119329

Basir, M. K., Amin, A., & Naeem, M. K. (2010). Micro-credit and poverty alleviation in Pakistan. *World Applied Sciences Journal*, *8*(11), 1381–1386.

Basu, A., Rodolphe, B., & Yulet, M. (2004). *Microfinance in Africa: Experience and lessons from selected African countries*. International Monetary Fund Working Paper, WP/04/176.

Basu, J. P. (2006). *Microfinance and Women Empowerment: An Empirical Study with special Reference to West Bengal.* Mumbai, India: Indira Gandhi Institute of Development Research.

Bateman, M. (2011). *Microfinance as a Development and Poverty Reduction Policy: Is It Everything It's Cracked Up To Be?* Background Note, Overseas Development Institute. Retrieved from https://www.odi.org/resources/docs/6291.pdf

Bateman, M. (2010). *Why Doesn't Microfinance Work?: The Destructive Rise of Local Neoliberalism.* London: Zed Books Ltd.

Batliwala, S. (1994). The Meaning of Women's Empowerment: New Concepts from Action.

Batliwala, S. (1994). The Meaning of Women's Empowerment: New Concepts from Action. In G. Sen, A. Germain & L.C. Chen (Eds.), Population Policies Reconsidered: Health, Empowerment and Rights. Cambridge: Harvard University Press.

Batliwala, S. (1994). The meaning of women's empowerment: new concepts from action. In Population Policies Reconsidered: Health, Empowerment & Rights. Cambridge, MA: Harvard University Press.

Beatriz, A., & Jonathan, M. (2005). *The Economics of microfinance.* MIT Press.

Beck, T., Demirguc-Kunt, A., & Levine, R. (2004). *Finance, Inequality and Poverty: Cross country evidence.* NBER working paper, 10979.

Beck, T., Demirgüç-Kunt, A., & Levine, R. (2004). *Finance, inequality and poverty: Cross-country evidence.* NBER working paper 10979.

Beck, T., Demirgüç-Kunt, A., & Levine, R. (2007). Finance, inequality and the poor. *Journal of Economic Growth, 12*(1), 27–49. doi:10.100710887-007-9010-6

Beck, T., & Maimbo, S. M. (Eds.). (2013). *Financial sector development in Africa: Opportunities and challenges.* Washington, DC: World Bank.

Behrman, J. R. (1997). Intrahousehold Distribution and the Family. In M. Rosenzweig & Stark (Eds.), The Handbook of Population and Family Economics (Vol. 1, Part A). Elsevier.

Bennett, L. (1997). *A Systems Approach to Social and Financial Intermediation with the Poor.* Paper presented at the Banking with the Poor Network/World Bank Asia Regional Conference on Sustainable Banking with the Poor, Bangkok, Thailand.

Bennett, L. (2002). *Using empowerment & social inclusion for pro-poor growth: A theory of social change. Working Draft of Background Paper for the Social Development Strategy Paper.* Washington, DC: World Bank.

Berg, C., & Emran, M. S. (2015). *Does Microfinance help the Ultra-Poor cope with Seasonal Shocks? Evidence from Seasonal Famine (Monga) in Bangladesh.* Working Paper.

Berg, G., & Schrader, J. (2009). *Can Microcredit help to cope with Aggregate Shocks? Evidence from Ecuador.* First European Research Conference on Microfinance, Brussels, Belgium.

Bertola, G. (1991). *Factor shares and savings in endogenous growth (No. w3851).* National Bureau of Economic Research. doi:10.3386/w3851

Bhadra, B. (2001, August). Janani O Prayukti: Lingakaran O Kshamatayaner Sahabastan [Mother and Technology: Co-existence of Sexualisation and Empowerment]. Yojana. (in Bengali)

Bhaduri, L. (2016). La importancia de la responsabilidad social empresarial, Evolucion del concepto. *Negocios y entorno, 32*(4), 7-17.

Bharali, R. K., Chiring, A. J., & Konwar, D. (2013). Empowering women through self-help groups (SHGs). In Financial Inclusion, Self-help Groups (SHGs) & Women Empowerment. New Delhi: New Century Publications.

Bhatt, A., & Bhatt, S. (2016). *Microfinance Institutions: Do they Empower Women? A Case Study of Light Microfinance Pvt. Ltd. NMIMS Management Review, 28.*

Bhattacharya, G., & Haldar, S. K. (2014). Trend, Differential and Determinants of Deprivation of Reproductive and Child Health in the Districts of West Bengal, India. *Journal of Health Management, 16*(1), 93–112. doi:10.1177/0972063413518686

Bhaumik, S. K. (2015). *Principles of Econometrics: A Modern Approach using Eviews*. New Delhi: Oxford University Press.

Bhuiya, M. M., Khanam, R., Rahman, M. M., & Nghiem, H. S. (2016). Impact of Microfinance on Household Income and Consumption in Bangladesh: Empirical Evidence from a Quasi-Experimental Survey. *Journal of Developing Areas, 50*(3), 305–318. doi:10.1353/jda.2016.0111

Bhusal, M. (2010). *Does Microfinance Really Empower? A study on the contribution of microfinance in empowering the poor women of northern Bangladesh*. Retrieved from www.theseus.fi/bitstream/handle/.../.202010.pdf

Bhuyan, S. (2008). *Micro finance and Self Help Groups; A case study of Assam* (Unpublished M.Phil dissertation). NEHU.

Bird, K., Hattel, K. E., Sasaki, & Attapich, L. (2011). *Poverty, income inequality and Microfinance in Thailand*. ADB Southeast Asia Working Paper Series, 6.

Bisnath, S., & Elson, D. (1999). *Women's empowerment revisited, Background paper, Progress of the World's Women*. UNIFEM. Retrieved from www.unifem.undp.org/progressww/empower.html

Biswas, M. P., & Rao, M. R. M. (2014). Role of NGO in Empowering Women through Microfinance: A Conceptual Study. *Journal of the Humanities and Social Sciences, 19*(5).

Biswas, S. (2010). *India's Micro-finance Suicide Epidemic*. BBC News.

Biswas, T. (2008). Women Empowerment through Micro Finance: A Boon for Development. *Social Welfare, 55*(8).

Bi, Z., & Pandey, S. L. D. (2011). Comparison of performance of microfinance institutions with commercial banks in India. *Australian Journal of Business and Management Research, 1*(6), 110.

Blumberg, R. L. (2005). Women's Economic Empowerment as the "Magic Potion" of Development? University of Virginia and University of California, San Diego, Paper presented at the 100th Annual Meeting of the American Sociological Association Philadelphia, August 2005.

Blumstein, P., & Schwartz, P. (1983). *American Couples: Money, Work and Sex*. New York: William Morrow.

Boateng, G. O., Boateng, A. A., & Bampoe, H. S. (2015). Microfinance and Poverty Reduction in Ghana: Evidence From Policy Beneficiaries. *Review of Business and Finance Studies, 6*(1), 99–107.

Borah, A. (2014). Women empowerment through Self Help Groups-A case study of Barhampur Development Block in Nagaon District of Assam. *IOSR Journal of Economics and Finance, 4*(3), 56-62. Retrieved from www.iosrjournals.org

Bostman, R., & Rogers, R. (2010). *What's mine is yours: the rise of collaborative consumption*. New York: Harper Business.

Bourguignon, F. (2003). The growth elasticity of poverty reduction: explaining heterogeneity across countries and time periods. *Inequality and Growth: Theory and policy implications, 1*(1).

Bourguignon, F., & Thierry, V. (2000b). Oligarchy, Democracy, Inequality and Growth. *Journal of Development Economics, 62*(2), 285–313. doi:10.1016/S0304-3878(00)00086-9

Bradshaw, Y. W. (1998). Small Enterprises: Flexibility and Networking in an African Context.

Brahmachary, A. (2013). Gender Discrimination: A Decomposition Analysis of Income Gap between Male and Female SHG Members. In *Proceedings of Women Empowerment And Rural Development: Role of Microfinance*. Berhampore Girls College.

Brahmachary, A. (2015). Female Work Force Participation in India: Present Trends and Underlying Processes. *Look East, 5*(1).

Brahmachary, A. (2014). *For a Better World: Livelihood Security Measurement of the SHG Members. In Microfinance, Risk-taking Behaviour and Rural Livelihood.* Springer.

Brush, C. G. (1992). Research on women business owners: Past trends, a new perspective, and future directions. *Entrepreneurship Theory and Practice, 16*(4), 5–30. doi:10.1177/104225879201600401

Buvinic, M., Gwin, C., & Bates, L. (1996). *Investing in women: Progress and prospect for the World Bank.* Washington, DC: World Bank.

Calvo, C., & Dercon, S. (2005). *Measuring Individual Vulnerability.* Department of Economics Working Paper Series, 229. Oxford, UK: Oxford University.

Calvo, C. (2008). Vulnerability to Multidimensional Poverty: Peru, 1998-2002. *World Development, 36*(6), 1011–1020. doi:10.1016/j.worlddev.2007.10.001

Canadian International Development Agency (CIDA). (1999). *CIDA's Policy on Gender Equality.* Quebec: CIDA.

Canals, J. (1994). *La internacionalización de la empresa.* Madrid: McGraw-Hill.

Cañigueral, A. (2015). Consumo colaborativo. *Leaners Magazine*, 18-22.

Cannon, T. T., & Rowell, J. (2003). Social Vulnerability, Sustainable Livelihoods and Disasters. Report to DFID. Conflict and Humanitarian Assistance Department (CHAD) and Sustainable Livelihoods Office.

Cappellari, L., & Jenkins, S. P. (2003). Multivariate Probit Regression Using Simulated Maximum Likelihood. *The Stata Journal, 3*, 278–294.

Caramela, S. (2017). *Microfinance: What it is and why it matters.* Retrieved on November 27, 2017 from http//www.businessnewsdaily.com/4286-microfinance.html

Carbaugh, R. J. (2005). La globalización de la actividad económica. In R. J. Carbaugh (Ed.), Economía Internacional (pp. 4-8). Thompson.

Cardona, O. D. (2004). The Need for Rethinking the Concepts of Vulnerability and Risk from a Holistic Perspective: a Necessary Review and Criticism for Effective Risk Management. In G. Bankoff, G. Frerks, & D. Hilhorst (Eds.), *Mapping Vulnerability: Disasters, Development and People* (pp. 37–51). London: Earthscan publications.

Carlosn, S., Dabla-Norris, E., Saito, M., & Shi, Y. (2015). *Household Financial Access and RiskSharing in Nigeria.* IMF Working Paper. WP/15/169

Carol, J. R. (1982). Adapting for Heteroscedasticity in Linear Models. *Annals of Statistics, 10*(14), 1224–1233. doi:10.1214/aos/1176345987

Carrl, O. & Agboola, G.M. (2012) Microfinance and Entrepreneurial Development in Nigeria. *JORIND, 10*(3).

Carter, M., Little, P., Mogues, T., & Negatu, W. (2007). Poverty Traps and the Long term consequences of Natural Disasters in Ethiopia and Honduras. *World Development, 35*(5), 835–856. doi:10.1016/j.worlddev.2006.09.010

Cattell, R. B. (1966). The scree test for the number of factors. *Multivariate Behavioral Research, 1*(2), 245–276. doi:10.120715327906mbr0102_10 PMID:26828106

Census. (2001). *Primary Census Abstract.* Census of India, Office of the Registrar General, India.

Central Bank of Nigeria (CBN). (2005). *Microfinance policy regulatory and supervisory framework for Microfinance*. Abuja, Nigeria: Author.

Centro Mexicano para la Filantropía (Cemefi). (2017). *CEMEFI, Servicios*. Recuperado de https://www.cemefi.org/

Chafkin, M. (12 de 1 de 2016). *Fast Company*. Obtenido de Fastcompany.com: http://www.fastcompany.com/3054873/can-airbnb-unite-the-world

Chakrabarti, R. (2004). The India Microfinance Experience – Accomplishments and Challenges. In Integrating the Rural Poor into Markets. Academic Foundation.

Chakrabarti, R., & Ravi, S. (2011). *At the crossroads: Microfinance in India*. Academic Press.

Chakraborty, I., & Chakraborty, A. (2009). *Female Work participation and Gender Differential in Earning in West Bengal*. Occasional Paper, No. 18. Institute of Development Studies.

Chambers, R. (1997a). Editorial: Responsible wellbeing: a personal agenda for development. *World Development*, *25*(11), 1743–1754. doi:10.1016/S0305-750X(97)10001-8

Chambers, R. (1997b). *Whose reality counts? Putting the first last*. London: Intermediated Technology Publications. doi:10.3362/9781780440453

Chandramouli, C. (2011). *India 2011 Census Data*. Office of the Registrar General & Census Commissioner, Ministry of Home Affairs, Govt. of India.

Chen, M. A., & Donald, S. (2001). *Managing Resources, Activities, and Risk in Urban India: The Impact of SEWA Bank*. Washington, DC: AIMS.

Cheston, S., & Kuhn, L. (2001). *Empowering Women through Microfinance*. Academic Press.

Cheston, S., & Kuhn, L. (2002). Empowering women through microfinance. In Pathways Out of Poverty: Innovations in Microfinance for the Poorest Families. Bloomfield, CT: Academic Press.

Cheston, S., & Kuhn, L. (2002). Empowering Women through Microfinance. In S. Daley-Harris, (Ed.), Pathways out of poverty: Innovations in Microfinance for the Poorest Families (pp. 167-228). Bloomfield, CT: Kumarian Press.

Chettri, D. (2012). Empowering women of rural Kalimpong through Self Help Group. In Microfinance & Self-Help Group: Policy & Practice. Kolkata: Readers Service.

Chippa, M. L., Sharma, S., & Dubey, R. K. (2014). Impact of Microfinance on Women Empowerment, Poverty Alleviation and Employment Security in Rural Areas of Rajasthan. *International Journal of Innovative Research in Science Engineering and Technology*, *3*(2), 9073–9080.

Chitagubbi, G., Shivalli, R., & Devendrappa, S. (2011). A study on the usefulness of Self Help Group membership to women for empowerment. *Journal of Farm Sciences*, *1*(1), 112–119.

Choubey, B. N. (1983). *Agricultural banking in India*. National.

Chowdhury, A. (2009). *Microfinance as a poverty reduction tool-A critical assessment*. DESA Working Paper No. 89ST/ESA/2009/DWP/89.

Chowdhury, A. (2009). *Microfinance as aPoverty Reduction Tool – A Critical Assessment*. Retrieved June 20, 2017 from www.un.org/esa/desa/papers/2009/wp89_2009.pdf

Chowdhury, A. M. R., & Bhuiya, A. (2004). The wider impacts of BRAC poverty alleviation programme in Bangladesh. *Journal of International Development*, *16*(3), 369–386. doi:10.1002/jid.1083

Chowdhury, M., & Simanowitz, A. (2004). The Social impact of Microfinance. *Journal of International Development*, *16*(3), 30.

Christabell, P.J., & Vimal, R. A. (2012). Financial Inclusion in Rural India: The role of Microfinance as a Tool. *Journal of the Humanities and Social Sciences*, *2*(5), 21–25.

Christen, R. P. (2006). Microfinance and sustainability: International experiences and lessons for India. In *Towards a sustainable Micorfinance outreach in India* (pp. 43–68). Mumbai: NABARD, GTZ & SDC.

Christensen, C., & Raynor, M. (2003). *The innovator's solution: creating and sustaining successful growth*. Boston: Harvard Business Press.

Chun, S. (2013). Why do Microfinance Institutions Charge High Interest Rates? An Empirical Assessment of the Fixed Cost Theory. Michigan State University.

Clarke, G. L. C., Xu, & Zou, H. (2003). F*inance and income inequality: Test of alternative Theories*. Washington, DC: World Bank Policy Research Working Paper, 2984.

Clydesdale, G. (2007). Cultural evolution and economic growth: New Zealand Maori. *Entrepreneurship and Regional Development*, *19*(1), 49–68. doi:10.1080/08985620601002204

Coase, R. (1937). The nature of the firm. *Economica*, *4*(16), 386–405. doi:10.1111/j.1468-0335.1937.tb00002.x

Coleman, B. (1999). The Impact of Group Lending in Northeast Thailand. *Journal of Development Economics*, *60*(1), 105–142. doi:10.1016/S0304-3878(99)00038-3

Collings, D. G., & Mellahi, K. (2009). Strategic talent management: A review and research agenda. *Human Resource Management Review*, *19*(4), 304–313. doi:10.1016/j.hrmr.2009.04.001

Compartamos Banco. (2013). *Reporte anual 2013*. Author.

Compartamos, S. A. B. (2013a). Recuperado el 07 de mayo de 2014, de http://www.gentera.com.mx/wps/portal/Gentera/Acerca/QuienesSomos

Compartamos, S. A. B. (2013b). Recuperado el 2014 de mayo de 02, de http://www.gentera.com.mx/wps/portal/Gentera/Sustentabilidad/NuestraCausa

Compartamos, S. A. B. (2013c). Recuperado el 02 de mayo de 2014, de http://www.compartamos.com.mx/wps/portal/Banco/AcercaCompartamos/NuestroProposito

CONEVAL. (2012a). *CONEVAL - Informe de pobreza y evaluacion en el Estado de Jalisco 2012*. Author.

CONEVAL. (2012b). *Informe de pobreza y evaluacion en el Estado de Jalisco 2012*. Author.

CONEVAL. (2013). *Informe sobre la pobreza y evaluación en México*. Author.

Consultative Group to Assist the Poor (CGAP). (2009). *Financial Access Report*. CGAP. Accessed from www.cgap.org/publications/financial-access-2009

Consultative Group to Assist the Poor (CGAP). (2009). *What do we know about the impact of Microfinance*. Accessed from www.cgap.org/p/site/c/template.rc/1.26.1306/

Cooke, E., Hague, S & McKay A. (2016). *The Ghana Poverty and In equality Report: The 6th Ghana Living Standards Survey*. Academic Press.

Copestake, J. (2002). Inequality and the polarizing impact of microcredit: Evidence from Zambia's copperbelt. *Journal of International Development*, *14*(6), 743–755. doi:10.1002/jid.921

Cornwall, A., & Edwards, J. (2016). Introduction: Negotiating empowerment. *IDS Bulletin*, *47*(21A). Retrieved from http://bulletin.ids.ac.uk/idsbo/article/view/1355/PDF doi:10.19088/1968-2016.123

Correa, F. Vasco, A. & Pérez, C. (2005). La curva medioambiental de Kuznets: evidencia empírica para Colombia. *Semestre económico, 8*(15), 13-30.

Corsi, M., Botti, F., Rondinella, T., & Zacchia, G. (2006). Women and Microfinance in Mediterranean Countries. *Development*, *49*(2), 67–74. doi:10.1057/palgrave.development.1100247

Cruz, C. (2006). Valoración de bienes y recursos ambientales y naturales: El problema de la medición. *Registro Colombia*, *21*(2), 11–17.

Cull, R., Demirgüç-Kunt, A., & Morduch, J. (2009). Microfinance meets the market. In *Moving Beyond Storytelling: Emerging Research in Microfinance* (pp. 1–30). Emerald Group Publishing Limited. doi:10.1108/S1569-3759(2009)0000092004

Cuong, N. V., Bigman, D., Van den Berg, M., & Thieu, V. (2007). Impact of micro-credit on poverty and inequality: The case of the Vietnam Bank for Social Policies. Paper submitted to Microfinance: What Do We Know? Groningen, Netherlands.

D'Agostino, R. B. (1998). Tutorial in Biostatistics: Propensity Score Methods for Bias Reduction in the Comparison of a Treatment to a Non-Randomized Control Group. *Statistics in Medicine*, *17*(19), 2265–2281. doi:10.1002/(SICI)1097-0258(19981015)17:19<2265::AID-SIM918>3.0.CO;2-B PMID:9802183

Dabir-Alai, P. (2004). The Economics of Street-Vending: An Empirical Framework for Measuring Vulnerability in Delhi in the Late 1990s. Paper presented in EGDI and UNU – WIDER Conference, Helsinki, Finland.

Das, D. (2006). *SHG-Bank Linkage Programme in NER with special reference to Assam- an Evaluative Study* (Unpublished Project Report). Deptt. of Commerce, Gauhati University.

Das, P. (2010). *Rural Non-Farm Employment in India-Pattern of Growth and determinants*. Firma KLM Private limited.

Das, S., Chandra, S., Kochhar, K., & Kumar, N. (2015). Women Workers in India: Why So Few Among So Many? (Working Paper, WP/15/55). IMF.

Dasgupta, R. & Rao, K.D. (2003). Microfinance in India: Issues, Challenges and Policy Options. *Savings and Development, 2*(37).

Dasgupta, R. (2001). An Informal Journey through Self Help Groups. *Indian Journal of Agricultural Economics, 56*(3).

Dasgupta, R. (2005). Microfinance in India - Empirical Evidence, Alternative Models and Policy Imperatives. *Economic and Political Weekly*, *40*(12), 1229–1237.

Dasgupta, R. (2005). Microfinance in India: Empirical evidence, alternative models and policy imperatives. *Economic and Political Weekly*, 1229–1237.

Das, S. K. (2012). Socio-Economic Empowerment of Women through SHG-Banking Linkage Programme: A Boon for Development. *International Journal of Management and Business Studies*, *2*(1).

Datta, S. R., & Mukherjee, S. R. (2009). *Women in the changing world-Global Experiences and Challenges*. Kolkata: Levan Books.

Davis, K. (1973). The Case for and against business assumption of social responsibilities. *Academy of Management Journal, 16*(2), 312–322. doi:10.2307/255331

De Aghion, B. A., & Morduch, J. (2004). Microfinance: Where do we stand? In *Financial development and economic growth* (pp. 135–148). Palgrave Macmillan. doi:10.1057/9780230374270_5

Deaton, A. (1992). *Understanding Consumption.* New York: Oxford University Press. doi:10.1093/0198288247.001.0001

Deaton, A. (1997). *The Analysis of Household Survey: A Microeconomic Approach to Development Policy.* Baltimore, MD: Johns Hopkins Press for the World Bank. doi:10.1596/0-8018-5254-4

Decile ratios of gross earnings. (n.d.). *OECD Statistics.* Retrieved from https://stats.oecd.org/Index.aspx?DataSetCode=DEC_Ioecd.org/Index.aspx?DataSetCode=DEC_I

Dehejia, R. H., & Wahba, S. (2000). Causal Effects in Non-Experimental Studies: Re-evaluating the Evaluation of Training Programmmes. *Journal of the American Statistical Association, 4*(10), 53–62.

Deininger, K., & Squire, L. (1996). A new data set measuring income inequality. *The World Bank Economic Review, 10*(3), 565–591. doi:10.1093/wber/10.3.565

Deloach, S. B., & Lamanna, E. (2009). *Measuring the Impact of Microfinance on Child Health Outcomes in Indonesia Revision 3.* Department of Economics Elon Univerity Working Paper Series, 2009-02r3.

Demirguc-Kunt, A., Klapper, L., Singer, D., & van Oudheusden, P. (2014). Measuring Financial Inclusion around the World. The Global Findex Database 2014. Policy Research Working Paper 7255.

Dercon, S., & Hoddinott, J. (2005). *Health, Shocks and Poverty Persistence.* Oxford, UK: Oxford University Press.

Desai, N., & Usha, T. (2001). *Women in Indian Society.* Delhi: National Book Trust of India.

Deshmukh-Randive, J. (2004). *Women's self-help groups in Andhra Pradesh: participatory poverty alleviation in action.* Washington, DC: World Bank. Retrieved from http://document.worldbank.org/curated/en/402521468752429977/women's-self-help-groups-in-Andhra-Pradesh-participatory-poverty-alleviation-in-action

Devaraja, T. S. (2011). *Microfinance in India-A tool for poverty reduction.* Mysore: University Grants Commission of India.

Devi, R., & Devi, V. N. (2017). Economic empowerment of rural women throughSHGs with reference to Coimbatore district. *International Journal of Engineering Development & Research, 5*(3), 1111–1113.

DFID. (2000). *Poverty Elimination and the Empowerment of Women: Strategies for Achieving the International Development Targets.* London: DFID.

Dhanya, M. B., & Sivakumar, P. (2010). *Women Empowerment and Microfinance: Case Study from Kerala.* Retrieved from http://mpra.ub.uni-muenchen.de/25337/1/MPRA_paper_25337.pdf

Dhar, A., & Dasgupta, B. (2014). When Our Lips Speak —genderlabour together. In S. Sen & A. Chakrabarti (Ed.), Development on Trials. Orient Blackswan: New Delhi.

Dhar, P. (2016). Microfinance Penetration in India: A State Wise Analysis. *International Journal of Interdisciplinary Research in Science Society and Culture, 2*(2).

Dhavamani, P. (2010). Empowerment of Rural Women through Self Help Groups in Sattur Taluk of Virudhunagar District. *Journal of Bloomers of Research, 2*(2).

Dichter, T. (1999). *Non-Governmental Organizations (NGOs) In Microfinance: Past, Present and Future–An Essay, Case Studies in Microfinance.* Retrieved from www.esd. worldbank.org/ sbp/ end/ ngo.htm

Dichter, T. W. (1999). Globalization and its effects on NGOs: Efflorescence or a blurring of roles and relevance?. *Nonprofit and Voluntary Sector Quarterly, 28*(1_suppl), 38-58.

Dobra, A. (2011). Microfinance: Champion in Poverty Alleviation and Failure in Female Empowerment. *International Politik und Geseflschaft, 3*(3), 134-144.

Doçi, E. (2016). Microfinance and the interaction of Macroeconomic factors in poverty reduction. *Academic Journal of Interdisciplinary Studies, 5*(2), 209–218. doi:10.5901/ajis.2016.v5n2p209

Draper, N. R., & Smith, H. (1998). *Applied Regression Analysis.* Wiley Series in Probability and Statistics. doi:10.1002/9781118625590

Duku, O. P. (2002). A critical assessment of Jamaica's national poverty eradication programme. *Journal of International Development, 14*(6), 773–788. doi:10.1002/jid.923

Dumitrescu, E. I., & Hurlin, C. (2012). Testing for Granger non-causality in heterogeneous panels. *Economic Modelling, 29*(4), 1450–1460. doi:10.1016/j.econmod.2012.02.014

Dunford, C. (2013). *Evidence that Shocks are Managed Better with the Help of Microfinance.* Retrieved from http://microfinanceandworldhunger.org/2013/01/evidence-that-shocks-are-managed-better-with-the-help-of-microfinance-the-recent-rcts/

Eboh, E. F. (2008). Changing Development Paradigms via Microfinance Banks. *African Journal of Entrepreneurship, 1*(1), 52–63.

ECA/SRO-WA. (2015). *West Africa Regional Integration Report, Inclusive green growth to accelerate socio-economic development in West Africa.* Author.

ECOWAS. (2015). *Rapport Annuel 2015: La CEDEAO après 40 années: réalisations, défis et perspectives.* CommunautéÉconomique des États de l'Afrique de l'Ouest.

Edwards, C. H. (1991). Quality of life. In C. Edwards (Ed.), *Human ecology: Interactions of man with his environment* (pp. 97–111). Dubuque, IA: Kendall Hunt.

Ekpe, I., Mat, N.B. & Razaq, R.C. (2010). The Effect of Microfinance Factors on Women Entrepreneurs' Performance in Nigeria: A Conceptual Framework.

Elder, J., & Kennedy, P. E. (2001). *Testing for Unit Roots: What Should Students Be Taught?* Retrieved from http://citeseerx.ist.psu.edu/viewdoc/download?doi=10.1.1.140.8811&rep=rep1&type=pdf

Election Commission of India. (2015). Retrieved from http://eci.nic.in/eci/eci.html

Emeka, E. O. (2011). Youth unemployment and implications for stability of democracy in Nigeria. *Journal of Sustainable Development in Africa, 13*(1).

Endeavor Insight. (2014). What Do the Best Entrepreneurs Want in a City?" *Endeavor Insight,* February 4.

EPA. (2014). *African Economic Outlook: West Africa.* EPA.

Escobal, J. (2001). The Determinants of Non-farm Income Diversification in Rural Peru. *World Development, 29*(3), 497–508. doi:10.1016/S0305-750X(00)00104-2

Everett, J. (1991). *The global empowerment of women.* Summary of the annual conference of the Association for Women in Development, Washington, DC.

FAO (Food and Agricultural Organization). IFAD (International Fund for Agricultural Development) and ILO (International Labour Organization) (2010). Gender Dimensions of Agricultural and Rural Employment: Differentiated Pathways Out of Poverty. Status, Trends and Gaps; FAO, IFAD and ILO: Rome.

Farr-Wharton, R., & Brunetto, Y. (2007). Women entrepreneurs, opportunity recognition and government-sponsored business networks: A social capital perspective. *Women in Management Review, 22*(3), 187–207. doi:10.1108/09649420710743653

Feldbrügge, T., & von Braun, J. (2002). *Is the World Becoming A More Risky Place? Trends in Disasters and Vulnerability to Them. Discussion Papers on Development Policy No.46.* Bonn: Center for Development Research.

Fernando, A. R. R., & Azhagaiah, R. (2015). Economic empowerment of women through self help groups. *Pacific Business Review International, 8*(5), 91–98.

Ferreira, F. H. (1999). *Inequality and economic performance: a brief overview to theories of growth and distribution.* World Bank.

Field, E., Pande, R., Papp, J., & Rigol, N. (2013). Does the Classic Microfinance Model Discourage Entrepreneurship Among the Poor? Experimental Evidence from India. *The American Economic Review, 103*(6), 2196–2206. doi:10.1257/aer.103.6.2196

Financial Inclusion in India. (n.d.). *A road map towards future growth | sumanjeetkaur - Academia.edu.* Retrieved December 16, 2017, from https://www.academia.edu/4018810/Financial_Inclusion_in_India_A_road_map_towards_future_growth

Fisman, R., & Tarun, K. (1998). *Facilitating Development: The role of Business Groups.* HBS, Working Paper.

Forbes, K. J. (2000). A Reassessment of the Relationship between Inequality and Growth. *The American Economic Review, 90*(4), 869–887. doi:10.1257/aer.90.4.869

Foster J, Greer J & Thorbeke E (1984). A class of decomposable poverty measure. *Econometrica, Journal of Econometric Socity*, 761-763.

Foster, J., Greer, J., & Thorbecke, E. (1984). A Class of Decomposable Poverty Measures. *Econometrica, 52*(3), 761–766. doi:10.2307/1913475

Fosu, A. K. (2017). Oil and Ghana's Economy. In E. Aryeeetey & R. Kanbur (Eds.), *The Economy of Ghana Sixty Years after Independence* (pp. 137–154). Oxford, UK: Oxford University Press. doi:10.1093/acprof:oso/9780198753438.003.0009

Fraad, H., Resnick, S. A., & Wolff, R. D. (2009). For Every Knight in Shining Armour, There's a Castle Waiting to be Cleaned. In G. Cassano (Ed.), Class Struggle on the Home Front: Work, Conflict and Exploitation in the Household. London, UK: Palgrave-Macmillan.

Fraad, H., Resnick, S. A., & Wolff, R. D. (1994). *Bringing it All Back Home: Class, Gender and Power in Modern Household.* London, Boulder, Colorado: Pluto Press.

Friedman, M. (1970, September 13). The Social Responsibility of Business Is to Increase Profits. *The New York Times Magazine.*

Friedman, M. (1957). *A Theory of Consumption Function.* Princeton, NJ: Princeton University Press.

Friedmann, J. (1992). *Empowerment: The politics of alternative development.* Oxford, UK: Blackwell.

Frimpong, D.K & Kalbersonn, N.J (2014). Assessing the Contribution of Microfinance Institutions to Poverty Reduction in Ghana: A Case Study of the Christian Rural Aid Network (CRAN), Hohoe, Ghana. *International Journal of ICT and Management.*

Fundacion Genetera. (2013). *Informe de Actividades.* Fundación Gentera.

Gaiha, R., Imai, K., & Nandhi, M. Adhi. (2009). Millennium development goal of halving poverty in Asia: Progress, prospects and priorities. *Journal of Asian and African Studies, 44*(2), 215–237. doi:10.1177/0021909608101411

Gaiha, R., & Kulkarni, V. S. (2013). *Credit, Microfinance and empowerment, invited contribution to expert group meeting on policies and strategies to promote empowerment of people in achieving poverty eradication, social integration and full employment and decent work for all, September 10 -11.* New York: United Nations Secretariat Building.

Galab, S., & Rao, N. C. (2003). Women's Self-Help Groups, Poverty Alleviation and Empowerment. *Economic and Political Weekly, 38*(12/13), 1274–1283.

Galor, O., & Zeira, J. (1993). Income distribution and macroeconomics. *The Review of Economic Studies, 60*(1), 35–52. doi:10.2307/2297811

Gangadhar, S., Bhat, M. S., & Malyadri, P. (2017). An Empirical Study on Microfinance and Women Empowerment in Karimnagar District of Telangana State, India. *CSCanada International Business and Management, 14*(2), 65–69.

Gaonkar, R. R. (2001). Working and impact of Self-Help Groups in Goa. *Indian Journal of Agricultural Economics, 56*(3), 471.

Garg, C. P. (2016). A robust hybrid decision model for evaluation and selection of the strategic alliance partner in the airline industry. *Journal of Air Transport Management, 52*, 55–66. doi:10.1016/j.jairtraman.2015.12.009

Garg, C., Sharma, A., & Goyal, G. (2017). A hybrid decision model to evaluate critical factors for successful adoption of GSCM practices under fuzzy environment. *Uncertain Supply Chain Management, 5*(1), 59–70. doi:10.5267/j.uscm.2016.7.002

Garikipati, S. (2008). The Impact of Lending to Women on Household Vulnerability and Women's Empowerment: Evidence from India. *World Development, 36*(12), 2620–2642. doi:10.1016/j.worlddev.2007.11.008

Garriga, E., & Melé, D. (2004). Corporate social responsibility theories: Mapping the territory. *Journal of Business Ethics, 53*(1/2), 51–71. doi:10.1023/B:BUSI.0000039399.90587.34

GDP per capita economic growth. (n.d.). Retrieved from https://tradingeconomics.com/gdp-per-capita

Gertler, P., Levine, D. I., & Moretti, E. (2003). *Do Microfinance Programs help Families insure Consumption against Illness?* Centre for International and Development Economics Research.

Ghate, P. (2007). *Microfinance in India: A State of the Sector Report.* Retrieved from https://www.microfinancegateway.org/sites/default/files/mfg-en-paper-microfinance-in-india-a-state-of-the-sector-report-2007-2007.pdf

Ghorude, K. N. (2009). Microfinance for Financial Inclusion and Sustainable Rural Development. *Southern Economist, 48*(1), 47–50.

Ghosh, R. (2005). *Microfinance in India: A critique.* Retrieved from http://unpan1.un.org/intradoc/groups/public/documents/APCITY/UNPAN024232.pdf

Giné, X., & Karlan, D. S. (2009). *Group versus individual liability: Long term evidence from Philippine microcredit lending groups.* Academic Press.

Goetz, A. M., & Sen Gupta, R. (1996). Who takes the Credit? Gender, Power and Control over Loan use in Rural Credit Programs in Bangladesh. *World Development, 24*(1), 45–63. doi:10.1016/0305-750X(95)00124-U

Goetz, A., & Sen Gupta, R. (1996). Who Takes the Credit? Gender, Power & Control Over Loan Use in Rural Credit Programs in Bangladesh. *World Development, 24*(1).

Goetz, A., & Sen Gupta, R. (1996). Who takes the credit? Gender, power and control over loan use in rural credit programs in Bangladesh. *World Development, 24*(1), 45–63.

Goldberg, N. (2005). *Measuring the Impact of Microfinance: Taking Stock of What We Know*. Grameen Foundation. Retrieved from www.gfusa.org

Gonzales, C., Jain-Chandra, S., Kochhar, K., Newiak, M., & Zeinullayev, T. (2015). *Catalyst for change: Empowering women and tackling income inequality. Staff Discussion Note*. Washington, DC: IMF.

Gough, K. V., & Yankson, W. K. P. (2000). Land Markets in African Cities: The Case of Peri-urban Accra, Ghana. *Urban Studies (Edinburgh, Scotland), 37*(13), 2485–2500. doi:10.1080/00420980020080651

Government of Assam. (2003). Socio-Economic Survey Report of Char Areas of Assam 2002-2003. Directorate of Char Area Development of Assam, Guwahati.

Government of India. (2011). *Population Census Report, 2011, Registrar General & Census Commissioner*. Ministry of Home Affairs.

Government of India. (2014). Micro, Small and Medium Enterprises (MSMEs) Report 2014.

Government of West Bengal (1991). *District Statistical Hand-Books: Murshidabad.*

Government of West Bengal (2001). *District Statistical Hand-Books: Murshidabad.*

Government of West Bengal (2009). *District Statistical Hand-Books: Murshidabad.*

Government of West Bengal. (1951). *District Statistical Hand-Books: Murshidabad.*

Government of West Bengal. (1961). *District Statistical Hand-Books: Murshidabad.*

Government of West Bengal. (1971). *District Statistical Hand-Books: Murshidabad.*

Government of West Bengal. (1981). *District Statistical Hand-Books: Murshidabad.*

Govt of Assam. (2011). Assam: District Census Handbook, Director of Census.

Govt of Assam. (2012). *Statistical Handbook*. Deputy Director of Economics and Statistics, Dhubri.

Granger, C. W. J. (1969). Investigating Causal Relations By Econometric Models and Cross-spectral Methods. *Econometrica, 37*(3), 424–438. doi:10.2307/1912791

Green, C. J., Kirkpatrick, C. H., & Murinde, V. (2006). Finance for small enterprise growth and poverty reduction in developing countries. *Journal of International Development, 18*(7), 1017–1030. doi:10.1002/jid.1334

Greenwood, J., & Jovanovic, B. (1990). Financial development, growth, and the distribution of income. *Journal of Political Economy, 98*(5), 1076–1107. doi:10.1086/261720

Grosh, M., del Ninno, C., Tesliuc, E., & Ouerghi, A. (2008). *For Protection and Promotion: The Design and Implementation of Effective Safety Nets*. Washington, DC: The International Bank for Reconstruction and Development /The World Bank. doi:10.1596/978-0-8213-7581-5

Gudynas, E. (2009). La ecología política de la crisis global y los límites del capitalismo benévolo. *Iconos de Ciencias Sociales*, *6*(36), 53–67.

Guo, S., & Fraser, M. W. (2010). *Propensity Score Analysis: Statistical Methods and Applications*. Sage Publications.

Gurumoorthy, T. R. (2000). Self-Help Groups Empower Rural Women. *Kurukshetra, 48*(5), 31-37.

Guruprasad, L. (n.d.). *Sustainability & growth of Microfinancing in India*. Retrieved from http://www.academia.edu/4364486/Sustainability_and_growth_of_Microfinancing_in_India

Haneke, D., Glosw, R., & Hernand, S. (1998). Medio Ambiente y desarrollor sustentable. *Revista sustentable LDC, 3*(2), 18-24.

Harika, K., Chiranjeevi, Ch., & Reddy, S. M. (2015). Income Inequalities of SHG Households: An Empirical Analysis. *Economic Affairs*, *60*(3), 467–471. doi:10.5958/0976-4666.2015.00066.2

Hasan, S. (2005). Social capital and social entrepreneurship in Asia: Analysing the links. *Asia Pacific Journal of Public Administration*, *27*(1). doi:10.1080/23276665.2005.10779296

Hashemi, S. M., Schuler, S. R., & Riley, A. P. (1996). Rural Credit Programs and Women's Empowerment in Bangladesh. *World Development*, *24*(4), 635–653. doi:10.1016/0305-750X(95)00159-A

Hashemi, S., & Rosenberg, R. (2006). *Graduating the Poorest into Microfinance: Linking Safety and Financial Service, CGAP*. Washington, DC: World Bank.

Hazarika, G., & Guha-Khasnobis, B. (2008). *Household access to microcredit & children's food security in rural Malawi: A gender perspective*. Discussion Paper No. 3793. Institute for the Study of Labor.

Heckman, J. (1978). Dummy Endogenous Variables in A Simultaneous Equations System. *Econometrica*, *46*(4), 931–961. doi:10.2307/1909757

Heckman, J. J. (1979). Sample Selection Bias as A Specification Error. *Econometrica*, *47*(1), 153–161. doi:10.2307/1912352

Henderson, J. (2002). Building the rural economy with high-growth entrepreneurs. *Economic Review (Federal Reserve Bank of Atlanta)*, *87*(3), 45–70.

Herath, H. M., Guneratne, L. H., & Sanderatne, N. (2015). Impact of microfinance on women's empowerment: A case study on two microfinance institutions in Sri Lanka. *Sri Lanka Journal of Social Sciences*, *38*(1), 51–61. doi:10.4038ljss.v38i1.7385

Hermes, N. (2014). Does microfinance affect income inequality? *Applied Economics*, *46*(9), 1021–1034. doi:10.1080/00036846.2013.864039

Hewlett, S. (1986). *A Lesser Life*. New York: William Morrow.

Hofstede, G. (1997). *Cultures and organization: Software of the mind*. New York: McGraw Hill.

Holloway, K., Niazi, Z. & Rouse, R. (2017). Women's Economic Empowerment Through Financial Inclusion: A Review of Existing Evidence and Remaining Knowledge Gaps. Financial Inclusion Program Innovations for Poverty Action (IPA).

Holt, S. L. (1994). The Village Bank Methodology: Performance and Prospects. In M. Otero & E. Rhyne (Eds.), *The New World of Micro-Enterprise Finance* (pp. 156–204). London: IT Publications.

Holvoet, N. (2003). The Impact of Microfinance on Decision-Making Agency: Evidence from South India. *Development and Change*, *36*(1).

Holvoet, N. (2005). The Impact of Microfinance on Decision-making Agency: Evidence from South India. *Development and Change*, *36*(1), 75–102. doi:10.1111/j.0012-155X.2005.00403.x

Honohan, P., & Beck, T. (2007). *Making Finance Work for Africa*. Washington, DC: World Bank.

Horridge, P. E., & Craig, J. S. (2001). Female business owners in apparel manufacturing: An integrative perspective. *Clothing & Textiles Research Journal*, *19*(3), 89–102. doi:10.1177/0887302X0101900301

Hosmer, D. W., & Lemeshow, S. (1989). *Applied Logistic Regression* (2nd ed.). New York: Wiley.

Hossain, M. (1988). *Credit for the Alleviation of Rural Poverty: The Grameen Bank in Bangladesh*. Washington, DC: IFPRI, Research Report No. 65 1988.

Hulme, D., & Mosley, P. (1996). *Finance against poverty* (Vol. 1 & 2). London: Routledge.

Hunter, W. W. (1875). *A statistical account of Bengal*. London: Trübner & Co.

Hunt, J., & Kasynathan, N. (2002). Reflections on Microfinance and Women's Empowerment. *Development Bulletin (Canberra)*, *57*, 71–75.

Hussain, F. D. (1987). *Public Sector Commercial Banking in India-Development-Constraints-Recent trends*. New Delhi: Deep & Deep Publications.

Hussein, M. H. (2009). *State of microfinance in Bhutan*. Prepared for Institute of Microfinance (InM) as part of the project on State of Microfinance in SAARC Countries.

Hussein, M. H. (2009). *State of Microfinance in Afghanistan*. Dhaka, Bangladesh: Institute of Microfinance.

Iakovleva, T., Solesvik, M., & Trifilova, A. (2013). Financial availability and government support for women entrepreneurs in transitional economies: Cases of Russia and Ukraine. *Journal of Small Business and Enterprise Development*, *20*(2), 314–340. doi:10.1108/14626001311326752

Iganiga, B. O. (2008). Much Ado about Nothing: The Case of the Nigerian Microfinance

Ikpe, O. U. (2017). *Effects of Access to Microcredit on the Food Security Status of Crop Farm Households in Niger Delta, Nigeria* (Doctoral dissertation).

Ilmakunnas, P. (1990). Aggregation versus disaggregation in forecasting construction activity. In T. Barker & M. H. Pesaran (Eds.), *Disaggregation in Econometric Modelling*. London: Routledge.

INEGI. (2010). Mexico en cifras. Retrieved from http://www.inegi.org.mx/Censos

INEGI. (2012). *Encuesta poblacion y vivienda*. INEGI.

Interian, J. (2016). Up in the air: Harmonizing economy through airbnb regulations. *Boston College International and Comparative Law Review*, 129–161.

International Finance Corporation (IFC). (2014). *Microfinance in Africa banking for the smallest Businesses inclusion and their impact on GDP and inequality*. IMF Working Paper 15/22. International Monetary Fund.

International Household Survey Network (IHSN). (2013). The NSS Report (68th Round), 2011-12. Retrieved from http://catalog.ihsn.org/index.php/catalog/3281

International Monetary Fund (IMF). (2014). *Regional Economic Outlook: Sub-Saharan Africa*. Author.

Islam, A., & Maitra, P. (2008). *Health Shocks and Consumption Smoothing in Rural Households: Does Microcredit have a Role to Play?* Department of Economics, Monash University Discussion paper 22/08.

Islam, M., & Sarmah, J. K. (2014). Impact of self help groups in empowering women:A study of rural Assam. *Social Change & Development, 11*(2), 90–98.

Iyer, L. (1991). *Women entrepreneurs challenges and strategies.* New Delhi: Federich, Ebert Stiftung.

Jahan, R. (1995). *The Elusive Agenda: Mainstreaming Women in Development.* Atlantic Highlands, NJ: Zed Books Ltd.

Jahan, R. (1995). *The Elusive agenda: Mainstreaming women in development.* Zed Books Ltd.

Jain, D. (1989). Letting the Worm Turn: A Comment on Innovative Poverty Alleviation. In Assessing Participatory Development: rhetoric versus Reality. Westview Press.

Jalilian, H., & Kirkpatrick, C. (2002). Financial development and poverty reduction in developing countries. *International Journal of Finance & Economics, 7*(2), 97–108. doi:10.1002/ijfe.179

Jamali, D., & Mirshak, R. (2007). Corporate social responsibility (CSR): Theory and practice in a developing country context. *Journal of Business Ethics, 72*(3), 243-262. doi: 10.1007A10551-006-9168-4

Janzen, S. A., & Carter, M. R. (2013). *The impact of microinsurance on consumption smoothing and Asset Protection: Evidence from A Drought in Kenya.* Selected paper prepared for presentation at the Agricultural & Applied Economics Association's 2013 AAEA & CAES Joint Annual Meeting, Washington, DC.

Jappelli, T. (2005). *The Life-cycle Hypothesis, Fiscal Policy, and Social Security.* CSEF Working Paper 140.

Jayadev, M. (2016). Microfinance in India. *Changing Contours of Microfinance in India*, 8.

Joffe, M. M., & Rosenbaum, P. R. (1999). Propensity Scores. *American Journal of Epidemiology, 150*(4), 327–333. doi:10.1093/oxfordjournals.aje.a010011 PMID:10453808

John, G.M. (2008, March 1). Women empowerment through self help groups. *Southern Economist*, 234-54.

Johnson, S., & Rogaly, B. (1997). *Microfinance and poverty reduction.* Oxfam. doi:10.3362/9780855988005

Jordan, B. (2008). *Welfare and well-being: social value in public policy.* The Policy Press.

Julien, K. (2009). A Look at Interest Rates in Microfinance. Retrieved from https://www.academia.edu/1044113/A_Look_at_Interest_Rates_in_Microfinance

Kabeer, N. (2001). Discussing Women's Empowerment. SIDA Studies 136 (2001).

Kabeer, N. (2005). Is microfinance a magic Bullet for Women's Empowerment? Analysis of Findings in South Asia.

Kabeer, N., & Noponen, H. (2004). *Social and Economic Impacts of PRADAN's Self-Help Group Microfinance and Livelihoods Promotion Programme: Analysis from Jharkhand, India.* Imp-Act Working Paper No. 11, IDS, Brighton. Retrieved from www.ids.ac.uk/impact/publications/working_papers.html

Kabeer, N. (1997). Women, wages & intra-household power relations in urban Bangladesh. *Development and Change, 28*(2), 261–302. doi:10.1111/1467-7660.00043

Kabeer, N. (2001). Conflicts over credit: Re-evaluating the empowerment potential of loans to women in rural Bangladesh. *World Development, 29*(1), 63–84. doi:10.1016/S0305-750X(00)00081-4

Kabeer, N. (2005). Gender Equality and Women's Empowerment: A Critical Analysis of the Third Millennium Development Goal. *Gender and Development*, *13*(1), 13–24. doi:10.1080/13552070512331332273

Kabeer, N. (2005). Is Microfinance a 'Magic Bullet' for Women's Empowerment? Analysis of Findings from South Asia. *Economic and Political Weekly*, 4709–4718.

Kabeer, N. (2005, October 29). Is micro finance a 'magic bullet' for women's empowerment? Analysis of findings from South Asia. *Economic and Political Weekly*, 4709–4718.

Kai, H., & Hamori, S. (2009). Globalization, financial depth, and inequality in Sub-Saharan Africa. *Economic Bulletin*, *29*(3), 2025–2037.

Kaiser, H. F. (1958). The varimax criterion for analytic rotation in factor analysis. *Psychometrika*, *23*(3), 187–200. doi:10.1007/BF02289233

Kakwani, N., & Son, H. H. (2016). Measuring Social Tension. In *Social Welfare Functions and Development* (pp. 45–76). Palgrave Macmillan. doi:10.1057/978-1-137-58325-3_3

Kaladhar, K. (1997). Microfinance in India: Design, structure and governance. *Economic and Political Weekly*, 2687–2706.

Kalbagh, C. (1991). *Women and development* (Vol. I). New Delhi: Delhi Discovery Publishing House.

Kalirajan, K., & Singh, K. (2009). The pace of poverty reduction across the globe: An exploratory analysis. *International Journal of Social Economics*, *36*(6), 692–705. doi:10.1108/03068290910956921

Kaliranjan, K., & Singh, K. (2012). *Self Help Group-Banking-Poverty Reduction Nexus: A Case Study of Uttrakhand State, India*. ASARC Working Paper, 2012/2.

Kamanou, G., & Morduch, J. (2005). *Measuring Vunerability to Poverty in: Stefan Dercon* (I. A. Poverty, Ed.). Oxford, UK: Oxford University Press.

Kamath, R., Dattasharma, A., & Ramanathan, S. (2013). *MFI (Microfinance Institutes) Borrowers: Their loans and Repayments – A study in Ramanagaram, India*. Working Paper No. 397. Indian Institute of Management, Bangalore.

Kanoria, H. P. (2012). *Swami Vivkananda's thoughts on women*. Retrieved from http://indiansrgr8.blogspot.com/2012/01/swami-vivekanandas-thoughts-on-women.html

Kapoor, S. (2011). *Management Development Programme on Microfinance, Reading Material*. IIM Lucknow.

Kapur, P. (2001). *Empowering the Indian Women*. New Delhi: Ministry of Information and Broadcasting, Government of India.

Karlan, D. S. (2001). Microfinance Impact Assessments: The Perils of Using New Members as a Control Group. *Journal of Microfinance*, *3*(2), 75–85.

Karmakar, K. G. (2009). Emerging Trends in Microfinance. *Economic and Political Weekly*.

Kasali, T. A., Ahmad, S. A., & Lim, H. E. (2015). The role of Microfinance in poverty alleviation: Empirical evidence from South-West Nigeria. *Asian Social Science*, *11*(21). doi:10.5539/ass.v11n21p183

Kato, M. P., & Kratze, J. (2013). Empowering Women through Microfinance: Evidence from Tanzania. *ACRN Journal of Entrepreneurship Perspectives*, *2*(1), 31-59.

Kazi, M. H., & Leonard, J. E. (2012). Microfinance, poverty and youth unemployment of Nigeria: A Review. *Global Journal of Human Social Science, Sociology, Economics & Political Science (Wellington, N.Z.)*, *12*(13), 45–59.

Kefas, S.D. (2006), Fighting Poverty through Empowering Women with Microfinance, *A Quarterly Newsletter of International Year of Microcredit, 2.*

Kellett, N. C. (2011). Microfinance and economic inequality in the Peruvian highlands. *Ethnology, 50*(3), 59–78.

Kessides, C. (2005). Contributions of urban development to economic growth and poverty reduction in Sub-Saharan Africa. Washington, DC: World Bank.

Key, R. J., & Firebaugh, F. M. (1989). Family resource management: Preparing for the 21st century. *Journal of Home Economics, 81*(1), 13–17.

Khan, Khalily, & Scheyvens. (2015). *Impact of Ex-Ante Access to Microfinanceon the Coping Strategies to cope with Monga of Poor Households in North-Western Bangladesh.* Institute of Microfinance (InM) Working Paper. No 43.

Khandker, S. R. (1998). *Fighting poverty with microcredit: Experience in Bangladesh.* New York: Oxford University Press.

Khandker, S. R. (1998). *Fighting Poverty with Microcredit: Experience in Bangladesh.* New York: Oxford University Press.

Khandker, S. R. (2005). Microfinance and poverty: Evidence using panel data from Bangladesh. *The World Bank Economic Review, 19*(2), 263–286. doi:10.1093/wber/lhi008

Khandker, S. R., Hussain, S., & Zahed, K. (1998). Income and Employment Effects of Micro-Credit Programmes: Village-level Evidence from Bangladesh. *The Journal of Development Studies, 35*(2), 96–124. doi:10.1080/00220389808422566

Khanna, T. (2000). Business groups and Social welfare in emerging markets: Existing evidence and unanswered questions. *European Economic Review, 444*(6), 748–761. doi:10.1016/S0014-2921(99)00059-8

Kimotho, M. W. (2007). The Key Success Factors in Microfinance: Wide Outreach and Long-Term Sustainability. The Nigerian Microfinance, 4.

Kim, S. H., Sharpe, D. L., & Kim, H. (2002). Factors influencing the likelihood of leaving self employment in Korea. *Family and Consumer Sciences Research Journal, 30*(4), 554–569. doi:10.1177/1077727X02030004007

King, E. M., & Mason, D. A. (2001). Engendering Development Through Gender Equality. Development Outreach, 3(2).

Kirkpatrick, C., & Maimbo, S. (2002). The implications of the evolving microfinance agendafor regulatory and supervisory policy. *Development Policy Review, 20*(3), 293–304. doi:10.1111/1467-7679.00172

Klasen, S. (2006). UNDP's Gender-Related Measures: Some Conceptual Problems and Possible Solutions. *Journal of Human Development, 7*(2), 243–274. doi:10.1080/14649880600768595

Klasen, S., & Schüler, D. (2011). Reforming the Gender-related Development Index and the Gender Empowerment Measure: Implementing some specific proposals. *Feminist Economics, 17*(1), 1–30. doi:10.1080/13545701.2010.541860

Kleinbaum, D. G., Sullivan, K. M., & Barker, N. D. (2007). *A Pocket Guide to Epidemiology.* New York: Springer Science and Business Media, LLC.

Kline, K., & Sadhu, S. (2012). *Microfinance in India: A new regulatory structure.* Centre for Microfinance.

Koponen, D. (n.d.). *Social entrepreneurship perspective for quality of life improvement at national business system level.* Kaunas University of Technology, Lithuania.

Koveos, P., & Randhawa, D. (2004). Financial Services for the Poor: Assessing Microfinance Institutions. *Managerial Finance, 30*(9), 70–95. doi:10.1108/03074350410769281

K-REP. (1995). Employment and Income in Micro and Small Enterprises in Kenya. Results of a 1995 Survey (Research Paper No. 26).

Krishna, A. (2003). Social Capital, Community driven Development and Empowerment: A Short Note on Concepts and Operations (*Working Paper* 33077). *World Bank.*

Krishna, A. (2003). Social Capital, Community Driven Development, and Empowerment: A short note on concepts and operations (*Working Paper* 33077). *World Bank.*

Kumar, S. & Anand, S. (2007). Journey of Rural Credit in India over the Past Sixty Year. *Kurukshetra, 55*(12), 52-54

Kumar, S. N. (2006, April 20). The Making of Debt Trap in Andhra Pradesh. The Hindu. Retrieved from www.hindu.com/2006/04/20/stories/2006042005220900.htm

Kumarankandath, A. (2017, April 28). *Microfinance and energy access*. Retrieved December 16, 2017, from http://www.downtoearth.org.in/blog/microfinance-and-energy-access-57720

Kumaran, P. K. (2002). Role of Self-Help Groups in Promoting Micro-enterprises Through Micro Credit: An Empirical Study. *Journal of Rural Development, 21*(2), 231–250.

Kumar, I., & Kondeti, S. (2014). Impact of micro finance on dairy enterprise women – A case study in Rayalaseema region of Andhra Pradesh. *Economic Affairs, 59*(4), 489. doi:10.5958/0976-4666.2014.00017.5

Kumari, G. L., & Subrahmanyam, S. (2017). Women Empowerment through Financial Inclusion – A Study with Reference to YSR Kadapa District of Andhra Pradesh. *International Journal of Applied Research, 3*(4), 509–513.

Kumar, N. (2013). Financial inclusion and its determinants: Evidence from India. *Journal of Financial Economic Policy, 5*(1), 4–19. doi:10.1108/17576381311317754

Kumar, R. (1993). *The History of doing: An illustrated account of movements for women's rights and feminism in India, 1800-1990.* New York: Verso.

Kumar, R. (1993). *The History of Doing: An Illustrated Account of Movements for Women's Rights and Feminism in India, 1800-1990.* New York: Verso.

Kundu, A. (2009). *Joint versus Individual Liability in Microfinance-A Comparative Impact Evalutation Through Natural Experiment.* Retrieved from http://mpra.ub.uni-muechen.de/32695.pdf

Kundu, A. (2011). Savings, lending rate and skill improvement in microfinance operating through public-private cooperation. *IUP Journal of Managerial Economics, 9*(4), 33–52.

Kuzilwa, J. (2005). The role of credit for small business success: A study of the National Entrepreneurship Development Fund in Tanzania. *The Journal of Entrepreneurship, 14*(2), 131–161. doi:10.1177/097135570501400204

Kuznets, S. (1955). Economic growth and income inequality. *The American Economic Review, 45*(1), 1–28.

Kuznets, S. (1963). Quantitative aspects of the economic growth of nations: VIII. Distribution of income by size. *Economic Development and Cultural Change, 11*(2), 1–80. doi:10.1086/450006

Lakshmi, R., & Vadivalagan, G. (2012). Impact of self help groups on empowerment of women: A study in Dharmapuri district, Tamilnadu. *Journal of Management & Sciences, 1*(2), 43–55.

Lalita, R. (1996). Women entrepreneurs. New Delhi: A.P.H. Publishing Corporation.

Laws, E. (2016). *Social Assistance and Idiosyncratic Shocks*. GSDRC Helpdesk Research Report, 1383.

Ledgerwood, J. (1999). *Microfinance Handbook: An Institutional and Financial Perspective*. Washington, DC: World Bank.

Leikem, K. (2012). *Microfinance: A tool for poverty reduction?* A Project submitted to University of Rhode Island.

Levin, A., Lin, C. F., & Chu, C. S. J. (2002). Unit root tests in panel data: Asymptotic and finite- sample properties. *Journal of Econometrics, 108*(1), 1–24. doi:10.1016/S0304-4076(01)00098-7

Levine, R. (2005). Finance and Growth-Theory and Evidence. In P. Aghion & ... (Eds.), *Handbook of Economic Growth*. Elsevier North Holland.

Ligon, E., & Schechter, L. (2003). Measuring Vulnerability. *Economic Journal (London), 113*(486), 95–102. doi:10.1111/1468-0297.00117

Littlefield, E., Morduch, J., & Hashemi, S. (2003). Is microfinance an effective strategy to reach the Millennium Development Goals? *Focus note, 24*(2003), 1-11.

Lizarzaburu, E., & Del Brio, J. (2016). Responsabilidad social corporativa y reputación corporativa en el sector financiero de países en desarrollo. *GCG: Revista De Globalización. Competitividad & Gobernabilidad, 10*(1), 42–65. doi:10.3232/GCG.2016.V10.N1.02

Madan, G. R. (1980). *Indian Social Problem*. Kolkata: Allied Publishers Private Limited.

Mader, P. (2013). Rise and fall of microfinance in India: The Andhra Pradesh crisis in perspective. *Strategic Change, 22*(1-2), 47–66. doi:10.1002/jsc.1921

Mahajan, V., & Nagasri, G. (2000). *Building sustainable microfinance institutions in India*. Internal Document.

Mahajan, V., & Ramola, B. G. (2003). *Microfinance in India: Banyan Tree and Bonsai. Background Paper Prepared for the World Bank*. Washington, DC: World Bank.

Mahanta, P., & Panda, G. (2012). Status of microfinance in India- A review. *International Journal of Marketing, Financial Services & Management Research, 1*(11).

Mahanta, P., & Panda, G. (2012). Sreekumar (2012). Status of microfinance in India: A review. *International Journal of Marketing. Financial Services & Management Research, 1*(11), 142–155.

Mahanta, P, & Panda, G. & Sreekumar. (2012). Status of Microfinance in India - A review, International Journal of Marketing. *Financial Services & Management Research, 1*(11), 142–155.

Mahjabeen, R. (2008). Microfinancing in Bangladesh: Impact on households, consumption and welfare. *Journal of Policy Modeling, 30*(6), 1083–1092. doi:10.1016/j.jpolmod.2007.12.007

Mahmud, S. (2003). Women and transformation of the domestic spaces for income generation in Dhaka bustees. *Cities (London, England), 20*(5), 321–329. doi:10.1016/S0264-2751(03)00049-0

Mahmud, S., Shah, N. M., & Becker, S. (2012). Measurement of Women's Empowerment in Rural Bangladesh. *World Development, 40*(3), 610–619. doi:10.1016/j.worlddev.2011.08.003 PMID:23637468

Mahoney, J. (2012). *The theoretical building blocks of organizational economics. Economic Foundation of Strategy*. SAGE.

Maity, S., & Sarania, R. (2017). Does microfinance alleviate poverty and inequality? Studying self-help groups in Bodoland, Assam. *Development in Practice, 27*(7), 1006–1019. doi:10.1080/09614524.2017.1355353

Makarfi, A. M., & Olukosi, J. O. (2011). Microfinance institutions as vehicles for sustainable credit access by the poor in Kano state, Nigeria. *European Journal of Finance & Banking Research*, *4*(4), 34–48.

Malhotra, A., S.R. Schuler & C. Boender (2002.) Measuring women's empowerment as a variable in international development. *Paper for World Bank Workshop on Poverty and Gender: New Perspectives*, May 7.

Malhotra, A., Schuler, S. R., & Boender, C. (2002). *Measuring women's empowerment as a variable in international development.* Background paper for World Bank Workshop on Poverty & Gender: New Perspectives.

Malik, B.S., & Vani, S. (2006). Micro-enterprises for empowerment of women. *Kissan World*, *33*(5).

Mandal, K. (2012). *Gender and Empowerment- A comparative Analysis of India and USA*. Kolkata: Levant Book.

Manjoor, H., & Manders, J. (2009). *Women Empowerment: Comparing concepts & Assessment Implications for microfinance*. Commissioned by Oiko Credit.

Manser, M., & Brown, M. (1980). Marriage and Household Decision-Making: A Bargaining Analysis. *International Economic Review*, *21*(1), 31–44. doi:10.2307/2526238

Marcketti, S. B., Niehm, L. S., & Fuloria, R. (2006). An Exploratory Study of Lifestyle Entrepreneurship and Its Relationship to Life Quality. *Family and Consumer Sciences Research Journal*, *34*(3), 241–259. doi:10.1177/1077727X05283632

Market Insights. (n.d.). Retrieved from http://finclusionlab.org/market-insights/india

Marr, A. (2002). Studying Group Dynamics: An Alternative Framework for the Study of Microfinance Impacts on Poverty Reduction. *Journal of International Development, 14(4), 511-534.*

Marr, A. (2004). A challenge to the orthodoxy concerning microfinance and poverty reduction. *Journal of Microfinance*, *5*(2).

Mayoux, L. (1997). The Magic Ingredient? Microfinance and Women's Empowerment, A Briefing. Paper prepared for the Micro Credit Summit, Washington.

Mayoux, L. (1997). *The Magic Ingredient? Microfinance and Women's Empowerment*. Paper for Micro Credit Summit. Retrieved from www.gdrc.org

Mayoux, L. (1999). Questioning virtuous Spirals: Microfinance and Women's Empowerment in Africa. *Journal of International Development*.

Mayoux, L. (2000). *Microfinance and the empowerment of women: A review of the key issues*. Social Finance Unit Working Paper, 23. Geneva: ILO.

Mayoux, L. (2005). Women Empowerment through Sustainable Micro-Finance: Rethinking Best Practice.

Mayoux, L. (2006, February). *Women's Empowerment through Sustainable Micro-finance: Rethinking Best Practice.* Retrieved from http://lindaswebs.org.uk

Mayoux, L., & Hartl, M. (2009). Gender and Rural Microfinance: Reaching and Empowering Women, Guide for practitioners. International Fund for Agricultural Development (IFAD), Powerguda, India.

Mayoux, L. (1997). *Micro-finance and the empowerment of women - A review of the key issues*. MFIN Micrometer.

Mayoux, L. (1998). Participatory learning for women's empowerment in micro-finance programmes: Negotiating complexity, conflict and change. *IDS Bulletin*, *29*(4), 39–51. doi:10.1111/j.1759-5436.1998.mp29004005.x

Mayoux, L. (2001). *Impact assessment of microfinance: Towards a sustainable learning process. Enterprise Development Impact Assessment Service*. EDIAS.

Mazumder, R. (2005). *Introduction to Feminist Theory*. Kolkata: Towards Freedom.

McCann, J. (2000). Quality of Life Scores Highest for Florida Entrepreneurs. University of Florida (2000).

McElroy, M. B., & Horney, M. J. (1981). Nash-Bargained Household Decisions: Toward a Generalization of the Theory of Demand. *International Economic Review*, *22*(2), 333–349. doi:10.2307/2526280

McGregor, S. L., & Goldsmith, E. B. (1998). Expanding our understanding of quality of life, standard of living, and wellbeing. *Journal of Family and Consumer Sciences*, *90*(2), 2–6.

McGuire, J. W. (1963). *Business and society*. New York: McGraw-Hill.

McKay, A., & Osei-Assibey, E. (2017). Inequality and Poverty in Ghana. In E. Aryeeetey & R. Kanbur (Eds.), *The Economy of Ghana Sixty Years after Independence* (pp. 317–331). Oxford, UK: Oxford University Press. doi:10.1093/acprof:oso/9780198753438.003.0017

McNabb, T. (2004). FCS students learn how to achieve a balance. *Journal of Family and Consumer Sciences*, *96*(1), 15–16.

McWhirter, E.H. (1991). Empowerment, in Counselling. *Journal of Counselling and Development*, *69*, 222-227.

McWilliams, A., Siegel, D. S., & Wright, P. M. (2006). Guest editors introduction: Corporate social responsibility: Strategic implications. *Journal of Management Studies*, *43*(1), 1–18. doi:10.1111/j.1467-6486.2006.00580.x

Meagher P. (2002). *Microfinance regulation in Developing Countries: A comparative review of current practice*. IRIS Center, University of Maryland.

Meenai, Z. (2003). *Empowering Rural Women: An Approach to Empowering Women Through Credit –Based, Self- Help Groups, Aakar*. Delhi: Books.

Mees, M, (2015). The effects of regulation on microfinance in West Africa. *Zoom Microfinance*, *43*.

Mehta, L., Jindal, S., & Singh, K. (2015). Financial Inclusion in India: Shifting the Base towards Crowning Glory. *Arabian Journal of Business and Management Review*, *5*(6). Retrieved from https://www.omicsonline.org/open-access/financial-inclusion-in-india-shifting-the-base-towards-crowning-glory-2223-5833-1000158.php?aid=61775

Mehta, S. K., Mishra, H. G., & Singh, A. (2011). Role of Self-Help Groups in Socio-Economic Change of Vulnerable Poor of Jammu Region. *International Conference on Economics and Finance Research IPEDR*, 4, 519-523.

Mhango, M. W., Marcketti, S. B., & Niehm, L. S. (2005). Small retailers' integration of e-commerce technology: Personal and business perspectives of Iowa business owners. *Journal of Business and Entrepreneurship*, *17*(2), 70–90.

Michael, S. C., & Pearce, J. A. II. (2009). The need for innovation as a rationale for government involvement in entrepreneurship. *Entrepreneurship and Regional Development*, *21*(3), 285–302. doi:10.1080/08985620802279999

Micro, S., & Enterprises, M. (MSME). (2018, March 6). Registered SSI Sector – Review of the results. Retrieved from http://www.dcmsme.gov.in/ssiindia/census/ch2.htm

MicrocreditS. C. R. (2015). Accessed from www.mfw4a.org/access-to-finance/microfinance.html

Microfinance Information Exchange. (n.d.). Retrieved from https://www.themix.org

Miled, K. B. M., & Rejeb, J. B. (2015). Microfinance and poverty reduction: A review and synthesis of empirical evidence. *Procedia: Social and Behavioral Sciences*, *195*(3), 705–712. doi:10.1016/j.sbspro.2015.06.339

Millennium Development Goals. (MDGs). (2015). The Millennium Development Goals Report 2015. New York: United Nations.

Ministry of Child and Women development, Govt. of India. (2017). Annual Report. 2016-17. Retrieved from http://www.wcd.nic.in/sites/default/files/FINAL%20WCD_AR_English%202016-17.pdf

Ministry of Statistics and Programme Implementation (MOSPI). (2011). *Census of India*. Retrieved from www.mospi.gov.in

Mintzberg, H., Quinn, J., & Voyer, J. (1997). Capítulo 4: Análisis de estratega a nivel empresa. En el proceso estratégico. Pearson.

Mitchelmore, S., & Rowley, J. (2013). Entrepreneurial competencies of women entrepreneurs pursuing business growth. *Journal of Small Business and Enterprise Development*, *20*(1), 125–142. doi:10.1108/14626001311298448

Mitra, S. K. (2005). Asking Price of Microfinance Loan to Poor Borrowers (Working Paper 191). Institute of Rural Management, Anand, India.

Mlachala, M., Cui, L., Jidoud, A., Newiak, M., Radzewicz-Bak, B., Takebe, M., . . . Zhang, J. (2016). Financial Development in Sub-Saharan Africa: Promoting inclusive and sustainable growth. International Monetary Fund, 61.

Modigliani, F., & Brumberg, R. H. (1954). Utility Analysis and the Consumption Function: An Interpretation of Cross-section Data in Post-Keynesian Economics. Rutgers University Press.

Mohamed, I. E. (2008). *The Augmented Dickey – Fuller (ADF) Test*. Retrieved from: http://www.lexjansen.com/nesug/nesug08/po/po05.pdf

Mokta, M. (2014). Empowerment of Women in India: A Critical Analysis. *The Indian Journal of Public Administration*, *60*(3), 473–488. doi:10.1177/0019556120140308

Montgomery, H., & Weiss, J. (2005). Great Expectations: Microfinance and Poverty Reduction in Asia and Latin America (Research Paper Series No. 63). ADB Institute, Manila.

Morck, Wolfenzon, & Yeung. (2004). *Corporate governance, economic entrenchment and Growth*. NBER, Working Paper 10692.

Morduch, J. (1998). *Does Microfinance Really Help the Poor? New Evidence from Flagship Programs in Bangladesh*. Princeton University Working Paper 1998.

Morduch, J. (1999, December). The Microfinance Promise. *Journal of Economic Literature*, *37*(4), 1569–1614. doi:10.1257/jel.37.4.1569

Morduch, J. (2000). The microfinance schism. *World Development*, *28*(4), 617–629. doi:10.1016/S0305-750X(99)00151-5

Morduch, J. (2005). *Consumption Smoothing Across Space: Testing Theories of Risk-Sharing in the ICRISAT Study Region of South India*. Oxford, UK: Oxford University Press.

Morris, M. (1998a, Fall). What is microenterprise development? (Editor's commentary). *Journal of Developmental Entrepreneurship*, *3*(2), 5–8.

Morris, M. (1998b). *Entrepreneurial intensity sustainable advantages for individuals, organizations, and societies*. Westport, CT: Quorum Books.

Morris, M., & Lewis, R. J. (1991). Entrepreneurship as a Significant Factor in Societal Quality of Life (1991). *Journal of Business Research*, *23*(1), 21–36. doi:10.1016/0148-2963(91)90056-4

Mosley, P., & Arun, T. (2003). *Improving access to rural finance in India: Supply side constraints.* Unpublished background paper to the economic and sector work study on access to finance. Washington, DC: World Bank, South Asia Finance and Private Sector Development Unit.

Mosley, P. (2001). Microfinance and Poverty in Bolivia. *The Journal of Development Studies, 37*(4), 101–132. doi:10.1080/00220380412331322061

Moyle, T. L., Dollard, M., & Biswas, S. N. (2006). Personal and Economic Empowerment in Rural Indian Women A Self-help Group Approach. *International Journal of Rural Management, 2*(2), 245–266. doi:10.1177/097300520600200207

Muhumed, M. M. (2016). The impact of microfinance on consumption in Bangladesh. *Journal of Economics and Sustainable Development, 7*(12).

Mukherjee, A. K., & Kundu, A. (2011). Impact of Swarna Jayanti Gram Swarojgar Yojona (SGSY) on Health, Education and Women's Empowerment. *Microfinance Review, 3*(1), 36–52.

Mukherjee, S. (2017). Anatomy and Significance of Public Healthcare Expenditure and Economic Growth Nexus in India: Its Implications for Public Health Infrastructure Thereof. In *Social, Health, and Environmental Infrastructures for Economic Growth* (pp. 120–144). IGI Global. doi:10.4018/978-1-5225-2364-2.ch007

Mukherjee, S. (2017). India's Looming Power Crisis and the Way Forward: An Ode to Sustainability. *International Journal of Sustainable Economies Management, 6*(1), 64–81. doi:10.4018/ijsem.2017010104

Mula, G. (2012). Micro finance scenario of eastern part of India under SGSY. *ARPN Journal of Agricultural and Biological Science, 7*(3), 182–187.

Muller, C., & Bibi, S. (2010). Refining targeting against poverty. Evidence from Tunisia. *Oxford Bulletin of Economics and Statistics, 72*(3), 381–410. doi:10.1111/j.1468-0084.2010.00583.x

Murdoch, J., & Roodman, D. (2009). *The Impact of Microcredit on the Poor in Bangladesh: Revisiting the Evidence.* Working paper 174, 2009 (June).

Muthiah, M. P., & Muthiah, K. (2010). Financial Inclusion in the Indian Rural Area Context–A Micro Level Study. *Research Highlights, 20*(2), 71–74.

NABARD. (1999). *Microfinance Scenario in the country.* NABARD. Retrieved from www.nabard.org

NABARD. (2000). NABARD and microfinance. National Bank for Agricultural and Rural Development.

NABARD. (2002). *NABARD & microfinance 2001-2002: Ten Years of SHG-Banking Linkage.* Retrieved from https://www.microfinancegateway.org/sites/default/files/mfg-en-paper-nabard-and-microfinance-2002.pdf

NABARD. (2005). *Progress of SHG – Bank Linkage in India, 2004-2005.* Microcredit.

NABARD. (2013). *Status of Microfinance in India 2012-13.* Retrieved from http://indiamicrofinance.com/status-microfinance-india-2012-2013-pdf-report-nabard.html

NABARD. (2014). *Status of Microfinance in India 2013-14.* Retrieved from www.nabard.org

NABARD. (2015). *Status of Microfinance in India 2014-15.* Retrieved from www.nabard.org

NABARD. (2016). *Status of Microfinance in India 2015-16.* NABARD.

NABARD. (2016). *Status of Microfinance in India 2015-16.* National Bank for Agricultural and Rural Development. Retrieved from https://www.microfinancegateway.org/sites/default/files/publication_files/smfi_2015-16.pdf

NABARD. (2016). *Status of Microfinance in India 2015-16*. Retrieved from https://www.microfinancegateway.org/sites/default/files/publication_files/smfi_2015-16.pdf

NABARD. (2016). *Status of microfinance in India report 2014-15*. Author.

NABARD. (2017). *Status of Microfinance in India 2016-17*. Retrieved from https://www.nabard.org/auth/writereaddata/tender/1307174808Status%20of%20Microfinance%20in%20India%202016-17.pdf

NABARD. (2017, March 31). *Status of Microfinance in India 2016-17*. Retrieved from http://www.nabard.org/auth/writereaddata/Flipbook/2017/Publication/Nabard-17-Status-of-Microfinance-in-India-2016-17/files/assets/basic-html/page6.html

NABARD. (n.d.). *Micro-Credit Innovation Department*. Retrieved from https://www.nabard.org/english/shgs.aspx

Nagayya, D. (2000). Micro-finance for self help groups. *Kurukshetra*, *48*(11), 10-15.

Naidu, M. C., Jayaraju, M., & Dasaatharamaiah, K. (2006). Women's empowerment through DWCRA – empirical study. *Social Welfare*, *51*(12), 32–38.

Nair, T. S., & Tankha, A. (2014, December). The Inclusive Finance Report. Retrieved from https://www.microfinancegateway.org/library/inclusive-finance-india-report-2014

Nair, A. (2005). Sustainability of micro finance self help groups in India; would federation help. *World Bank Policy Research Working Paper*, *3516*. doi:10.1596/1813-9450-3516

Nair, T. (2012). Financing of Indian microfinance evidence and implications. *Economic and Political Weekly*, *67*(25), 33–40.

Nair, T. S. (2001). Institutionalising microfinance in India: An overview of strategic issues. *Economic and Political Weekly*, 399–404.

Namboodiri, N. V., & Shiyani, R. L. (2001). Potential Role of Self-Help Groups in Rural Financial Deepening. *Indian Journal of Agricultural Economics*, *56*(3), 401–409.

Nana, O. (2008). Microfinance Product Development in Ghana: The Innovative And Unique Dimensions of Kraban Support Foundation's Microloan Products. *Paper presented at the Third Microfinance Conference*, January 10-11, Elmina Beach Resort, Ghana.

Nanda, P. (1999). Women's participation in rural credit programs in Bangladesh and their demand for formal health care: Is there a positive impact? *Health Economics*, *8*(5), 415–428. doi:10.1002/(SICI)1099-1050(199908)8:5<415::AID-HEC450>3.0.CO;2-L PMID:10470548

Nandy, S., & Kumar, S. (2014). Women entrepreneurship in 21st century India. *Global Journal of Finance and Management*, *6*(9), 967–976.

Narayanasamy, N., Manivel, S., & Bhaskar, B. (2003). Networking SHGs and Co-operatives—An Analysis of Strengths and Weaknesses. *Journal of Rural Development*, *22*(3), 333–343.

Narayan, D., Chambers, R., Meera, K., Shah, M. K., & Petesch, P. (2000a). *Voices of the Poor: Crying out for change*. Oxford, UK: Oxford University Press. doi:10.1596/0-1952-1602-4

Narayan, D., Patel, R., Schafft, K., Rademacher, A., & Koch-Schulte, S. (2000b). *Voices of the poor: Can anyone hear us?* Oxford, UK: Oxford University Press. doi:10.1596/0-1952-1601-6

Narender, K. (2007). Microfinance for poverty reduction-the Dhan Foundation Experience. In M. Self-employment & P. Alleviation (Eds.), *Kamdar* (pp. 205–226). Mumbai: Himalaya Publishing House.

Nasir, S. (2013). Microfinance in India: Contemporary Issues and Challenges *Middle East Journal of Scientific Research, 15*(2), 191–199.

Nasir, S. (2013). Microfinance in India: Contemporary issues and challenges. *Middle East Journal of Scientific Research, 15*(2), 191–199.

NCSS Statistical Software. (2017). *Statistical, Graphics, and Sample Size Software*. Retrieved from: https://www.ncss.com/

Nessa, T., Ali, J., & Hakim, R. A. (2012). The Impact of Microcredit Programme on Women Empowerment: Evidence from Bangladesh. Ontario International Development Agency. Retrieved from http://www.ssrn.com/link/OIDA-Intl-JournalSustainable-Dev.html

Nirmala, C. R., & Debasish, B. (2016). Women Empowerment through SHGs and Financial Inclusion: A Case Study on Lataguri Region in West Bengal. *International Journal of Management Research and Review., 6*(6), 827–834.

Nithyanandhana, S. H., Mansorb, N., & Nairc, S. (2015). Self Help Groups as Modalities for Poverty Alleviation for Women in India. *Institutions, Etc., 7*(3), 67–94.

North, D. C. (1990). *Institutions, institutional Change, and economic performance*. New York: Norton. doi:10.1017/CBO9780511808678

North, D. C. (2005). *Understanding the Process of Economic Change*. Princeton, University Press. doi:10.1515/9781400829484

Norton, S. W. (2002). Economic growth and poverty: In search of trickle-down. *The Cato Journal, 22*, 263.

Nyantakyi, E., & Sy, M. (2015). The Banking System in Africa. *Main Facts and Challenges, AEB, 6*(5), 28–29.

Nyiatahger, Z.T., Umeh, J.C., & Ocholi, A. (2015). Socio-Economic Effects of Malaria on Households' Consumption in North-Central Nigeria. *Journal of Agriculture and Veterinary Science, 8*(7), 65-72.

O'Gorman, M. (2010). Microfinance in India. *Canadian Journal of Development Studies/Revue Canadienned'études Du Développement, 31*(1–2), 225–227.

O'Neil, T., Domingo, P., & Valters, C. (2014). *Progress on women's empowerment: From technical fixes to political action*. London: ODI.

Oduro, A. D., & Ackah, C. G. (2017). Closing the Gender Gaps in Ghana. In E. Aryeeetey & R. Kanbur (Eds.), *The Economy of Ghana Sixty Years after Independence* (pp. 317–331). Oxford, UK: Oxford University Press. doi:10.1093/acprof:oso/9780198753438.003.0019

OIT. (2007). *Organización Internacional del Trabajo, ¿Quiénes somos?* Recuperado de http://www.ilo.org/inform/online-information-resources/research-guides/lang--es/index.htm

Okon, D.P., Etim, N., & Offiong, A.A.A. (2012). Impact of Micro Credit Scheme on Rural Farmers in Akwa-Ibom State, Nigeria. *Journal of Agriculture & Social Sciences, 8*(2).

Onwumere, J.U.J. (2008). Microfinance and Developing the Nigerian Economy. The Nigerian Banker, October – December.

Ostry, J. D., Berg, A., & Tsangaride, C. (2014). *Redistribution, inequality, and Growth, IMF Staff Discussion Note 14/02*. Washington, DC: International Monetary Fund.

Otero, M. (1999). Bringing Development Back into Microfinance. Latin America: ACCION International.

Ouattara, K. (2005). *Microfinance regulation in Benin-Implications of the PARMEC Law for Development and performance of the industry. Africa Region Working Series*. Washington, DC: World Bank.

Overseas Development Council Census of India. (2001). *2001 Data*. Office of the Registrar General & Census Commissioner, Ministry of Home Affairs, Govt. of India.

Owojori, A. A. & Oladejo, M. O. (2009). Re-engineering cooperative societies for sustainable small and medium business growth and development in Nigeria.

Owusu-Danso, T. (2015). *Implications of Microfinance for gender inequality in Ghana*. Accessed from https://www.aeaweb.org/conference/2015/retrieve.php?pdfid=983

Padró, F. (2004). *Statistical Handbook on the Social Safety Net*. London: Greenwood Press.

Panwar, J. S., &Carmody, L. (2011). *Microfinance in India*. Academic Press.

Pati, A. P. (2006). Financial Sustainability of Micro Lending Through SHG-Bank Linkage Programme. ICSSR.

Patil, V. G., & Karjat, Y. (2011). Microfinance in India. *Golden Resrach Thoughts*, *1*, 1–4.

Pedroni, P. (1999). Critical values for cointegration tests in heterogeneous panels with multiple regressors. *Oxford Bulletin of Economics and Statistics*, *61*(S1), 653–670. doi:10.1111/1468-0084.61.s1.14

Peng, M. (2012). *Global strategy*. Cincinnati, OH: Thomson South Western.

Peng, M. (2012). *Estrategia Global*. Queretaro, Mexico: Cengage.

Peng, M. W. (2000). *Business strategies in transition Economies. Thousand Oaks,* CA: Sage.

Peng, M. W. (2012). *Estrategia global*. México: Cengage Learning.

Pennings, J. M. (1982). The Urban Quality of Life and Entrepreneurship. *Academy of Management Journal*, *25*(01), 63–71. doi:10.2307/256024

Penrose, E. (1959). *The theory of the growth of the firm. Nueva York, EstadosUnidos*. John Wiley and Sons.

Perotti, R. (1994). Income distribution and investment. *European Economic Review*, *38*(3), 827–835. doi:10.1016/0014-2921(94)90119-8

Peters, M., Frehse, J., & Buhalis, D. (2009). The importance of lifestyle entrepreneurship: A conceptual study of the tourism industry. *Revista de Turismo y Patrimonio Cultural*, *7*(2), 393-405.

Piketty, T., & Saez, E. (2003). Income inequality in the United States, 1913–1998. *The Quarterly Journal of Economics*, *118*(1), 1–41. doi:10.1162/00335530360535135

Pistaferri, L. (2009). The Life-cycle Hypothesis: An Assessment of Some Recent Evidence. *Rivista di Politica Economica*, 35–65.

Pitt, M. M., Khandker, S. R., & Cartwright, J. (2003). D*oes Micro-Credit Empower Women? Evidence from Bangladesh*. Policy Research Working Paper 2998, World Bank. Retrieved from http://econ.worldbank.org

Pitt, M. M., & Khandker, S. (1998). The impact of group-based credit programs on poor households in Bangladesh: Does the gender of participants' matter? *Journal of Political Economy*, 2.

Pitt, M. M., & Khandker, S. R. (1998). The Impact of Group-Based Credit Programs on Poor Households in Bangladesh: Does the Gender of the Participant Matter? *Journal of Political Economy*, *106*(5), 958–996. doi:10.1086/250037

Pitt, M. M., Khandker, S. R., & Cartwright, J. (2006). Empowering Women with Microfinance: Evidence from Bangladesh. *Economic Development and Cultural Change*, *54*(4), 791–831. doi:10.1086/503580

Pitt, M. M., Khandker, S. R., Choudhury, O., & Millimet, D. (2003). Credit Programs for the Poor and the Health Status of Children in Rural Bangladesh. *International Economic Review*, *44*(February), 87–118. doi:10.1111/1468-2354.t01-1-00063

Pitt, M. M., Khandker, S. R., McKernan, S., & Latif, M. A. (1999). Credit Programs for the Poor and Reproductive Behavior in Low-Income Countries: Are the Reported Causal Relationships the Result of Heterogeneity Bias? *Demography*, *36*(1). doi:10.2307/2648131 PMID:10036590

Pitt, M. M., Khandker, S. R., McKernan, S.-M., & Latif, M. A. (2000). The Effect of Non-agricultural Self-Employment Credit on Contractual Relations and Employment in Agriculture: The Case of Microcredit Programs in Bangladesh. *Bangladesh Development Studies*, *26*(2–3), 15–48.

Planning Commission. (2014). *Data-book Compiled for Use of Planning Commission*. New Delhi: Planning Commission, Government of India.

Planning Commission. (2014). *Government of India, Report of The Expert Group to Review The Methodology for Measurement of Poverty*. Retrieved from http//www.planning commission.

Pokhriyal, A. K., Rani, R., & Uniyal, J. (2014). Role of Micro-Finance in the Empowerment of the Women. *Journal of Business and Finance*, *02*(01), 21–31.

Politis, D.N. & Poulis, S. (2014). *Heteroskedastic Liner Regression: Steps Towards Adaptivity, Efficiency, and Robustness*. Retrieved from: file:///G:/PhD_Quantative%20Research%20Methods%20and%20Computer%20Applications/Heteroskedasticity%20linear%20regression__%20steps%20towards%20adaptivity,%20efficiency,%20and%20robustness%20__%2001+.pdf

Porter, E. G., & Nagarajan, K. V. (2005). Successful women entrepreneurs as pioneers: Results from a study conducted in Karaikudi, Tamil Nadu, India. *Journal of Small Business and Entrepreneurship*, *18*(1), 39–52. doi:10.1080/08276331.2005.10593331

Prakash, C., & Barua, M. K. (2015). Integration of AHP-TOPSIS method for prioritizing the solutions of reverse logistics adoption to overcome its barriers under fuzzy environment. *Journal of Manufacturing Systems*, *37*, 599–615. doi:10.1016/j.jmsy.2015.03.001

Pramod, B. (2006). SHG-Bank linkage programme: Future scenario. In *Towards a sustainable microfinance outreach in India - Experiences and perspectives* (pp. 69–82). Mumbai: NABARD, GTZ & SDC.

Programa Nacional de Financiamiento al Microempresario. (2014). *Benchmarking de las finanzas en México 2012-2013*. Author.

PROMUSAG. (2012). *promusagg-fappa-proyectos-sra.blogspot*. Retrieved from www.promusagg-fappa-proyectos-sra.blogspot.mx

Prowse, M. (2003). *Towards a Clearer Understanding of 'Vulnerability' in Relation to Chronic Poverty*. CPRC Working Paper No 24, University of Manchester.

Puhazhendhi, V., & Satyasai, K. J. S. (2000). Micro Finance for Rural People: An impact Evaluation. Microcredit Innovations Department, National Bank for Agriculture and Rural Development.

Puhazhendi, V., & Badatya, K. C. (2002). *SHG-Bank linkage programme for rural poor – An impact assessment*. Paper presented at the SHG-Bank Linkage Programme Seminar, New Delhi, India.

Punitha, M., Sangeetha, S., & Padmavathi, K. (1999). Women entrepreneurs: Their problems and constraints. *The Indian Journal of Labour Economics*, *42*(4), 707–716.

Purchasing power parities (PPP). (n.d.). Retrieved from https://data.oecd.org/conversion/purchasing-power-parities-ppp.htm

Putnam, R. (1993). *Making Democracy Work: Civic Traditions in Modern Italy*. Princeton, NJ: Princeton University Press.

Qazi, M. (2007). Microfinance and Woman's Empowerment. In M. Self-Employment & P. Alleviation (Eds.), *Kamdar* (pp. 158–177). Mumbai: Himalaya Publishing House.

Rahman, A. (1999). Micro-Credit Initiatives for Equitable and Sustainable Development. *World Development*, *27*(1), 67–82. Retrieved from http://EconPapers.repec.org/Repec:wdevel:v:27:1999:i:1:67-82 doi:10.1016/S0305-750X(98)00105-3

Rajagopalan, T. (1989). *Farm credit in dry land areas: A study of credit needs & problems of small & marginal farmers in Chityal Mandal, AP, India* (Unpublished Thesis). Asian Institute of Technology, Bangkok, Thailand.

Rajendran, K., & Raya, R. (2010). *Impact of Micro Finance - An empirical Study on the Attitude of SHG Leaders in Vellore District*. Tamil Nadu, India: Global Journal of Finance and Management.

Ramachandran, T., & Seilan, A. (2005). Socio-economic empowerment and self help groups. *Social Welfare*, *52*(6), 26.

Ramanajaneyulu, M. (2006). *Economic empowerment of women in India*. New Delhi: Anmol Publications Pvt. Ltd.

Ramasamy, B., & Yeung, M. (2009). Chinese consumers' perception of corporate social responsibility (CSR). *Journal of Business Ethics*, *88*(S1), 119-132. doi: 10.1 007/sl 055 1 -008-9825-x

Rangarajan, C. (2008). *Report of the Committee on Financial Inclusion*. Retrieved from www.sidbi.in

Rangarajan, L. N. (Ed.). (1992). *The Arthashastra*. Penguin Books India.

Ranjani, K. S. (2012). Regulating Microfinance Institutions in India: A Conceptual Framework. *Synergy* *10*(1), 51-62.

Rankin, K. N. (2002). Social capital, microfinance and the politics of development. *Feminist Economics*, *8*(1), 1–24. doi:10.1080/13545700210125167

Rao, B. B. & Sharma, K. L. (2007). *Testing the Permanent Income Hypothesis in the Developing and Developed Countries: A Comparison between Fiji and Australia*. MPRA Paper 2725.

Rao, K. M. (2008). MFIs in India: An overview. *Microfinance in India*, 57–66.

Ravallion, M. (2004). *Pro-poor growth: A primer*. Academic Press.

Ravallion, M., & Chen, S. (2001). *Measuring pro-poor growth, Policy Research Working Paper no. WPS2666*. Washington, DC: World Bank.

Ravallion, M. (2001). The Mystery of the Vanishing Benefits: An Introduction to Impact Evaluation. *The World Bank Economic Review*, *15*(1), 115–140. doi:10.1093/wber/15.1.115

Rawlings, L., & Schady, N. R. (2002). Impact Evaluation of Social Funds: An Introduction. *The World Bank Economic Review*, *16*(2), 213–217. doi:10.1093/wber/16.2.213

Ray, S., & Mahapatra, S. K. (2014). Penetration of MFIs among Indian States: An Understanding through Macro Variables (working paper 2014-01). Centro de Economia e Financas da UP.

Ray, D. (1998). *Development economics*. New Jersey: Princeton University press.

Reddy, B. S., & Nathan, H. S. K. (2011). *Emerging Energy Insecurity - The Indian Dimension*. Academic Press.

Reddy, C. S., & Manak, S. (2005). Self-help groups: A keystone of microfinance in India-women empowerment and social security. Andhra Pradesh MahilaAbhivruddhi Society (APMAS). India: Hyderabad.

Reddy, G. N. (2002). Empowering Women Through Self-Help Groups and Micro-Credit: The Case of NIRD Action Research Projects. *Journal of Rural Development*, *21*(4), 511–535.

Report of the United Nations. (1995). Retrieved from: www.laghuudyog.com/schemes/microfinance.htm

Report, A. A. (2012). *Backward Classes Welfare Department* (pp. 2010–2011). Kolkata: Government of West Bengal.

Reserve Bank of India (RBI). (2017, September 15). RBI's Handbook of Statistics on Indian Economy, 2016, 2017. Retrieved from https://rbi.org.in/Scripts/AnnualPublications.aspx?head=Handbook%20of%20Statistics%20on%20Indian%20Economy

Responsibility. (2016). *Microfinance market outlook: Development, forecasts and trend.* Accessed from https://www.microfinancegateway.org/.../microfinance-market-outlook-2016-develop

Rhyne, E. (2001). *Mainstreaming Microfinance: How Lending Began, Grew and Came of Age in Bolivia.* Bloomfield: Kumarian Press.

Rice, R. W. (1985). Organizational work and the perceived quality of life: Toward a conceptual model. *Academy of Management Review*, *10*, 296–310.

Rifkin, J. (2014). *La sociedad de coste marginal cero: el internet de las cosas, el procomún colaborativo y el eclipse del capitalismo.* Barcelona: Paidós.

Rogers, B., & Youssef, N. (1988). The importance of women's involvement in economic activities in the improvement of child nutrition & health. *Food and Nutrition Bulletin*, 10.

Romero, J. M., & Nagarajan, G. (2011). *Impact of Micro-Savings on Shock Coping Strategies in Rural Malawi.* Retrieved from http://www.fsassessment.umd.edu/

Rona, M. (2006, April). Financial Inclusion: Meeting The Challenge. *People's Democracy*, 22.

Roodman, D., & Morduch, J. (2014). The impact of microcredit on the poor in Bangladesh: Revisiting the evidence. *The Journal of Development Studies*, *50*(4), 583–604. doi:10.1080/00220388.2013.858122

Roomi, M. A., & Parrot, G. (2008). Barriers to development and progression of women entrepreneurs in Pakistan. *The Journal of Entrepreneurship*, *17*(1), 59–72. doi:10.1177/097135570701700105

Rosenbaum, P. R. (2002). Observational studies (2nd ed.). New York: Springer. doi:10.1007/978-1-4757-3692-2

Rosenbaum, P. R., & Rubin, D. B. (1983). The Central Role of the Propensity Score in Observational Studies for Causal Effects. *Biometrika*, *70*(1), 41–45. doi:10.1093/biomet/70.1.41

Rosenberg, R. (2007). CGAP Reflections on the Compartamos Initial Public Offering: A Case Study on Microfinance Interest Rates and Profits (Focus Note 42). CGAP.

Rout, R. K., Das, L. K., Ranasingh, N., & Behera, S. (2015). Impact of Microfinance on household income: Evidence from village level study in Orissa. *International Journal of Management &Economics Invention*, *1*(10), 436–441.

Rowland, Jo. (1997). *Questioning Empowerment.* Oxford: Oxfam. doi:10.3362/9780855988364

Roy, K., & Haldar, S. K. (2010). Measuring Poverty and Socio-Economic Deprivation Inequalities in India at Sub-National Level. *Asia-Pacific Social Science Review*, *10*(1).

Roy, S. K. (2012). Financial inclusion in India: An overview. *Asian Journal of Multidimensional Research, 1*(5), 136–138.

Rubin, D. B. (1974). Estimating Causal Effects to Treatments Randomized and Nonrandomized Studies. *Journal of Educational Psychology, 66*(5), 688–701. doi:10.1037/h0037350

Rubin, D. B. (1980). Bias Reduction using Mahalanobis - Metric Matching. *Biometrics, 36*(2), 293–298. doi:10.2307/2529981

Rudd, A. (2011). *Microfinance as a Poverty Alleviant: Have We Given it Too Much Credit? An Analysis of Variance in Welfare Outcomes.* Retrieved from econweb.ucsd.edu/.../MICROFINANCE%20AS%20POVERTY%2

Russo, A., & Quaglieri, A. (2014). La lógica espacial del intercambio de casas: una aproximación a las nuevas geografías de lo cotidiano en el turismo contemporáneo. *Revista electrónica de georgrafía y ciencias sociales*, 324-331.

Sa-Dahn. (2015). Bharat Micro Finance Report 2015. Retrieved from https://www.microfinancegateway.org/library/bharat-microfinance-report-2015

Sa-Dahn. (2016). Bharat Microfinance Report 2016. Retrieved from http://indiamicrofinance.com/wp-content/uploads/2016/09/The-Bharat-Microfinance-Report-2016.pdf

Sa-Dhan. (2014). *The Bharat microfinance report 2014.* Accessed at http://www.sa-dhan.net/Resources/Finale%20Report.pdf

Sa-Dhan. (2015). *Bharat Microfinance Report-2015.* New Delhi: The Association of Community Development Finance Institutions.

Sa-Dhan. (2016). Microfinance Directory (2nd ed.). Sa-Dhan, The Association of Community Development Finance Institutions.

Sa-Dhan. (2016). *The Bharat microfinance report 2016.* Accessed at https://www.microfinancegateway.org/ sites/ default/ files/ publication_files/ the_ bharat_microfinance_report_2016-min.pdf

SAGARPA. (2016). Programas fappa y promete. sagarpa. Retrieved from http://www.sagarpa.gob.mx/Programas-SAGARPA/2014/Documents/Resumen%20de%20ROP%20FAPPA%20y%20PROMETE%202014.pdf

Saha, G. (2015). Microfinance sector towards rural Development in North East. *International Journal of Recent Scientific Research, 6*(6).

Sahay, R., Cihak, M., N'Diaye, P., & Barajas, A. (2015a). *Financial inclusion: Can it meet multiple macroeconomic goals? IMF Staff Discussion Note 15/17.* Washington, DC: International Monetary Fund.

Sahay, R., Cihak, M., N'Diaye, P., Barajas, A., Bi, R., Ayala, D., ... Yousefi, S. R. (2015b). *Rethinking Financial deepening: Stability and growth in emerging markets, IMF Staff Discussion Note 15/08.* Washington, DC: International Monetary Fund.

Sahay, S. (1998). *Women and empowerment approaches and strategies.* New Delhi: Discovery Publishing House.

Sahu, A. B., & Das, S. R. (2006). *Women Empowerment Through Self Help Groups- A Case Study.* Retrieved from www.isical.ac.in

Salinas, C. (2007). El desarrollo Sustentable. *Memorias del Segundo Congreso de In- vestigación sobre Sustentabilidad y Calidad de Vida, UAEM, 2*(2), 12-21.

Sane, R., & Thomas, S. (2013). Regulating microfinance institutions. *Economic and Political Weekly, 18*(5), 59–67.

Santos, I., Sharif, I., Rahman, H. Z., & Zaman, H. (2011). *How do the Poor cope with Shocks in Bangladesh? Evidence from Survey Data?* Policy Research Working Paper 5810.

Sarangadharan, M., & Rasia Begum, S. (1995). *Women entrepreneurship.* New Delhi: Discovery Publishing House.

Sarangi, N. (2007). *Microfinance and Rural Poor: Impact Assessment Based on Field Work in Madhya Pradesh, India.* New Delhi, India: CSRD, Jawhar Lal Nehru University.

Saravanan, M. (2016). The Impact of Self-Help Groups on the Socio-Economic Development of Rural Household Women in Tamil Nadu- A Study. *International Journal of Research – Granthaalayah, 4*(7), 22-31.

Saravanan, S., & Dash, D. P. (2017). Microfinance and Women Empowerment-Empirical Evidence from the Indian States. *Regional and Sectoral Economic Studies., 17*(2), 61–74.

Sarkhel, J., & Dutta, S. (2010). *An insight into statistics. Book syndicate PVT.* LTD.

Sarma, A. (2006). Microfinance: Hope for the Poor. *Yojona, 50.*

Sarmah, G. N., & Das, D. K. (2012). Micro finance, self help groups (SHGS) and the Socio- Economic development of rural people (A case study with special reference to the Lakhimpur district of Assam). *Asian Journal of Research in Business Economics and Management, 2*(4), 145–159.

Sarumathi, S., & Mohan, K. (2001). Role of Microfinance in Women's Empowerment. *Journal of Management and Science, 1*(1).

Satish, P. (2005). Mainstreaming of Indian Microfinance. *Economic and Political Weekly, 40*(17).

Scarborough, N. M., & Zimmerer, T. W. (2003). *Effective small business management: An entrepreneurial approach* (7th ed.). Upper Saddle River, NJ: Prentice Hall.

Schicks, J. (2010). Microfinance Over-Indebtedness: Understanding its Drivers and Challenging the Common Myths (Working Paper N° 10/048 2010). Centre Emile Bernheim (CEB).

Schicks, J. (2011). *Over-Indebtedness of Micro-Borrowers in Ghana: An Empirical Study from a Customer Protection Perspective.* Retrieved from: https://centerforfinancialinclusionblog.files.wordpress.com/2011/11/111108_cfi_over-indebtedness-in-ghana_jessica-schicks_en_final.pdf

Schmidheiny, S. (2006, Spring). A view of corporate citizenship in Latin America. *Journal of Corporate Citizenship, 2006*(21), 21–24. doi:10.9774/GLEAF.4700.2006.sp.00004

Schmidt, R. (2010). Microfinance, Commercialization and Ethics. *Poverty & Public Policy, 2*(1). doi:10.2202/1944-2858.1020

Scott, W. (2013). Chapter 3: Crafting an analytic framework 1, Three pillars of institutions. Institution and organization, ideas, interest, and identities. SAGE cuarta edición.

Scully, N. (2004). *Microcredit: 'No panacea for the poor women.* Washington, DC: Global DevelopmentResearch Centre.

SE. (2017). *Definición de Responsabilidad Social Empresarial.* Recuperado de https://www.gob.mx/se/articulos/responsabilidad-social-empresarial-32705

Seddoh, J. (2014). The Impact of Plan Ghana's Microfinance Scheme on Poverty Reduction Among Women in Lower Manya Krobo. *Journal of African Studies and Development, 6*(8), 132–139. doi:10.5897/JASD2014.0285

Selvi, R. R., & Shanmughun, R. (2016). A study on women empowerment through self-help groups in Erode district. *International Journal of Multidisciplinary Research & Modern Education, II*(I), 383–388.

Sen, A. K. (1993). Capability and well-being. In: Nussbaum and Sen, eds. The quality of life. Helsinki: World Institute of Development Economics Research. doi:10.1093/0198287976.003.0003

Sen, A. (1973). *On economic inequality*. Delhi: Oxford University Press. doi:10.1093/0198281935.001.0001

Sen, A. (1992). Missing Women. *British Medical Journal*, *304*, 586–587. PMID:1559085

Sen, A. K. (1990). Gender and co-operative conflict. In I. Tinker (Ed.), *Persistent inequalities*. New Delhi: Oxford University Press.

Sendhilvelan, M., & Karthikeyan, K. (2006). No Frills Account: A basic drive for financial inclusion. *Southern Economist*, *45*(3), 13–14.

Sen, G., & Grown, C. (1987). *Development, crises and alternative visions: Third world women's perspectives*. New York: Monthly Review Press.

Sen, G., & Grown, C. (1987). *Development, Crises, and Alternative Visions: Third World Women's Perspectives*. New York: Monthly Review Press.

Sen, K. M., & Kumar, A. K. S. (2001). Women. In *India, How Free? How Equal?* New Delhi: Office of the United Nations Resident Coordination in India.

Servon, L. J. (1998). Credit and Social Capital: The Community Development Potential of U.S. Microenterprise Programs. *Housing Policy Debate*, *9*(1), 115–149. doi:10.1080/10511482.1998.9521288

Shah, P., & Dubhashi, M. (2015). Review Paper on Financial Inclusion-The Means of Inclusive Growth. *Chanakya International Journal of Business Research*, *1*(1), 37–48. doi:10.15410/cijbr/2015/v1i1/61403

Sharma, K. C. (2001). Micro financing through self help groups. *Journal of Agricultural Economics*, *56*(3), 460–461.

Sharma, P. R. (2007). Micro-finance and Women Empowerment. *The Journal of Nepalese Business Studies*, *4*(1), 16–27. doi:10.3126/jnbs.v4i1.1026

Sharma, Y. (2013, November-December). Women Entrepreneur in India. *IOSR Journal of Business and Management*, *15*(3), 9–14. doi:10.9790/487X-1530914

Shaver, K. G., Gartner, W. B., Crosby, E., Bakalarova, K., & Gatewood, E. J. (2001). Attributions About Entrepreneurship: A Framework and Process for Analyzing Reasons for Starting a Business. *Entrepreneurship Theory and Practice*, *26*(2), 5–32. doi:10.1177/104225870102600201

Shedecor, G. W., & Cochran, W. G. (1989). Statistical Methods. Iowa State University Press.

Shepard, E. (n.d.). *Situating Micro-Finance on a Theoretical Spectrum: The Case of Bolivia*. Retrieved from https://atlismta.org/online-journals/0607-journal-development

Shetty, N. K. (2009). The microfinance promises in financial inclusion: Evidence from India. *IUP Journal of Applied Economics*, *8*(5/6), 174.

Shylendra, H. S. (2006, May 20). Microfinance institutions in Andhra Pradesh: Crisis and diagnosis. *Economic and Political Weekly*, 1959–1963.

Simanowitz, A. (2002). *Microfinance for the poorest: A review of issues and ideas for contribution of Imp-Act*. An action Research Programme.

Simanowitz, A., & A. Walker (2002). Ensuring impact: reaching the poorest while building financially self-sufficient institutions, and showing improvement in the lives of the poorest women and their families. *Paper for the Microcredit Summit*, New York, November 10-13.

Simon, H. A. (1957). *Models of Man*. John Wiley.

Sing, G (2009). Microfinance – An Innovation in Rural Credit System. *Kurukshetra*, Feb., 3-6.

Singh, K. (1992). Women entrepreneurs. Ashish Publishing House.

Sinha, F. (2009). State of Microfinance in India. Retrieved from http://www.inm.org.bd/publication/state_of_micro/India.pdf

Sinha, F. (2005). Access, use and contribution of microfinance in India: Findings from a national study. *Economic and Political Weekly*, 1714–1719.

Sinha, M., Sengupta, D., Roy, O., Banerjee, J., & Sengupta, P. P. (2017). Determinants of Participation of Women in Labour Market: An Empirical Evidence from Nadia District of West Bengal in India. *Man in India*, *97*(2), 239–255.

Sinha, S., & Matin, I. (1998). Informal Credit Transactions of Microcredit Borrowers in Bangaldesh. *IDS Bulletin*, *29*(4), 66–80. doi:10.1111/j.1759-5436.1998.mp29004008.x

Sirgy, M. J., Morris, M., & Samli, K. C. (1985). The question of value in social marketing: Use of a quality of life theory to achieve long-term life satisfaction. *American Journal of Economics and Sociology*, *44*(2), 797–814. doi:10.1111/j.1536-7150.1985.tb02336.x

Sivaramakrisnan, K. (2003). Poverty alleviation through Self Help Groups. *Cooperation*, *3*(5).

Siyoum, A. D., Hilhorst, D. J. M., & Pankhurst, A. S. A. (2012). The Differential Impact of Microcredit on Rural Livelihoods: Case Study from Ethiopia. *International Journal of Development and Sustainability*, *1*(3), 1–19.

Srinivasan, N. (2009). *Microfinance India, State of the Sector Report 2009*. New Delhi: Sage Publications.

Srinivasan, N. (2010). *Microfinance India: state of the sector report 2009*. SAGE Publications India.

Sriram, M. S. (2010). Commercialisation of Microfinance in India: A Discussion of the Emperor's Apparel. *Economic and Political Weekly*, 65–73.

Sriram, M. S., & Upadhyayula, R. (2002). *The transformation of microfinance in India: Experiences, options and future*. Indian Institute of Management Ahmedabad, Research and Publication Department.

Srivastava, R. S. (2001). Women Empowerment: Some Critical issues. In A. Avasti & A.K. Srivastava (Ed.), Modernity, Feminism and Women Empowerment. New Delhi: Rawat Publications.

Stanforth, N., & Muske, G. (1999). Family and consumer science students' interest in entrepreneurship education. *Journal of Family and Consumer Sciences*, *91*(4), 34–38.

Streitfeld, D. (2014, October 15). Airbnb listing mostly illegal. *New York Times*.

Stuart, E. A., & Rubin, D. B. (2007). Best Practices in Quasi-Experimental Designs: Matching Methods for Causal Inference. In J. Osborne (Ed.), *Best Practices in Quantitative Social Science* (pp. 155–176). Thousand Oaks, CA: Sage Publications.

SU. (2007). From marginal tinkering to major changes: Microfinance and poverty alleviation. *Economic and Political Weekly*, *42*(5), 3.

Sugiyanto, S., Kusumastuti, Y. S., & Donna, D. R. (2012). *Managing Risks: How do Poor Households Smooth their Income and Consumption? An Examination of Poor Households in Yogyakarta, Indonesia.* IMTFI Working Paper.

Suja, S. (2012). Women empowerment through self-help group – An evaluative study. *Sona Global Management Review, 6*(3), 68–83.

Sujatha, B. (2007). *Financial Inclusion: Concepts and Strategies.* ICFAI University Press.

Suprabha, K. R. (2014). Empowerment of Self-Help Groups (SHGs) towards Microenterprise Development. *Procedia Economics and Finance, 11*, 410–422. doi:10.1016/S2212-5671(14)00208-1

Swain, R. B. (2007). Impacting Women through Microfinance. *Dialogue, Appui au Developpement Autonome*, 37.

Swain, R. B., & Floro, M. (2012). Assessing the Effect of Microfinance on Vulnerability and Poverty among Low Income Households. Journal of Development Studies.

Swain, R. B., & Floro, M. (2015). *Effect of Microfinance on Vulnerability, Poverty and Risk in Low Income Households.* American University.

Swain. (2007). Can Microfinance Empower Women? Self-Help Groups in India. Retrieved from http://mfg-en-paper-can-microfinance–empower- women-self-help-groups-in-india-may-2007.pdf

Swain, R. B., & Wallentin, F. Y. (2009). Does Microfinance Empower Women Evidence from Self-Help Groups in India. *International Review of Applied Economics, 23*(5), 541–556. doi:10.1080/02692170903007540

Swiss Agency for Development and Cooperation (SDC). (2004). *Creating the Prospect of Living a Life in Dignity – Principles Guiding the SDC in its Commitment to Fighting Poverty.* Berne: SDC.

Taha, S.G.A. (2010). *The Effectiveness of Microcredit Programmes on Alleviating Poverty and Empowering Women in Cairo.*

Taylor, G., & Pereznieto, P. (2014). *Review of evaluation approaches and methods used by interventions on women and girls' economic empowerment.* London: ODI.

Tchouassi, G. (2011). Microfinance, inequality and vulnerability: Empirical analysis from Central American countries. *Journal of Development and Agricultural Economics, 3*(4), 150-156.

Tchouassi, G. (2011). Microfinance, inequality and vulnerability: Empirical analysis from Central African countries. *Journal of Development and Agricultural Economics, 3*(4), 150–156.

Teye, J. K., Teye, I., & Asiedu, M. O. (2015). Financing Housing in Ghana: Challenges to the Development of Formal Mortgage System. *Journal of Housing and the Built Environment, 30*(1), 1–16. doi:10.100710901-013-9376-z

Thapa, S. (2012). Self-help group and women empowerment: Problems and prospects (A Study in Sikkim). In Microfinance and self-help group: Policy and practice. Kolkata: Readers Service.

The Mahatma Gandhi National Rural Employment Guarantee Act. 2005 (MGNREGA). (2014). Retrieved from http://www.nrega.nic.in/netnrega/home.aspx

Thorat, Y. S. P. (2006). Microfinance in India; Sectoral issues and challenges. *Towards a Sustainable Microfinance Outreach in India*, 27–42.

Thorat. Y.S.P. (2005). Microfinance in India: Sectoral issuses and challenges. *High level policy conference on Microfinance in India.*

Tiwari, A. (2012). Is microfinance working for what it is meant to be? A comparative study on Bangladesh and India. *International Journal of Multidisciplinary Research, 2*(3), 148-164.

Tiwari, A. (2012). Is microfinance working for what it is meant to be? A comparative study on Bangladesh and India. *ZENITH International Journal of Multidisciplinary Research*, 2(3), 148–164.

Todd, H. (2001). *Paths out of Poverty: The Impact of SHARE Microfin Limited in Andhra Pradesh, India*. Unpublished Imp-Act Report 2001.

Townsend , J., Zapata, E., Rowlands, J., Alberti, P. and Mercado, M. (1999). Women and Power: Fighting Patriarchies and Power. London, New York: Zed Books.

Tranmer, M., & Elliot, M. (2008). *Multiple Linear Regression*. Retrieved from: http://www.ccsr.ac.uk/publications/teaching/mlr.pdf

Tressel, T. (2003). Dual financial systems and inequalities in economic development. *Journal of Economic Growth*, *8*(2), 223–257. doi:10.1023/A:1024464506029

Tzannatos, Z. (1999). Women and labour market changes in the global economy: Growth helps: Inequalities hurt and public policy matters. *World Development*, *27*(3), 551–569. doi:10.1016/S0305-750X(98)00156-9

Udry, C. (1994). Risk and Insurance in a Rural Credit Market: An Empirical Investigation in Northern Nigeria. *The Review of Economic Studies, 61*(3), 495-526.

Udry, C. (1990). Credit Markets in Northern Nigeria: Credit as Insurance in A Rural Economy. *The World Bank Economic Review*, *4*(3), 251–269. doi:10.1093/wber/4.3.251

Umdor, S. (2006). An Assessment of the Self Help Groups Credit Programme in Meghalaya (Unpublished Ph.D. Thesis). Deptt. of Economics, North Eastern Hill University, Shillong.

UN Division for the Advancement of Women (UNDAW), Department of Economic and Social Affairs. (2001). Empowerment of Women Throughout the Life Cycle as a Transformative Strategy for Poverty Eradication. *Report of the Expert Group Meeting*, New Delhi, India, November 26-29.

UN Division for the Advancement of Women (UNDAW). Department of Economic & Social Affairs. (2001). *Empowerment of women throughout the life cycle as a transformative strategy for poverty eradication.* Report of the Expert Group Meeting, New Delhi, India.

UN-DESA. (2015). *World Economic Situation and Prospects*. Author.

UNDP. (2013). *Microfinance in Africa: Overview and suggestions for action by stakeholders*. Author.

UNIFEM. (2000). *Progress of the world's women*. New York: United Nations Development Fund for Women.

United Nation. (2011). *United Nation's Human Development Report 2011*. New York: United Nations Development Programme.

United Nations (2013). *Microfinance in Africa: Overview of Suggestions for Action by Stakeholders.* Office of Special Adviser on Africa. Author.

United Nations Children's Fund (UNICEF). (1999). *Human rights for children & women: How UNICEF helps make them a reality*. Retrieved from http://www.unicef.org/pubsgen/humanrights-children/index.html

United Nations Children's Fund (UNICEF). (1999). Human rights for children and women: How UNICEF helps make them a reality. Retrieved from http://www.unicef.org/pubsgen/humanrights-children/index.html

United Nations. (2000). *Millennium Development Goals (MDGs)*. Author.

United Nations. (2001). *Guidelines on Women's Empowerment for the UN Resident Coordinator System. Secretariat of the UN Inter-Agency Task Force on the Implementation of the ICPD Program of Action*. New York: United Nations.

United Nations. (2006). The Millennium Development Goals (MDG) Report (2006).

United Nations. (2015). *The World's Women 2015: Trends and Statistics*. United Nations, Department of Economic and Social Affairs, Statistics Division.

Urbado, D., Díaz, J., & Hernández, R. (2007). Evolución y principios de la teoría económica institucional. Una propuesta de aplicación para el análisis de los factores condicionantes de la creación de empresas. *Investigaciones Europeas de Dirección y Economía de la Empresa, 13*(3), 183–198.

USAID. (2004). *Assessment of the Micro, Small and Medium Enterprises Sector in Nigeria: PRISMS: Promoting Improved Sustainable Microfinance Services*. Retrieved from http://www.usaid.gov/ng/downloads/reforms/ assessmentofthemsmesectorinnigeria.pdf

Vachya, L., Pesala, B., & Nagarjuna, B. (2009). Impact of Micro Finance Inequality Among the SHG Women: Selected Villages in Andhra Pradesh. *Small Enterprises Development, Management & Extension (Sedme) Journal, 36*(4). Retrieved from http://ojs.nimsme.org/)

Vallaeys, F. (2012). Observatorio Regional de Responsabilidad Socila para America Latina y el Caribe. In *Observatorio Regional de Responsabilidad Socila para America Latina y el Caribe* (p. 13). IESALC-UNESCO.

Vargas-Hernández, J. G. (2014). *Capítulo VIII. ¿Cómo los agentes y como los administradores confunden las cosas? Teoría de la agencia. Gestión estratégica de organizaciones*. Buenos Aires, Argentina: Elaleph.

Vasal, V. (2009). Corporate Social Responsibility & Shareholder Returns - Evidence from the Indian Capital Market. *Indian Journal of Industrial Relations, 44*(3), 376–385. Recuperado de http://www.jstor.org/stable/27768210

Vasantha. (2015). Microfinance through self-help group as catalyst for poverty reduction and women empowerment. *Asian Journal of managerial Research, 6*(2), 243-257.

Veblen, T. (1965). *La teoría der la empresa de negocios (1904)*. Buenos Aires: Eudeba.

Vella, S. (2011). *The Link between Microfinance and Social Safety Net Programmes* (Bachelor's dissertation). University of Malta.

Vengroff, R., & Creevey, L. (1994). Evaluation of Project Impact: ACEP Component of the Community Enterprise Development Project (Report to USAID/Dakar).

Verma, S., & Aggarwal, K. (2014). Financial Inclusion through Microfinance Institutions in India. *International Journal of Innovative Research and Development, 3*(1). Retrieved from http://www.ijird.com/index.php/ijird/article/view/46389

Vichore, S., & Deshpande, S. (2012). Microfinance in India — A comprehensive analysis of the growth and performance MFIs. *Research Journal of Social Science and Management, 2*(1), 51–56.

Vijender, A., Rachna, A., & Parul, K. (2012). Micro finance and risk management for poor in India. *Research Journal of Recent Sciences, 1*(2), 104–107.

Villarreal, O. (2005). La internacionalización de la empresa y la empresa multinacional: Una revisión conceptual contemporánea. *Cuadernos de Gestión, 5*(2), 55–73.

Visser, W. (2008). Corporate Social Responsibility in Developing Countries. In A. Crane, A. McWilliams, D. Matten, J. Moon & D. Siegel (Eds.), The Oxford Handbook of Corporate Social Responsibility (pp. 473-499), Oxford, UK: Oxford University Press.

Vong, J. (2013). Impact of microfinance on gender inequality in Indonesia. In *Proceeding of the International Conference on Managing the Asian Century*. Springer. doi:10.1007/978-981-4560-61-0_23

Voola, A. (2014). *Beyond the economics of gender inequalities in microfinance: Comparing problem representations in India and Australia* (PhD thesis). Sydney School of Education and Social Work.

Vyas, P. (2004). A Step towards joint tiger census with Bangladesh. West Bengal, India: Academic Press.

Wadhera, K., & George, K. (2012). *Empowering rural women: Micro enterprise through achievement Motivation, New-Delhi*. SAGE Publications.

Walker, E., & Webster, B. (2006). Management competencies of women business owners. *The International Entrepreneurship and Management Journal*, *2*(4), 495–508. doi:10.100711365-006-0009-9

Weiermair, K., & Peters, M. (1998a). Entrepreneurial Small- and Medium Sized Tourism Enterprises. In K. S. Chon (Ed.), *Tourism and Hotel Industry in Indo-China and Southeast Asia: Development, Marketing and Sustainability* (pp. 235–243). Houston: Hilton College.

Weiermair, K., & Peters, M. (1998b). The internationalization behavior of service enterprises. *Asia Pacific Journal of Tourism Research*, *2*(2). doi:10.1080/10941669808721992

Welsh, D. H., & Krueger, N. (2012). The evolution of social entrepreneurship: What have we learned? *Journal of Technology Management in China*, *7*(3), 270–290. doi:10.1108/17468771311325176

Wen, I. (2009). Factors affecting the online travel buying decision: A review. *International Journal of Contemporary Hospitality Management*, *21*(6), 752–765. doi:10.1108/09596110910975990

White, H. (1980). A Heteroskedasticity-consistent Covariance Matrix Estimator and a Direct Test for Heteroskedasticity. *Econometrica*, *48*(4), 817–838. doi:10.2307/1912934

White, S. (1991). *Evaluating the impact of NGOs in rural poverty alleviation: Bangladesh country study*. London: ODI.

Williamson, O. (1979). Transaction cost economics: The governance of contractual relations. *Journal of Economics*, *22*(2), 233–261. Recuperado de http://www.jstor.org/stable/725118

World Bank (2014). *Micro Data on Financial Inclusion Survey for 2014 (the Global Fundex Survey Data Set)*. Author.

World Bank Policy Paper (1994). *Enhancing women's participation in economic development*. No.13415. World Bank.

World Bank. (1990). *World Development Report 1990: Poverty*. New York: Oxford University Press.

World Bank. (2001). *Engendering Development: Through Gender Equality in Rights, Resources and Voice, World Bank Policy Research Report*. Oxford: Oxford University Press.

World Bank. (2001). Social Capital for Development. Retrieved from http://www.worldbank.org/poverty/scapital/

World Bank. (2001). *World Development Report 2000/2001*. New York: Oxford University Press.

World Bank. (2006). *World development indicators database*. Author.

World Bank. (2011). *World development indicators database*. Author.

World Bank. (2012). *World Development Report, (2012)- Gender Equality and Development*. Washington, DC: The World Bank.

World Bank. (2015). *GDP Growth (annual %)*. Data - World Bank Data. [Online], Available Data.worldbank.org/indicator/NY.GDP.MKTP.KD.ZG

World Bank. (2015). *Global Monitoring Report 2015/16*. Accessed at http://www.worldbank.org/en/publication/global-monitoring-report

Wrenn, E. (2005).Microfinance: Literature Review. www.dochas.ie/Shared/Files/2/MicroFinance_literature_review.pdf. Retrieved 8 July 2017.

Wry, T. (2015). *What impact does microfinance have on inequality?* Accessed from https://www.weforum.org/.../12/what-impact-does-microfinance-have-on-inequality

Yang, B., Jialali, P., & Wei, X. (2011). Microfinance in China's poor area and its impact to loan type-evidence from Xinjiang Uygur autonomous region. *Fourth International Conference on BusinessIntelligence and Financial Engineering*, 486-490, 10.1109/BIFE.2011.82

Yaron, J. (1991). *Successful Rural Financial Institutions*. Washington, DC: World Bank.

Yasuharu, S., & LaStarria-CorNhieL, S. (2015). Agricultural Microcredit and Household Vulnerability in Rural Malawi. *Journal of International Cooperation Studies*, *22*(2), 3.

Yin, R. K. (2003). *Case Study Research: Design and methods* (3rd ed.). Thousand Oaks, CA: Sage.

Yunus, M., & Jolis, A. (1998). Banker to the poor: the autobiography of Muhammad Yunus, founder of the Grameen Bank. Aurum. Official Records of NABARD Regional Office, Guwahati.

Yunus, M. (1999). *Banker to the Poor*. New York, NY: Public Affairs.

Zaman, H. (1999). *Assessing the Impact of Micro-credit on Poverty and Vulnerability in Bangladesh*. Policy Research Working Paper 2145. World Bank.

Zaman, H. (2001). *Assessing the poverty and vulnerability impact of micro-credit in Bangladesh, A case study of BRAC*. Background paper for the WDR 2000/2001.

Zaman, H. (2001). *Assessing the poverty and vulnerability impact of micro-credit in Bangladesh: a case study of BRAC. Background paper for World Bank World Development Report 2000/2001*. Washington, DC: World Bank.

Zang, Q. (2017). Does microfinance reduce poverty? Some international evidence. *The B.E. Journal of Macroeconomics*, *17*(2). doi:10.1515/bejm-2016-0011

Zeller, M. (1999). *The Role of Micro-Finance for Income and Consumption Smoothing*. Paper presented at the Inter-American Development Bank Conference on Social Protection and Poverty, Washington, DC.

Zeller, M. (2001). The Safety Net Role of Microfinance for Income and Consumption Smoothing. *Shielding the Poor: Social Protection in the Developing World*, 217-238.

Zellner, A. (1962). An Efficient Method of Estimating Seemingly Unrelated Regressions and Tests for Aggregation Bias. *Journal of the American Statistical Association*, *57*(298), 348–368. doi:10.1080/01621459.1962.10480664

Zhang, Q., & Posso, A. (2017). *How Microfinance reduces gender inequality in developing countries*. Accessed from www.huffingtonpost.com/.../how-microfinance-reduces-gender-inequality-in-develop

About the Contributors

Ramesh Chandra Das is currently Associate Professor of Economics at Katwa College, West Bengal, India with eighteen years of teaching and research experience in different fields of the subject. He has obtained Masters, M. Phil and Ph. D Degree in Economics from the University of Calcutta. Dr. Das has contributed several research papers to national and international journals with reputations along with completions of three minor research projects sponsored by UGC, India. He has written one text book on Microeconomics for different fields of students and academicians and edited Handbook of Research on Globalization, Investment and Growth-Implications of Confidence and Governance, and Handbook of Research on Global Indicators of Economic and Political Convergence, Handbook of Research on Economic, Financial, and Industrial Impacts on Infrastructure Development and Social, Health, and Environmental Infrastructures for Economic Growth, all published by IGI Global, USA. He has been acting as editor-in-chief in Asian Journal of Research in Business Economics and Management and one of the editorial advisory board members of Society for the Study on Business and Finance.

* * *

Maniklal Adhikary has been teaching Economics at The University of Burdwan, India for 35 years besides guiding research scholars working in varied fields related to Economics. His areas of interest include Macroeconomic Theory, Mathematical Economics, Theory of Economic Growth and Planning, Economics of Water (Resource and Environment), Econometrics – Theory and Applications, Time Series Econometrics, Financial Econometrics, Production Function and Stochastic Frontier Production Function besides training his students in dealing with different econometric software. Prof. Adhikary has more than one hundred academic papers in various journals of national and international repute and five books of which two are edited.

Henry Thomas Asogwa was born on 2nd September, 1982 at Otukpo, Benue State, Nigeria. He has M.Sc in Economics from University of Nigeria, and is currently a Ph.D Student at Nnamdi Azikiwe University, Awka in Anambra State, Nigeria and also an Assistant Research Fellow at the Institute of Development Studies, University of Nigeria, Nsukka.

Supravat Bagli is Assistant Professor, Department of Economics, Presidency University, Kolkata, India. He has done his M. Phil and Ph. D. from the University of Burdwan, West Bengal. His areas of interest in research are application of econometric theory, Economics of microfinance, Poverty and inequality studies. He has teaching experience of more than a decade. Dr. Bagli, in his credit, has twenty five research papers published in different reputed journals and books. He regularly presents papers relating to microfinance, financial inclusion and poverty in different national and international seminars.

Indrani Basu is presently Assistant Professor in Economics, Berhampore College, under the University of Kalyani, India. She has fourteen years of experience in teaching and research. She was awarded M. Phil and Ph. D by the University of Kalyani. She has published a number of research papers in peer reviewed journals and books. She has acted as 'external monitoring officer' in a project seeking the evaluation of 'Pulse-Polio Immunization programme' financed by Government of India and World Health Organization during 2003 – 2006 in West Bengal. Apart from this, her areas of interest to do something for the women, who serve the world a lot, but get very meager recognition from the society.

Kinkini Bhattacharjee has obtained her bachelor and master degree in Economics from the University of Burdwan with good marks. She is presently working as guest lecturer in the Department of Economics, Katwa College, West Bengal, India. She has research interests on quantitative economics. Besides, she is doing bachelor degree in education.

Rajib Bhattacharyya has got his bachelor and master degree in Economics from the University of Calcutta. He obtained his M. Phil degree from the same University. He was awarded the Ph. D in Economics and his thesis was on Growth of Outsourcing in India. He has been serving as a full-time lecturer in Economics since 2001 and presently serving as an Assistant Prof. in Economics (W.B.E.S.), Hooghly Mohsin College. He has more than 7 years of teaching experience at PG level. He made several publications in different areas of international economics and women entrepreneurship development.

Santanu Bisai is presently an Assistant Professor in Economics at Shyamaprasad College, Kolkata, India. He has also worked in the same post in Prasanta Chandra Mahalanobis College, Kolkata, India. He has obtained masters and doctoral degree in Economics respectively from the University of Calcutta and Vidyasagar University. He has been working for long in the areas of Agricultural and Rural Economics, Microfinance, Self-help Groups, among others. He has produced many research articles published in reputed journals.

Avijit Brahmachary is currently Assistant Professor at Kandi Raj College, Kandi, Murshidabad in the state of West Bengal, India. He is a post-graduate in Economics from the University of Kalyani, West Bengal. He was awarded the Ph.D degree in Economics on 2008. He has special interest in the field of microfinance and behavioral finance and has several publications in national and international publication house. He has presented several research papers on microfinance and behavioral finance in different national and international conferences.

Sumanta Kumar Das has been serving as an assistant teacher in a Government sponsored school of West Bengal since 2008. He has submitted his Ph.D. thesis in 2017 under the supervision of Dr. Maniklal Adhikary. He has research interests on Self-Help Groups, Women Empowerment, Applied Economics, Agriculture Economics, Informal Economics, etc.

Kanchan Datta is an Associate Professor of Economics in the University of North Bengal. He obtained his Ph.D degree in the year 2010 from the University of North Bengal. Dr. Datta has published many research papers in various journals and also has participated in many national and international conferences. His special interest is in Time series Econometrics. In the University he teaches Basic plus Advanced Econometrics, and Advanced International Economics. He was the Head of the Department during the time period 8th July 2015 - 7th July 2017. He is an editorial board member of UGC affiliated Journal 'Economic Affairs'.

Onyinye Maria David-Wayas is a Lecturer II and Ph.D Student at the Department of Economics, University of Nigeria, Nsukka, Enugu State, Nigeria. She has B.Sc and M.Sc degrees in Economics and had some awards due to her performance in those results.

Ratan Dey is an MA in Economics from Sidho-Kanho-Birsha University, Purulia West Bengal, India. He has done PG project at Sidho-Kanho-Birsha University. He is currently doing B. Ed. at Institute of Advanced Study in Education, Bhopal. He is also a part-time worker of ICICI bank at Port Blair, Andaman and Nicobar Islands, India.

Abhijit Dutta is currently Professor of Commerce at the Department of Commerce, Sikkim (Central) University, Gangtok, India. He obtained the degree of PhD in Commerce from Utkal University, India. He has joined this university in 2015 and he is having more than twenty years of teaching experience at UG and PG levels in various reputed institutes across India and serving as also doctoral supervisor. He published a good numbers of papers in various reputed national and international journals. His areas of research interest include Capital Market, Infrastructure Finance and Behavioural Finance.

Richardson Kojo Edeme is a Lecturer in the Department of Economics, University of Nigeria, Nsukka. He obtained a PhD in Economics in 2011 from University of Nigeria, specializing in Public Finance and Fiscal Policy. His area of research interest includes Public Economics and Policy, Applied Microeconomics and Macroeconomics Analyses, Industrial/Trade Policies, Health Economics.

Chisom Emecheta was born on the 13th of April 1987. She is a Lecturer II in the Department of Economics, University of Nigeria, Nsukka. She has keen interest in the area of development issues and has obtained a Master Degree in Development Economics.

Asim Kumar Karmakar is Assistant Professor, Department of Economics, Jadavpur University, India. He is presently the Executive Member of both the Indian Economic Association (IEA) and The Indian Econometric Society (TIES); formerly the Managing Editor (2011-2014) of the Quarterly Referred Journal Artha Beekshan of Bengal Economic Association. He has completed three minor research projects sponsored by the CAS, Jadavpur University and the UGC. He has contributed many research papers in reputed journals at home and abroad, and written books on different fields of economics; titles include Balance of Payments Theory and Policy: The Indian Experience, Capital Account Convertibility in India, Analytical Issues in Trade, Development and Finance.

Napoleon Kurantin is a Lecturer at the School of Public Service and Governance, Ghana Institute of Management and Public Administration, Accra, Ghana. His recent works include: The Role of Land Administration in Support of Sustainable Socio-economic Governance, Security and Development: The Experience of Ghana Land Administration Project, 2015; The Effects of Budget Deficit on Economic Growth and Development: The Experience of Ghana (1994 – 2014), 2015.

Sudhansu Sekhar Mahapatra is presently functioning as Professor in the Department of Commerce, Sikkim University, Gangtok, India. Prior to his joining Sikkim University in 2014, he was working as Associate Professor and Head, Department of Commerce in Sikkim Government College. For a brief period, he was Principal of Sikkim Government College, West Sikkim. A doctorate in Commerce, Dr. Mahapatra has 28 years of teaching experience at College and University level. He has published a number of articles in reputed journals. He was a member of Academic Council of Sikkim University.

Amit Majumder is presently working as Assistant Professor & Head of the Department of Commerce (UG &PG), Bijoy Krishna Girls' College, Howrah since. He is also a visiting Faculty, Department of Commerce, University of Calcutta. Dr. Majumder had sole authored 2 books from international publisher from Germany and contributed in 52 edited volumes, 32 nationally and internationally acclaimed peer-reviewed and referred journals. He is successfully supervising the Ph.D. Scholars of University of Calcutta and other national Universities and institutions. His areas of interests are Strategic Management, Corporate Governance, Corporate Social Responsibility, etc.

Amir Manzoor holds a PhD in management sciences. He is a graduate of NED University, Pakistan, Lahore University of Management Sciences (LUMS), Pakistan and Bangor University, United Kingdom. He has more than 15 years of diverse professional and teaching experience working at many renowned national and internal organizations and higher education institutions. His research interests include E-commerce, Strategic Management, Enterprise Resource Planning (ERP), Project Management, Supply Chain Management, Data Analysis, Technology applications.

Debashis Mazumder has done his MA in Economics from Jadavpur University, Kolkata; M.Phil in Economics from Calcutta University, and Ph. D in Economics from Rabindra Bharati University, Kolkata, India. At present, he is working as Professor of Economics at The Heritage College, Kolkata. Dr. Mazumder was Associate Professor in Bangabasi College under Calcutta University. He is also acting as visiting faculty in the Post Graduate Department of Commerce at Nababullygunge Mahavidyalaya Kolkata, and in the PG (Economics) Section of Indira Gandhi National Open University (IGNOU), Muralidhar Girs' College Center, Kolkata. He has written a good number of text books on Managerial Economics and contributed articles in many national and international journals.

Sovik Mukherjee is at present a Lecturer in Economics, Department of Commerce (Evening) at Shri Shikshayatan College, Kolkata, India. He is also pursuing his research in the Department of Economics, Jadavpur University, Kolkata, India. Mr. Mukherjee has a B.A (Hons.) degree in Economics from Jadavpur University and was awarded the Ujjayini Memorial Gold Medal, an M.A degree and an M.Phil degree in Economics from Jadavpur University, Kolkata, India. His research interests lie in the areas like public economics and taxation, applied game theory, environment and health economics and the econometric analysis of financial crises. He is a Life Member of the Indian Economic Association, The Indian Econometric Society and the Bengal Economic Association.

Partha Mukhopadhyay is a PhD Scholar at Department of Humanities and Social Sciences, National Institute of Technology Durgapur, India. He has been working in Durgapur Steel Plant, Steel Authority of India Limited since 1993. Having the degree of MBA (Finance), he has also completed a post graduate degree in Human Resource area. Till date he has published and presented more than fifteen research papers in national and international level seminars and conferences. He owns the credit of some papers published in international journals and books including Scopus indexing etc. His research interests include Time Series Econometrics, Agricultural Economics and Applied Econometrics, etc.

Johnson Ezema Nchege was born on October 2nd, 1988 at Amaekpu in Ohafia Local Government Area of Abia State, Nigeria. He obtained his Bachelor of Science (B.Sc.) and Master degree in Economics respectively in 2012 and 2016. He is currently employed as an Assistant Lecturer in the Department of Economics, University of Nigeria, Nsukka.

Anindita Neogi passed M.A in Economics from University of Kalyani and then completed research in 'Monetary Economics' from University of Kalyani, India. She served as Part-time Lecturer in Economics at Rishi Bankim Chandra College, 24 PGS, Kalyani Mahavidyalaya, Nadia and Chakdaha College, Nadia of West Bengal successfully for about eight years. Dr. Neogi presently serving as Assistant Professor in Economics at Kandi Raj College, Murshidabad, West Bengal since 2010. She is also acting as Counsellor of IGNOU for UG and PG courses since 2015. Published some papers at National and State level seminars.

Chigozie Nelson Nkalu is a Lecturer in the Department of Economics, University of Nigeria, Nsukka-Nigeria. He obtained an MSc in Economics from University of Nigeria, specializing in Development Economics. His research interest is in the area of Development and Monetary Economics.

Augustine Chika Odo is presently a Lecturer in the Department of Economics, Godfrey Okoye University, Enugu State, Nigeria. Currently, he is a Ph.D scholar in the Department of Economics, University of Nigeria Nsukka, Enugu State, Nigeria. His areas of research are development economics and quantitative economics.

Bertha Z. Osei-Hwedie is a Professor of International Relations in the School of Public Service and Governance, Ghana Institute of Management and Public Administration, Accra, Ghana. Her recent works include "China-Japan Rivalry in Africa", 2015; "Continuity and Change: The Influence of the Presidents on Botswana's Foreign Policy"{co-author}, 2014; "The Quest for Gender Parity in Southern African Politics", 2013;"Peace, Security and Governance in Sub-Saharan Africa", 2013; "China's Re-engagement with Africa: The Search for Peace and Security", 2012;"China's Role in Africa's Conflict Resolution, Peacekeeping and Peacebuilding", 2011.

Anjan Ray Chaudhury obtained his Master Degree in Economics from the University of Calcutta. He got the Research Fellowship offered by University Grants Commission and worked as a full-time Research Fellow at the Institute of Development studies, Kolkata. His PhD work was on 'Horizontal Inequality: The Concept, Measurement and Determinants', later on the completion of his PhD work, he has been continuously working on Welfare Economics and International Economics. Some papers of Dr. Ray Chaudhury in this area have been published in some reputed international and national journals. He has also attended some international and national seminars/conferences/workshops.

María Alejandra Santos Huerta is presently associated to the Department of University administrative center of economic sciences. University of Guadalajara, Mexico. Dr. Santos Huerta has research interests on managerial sciences, administrative sciences, managerial economics, among others. She has many publications in different journals and books with repute.

Partha Pratim Sengupta is Professor of Economics and Head, Department of Humanities and Social Sciences, National Institute of Technology Durgapur, India. He has been teaching at the institute since thirty-five years, out of which twenty years of teaching at PG level and Research. Till now more than twenty students have been awarded Doctorate degree under the supervision of Professor Sengupta. He published more than one hundred research papers in national and international level peer reviewed journals. His areas of research interest include International Economics, Business Economics, Development Economics, and Entrepreneurship Management.

Shahjahan Ali Sheikh is presently Assistant Professor in Economics, Ratnapith College of Assam in India. Besides, he is associated to the Department of Economics, North Bengal University, India as research fellow. His areas of research include rural economics, informal economics, microfinance, etc and he has some published papers in journals and books in his credit till date.

Madhabendra Sinha is currently a Senior Research Fellow in Economics at the Department of Humanities and Social Sciences, National Institute of Technology Durgapur, India. He has obtained the degree of MSc and MPhil in Economics from the University of Calcutta, India. His research interests include International Economics, Time Series Econometrics, Open Economy Macroeconomics, Development Economics and Applied Econometrics etc. He has published and presented more than thirty-five research papers in national and international level journals, seminars, workshops and conferences in India and abroad also.

Ezebuilo Romanus Ukwueze was born on 11th November, 1972 at Umukabi Village, Ede-Oballa, Nsukka in Enugu State, Nigeria. He has PhD in Economics (bias Development Economics) and is a Senior Lecturer at the Department of Economics, University of Nigeria, Nsukka in Enugu State, Nigeria. He has produced a list of research articles in national and international journals and books with reputations.

José G. Vargas-Hernández, MBA, PhD, is a member of the National System of Researchers of Mexico and a research professor at University Center for Economic and Managerial Sciences, University of Guadalajara. Professor Vargas-Hernández has a Ph. D. in Public Administration and a Ph.D. in Organizational Economics. He has undertaken studies in Organizational Behavior and has a Master of Business Administration, published four books and more than 200 papers in international journals and reviews (some translated to English, French, German, Portuguese, Farsi, Chinese, etc.) and more than 300 essays in national journals and reviews. He has obtained several international Awards and recognition.

Index

H

I

L

M

N

O

P

Q

R

S

T

U

V

W

www.ingramcontent.com/pod-product-compliance
Lightning Source LLC
LaVergne TN
LVHW060354300926
849162LV00006B/1264